AMERICAN HISTORY
VOLUME I
Pre-Colonial Through Reconstruction

Eleventh Edition

A Library of Information from the Public Press

Editor

Robert James Maddox
Pennsylvania State University
University Park

Robert James Maddox, distinguished historian and professor
of American history at Pennsylvania State University,
received a B.S. from Fairleigh Dickinson University in 1957,
an M.S. from the University of Wisconsin in 1958, and a
Ph.D. from Rutgers in 1964. He has written, reviewed, and
lectured extensively, and is widely respected for his
interpretations of presidential character and policy.

Cover illustration by Mike Eagle

The Dushkin Publishing Group, Inc.
Sluice Dock, Guilford, Connecticut 06437

The Annual Editions Series

Annual Editions is a series of over fifty volumes designed to provide the reader with convenient, low-cost access to a wide range of current, carefully selected articles from some of the most important magazines, newspapers, and journals published today. Annual Editions are updated on an annual basis through a continuous monitoring of over 200 periodical sources. All Annual Editions have a number of features designed to make them particularly useful, including topic guides, annotated tables of contents, unit overviews, and indexes. For the teacher using Annual Editions in the classroom, an Instructor's Resource Guide with test questions is available for each volume.

VOLUMES AVAILABLE

Africa
Aging
American Government
American History, Pre-Civil War
American History, Post-Civil War
Anthropology
Biology
Business and Management
Business Ethics
Canadian Politics
China
Comparative Politics
Computers in Education
Computers in Business
Computers in Society
Criminal Justice
Drugs, Society, and Behavior
Early Childhood Education
Economics
Educating Exceptional Children
Education
Educational Psychology
Environment
Geography
Global Issues
Health
Human Development
Human Resources
Human Sexuality

Latin America
Macroeconomics
Management
Marketing
Marriage and Family
Microeconomics
Middle East and the Islamic World
Money and Banking
Nutrition
Personal Growth and Behavior
Psychology
Public Administration
Race and Ethnic Relations
Social Problems
Sociology
Soviet Union and Eastern Europe
State and Local Government
Third World
Urban Society
Violence and Terrorism
Western Civilization,
    Pre-Reformation
Western Civilization,
    Post-Reformation
Western Europe
World History, Pre-Modern
World History, Modern
World Politics

Library of Congress Cataloging in Publication Data
Main entry under title: Annual editions: American history, volume one.
        1. United States—History—Periodicals. 2. United States—Historiography—Periodicals.
3. United States—Civilization—Periodicals. I. Title: American history, volume one.
E171.A75   973'.05   74–187540
ISBN 1–56134–010–3

Eleventh Edition

Manufactured by The Banta Company, Harrisonburg, Virginia 22801

Editors/ Advisory Board

To the Reader

In publishing ANNUAL EDITIONS we recognize the enormous role played by the magazines, newspapers, and journals of the *public press* in providing current, first-rate educational information in a broad spectrum of interest areas. Within the articles, the best scientists, practitioners, researchers, and commentators draw issues into new perspective as accepted theories and viewpoints are called into account by new events, recent discoveries change old facts, and fresh debate breaks out over important controversies.

Many of the articles resulting from this enormous editorial effort are appropriate for students, researchers, and professionals seeking accurate, current material to help bridge the gap between principles and theories and the real world. These articles, however, become more useful for study when those of lasting value are carefully *collected, organized, indexed,* and *reproduced* in a *low-cost format*, which provides easy and permanent access when the material is needed. That is the role played by *Annual Editions*. Under the direction of each volume's *Editor*, who is an expert in the subject area, and with the guidance of an *Advisory Board*, we seek each year to provide in each *ANNUAL EDITION* a current, well-balanced, carefully selected collection of the best of the public press for your study and enjoyment. We think you'll find this volume useful, and we hope you'll take a moment to let us know what you think.

Recent trends in historical writing have been to emphasize the lives of ordinary people, and to recognize the diversity of our society by calling attention to the contributions and problems of ethnic and racial minority groups. This development supplements and enriches our understanding of the past, but does not render obsolete the need to understand significant events and leaders. That the Constitution was written one way and not another profoundly affected the course of American history, and individuals such as Franklin D. Roosevelt and Martin Luther King, Jr., *did* make a difference.

American History offers a selection of essays on both traditional and nontraditional subjects. Articles on various aspects of both social and cultural history are included along with those dealing with politics, diplomacy, and military conflicts. Some present analyses of large events, some offer insights on everyday life, and still others convey the "feel" of things through eyewitness accounts. We hope this combination of writings will provide a useful supplement to textbooks, which of necessity have to provide broad coverage at the expense of treating particular topics at length.

This volume contains a number of features designed to be helpful to students, researchers, and professionals. These include a *topic guide* for locating articles on specific subjects; the *table of contents abstracts* that summarize each essay, with key concepts in bold italics; and a comprehensive *index*. Articles are organized into four units. Each unit is preceded by an overview that provides a background for informed reading of the articles, emphasizes critical issues, and presents *challenge questions*.

Every succeeding edition of *American History* includes new articles to replace some old ones. We are eager to continue to improve the quality of the selections, and to consider possible alternatives that might have been missed. If you come across an article that you think merits inclusion in the next edition, please send it along. We welcome your comments about the readings in this volume, and a post-paid reader response card is included in the back of the book for your convenience. Your suggestions will be carefully considered and greatly appreciated.

Robert James Maddox
Editor

Contents

Unit 1

The New Land

Six selections discuss the beginnings of America, the new land—from the early English explorers, early life of the colonists, and religious intolerance, to the stirrings of liberty and independence.

To the Reader	iv
Topic Guide	2
Overview	4

1. A New World . . . and a New Era in World History, 6
Arturo Uslar Pietri, *The UNESCO Courier,* March 1988.
Christopher Columbus was searching for a water route to Asia when he and his crew landed on the tiny island he named San Salvador. The date was October 12, 1492. More than the beginning of a new era in history, according to Venezuelan writer Arturo Uslar Pietri, the event set the stage for history itself to take on a "universal dimension."

2. Roanoke Lost, Karen Ordahl Kupperman, *American Heritage,* August/September 1985. 10
Founded by Sir Walter Raleigh, *the first settlement at Roanoke Island* had to be evacuated by Sir Francis Drake. The second group to settle there was never heard from again.

3. Who Were the Pilgrims? Richard Ellison, *New England Monthly,* November 1988. 17
Whether the Pilgrims actually landed near what became known as Plymouth Rock is doubtful, as are many other "facts" about these early settlers. *The Pilgrim myth*, according to Richard Ellison, "has far more to do with who we want them to be than who they really were."

4. Colonists in Bondage: Indentured Servants in America, Barbara Bigham, *Early American Life,* October 1979. 20
Indentured servitude preceded *slavery* as a means of providing labor for the colonies. Barbara Bigham discusses the similarities and differences between these institutions.

5. Anne Hutchinson: "A Verye Dangerous Woman," Stephanie Ocko, *Early American Life,* August 1979. 25
Anne Hutchinson, the focus of this article, was an outspoken woman who claimed to have revelations from God. Her preaching of unorthodox sermons got her into trouble and eventually forced her to leave Boston. "Neither martyr nor successful reformer," Hutchinson challenged the *religious intolerance* of the day.

6. Remapping American Culture, *U.S. News & World Report,* December 4, 1989. 28
David Hackett Fischer's recent book, *Albion's Seed,* has been described as "the finest work of synthesis in *early American history* in more than 50 years," but also one that is sure to "raise a firestorm." Alvin Sanoff and Sharon Golden explain Fischer's theory that separate waves of immigration from England produced four distinct political and cultural regions in America.

The concepts in bold italics are developed in the article. For further expansion please refer to the Topic Guide and the Index.

Unit 2

Revolutionary America

Six articles examine the start of the American Revolution. The new land offered opportunities for new ideas that led to the creation of an independent nation.

Overview 32

7. **The Shot Heard Round the World,** Henry Fairlie, *The New Republic,* July 18 & 25, 1988.   34
   "Here once the embattled farmers stood," wrote Ralph Waldo Emerson, "And fired the shot heard round the world." In this article Henry Fairlie shows that Emerson's words were more than poetic boasting. News of the **American Revolution** stirred great interest in the capitals of Europe. "Both rulers and their subjects," Fairlie claims, "saw it as a revolution of universal appeal."

8. **Life, Liberty, and the Pursuit of Happiness: America's Modest Revolution,** John R. Kayser, *USA Today Magazine (Society for the Advancement of Education),* July 1990.   39
   The French Revolution, according to John Kayser, sought nothing less than to "transform human nature, recast the world, and bring about entirely new relationships among individuals." That tradition, he argues, has collapsed with the communist regimes in the Soviet Union and in Eastern Europe. The very modesty of the American revolutionary tradition, he claims, "is the core of its phenomenal success."

9. **General George Washington, Espionage Chief,** Walter R. Haefele, *American History Illustrated,* November/December 1989.   41
   George Washington may not have been able to lie about chopping down the cherry tree, but he was perfectly willing to employ deceit against the British. Walter Haefele analyzes the role of **espionage during the American Revolution**.

10. **'It Is Not a Union,'** Peter Onuf, *The Wilson Quarterly,* Spring 1987.   46
    Americans celebrated the end of the war with England, and looked confidently to the future. A host of foreign and domestic problems soon began plaguing the new nation. Peter Onuf tells how these problems led to the demand for **revision of the Articles of Confederation**. Calls for a convention to strengthen the Articles alarmed Patrick Henry, who "smelt a rat." He correctly feared the delegates would create an entirely new government.

11. **Philadelphia Story,** Jack N. Rakove, *The Wilson Quarterly,* Spring 1987.   50
    The 55 men who met in Philadelphia during the spring and summer of 1787 constituted a diverse group. This article explains the various compromises—including one on slavery—that enabled the delegates **to forge a new constitution**.

12. **The American Revolution: A War of Religion?** Jonathan Clark, *History Today,* December 1989.   58
    Was the American Revolution a product of political repression and constitutional differences? As this article suggests, **the role religion played in 1776** was considerable.

Unit 3

National Consolidation and Expansion

Sixteen selections examine the developing United States, the westward movement of people seeking a new life, and the realities of living in early nineteenth-century America.

Overview   **64**

13. **James Madison and the Bill of Rights,** Jack N. Rakove, *This Constitution,* Spring/Summer 1988.   **66**
James Madison can rightly be regarded as the principal framer of the Bill of Rights. His dedication to the principles of the rights of citizens was expressed in his writing of *The Federalist Papers.*

14. **Slaves and Freedmen,** Keith Melder, *The Wilson Quarterly,* New Year's 1989.   **72**
Washington, D.C. became the nation's capital in 1790 as part of a political deal. That a thriving slave market should develop in the city appalled some white Americans. Others were appalled at the number of freed blacks who settled there.

15. **The Lives of Slave Women,** Deborah Gray White, *Southern Exposure,* November/December 1984.   **78**
Slave women, in the American South, were worked as hard as men. They did the same field work, either with men or in segregated gangs. This article examines some of the dynamics of *Southern slave women.*

16. **The Great Chief Justice,** Brian McGinty, *American History Illustrated,* September 1986.   **84**
The *U.S. Constitution* was ambiguous about the role of the *Supreme Court.* During the first 11 years of its existence, the Court was ineffectual, an "inconsequential junior partner" of the executive and legislative branches. Under John Marshall's leadership, according to this article, the body became a court "supreme in fact as well as name."

17. **A Shadow of Secession? The Hartford Convention, 1814,** James M. Banner, Jr., *History Today,* September 1988.   **92**
By the summer of 1814 the war with Great Britain was going badly, and the United States appeared on the brink of commercial and financial ruin. In September a call went out for a convention of delegates from the New England states to meet that winter, a convention some hoped might lead to secession. Banner shows there was little danger of that, but he explores some of the deeper issues involving *the very nature of the union.*

The concepts in bold italics are developed in the article. For further expansion please refer to the Topic Guide and the Index.

18. **Russia's American Adventure,** Lydia T. Black, *Natural History,* December 1989.   **98**

A group of New Englanders founded *an industrial community in Lowell, Massachusetts,* which appeared as a kind of utopia for labor. The workers were women, most of whom had previously worked on farms, and whose lives were strictly ordered and supervised. This article describes how the experiment failed to live up to its promise.

In 1867 the United States acquired *Alaska* from the Russian empire. Black shows how the Russian American Company influenced Alaskan culture, particularly after 1818. "Today," she writes, "partly because Alaskan native groups have called for better teaching of their own history, a new generation is examining this heritage."

19. **From Utopia to Mill Town,** Maury Klein, *American History Illustrated,* October 1981.   **103**

A group of New Englanders founded *an industrial community in Lowell, Massachusetts,* which appeared as a kind of utopia for labor. The workers were women, most of whom had previously worked on farms, and whose lives were strictly ordered and supervised. This article describes how the experiment failed to live up to its promise.

20. **The Secret Life of a Developing Country (Ours),** Jack Larkin, *American Heritage,* September/October 1988.   **108**

The author describes *everyday life in early nineteenth-century America.* In appearance, manners, and morals, he finds, "we were not at all the placid, straitlaced, white-picket-fence nation we imagine ourselves to have been."

21. **The Jacksonian Revolution,** Robert V. Remini, *The World & I,* January 1988.   **123**

Andrew Jackson presided over the creation of the second American party system. Robert V. Remini evaluates *Jackson's presidency* and finds it did amount to a "revolution." The author concludes with an overview of the major interpretations of "Jacksonian Democracy."

22. **Lone Star Rising: Texas Before and After the Alamo,** Archie P. McDonald, *American History Illustrated,* March 1986.   **130**

This essay traces the *history of the region that is now Texas* from the period of Spanish explorations, through independence, to statehood.

23. **Eden Ravished,** Harlan Hague, *The American West,* May/ June 1977.   **134**

The threat of *exhausting our natural resources* has become obvious in recent decades. Hague shows that some voices were raised on this issue even before the Civil War. In spite of these warnings, however, the belief in the inexhaustibility of resources in the West generated the unique American acceptance of waste as the fundamental tenet of a life-style.

The concepts in bold italics are developed in the article. For further expansion please refer to the Topic Guide and the Index.

24. **Act One,** Lois W. Banner, *The Wilson Quarterly,* Autumn 1986.   **142**

In July 1848 a "Woman's Rights Convention" opened in Seneca Falls, New York. Its organizers, Lucretia Mott and Elizabeth Cady Stanton, issued an astounding proclamation: "We hold these truths to be self-evident, that all men and women are created equal." However, as Lois W. Banner reports, *the early woman's rights movement* never attained great popularity, and was overwhelmed by the Civil War.

25. **El Presidente Gringo: William Walker and the Conquest of Nicaragua,** Roger Bruns and Bryan Kennedy, *American History Illustrated,* February 1989.   **145**

In 1856 *William Walker made himself president of Nicaragua*. Four years later he was executed by a Honduran firing squad. Bruns and Kennedy show how this daring filibuster, who believed he was the legendary "Gray-eyed Man of Destiny," left a legacy that still lives.

26. **The War Against Demon Rum,** Robert Maddox, *American History Illustrated,* May 1979.   **153**

European visitors were shocked at the amount of alcohol that early Americans consumed. As time went on, more and more people became alarmed at the habits of their fellow citizens. This article traces the evolution of the *temperance and prohibition movements*.

27. **Last Stop on the Underground Railroad: Mary Ann Shadd in Canada,** Cheryl MacDonald, *The Beaver,* February/March 1990.   **158**

Mary Ann Shadd was celebrated as *the first black woman in North America to edit a newspaper*. She devoted her life to the struggle against slavery in the South and segregation in the North.

28. **The Cry Was: Go West, Young Man, and Stay Healthy,** Bil Gilbert, *Smithsonian,* March 1983.   **164**

By today's *health standards*, nineteenth-century Americans were a sickly lot. In addition to all the ills we now suffer, they were afflicted by malaria, cholera, diphtheria, typhus, and smallpox. Gilbert suggests that many people traveled west to the *frontier* in search of health and wealth.

The concepts in bold italics are developed in the article. For further expansion please refer to the Topic Guide and the Index.

Unit 4

The Civil War and Reconstruction

Nine articles discuss the tremendous effects of the Civil War on America. With the abolishment of slavery, the United States had to reconstruct society.

Overview   168

29. **Dred Scott in History,** Walter Ehrlich, *Westward,* Winter 1983.   170
The **Dred Scott** case resulted in one of the most momentous decisions ever rendered by the **Supreme Court**. This article clears away some of the myths surrounding the origins of the case and discusses its impact upon the **slavery** question, the **Republican party**, and the Court itself.

30. **How We Got Lincoln,** Peter Andrews, *American Heritage,* November 1988.   176
When the Republican party held its convention in Chicago in 1860, Senator William Henry Seward of New York was the odds-on favorite to be nominated for the presidency. Andrews shows **how Abraham Lincoln won** instead.

31. **There, in the Heat of July, Was the Shimmering Capitol,** Thomas A. Lewis, *Smithsonian,* July 1988.   185
By 1864 the South was close to defeat, but Lieutenant General Jubal Early of the Confederate States Army had Washington, D.C., within his grasp. This article reviews this interesting event, and examines the confusion typical of the battles fought during the **American Civil War.**

32. **Family and Freedom: Black Families in the American Civil War,** Ira Berlin, Francine C. Cary, Steven F. Miller, and Leslie S. Rowland, *History Today,* January 1987.   190
Emancipation freed approximately 4 million slaves and constituted a social and economic revolution. These documents written by former slaves depict their struggle to attain freedom for themselves and their families.

33. **Why The Confederacy Lost,** Brian Holden Reid and Bruce Collins, *History Today,* November 1988.   199
Was it possible for the **American Civil War** to have continued in one form or another? This article discusses the possibility that the South, in failing to use revolutionary methods to full advantage, might have helped in shortening the war.

34. **A Union Officer at Gettysburg,** Frank Aretas Haskell, *American History Illustrated,* Summer 1988.   206
This is an eyewitness account of the **Battle of Gettysburg**, including Pickett's famous charge. The officer who wrote it died in combat one year later.

The concepts in bold italics are developed in the article. For further expansion please refer to the Topic Guide and the Index.

35. **The Hard Fight Was Getting Into the Fight at All,** Jack   215
    Fincher, *Smithsonian,* October 1990.
    "During the Civil War," Fincher writes, "the hardest problem for
    black men was not in being brave; it was in getting a chance to
    fight at all." He describes their struggle to bear arms and their
    magnificent performance in battle.

36. **What Did Freedom Mean? The Aftermath of Slavery as   223
    Seen by Former Slaves and Former Masters in Three
    Societies,** Dean C. Brink, *Magazine of History,* Winter
    1989.
    "Most anyone ought to know that a man is better off free than as a
    slave," a former house servant wrote to a congressional commit-
    tee in 1883. But many impediments to full equality remained. This
    article presents **accounts written by former slaves and former
    masters** in several societies.

37. **The New View of Reconstruction,** Eric Foner, *American   235
    Heritage,* October/November 1983.
    Prior to the 1960s, according to Eric Foner, **Reconstruction** was
    portrayed in history books as "just about the darkest page in the
    American saga." This article presents a balanced view of the era
    and suggests that even though Reconstruction failed to achieve
    its objectives, its "animating vision" still has relevance.

Index   241
Article Review Form   244
Article Rating Form   245

The concepts in bold italics are developed in the article. For further expansion please refer to the Topic Guide and the Index.

Topic Guide

This topic guide suggests how the selections in this book relate to topics of traditional concern to American history students and professionals. It is useful for locating articles that relate to each other for reading and research. The guide is arranged alphabetically according to topic. Articles may, of course, treat topics that do not appear in the topic guide. In turn, entries in the topic guide do not necessarily constitute a comprehensive listing of all the contents of each selection.

TOPIC AREA	TREATED IN:	TOPIC AREA	TREATED IN:
African Americans	14. Slaves and Freedmen 15. Lives of Slave Women 27. Last Stop on Underground Railroad 29. Dred Scott 32. Black Families in the American Civil War 35. Hard Fight 36. What Did Freedom Mean? 37. New View of Reconstruction	Exploration	1. A New World 2. Roanoke Lost 18. Russia's American Adventure
American Revolution	7. Shot Heard Round the World 8. Life, Liberty, and the Pursuit of Happiness 9. General George Washington 12. American Revolution: War of Religion?	Government	10. 'It Is Not a Nation' 11. Philadelphia Story 13. James Madison and the Bill of Rights 16. Great Chief Justice 17. A Shadow of Secession? 21. Jacksonian Revolution 29. Dred Scott 30. How We Got Lincoln 32. Black Families in the American Civil War 37. New View of Reconstruction
Articles of Confederation	10. 'It Is Not a Union'	Hartford Convention	17. A Shadow of Secession?
Civil War	31. There, in the Heat of July 32. Black Families in the American Civil War 33. Why the Confederacy Lost 34. A Union Officer at Gettysburg 35. Hard Fight	Health	28. Cry Was: Go West Young Man
		Hispanics	1. A New World 22. Lone Star Rising
		Immigration	6. Remapping American Culture
Constitution	10. 'It Is Not a Union' 11. Philadelphia Story 13. James Madison and the Bill of Rights 16. Great Chief Justice 29. Dred Scott	Indentured Servants	4. Colonists in Bondage
		Labor	4. Colonists in Bondage 19. From Utopia to Mill Town
Culture	3. Who Were the Pilgrims? 6. Remapping American Culture 20. Secret Life of Developing Country	Latin America	25. El Presidente Gringo
		Lincoln, Abraham	30. How We Got Lincoln
Environment	23. Eden Ravished		

TOPIC AREA	TREATED IN:	TOPIC AREA	TREATED IN:
Madison, James	13. James Madison and the Bill of Rights	**Supreme Court**	16. Great Chief Justice 29. Dred Scott
Native Americans	1. A New World 18. Russia's American Adventure	**Temperance**	26. War Against Demon Rum
Pilgrims	3. Who Were the Pilgrims?	**Underground Railway**	27. Last Stop on Underground Railroad
Reconstruction	37. New View of Reconstruction	**Washington, George**	9. General George Washington
Religion	3. Who Were the Pilgrims? 5. Anne Hutchinson 12. American Revolution: War of Religion?	**Western Expansion**	22. Lone Star Rising 23. Eden Ravished 28. Cry Was: Go West Young Man
Slavery	14. Slaves and Freedmen 15. Lives of Slave Women 27. Last Stop on Underground Railroad 29. Dred Scott 35. Black Families in the American Civil War 36. What Did Freedom Mean?	**Women**	5. Anne Hutchinson 15. Lives of Slave Women 24. Act One 26. War Against Demon Rum 27. Last Stop on Underground Railroad

The New Land

The year 1992 will mark the 500th anniversary of Christopher Columbus's landing on a Caribbean island he named San Salvador. His and other voyages during the fifteenth and sixteenth centuries opened up what was to Europeans a "new world." Early explorers came in search of direct routes to Asia, or to acquire the fabulous treasures of gold, silver, and jewels, rumored to be there for the taking. Only later did people, mostly English, come to create permanent settlements in the wilderness. These early colonies were little more than tiny outposts dotting the coastlines.

What was new to Europeans was very old to native inhabitants. Referred to by explorers as "Indians," these peoples lived in diverse cultures ranging from the "advanced" civilizations of the Incas and Aztecs to nomadic groups possessing only the most primitive tools and weapons.

For Europeans the New World opened possibilities undreamed of before: from finding the Garden of Eden to the Fount of Eternal Youth. In "A New World," Arturo Uslar Pietri describes how the explorations changed the course of history. Aware of the cruelties, disease, and devastation Europeans visited upon native inhabitants, which he discusses, he nonetheless celebrates Columbus's achievement. "For with the active merging of four continents and the major oceans," he writes, "history itself took on a universal dimension."

Although a latecomer to the New World, England became more involved than other nations in settling North America. One early effort, as described in "Roanoke Lost," was originally intended as a base for privateering against Spanish ships. Forty years later the Pilgrims came in order to build a separate religious community that would conform to their idea of early Christianity. "Who Were the Pilgrims?" discusses the many myths that later arose about this small community. Religion played an important part in the colonies, as shown in "Anne Hutchinson: 'A Verye Dangerous Woman.'"

Land was abundant in the New World, but there was a chronic shortage of people to work it. One means of solving the problem was to import slaves from Africa; another widely used way was to employ "indentured" servants. In return for the cost of transportation, food, clothing, and housing, needy people contracted to work for a stipulated period in the colonies, after which they would be free. "Colonists in Bondage: Indentured Servants in America" describes how this system worked.

Regional differences have affected the United States throughout its history. The final reading in this unit, "Remapping American Culture," discusses a provocative book that attributes many of these differences to successive waves of immigration from England, northern Ireland, and Scotland during colonial days. Immigration from other areas has since had an impact, but the original folkways still exert strong influence.

Looking Ahead: Challenge Questions

How did European views about the use of land differ from those of Native Americans? How did these differences lead to conflict?

Evaluate the impact of European conquest on native groups, and also its implications for the future of world history.

Many myths about the Pilgrims have made their way into American history. What needs did these myths satisfy?

Why did early colonial leaders try to impose religious conformity?

Why was the practice of indenture replaced by slavery?

What regional characteristics are used to explain the thesis that waves of immigration from various parts of England established lasting cultural and political patterns?

A New World

... and a new era in world history

In 1992 the fifth centenary of an event that had an enormous influence on the history of the modern world will be commemorated, notably in the Spanish- and Portuguese-speaking countries: the arrival of Christopher Columbus and his Spanish crew, on 12 October 1492, in a land which would later be named "America". On that day a far-reaching process of cultural cross-fertilization was set in motion, which, although marked by the violence of conquest and colonization, was to create a new reality, justly called the "New World", that would radically transform the whole planet. The **Unesco Courier** *will be devoting more space to this theme in later issues; meanwhile we publish an evocation of that new world by the Venezuelan writer Arturo Uslar Pietri.*

Arturo Uslar Pietri

ARTURO USLAR PIETRI, *Venezuelan writer and politician, taught Latin-American literature at Columbia University, United States, before serving as his country's ambassador to Unesco and as a member of the Organization's Executive Board. His wide range of published works includes the historical novels* El camino de el dorado *(1947) and* Oficio de difuntos *(1974); the short story collections* Red *(1936) and* Pasos y pasajeros *(1965); and essays among which are* La otra América *(1974),* Fantasmas de dos mundos *(1979) and* Giotto y compañía *(1987).*

IN less than five years' time, day will break on 12 October 1992. The Earth will come into view as the Sun progressively casts its light on a succession of regions, climates and peoples until the planet has come full circle. This is what, symbolically, has happened in the course of five centuries since that day when, with the first light, a new age dawned in the life of man.

It all began with the most auspicious of voyages: three sailing ships, with their eighty-eight crew members and a man of vision who, without knowing it, was trailing the destiny of the world behind him. Their initial reaction was one of mild surprise, but the Europeans soon came to realize that new lands and new peoples had been discovered. They did not know the extent of what they had found, and even today it is an effort for us to grasp the full significance and magnitude of the event. Some considerable time was to elapse before they perceived that they were dealing with a new continent that had never been known in Europe before. Christopher Columbus, the "admiral of the ocean sea", thought that he had found the western route to the Indies; he was searching for Asia and was carrying letters for Prester John, the legendary ruler of the East.

When we speak of the discovery of the Americas, we think of the first fleeting impression which it conjured up in the minds of the Europeans. What actually happened—and this came to be realized as one surprise followed another—was that a new age had begun. The things that Europeans saw or thought they saw, the things they sought and found, the things that were coming to an end or were only just beginning, all represented a new age for mankind as a whole.

The news of the discovery spread like a revelation: it stimulated people's imaginations and gave the humanists grounds for rediscovering the remote myths of classical Antiquity. No document had more influence on the turn taken by the European mind than the letter written by Columbus recording the birth of a new era. The immeasurable magnitude of the discovery was unfurled step by step—from the Antilles, with their mythological name, it ranged over the Costa Firme (or mainland), the Darién isthmus, the marvel of the Pacific seaboard, the conquest of Mexico and Peru, the search for El Dorada, the circumnavigation of the globe, and the control of the two immense seas surrounding the new and prodigious land.

It took a long time to learn what the Europeans had found, if indeed we have ever really succeeded in learning: it may have been the Earthly Paradise, the long-lost Golden Age of Greek mythology; or it may have been the Amazons they were looking for on the world's largest river and on the vast sun-lit coast which they called California.

What they above all discovered was the boundless possibilities of the imagination. There emerged from the writings of Columbus, Amerigo Vespucci and Pedro Mártir de Anglería not only the promise of an inexhaustible source of novelty but an irresistible invitation to engage in intellectual creation. In the end, it was to prove possible to find everything that people had ever dreamt of: from the Garden of Eden to the headless men; from the lost tribes of Israel to the imaginary city of Manoa, resplendent with gold and precious stones; from hallucinogenic plants to the Fount of Eternal Youth.

The Old World meets the New

That day marked the start of a new mutation of the Western world. The great culture which had slowly evolved and spread from the Mediterranean to the Baltic and was steeped in the fertile mix composed of the Greek, Latin and Judeo-Christian heritages, took a giant stride to the far shore of the *mare tenebrosum*, in order to embark on a new stage in its immense creative movement. The Iberians in South America and the Anglo-Saxons in the North, together with the Spaniards, Englishmen, Frenchmen, Dutchmen and Danes who converged on the open space of the Caribbean and turned it into a strange *mare nostrum*, all brought with them an image of Europe that was to change its appearance and significance. In the North, the narrowly circumscribed transplantation of the Puritan colonies was to predominate, whereas in the South there was an unrestricted and mutually rewarding coming-together of different heritages and cultures.

The very same line that had divided the Old World into two spheres of Christianity, with differing conceptions of man and his destiny, was carried over to the other hemisphere, complete with the differences and conflicts emerging from European history between the Protestant North and the Catholic South, between a pragmatic conception of life dedicated to work, thrift and peace-loving virtues and another conception, dazzled by the call of heroism, the tragic and adventurous sense of life, and contempt for passive servility. In the North, they went patiently about their work, sow-

ing the seeds from which Montreal, Ottawa, New York, Chicago and Los Angeles would one day spring. In the South, cities, kingdoms, universities, palaces and convents were to be created in an open-minded attitude to the mixing of cultures, from which a new form of community was to emerge.

What came into being was not so much a new Spain or a new Portugal as a new dimension of the historical estate in a new setting and with different protagonists. At the beginning of the eighteenth century, the New World was that which had been formed in Ibero-America, with which Europe was not very familiar and which it did not readily understand. It was a new society situated not only on one shore of the common sea, but on both shores. It was a community that was to transform the common heritage and to have an influence on its component parts on either side of the Atlantic. The day the King of Portugal set up his court in Rio de Janeiro, it became quite clear that such a community existed, that it did not have a privileged focal point, and that it was consistent with a new age. Had it been possible to carry out the plan put forward by the Count of Aranda,[1] or some such similar plan, the traumatic rift of independence would not have occurred and the powerful affirmation of the Ibero-American community would not have been retarded for more than a century.

The community was created by a growing pattern of exchanges and mutual influence between its two component parts, ranging from mental attitudes and legal systems to customs, diet, the economy, society and the concept of identity.

The Earth becomes one

Had the voyage merely involved the discovery of new lands and peoples, it would not have had such enormous consequences. Many irrevocable changes took place at that "watershed" date, which was also the starting-point for many other changes that are still taking place today. The time when mankind lived separate existences came to an end and a comprehensive view of the planet was obtained for the first time. The cosmography of Ptolemy collapsed; the *mare tenebrosum* became a highway; the centre of the world was shifted from the Mediterranean to the Atlantic; the entire globe was covered by sea routes; and the Earth became one. It has frequently been said that this represented the beginning of a new era in world history, but it is necessary to go further, for with the active merging of four continents and the major oceans, history itself took on a universal dimension.

People came from every imaginable place, attracted by the promise of the immense discovery. The historian Gonzalo Fernández de Oviedo, who saw them

arrive, had this to say: "Here, none of the languages spoken in all those parts of the world where there are Christians are missing, whether it be Italy, Germany, Scotland or England, or whether they be Frenchmen, Hungarians, Poles, Greeks, Portuguese or all the other peoples of Asia, Africa and Europe."

Not only were the great European powers stirred into action in order to exploit the new opportunities, but trade also started with the Chinese ports across the Pacific, in the bid to extend the dialogue between civilizations. Africa, isolated as it was and with no means of taking action on its own, suffered harshly from the discovery. In the space of one century, millions of Africans, bringing their cultural background with them, were to be transported and unjustly put to work performing the basic tasks required to create a new reality.

It was at this time, in fact, that the New World began to steer a new course, not only in the narrow sense used by the humanists of the period, but also in two other real and creative senses that were complementary to one another. There was certainly a New World of the Americas which took shape in a centuries-long development involving the taking-over of the land, the existence side by side of peoples and cultures, the mixing of races and mental attitudes, and the adaptation to new places and new partners in dialogue.

From that moment onwards, neither Europeans, nor Indians nor Africans could go on being the same as they had been. A far-reaching process of cross-fertilization, especially of a cultural nature, was set in motion. The end product was not—and could not be—European, neither could it be Indian or African. To varying degrees, the three cultures were combined with one another and blended to create a different pattern which, although still not fully recognized or precisely defined today, was reflected in all the forms assumed by people's lifestyles, attitudes and relationships.

Whenever a world is created there is something of a cataclysm, whether it be the "Big Bang" of modern astrophysics or the global revolutions of our time. There was a great deal that was cataclysmic about the creation of the New World, what with the bloody struggles, the violence, the heart-breaking rifts, the unaccustomed circumstances in which people were transplanted and had to adapt, the ordeals of living and dying, and the examples of cruelty and magnanimity. Yet they all contributed to a development lasting less than a century in which people of differing and alien origins came to create a new human scheme of things against the huge and varied backcloth of a new continent.

When Cortés, with blood-curdling conviction, tore down the representations of the Aztec deities from their altars and put the cross and the image of the Virgin Mary in their place, he engaged in an act of the most physical and spiritual violence. His attitude, which we are now reluctant to understand, was one that was to spell out the singular nature of the process by which the New World came to be formed. The discoverers did not come to live side-by-side with the Indians or to superimpose their own system: they came to lay foundations, to replant and to create. The priest and contemporary historian Lucas Fernández de Piedrahita spoke with terrible candour of the unwavering intention to "stamp out the idolatry that has been deeply rooted in the barbarous practices of the natives for so many centuries".

The creation of the New World was indeed cataclysmic and a new human scheme of things was to emerge from it. In less than a century, the Spanish, the Indians and the Africans all became brothers in Christ and the spiritual descendants of Abraham, Moses and the Fathers of the Church. This was to form the main basis for the striking cultural unity which spiritual communion was to impart to this new incarnation born of old and separate cultures. The New World, with all its specific features and nuances, became Christian and part of Western culture, which would define its identity and destiny for ever more. Thus was formed the life-enhancing clay from which "the Inca" Garcilaso de la Vega, Simón Bolívar, Benito Juárez and Rubén Darío were to spring.

Far-reaching transformations

The date of 12 October 1492 marked not only the beginning of a New World in the Americas, but also that of the most far-reaching change ever experienced by the rest of the planet in its entire history. The historians of science, thought, economics and society have all stressed the immensity of these new developments. The avalanche of precious metals from the Americas, for example, was behind the rise of capitalism and present-day monetary systems, in that the thousands of tons of gold and silver shipped back went beyond the confines of medieval-style banking transactions and created a transnational financial market.

Population growth in Europe, which was instrumental in bringing about major urban concentrations, national consolidation and the subsequent development of the industrial revolution, had its roots not only in worldwide market expansion but also in the fact that the famines which had decimated the Europeans for centuries had finally come to an end. The role played in this development by some of the non-human factors arising out of their discovery of the Americas, such as maize and potatoes, was

decisive. Eating habits and social practices alike were transformed by the introduction of tobacco, cocoa, rubber, quinine and Brazilwood. The red macaw and the plumed Indian featuring in the multi-coloured decors of the baroque painters are a spectacular manifestation of this definitive presence.

The novel concept of the Americas and all that it implied was to change the science and thinking of the West. In their view of the planet and the cosmos, people had to abandon Ptolemy's ingenuous cosmological mechanism in favour of the heliocentric conception of the planetary system, with all its far-reaching consequences. The new climates, the new skies, the reality of the Antipodes, the inexhaustible variety of plant and animal life never seen before, were all to give rise to doubts and debate and to lead to further questions, such as whether those animals had not been known in Noah's Ark and, if they had, how they had come to disappear from the Old World.

The advances made in science in the nineteenth century have their roots in the Americas. The book by Acosta,[2] Alexander von Humboldt's travels, and the arrival of the *Beagle*—the boat on which Charles Darwin made his celebrated voyage—off the coast of South America and the Galapagos, were all key background material for Darwin's formulation of the doctrine on the origin of species.

'Utopia is American'

The ideas of independence and revolution that have dominated the history of the modern world have their origin in the experience of the Americas. Utopia is American. Columbus's letter and the publications of the first chroniclers of the discovery were to come as a shock to European thought. The devastating impact of that scarcely understood revelation can be seen in the essays of Michel de Montaigne.

Thomas More's famous book *Utopia* (1516) is plainly the ideological consequence of this first view of the American world. More, the Chancellor-saint, looked with disgust on the England of his time. Poverty, injustice, war, hatred and power struggles had only served to spread misfortune everywhere. His main character, Raphael Hythloday, confirmed what Columbus and Vespucci had already announced, namely that there was another world where people lived in peace, plenty, justice and honesty. The conclusion was inevitable: the Europeans had in many ways departed from the true path and had been condemned to live in an abominable form of society.

In this connection, some years ago Paul Hazard, the historian of ideas, spoke authoritatively of the crisis of European consciousness, which is nothing but the harrow-

ing and painful reflection on their own situation inspired in Renaissance thinkers by the vision of the "noble savage". This fundamental contradiction between what exists and what is possible was to feed the revolutionary thinking which culminated in the Enlightenment with Jean-Jacques Rousseau and the Encyclopaedists and with the great and bloody baptismal rite of the French Revolution. In this sense, Robespierre, Marx, Lenin and Mao can be said to have followed earlier thinking on the discovery of the Americas.

There has been an overwhelming tendency to look upon the history of political ideas from the European standpoint. Yet it was on American soil that the idea of independence was raised for the first time and that reference was first made in a fundamental historical document [Declaration of Independence, 1776] to the self-evident truths: "... that all men are created equal, that they are endowed by their Creator with certain unalienable Rights, that among these are Life, Liberty and the pursuit of Happiness". It was likewise on American soil, in the Preamble to the world's first written Constitution—that of the United States of America—that there first appeared a figure whose unwonted presence was asserted by a phrase that was subsequently to echo as far as the furthest corners of the Earth: "We the people ... "

There is nothing that exists today by way of civilization, politics or thought that is not a consequence, in some way or another, of the great event which had Columbus's voyage as its point of departure, whether it concerns the arts or the sciences, ideologies or customs, or the concept of the universe and the concept of mankind itself.

If the discovery is confined to only one of its aspects, or if it is simplified into only one of the infinite number of facets which it has continually displayed over half a millennium, then it is condemned not to be understood. If it is reduced to the elementary idea of a discovery and conquest, then it will be mutilated and deformed until it becomes unrecognizable. There can be no denying that there was a discovery in a fleeting and piecemeal fashion, and that there was also a conquest, with all its terrifying inhuman—or perhaps only too human—consequences. But this was only part, albeit a necessary and inevitable part, of an immense process that has no parallel in history.

Matters of conscience

There was a bloody stage of conquest, and that word alone conjures up frightful images in the memories of peoples, especially among the weakest. However, while it was unfortunately not the first time, nor the last, that one nation has imposed itself by force on others, it was, outstandingly, the one exemplary occasion in history when a conquering power stopped in its tracks to give thought to the legitimacy and justice of what it was doing.

The debate that took place in Valladolid in 1550 and the royal edicts stemming therefrom[3] represented the first occasion on which a major power called a halt to its expansion in order to resolve the issues of justice and conscience entailed by that fact. It was on that occasion that a proclamation was made for the first time from the highest level of the State, to the effect that "all peoples are nations" (Bartolomé de las Casas), that all nations have rights that have to be respected, and that they form an international community. What was no less important was the fact that because they were men, those remote and unknown Indians had the same rights as the conquistadors. Is there any human being on Earth today who would be prepared to disavow and reject this heritage?

Mankind as a whole should be convened to commemorate with proper dignity the fifth centenary of that symbolic date and all its implications, without exception and without confining it to only one of its aspects.

By the time 12 October 1992 comes, the enlightened words verging on blasphemy which the cleric and historian Las Casas wrote to the Emperor Charles V may not sound so much like hyperbole: "The best thing since the creation of the world, other than the incarnation and death of Him who created it, is the discovery of the Indies, which is why they are called the New World."

1. At the end of the eighteenth century, this reform-minded Spanish governor proposed that three vassal but self-governing kingdoms—Mexico, Peru and Tierra Firme—be created in Spanish America, with only Cuba, Puerto Rico and some points of the mainland continuing to be colonies.
2. *Historia natural y moral de las Indias* (1590; *Natural and Moral History of the Indies*, 1604), the earliest survey of the New World and its relation to the Old, by the Spanish theologian, missionary and historian José de Acosta.
3. In 1550 the Emperor Charles V convoked a meeting of theologians, the Council of Valladolid, to discuss the questions raised by the anti-colonial writings of Las Casas. One of the most positive outcomes of the debate was a revised version of the "Laws of the Indies". This legislation, extremely liberal for its day and intended to protect the American Indians from colonial excesses, was not always enforced in practice. *Editor.*

Roanoke Lost

Four hundred years ago the first English settlers reached America. What followed was a string of disasters ending with the complete disappearance of a colony.

Karen Ordahl Kupperman

Karen Ordahl Kupperman is Associate Professor of History at the University of Connecticut. Her book Roanoke: The Abandoned Colony *was published by Rowman & Allanheld.*

Roanoke is a twice-lost colony. First its settlers disappeared—some 110 men, women, and children who vanished almost without a trace. Ever since, it has been neglected by history, and few Americans of today are aware that the English tried and failed to colonize this continent long before the Pilgrims landed at Plymouth. Four hundred years ago, between 1584 and 1587, Sir Walter Raleigh and his associates made two attempts to establish a settlement on Roanoke Island, in North Carolina's Outer Banks. One colony returned to England; the other disappeared in America. The effort at plantation was a dismal failure; later colonies survived, however, partly because of Roanoke's costly lessons.

Sir Walter Raleigh was a rising young man of thirty in 1584, when he decided to found the first English colony in North America. He was a younger son of a distinguished but impoverished family, and his parents had managed to give him the education of an aristocrat. He had spent his youth serving in the French civil wars, had seen action in England's brutal effort to solidify its control over Ireland, and had been commander of a ship in the fleet of Sir Humphrey Gilbert, his much older half brother.

By 1581, when he was twenty-seven, Raleigh was a veteran of the kind of experiences that had prepared countless other sons of the gentry for lives as country gentlemen. But at this point he was noticed by Queen Elizabeth, and he became a member—for a while the most important member—of a charmed circle of young men who played her lovestruck suitors. Raleigh was a master at the punning word games she loved. His poetry was prized, and his exotic good looks, enhanced by flamboyant clothes, made him stand out. The queen loved him; most people found him too arrogant, "damnable proud," as John Aubrey wrote.

Becoming the queen's favorite meant wealth beyond imagining. Over the next several years Elizabeth bestowed on Raleigh land and houses all over England and Ireland. Moreover, she gave him monopoly control of the wine and woolen-cloth industries, and his agents raked off a percentage of the profits to subsidize his extravagant life.

In 1583 Sir Humphrey Gilbert died at sea, attempting to start a colony in Newfoundland, and Raleigh asked the queen to transfer to him his half brother's exclusive right to colonize in North America. In 1584, with his patent in hand, Raleigh sent two ships to reconnoiter the southern coast of North America.

That year was a turning point in Queen Elizabeth's foreign policy; it was no accident that Raleigh's colonizing activities began then, for that was when the growing animosity between Spain and England erupted into open war. The immense wealth flowing from its American possessions had helped make Spain the superpower of the sixteenth century; England was seen even by its own citizens as a scrappy underdog. Moreover, the English saw Spain, "the swoorde of that Antychryste of Rome," as the leader of an international conspiracy to crush Britain and restore it to papal control. Spanish agents were in fact active in the country, focusing their plans on the imprisoned Mary Queen of Scots; they assumed that an English majority loyal to the old religion would greet Spanish "liberators" with joy.

In 1584 these tensions came to a head. The Spanish ambassador, whose plotting had become intolerable, was expelled from England. The next year all English ships in Spanish harbors were seized. The breach was irreparable, and a sea war was on.

Elizabeth conducted it as she did her other enterprises: by issuing licenses and patents to private citizens. In theory, commissions to go after Spanish ships were strictly controlled; in practice, corruption allowed wide access to privateering licenses, and legalized piracy became big business for the next decade and a half, sometimes bringing in 10 percent of the nation's imports. Gentlemen like Raleigh, joining forces with merchants to field large fleets, saw themselves as patriots, and history has celebrated their exploits.

Though all Spanish ships were vulnerable, attention focused on the treasure fleet, heavily laden cargo ships that annually carried the wealth of the Indies to Spain. By the mid-1580s Spain was so overextended that this treasure was no longer a luxury. By seizing Spanish ships, English privateers could set themselves up for life and cripple the enemy at the same time.

Roanoke initially was planned purely to make preying on the treasure fleet easier. A base near the West Indies, yet hidden away, could make privateering a year-round occupation, even during fall and winter storms. Colonization, like privateering, was licensed by the government, but since each expedition had to pay its own way, a colony at Roanoke would never have been attempted without the tie to privateering. Spanish treasure partially repaid Roanoke's investors, yet privateering also killed the plantation and led to the tragedy of the Lost Colony.

Raleigh's reconnaissance fleet, commanded by Arthur Barlowe and Philip Amadas, was sent in April 1584. They followed the route normal at the time: south along the coast of Europe to pick up the trade winds off the Canaries and then west to the Caribbean and the coastal current that helped propel them northward. After several weeks of exploration around the Outer Banks, Amadas and Barlowe were sure they had found a perfect location for the new settlement: sheltered yet providing easy access to the treasure fleet's homeward path.

Barlowe, who wrote the official account of the voyage, described the land in the most glowing terms: "The soile is the most plentifull, sweete, fruitfull and wholesome of all the worlde." Though the expedition had done little real exploring or testing, Barlowe recklessly compared Roanoke to Eden: "The earth bringeth foorth all things in aboundance, as in the first creation, without toile or labour." In reality the Outer Banks are relatively infertile, and the location was a poor one for a settlement.

Even before the reconnaissance fleet returned, backers were being signed up for a full colony. Elizabeth gave the project many marks of favor. Though she declined to put government money behind it, she invested her own money and a ship and even allowed the territory to be called Virginia in her honor. She refused to let Raleigh go on such a dangerous voyage, so he chose his hotheaded cousin Sir Richard Grenville to command the expedition.

The composition of the fleet bearing the colony of 108 men, which sailed in April 1585, clearly indicated the investors' expectations: five large and two small ships carried almost three hundred sailors and as many soldiers. Such huge crews were a sure sign of an intention to go privateering: prize ships were to be boarded and conquered in hand-to-hand fighting and then sent home to England manned by the privateers.

The 1585 venture followed the same course as Amadas and Barlowe's but remained several weeks in the West Indies while the prospective colonists grew anxious about reaching Roanoke in time to build a settlement before winter. Ralph Lane, who was to be governor of the colony, quarreled so bitterly with Grenville that the admiral threatened to execute him for mutiny. At the end of June the fleet finally moved on.

As soon as the ships arrived off the Outer Banks, it became clear that the location was a mistake. The flagship was driven repeatedly against the shore and was almost lost, and most of the colonists' food supplies were destroyed. The inlet that gave access to Roanoke Island was so shal-

low and treacherous that only the tiny pinnaces could be taken through, and then only with extreme care. Medium-size ships could shelter along the Banks, but the largest vessels were forced to anchor several miles out to sea, exposed to dangerous storms.

It must have been a grim council that sat down to decide what to do. There is some evidence that Grenville and his entire fleet were supposed to stay and inaugurate the colony's use as a privateering base, but that was now clearly impossible. Grenville promised that he would bring supplies in the spring, just as soon as the Atlantic was safe, so Lane and his colonists agreed to stay, spending the winter looking for a better location and learning about the territory. The colonists set to work building a fort, and Grenville and his men went exploring on the Carolina mainland.

We know a great deal about the Carolina Algonquians, on whom the colonists were intruding, because Raleigh was a true Renaissance man whose scholarly interests were as important to him as fighting Spain and making money. He had sent along Thomas Hariot, a young scientist and mathematician recently graduated from Oxford, to study the land and its resources and make a full report on Indian culture. Amadas and Barlowe had returned from their reconnaissance with two Indians, named Manteo and Wanchese, and Hariot had spent a year learning their language and teaching them English. An artist named John White accompanied Hariot to Virginia to illustrate his findings.

Together, White and Hariot

Roanoke initially was planned purely to make preying on Spanish treasure ships easier.

created a remarkable record; their maps are said to be the most accurate done in America in the sixteenth century, and White's paintings of Indian life were not equaled before the advent of photography. They show strong, dignified Indians and a highly successful culture. Hariot's descriptions allow us to see that culture from the inside.

The coastal Carolina Algonquians were organized in tribal groupings consisting of several towns of approximately one to two hundred people each. The Roanoke Indians had their capital on the mainland opposite the island, under a werowance named Wingina. Werowance means "he who is rich," but the Indians' meaning of riches was different from the colonists'. The tribe's goods, including the novel European trade items, all flowed into the hands of the chief, but his role was redistributing, so that all shared the bounty. If he had tried to control the wealth, he would have lost his people's respect. Though he moved among his subjects in great state, the werowance lacked coercive power and led by moral authority alone.

Justice and war were also governed by a principle of balance. When an individual or a tribe sustained injury, redress was sought through compensation or the infliction of a similar injury. Warfare was therefore limited and controlled, and generosity was rewarded. Barlowe and Amadas had seen a vivid illustration of this principle in their first contact with the Roanokes. A single man approached their ships and

greeted them. He was taken aboard and given a hat and shirt and a taste of wine and meat. When he left, they saw him fishing a short way off; soon he returned, divided his catch into piles, and told the colonists in sign language that one pile was to go to each ship. He would not leave until he had reciprocated their hospitality.

Hariot was particularly interested in Indian religion, and his description allows us to understand some of their theology. The priest, a man chosen for his wisdom, was responsible for overseeing his people's relationship to the deity and maintaining the round of ceremonies that helped the crops grow. Another figure, whom White called the Flyer, was a much younger man, chosen for his magical powers, which derived from a personal relationship with a supernatural being. This conjurer wore a small black bird on the side of his head and a skin with an animal's face on his front. Because disease was thought to be caused by the vengeful spirits of improperly killed animals and because the conjurer had magical relationships with animals, he was considered able to effect cures. The Flyer probably represented an older, individualistic hunting cult that was being edged out by the newer, more abstract religion of the priest.

The English were pleased to find that the Indians lived in towns organized around village greens and surrounded by cornfields just like familiar towns at home. Yield was, to Hariot's mind, almost mi-

raculous: "at the least two hundred London bushelles . . . [whereas] in England fourtie bushelles of our wheate yeelded out of such an acre is thought to be much." Corn was planted in hills, with beans growing up the stalks; the beans, with their nitrogen-fixing properties, fertilized the corn as it grew, and the two crops eaten together formed superior protein. There is incontrovertible evidence of the efficiency of Indian agriculture: the Carolina Algonquians had on hand enough surplus food to keep more than one hundred colonists alive during the winter of 1585–86.

Praise for Indian society did not imply a vision of coexistence; even Europeans like Hariot who were truly interested in the natives saw themselves as bringing the priceless gifts of Christianity and civilization. Indian sophistication simply meant that the job of conversion would be easier; the natives would see the superiority of English culture and spontaneously choose it for themselves.

The Indians showed interest in Hariot's magnet, compass, and books and in the colonists' guns and "spring clocks that seeme to goe of themselves," and according to Hariot, they assumed such technology was a divine gift. When many Indians died of European diseases to which they had no immunity while the English did not suffer, the natives saw the hand of a powerful god at work.

The Indians were not, however, ready to give up their own culture wholesale. Like

Indians all over America, the Carolina Algonquians picked and chose from the Europeans those items of technology, particularly metal tools, that made tasks within their own economy easier; they wanted to enhance their way of life, not relinquish it. Moreover, it is easy for us to exaggerate the apparent superiority of European technology; what the Indians saw at Roanoke was a large party of men who were so helpless that Gov. Ralph Lane at one point accused the Indians of making war simply by cutting off all contact with the English.

While the Roanoke colonists were learning about the Indians, they were revealing a great deal about themselves. The Indians must have been deeply disturbed by what they saw. Almost as soon as the first colony arrived, in 1585, Grenville took his small boats and went exploring on the mainland. The explorers at one point discovered a silver cup missing from their baggage and returned to a village they had visited two days previously to demand its return. When they found that all the inhabitants had fled, they "burnt, and spoyled their corne, and Towne. . . ."

It is hard for us to understand why Grenville would have ordered an act so damaging to friendly relations—especially since the colonists, whose supplies had been destroyed in the accident to the flagship, would be totally dependent on the Indians until spring. His thinking rested on a view of human nature prevalent in that age: All relationships, even among

The English admired Indian society, but they did not entertain a vision of coexistence.

Europeans, were seen as involving domination and submission. The colonists revealed again and again their assumption that anyone who showed vulnerability would be a victim of treachery and would deserve it. Grenville thought that by exacting severe vengeance on those he suspected of stealing, he was protecting the colonists, not damaging their chances. And though the backers in England had counseled the colonists to win the Indians through loving kindness, they had ensured the policy of intimidation by sending over veterans of the Irish and continental wars as colonists. We will never know if a peaceful relationship might have been possible; it was not given a chance.

The English were also obsessed with control within their own settlement. The relation between leaders and the "meaner sort" was expected to be one of iron discipline; the rank-and-file colonists, whom Gov. Ralph Lane referred to as "wild men of mine own nation," would be mutinous if given a chance. Lane believed that the low rate of disease in his colony's year in America was a direct product of his "severely executed" discipline. We have veiled hints of trouble in the colony; apparently the taverns of England rang with complaints once the soldiers returned home, and Hariot pointed out that those who complained were men who had been disciplined in America.

Lane had three missions to accomplish during the winter:

to find a good base with a deepwater port; to find a passage to the Pacific, which was called the South Sea and was assumed to be just a few days' march to the west; and to find gold. He sent a party of men north to make a preliminary search for the privateering base they needed. These men spent the winter at Chesapeake Bay, meeting with many Indian leaders, and returned convinced that it would make a better location. The account of their activities is very brief; presumably Raleigh wanted to keep their findings away from competitors, though the excellence of Chesepeake Bay was already as well known to the Spanish as to the English.

Lane himself took on the other two jobs. He learned from Wingina, the Roanoke chief, of a large and powerful tribe to the west, the Choanokes, under Menatonon. Lane arrived at Menatonon's headquarters during a great council of tribes, which Wingina had said was being held to conspire against the English. Menatonon and his son were captured; the chief was held for two days, during which he and Lane held long conversations about the region. The governor was greatly impressed with Menatonon, who confirmed that Chesapeake Bay was the best site for an English base but warned that the Indians there would resist an incursion. Menatonon also described a rich mine on a huge body of water somewhere to the west.

Lane determined to travel west and find that fortune. He kept Menatonon's son prisoner to forestall treachery and

took a select party upriver. The inability of the English to deal with the wilderness quickly became apparent; the Indians along the route withdrew into the interior, and food ran out, forcing Lane to turn back. The English policy of overawing Indians and forcing their aid must have looked rather hollow by then.

Meanwhile, as spring came on, the Roanokes' food supply was stretched beyond endurance. Both Indians and English split up into small groups to live off the land, vastly increasing English vulnerability. At the same time, the goods traded to the Roanokes in return for their corn gave them unprecedented power to attract alliances with other tribes.

Spring brought the death of Wingina's brother Granganimeo, the man most friendly to the English in Roanoke councils; Wingina changed his name to Pemisapan, which implied a watchful, wary attitude. It may have been a war name. The colonists became convinced he was planning a conspiracy with other tribes to get rid of the settlement. Lane struck first, and Pemisapan died in an attack that began with the battle cry "Christ our victory!"

Though the immediate threat was ended, the colonists were desperate: there would be no harvest for weeks, and they could expect no Indian aid. A week after the death of Pemisapan, long after Lane had expected relief from home, his lookout sighted an English fleet; the colonists knew they were saved.

The fleet was that of Sir Francis Drake, who had been privateering in Spanish America almost as long as the settlers had been at Roanoke. He came expecting to make use of their base, but what he found was quite different: a colony in disarray and an anchorage that kept his ships two miles out to sea. He and Lane discussed the possibility of his leaving ships, men, and supplies so that Lane could continue his explorations over the summer, but a great storm so damaged Drake's fleet that he was forced to leave. The colonists all went with him. The sailor hosts were so anxious to get under way that most of the settlers' baggage, including Hariot's notes and specimens and many of White's drawings, was thrown overboard.

More than possessions were lost; three colonists on a mission into the interior were abandoned. Moreover, Drake had liberated a large force of African slaves and Indians from Spanish control, and they were apparently left behind to make room on the ships for the colonists. Raleigh's relief fleet finally arrived three weeks later, after a long diversion for privateering, and left a holding party of fifteen men in the deserted settlement. None of them was ever heard of again.

Once the colonists were safely back home, all agreed that a new site on Chesapeake Bay should be tried. Though farsighted men such as Thomas Hariot and the great promoter Richard Hakluyt argued for the development of identified American resources, the

The colonists became desperate. When Drake was forced to leave, they all went with him.

governor and many of his colonists were contemptuous of the possibilities of the new land unless gold was found. Lane now saw the land as a barrier and wrote that the best hope was for discovery of a passage through to the East. Potential backers saw clearly that all income so far had flowed from privateering.

Nonetheless, there were those who felt strongly that with a new site and the proper backing a colony could become self-sustaining and ultimately provide a rich trade for England. John White was preeminent among them. He and Thomas Hariot hoped their findings would help attract new backing. Hariot's *A briefe and true report of the new found land of Virginia*, a careful survey of resources, was published on its own in 1588 and with woodcuts of White's paintings in 1590.

Hariot's work must have circulated in manuscript before publication; by 1587 a new colonial venture had been set up, and White, the man who had worked hardest for it, was the new governor. Its promoters set out to correct all the obvious errors made in 1585, but the legacy of the first colony, particularly its connection with privateering, was to haunt the new effort and ultimately to destroy it.

Raleigh, with his estates and concerns all over England, was losing interest in running a colonial venture the future of which seemed dim. He encouraged White to organize a corporation in which the colonists themselves would take a leading role. The City of Raleigh, as the corporation was called, was to be governed by White and a board of directors known as the assistants, most of whom intended to emigrate. The leadership would be much less authoritarian than that of the earlier colony, and the settlement would be on Chesapeake Bay, on fertile land approachable by oceangoing ships—probably very near where Jamestown was to be founded in 1607.

The colonists—men, women, and children—were people with something to invest, at least to the extent of outfitting themselves for the journey. Each family was to receive five hundred acres in the new land, and they came to America planning to stay, to re-create English culture. There were seventeen women and nine children. Two of the women were so heavily pregnant that they gave birth within weeks of their arrival at Roanoke. Several of the families consisted of men and their sons; presumably mothers and other children were to join them later. In its population as well as in its corporate organization, the City of Raleigh pointed to the future: all successful colonies were built on this family-centered model.

The colony set out on three small ships in the spring of 1587. Simon Fernandes, a Portuguese navigator who was one of the corporation's assistants, was in charge of the voyage and saw no reason not to place top priority on privateering. Almost three months elapsed before the ship finally landed in America.

Shipboard life was miserable. Only the highest officers had bunks; ordinary seamen and passengers rolled up in blankets between decks. Rations were salt meat and fish and hardtack, with some oatmeal, butter, and cheese. The water and beer began to go bad after the first four weeks. During storms the passengers stayed belowdecks, where rats and cockroaches, stirred up by the ship's motion, scuttled over them. Vomit, feces, and urine mixed with the seawater leaking into the ship. The stench quickly became overpowering.

Also, the passengers' lives were in danger as long as their little fleet attacked other ships. White raged impotently at Fernandes, who gambled with the entire venture. Fernandes refused to take the colonists north to Chesapeake Bay and dumped them instead at Roanoke. According to White, the explanation from "our Simon" was that "the summer was farre spent" and he wanted to get back to privateering. But the ships stayed with the colonists for a month, until they were settled for the winter, and, in fact, Fernandes may have felt it was too late in the year to begin a wholly new settlement—the houses on Roanoke were still standing—and White may have been secretly pleased to be back on familiar ground.

Once the houses were cleaned up, the settlers began to assess their situation. From the beginning there was evidence of Indian hostility: not only were Grenville's men missing, but George Howe, one of the assistants, was killed when he went off alone to catch crabs. White decided to approach the Croatoans, Manteo's people, who had always been friendly. Manteo had made a second trip to England with Lane's men and had just now returned to his land with White's colonists.

The Croatoans, though fearful at first, welcomed the colonists and gave the delegation a feast. There were signs of tension, though: the Croatoans asked the colonists "not to gather or spill any of their corne, for that they had but little." They also hesitantly mentioned the fact that some of their people had been wounded when Lane's men mistook them for enemies, and they asked for some badge to indicate their friendly status.

The Croatoans confirmed what the colonists already knew—that the nearby mainland Indians were now implacably hostile and had been responsible for the fate of Grenville's holding party. Moreover, their description of the battle made clear the clumsiness of English military technology against Indian bowmen, who had moved nimbly among the trees while the English, with their cumbersome, slow-loading muskets, became standing targets.

The delegation asked Manteo's people to organize a meeting between the settlers and their enemies in one week. When no word came, the English, true to their view of human nature, saw it as a challenge they could not ignore. They decided to surprise the Roanokes at their mainland capital, Dasemunkepeuc, and avenge the deaths

The legacy of the first colony would haunt, and ultimately destroy, the second.

of George Howe and Grenville's men. The attack was a fiasco. The village was inhabited only by Croatoans, including women and children, who had moved in after the Roanokes had fled. The colonists thus offended their only friends while failing to prove that Indians could not kill Englishmen with impunity.

The colonists must have been heavyhearted as they observed the mariners cleaning and recaulking their ships for the return voyage. White said they kept busy writing letters and preparing "tokens" for family and friends back home. He proudly recorded the birth of his own granddaughter, Virginia Dare, the first baby born in America of English parentage, and noted that Margery Harvie was also delivered successfully. As the fleet's departure approached, the colonists grew fearful; they wanted to make sure that they were not forgotten and begged White to go along as their representative. He held out for days, fearing he would be accused of desertion, but finally agreed after getting the request in writing.

As soon as he was back in England, White rushed to Raleigh, and plans were laid for a great supply fleet of seven or eight ships to sail in the spring under Sir Richard Grenville. Raleigh arranged for the publication of Hariot's report to encourage investment. White devoted the winter to gathering the necessary supplies and more colonists. Everything was ready for an early departure.

Suddenly the connection with privateering intervened in the most fateful possible way: Spain decided to cut off harassment at the source, assembling the great Spanish Armada of one hundred and thirty ships manned by eight thousand sailors and nineteen thousand soldiers. Elizabeth and her advisers were afraid; the Privy Council announced that no ships capable of service in war were to leave England. Grenville's great fleet was diverted to defense, and throughout the summer of 1588 England focused on its own danger.

White alone continued to think exclusively of his colonists. He persuaded the authorities to free two tiny ships to take him and a few new settlers and supplies to Roanoke. But these little ships careered around the ocean, attacking other vessels. After two French ships had routed them, White's company felt lucky to limp back to England alive.

Early in 1589 the corporation backing Roanoke was reorganized again, and this time Raleigh signed over most of his rights. Additional investors were recruited, and they took a somewhat leisurely attitude toward the colony. Nothing was done all year. In 1590 the Privy Council, fearing a renewed attack by Spain on the homeland, issued another general stay of shipping. White, desperately impatient, managed to get some privateers an exemption if they would promise to take him to Roanoke.

Long weeks were spent preying on ships in the West Indies. Finally, in August 1591, two of the ships moved northward to the Outer Banks. When they finally anchored off Roanoke, White was excited to see smoke rising from the settlement. After several false starts they reached the island in their rowboats just as night fell. To reassure the colonists that they were a friendly party, they sounded a trumpet call and sang folk songs.

White and his companions were astounded to find the colony deserted. The fire had apparently been kindled by lightning. They concluded, though, that the settlers had clearly not gone away in distress. Everything left behind, including all of White's books and pictures and his armor, had been neatly buried. The colonists had left a message: CROATOAN was carved on a post, and CRO was found on a nearby tree. The governor recalled that before he had left, nearly three years earlier, the settlers had decided to try to go overland to a better location, so he was not downcast. The message had been planned, moreover, and there would have been a Maltese cross added if the colonists had left in distress. White was reassured that they were safe at Croatoan, "the place where Manteo was borne, and the Savages of the Island our friends."

White's next step, obviously, was to go to Croatoan for a joyful reunion. At this point nature once more intervened and crushed the last hope of seeing the colonists alive. The two ships were battered by a gale; then, as the anchor was being raised on White's vessel, the chain broke. A second anchor was lost in an attempt to prevent the ship from being driven aground. Only one anchor remained. Plans to replenish supplies in the West Indies and return in the spring were shelved when another storm blew the vessels to the east, and the party decided to head home. John White had made his last attempt to find his colonists. Years later he wrote of his hope that God would comfort them; he could do no more.

Raleigh's days of great power were almost over. His secret marriage in 1592 so enraged Elizabeth that she first imprisoned him and then exiled him from London. He began to concentrate his American schemes on Guiana, rumored to be the site of gold mines, hoping that a rich strike would restore him to royal favor. He made his first transatlantic voyage there in 1595 but found nothing. The next year his participation in the English attack on Cádiz earned him admittance to the queen's circle once again.

In 1603 Queen Elizabeth died, and the anti-Spanish policy died with her. Her successor, James I, the Stuart king of Scotland, wanted to avoid war at all costs and quickly signed a treaty with Spain. Privateering was now the work of outlaws. Raleigh had lost most of his fortune in his various ventures; he now lost everything. James, convinced that Raleigh was plotting against him, threw him into the Tower of London.

Raleigh was allowed contact with the outside world during his imprisonment and became famous as a scientist and writer. He was allowed

The Jamestown settlers heard rumors of people who might be the lost colonists of Roanoke.

to maintain a small herb garden and a laboratory, and many fashionable people, including Queen Anne, came to him for his "Great Cordial."

Finally he persuaded the king, who was deeply in debt, to allow him another chance to find his Guiana gold. The expedition, plagued by tropical sickness, failed, and contrary to royal instructions, some Spanish subjects were killed. Raleigh, on his return to England, was executed on the original treason warrant. He came to be seen as a martyr by those who opposed James I and his son Charles; when Charles was beheaded in 1649 by a victorious Parliament, Raleigh's vision of England's future greatness once more ruled.

Meanwhile, once privateering was closed off as an outlet, patriotic gentry and merchants poured money into colonization in America. In 1607 Jamestown was founded near Chesapeake Bay. Whereas Roanoke had had a few investors, Jamestown had hundreds. Many mistakes were made, there was great suffering in the new Virginia colony, and investors saw little or no return; but since this was all that prevented Spain from dominating the whole of America, investment and reinvestment poured in. Both Hariot and Raleigh lived to see Jamestown established; they must have reflected on how Roanoke might have done with such support. By the time Hariot died in 1621, tobacco was firmly established as Virginia's cash crop, and he surely drew satisfaction

from seeing an American product emerge triumphant. Local commodities were indeed America's gold.

The Jamestown settlers heard rumors of people who looked and dressed like them and hoped they could locate the lost colonists of Roanoke, whose twenty years' experience in the country could have been very useful. The story, as finally pieced together, was that most of White's settlers had made their way overland to Chesapeake Bay and had been taken in by the Chesapeake tribe. Powhatan, the father of Pocahontas, dominated many of the tribes in Jamestown's neighborhood but was resisted by the Chesapeakes. At about the time Jamestown was founded, he attacked and wiped out the Chesapeakes, including their English mem-

bers. This reconstruction was accepted by the Virginia Company, and historians believe it is probably near the truth.

Some part of the colony must have remained with the Croatoans so it could guide White and the supply fleets; the CROATOAN legend was meant to direct White to them. This party, like the main group, was never seen again. There were persistent rumors that some English people had escaped the attack on the Chesapeakes and were with other tribes. John Smith claimed that Powhatan showed him "divers utensils of theirs," and another Virginian, George Percy, reported seeing an Indian boy whose hair was "a perfect yellow." But that was all.

Who Were the Pilgrims?

Well, they weren't called Pilgrims, they wore colorful clothing, and Plymouth Rock wasn't "discovered" until 121 years after the fact. But when a nation needs a myth, it makes one.

Richard Ellison

Richard Ellison is an independent television producer.

THE MARE was the first to die. They led her to the edge of the pit and cut her throat. Then, as her forelegs buckled, they pushed her over the edge. Next came the cow, then the two goats. As for the sheep, it was unclear from the youth's description which ones were guilty; so the entire flock was paraded before him and he picked out the five. The two calves were killed next, followed by the turkey. Finally it came time for the young man himself.

Thus the law was fulfilled as it was written in Leviticus 20:15: *And if a man lie with a beast, he shall surely be put to death, and ye shall slay the beast.*

These executions were not carried out in biblical Palestine, or medieval Germany, or Spain under the Inquisition. The year was 1642, the place was Plymouth Colony, and the condemned sodomist was a Pilgrim's servant, a Scituate youth named Thomas Granger. Having been caught in flagrante delicto with the mare and having confessed his other unnatural amours, young Thomas was tried and convicted by a jury of fellow colonists.

It is hardly surprising that Granger was put to death for sodomy, although the sacrifice of his sexual partners— "no use made of any part of them"— was a very literal reading of scriptural law. It is surprising, however, that the incident has remained so obscure. The execution of Granger is one of the most graphic and dramatic scenes in Governor William Bradford's *Of Plym-*

outh Plantation, our most complete account of the Pilgrims' life, yet subsequent chroniclers have preferred to ignore the episode.

The Granger affair was simply not compatible with the Pilgrim myth. The story of the Pilgrims as we know it today—their creation of a nascent democracy, their feast with the Indians—was fashioned in the eighteenth and nineteenth centuries, much of it out of whole cloth. There is far more documented detail about Thomas Granger and his animals than about such well-worn tales as the landing on Plymouth Rock and Miles Standish's surrogate courtship of Priscilla Mullens. But white, Protestant, middle-class Americans, particularly those of the Victorian era, did not want to be reminded that their forebears' roots were in the Middle Ages. Nor do most of us. Indeed, the Pilgrim myth has far more to do with who we want them to be than who they really were.

IF THE PILGRIMS were to come back to Plymouth now, they would be astonished to discover that they are famous. Most history is written by winners, and the Pilgrims, after all, were losers in their battle for independence. By the late 1600s, they had been dominated, overshadowed, and eventually absorbed by Massachusetts—mere footnotes to the historians of Puritan Boston.

The notion of the Pilgrims as founding fathers and democratic nation-builders began after the Revolutionary War in a young country hungering for a democratic account of its genesis. Actually, Pilgrim history as recounted by Governor Bradford testifies to the

modest view they held of their place in the world. Their avowed purpose was quite simple: to construct a separate religious community conforming to their idea of the primitive Christian church.

The Pilgrims may have nudged their new land closer to nationhood, but they did so inadvertently while setting their sights on a better kingdom. "As one small candle may light a thousand, so the light here kindled hath shone unto many, yea in some sort to our whole nation" is one of the most-quoted passages in Bradford's history. He was referring, however, to the growth of Congregationalism, not nationalism.

Nevertheless, the idea of Manifest Destiny eventually became associated with the Pilgrims. The Mayflower Compact, an impromptu agreement drawn up to ward off incipient anarchy among the planters when their ship reached the shores of ungoverned New England instead of Virginia, was inflated into one of history's great democratic statements despite its emphasis on communal responsibilities rather than individual rights. And Bradford's *Of Plymouth Plantation,* written as a straightforward chronicle of his times, came to be compared— and not unfavorably—to the New Testament Gospels.

The *Mayflower* itself, a ship whose name Bradford never used and whose remains were scrapped in England, became as famous as Noah's ark. Plymouth Rock, also unmentioned by Bradford or any of his contemporaries, entered history in 1741, when Elder John Faunce, at ninety-five, took tearful farewell of a huge granite boulder on which, he said he had been told, his Pilgrim forebears first landed. Although exhaustive research has failed either to prove or disprove Faunce's account, that did not matter. As Tocqueville observed in *Democracy in America:* "The Rock has become an object of veneration in the United States. . . . Here is a stone which the feet of a few outcasts pressed for an instant; and the stone becomes famous; it is treasured by a great nation; its very dust is shared as a relic."

By the time Tocqueville wrote this, in the 1830s, the myth-making process was well advanced. Regular observance of Forefathers' Day—the local annual celebration of the Plymouth landing—began in 1769 (almost 150 years after the event itself). The historical record suggests that the Plymouth colonists did not become known as "Pilgrims" until a Forefathers' Day celebration in the 1790s.

And on Forefathers' Day 1820, the two hundredth anniversary of the *Mayflower* landing, Pilgrim hagiography got a big boost from Daniel Webster, considered the greatest orator of his time, who celebrated the Pilgrims with a rousing three-hour speech. Among many other things, he undertook to fill a lacuna in Bradford's history. This, according to Webster, is what the forefathers *ought* to have said as they stepped onto the famous rock: "If God prosper us, we shall here begin a work which shall last for ages. We shall plant here a new society, in the principles of the fullest liberty, and the purest religion; . . . the temples of the true God shall rise, where now ascends the smoke of idolatrous sacrifice." Generations of schoolchildren were compelled to recite portions of Webster's oration, which helped fix the impression of the Pilgrims as a people of unlimited horizons and grandiose objectives.

JUST AS THE YOUNG revolutionaries had transformed the Pilgrims into idealists with democratic yearnings, so the Victorians, flush with pride in their own industry, reinvented their forefathers as divinely blessed capitalists. What the Victorians managed to ignore was that, to the Pilgrims, material success had spelled spiritual failure. As Bradford saw it, progress was "that subtle serpent" who "slyly wound in himself

---

The Victorians, flush with pride in their own industry, reinvented the Pilgrims as divinely blessed capitalists

---

under fair pretences of necessity" to weaken the bonds of the loving community. When a portion of the Plymouth congregation moved to Cape Cod, Bradford thought "that it was not for want or necessity so much that they removed as for the enriching of themselves." He went on, plaintively: "And thus was this poor church left, like an ancient mother grown old and forsaken of her children, . . .left only to trust in God. Thus, she that had made many rich became herself poor."

While some of our best nineteenth-century writers, including Hawthorne, Thoreau, and Twain, indulged in Puritan-bashing, politicians and the popular press continued to romanticize the Pilgrims. The legend was articulated in painting, souvenirs, advertisements, fanciful images (the "stern and rock-bound coast" of Felicia Hermans's famous hymn "The Landing of the Pilgrim Fathers"), and poetry, most notably Henry Wadsworth Longfellow's "The Courtship of Miles Standish."

As the myth took on greater momentum, it combined nationalistic and Anglo-Saxon Protestant sentiments with straightforward ancestor worship. Monuments to the Pilgrim Fathers accumulated. The Rock, which was moved several times, was protected by an elaborate stone canopy (replaced in 1921 by the present granite portico). The national Monument to the Forefathers—a pedestal topped by a thirty-six-foot figure personifying Faith, with Morality, Education, Law, and Liberty at her feet—was completed in the 1880s.

Not to be outdone, nearby Duxbury—where Miles Standish, John Alden, and others had moved early in the history of Plymouth—erected a monument to the doughty captain. And Provincetown, where the *Mayflower* first dropped anchor, belatedly put up the tallest of the Pilgrim monuments, a campanile more than 250 feet high. President Theodore Roosevelt laid the cornerstone, and President William Howard Taft dedicated the tower.

Meanwhile, the popular culture was creating its own store of Pilgrim monuments. The Landing on the Rock was repeated through every conceivable medium, including plates and mugs. Fair Priscilla, comely Alden, brave Standish, and studious Bradford were represented again and again (although no portrait of any of them exists). And as genealogy flourished, more and more Americans joined the ranks of the *Mayflower* descendants.

To be sure, no sooner did the myths triumph than they were challenged. Historian Charles Beard gave a sardonic welcome to Pilgrim-inspired oratory at the tercentenary of the landing, in 1920: "We shall hear again how it was the Puritans who created on these shores representative and democratic republics, wrested the sword of power from George III, won the Revolutionary war, and freed the slaves. It has ever been thus."

Such reassessments had no immediate impact on popular representations of the Pilgrims, but the altered atmosphere of the 1920s gave impetus to a scholarly effort to see the forefathers less nostaligically and not project backward upon them modern values and concerns. It received artistic expression in Stephen Vincent Benét's *Western Star:* "In fact, there were human beings aboard the Mayflower/Not merely ancestors."

THE EFFORT to understand the Pilgrims as human beings rather than ancestors distinguishes revisionist Pilgrim scholars from the traditionalists, and recent scholarship has radically altered the "living museum" at Plimoth Plantation.

The plantation was begun in the 1940s as an attempt to replicate the physical colony on a site similar to the original. Houses were built, furnished with donated objects, and peopled with mannequins. By the late 1960s historical and archaeological research began to reveal that the Pilgrims' concepts of time, space, privacy, childhood, and individuality were as different from ours as their belief in an earth-centered universe and their fears of vapors, comets, and witchcraft.

These discoveries led to changes in the plantation, including a decision to dispense with the mannequins and put real people in the village. Today, the Pilgrims at the plantation, called "interpreters," undergo intensive training based on two decades of research into many aspects of seventeenth century society. They wear the clothing and are taught to use the implements, speak the language, and, to the greatest extent possible, think the thoughts of specific individuals who were in the colony in 1627.

Meanwhile, other scholars have worked to place the Pilgrims in the context of America's spiritual history. Some see them as the initiators of a tradition of religious fervor that can be traced through the revivalist movement of the mid-1700s to today's moral majoritarians, some of whom might approve of the sentence passed on Thomas Granger and his animals in 1642. Others see them as the country's first utopians, forerunners of the commune dwellers of the 1960s.

And yet, despite scholarship that might have added ambiguity and complexity to our picture of the Pilgrims, most Americans have continued to see them as they were seen in the nineteenth century. Then, as now, tradition dressed the Pilgrims in sober black, with white collars, wide-brimmed hats, and buckled shoes, although their actual apparel was much more varied and colorful. Tradition moved the Pilgrims up the social scale and converted the *Mayflower* descendants into a native elite, although their origins were humble.

NO PART OF the Pilgrim myth is more appealing to the heart than the notion of an easy harmony between Pilgrims and Indians, romantically symbolized by a feast at Thanksgiving, yet no part is more unreliable. The Pilgrims did want to live at peace with the Indians—but only on Pilgrim terms. The give-and-take between the two cultures was all in one direction—toward the

Daniel Webster gave the myth a big boost by suggesting what the Pilgrims **ought** *to have said when they stepped onto the famous rock.*

destruction of the Indian way of life and the domination of the European. When the Pilgrims felt threatened by a northern Massachusetts tribe, for instance, a company under Miles Standish massacred seven of its leaders. Despite a gentle reprimand from their minister, the Pilgrims believed themselves divinely justified. Moreover, they assumed that God, rather than European fur traders and fishermen, had brought the plague that nearly wiped out the coastal Indian tribes, clearing the way for English settlement. They took literally God's injunction in Genesis 1:28: "Be fruitful and multiply, and fill the earth, and subdue it, and have dominion over the fish of the sea and over the fowl of the air, and over every living thing that moveth upon the earth."

As one of the leading Pilgrims put it, the Indians "do but run over the grass, as do also the foxes and wild beasts." From that it was easy to decide that they should be subjected to English rule.

According to tradition, the Indians fell easily into two categories. There were the good ones, like Squanto, who helped the Pilgrims, and there were bad ones, like Wituwamet, who opposed them and lost his head for it. The reality, of course, was that the Indians led lives every bit as complex as the Pilgrims, sometimes more so. Squanto, for instance, was familiar with the world in a way most Pilgrims

could never hope to be. Six years before the Pilgrims landed at Plymouth, Squanto had been abducted to Spain in an effort to sell him as a slave, rescued by priests, and spirited to England, where he lived for three years and learned to speak English.

The Indians have left few recorded voices, but the surviving ones reveal a sad understanding of the threat to their way of life. From the Narragansett sachem Miantonomo we have this: "These English having gotten our land, they with scythes cut down the grass, and with axes fell the trees; their cows and horses eat the grass, and their hogs spoil our clam banks, and we shall all be starved."

Whether it was called God's will, Manifest Destiny, progress, or civilization, the march went on to almost universal applause. Few observers had the foresight of Swedish botanist Pehr Kalm, who wrote of the settlers as cultivators: "In a word, the corn-fields, the meadows, the forests, the cattle, et cetera are treated with great carelessness. . . . This kind of agriculture will do for some time; but it will afterwards have bad consequences, as every one may clearly see."

In glaring hindsight from the end of the twentieth century, everyone now sees that the Indians' way of relating to the environment had value, and we have only begun to measure the consequences of three and a half centuries of carelessness. American Indians and sympathizers now gather annually around a statue of Massasoit, the Wampanoag sachem who made a peace with the Pilgrims when he might have driven them into the sea. The statue looks down on Plymouth Rock. The demonstration, held on Thanksgiving, is called the National Day of Mourning.

Colonists in Bondage:
Indentured Servants in America

Barbara Bigham

A ship docked at a Virginia harbor in 1635, and from its decks emerged nearly two-hundred newcomers from England, among them twenty-five-year-old Thomas Carter. For some the voyage had cost over £5 sterling. For others, the price was higher still: several years of their lives. Carter, like thousands of other penniless Europeans, had sold himself into bondage as an indentured servant to pay his passage to the colonies. Once there, he lived the life of a virtual slave—the property of his master. But when his indenture was over, he became a free man, and with his "freedom dues" of some clothes and tools, he worked to rise above his humble beginnings and serve as a respected member of the community. Eventually, he had four servants indentured under him at his estate in Isle of Wight County, Virginia. His descendants took an active part in colonial affairs and went on to fight in the Revolution. Some were involved in noble pursuits, others in scandalous incidents, and one—a ninth-generation grandson—became the thirty-ninth president of the United States.

Few Germans arriving in America under indenture knew the English language. This indenture, written in German, is dated 1736. Courtesy of the Pennsylvania Historical and Museum Commission, Harrisburg, Pennsylvania.

Land was plentiful in the New World, and fertile, but without a large number of laborers to fell trees and work the soil, it was as useless as a desert. Few new settlers could afford to hire a work force of free men, nor could they afford to buy slaves. Of the several schemes employed to entice workers to the colonies, none worked so well as the system of indentured servitude, which established itself almost as soon as the first colonists landed.

The earliest surviving indenture contract is dated 1619, when four owners of a Virginia plantation signed an agreement with Robert Coopy, of Gloucestershire, England. Coopy promised "faythfully to serve . . . for three years from the daye of his landing in the land of Virginia" in return for his benefactors' promise to "transport him (with gods assistance) with all convenient speed into the said land of Virginia at their costs and charges in all things, and there to maintayne him with convenient diet and apparell meet for such a servant, And in the end of the said terme to make him a free man of the said Cuntry . . . And to grant to the said Robert thirty acres of land within their Territory . . ."

The system caught on immediately, and by 1625 there were 487 indentured servants out of a population of 1,227 in the Virginia Company. During the next decade the wording of indenture contracts became fairly uniform, and by 1636, printed forms were available with blank spaces for the names of the servant and master and the details of the contract.

Indentured servitude grew as thousands of men and women in England crammed into cities competing for the few low-paying jobs open to them and for a precariously short food supply. Religious and political pressures, aggravated by famine and disease, made people restless and receptive to the prospect of a better existence elsewhere. Handbills and broadsides written by promoters (many of whom had never been to America) to stimulate migration painted the rosiest possible picture of the American colonies, promising abundant land for all and high wages for craftsmen. They neglected to mention the hardships of living in the still-wild country. As the colonies grew, those who had already made the transition sent tantalizing letters home. Robert Parke wrote to his sister in 1725, "There is not one of the family but what likes the country very well and would if we were in Ireland again come here directly; it being the best country for working folk and tradesmen in the world." With such encouragement, "emigration fever" swept through Europe, keeping ships filled with would-be settlers. Those who could afford to do so paid their own passages, arriving in the colonies as free men. Thousands more, with a yearning for the colonies, but no gold in their pockets to pay for the trip, were satisfied by enterprising colonists willing to invest in their passage and maintenance in return for several years of labor.

These early capitalists usually hired an agent (a ship captain was a frequent choice, as were merchants who traveled between the two continents) to contact discouraged workers in England and sign them on as indentured servants. An agreement written in duplicate on a large sheet of paper was signed by both master and servant, then "indented" or cut, in two—one copy for each party. The terms of the contract seldom varied; besides transporting the servant, the master agreed to feed, clothe, and house him for a certain number of years, usually between four and fourteen. At the end of the stipulated time, he was to pay the servant with a small stake and his freedom. Details of the treatment the servant could expect, the rules governing his life, and the freedom dues were rarely set down in writing. They were, instead, to be "according to the custom of the country," which could change with the prosperity, or the personality, of the master.

It was soon evident that great profits were to be made, and many a "middle man" turned professional agent and combed the cities and farm regions in England for men and women willing to become bound servants. He signed their indentures as master and transported them, a shipload at a time, to the colonies. The total cost, including transportation and a few pieces of clothing per person, was seldom more than £10 per head. In the colonies the agent could count on getting £15 to £30 for each servant "set over." (The word sell was consciously avoided when it referred to white men, yet the new owner bought a servant in much the same way he bought a slave.)

Substantial profits to be made in the servant trade led to notoriously deceitful, as well as illegal, methods of recruitment. Agents came to be known as "spirits," with reputations for having no qualms about lying to a man or getting him so drunk that he would put his mark on any piece of paper shoved in front of him. If lies and gin didn't work, a whack on the head usually would. Many men and women were forced to the ship and shoved into the hold not to see daylight again until the shores of England were out of sight.

Public outrage over such forced migration, particularly when it involved children, spurred Parliament to enact laws that protected the citizen from the spirits and, at the same time, protected the honest agent from false accusations of kidnapping by a servant with second thoughts about honoring his indenture. Agents and servants were required to sign the contract before a magistrate, a registry of servants being transported to the colonies was kept, and in some cases, outbound ships were searched so that any passengers with a change of mind could return home. Although these measures were not entirely successful, they helped ensure that most men and women who bound themselves as servants and sailed for America did so because they wanted to.

The English Parliament used indentured servitude to rid the country of vagrants roaming England in that

JUST ARRIVED, *in the* Ship JOHN, *Capt.* ROACH, *from* DUBLIN,

A NUMBER of HEALTHY, INDENTED MEN and WOMEN SERVANTS:

AMONG THE FORMER ARE,

A Variety of TRADESMEN, with some good FARMERS, and stout LABOURERS: Their Indentures will be disposed of, on reasonable Terms, for CASH, by

GEORGE SALMON.

Many Europeans could afford to come to America only by offering themselves as indentured servants or redemptioners. Newspaper advertisements like the one above regularly announced the arrival of indentured servants.

time of social upheaval. Frequently these rootless vagabonds were farmers who had been dispossessed of their lands; and unable to find work, they turned in desperation or bitterness to lives of petty crime and theft. Convicted criminals, many from Newgate Prison, were sent by the state to the colonies as bound servants. Most had a choice of sorts: hanging or America. America was the favored alternative. Prior to 1717, forced exile did not exist in England, but convicts who would ordinarily be sentenced to die (and a large number of minor crimes were punishable by that harsh sentence) could be pardoned on condition that they leave the country. After 1717, most offenders could be legally transported to America or the West Indies as indentured servants for not less than seven years.

Besides clearing out overcrowded English jails, bondage supplied much needed labor for the colonies. Of the prisoners convicted at Old Bailey from 1729 to the American Revolution, at least 70 percent were sent to America. Such deportation of criminals did not win favor with colonists who likened it to having England "emptying their jakes (privies) on our tables." Maryland

and Virginia, destinations for most criminal-immigrants, passed restrictive laws forbidding convict ships to land, but such laws were quashed by the British crown. Although they complained bitterly, colonists desperate for cheap labor could not afford to be too particular about the past indiscretions of available servants: convict indentures never lacked buyers. About 30,000 convicts (in reality a small part of those who arrived under indenture) were transported to the colonies, many for petty crimes.

Whether the ships crossing the Atlantic were filled with convicts or willing bondsmen, they were filled to overflowing. As many as 800 persons might be crowded aboard a single vessel, and even the smaller ships often carried 200 or 300 people. One ship, measured for a safe load of 223, made the crossing with 322 on board; when criticized, the ship owner claimed his craft was far less crowded than many others.

Except for the convict ships, servants rarely had to endure the horrors common on slavers. Still, the voyage was unpleasant at best. Food supplies were as limited as space, and although ships were usually provisioned for a twelve-week voyage, many crossings delayed by bad weather or poor navigation ended as the last rations of wormy food and rancid water were being handed out. Less fortunate voyagers came to the end of provisions before they sighted land.

Ship captains were notoriously neglectful of cleanliness. Even when they did periodically wash out the ship with vinegar, the vessels were normally steeped in filth. Jammed into cargo holds with few sanitary facilities, the mass of passengers suffered from diseases and sickness made worse by the lack of ventilation. Although they were free to go above deck for fresh air during fair weather, when rough seas or stormy skies threatened, all were sent below the battened-down hatches. One German immigrant cataloged the suffering of fellow passengers during a 1751 crossing as "terrible misery, stench, fumes, horror, vomiting, many kinds of seasickness, fever, dysentery, headache, heat, constipation, boils, scurvy, cancer, mouth-rot, and the like." Another voyager reported that "we had enough in the day to behold the miserable sight of blotches, pox, others devoured with lice til they almost at death's door. In the night fearful cries and groaning of sick and distracted persons. . . ."

By the time the servants reached the colonies they were dirty, sick, and weak. Those with prearranged indentures were taken off the ship by their new masters, while those indentured to agents were readied for sale. Fresh clothing, clean water, and good food were enough to erase most of the visible ill effects of the voyage, and within a few days the cargo was ready for sale. Newspaper advertisements or broadsides announced the arrival of "a number of healthy indented men and women servants . . . a variety of tradesmen, good farmers, stout laborers . . . whose indentures will be disposed of, on reasonable terms, for cash."

The buyers arrived on the day of the sale, and the servants were brought out for inspection. Strong young

---

RUN away the 27th of *August* laſt, from *James Anderſon* Miniſter of the Goſpel in *Donigal*, in the County of *Lancaſter* in *Penſilvania*, a Servant Man named *Hugh Wier*, aged about 30 Years of a middle Stature and freſh Complexion, ſandy Beard, and ſhort dark brown Hair, he went off very bear in Cloathing, and is ſuppoſed to have got himſelf dreſs'd in *Indian* Habit, (He having been uſed among *Indians*, when he run away from other Maſters before) He is by Trade a Flax-dreſſer, Spinſter and Woolcomber, and it is ſuppoſed he can Weave; He alſo does moſt ſort of Women Work, ſuch as waſhing of Cloaths or Diſhes, milking of Cows, and other Kitchen Work, and uſually changes his Name, Whoever takes up ſaid Servant and ſecures him either in this or any of the neighbouring Provinces and let his Maſter know of it, by Poſt or otherways, ſo as his ſaid Maſter may have him again, ſhall have *Three Pounds* as a Reward, and all reaſonable Charges paid by me, *James Anderſon*

Advertisement for a runaway indentured servant in the "American Weekly Mercury" of Philadelphia, December 14, 1733.

men, skilled workers, and comely women sold quickly, but the sick or old were harder to dispose of, and at times were given away as a bonus with more desirable servants. In later years, it was not uncommon for one buyer to purchase the indentures of all, or a large part, of the human cargo. These "soul-drivers" loaded their merchandise on wagons and drove through the countryside selling it door-to-door the way the drummer sold sewing needles.

A Pennsylvania soul-driver named McCullough got more than he bargained for when he bought a group of servants in Philadelphia and began a circular swing through the farmlands and towns of the backcountry. He sold all but one of the servants, an Irishman whose rowdy behavior frightened away any potential buyers. The two men stayed one night at an inn but the Irishman woke early and, passing himself off as the master, sold McCullough—still asleep upstairs—to the innkeeper. Before he left the inn he warned the innkeeper that his newly acquired servant was a clever rascal, fond of telling lies and even of persuading gullible people that he was the master.

There were other passengers on those ships who found their way into servitude, although they had not begun their voyages with that in mind. Whole families of German and Swiss immigrants left home to build new lives in the American colonies, making their way down the Rhine to book passage in Rotterdam. But overly-enthusiastic recruitment pamphlets didn't mention the opportunists who overcharged for provisions along the route, or the long waits at the docks until space could be found on some America-bound vessel. Many found that

their money would not stretch far enough to pay their passage. An agent, merchant, or ship captain would step forward to advance the money needed for the voyage, granting the prospective colonist a period of time, usually two weeks, to raise the balance due when he arrived in the colonies. Some managed to find friends or relatives to redeem them, or had the good fortune to fall into the hands of one of the relief societies set up by their countrymen for the unwary victims. Many did not and so, to repay the agent, were sold into servitude. The redemptioner was in no position to quibble over the terms of his indenture, and often had to accept a situation no willing servant would have agreed to before leaving home.

Willing servant, transported convict, or disappointed redemptioner—once bound to a master he was his property, like his house, or horse, or slave. Yet his status was a curious mixture of slave and free man. His services could be bought or sold, rented or even inherited, but the terms of his contract remained the same under each master. He could own property but could not engage in trade. Marriage without his master's consent was strictly forbidden, and fornication and illegitimate pregnancy were serious offenses. Runaway servants were tracked down like runaway slaves and punished just as severely, although a white complexion made eluding capture much more possible. Posters and advertisements offered rewards for their return and warned of the consequences of harboring fugitives. Corporal punishment, including whipping, was accepted practice, often accompanied by a punishment even more hated: the addition of months or even years to the indenture period. A thwarted runaway could expect one month to be added to his term for every week he was gone. Sometimes the extension was confirmed with a whipping or the gift of a heavy iron collar engraved with the master's initials.

But indentured servants were not black slaves—they were white and Christian and as such had an edge over their African counterparts. The most important difference was the right to petition the courts against abuse, a right that was exercised freely and frequently.

At first, the rules regulating the lives of the servants and their treatment were governed by local custom. As the number of servants soared, many of these customs were incorporated into law. Any servant who felt his master was defying a 'custom of the country' or breaking a law could visit the local magistrate and file a petition of grievance.

In 1700, Catherine Douglas of Lancaster County, Virginia, learned that the courts would listen to and judge a case impartially, without bias against a penniless bonded servant. She filed a petition claiming that in England she had signed a four-year indenture with John Gilchrist in exchange for her passage, Gilchrist in turn sold her to Mottron Wright for a seven-year term. Although her own copy of the indenture had been destroyed, Catherine was able to produce three witnesses who testified that they had seen the original and that it had indeed specified four years. Wright argued that his seven-year contract had to be upheld, but the court decided in Catherine's favor; she was set free after serving her four years.

Until the middle of the 17th century, when laws governing black slavery began to be passed, Africans were also imported into the colonies under indenture. Until then, and occasionally after, redress was afforded blacks through the courts. In 1691, a Stafford County, Virginia, court heard an unusual case when black servant Benjamin Lewis petitioned for his freedom, claiming that before leaving England he had been indentured for four years. His term was over but his master refused to set him free, saying that as a Negro, Lewis was not a servant but a slave. The master produced another indenture signed by Lewis for a fourteen year term, but admitted it had been written while the first contract was still in effect. The jury ruled that the original contract was valid and proclaimed Lewis a free man.

Most cases brought before the courts by servants dealt with poor treatment and physical abuse. As with black slaves, the treatment of bonded servants was as varied as the personalities of their masters. Most were dealt with fairly and well, for humanitarian as well as practical reasons, but for some servants, life became a nightmare. Elizabeth Sprigs, indentured in Maryland, wrote of "toiling day and night, and then [being] tied up and whipped to that degree you would not beat an animal, scarce anything but Indian corn and salt to eat and that even begrudged." Some observers reported that when white servants worked side by side with black slaves, the slaves were often fed better and treated with more care since they represented a life-time investment.

The relatively minor charge of providing insufficient clothing was brought against William Miller by his servant William Hust. Court officials in Spotsylvania, Virginia, heard the case in 1758 and issued detailed orders to Miller. "The said Miller [shall] give him one cotton and kersey jacket and britches, 3 Ozanb shirts and sufficient diet and 1 pair of shoes and stockings, 1 hat. . . ." Usually the court found it adequate to reprimand the master and instruct him to properly provide for his servant.

A more serious charge was filed against plantation owners Francis Leaven and Samuel Hodgkins. Their servant, John Thomas, had commited some minor offense, and for punishment, the two hung him up by his hands and placed lighted sticks between his fingers, permanently injuring his hands. The court awarded Thomas not only his freedom, but 5,000 pounds of cotton from each of the masters, who were jailed for the assault.

Most indentured servants lived out their indenture periods without having need to petition the courts, and without the inclination to abscond. They worked hard, as did the free settlers, often learning a trade and gaining valuable experience. When their indenture period ended, freedom dues helped them begin life as free men. The dues varied with locale, but its intent was to give the servant a stake to start out on his own. In 1640, Maryland law required a freedom dues of "one good cloth suit of kersey or broadcloth, a shift of white linen, one new pair of stockings and shoes, two hoes, one axe, 3 barrells of corne and fifty acres of land. . . ." Land as part of the freedom dues was an important incentive for immigration, but as the more desirable tracts were taken up in populated areas, the promise of acreage virtually ended except for wilderness or scrub land. In 1683, the Maryland law dropped the land requirement. In Virginia, a 1748 law gave freed servants a freedom dues of three pounds, ten shillings. The tendency toward cash increased as the colonies prospered.

With his freedom dues, the former servant could make his way in the colonies as a hired laborer or even as a landowner. No stigma attached to his past bondage; with diligent hard work he could become as prosperous and respected as any settler who had paid his own way from Europe with cash. Those who had been lazy and dishonest in Europe before they were bound out probably continued to be so after they were free. Former convicts often ended up on American rather than English gallows, but many others became distinguished citizens and property holders. Seven burgesses in the Virginia assembly of 1629 had been indentured servants, as had fifteen members of the 1637 Maryland Assembly. Charles Thomas, later to serve as Secretary of the Continental Congress, started his American life in bondage, as did Matthew Thornton, a signer of the Declaration of Independence for the colony of New Hampshire. Like many other Americans who could trace their roots to humble beginnings, they had bought their dreams with the most precious commodity they owned: themselves.

Anne Hutchinson
"A Verye Dangerous Woman"

Stephanie Ocko

Even before the *Griffin* docked in Boston harbor in September, 1634, Anne Hutchinson had preached and "vented her opinions" to other passengers aboard. "The fear of man is a snare," she said, as the ship sailed into port, "but they that trust upon the Lord shall be safe." Later, a fellow passenger claimed she uttered these words when she saw the "meanness" of Boston. This she dismissed as absurd, because she had been prepared for Boston. She had said it because "having seen him which is invisible, I fear not what man can do unto me." Anne Hutchinson had had a revelation of the days she would spend in Massachusetts Bay Colony.

The "masterpiece of woman's wit" arrived from Alford, Lincolnshire, with her husband and eleven of her children, of whom the oldest was twenty-one, and the youngest an infant. No stranger to religion, Anne had grown up during the persecution of the Catholics and Separatists under Elizabeth and James I. Her father, Reverend Francis Marbury, had been imprisoned for preaching against the incompetence of English ministers. Now forty-three years old, Anne had undergone her own religious conversion and had followed her beloved minister Reverend John Cotton, whose removal to New England a year earlier had been "a great trouble to me. . . . I could not be at rest but I must come thither."

Merchant William Hutchinson, "a man of very mild temper and weak parts, and wholly guided by his wife," as Governor John Winthrop was later to describe him, settled his family in a spacious house in the center of Boston, a community of about five hundred. Anne, well-bred and wealthy, turned her attention to helping the women of Boston as a midwife.

The religious climate in the six-year-old colony was oppressive. In the rough first days of settlement, religion had served to turn people from asking how they could go back to England to how they could go to heaven. As the colony took hold, ministers emphasized everyone's pious duty to pray, fast, and discipline oneself. Reminded that hypocrites could appear to be "saved," colonists were urged to examine their hearts daily as their only means to salvation.

Under the anxiety of never being sure they were saved, women in particular suffered. One Boston woman threw her child into a well because "now she was sure she should be damned."

It was not long before Anne Hutchinson began to hold women's meetings. At first the women discussed the previous Sunday's sermons, but before long, Anne began interpolating her own beliefs which differed from those of the Boston ministers. Those who would be saved, she said, were those in whom the Holy Spirit lived; this was signalled by a personal love of Christ and an inner light. The ministers of Boston, she said, preached too much that people could be saved only by "works," that is, by following the Scriptures and the Ten Commandments.

In what was to become known as the argument between a covenant of grace versus a covenant of works, Anne further exacerbated the local elders by claiming that only two Boston ministers were "elect," or saved, John Cotton and her brother-in-law John Wheelwright.

Anne's Thursday night meetings took on a new importance. As many as eighty people filled her house, including "some of the magistrates, some gentlemen, some scholars and men of learning, some burgesses, . . . some of our captains and soldiers. . . . She had more resort to her for counsell about matters of conscience," Winthrop observed, "than any minister in the country."

Among them was Sir Henry Vane, who became governor of the colony in 1636.

What started as an ecclesiastical point of difference grew into a schism that threatened the political stability of the colony. When Anne, with the support of Governor Vane and John Cotton, attempted to have her brother-in-law installed as minister of the Boston church, most of the congregation supported her. But the pastor of the church, Reverend John Wilson, a man "whom orthodoxy in New England had no champion more cruel and more ungenerous," gave a speech on the "inevitable dangers of separation" caused by the religious dissensions, and joined with John Winthrop.

Reprinted with permission from the August 1979 issue of *Early American Life*.

25

1. THE NEW LAND

Because they feared that England would hear of their troubles and cut off the colony (Charles I had tried to squelch it in 1635), a meeting was called with Vane, Cotton, Wheelwright, and Hutchinson to try to settle their religious differences. Cotton conceded that their differences were slight, but the others still maintained that a personal union with the Holy Spirit was possible.

"It began to be as common here," Winthrop said early in 1637, "to distinguish between men, by being under a covenant of grace or a covenant of works, as in other countries between Protestants and Papists." Thomas Weld complained, "Now after our sermons were ended, you might have seen half a dozen pistols discharged at the face of the preacher, (I mean) so many objections were made by the opinionists in the open assembly." When a call to arms went out for men to fight in the Pequot War, a contingent from Boston "came near refusing to march" because the chaplain (Reverend Wilson) was under a covenant of works.

By now Anne Hutchinson's followers were called Antinomians, a term coined originally by Martin Luther to designate those who believed they were above the Mosaic Law, or the Ten Commandments. In fact, the term, intended to be derogatory, was erroneously applied to Hutchinson's followers, who did not believe that the indwelling of the Holy Spirit released them from obligation to moral law.

In May 1637, a general election was called, and Vane lost to John Winthrop, who took command of the divided colony. To prevent new Antinomians from settling Winthrop imposed a restriction on immigrants, among them Anne's brother and several of her friends who were forced to return to England. In August, eighty-two "heresies" committed by the Antinomians were read at a synod, and a ban was placed on all private meetings.

But Wheelwright continued to preach, and Anne now held her meetings twice a week. Therefore, in November, Wheelwright and Anne were charged and called to account at a meeting of the General Court.

Intending to prove that Anne's behavior was immoral, Winthrop described her meetings as "a thing not tolerable nor comely in the sight of God, nor fitting for your sex," and accused her of breaking the Fifth Commandment by not honoring her father and mother (in this case, the magistrates of the colony).

Answering deftly, Anne came close to clearing herself of all charges. But suddenly, she mentioned that she had had several revelations, including one in which she saw that she "should be persecuted and suffer much trouble" in Boston. The Lord revealed himself to her, she said, "upon a Throne of Justice, and all the world appearing before him, and though I must come to New England, yet I must not fear nor be dismaied," she said. "Therefore, take heed. For I know that for this that you goe about to doe unto me," she threatened, "God will ruin you and your posterity, and this whole State."

Winthrop answered quickly. "I am persuaded that the revelation she brings forth is delusion," he said.

"We all believe it!" the other members cried.

The court voted to banish her.

"I desire to know wherefore I am banished," she demanded.

"Say no more, the court knows wherefore, and is satisfied," Winthrop replied.

Wheelwright was exiled and shortly left for New Hampshire, and Hutchinson was put under house arrest for the winter to await a church trial in the spring. Fearing that the Antinomians would "make some suddaine irruption upon those that differ from them in judgment," the court ordered that all their arms be seized.

The winter was particularly harsh. Snow stood one-and-a-half feet deep from November to March, 1638. In February Winthrop reported that local Indians repeatedly saw the devil, who told them to desert the English. If Winthrop was uneasy about Anne's revelation of disaster to the colony, he did not have far to look to find a sign of the devil connected to her. Sometime during the winter it was revealed that Anne's friend, Mary Dyer, "notoriously infected with Mrs. Hutchinson's errors," had given birth to a monster described by the midwife as a horned, scaly creature with its facial features scattered over its torso. At the first thaw, Winthrop and "above a hundred persons" opened the monster's grave and were satisfied to see "horns, and claws, . . . and some scales, &c."

On March 15, 1638, Anne was brought to trial before the elders of the church of Boston. Charged with sixteen ecclesiastical errors, she acknowledged some misunderstandings. But when her sons and sons-in-law attempted to speak on her behalf, John Cotton cautioned them against "hindering" the work of God in healing her soul. To the women of the congregation, he said to be careful in listening to her "for you see she is but a woman and many unsound and dayngerous Principles are held by her."

If Cotton had once been her friend, he now turned full force against her, attacked her meetings as a "promiscuous and filthie coming together of men and women without Distinction or Relation of Marriage," and accused her of believing in free love.

"Your opinions frett like a Gangrene," Cotton mercilessly pursued, "and spread like a Leprosie, and will eate out the very Bowells of Religion."

The elders admonished her and gave her a week in which to repent. She was sent to Cotton's house.

On March 22, the interrogation was resumed. She admitted several errors, but denied that she was not bound to the Law and held to her belief in inherent grace. Several elders expressed doubt that she had fully repented her "fowle and Damnable Herisies." One called her a "Notorious Imposter."

Then Reverend Wilson, whom she had once tried to evict from the Boston church, delivered her excommunication. "I doe cast you out and in the name of Christ I doe deliver you up to Satan, that you may learne no more to blaspheme, to seduce, and to lye."

A crowd was gathered at the church as she left with Mary Dyer. "Who is that young woman?" someone in the crowd asked. "It is the woman who had the monster!" someone replied.

To Anne, a bystander shouted, "The Lord sanctify this unto you."

"The Lord judgeth not as man judgeth," she replied. "Better to be cast out of the church than to deny Christ." Winthrop reported that after the excommunication, "her spirits . . . revived again, and she gloried in her sufferings, saying that it was the greatest happiness, next to Christ, that ever befel her."

Within a week, Anne left Boston and walked with several of her children to the Island of Aquidneck in Rhode Island where she joined her husband and several others. On land purchased from the Indians, the small band of Antinomians set up a colony which they named Portsmouth.

Shortly after arriving, Anne "perceived her body to be greatly distempered, and her spirits failing, and in that regard, doubtful of her life." With Dr. John Clarke as attending physician, she expelled what a modern pathologist has termed a hydatidiform mole, or a uterine growth. Word quickly reached Boston, and John Cotton announced that she had given birth to "twenty-seven lumps of man's seed without any mixture of anything from the woman." Governor Winthrop perceived that she had had not one, but "30 monstrous births."

Now forty-eight years old, cast out by the minister she had followed to America, and in exile, Anne Hutchinson did not retire. Winthrop kept his eye on her and on the "Isle of Errours," as well as on the strange happenings in Boston. A day after his re-election in May, 1638, he fell ill with a fever that "brought him near death" for a month. Corn planted in the spring "rotted in the ground." And on June 1, a great earthquake roared "like a continued thunder or the rattling of coaches in London." At Portsmouth, he noted, it had come while Mrs. Hutchinson and some friends were at prayer. "The house being shaken thereby, they were persuaded (and boasted of it)," he said, "that the Holy Ghost did shake it in coming down upon them, as he did upon the apostles."

Early in 1639 the Boston church sent a delegation to Portsmouth to dissuade Anne from preaching, but she refused to acknowledge the presence of a church in Boston. When they tried to talk to her husband, William, "he told us that he was more nearly tied to his wife than to the church and he thought her a dear saint and servant of God."

In 1642 William died. Always her supporter, he left her at a time when Massachusetts Colony was threatening to gain possession of Rhode Island, because of an ill-defined boundary. In the company of fifteen members of her family, including her three youngest children, all under ten, and her grandchildren, Anne headed for the Dutch colony in New York. Despite the fact that Governor Winthrop claimed she left Aquidneck because she was weary of the island, "or rather, the island being weary of her," Anne sought a friendlier atmosphere near present-day Eastchester Bay, New York.

But a few months later, fifteen Dutchmen were slain in a battle between the Mohegans and the Narragansetts. In August, 1643, having swept across Long Island, the Mohegans raided the Hutchinson house. They killed cattle, set fire to the house, and slaughtered Anne and thirteen members of her family.

The reaction in Boston was predictable. "I never heard that the Indians in those parts did ever before this commit the like outrage upon any one family," Governor Winthrop said, "and therefore God's hand is more apparently seene herein, to pick out this wofull woman, to make her and those belonging to her, an unheard of heavie example of their cruelty above al others. Thus," he concluded, "the Lord heard our groanes to heaven, and freed us from this great and sore affliction."

Neither martyr nor successful reformer, Anne Hutchinson nevertheless identified and challenged the colony's palpable weakness. Her "ready wit and bold spirit" aroused a fear that moved the founding fathers to an inelegant harshness. Confounded, Winthrop saw her eloquence as the work of the devil, her cleverness in answering the ridiculous charges at her trials as "circumlocutions," her religious differences as atheism. To him, she was a "Prophetesse, . . . an American Jesabel." Had she been a man, she might have wrested political power from Governor Winthrop. As it was, she used her considerable influence as a woman to test the colony's religious tolerance, which, ironically, had been the reason for settlement.

Remapping American culture

A new U.S. history traces today's regionalism to colonial days

For nearly a century, historians have searched for the wellspring of American politics and culture. Herbert Baxter Adams found it in the Teutonic forests, where Saxon warriors had gathered in an early version of the New England town meeting. Frederick Jackson Turner looked westward to the American frontier, while Richard Hofstadter and Daniel Boorstin looked to the economic abundance and inventiveness that produced a broad-based middle class. Now, historian David Hackett Fischer is bidding to join their ranks with a provocative new theory of the roots of the American experience.

The Brandeis University historian has uncovered America's political and cultural roots in the countryside of Britain. In his new book, *Albion's Seed* (Oxford University Press, $39.95), Fischer argues that settlers from different sections of England—called Albion by the ancient Greeks—brought divergent values to the new world, where they established distinctive regional cultures that remain central to the nation's fabric even today. Fischer contends that everything from contrasting New England and Southern accents to what makes the South far more politically conservative than the Northeast can be explained by looking at the differences among the early settlers.

This bold thesis, called "a revisionist blockbuster" by one critic, is nothing less than an attempt at a new synthesis of U.S. history. Before the 1960s, American history had been written as a smooth narrative of the achievements of the famous and powerful that left little room for the lives of ordinary citizens. But the '60s turned American history—and the nation itself—on its head, and shattered the old scholarly synthesis. The once neglected masses became the focus of research as "the new social history" moved to the fore and historical scholarship fragmented into numerous subspecialties. Many leading historians wondered whether, like Humpty Dumpty, U.S. history could ever be put back together again. Fischer is trying to do just that.

His America, hardly the "melting pot" described in many history texts, is a land that from its very beginning was marked by diversity, not homogeneity. It is a land in which the early settlers all spoke English but otherwise had remarkably little in common. They arrived here at different times and from different regions of England, each fleeing a different form of oppression. Most of the Puritans came from the east of England to Massachusetts between 1629 and 1641. A small Royalist elite and large numbers of indentured servants arrived in the Chesapeake region from the south and west of England between 1642 and 1675. Quakers from England's north midlands and Wales arrived in the Delaware Valley between 1675 and 1725, and immigrants from Northern Ireland, parts of Scotland and the border area of north England settled in Appalachia from 1717 to 1775. "They carried across the Atlantic four different sets of British folkways which became the basis of regional cultures in the New World," says Fischer.

Almost from the beginning, there was little love lost among the colonists. The Anglicans of Virginia and the Puritans of New England agreed on little other than their loathing of Quakers, who were regarded as dangerous radicals. The Puritans and Quakers, in turn, disliked the Virginians. In 1651, one Puritan observed of Virginians: "I think they are the farthest from conscience and moral honesty of any such number together in the world." And Puritans, Virginia cavaliers and Quakers united in the view that the backcountry settlers of Appalachia were barbarians.

These sometimes feuding groups left 20th-century America a rich and diverse legacy, especially when it came to regional tongues. Fischer traces the unique dialect of Massachusetts and much of New England to a high-pitched nasal accent called the "Norfolk whine" that the Puritans brought to the new world. Even today, the distinctive pronunciation of the letter *r* that characterizes Yankee speech, transforming a word such as *Harvard* into *Haa-v'd*, can be heard in England's East Anglia region. In contrast, the slow drawl of the South comes from the south and west of England, where ancestors of the Virginia cavaliers uttered such words as *chitlins* and *no-count*.

Even what is controversially labeled today as black dialect may have been an English import. The people of Virginia, even those of high rank, preferred "I be," "she ain't," "it don't" and "I hain't" to such phrases as "I am" and "you are," says Fischer, who found that American travelers to England in the 19th century were startled by the resem-

From *U.S. News & World Report*, December 4, 1989, pp. 60-62, 63-64. Copyright © 1989 by U.S. News & World Report.

blance of the dialect of rural Sussex to Virginia speech. A different and equally persistent language variation was introduced into Appalachia by Scottish and Irish settlers who pronounced *where* as *whar* and *there* as *thar* and used such constructions as *he come in* and *she done finished,* which show up today in everything from country music to comedy routines. The more subtle linguistic peculiarities of the Quakers sowed the seeds of the flat accent of the Midwest.

Not only did the early settlers speak differently, they also held dramatically different attitudes toward education. The Puritans were members of a sturdy middle class steeped in the Bible who transmitted to their descendants the importance they placed on literacy and learning. That is why even today there are exceptionally high levels of college attendance in New England, home to some of the nation's finest colleges. The Quakers, ambivalent about education, were slower to found colleges, but put more emphasis on schooling than residents of the Southern highlands—West Virginia, Arkansas, Kentucky, Alabama and Mississippi— where even now levels of educational attainment are comparatively low. Fischer traces this to educational practices brought from Northern Ireland, the north of England and parts of rural Scotland to the backcountry, "where there were no institutions comparable to New England's town schools or even to Virginia's system of parish education."

In domestic matters—sexual relations and family violence, especially—the past was also prologue. Violence was much greater in the patriarchal cultures of the backcountry and the Chesapeake than among the Puritans and Quakers. This colonial pattern manifests itself today in regional variations in the homicide rate, which is much lower in the North than in the South and Southwest. And from the beginning, it appears, there was an intimate connection between domestic violence and attitudes toward women. In Puritan Massachusetts, for instance, the

---

The Puritan legacy

Centuries later, the imprint of an austere, sober people remains indelible

COURTESY OF SANDAK/G. K. HALL & CO.

Modern New England may be best known for leafy autumns and high tech, but the legacy of the Puritans lives on in the form of boiled dinners, town meetings and Cape Cod houses. Puritans associated their diet with piety, not the palate, so they preferred cold baked beans and boiled vegetables to bountiful seafood. The austerity of the diet was leavened, however, by the baked pie, which became a special culinary delight. For housing, the Puritans utilized two styles from East Anglia, the saltbox—boasting two stories in front and one in back—and the 1½-story Cape Cod, which remains popular today.

Their fashion statement came in the form of such "sadd colors" as tawny, russet and purple, which continue as part of the region's official culture. They show up in ceremonies at institutions like Brown University, whose idea of high color is dark brown trimmed with black.

Ordered liberty, the belief that individual liberties belong to all within a framework of an active town-meeting government, became a Puritan bench mark. John Quincy Adams and his father, John Adams, before him were among 16 U.S. Presidents descended from the settlers.

Cavaliers and servants

The rich led an opulent life, while the rest settled for much slimmer pickings

COLONIAL WILLIAMSBURG PHOTOGRAPH, WILLIAMSBURG, VA.

The Civil War notwithstanding, the "distressed cavaliers" and their plantation style remain a cornerstone of Southern culture. Stately mansions with large rooms, high ceilings and elaborate gardens were built by Virginians who were accustomed to housing extended patriarchal families. The homes served as reminders of the manors of southern England. Not surprisingly, the cavaliers did not stint on their dining pleasure. Prosperous planter William Byrd enjoyed fried chicken, often cooked with bacon or ham, now a staple of the American diet. A favorite of many Virginians was "frigacy," or fricassee, chicken or meat simmered with herbs in an open pan.

In the colony, clothes did not make the man, they showed who he was. While servants and commoners wore garments of canvas, the elite dressed in bright silks and satins, often displaying family coats of arms on rings, silverware and furniture.

Virginians believed in the hierarchical concept of freedom. Liberty belonged to free-born Englishmen, not to all people. George Washington and Thomas Jefferson are among the 10 Chief Executives from their ranks.

Christian ideal of spiritual equality between the sexes held sway, and every woman was entitled by law to physical protection from both physical and verbal abuse. Men and women were also punished equally for sexual transgressions. The Quakers went further. They held the revolutionary view that the family was a union of individuals who were equal in the sight of God, and Quaker law was the first to routinely use the pronouns "he or she."

In the backcountry, by contrast, men were considered warriors and women workers—an inequitable domestic relationship that led to high levels of household violence. And in the Chesapeake region, women were held inferior even by the law. While rape was a hanging crime in New England, in the Southern colonies it was sometimes punished less severely than petty theft.

This history helps explain why support for women's suffrage and for the equal-rights amendment has been strongest across the Northern tier of the nation and weakest in the South and Southwest, Fischer contends. Most states in the Southern highlands voted against the ERA, while every state in the Northern tier supported it. The nation's politics, he believes, reflect at heart the philosophical differences spread by Albion's seed.

Even the participation of Americans in wars of all kinds may be traceable to unique regional experiences. Fischer offers the controversial argument that Northeastern liberals joined World War II because they saw it as a moral crusade against Fascism and militarism, while Southern conservatives were drawn by a kinship with Britain that dated back to the cavaliers. Backcountry descendants fought for national honor, while Quakers nonviolently supported what they saw as a battle against the warrior spirit.

What is most remarkable is that these differences have persisted through waves of subsequent immigration. Although fewer than 20 percent of Americans now have British ancestors, says Fischer, the nation remains a product of Albion's

DELAWARE VALLEY

Quaker simplicity

They brought a social conscience to their dining table and abhorred excess in all things except moderation

Function, not frills, marked the Quaker way of life. The Quakers opposed excess and refused to touch foods they regarded as tainted by social evil, a harbinger of such modern movements as the grape boycott. Their main culinary contribution was a special form of food preservation that spawned products like cream cheese.

Their homes were built of stone and brick and came primarily in the "Quaker plan" (three rooms on the first floor and a full second story) and the "four-over-four" (four large rooms with central halls on both the top and bottom floors).

Quakers believed that costly costumes created envy and divisiveness. A man's wardrobe often consisted of leather breeches and a wide leather apron, derived from the folk costume of England's North Midlands. Women wore modest dresses and put no powder or color on their faces.

Reciprocal liberty, in which every freedom demanded for oneself should be extended to others, was a credo of the Quakers. They did not approve of politics, and hence the culture sired few Presidents, among them Herbert Hoover.

APPALACHIA

Backcountry folk

Although they were the last of Albion's seed to arrive, they have given the nation 18 Presidents

The settlers of Appalachia were hard-living and hard-working and believed in self-reliance and individual responsibility. Their diet would shock today's cholesterol-sensitive citizenry; it leaned heavily to milk, butter and clabber, a blend of sour milk, curds and whey. They brought with them their beverage of choice: Whisky. But they had to adapt to their new home's native grains, replacing Scotch with bourbon.

Privacy was not a concern, so families lived in stone or log cabins, made into one large room, that were similar in style to homes in England's northern border country. Clothing emphasized the differences between the sexes in a culture that stressed sensuality. Single women often wore a full bodice with deep décolletage, a short full skirt and a hem high above the ankle. The men wore shirts cut full in the chest and shoulders and pants that were loose and flowing. This attire, considered the prototype of frontier dress, was similar to clothing in Britain's borderlands.

The idea of natural liberty flourished in their remote environs. Although back-country residents were the last of the immigrant groups to arrive, they produced 18 Presidents, including Lyndon Johnson.

seed because newer waves of immigrants "tended to adopt the folkways of the regions in which they settled." He draws on his own experience teaching at Brandeis, a predominantly Jewish school, where his Protestant stereotypes about the culture of Judaism were exploded by encountering everything from Yankee Jews to "backslapping Texas Jews in cowboy boots and 10-gallon hats."

Still, Fischer readily acknowledges that since the 18th century the original four cultures of British America have commingled with others. Today, he finds at least seven regional cultures in the U.S., and perhaps more. The Albion four, which have spread out across the nation, have been joined by the cultures of Greater New York—"a very heavy infusion of Middle European and Jewish culture grafted on the old Dutch root"—the predominantly Mormon Great Basin and heavily Hispanic Southern California.

Myth of homogeneity. By focusing on England, Fischer opens himself to the charge that he is offering nothing more than a WASP's-eye view of history while slighting the centuries-old contributions of other cultures, most notably that of African Americans. Fischer will deal with African American culture in the second volume of his projected five-volume series. The 53-year-old scholar, who has been working on the project for almost two decades, has finished drafts of two volumes and rough drafts of the others.

The second volume, tentatively titled *American Plantations,* will focus on two strains of black culture, one brought to the Chesapeake region from West Africa and the other to South Carolina from the Congo basin. The book will also examine native-American culture and the Dutch culture that was instrumental in the development of New York. Hispanic culture is several volumes away, since Fischer argues that its impact was not significant until the 19th century.

Critics fault Fischer for sometimes offering fuzzy evidence to back up claims of the continuing strength of Albion's seed in the 20th century. He has also been accused of underplaying differences within a regional culture and of presenting a framework that, all in all, is a little too tidy. But whatever the shortcomings of his encyclopedic, 946-page work, historians who have read it generally agree that the book is a masterpiece of scholarship. Cornell University's Michael Kammen lauds the Brandeis scholar for producing "the finest work of synthesis in early American history in more than 50 years." The University of Florida's Bertram Wyatt-Brown predicts that the book will "raise a firestorm," but he believes that Fischer's overall "thesis and its proof are so sweeping that critics will find it hard to refute."

What Fischer has done is to shatter the myth that America has evolved into one homogeneous mass culture. As his portrait shows, although we share the same films, TV shows and fast-food restaurants, we remain a remarkably diverse people.

Alvin P. Sanoff with Sharon F. Golden

Revolutionary America

How "revolutionary" was the American Revolution? Some scholars have seen it primarily as an attempt to throw off British rule rather than as an attempt to create a new society. Perhaps it was both. Although the United States has long since been politically conservative, the ideals on which the nation was founded have struck responsive chords throughout the world.

Relations between the American colonies and England ran fairly smoothly for generations. The British government had worldwide interests and its own domestic problems to deal with, resulting in what became known as a policy of "benign neglect" toward the colonies. This meant, in practice, that many colonies virtually ran their own affairs with minimal interference or regulation from England.

What Americans called the French and Indian War, which ended in 1763, radically altered the situation. England emerged from the conflict with its treasury depleted, and its efforts to get the colonists to pay a share of the burden struck many Americans as an intolerable violation of traditional rights. These economic grievances, combined with differences over political and religious issues—scholars still debate the relative importance of each—ultimately led to rebellion.

"The Shot Heard Round the World" shows that the Declaration of Independence was heard throughout Europe at the time. Most European nations were ruled by monarchs, to whom the Declaration's principles were threatening. The British, at whom the document was aimed, were less alarmed and "on the whole they took it like gentlemen."

"Life, Liberty, and the Pursuit of Happiness: America's Modest Revolution" compares the American experience with that of the French Revolution, which was committed to a complete restructuring of society. The Declaration of Independence, according to the author, "appeals to everyone [but] does not offer everything to all men." The very modesty of its aims accounts for the American Revolutionary tradition's success, and the immodesty of its aims doomed to failure those who followed the French Revolutionary tradition. Was the American Revolution a product of political repression and constitutional differences as suggested in "The American Revolution: A War of Religion?" The essay "General George Washington, Espionage Chief," analyzes his effective use of spies during the war.

Independence from England brought a great sense of achievement to the former colonists, but also a host of problems. Many became disenchanted with the existing system as time wore on. " 'It Is Not a Union' " describes how momentum built for revising the Articles of Confederation, and "Philadelphia Story" analyses the various compromises that were necessary to draw up the new Constitution.

Looking Ahead: Challenge Questions

Most of the revolutionary leaders were men of moderation. Why did their proclaimed ideals frighten some Europeans and inspire others? Is it true, as the second essay maintains, that these ideals have worldwide attraction today precisely because they were so modest?

Was the system established by the Articles of Confederation so unworkable as to require a new constitution? Or did the Founders exploit some obvious weaknesses in order to create a government to their liking?

THE SHOT HEARD ROUND THE WORLD

HENRY FAIRLIE

"Here once the embattled farmers stood
And fired the shot heard round the world."
—Hymn sung at the completion of the Battle Monument
Concord, July 4, 1837

The claim in Emerson's line is expansive. Can it be true that the shot was heard round the world—when there were no satellites, no television, no radio, no telephone? Let us see.

It then took from five to six weeks for news to cross the Atlantic. (The first regular passenger service between England and the colonies was instituted in 1755.) Thus the news of the "battles" of Lexington and Concord, fought on April 19, 1775, appeared on May 29 in the London press, from which the French papers, as usual, took their news of America; and from them the press in the rest of Europe picked up the story. By June 19 it appeared in a newspaper as far away as St. Petersburg. Similarly the news of the Declaration of Independence was first published in a London newspaper on August 17, 1776; a week later it appeared in papers in Hamburg, on August 30 in Sweden, and on September 2 in Denmark. The actions in Lexington and Concord had been no more than skirmishes in two villages whose names Europeans can never have heard before. Yet the news excited editors across Europe, and they knew it would arouse their readers. The saw *at once* the size of the event.

In 1775-76 the French Revolution had not sounded its tocsin to the peoples of Europe. Most of them lived under the rule of a few absolute monarchs: Louis XVI in France; Maria Theresa (as dowager empress) and her son Joseph II in Austria and the Holy Roman Empire; Frederick the Great in Prussia; Catherine the Great in Russia; and Christian VII in Denmark. It was the age of the "enlightened despots," who genuinely had the welfare of their subjects at heart, but though they proclaimed the right of their peoples to be well governed, they did not acknowledge their right to govern themselves. The only monarch who had (sourly) learned the ABCs of freedom was, paradoxically, the one against whom the colonists were rebelling. The English were far freer than any peoples on the Continent. But the English reaction to the news from America is more interesting if we know how the shot was heard on the other side of the English channel.

Maria Theresa had ascended the throne in 1740 at the age of 23. Even then she realized that the old order could not survive, and set about instituting a series of effective reforms. Her scarcely less remarkable son, who succeeded his father as co-regent in 1765, produced the most thought-out exposition of the duties of an enlightened despot. They received the news of the Declaration at about the same time it reached London, and two weeks before it found its way through the heavy censorship into the daily press in Vienna. Taking a dim view of popular uprisings, Maria Theresa expressed to George III her "hearty desire to see the restoration of obedience and tranquility in every quarter of his dominions," and Joseph told the British ambassador, "The cause in which England is engaged . . . is the cause of all sovereigns who have a joint interest in the maintenance of due subordination . . . in all the surrounding monarchies."

The rulers feared that their subjects would see the American action not as a rebellion against a rightful monarch in his own territories—there had been plenty of rebellions against European sovereigns—but as the proclamation of a revolutionary doctrine of universal application, as the Declaration indeed announced it to be. Thus, although the Declaration was at last allowed through the censorship in Vienna, when the *Wienerisches Diarium* the next year explained the War of Independence as a clash between two political principles—monarchy and popular sovereignty—Maria Theresa was outraged, even though the paper had covered itself by printing an editorial saying that this view of the rebellion was mistaken.

Similarly, when the news of Lexington and Concord got through the censors into the *Sanktpeterburgskie Vedemosti*, the Americans were, in deference to the Empress Catherine, firmly called "rebels." In 1780, when Catherine read the Abbé Raynal's history of Europe's dominions overseas and came to his chapter on the American Revolution, she wrote to a friend: "The American record is filled with declarations in which there is too little that is reasonable and too much that is unbecoming impertinence."

IN BELGIUM, which was then under the rule of Austria, it was clear that the subjects of the enlightened despots might take the American "impertinence" as an example. From as early as 1766, when the *Gazette des Pays-Bas* in Brussels reported the remonstrations of colonial assemblies in America, the Belgian press followed American affairs intently. In four Belgian newspapers and journals the Maryland Constitution was printed in 1777, the Massachusetts Constitution in 1780, some of a collection of the constitutions of all 13 states in 1783, Virginia's Code of Civil and Criminal Laws in 1786, and in the following year the U.S. Constitution in full. This steady flow of news (including the reports of the war and of American victories) could only stir up the middle class in Belgium. They enjoyed neither national independence nor a constitution guaranteeing any basic political rights, while each day the Americans were remaking their political and civil society before the eye of the world. By 1787 a strong movement for independence and a new constitution was growing in Belgium.

In the debates that were provoked in Europe we can see how the shot was heard. We can follow them (as they were conducted in the press) through the 25 or so out-of-the-way historical monographs, memoirs, and so on, that are the main source of this story. Throughout the debates a constant appeal was made to the example of America. Liberty had been crushed in Poland, was struggling in Holland, said Lambert d'Outrement, a lawyer in Liege, but it had been maintained in England, and triumphed in America: "What will be the lot of the Austrian Low Countries?" There could be only one answer. Belgium would try itself. Toward the end of 1789 the States-General of the Austrian Netherlands deposed Joseph II and proclaimed the *United States* of Belgium. The Belgian Declaration of Independence (and the equivalent declarations of the provinces of Belgium, like the states in America) followed the American Declaration faithfully. In the Manifeste de la Province de Flandre (1790), "the Course of Human Events" became *"un Concours de circonstances . . . extraordinaires,"* and continued: *"En conséquence . . . au juge suprême de l'Univers . . . a droit d'être un Etat libre et indépendant"*—almost word for word the American original.

Thus, although the French Revolution had by then erupted, the inspiration was coming from America. The working people of Europe, it was said in the Belgian debates, must inevitably look to America. They had learned that conditions for the likes of them were better there, and many were emigrating. A telling use was made of America's distance from the mother country, since Belgium, like many of the territories of the Austrian Empire, was remote from the imperial capital and government in Vienna. Moreover when, during the War of Independence, the absolute monarchs of Europe entered into relations (and even alliances) with the Americans, they were in effect endorsing revolution. The monarchs might say that the American Revolution was intolerable, but by their actions they were telling their peoples that revolution was not a crime, but as d'Outrement said, *"un beau monument élevé à la liberté."*

THE SIGNIFICANCE Europeans attached to America was underlined by the deftness and even courage with which editors across the Continent managed to circumvent the censorship. In 1775-76 Denmark was a significant power. It included Norway (and Greenland, a Norwegian possession), Schleswig and Holstein, Iceland, and three West Indian islands, St. Croix, St. Thomas, and St. John (which were later sold to the United States). Given the insanity of Christian VII, it was governed by a court party as an enlightened despotism, and as usual a significant part of the extensive bureaucracy was the ever watchful censorship.

On August 23, 1776, the *Altonaischer Mercurius* (a German-language newspaper published in Altona in Holstein) printed an edited version of the Declaration, which was then translated and printed at the top of the front page of the *Kiobenhavske* [Copenhagen] *Tidender*, the newspaper with the largest circulation in Denmark. In both papers it appeared uncut as far as the sentence "The History of the present King of Great-Britain is a History of repeated Injuries and Usurpations, all having in direct Object the Establishment of absolute Tyranny over these States." The trouble was that the intermittently insane George III was one of the demented Christian's closest allies. So in the above sentence, the words "King of Great-Britain" were replaced by "the present ministry of Great Britain." But the Declaration continued with the long list of grievances against George, and it was all too likely that any Danish reader would have begun ticking off in his mind his own grievances against the Danish monarchy. Ingeniously, the *Mercurius* solved the problem by publishing the Declaration in two halves, the second (with the grievances) appearing on August 26, in which all the references to King George were replaced by the anonymous *"Er"* (he). This appeased the censors; it cannot have fooled the readers.

How different it was in the New World. Over in the West Indies, the only Danish newspaper, the *Royal Danish American Gazette*, published (significantly) in English, printed the complete Declaration as early as August 17, even placing it prominently on the front page, which was otherwise reserved for advertising. The Danes in the colonies seemed themselves to have become Americans.

It was not only the editors in Denmark (and elsewhere), nosy for news, who were excited by the events in America. As early as October 22, 1776, A. P. Bernstorff, the great Danish minister for foreign affairs, wrote to a friend: "The public here is extremely occupied with the rebels [in America], not because they know the cause, but because the mania of independence in reality has infected all the spirits, and the poison has spread imperceptibly from the works of the philosophes all the way out to the village schools." Those last eight words, from such a source, tell us something we need to know.

So does a firsthand glimpse of the popular mood in Copenhagen. The *Aftenpost* carried a column—as we would now call it—by one Edmund Balling, describing life in the city; it sounds like a city column by Jimmy Breslin or Mike Royko. Balling dropped into alehouses, which he described as "our political schools of Fencing, those bourgeois Art of War Listening Rooms, where our little Politici, during a Glass of Ale, a Pinch of Snuff and a Pipe of Tobacco," tossed about the issues of the day. At the end of 1776 he found them debating the War of Independence. One said the Americans were rebels, and "ought to be beaten over the Forehead like Bullocks"; another countered that "the English ought to be thrashed"; a third had no doubt that the English had got "something to chew on"; and a sausage-stuffer called it an "accursed War" because the rice from South Carolina had become so dear, and what could he now stuff his sausages with in place of meat? On January 12, 1778, Balling told of a man entering an alehouse (after reading the news, one guesses, of Burgoyne's defeat): "Good evening, Gentlemen! Ha! Ha! Have we the newspapers? Well, what does England say now? . . . Yes, this War will likely make a rather considerable Change in Europe."

As in Belgium, the impact did not lessen even after America achieved its independence. In 1820 a Danish civil servant, C. F. von Schmidt-Phiseldeck, called the Fourth of July "this forever memorable day." And in our own time a Danish historian has said that "the Declaration of Independence had a decisive impact on the course of events leading to the attainment in 1849 of Denmark's first democratic constitution."

BUT AS WE come across the editors, their newspapers, and their readers, the European response is telling us something very important about the American Revolution itself. It was carried in the colonies and overseas by the assertiveness of the American middle class. One of George III's more apt comments was that his sovereignty was being challenged by a lot of "grocers." Marx was really saying no more when he declared that "the American Revolution sounded the tocsin for the European bourgeoisie," and gave "the first impulse to the European Revolution." Lenin later said the War of Independence was "one of those great, truly liberating, truly revolutionary wars"—something that cannot be said of the revolution he wrought in Russia.

Two vigorous merchant cities—Hamburg and Dubrovnik—illustrate the response of a newly aggressive merchant class in Europe. Hamburg was a free port, as most of its dock area still is (its official name even now is the Free and Hanseatic City of Hamburg), and since the Reformation had been the proud refuge of Protestants, other dissidents, and refugees. Ports are naturally liberal, being used to strangers, with their different cultures and ideas. When the Declaration was published in the *Staats und Gelehrte Zeitung*, its citizens naturally sympathized with the colonies in their claim to be a free trading nation, with which Hamburg could expand its commercial ties (as it did after the war), greatly reinforcing its prosperity. Completing the story, another cargo would eventually stream through Hamburg: a vast number of immigrants to the New World from Russia and Eastern Europe. Dubrovnik had risen to be a powerful merchant republic in the Middle Ages, and had existed since then (virtually independent) under the protection, in suc-

cession, of Venice, Hungary, and Turkey—until Napoleon, with his usual disrespect for history, abolished the republic in 1806, the same year in which he occupied Hamburg. Again, far away on the Adriatic, the citizens of a strong merchant port were stimulated by the news from America, a point made in a book published by the city of Dubrovnik to celebrate the bicentennial of the Declaration.

IT IS the response of the middle class in Europe that throws light on the attitudes in England. To the ruling class in England the Declaration of Independence did not herald the dawn of a new age, or introduce new abstract principles of freedom and equality that had a universal application. In fact, it seemed to them less of a threat than it did to the ruling monarchs on the Continent, since they enjoyed many of the freedoms the Americans were claiming. It was to them a very local document, a list (as indeed it was) of very local grievances. Neither it nor any shot, in their view, was heard round the world. Both had been aimed, after all, at them; and on the whole they took it like gentlemen.

Here was a war in which the First British Empire, as it is known to history, was falling, and it is natural we should wish that the author of *The Decline and Fall of the Roman Empire*, who was a member of Parliament throughout the war, had offered a long historical perspective or a few grand philosophical reflections on so great an event. But Edward Gibbon's attitude was not only devious; it was corrupt, even if in the accepted manner of the day. No one can blame him for wishing to write the great book, or for wishing to receive some patronage as he labored at his task. He looked, of course, to the government for an appointment, and accepted the post of one of the Lords Commissioner of Trade and Plantations. With this sinecure, his voice and vote were bought by George III and his ministers, which makes one appreciate even more the king's dig at him one day, "Scribble, scribble, scribble, eh, Mr. Gibbon?"

At the end of the difficult parliamentary session in 1775, Gibbon was glad to get away, saying that "having saved the British I must destroy the Roman Empire." But this little jest was capped by an American. Horace Walpole reported with delight in a letter in 1781: "Dr. [Benjamin] Franklin . . . said he would furnish Mr. Gibbon with materials for writing the History of the Decline of the British Empire." A lampoon went the rounds in London during the war. Attributed to Charles James Fox, a dauntless leader of the opposition and staunch friend of the Americans, two verses ran:

King George in a fright
Lest Gibbon should write
The history of England's disgrace
Thought no way so sure
His pen so secure
As to give the historian a place.

His book well describes
How corruption and bribes
O'erthrew the great empire of Rome;

And his rantings declare
A degeneracy there
Which his conduct exhibits at home.

We do not get wit like that from our politicians now.

Whether in Gibbon's own jest, Franklin's quip, or Fox's lampoon, there is nothing to suggest that the governing class in London could work itself into any great passion over the American war—neither the supporters nor the opponents of the American cause. (Though the consummate and by then aged orator William Pitt, for whom Pittsburgh was named, reinforced his impassioned philippic in defense of the American colonists by collapsing unconscious on the floor of the House at the end.)

W E ALSO KNOW how the American news was received outside London. In December 1775 the daily journal of the Rev. James Woodforde (a country parson in Weston, Norfolk, of ordinary loyalty to the Crown) gave "notice of a Fast being kept on Friday next concerning the present war between America and us." Note that the colonists are not called subjects or rebels, as on the Continent, but *America*, as if they were already a nation. The war then seems to have aroused little interest until there was another official Day of Prayer in 1780, for it was by then clear that God was not pulling his weight. So the good parson "read the proper prayers on the Occasion, but there was no sermon preached. My Squire and Lady at the Church. . . . Sister Clarke, Nancy, Sam and myself all took it into our heads to take a good dose of Rhubarb on going to bed." Rhubarb is an astringent purgative—a very English way of disposing of the news of fresh disasters, rather like taking a "nice cup o' tea" in the Blitz.

In 1781 he recorded the news that "Cornwallis and his whole army . . . are all taken by the Americans and French in Virginia." That is all; not dismay, no commotion, no anger. When it was all over, the news of the Treaty of Versailles was a "joyful" event, though England had suffered a great defeat and lost a vast possession. There remained only the aftermath, an entry as late as December 9, 1785: ". . . to a poor soldier laterly [sic] arrived from America that had been wounded & is now ill gave 1 [shilling] and 6 [pence]"—a neglected veteran of an unpopular, unsuccessful war.

Throughout the war we could have found Horace Walpole at home in London, writing to his friends the letters that now fill 36 volumes in the Yale edition. One of Europe's most intelligent and cultivated men, he chose (happily for us) to be a spectator of great events rather than an actor in them. He returned again and again to the American question, urbane, tart, and outraged. Why are we in America? he asked, as 200 years later he might have asked about Vietnam. "We could even afford to lose America," he wrote as early as March 28, 1774. After Washington's victory at Trenton he wrote: "What politicians are those that have preferred the empty name of *sovereignty* to that of *alliance*! and forced subsidies to the golden age of oceans and commerce." The Americans, he pointed out to a friend,

"do not pique themselves upon modern good breeding, but level at the officers, of whom they have slain a vast number." This savage amusement at the fact that the Americans "impertinently" fired on English officers is a wholly accurate reflection of "the amazing heights which pro-Americanism could reach in London," as one researcher found it in even the popular novels of the day. The Boston Tea Party was to him the symbol of English official stupidity: "Mrs. Britannia orders her senate to proclaim America a continent of cowards, and vote it should be starved unless it drink tea with her."

By the end of 1777 Walpole was writing: "We have been horribly the aggressors." A week after the capitulation at Yorktown, but before he had news of it, he proclaimed: "The English in America are as much my countrymen as those born in the parish of St. Martin's in the Field; and when my countrymen quarrel, I think I am free to wish better to the sufferers than to the aggressors; nor can I see how my love of my country obliges me to wish well to what I despise. . . . Were I young and of heroic texture, I would go to America." It is clear from all the evidence that the English people as a whole could not have their hearts in a war against their "countrymen."

B UT THERE WAS one exception to this generally unexcited and unideological response in England, and it is illuminated by the reaction on the Continent. The merchants of the City of London and of other expanding cities of the new middle class in England identified their own interests closely with those of the colonists. The London press, almost without exception, was the voice of this class. With the introduction of the tax on the colonists' trade in molasses and sugar in 1764, the *London Chronicle* at once reported from the west coast port of Bristol, which depended on the American trade, that "the principal merchants of the city intend to support with all their interest the independent free trade of the American colonies." In the numerous and remarkably free English newspapers we can trace how this argument from interest developed steadily into an ideological assertion. As the Americans, during those extraordinary ten years from 1765 to 1775, worked out the philosophical grounds on which they would claim independence, the English merchant class found itself examining and then adopting the same arguments.

In resisting taxation "without representation" by the English Parliament, the Americans (those "grocers") argued that in *English custom* and "natural law" there was a power above Parliament—in short, the Constitution in revolutionary thinking, in the work of the Founding Fathers, and forever afterward in the mind of America. The idea that Parliament was sovereign was then a fairly new development, and there were many at home who objected to it, but it was the American colonists who clarified the issue by their dogged resistance. Moreover, the English middle class had its own doubts about the justice of the parliamentary system as it then existed. The Industrial Revolution was reaching its flood, and beyond London many of the rising middle-class cities such as Manchester and Sheffield were not represented at all. So the American cry of "no taxation without representation" drew a strong echo from them.

When the news of the Boston Tea Party reached England, the *London Packet* called such resistance lawful and even honorable against "tyrannic" measures. After Lexington and Concord the *London Evening Post* said that "the prevailing toast in every company of true Englishmen is, 'Victory to the Americans, and re-establishment to the British Constitution.'" (No one was arrested or imprisoned in England for supporting the Americans.) Thus in England as in Europe the American cause had been translated into a universal cause—by a rising class. The American Revolution represented the spontaneously international ideology of this class, which was feeling its strength in Europe, growing assertive in England, and already established in America, even able to organize and arm itself for war.

Of all the dramatic assertions in the Declaration of Independence, none is more "impertinent" than the assurance with which the 13 colonies said they had decided to "assume among the Powers of the Earth, the separate and equal Station" to which they were entitled. Yet the presumption was not as great as it seems. As early as 1765 a correspondent in the *London Magazine* said: "Little doubt can be entertained, that this vast country will in time become the most prosperous empire that perhaps the world has ever seen." This was widely appreciated, and both the English and Europeans were aware of the rapid increase in America's population, and of Franklin's estimate that it would double every 25 years. Shortly after Lexington and Concord the *Chester Chronicle* quoted Bishop Berkeley's poem, "Westward the course of Empire takes its way."

ONCE THE NEWS of the fateful shot reached the courts of Europe, the monarchs were alert to the effect the American rebellion might have on the balance of power in Europe. George III at once dispatched a personal envoy to Catherine the Great, to request fewer than 20,000 Russian troops for help in suppressing the American insurrection. But Catherine did not have a high opinion of George, and refused to supply any soldiers or to make the treaty that Britain wanted. She and her government were extremely well informed about American affairs, and on receiving news of the Declaration, the counselor of the Russian Embassy in London wrote to the Russian foreign minister, N. I. Panin, saying that both it and the prosecution of a formal war against Britain "offer evidence of all the courage of leadership" in America.

King George had no better luck in Vienna. Austria had been allied with France since 1756, but by 1775 it was exhausted by the Seven Years' War, and urgently trying to resist the rise of Prussia in the east under Frederick the Great. Maria Theresa saw that Austria needed to secure its position in the west by friendship with both England and France, and by 1776 wished to revive her earlier friendship with England. In 1777 she wrote to her daughter Marie Antoinette (who had none of her inquiring intelligence or even savvy, and paid the price at the guillotine) that the "war in America" troubled her, as well it might since it pitted France and England against each other. She therefore skillfully maintained Austria's neutrality throughout the war, and forbade both English and American recruiting in Hapsburg lands.

This response of the European monarchs—Denmark also remained neutral, in spite of its alliance with England and its far-flung shipping and trading interests—was the clearest recognition that America had indeed become a new nation on something like equal terms with the oldest and most imperious in the Old World, at once acting and being accepted on the stage of Europe as one of the "Powers of the Earth."

It must be remembered that the enlightened despots were significant figures of the Enlightenment; Catherine corresponded regularly with Voltaire. There was therefore nothing particularly remarkable in the fact that the chief assistant to Panin as the Russian foreign minister was D. I. Fonvizin, whose plays boldly satirized the Russian aristocracy and the institution of serfdom. When Fonvizin traveled through Europe in 1777-78, he met Benjamin Franklin at a *rendez-vous des gens de lettres*, calling him in a letter to his sister "the glorious Franklin." (Franklin wrapped the European intellectuals around his little finger.) Another Russian, commenting on this meeting, wrote: "The representative of the young enlightenment of Russia was an interlocutor with the representative of young America." The excitement at such a meeting demonstrates yet another way in which the new United States, a child of the Enlightenment, impressed itself on Europe as already a mature nation.

THE STORY of how the shot was heard round the world carries obvious instructions. Any notion that the War of Independence was only a rebellion falls to the ground. Both rulers and their subjects saw it as a revolution of universal appeal. The dynamism of that appeal was derived from the fact that the Americans had already built a great trading nation and created not only a strong middle class in the process, but a society that as a whole was middle-class in its temper and energy. What is more, as a result of the preparation between 1765 and 1775—ten of the most creative years in political thinking in the history of the world—the Americans entered the War of Independence with a profound political philosophy that immediately lit fires round the world. They are not yet extinguished.

The names of two unknown villages, Lexington and Concord, became household words even as far as Dubrovnik and St. Petersburg. And on any Fourth of July one cannot help thinking of the few minutemen who took their stand on a bridge and sent the drilled Redcoats running with their tails between their legs back into Boston.

Life, Liberty, and the Pursuit of Happiness: AMERICA'S MODEST REVOLUTION

"Unlike the French revolutionary tradition, the American Revolution was far more modest. This very modesty is the core of its phenomenal success. . . ."

John R. Kayser

Dr. Kayser is associate professor of political science, University of New Hampshire, Durham.

WHEN Soviet Premier Nikita S. Khrushchev boasted, "We will bury you," he was not simply premature, he was totally wrong. There is a fitting historical irony to the fact that 1989 marked both the bicentennial of the French Revolution and the collapse of the French revolutionary tradition in the East. (Lenin claimed that the communist revolutionaries were 20th-century versions of the radicals of the French Revolution.) Today, events in Eastern Europe signal the failure of the French revolutionary tradition. As thousands of citizens from communist nations pour into the West, lured as much by our principles as our prosperity, we must resist the temptation to imitate Khrushchev and gloat. Instead, we should take this historical moment to reflect on the cause of our victory.

The triumph of the West in 1989 began in 1776, the year of the American Revolution. Ours was the first of the great egalitarian revolutions of the 18th century; the other was the French. To a large extent, the modern world has been shaped by these upheavals.

The French revolutionary tradition is the more radical of the two. With its surface idealism, cry for total commitment, and vision of a completely restructured society peopled by totally restructured human beings, it well serves the interests of modern radical revolutionaries. However, the French revolutionary tradition is beset with failure. In its original form, it hardly can be considered successful. Since its crystalization, France has had five different republics, one empire, a restored monarchy, and various other short-lived regimes. Added to this is the deep divisiveness the revolution caused within French society.

The waning of the French revolutionary tradition is not difficult to understand. Its aim goes well beyond politics. Seeking to transform human nature, recast the world, and bring about entirely new relationships among individuals, it is a "total" revolution. Moreover, it claims to be enlightened and scientific, and hence reasonable. Inability to achieve its goals—so clearly "reasonable"—must be the result of a counter-revolutionary conspiracy. Such conspiracies must be rooted out and conspirators destroyed. Thus, the fictional Sidney Carton is led to the guillotine, the fictional Rubashov shot in the basement of a Moscow prison, and the all too non-fictional Chinese students murdered in Tiananmen Square. The revolution is not allowed to fail, and those who reveal its failure are disregarded if they are foreigners or silenced if they are citizens. There is, however, a limit to those who can be silenced and to concealing failure. That limit seems to have been reached in 1989.

The success of the American revolution, on the other hand, is evident in a variety of ways. Since the first operation of our government under the Constitution in March, 1789, we have had but one regime—a democratic republic. Granted, it sorely was tested in a horrible civil war, but the foundation, as Lincoln pointed out, prevailed. We are the oldest, continuous revolutionary republic in the world. We indeed have become, in the words of our founders, "a new order for the ages."

Our economic prosperity has kept pace with our political stability. In economic terms, we are the showcase of modernity. Nor is our wealth confined to the few. We have a general standard of living the rest of the world seeks to duplicate and which would evoke the envy of the nobility of preceding ages.

Intellectually, we stand second to none. Our great universities sponsor scientific advancement as they safeguard the past. These centers of learning not only are open to the privileged few, but are accessible to a vast majority of Americans.

In sum, the way of life produced by our revolution has exceeded that produced by other revolutionary traditions by so far that the question is not so much why others failed, but why ours succeeded.

"The real American revolution," said John Adams, "was the radical change in the principles, opinions, sentiments and affections of the people." We must seek these out if we are to discover the secret of our success. We do not have to look very far. We have a public document—indeed, the first law in the United States Code—which sets forth these principles, opinions, sentiments, and affections. This document, the anniversary of which we celebrate as our national birthday, is The Unanimous Declaration of the Thirteen

United States of America, better known as The Declaration of Independence.

The first significant principle of the American Revolution clearly is included in the proper title—unanimity. Indeed, it proves to be a harbinger of the success of our revolutionary regime. The great stumbling block to unanimity was the issue of slavery, which would haunt the republic until 1865. In his original draft of the document, Jefferson had inserted a strongly worded anti-slave clause denouncing the King for having compelled the colonists to adopt this inhuman practice. Only two of the 13 states were opposed to the clause, and it was at their behest that the other 11 compromised and deleted it from the document. Why compromise for only two states? Was unanimity so necessary?

For the framers, it was needed for two reasons—one practical, the other principled. In practical terms, adoption of the Declaration meant war. A divided nation was less apt to conclude that war successfully, hence the willingness to compromise. In terms of principle, unanimity reveals the basis of the political ideas animating the Declaration, and thus the revolution.

These concepts have a variety of sources, but the clearest is the English philosopher, John Locke. He stated that men originally are in a "state of nature," a condition in which there is no established authority and each man may act properly as his own judge, lawgiver, and executor. We may act in these capacities because we are all equal. According to Locke, "there being nothing more evident than that creatures of the same species . . . should be equal one amongst each another." Yet, such a state produces chaos. Each of us properly seeking his own preservation comes into conflict with everyone else. This leads naturally to a sort of war of all against all. Since we are all equal in the "state of nature" and each has all the rights of any other, movement toward legitimate authority—government—only can come about by consent. That acquiescence is the basis of a common identity, but such consent must be unanimous. Those who do not wish to become part of the new identity—to become one of the new people—don't. In more modern terms, this unanimous consent forms the basis of society, but not government. This is, of course, precisely what the Declaration does—it creates a people. This is why we use it as the date upon which to commemorate our national birthday.

Lest it be argued that the anti-slave cause was sacrificed on the altar of unanimity, we should be aware that the society created by the Declaration did not then have the power to abolish slavery. The inclusion of the anti-slave clause would not have freed a single slave. Yet, the adoption of the Declaration, as Lincoln stressed some four score and seven years later, made it morally impossible to maintain such a practice. Only by virtue of the revolutionary principles of the Declaration were men able to "see" the absolute injustice of slavery. Yet, between the "seeing" and the remedy lay a civil war. Looking back, we may marvel that the Framers' compromise was more apparent than real. Without the "compromised" Declaration, the slaves would have scant principles to which to appeal the injustice of their plight. The very compromise hints at both the practical and principled character of our founding—sacrifice what can not be achieved today in order that it may be achieved tomorrow.

Unanimity, in turn, hints at the *great* principle of the Declaration—equality. The first of the self-evident truths, it is the center of American political principles. This truth is self-evident in the sense in which axioms of geometry are—it is the reasonable basis of all other demonstrations and hence is not in need of proof itself. By equality, however, the Framers did not mean the obvious falsehood that we were equal in all respects or in talent. Following Locke, they declared that we were equal in the sense that no one of us had a natural or divinely granted right to rule another. All legitimate rule must be based upon consent. We are equal, then, in that no one is by nature or divine mandate superior to another. Any such political superiority must flow from the freely given consent of all parties.

We are equal in another "self-evident" way—in certain rights. Among these are life, liberty, and the pursuit of happiness. These rights are not given by the society created by the Declaration. Rather, the society is created to protect them better. They are so important that the Declaration goes beyond calling them natural, citing them as inalienable. That is, we can not relinquish them to government. These inalienable rights are to be seen as distant from civil rights. The latter stem not from our equal condition in the "state of nature," but from society. They are the *result of* the political process, while inalienable rights *create the necessity for* the political process.

The pursuit of happiness

The third inalienable right—to the pursuit of happiness—may be the clearest reason why our revolution proved so successful and the French and its heirs so unsuccessful.

The right to pursuit of happiness means exactly what it says. We are not guaranteed happiness, and the government is not to be judged according to whether it satisfies all we demand in the name of happiness—it guarantees us only the right to pursue that end.

In proclaiming this right, the Declaration takes a neutral stand with respect to the content of happiness. This is not as abstract or theoretical as it appears. At the time of the Declaration, governments did seek to promote a particular vision of happiness and that concept was necessarily part and parcel of government-sponsored religion. In practical terms, happiness meant a particular religious perspective. In the context of 1776, then, the pursuit of happiness meant no authoritative or state-supported vision of happiness, and hence no state religion. This is not to say the Framers were anti-religious or dogmatic atheists, as were their counterparts in the French and communist revolutions. Instead, they recognized the problems that dogma, religious or atheistic, posed for political society. Their toleration stemmed neither from an indifference to religion nor impiety, but from the profound fear of doctrinal warfare, a dread amply justified by an examination of the causes of the reign of terror in France or the purges in Stalin's U.S.S.R. and Mao's China.

Finally, the Declaration's principles conclude by affirming that government exists to protect these self-evident truths. Equality is protected by assuring that consent is at the heart of our politics. Such assent ranges from the unanimity of the Declaration, as well as the day-to-day majority rule in legislatures and in electing people to office. The rights are assured by provisions within the Constitution. The Declaration does not promise or seek to guarantee more than this.

Equality as consent does not lead necessarily to equivalence of condition. Indeed, equality as presented in the Declaration allows for the development of diverse talents with correspondingly different rewards. Rights as determined by the Declaration are limited to those essential for life and the pursuit of happiness. It thus creates a society characterized by limitations on what government can do to and for us. Above all, we are not to look to government as the remedy for all that ails humanity.

While the Declaration appeals to everyone, it does not offer everything to all men. Unlike the French revolutionary tradition, the American Revolution was far more modest. This very modesty is the core of its phenomenal success and has prevented government from becoming the big brother of communist revolutions. Moreover, it has averted the blood purge that usually follows those revolutions as a "cleansing" act. Such modesty should prevent us from imitating Khrushchev and boasting about burials. It is more apt that we imitate Tom Sawyer, who found his proudest moment in witnessing his own funeral.

SPIES IN THE REVOLUTION

GENERAL GEORGE WASHINGTON ESPIONAGE CHIEF

WALTER R. HAEFELE

Free-lance writer Dr. Walter R. Haefele is a retired California research chemist.

General George Washington's espionage system was a major factor in the Americans winning the Revolutionary War. Whether the commander of the Continental Army chose to fight or run, knowledge of British military strengths and movements was of crucial importance. Much of this information could be obtained only through the use of secret agents. On a number of occasions the possession of intelligence regarding enemy intentions tipped the scales to victory for the chronically outnumbered American forces. Deception also served Washington as an effective weapon, when on occasion he used his spy system in reverse to send misleading information to his opponents.

The American espionage system was primitive at first because Washington and his staff had little experience in covert operations. Fighting Indians in the woods during the French and Indian War had hardly prepared the Americans for spying on the British. But by 1777 Washington had smoothly functioning spy rings in Philadelphia, and from 1778 to the war's end several espionage groups were transmitting invaluable intelligence to him from New York City, site of the British headquarters. Within three years after the war began, Washington and his staff were employing spies, double agents, secret inks, and code books—all still basic intelligence techniques today.

Secrecy is paramount when running an intelligence operation, and Washington was especially careful to avoid betraying his agents. Today no Revolutionary War era secret files or day books about American espionage activities, such as those the British kept in New York during the war, exist to identify Washington's spies and agents. To gather information about American intelligence activities, historians have studied spies'

memoirs, incomplete expense accounts kept by Washington and his subordinates, and secret agents' letters that Washington and his staff copied. Spies destroyed letters that Washington wrote to them, but, fortunately for posterity, Washington saved facsimiles. Nevertheless, some of Washington's agents remain anonymous to this day.

Washington kept careful records of the government money he spent during the war. Of his total expenditures of $160,000, about $17,000—a great deal of money in those days—was spent for "reconnaissance." He paid his spies in cash, using bags of coins financier Robert Morris provided. These expenses increased rapidly as the war continued. For example, in 1777 Washington paid Nathaniel Sackett, who ran a spy ring in New Jersey and conducted counterespionage activities, $500 for expenses and $50 a month. But most secret agents served without pay and, for obvious reasons, without recognition.

From *American History Illustrated*, November/December 1989, pp. 22-27, 69-70. Reprinted through the courtesy of Cowles Magazines, publisher of *American History Illustrated*.

2. REVOLUTIONARY AMERICA

Early Experiences

In Boston during 1775 and early 1776, many patriots, including Paul Revere, were active amateur spies and saboteurs. They slipped through British lines in row boats, or sailed around them in their fishing boats, bringing Washington intelligence from within the British-occupied city. Washington welcomed the information but, still being inexperienced and unable to properly evaluate it, hesitated to act on it. Fortunately, no major action was needed in Boston at that time. After the Continental forces seized Dorchester Heights above Boston, their subsequent bombardments from there forced the British to leave the city in March 1776.

Early on, spying was a matter of finding an intelligent volunteer to send behind British lines. Captain Nathan Hale was a tragic example of this naïve policy. After the British landed on Long Island in late summer 1776 and soundly defeated the Continental Army there, Washington had to withdraw his troops to Manhattan. While his army regrouped, Washington needed to know British intentions and troop dispositions.

During an open meeting of his military unit, Hale, a twenty-one-year-old Yale graduate, volunteered to spy. He traveled to Long Island and behind the British lines without a cover name, money, contacts, or a safe house that might shelter him. He had no secret way to send back his observations and drawings, so that on September 21 the British caught him carrying in his shoe drawings and other intelligence information. The British hanged Hale, without a trial, in front of their artillery park near the Dove Tavern that stood near today's intersection of 66th Street and Third Avenue.

Appalled by the poorly-executed mission, Washington became almost fanatically secretive after Hale's death. The American commander grew convinced of the need to organize a "secret service." His officers were sworn to eternal secrecy, which is why many spies' identities remained unknown long after the war. Washington was well aware of the consequences of defeat or of his headquarters being overrun by the British. If records about his spies fell into British hands, the patriots would die on the gallows. Further, even a peace treaty might not end Tory reprisals against his wartime secret agents.

On July 26, 1777, Washington wrote to Colonel Elias Dayton, one of his intelligence officers, "The necessity of procuring good intelligence is apparent and need not be further urged. All that remains for me to add is, that you keep the whole matter as secret as possible. For upon Secrecy, Success depends in most enterprises of the kind, and for want of it, they are generally defeated. . . ."

Soon after the Hale fiasco, Washington had several spy masters and intelligence networks in operation. In addition to other duties, Colonel Elias Boudinot headed espionage in northern New Jersey, while Major Generals Israel Putnam and William Heath supervised the spies around New York. Nathaniel Sackett, a civilian, had a separate espionage network in Perth Amboy and New Brunswick, New Jersey. Washington ordered Major General Thomas Mifflin to establish one in Philadelphia.

Intelligence Success at Philadelphia

Mifflin's spy system started to deliver a few months later, after the Continental Army had to abandon Philadelphia and the British occupied it. By December 1776, Washington was headquartered at Valley Forge with his army confronting the British on an arc around Philadelphia.

Major John Clark, a brilliant intelligence officer who took over Mifflin's Philadelphia network, had among his informers there merchants, gentry, and a man aboard the British fleet, as well as old ladies, farmers, and tradesmen who passed through the city. Day and night Clark was on the move contacting his agents, who delivered a constant stream of information. His spy ring became so efficient that within a few hours after the battle of Germantown in October 1777 he was able to report the number of British casualties.

Other officers operated separate Philadelphia spy networks, and Washington personally directed some secret agents there.

Lydia Darragh, a Quaker housewife who had a son in the American army, lived on Second Street in Philadelphia, directly across from British headquarters. According to a tradition passed down by Lydia's descendants, her husband William wrote on bits of paper intelligence information she secured. She placed them in buttons, covered them with cloth, sewed them on her young son's coat, and sent him out through the British lines. The teen-ager sought out his brother, Lieutenant Charles Darragh, and soon the information was in Washington's hands.

After the British army usurped part of her house for conferences, Lydia listened one night through the wall of an adjacent closet. When she heard the British planning a December 4-5, 1777 surprise attack on a weak spot in Washington's lines at Whitemarsh, Pennsylvania, she used her British pass to walk through their lines to buy flour out in the country—and to warn the Americans. As a result, Washington entrenched his army at just the right place to defend against the attack. The British had intended a major breakthrough with more than five thousand men, but when they encountered strong resistance, they merely skirmished there, remaining for a few days before returning to Philadelphia.

Trying to find out why their plans had failed, the British questioned Lydia but took no action against her. This disappointment at Whitemarsh, reported in London by General Charles Cornwallis when he went on leave, discouraged the British there and in Philadelphia, and may have influenced British General William Howe's decision to resign his command and return to England. The brave woman in her prim, gray Quaker dress had scored a major intelligence coup.

Success at Trenton and Princeton

Washington's brilliant Christmas Day 1776 foray against the Hessians in Trenton, New Jersey achieved success largely because of the work of a brave spy named John Honeyman. A weaver, butcher, and British army veteran of the French and Indian War, Honeyman had met Washington earlier in Philadelphia and possibly spied for him there.

Honeyman's Trenton activities followed a prearranged scenario: he courageously allowed himself to be proclaimed a Tory and a traitor in his hometown of Griggstown, New Jersey. He then fled to British-occupied Trenton, posing as a butcher. Later he contrived to be arrested by the Americans as a suspected Tory spy, but only after he had specific information about Hessian strengths and troop dispositions. Washington insisted on questioning the captured Honeyman in his own tent.

To screen his intentions, Washington jailed Honeyman. Immediately afterward Honeyman escaped during a nearby fire, crossed the icy Delaware River, and bravely returned to Trenton. There he assured the Hessians that Washington's troops were disorganized; Honeyman then left town again. Although Washington's attack on Trenton the next day had its hazards, it was brilliantly successful because it was based on foreknowledge. The sleet storm that kept the Hessian mercenary troops indoors also helped. Within two hours the Continental army killed or wounded about one hundred and captured more than nine hundred Hessians without losing a single man. This victory boosted the patriots' morale—especially when the captured Hessians were paraded through the streets of Philadelphia.

In January 1777, one month after the battle of Trenton, Washington's spies provided him with extensive information about the British before the battle of Princeton, New Jersey. Anonymous today, these spies plotted all the approaches to Princeton, as well as the British defenses and their artillery and troop locations. Washington enjoyed the opportunity to chase fleeing British troops across an open field. The British retreated northward after the battle, and Washington's army settled into winter quarters in Morristown.

Spies Around New York

Because New York City housed British headquarters, important players in the American espionage game worked there and on nearby Long Island, setting up one of their first organized espionage networks.

At first Brigadier General Charles Scott supervised many of the spies on Long Island, but in 1778 Washington appointed Major Benjamin Tallmadge of the Second Regiment of Light Dragoons to take charge. Tallmadge, who had been Nathan Hale's close friend and classmate at Yale University, managed a highly effective team known as the Culper network. He also supervised other spies inside New York City; their identities are known only by initials in his record book. The intelligence they gathered came to him across Long Island Sound. He later wrote in his memoirs that he had "kept one or more boats constantly employed on this business."

To help him, Tallmadge, a native of Brookhaven, Long Island, enlisted his friends Abraham Woodhull and Robert Townsend, a Quaker and another member of Hale's 1773 Yale class. They were young men, financially well-off and of good social position, and thus able to mix easily with British officers. They set up a systematic information collection and transmission line that the British were never able to stop.

Townsend and a partner kept a general store in New York City. Following Washington's written instructions about espionage targets, he obtained information from British officers when they bought in his store and from Tories who unwittingly gossiped in coffee houses. To fool the British, he wrote articles for *The Royal Gazette*, a Tory newspaper owned by James Rivington, his partner in a coffee shop and, historians now believe, another of Washington's spies. Townsend had perhaps a dozen other sources in New York, including a woman known today only as "355." Woodhull occasionally visited New York to collect information, staying at his sister's house, where Townsend was a boarder.

In communications with Washington, Townsend became Samuel Culper, Jr., and Woodhull was Samuel Culper, Sr.; Tallmadge was John Bolton. Coded letters to and from Washington were usually written in invisible ink, and fragments of some messages are still preserved. John Jay, Continental Congress president and later the first chief justice of the United States, supplied bottles of the disappearing ink used for writing the letters, as well as the fluid used by Washington to make the writing visible again.

Tallmadge was an ingenious fellow. He devised a code book of 756 important words, including people's names, each having a number. He made only four copies—one each for Washington, the two Culpers, and himself. In this little book he also set up a substitution cipher, in which the letter "e" was "a," "f" was "b," "t" was "z," and so on. Here is an example, written originally in invisible ink, from one of Culper's letters: "Dqpeu Beyocpu agreeable to 28 met 723 not far from 727," which meant "Jonas Hawkins agreeable to appointment met Robert Townsend not far from New York."

To conceal what he was writing to Washington, Townsend (Culper, Jr.) extracted a blank sheet from the middle of a ream of paper, wrote on it with secret ink, then reinserted it carefully in the ream again. The stack of sheets was then wrapped carefully and sealed to resemble an unopened ream.

Culper spy ring courier Austin Roe brought instructions from Tallmadge to New York, periodically riding the fifty-five-mile distance on relays of horses. When he left, he added to his other purchases the ream of paper with Townsend's letter interleaved, braving the searches of British sentries at the Long Island ferry. Riding 110 miles in two days was exhausting, and on more than one of his missions Roe was assailed and robbed.

In Setauket he extracted the special sheet of paper from the stack and strolled over to see his cattle in Woodhull's (Culper Sr.'s) field; there Roe deposited the sheet in a concealed box. Woodhull retrieved Townsend's letter, added information from other spies on Long Island in a secret note of his own, and sent the intelligence across Long Island Sound on Caleb Brewster's whaleboat.

Woodhull knew where the rendezvous with Brewster's boat would be by watching Anna Strong's clothesline across the creek in Strongs' Neck. A black petticoat hanging on the line signalled that Brewster had arrived from Connecticut, and the number of handkerchiefs on the line indicated which of six landing places was being used. Woodhull delivered the messages there and Brewster ferried them across to Tallmadge, who sent the secret letters to Washington's headquarters by relays of special couriers spaced fifteen miles apart.

Washington relied heavily on the Culpers' information; he wrote in May 1781 that "of the Culpers' fidelity and ability I entertain the highest opinion." This network sent back a stream of intelligence about British ships and troop movements, destinations, arrivals of supplies and informed speculations about intentions. A British attack on New London, Connecticut was foiled by warnings from the Culpers.

Benedict Arnold and John André

The Culper network sent back the first intimations that something peculiar was going on at West Point, then commanded by Brigadier General Benedict Arnold. British Major John André was visiting at Townsend's father's home in Oyster Bay, Long Island, where other British officers were quartered. Townsend's sister Sarah saw a stranger leave a letter addressed to John Anderson on a kitchen shelf and saw André slip in and pick it up. Later, she overheard André and other British officers speaking in low voices about a man named Anderson and the advantages of seizing West Point and its great quantity of military stores. Suspicious, she informed her brother in New York, who promptly sent a message across the Sound to Tallmadge.

When the message reached him about a day later, Tallmadge learned that a man named Anderson, who soon admitted he was André, had recently been caught carrying in his boots intelligence information, including plans of West Point fortifications. When Tallmadge remembered hearing that Arnold had issued an order specifically permitting "Anderson" to pass through the American lines, he immediately realized what was happening. The sequence of events Tallmadge then triggered almost caused Arnold to be apprehended before he defected and boarded a British sloop.

With so many British officers quartered in his Long Island town and even in his house, Woodhull often feared discovery. He suffered a nervous collapse after two rollicking ladies burst into his room one night as he was writing a spy letter in invisible ink. But after some weeks and a visit from Tallmadge, he resumed his intelligence activities.

Arnold had been in Washington's confidence so long that everyone in the Culper spy network was terrified after Arnold defected and became a British general in New York City. Arnold apparently named several American spies, and the British subsequently seized them, including agent 355, Townsend's common-law wife. Condemned and imprisoned, she died a few months later aboard a British prison ship. Disheartened, Townsend left New York. But after a few months he returned and resumed gathering intelligence.

Townsend and Woodhull were truly master spies; their intrepid network operated from 1778 until the war's end, sending invaluable intelligence about the British to Washington. Secrecy became such a habit with Townsend and Woodhull that they carried their secrets to their graves. Diligent research by historians 150 years later eventually revealed the identities of these two agents.

Other New York Agents

Washington had other spies in New York City, some of whom he managed himself. Carefully following his own orders, he kept their identities secret even from Tallmadge and other American intelligence officers. Although some of Washington's spies traveled in and out of the city, he preferred those who had a long-standing cover there. Hercules Mulligan was a popular New York City tailor patronized by many British soldiers and Tories. For years Mulligan passed intelligence information to the Americans, enduring the hatred of his neighbors who thought he was a die-hard Tory. Later they were surprised to see Washington visit the tailor's house for breakfast on the morning after the American general entered New York to observe the British depart from the city on the First Evacuation Day, November 25, 1783.

As the war continued, Washington's spy system became truly sophisticated. He used several double agents to confuse the British. An agent named Captain Elijah Hunter was well-accepted in New York by General Henry Clinton, the British commander. The British thought Hunter was a Tory and asked him to spy on the Americans. Although suspicious of Hunter at first, despite John Jay's recommendation, Washington eventually accepted Hunter and used him to send false as well as accurate information to Clinton.

Davis Gray, a Continental Army captain, became another of Washington's double agents. He even talked the British into placing him in *their* secret service! Gray's work for the British involved carrying letters in and out of New York. While so doing, he took intelligence to Washington and brought back a mixture of accurate and false intelligence to the British. Occasionally he betrayed a few Tories. In September 1781, when he learned that traitor Benedict Arnold's new British legion was planning to attack New London, Connecticut, Gray commanded some American militia and fought bravely at Fort Groton. He then resumed his spy activities. To protect Gray, Washington for several years had the double agent specially listed as a deserter, but in May 1782 Gray was allowed to rejoin the Continental Army.

With Washington's approval, American Captain Caleb Bruen joined Clinton's British spy staff. The British general's secret records, now at the University of Michigan, reveal that the British asked Bruen to spy on the Americans and to act as a courier of information from other British spies in New Jersey and Rhode Island.

Alexander Bryan and Burgoyne's Defeat

Perhaps the most important single spy coup of the entire war was that of a courageous, inexperienced amateur, Alexander Bryan. In the fall of 1777 the American cause had its darkest hour. Washington's army had been beaten in the battles of Brandywine and Germantown, and Burgoyne's army was marching down from Canada. The British plan was to squeeze Washington's American Major General Horatio Gates's armies in a pincer movement between Burgoyne's and Howe's forces located at Philadelphia and New York.

Gates was lucky. He persuaded Bryan to enter the British lines near Saratoga, New York and investigate. Bryan bought some fabric from the British, then wandered around, posing as a man seeking a tailor. He brought back facts about British army strength and the news that Burgoyne planned to attack Bemis Heights; Gates prepared accordingly—and won a glorious victory.

At a time when American morale was at a low ebb, this astounding victory roused the country to further resistance and brought the French into the war on the American side. The success was a major turning point in the war—and Bryan, a rank amateur, had a large role in it.

Deception as a Weapon

Although Washington's integrity was absolute, he knew how to deceive when necessary. In the terrible winter of January to May 1778 that the Continental Army spent at Morristown, the force's numbers dwindled at one time to fewer than four thousand men. Enlistments expired and soldiers returned home. Food was scarce, and housing was scattered and wretched. Even ammunition was a problem. Washington was anxious lest the veteran British troops thirty miles away at Perth

Amboy, New Jersey would sally forth to destroy his tiny army.

Washington had his generals prepare false reports of the number of men under their command. He then had the reports sent to Congress via a route where the British were sure to capture the courier. Additional confirming "evidence" was leaked to the British from an "informed" source in Philadelphia. With this information in hand, the British commander refused to believe the account of a British officer, a former prisoner of war, who described the weakness of Washington's army after having just escaped from the American camp. The unusually cold winter caused the British to seize any excuse to stay in their warm quarters, leaving Washington's army unmolested.

In October 1777, after losing the battles of Brandywine and Germantown, Washington's army was in perilous condition. Although Burgoyne had surrendered to Gates at Saratoga, Washington needed time to rebuild his forces. He arranged to have spurious orders to Gates and two other generals intercepted by the enemy in order to deceive Clinton, the British commander in chief, into thinking that Gates was headed down the Hudson River to attack. Washington simultaneously used the clever Major Clark and his Philadelphia spy network to leak different false information about American strength to British General Howe.

This elaborate hoax tricked Howe into believing that papers "stolen" from American army files would be delivered to him secretly by a "trustworthy" Quaker who spied because he opposed all wars. Washington must have chuckled as he wrote some of the false documents, including one specifying his military intentions. The result: both Clinton and Howe kept their troops at home.

In July 1780 the Culper spy network in New York informed Wash-

ington of nine British ships preparing to board eight thousand troops and artillery and sail up Long Island Sound toward Newport, Rhode Island, where an outnumbered French fleet was disembarking troops. Because Washington realized that his army was too weak to attack Manhattan, he resorted to subterfuge: a well-respected Tory farmer delivered to the British a packet of letters he had "found" on the road. The letters detailed Washington's "authentic" plans for twelve thousand Continental troops to attack Manhattan. Clinton, the commander, was deluded; using special signal fires along Long Island Sound, he sent orders to his ships to return to defend New York. The French landed in Newport unhindered.

Using his spy system and other methods, Washington supplied false information to the British on still other occasions. Thus did espionage play a major role in assuring an American victory—and a new nation. The legend of young George Washington not lying about chopping down the cherry tree has survived through the years, but where military matters were concerned, Washington had a talent for deceit.

Recommended additional reading: General Washington's Spies on Long Island and in New York *by Morton Pennypacker (Brooklyn: Long Island Historical Society, 1939),* Turncoats, Traitors, and Heroes *by John Bakeless (Philadelphia: J.B. Lippincott Co., 1959), and* Secret History of the American Revolution *by Carl Van Doren (New York: Viking Press, 1941) are three classic studies of espionage during the Revolution. The* Encyclopedia of American Intelligence and Espionage From the Revolutionary War to the Present *by G.J.A. O'Toole (New York: Facts On File, 1988) is a fascinating, recently published compendium of information on spies and spying.*

'IT IS NOT A UNION'

Peter Onuf

Peter Onuf, 40, is associate professor of history at Worcester Polytechnic Institute. Born in New Haven, Connecticut, he received an A.B. (1967) and a Ph.D. (1973) from Johns Hopkins University. He is the author of The Origins of the Federal Republic: Jurisdictional Controversies in the United States 1775–87 *(1983), and* Statehood and Union: A History of the Northwest Ordinance *(1987).*

When news of the Peace of Paris reached the United States in the spring of 1783, war-weary Americans marked the event with jubilant parades. In Philadelphia, a writer in the *Pennsylvania Gazette* pleaded with his fellow citizens to restrain their revels during the celebratory "illumination of the city." It was the end of seven long years of deprivation and sacrifice, and an occasion for much pride: The United States (with crucial help from France) had just bested the mightiest power on earth.

Patriots looked forward to a new epoch of prosperity and growth. In a Fourth of July oration in 1785, a prominent Boston minister named John Gardiner declared that "if we make a right use of our natural advantages, we soon must be a truly great and happy people." The hinterland would become "a world within ourselves, sufficient to produce whatever can contribute to the necessities and even the superfluities of life."

Many Americans shared Gardiner's optimism. Their land was inherently rich in natural resources, still barely exploited. Virtually all of its three million inhabitants (including some 600,000 black slaves) still lived within 100 miles of the Atlantic Ocean, in a band of settlement stretching some 1,200 miles from Maine to Georgia. In 1790, the first U.S. census would establish the nation's demographic center at a point 25 miles *east* of Baltimore. At the time of the Revolution, that Maryland city, with a population of some 6,000, was the nation's fifth largest, behind Philadelphia (30,000), New York (22,000), Boston (16,000), and Charleston (14,000).

Directly or indirectly, city folk depended upon trade for their livelihood. Merchant ships set sail for Europe bearing wheat, corn, fur pelts, dried fish—or headed down the coast to pick up cargoes of tobacco, indigo, and rice from Southern plantations before crossing the Atlantic. They returned carrying calico, velvet, furniture, brandy, machinery, and often with new immigrants. Labor shortages in the cities pushed wages for servants, stevedores, and carpenters far higher than those prevailing in the cities of Europe. Many foreign visitors remarked on the new nation's general good fortune. "Nor have the rich the power of oppressing the less rich," said Thomas Cooper, a British scientist, "for poverty such as in Great Britain is almost unknown." (Such reports were not always reliable. One traveler wrote home about the amazing American Wakwak tree, with fruit that grew in the shape of a young woman.)

A Christian Sparta?

But the overwhelming majority of Americans—more than 90 percent—lived on farms. On a tract of 90 to 160 acres, the typical American farmer grew corn and other staples for home consumption, and raised chickens, pigs, and a dairy cow or two for his family, with perhaps a few extra animals to be bartered in the village market. Visits to town were weekly events at best; anyone who journeyed more than 50 miles from home was probably heading west, leaving for good. People and news traveled slowly. It took about a month for a Philadelphia newspaper to reach Pittsburgh, then a crude frontier outpost 250 miles inland.

Despite the general sparsity of population, local crowding and worn-out cropland in New England produced growing numbers of migrants. They crossed the Appalachians over rough wagon trails to the frontier in western Pennsylvania and Virginia, or to the future states of Kentucky, Tennessee, and Ohio. Other settlers moved South, to Georgia and the Carolinas. And all during the 1780s modest numbers of new

From *The Wilson Quarterly*, Spring 1987, pp. 97-103. Copyright © 1987 by The Woodrow Wilson International Center for Scholars.

immigrants from Europe continued to arrive at East Coast ports, chiefly from Ireland, Scotland, and Germany.

And yet, despite the outward signs of economic vitality during the mid-1780s, there was a growing alarm among many of the new nation's leaders—men such as George Washington, John Jay, and Alexander Hamilton. The states, only loosely bound together under the Articles of Confederation of 1781, were constantly bickering over conflicting territorial claims beyond the Appalachians, and Congress was powerless to mediate. Near Wilkes-Barre, Pennsylvania militiamen had even opened fire on Connecticut settlers.

Spain and Great Britain were poised to take advantage of the frontier's "anarchy." To the north, British troops still garrisoned forts along the Great Lakes, a violation of the Treaty of Paris. To the south, the Spaniards, who held New Orleans and claimed all the lands west of the Mississippi, had closed the great river to American shipping below Natchez. King Charles III's officers were actively encouraging American settlers in Kentucky to break away from the Union and establish political and commercial relations with Spain.

Washington and his allies worried less about America's outright conquest by a foreign power than the nation's fragmentation and decline into a state of degrading neocolonial dependency. A postwar consumer spree deepened that concern. Samuel Adams, the austere Bostonian, fretted that his countrymen's hunger for "luxury" goods imported from England—glassware, clocks, rugs—was "prostituting all our glory, as people." Few of his peers shared Adams's vision of a future America reigning as a virtuous "Christian Sparta," but they worried that the expensive imports would drain the nation of scarce hard currency and hinder the growth of domestic industry.

The states themselves were badly divided over these and other issues. The merchants, farmers, and fishermen of the North regarded the slave-owning plantation proprietors of the South with deep suspicion. Geographically and culturally, great distances separated them. Thomas Jefferson once drew up a list comparing the people of the two regions, describing Northerners as "chicaning," "jealous of their liberties and those of others," and "hypocritical in their religion." Southerners, he said, were "candid," "zealous for their own liberties but trampling on those of others," and devoted only to the religion "of the heart."

Economic issues were also divisive. Many Northern traders and politicians were angered by British laws that banned American merchantmen from the lucrative trade with the British West Indies, involving the exchange of Southern tobacco and rice for Caribbean sugar, molasses, and rum. But the Southerners feared a Northern monopoly on that traffic more than they did the relatively benign British one. Pierce Butler, later a South Carolina delegate to the Federal Convention, declared that the interests of North and South were "as different as the interests of Russia and Turkey."

Do-Nothing Congress

None of these challenges would have proved insurmountable for a strong national government. But the Continental Congress, operating under the Articles of Confederation, was ineffective. The Confederation was but "a firm league of friendship," as the 1781 document put it, that left the states their "sovereignty, freedom and independence, and every Power, Jurisdiction and right" not expressly delegated to the Continental Congress.

Among the many powers left to the states was that of taxing the citizenry. Congress received its revenues by levies on the state governments—"a timid kind of recommendation from Congress to the States," as George Washington described it. If a state chose not to pay, as often happened, Congress could do nothing.

Not only did the Articles grant Congress few powers, but they made it difficult for the legislature to exercise those that it did possess. There was no real executive, only a largely ceremonial president of Congress. The congressmen voted by states (there was thus no fixed number of legislators), and most important measures required the assent of nine of the 13 states to become law. Substantive amendments of the Articles could be adopted only by a unanimous vote in Congress and by the state legislatures. Every effort to strengthen the Confederation failed.

The history of the Articles themselves illustrates the difficulty of organizing concerted action by the states. A year after the Declaration of Independence, the Continental Congress, assembled in Philadelphia, had finally endorsed a draft of the Articles and sent it to the new state legislatures for ratification. Each of the ex-Colonies had strong objections, but, amid the pressures of wartime, they all swallowed their misgivings—except Maryland. It held out for four years, until March 1781. Meanwhile, the Continental Congress was forced to carry on the war effort without any constitutional authority. Laboring under enormous handicaps, it gave George Washington's beleaguered forces in the field little in the way of coherent support.

The 'Dogs of War'

By the mid-1780s, Congress was hard-pressed even to muster a quorum, and it suffered numerous indignities. In June 1783, after the Treaty of Paris, a band of mutinous soldiers surrounded the Pennsylvania State House in Philadelphia, where Congress was meeting, holding the legislators captive for a day. After the Pennsylvania authorities refused to call out the militia and restore order, the legislators decamped for Princeton, New Jersey, then moved to Annapolis, Maryland, before settling in New York City in 1785. The *Boston Evening Post* mocked the politicians for "not being stars of the *first* magnitude, but rather partaking of the nature of *inferior* luminaries, or *wandering* comets."

Victory, in short, had shredded many of the old wartime bonds. Without a common enemy to fight, Americans seemed incapable of preserving their Union. "Lycurgus," a pseudonymous writer in the *New Haven Gazette*, complained that the Union under the Articles "is not a union of sentiment;—it is not a union of interest;—it is not a union to be seen—or felt—or in any manner perceived."

Many local politicians—Congressman Melancton Smith of New York, Luther Martin of Maryland, George Mason of Virginia—dismissed such worries. The Antifederalists, as they were later called, believed that the preservation of republican liberties won by the Revolution depended on maintaining the sovereignty and independence of the states. They held, with Montesquieu, the great French *philosophe*, that republican government could survive only in small countries, where citizens could be intimately involved in politics. Maryland planter John Francis Mercer spoke for the Antifederalists when he declared that he was "persuaded that the People of so large a Continent, so different in Interests, so distinct in habits," could not be adequately represented in a single legislature.

With some justice, the Antifederalists could also claim that the states were managing quite well. Their citizens enjoyed the benefits of the most progressive constitutions the world had ever known and, by and large, they were prospering. Patrick Henry dismissed all the talk of trouble in the land. Had *Virginia* suffered, he asked?

But Washington, Virginia's James Madison, and other advocates of an "energetic" central government warned that the 13 states would not survive for long on their own, at least not as republics. These nationalists (later called Federalists) viewed the growing power of the states as a threat to peace. The state governments had begun to fill the vacuum left by Congress, adopting their own commercial policies, ignoring national treaties, and, at the behest of wealthy citizens who feared that they would never otherwise be repaid, even assuming some debts incurred by Congress. The nationalists feared that increasing conflicts among the states would unleash what the Old Dominion's Edmund Randolph called the "dogs of war."

Whispering Treason

Such warnings were not easily dismissed. In New York, Governor George Clinton was enriching the state treasury by taxing merchandise shipped through New York between New Jersey and Connecticut. Feelings ran so high that Congressman Nathaniel Gorham of Massachusetts worried that "bloodshed would very quickly be the consequence."

The weakness of the central government handicapped America diplomats. Britain had refused to abandon its outposts on U.S. soil, arguing (correctly) that Congress had failed to enforce some of *its* obligations under the Treaty of Paris, namely, guarantees that prewar debts owed to British creditors would be repaid and that American loyalists would be reimbursed for their confiscated property.* Several states had simply ignored these provisions.

On the frontier, the threats from foreign powers were a constant worry. Rufus King, a Massachusetts congressman, observed that if the nation's disputes with Spain over the Mississippi and other matters were not settled, "we shall be obliged either wholly to give up the western settlers, or join *them* in an issue of force with the Catholic king." Both prospects, he concluded, were unthinkable.

More troubling still to the nationalists were the activities of the American frontiersmen themselves. From the Maine District of Massachusetts to western North Carolina, various separatists since the time of the Revolution had been petitioning Congress for admission to the Union as new states. But the older states refused to relinquish their claims. Vermont, legally a part of New York, was the most durable—and dangerous—of these rebellious territories. Rebuffed by Congress during the Revolution, the Vermonters, led by a group including Governor Thomas Chittenden and Ethan Allen, hero of the Green Mountain Boys, had entered into not-so-secret negotiations with London to rejoin the British empire.

The nationalists were dismayed when these talks resumed in 1786. Washington wrote that the Vermonters might "become a sore thorn in our sides," adding, "the western settlements without good and wise management . . . may be equally troublesome."**

The Westerners, in Kentucky and Tennessee, were understandably frustrated by the weakness of the central government. Chief among their complaints was the absence of congressional help in fending off constant attacks by marauding Indians, often instigated by the British and the Spaniards. Nor could the state governments, they argued, effectively govern distant territories. "Nature has separated us," wrote Judge David Campbell of the would-be state of Franklin in western North Carolina. The frontiersmen's anger grew during 1786 and 1787 as rumors circulated that

---

*During the Revolution, some 100,000 Loyalists fled to Britain, Canada, and the British West Indies. Many of the exiles were well-to-do farmers or merchants, and they claimed to have left behind more than $40 million worth of property, which the state governments seized.

**Vermont finally gained statehood in 1791.

Congress was negotiating with Spain, offering to relinquish American claims to free navigation of the Mississippi in exchange for trade advantages. (These suspicions were justified, but the talks collapsed.) Kentucky's General James Wilkinson and other Westerners talked openly about leaving the Union and forming alliances with the Old World.

A Rat and a Gamble

All of the nationalists' apprehensions were dramatized by a shock in the summer of 1786: the outbreak of Shays's Rebellion.

The rebels were farmers in economically depressed western Massachusetts who faced ruinous new state taxes imposed to help retire the state's wartime debt. As distress turned to anger, Captain Daniel Shays, a veteran of the Revolution, emerged as the leader of a ragtag mob that gathered to close down the Massachusetts courthouses that oversaw farm foreclosures and sent debtors to jail.

Thomas Jefferson, serving abroad as the American minister to France, was unperturbed. "I like a little rebellion now and then," he wrote to Abigail Adams. "It is like a storm in the Atmosphere." But in the United States, the uprising could not be so airily dismissed. It sparked the first general alarm about the future of the Union. "I never saw so great a change in the public mind," observed Boston merchant Stephen Higginson that autumn.

Word of the insurrection spread quickly. In Annapolis, Maryland, the news came during the first week of September, just as delegates from five states were meeting to discuss the condition of the Confederation's commerce. Among them were two of the country's most ardent nationalists—James Madison and New York's Alexander Hamilton—who were desperately seeking ways to strengthen the central government.

The stage for the Annapolis Convention had been set two years earlier at Mount Vernon, at a meeting hosted by George Washington. There, in March 1785, commissioners from Virginia and Maryland had met to resolve their disputes over tolls and fishing rights on the Potomac River. The success of the meeting led the two state legislatures to call for a larger meeting of all the states, to be held at Annapolis, to consider granting Congress broader powers to regulate interstate commerce.

The Annapolis Convention was a failure. Eight of the 13 states sent no representatives. More out of desperation than careful forethought, Hamilton and Madison proposed yet another meeting to consider strengthening the Confederation, to be held in Philadelphia in May 1787.

So clear to the Annapolis delegates was the case for reform that they might well have agreed to the Philadelphia meeting even without the shocking news from Massachusetts. The six-month rebellion was effectively ended in January 1787, in a battle near the federal armory at Springfield. Four Shaysites lost their lives. But the insurrection had already persuaded many state and local leaders to put aside their doubts about the need for a stronger central government.

In February 1787, after several states had already elected delegates to the Philadelphia Convention, the Continental Congress in New York City endorsed the gathering, with the stipulation (added at the insistence of Massachusetts) that it meet "for the sole and express purpose of revising the Articles of Confederation."

Patrick Henry, the fierce opponent of a stronger Union, had already declined to be a delegate from Virginia, declaring that he "smelt a rat." Indeed, few of the American political leaders who recognized the need for reform harbored any illusions about merely patching up the Confederation. They did not know what would happen at Philadelphia, or even if, like the Annapolis meeting, it would prove to be a failure, but they were now prepared to gamble. As Madison put it one month before the Federal Convention, the hurdles confronting any reform were so great that they "would inspire despair in any case where the alternative was less formidable."

PHILADELPHIA STORY

Jack N. Rakove

Jack N. Rakove, 39, is associate professor of history at Stanford University. Born in Chicago, he received a B.A. from Haverford College (1968), and a Ph.D. from Harvard (1975). He is the author of The Beginnings of National Politics: An Interpretive History of the Continental Congress *(1979).*

"There never was an assembly of men, charged with a great and arduous trust, who were more pure in their motives, or more exclusively or anxiously devoted to the object committed to them."

It probably was shortly before his death, in 1836, that Virginia's James Madison, the sole surviving Framer of the Constitution, dictated those closing words of the preface to his notes of the debates at the Constitutional Convention. This was how Madison wanted his countrymen to imagine the Convention. In many ways we have followed his wishes—and will be asked to do so again during the bicentennial celebrations.

Yet, for most of this century, this popular image of the Founding has coexisted with another, less heroic portrait etched by scholars since Charles A. Beard published *An Economic Interpretation of the Constitution* (1913).

Rather than treat the Constitution as the product of a highly principled debate conducted by an extraordinary group of men who resolved *all* of the great questions before them, these historians have emphasized everything that was practical and tough-minded about the task of creating a national government: the threats and bargains that dominated the politics of the Convention, and the determination of the delegates to protect the interests of their states and, for that matter, of their own propertied class.

To strike an accurate balance between these two contrasting images is the great challenge that confronts anyone who studies the making of the Constitution.

That task is more important now than it has been at any point in our recent history. Today's controversy over constitutional jurisprudence, sparked by U.S. attorney general Edwin Meese III, requires that Americans ask again how much weight the "original intent" of the Framers should carry in interpreting the Constitution.

One thing is clear: The 55 delegates to the Philadelphia Convention were not all cut from the same cloth. Six had signed the Declaration of Independence, 14 were land speculators, 21 were military veterans of the Revolution, at least 15 owned slaves, and 24 served in Congress. Thirty-four were lawyers.

Present were many of the most outstanding men that the new Republic could muster. Among them were Benjamin Franklin, the president of Pennsylvania's Supreme Executive Council and the leading American scientist of the century, so disabled by gout and other ailments at the age of 81 that he was carried from his lodgings to the Convention in a sedan chair borne by four convicts; Virginia's George Washington, then 55, who came to Philadelphia very reluctantly after three years of retirement from public life at Mount Vernon; New York's Alexander Hamilton, 30, Washington's wartime aide; George Mason, a 60-year-old Virginia plantation owner and (said Thomas Jefferson) "the wisest man of his generation."

Also in attendance were men of somewhat less distinction. One of the more interesting examples was Luther Martin, "the rollicking, witty, audacious Attorney General of Maryland," as Henry Adams later described him, "drunken, generous, slovenly, grand . . . the notorious reprobate genius."

Missing from the Convention were Thomas Jefferson, 44, author of the Declaration of Independence 11 years earlier, who was overseas serving as the American minister to France, and former congressman John Adams, 51, likewise engaged in England. The great firebrands of the Revolution—Samuel Adams, Thomas Paine, Patrick Henry—were also absent.

A Humid Summer

No delegates came from Rhode Island. "Rogue Island," as a Boston newspaper called it, was in the hands of politicians bent on inflating the currency to relieve farm debtors; they would have nothing to do with a strong national

From *The Wilson Quarterly*, Spring 1987, pp. 105-121. Copyright © 1987 by Jack N. Rakove.

government and the monetary discipline it would impose. For lack of funds, New Hampshire's delegates arrived more than two months late, bringing the number of states represented to 12. Indeed, during the Convention's debates, the cost and difficulties of travel would occasionally be cited as looming obstacles to effective national government. Nearly a year, Madison predicted, would be "consumed in preparing for and travelling to and from the seat of national business."

The delegates were supposed to gather in Philadelphia on May 14, 1787, but it was the rare public assembly in 18th-century America that met on time. Only on Friday the 25th did delegates from seven states—a quorum—assemble in the spacious east room of the Pennsylvania State House, the same chamber where the Declaration of Independence had been signed. The delegates sat two or three to a desk. George Washington was immediately elected president of the Convention. Serious discussion began on the 29th. Thereafter, the delegates met six days a week until they finally adjourned on September 17, taking only one recess. It was, by contemporary standards, an arduous schedule. The delegates met for four, six, sometimes even eight hours a day.

In the afternoons, when the Convention adjourned, the delegates often repaired to local taverns—the Indian Queen, the George, the Black Horse—or turned to other amusements. These included visiting Mrs. Peale's Museum, with its fossils, stuffed animals, and portraits of the Revolution's heroes (by her husband, Charles), browsing through libraries and book and stationery shops, reading the city's eight newspapers, and watching the occasional horse race through the city streets, paved with bricks and cobblestones. Down by the busy docks and brick warehouses along the Delaware River, spectators could watch as inventor John Fitch demonstrated a novel contraption: a steam-powered boat.

Although there was a large and growing German population, the Quakers, in their broadbrim hats, still set the tone in Philadelphia, and the tone was sober but cosmopolitan. George Mason, from rural Virginia, complained after his arrival that he was growing "heartily tired of the etiquette and nonsense so fashionable in this city."

It was hot and humid that summer. "A veritable torture," moaned one French visitor. But the delegates had to keep their windows closed as they slept: Obnoxious stinging flies filled the air. The dyspeptic Elbridge Gerry of Massachusetts sent his family to the healthier clime of New York City, where the U.S. Congress was sitting. A few of his colleagues, such as Charles Pinckney, the young delegate from South Carolina, rented houses and brought their families to Philadelphia; others lived alone in rented rooms above the taverns or boarded in Mrs. Mary House's place at the corner of Fifth and Market streets near the State House. Most brought servants. George Washington was the guest of Pennsylvania delegate Robert Morris, Philadelphia's great merchant prince, who owned a large mansion a block from the State House.

A typical session of the Convention would find perhaps 35 or 40 delegates from 10 or 11 states in attendance. Some delegates came and went, others sat silently the entire time—

and a few would have been better advised to say less. Washington did not so much as venture an opinion until the last day of debate. But his stern presence in the chair did much to preserve the decorum of the meeting.

Madison's Fears

The debates were held in secrecy. Otherwise, candor would have been impossible, since the delegates knew that their opinions and votes, if made public, would become live ammunition in the hands of political foes back home. Moreover, the threat of deadlock would have quickly arisen had the dissidents within the Convention been allowed to stir up a hue and cry among their constituents. "Their deliberations are kept inviolably secret, so that they set without censure or remark," observed Francis Hopkinson, a Philadelphia musician and signer of the Declaration, "but no sooner will the chicken be hatch'd but every one will be for plucking a feather."

Nevertheless, we know a great deal about what was said at the Convention, thanks chiefly to the copious daily note-taking of Virginia's James Madison, then just turned 36, who is now generally regarded as the "father of the Constitution."

Were he alive today, the slight, soft-spoken Madison would probably be happily teaching history or political theory at his alma mater, Princeton University (or the College of New Jersey, as it was then known). He took a distinctively intellectual approach to politics, reinforced by a decade of experience in the Virginia legislature and the U.S. Congress. He had read deeply in the history of ancient and modern confederacies and pondered the shortcomings of the Articles of Confederation and the state constitutions. (It was Madison's frustration with the scanty archives left by earlier confederacies that prompted him to take meticulous notes at the Convention.) He arrived in Philadelphia 11 days early to begin drafting, with his fellow Virginians, the Virginia Plan. After the state's 34-year-old governor, Edmund Randolph, presented the plan on May 29, it became, in effect, the agenda of the Convention.

The starting point for all of Madison's proposals was his belief, based on the nation's unhappy experiences under the Articles and under the state constitutions, that the state legislatures could not be counted on to respect the national interest, the concerns of other states, or even the "private rights" of individuals and minorities.

Like most other Federalists, Madison thought that the legislatures were dominated by demagogues who sought office for reasons of "ambition" and "personal interest" rather than "public good." Such men—e.g., Patrick Henry, his great rival in Virginia—could always "dupe" more "honest but unenlightened representative[s]" by "veiling [their] selfish views under the professions of public good, and varnishing [their] sophistical arguments with the glowing colors of popular eloquence."

From this condemnation of state politics, Madison drew a number of conclusions that appeared in the Virginia Plan.

First, unlike the existing Congress, which relied upon the good will of the states to see its resolutions carried out, the new government would have to be empowered to impose laws and levy taxes directly upon the population, and to enforce its acts though its own executive and judiciary. Second, he hoped that membership in the new Congress would result from "such a process of elections as will most certainly extract from the mass of the society the purest and noblest characters it contains."

One State, One Vote?

Yet, because Madison also doubted whether popularly chosen representatives could ever be entirely trusted, he hoped to make an indirectly elected Senate (with members nominated by the legislatures but elected by the people) the true linchpin of government. Not only would this Senate thwart the passage of ill-conceived laws by the lower house, it would manage the nation's foreign relations and appoint all major federal officials. But since even the Senate could not always be counted upon to legislate wisely, Madison sought an additional check in the form of a joint executive-judicial Council of Revision that would possess a limited veto over all acts of Congress.

Most important of all, Madison wanted to arm the national government with a "negative in all cases whatsoever" over the acts of the states. This radical veto power would be shared jointly by Congress (or the Senate) and the Council of Revision.

In Madison's mind, the whole edifice of the Virginia Plan rested on the adoption of some form of proportional representation in Congress. If the Confederation's "one state, one vote" scheme were retained, for example, each citizen of tiny Delaware (population in 1790: 59,000) would, in effect, carry the same weight in the powerful new government as 12 Virginians. Delegates from Massachusetts and Pennsylvania, the Confederation's other two largest states, reached the same conclusion.

The Pennsylvanians, in fact, wanted to deny the small states an equal vote even within the Convention. But in a private caucus held before the Convention, the Virginians persuaded Pennsylvania's leading delegates—James Wilson (the Convention's finest legal mind), Gouverneur Morris (its wiliest advocate and its most talkative delegate, with 173 speeches), and Robert Morris (the former superintendent of finance for the Confederation)—that they could prevail over the small states by force of reason. And sooner rather than later. For the large states' delegates also agreed that the problem of representation had to be solved first.

Two of the small states' leaders tried to avoid the clash: Roger Sherman, a 66-year-old Connecticut farmer and storekeeper turned politician, and John Dickinson of Delaware, who had gained fame as the "penman of the Revolution" during the late 1760s for his antitax *Letters from a Farmer in Pennsylvania.* Sherman was among the signers of the Declaration of Independence; Dickinson had refused to put his name to it, still hoping for reconciliation with Great Britain.

Both men had taken leading roles in drafting the Articles of Confederation a decade before the Convention. Now, during the early days of debate in Philadelphia, they tried to head off full discussion of the dangerous issue of representation.

Let the Convention first determine what it wanted the national government to do, they suggested. Perhaps it might vest Congress with only a few additional powers; then there would be no need to propose any changes in the system of representation.

Toward the Great Compromise

Their opponents would not waver. "Whatever reason might have existed for the equality of suffrage when the union was a federal one among sovereign states," Madison flatly declared, "must cease when a national government should be put into the place."

Although interrupted by discussion of other issues, such as fixing the qualifications for legislative office, the struggle over representation would go on for seven grueling weeks. It lasted until July 16, when the Great Compromise, as scholars now call it, allowed the Convention to move forward.

The fight went through three phases. During the first (May 29–June 13), the large states exploited the initiative they had seized with the Virginia Plan to gain an early endorsement of the principle of proportional representation in both houses. The small-state men rallied after June 14, when William Paterson, 42, a diminutive country lawyer and New Jersey attorney general—"of great modesty," noted Georgia's William Pierce, "whose powers break in upon you and create wonder and astonishment"—presented the New Jersey Plan.* This second round of debate came to a dramatic end on July 2, when the convention deadlocked (five states to five, with Georgia divided, and thus losing its vote) over a motion by Oliver Ellsworth of Connecticut to give each state an equal vote in the Senate.

Round Three began immediately, with the appointment of a committee made up of one member from each delegation and explicitly charged with finding a compromise. The Convention received its report on July 5, debated it until the 14th, and finally approved it by a narrow margin two days later.

These seven weeks were the Convention's true testing time. The tension is apparent to anyone who reads Madison's daily notes. The character of debate covered a wide spectrum, from highly principled appeals to heavy-handed threats and pokerfaced bluffs.

In the speeches of the large states' leading advocates—Madison, Wilson, and Rufus King, the 32-year-old lawyer

---

*The New Jersey Plan would have amended the Articles of Confederation, leaving the unicameral Congress intact, but empowering it to elect a plural executive and granting the national government the power to impose taxes directly on the citizens of states that failed to meet the contributions quotas assigned them by Congress. The government would also have the power to compel the states to abide by its laws by force of arms. This was a crucial concession, for it acknowledged the fundamental weakness of confederation.

THE 'NEFARIOUS INSTITUTION'

James Madison was somewhat surprised by the intensity of the debates between the large and small states at Philadelphia. After all, he told the delegates on June 30, the states were really not divided so much by size as by "the effects of their having, or not having, slaves."

Yet slavery did not become a major issue at the Constitutional Convention. In August, Gouverneur Morris passionately denounced it as "a nefarious institution." But, as John Rutledge of South Carolina quickly reminded the delegates, "the true question at present is whether the Southern states shall or shall not be parties to the union."

As they would time and again during the Convention, the delegates turned away from divisive social issues to focus on what historian James MacGregor Burns has called the "mundane carpentry" of making a constitution.

•

Abolitionist sentiment was widespread but not deep in 1787. Traffic in imported African slaves was outlawed everywhere except in Georgia and the Carolinas, yet only Massachusetts had banned slave ownership. Many delegates, Northerners and Southerners alike, disliked slavery; some also believed, as Connecticut's Oliver Ellsworth said, that the arrival of cheap labor from Europe would ultimately "render slaves useless."

Such hopes, combined with the delegates' sense of the political realities, led them to reduce the slavery issue to a series of complicated tradeoffs.

Early in June, the large states accepted the famous "three-fifths" compromise: Slaves (carefully referred to as "all other Persons") would each count as three-fifths of a free white "person" in any scheme of representation by population. In return, the Georgians and Carolinians tacitly agreed to support the large states' ideas for a strong national government.

But on August 6, a report by the Committee of Detail upset the agreement. The Committee recommended several measures that would weaken the new national government, including a ban on national taxes on exports. More important, it proposed a ban on any federal regulation of the slave trade.

The debate was heated. Rufus King of Massachusetts reminded the Southerners of the earlier bargain and added that he could not agree to let slaves be "imported without limitation and then be represented in the National Legislature." A slave influx could give undue legislative power to the South.

Another committee—the Committee of Eleven—was named to mediate the dispute. After more haggling, the ban on export taxes was retained. The government would be empowered to halt the slave trade in 1808. But the new Constitution also mandated the return to their owners of escaped slaves.

Congress did abolish the slave trade in 1808, but the "peculiar institution" did not die. Inevitably, the North-South division that Madison saw in 1787 widened, while the heated conflict between the large and small states faded almost as soon as the delegates left Philadelphia. The Framers' artful compromises, later denounced by abolitionists as "A Covenant with Death and an Agreement with Hell," could not contain the nation's passions over slavery.

from Massachusetts—one finds powerful and profound briefs for the theory of majority rule. Indeed, the spokesmen for the other side rarely met the arguments on their own terms. Delaware's hot-tempered Gunning Bedford, Jr., claimed, for example, that the large states would "crush the small ones whenever they stand in the way of their ambitious or interested views." But when Madison and his allies demanded to know what common interest could ever unite societies as diverse as those of Massachusetts, Pennsylvania, and Virginia, the small-state men could not come up with an answer.

What was finally at issue was a question not so much of reason as of will. John Dickinson had made sure that Madison got the point immediately after the New Jersey Plan was introduced on June 15. "You see the consequences of pushing things too far," he warned, as the delegates filed out of the chamber at the end of the day. "Some of the members from the small states wish for two branches in the general legislature, and are friends to a good national government: but we would sooner submit to a foreign power, than submit to be deprived of an equality of suffrage in both branches of the legislature, and thereby be thrown under the domination of the large states."

Skepticism Abroad

When the large states hinted that perhaps they might confederate separately, or that the Union might dissolve if their demands were not met, Bedford retorted that the small states would "find some foreign ally of more honor and good faith, who will take them by the hand and do them justice."

In the end, it was the bluff of the large states that was called. Once the deadlock of July 2 demonstrated that the small states would not buckle, the necessity for compromise became obvious. And the committee, called the Grand Committee, that the Convention elected to that end was stacked in favor of the small states. The three members chosen for the most populous states—Elbridge Gerry of Massachusetts, Benjamin Franklin of Pennsylvania, and George Mason of Virginia—were less militant than others in their delegations.

While the Grand Committee labored, the other delegates observed the 11th anniversary of American Independence. Philadelphia marked the occasion in fine fashion. A fife-and-drum corps paraded about the city; the militia fired three cannonades. In the local taverns, revelers toasted the day.

The delegates kept their worries to themselves. "We were on the verge of dissolution," wrote Luther Martin, "scarce held together by the strength of an hair, though the public papers were announcing our extreme unanimity." Indeed, up and down the Atlantic seaboard, editors were speculating about the proceedings in Philadelphia. "With zeal and confidence, we expect from the Federal Convention a system of government adequate to the security and preservation of those rights which were promulgated by the ever memorable Declaration of Independency," proclaimed the *Pennsylvania Herald*. "The world at large expect something from us," said Gerry. "If we do nothing, it appears to me we must have war and confusion."

In Britain, France, and Spain, royal advisers awaited news from America with detached curiosity. The Spaniards were particularly interested in the proceedings at Philadelphia, for if an effective government were not formed, American settlers in the lands west of the Appalachians might fall into their orbit. Even after the adoption of the Constitution, wrote historians Samuel Eliot Morison and Henry Steele Commager, "most European observers believed that the history of the American Union would be short and stormy."

On July 5, the committee presented its report to a glum Convention. The compromise it proposed was one in name only. In return for accepting an equal state representation in the Senate, the large states would gain the privilege of having all tax and appropriations bills originate in the House of Representatives, whose members were apportioned on the basis of population, with no changes by the upper chamber allowed. (Later, the Convention decided to allow the Senate to alter tax and spending laws.) Madison and his allies dismissed the proposed tradeoff as worthless, neither desirable in theory nor useful in practice; the Senate, they said, could simply reject a bill it disliked.

Averting a Collapse

But, by this time, argument no longer mattered.

The key vote of July 16 found five states for the compromise, four against, and Massachusetts divided by Gerry and Caleb Strong, who insisted that "an accommodation must take place." The compromise won, but not by much.

Emotions were still running high. New York's two remaining delegates, Robert Yates and John Lansing, Jr., had departed on July 10, declaring that the Convention was exceeding its authority. This point was raised several times during the proceedings, and brushed aside. As James Wilson had put it, the Convention was "authorized to *conclude nothing*, but . . . at liberty to *propose anything*."

Next on the Convention's agenda for the afternoon of July 16th was the difficult task of beginning to define the extent of the legislative authority of Congress.

But the large states' delegates were unprepared to go on. The broad powers the Virginia Plan had proposed for Congress had rested on the expectation that both houses would be selected by proportional voting. "The vote of this morning had embarrassed the business extremely," Edmund Randolph declared during the afternoon of the 16th. He suggested that the Convention adjourn to give both sides a chance to rethink their positions. Mistakenly believing that Randolph was calling for an adjournment *sine die* (indefinitely), William Paterson of New Jersey immediately jumped to his feet and enthusiastically agreed that "it was high time for the Convention to adjourn, that the rule of secrecy ought to be rescinded, and that our constituents should be consulted."

But that, Randolph apologized, was not what he had meant. All he sought was an overnight adjournment. Tempers cooled, a few members hastened to remind their colleagues that even if "we could not do what was best, in itself, we ought to do something," and the Convention broke up for the day.

A Single Executive?

The next morning, the large states' delegates caucused to decide whether to pull out and confederate separately. "The time was wasted in vague conversation on the subject," Madison noted, "without any specific proposition or agreement." The Convention, despite the large states unhappiness, would continue.

The critical vote of July 16, then, was not a compromise as we ordinarily use the term. One side had won its point, the other had lost. But the outcome of this struggle did cause a series of other changes and "accommodations" that profoundly affected both the structure of the future U.S. government and its powers.

In its preoccupation with representation in Congress, the Convention had barely discussed the other two branches of government. Most of the delegates agreed with Madison that the central problem was to find a way to enable the executive and the judiciary to withstand the "encroachments" of the legislature. But how was that to be accomplished?

At an early point, the Convention had rejected Madison's scheme for a joint executive-judicial Council of Revision. The judiciary could simply overturn unconstitutional laws by itself, the members felt, and it would be most effective if "free from the bias of having participated" in writing the laws.

It is remarkable how little time the Framers spent discussing the role of the judiciary. Harvard's Raoul Berger noted some years ago that "the very casualness with which the [Convention's] leadership assumed that judicial review was available . . . suggests that the leaders considered they were dealing with a widely accepted doctrine." In their focus on the powers of the other branches of government, however, the Framers never sought to prescribe either the scope of the courts' power to declare laws unconstitutional or the basis on which this power could be exercised.

Far more of the Convention's time was devoted to the subject of executive power. But here, too, it is difficult to fathom exactly what the Framers intended.

Something of the uncertainty the convention had to overcome was illustrated when the subject of the executive was first raised on June 1. After James Wilson moved that "the executive consist of a single person," the delegates sat speechless in their chairs, reluctant to begin discussing so great an issue. "A considerable pause ensuing," noted Madison, "and the chairman asking if he should put the question, Dr. Franklin observed that it was a point of great importance and wished that the gentlemen would deliver their sentiments on it before the question was put." A lively debate began, and it immediately revealed two things.

The delegates agreed that a republican executive could not be modeled on the British monarchy. Second, most members thought that considerations of efficiency and responsibility alike required an executive headed by a single person—though a few dissenting members joined Randolph in fearing that such an office would prove "the foetus of monarchy." The dissenters variously favored either a plural executive, a kind of government by committee, or some form of ministerial government, akin to the British cabinet.

The great puzzle was how the executive was to be elected.

Today, Americans regard the strange device that the Framers finally invented, the electoral college, as evidence of how far they were prepared to go to prevent a popular majority from choosing a potential tyrant. What the Framers actually feared, however, was that a scattered population could never "be sufficiently informed of characters," as Roger Sherman put it, to choose wisely among what the Framers assumed would be a large field of candidates.*

Believing that popular election was impractical, then, many delegates saw no alternative to having Congress choose the executive. But this only raised other objections. An election by Congress would be "the work of intrigue, cabal, and of faction," Gouverneur Morris asserted. "Real merit" would be passed over.

Moreover, the executive could not be expected to discharge his duties conscientiously, free from improper legislative influence, unless he were made ineligible for reelection. But that, Morris noted, would "destroy the great motive to good behavior, the hope of being rewarded by a reappointment." Such an executive, he continued, would be tempted to "make hay while the sun shines."

The desire for reelection would be an incentive to good behavior. But would that not leave open the possibility that a leader's fondness for the powers and perquisites of office—or a public that had grown too used to a leader—might lead to the creation of a monarchy in everything but name?

*Article II, Section 1 of the Constitution grants each state "a Number of Electors, equal to the whole Number of Senators and Representatives to which the State may be entitled in the Congress." The small states thus enjoyed more influence than they would have under a strictly proportional system. It was hoped that the electors would be the wisest and ablest men of their states. The Constitution does not require electors to bind themselves to particular candidates: In 1968, a North Carolina elector designated as a Republican cast his vote for George Wallace.

Fishing for Trout

Just before it recessed on July 26, the Convention agreed (six states to three, with Virginia divided) to have Congress appoint a single executive, to serve for a single seven-year term. It then turned the task of recasting all the resolutions approved thus far over to a Committee of Detail composed of Randolph, Wilson, Ellsworth, John Rutledge of South Carolina, and Nathaniel Gorham of Massachusetts.

The muggy weather continued. "At each inhaling of air," wrote one visitor to Philadelphia, "one worries about the next one. The slightest movement is painful." Many of the delegates from nearby states took the opportunity to return home. Others fled to the countryside. General Washington, in his usual terse style, recorded in his journal: "In company with Mr. Govr. Morris and in his Phaeton with my horses, went up to one Jane Moore's (in whose house we lodged) in the vicinity of Valley Forge to get Trout."

When they reconvened on August 6, the delegates were eager to move the business toward a conclusion. During the remaining six weeks, the debates became more rushed—and more focused. They centered on specific clauses and provisions; decisions that would figure prominently in later controversies over the Constitution were reached with surprisingly little discussion, revealing far less about the Framers' intentions than modern commentators would like to know.

Far and away the most momentous changes that took place were those involving the powers of the executive.

In the report of the Committee of Detail, the major duties of the president (as the committee now named the executive) were confined to seeing that the laws were "duly and faithfully executed" and to serving as commander-in-chief of the armed forces. He would also enjoy a limited veto over acts of Congress. Two of the powers that provide the foundation for much of the political authority of the modern presidency remained in the Senate: the power to make treaties and the power to appoint ambassadors and justices of the Supreme Court (and perhaps even the heads of major executive departments, though this was left unclear).

In Britain, these powers were critical elements of the royal prerogative, and the Framers were reluctant to grant them to the president. Yet, with the report of the Committee of Detail in their hands, many began to reconsider. Madison, Wilson, Gouverneur Morris, and other delegates from the large states now opposed giving sole power over foreign affairs to the Senate, a body in which the small states would enjoy disproportionate influence, and whose members would be elected by the presumably reckless state legislatures.

Shaping the Presidency

From this unhappiness with the Great Compromise over representation in Congress, a new concept of the presidency began to emerge. Though many of the Framers worried about the potential abuse of executive power, some now described the president, in Gouverneur Morris's words, as "the general guardian of the national interests." He would not only carry out the national will as it was expressed by the legislature, but also act independently to define a national interest larger than the sum of the legislators' concerns.

The best evidence for this enlarged conception of executive power is circumstantial, resting less on anything the delegates said than on the final changes that led to the adoption of the electoral college. Unfortunately, the key discussions took place within the Committee on Postponed Parts, appointed on August 31 to consider a potpourri of unresolved issues. Very little is known about what was said during its debates.

In the Committee's major report, read September 4, the president suddenly enjoyed significant responsibility for foreign affairs and the power to appoint ambassadors, judges, and other officials, with the "advice and consent" of the Senate. At the same time, his election by an electoral college promised to make the president politically independent of Congress. The report also specified a four-year term and eligibility for reelection.

The Committee had clearly sought to preserve the Great Compromise. The large states, it was assumed, would enjoy the advantage in promoting candidates for the presidency. (None of the Framers anticipated the formation of powerful political parties.) But if an election failed to produce a majority—as many delegates thought it usually would—the election would fall to the Senate. There, the small states would have greater influence.

Saving the Day

James Wilson rose to object. If the Senate controlled the ultimate power of election, he warned, "the President will not be the man of the people as he ought to be, but the Minion of the Senate." Many members agreed, but nobody could find a solution that would not erode the Great Compromise.

It was only after the report had been adopted that Roger Sherman and North Carolina's Hugh Williamson had the idea of sending deadlocked elections into the House of Representatives, with the members voting by states. This had the ingenious effect of preserving both the president's independence from the Senate and the Great Compromise. The amendment was adopted almost without debate.*

On September 12, George Mason broached the subject of a Bill of Rights. "It would give great quiet to the people," he argued, if trial by jury and other rights were guaranteed in the new Constitution. Roger Sherman replied that a Bill of Rights was unnecessary. The states, he said, could protect

*The House of Representatives has been called upon to decide an election only twice: In 1800, it selected Thomas Jefferson over Aaron Burr; in 1824, John Quincy Adams over Andrew Jackson, Henry Clay, and William H. Crawford. The possibility that a candidate might prevail in the electoral college without winning a majority of the popular vote—which has occurred only once, when Benjamin Harrison defeated Grover Cleveland in 1888—has sparked many proposals for reform over the years.

these rights: Eight of them had already incorporated such provisions into their constitutions. The discussion was brief. The Convention voted against including a Bill of Rights, 10 states to none. Only later, after several state ratifying conventions demanded it, were the guarantees that Americans now associate with the Constitution introduced in Congress and ratified by the states as the first 10 amendments.

Despite this progress, Madison was gloomy. As he informed Jefferson seven weeks later, he was discouraged because the Convention had rejected the Virginia Plan's scheme for an unlimited national veto of all state laws, instead vesting the courts with narrower powers of review. Madison was convinced that an independent judiciary, as framed by the Convention, would lack the political strength to override the improper acts of the legislatures, which could always claim to express the will of the people.

Madison had entered the Convention with higher hopes and more ambitious goals than any of the other delegates. What they saw as compromises and accommodations he regarded as defeats. He privately thought that the worst "vices of the political system" would go unchecked even if the new national government worked as planned. He did not cheer the end result.

So it fell to Benjamin Franklin to claim the privileges of age and reputation to urge the 41 delegates still present as the Convention drew to a close to make their final approval of the Constitution unanimous. That would speed its ratification by Congress and the states.

A Hopeful Experiment

"When you assemble a number of men to have the advantage of their joint wisdom," Franklin reminded them, "you inevitably assemble with those men, all their prejudices, their passions, their errors of opinion, their local interests, and their selfish views. From such an assembly," he asked, "can a perfect production be expected? It therefore astonishes me, Sir, to find this system approaching so near to perfection as it does; and I think it will astonish our enemies, who are waiting with confidence to hear that our councils are confounded like those of the Builders of Babel. . . . Thus I consent, Sir, to this Constitution, because I expect no better, and because I am not sure that it is not the best."

On September 15, 1787, the delegates, voting by states, did endorse the Constitution. But Franklin's appeal failed to sway three of the delegates. Mason, Randolph, and Gerry refused, for various reasons, to sign the Constitution. Mason worried, among other things, about the extent of the president's powers and the absence of a Bill of Rights.

For what Franklin invoked was not simply the cumulative wisdom of what the Framers had wrought, but also the character of the deliberations themselves. No one could better gauge the range of intentions, honorable and otherwise, that had entered into the making of the Constitution than Franklin, who was perhaps the most worldly and calculating of all the Framers. No one could better grasp both the limits as well as the possibilities of human reason than the leading American experimental scientist of his century.

Franklin was bold enough to observe how "near to perfection" the completed Constitution came, yet he was just as prepared to concede that the objections against it might have merit. (Franklin himself favored a unicameral national legislature and a plural executive.) With his usual cleverness, he asked only that "every member of the Convention who may still have objections to it, would with me, on this occasion doubt a little of his own infallibility."

It took Madison a while to appreciate Franklin's wisdom. But when he dictated the final paragraphs of his preface to the Philadelphia debates, he took the same philosophical view. "Of the ability and intelligence of those who composed the Convention," he wrote, "the debates and proceedings may be a test." But, he went on, "the character of the work which was the offspring of their deliberations must be tested by the experience of the future, added to that of the nearly half century which has passed."

To see the Constitution as Franklin asked its very first critics to see it, or as Madison later learned to view it, does not require later generations to invest the Framers with perfect knowledge, to conclude that they had closely considered and conclusively resolved every issue and problem that they faced.

The Framers were patriotic men of varied capacities who rose above their passions and self-interest to forge a grand document. But they left Philadelphia viewing the Constitution as a hopeful experiment whose results and meanings would be made known only through time.

Nothing would have struck the Framers as more unrealistic than the notion that their original intentions must be the sole guide by which the meaning of the Constitution would ever after be determined. They did not bar future generations from trying to improve upon their work, or from using the lessons of experience to judge the "fallibility" of their reason. They asked only that we try to understand the difficulties that they had encountered and the broad array of concerns, variously noble and self-serving, that they had labored to accommodate during nearly four months of debate in the City of Brotherly Love.

THE AMERICAN REVOLUTION:
A WAR OF RELIGION?

Jonathan Clark probes the anti-Catholic actions and millenarian rhetoric of eighteenth-century America, challenging the assumption that 1776 was solely a product of secular and constitutional impulses.

Jonathan Clark is a Fellow of All Souls College, Oxford and author of Revolution and Rebellion: State and Society in England in the Seventeenth and Eighteenth Centuries *(Cambridge University Press, 1986).*

Thanks to our ruling picture of the American Revolution, a major premise of British and American history remains unrevised: the belief that both societies have pursued the uninterrupted evolution of a secular, libertarian, constitutional ideal, and that its progressive implementation has progressively freed them from internal revolutionary threat. A longer perspective is a crucial corrective: through all the vicissitudes of English politics from the 1530s to the 1820s and beyond, the most consistent theme both of popular sentiment and of ideological exegesis was anti-Catholicism. From the sixteenth century, Englishmen pictured the Roman Church not merely as a system of cruelty and intolerance, but as an international conspiracy operating through secret agents and with the covert sympathy of fellow travellers. Deliverances were attributed to direct divine intervention in favour of Protestant England. An apocalyptic or millenarian perspective on England's and America's history was generated principally in the context of Protestantism's conflict with Rome.

'An attempt to land a bishop in America'; a cartoon reflecting resistance to attempts at transplanting an Anglican state church into New England.

From *History Today*, December 1989, pp. 10-16. Reproduced by kind permission of History Today, Ltd., 83-84 Berwick Street, London W1V 3PJ, England.

By the late seventeenth century, anti-Catholic paranoia was even stronger in America than in England, despite the presence in the colonies of an even smaller Catholic minority. This heightened sensibility reacted strongly against the exercise of executive power by James II and produced a situation of extreme tension: in 1689 news of events in England triggered violent rebellions in three colonies – Massachusetts, New York and Maryland – and peaceful changes of government where the authorities did not resist the proclamation of William and Mary. The Massachusetts rebellion was aimed at restoring Puritan hegemony and local autonomy, enjoyed from Charles I's charter of 1629 until its cancellation when the colony was unwillingly incorporated in the Dominion of New England in 1684. This swift and violent reaction was in part a response to a theory of popish conspiracy, manifest in recent English history:

> We have seen more than a decade of Years rolled away since the English World had the Discovery of an horrid Popish Plot; wherein the bloody Devotees of Rome had in their Design and Prospect no less than the Extinction of the Protestant Religion… And we were of all Men the most insensible, if we should apprehend a Countrey so remarkable for the true Profession and pure Exercise of the Protestant Religion as New-England is, wholly unconcerned in the Infamous Plot.

In New York the rebellion, headed by Jacob Leisler, was in part an ethnic Dutch backlash against English encroachment since the conquest of the colony in 1664, in part an attempt by one set of magnates to dispossess another set of the spoils of office. Nevertheless, the popish phobia created a political idiom in New York and could be exploited.

All shortcomings in the administration of proprietary Maryland could be similarly attributed to the religion of its administrators, and political parties were already polarised on sectarian lines. By 1689, this division had generated paranoid complaints of 'Not only private but publick outrages, & murthers committed and done by papists upon Protestants without redress, but rather connived at and tolerated by the chief in authority'. In March 1689 the colony was gripped by a rumour that the Catholic ruling group was conspiring with the Indians to massacre the

Protestants. According to the Council's report to London, people had 'gathered themselves together in great parties to defend themselves, as they were persuaded, against a groundless and imaginary plott and designe contrived against them as was rumoured and suspected by the Roman Catholicks inviting the Indians to joyne with them in that detestable and wicked Conspiracy'

The American colonies rehearsed certain libertarian issues in 1689, but they had not obtained all or even most of what they had sought. The issues therefore remained; but their significance was transformed by the change of dynasty. No longer could antipopery sentiments transform practical objections to English rule: William III's Calvinism aligned him squarely with New England Puritanism, and the Lutheranism of George I and George II similarly established their credentials. The enemy was henceforth an external one. If the practical threat of popery receded, it did not disappear: in Europe the Protestant interest often seemed on the defensive until the Seven Years' War; French Canada and Spanish Florida similarly served as reminders to Americans. An added peril now began to prey on the psyche of the southern colonist: the fear that he would be murdered by the negro, either in an isolated incident or as part of a mass insurrection which would necessarily

result (as with anti-Catholic phobias) in a general massacre of white Protestants. Isolated incidents certainly occurred. Would they run together to constitute a revolution?

The early Hanoverian era saw a series of plots or uprisings by negro slaves in America, equally savage in their impact and in the punishments with which they were repressed. Conspiracies were discovered and rebellion prevented in Virginia in 1687 and 1709, South Carolina in 1720, New Jersey in 1734, Maryland in the late 1730s, South Carolina in 1740 and elsewhere. Violent rebellions occurred in New York City in 1712 and 1741, in South Carolina (the Stono Rebellion) in 1739 and on other occasions. In the 1730s and 40s slave disorder has been linked to the evangelical movement known as the Great Awakening: the first movement to sweep large numbers of negroes into sectarian participation, it acted to challenge hierarchical distinctions of white and black even more forcibly than those of white and white.

Despite the special circumstances of slave revolts, religion could appear both in their motivation and in the white response. In 1741 New York was convulsed by fears of a negro insurrection: outbreaks of arson and robbery seemed to be its preliminaries; informers fuelled the panic, and trials rehearsed the issues in the public eye.

Paranoia now inflated public disorder into a full-scale conspiracy. Much of the blame was attributed to revivalist religion, ignited by the recent visit of the Calvinist George Whitefield, and directed to the subversive end of the conversion of blacks as well as whites. Wartime conflict between Spanish Florida and the colony of Georgia soon introduced another ancient preoccupation into the mounting New York frenzy: the Catholic plot. Suspicion of the enthusiasm or superstition which was seen as common to both Methodism and Catholicism now joined with the ancient horror of a Catholic massacre. These events were seen as part of the divine scenario: 'so bloody and Destructive a Conspiracy was this, that had not the mercifull hand of providence interposed and Confounded their [the negroes'] Divices, in one and the Same night the Inhabitants would have been butcher'd in their houses, by their own Slaves, and the City laid in ashes'. Within such a context, New York's response to this fictional conspiracy is explicable as motive rather than mere rhetoric: four whites were hanged as conspirators; so were eighteen blacks; and thirteen more negroes were burnt at the stake. Similar conspiracies continued to be uncovered up to and long after the Revolution. Such was the emotional background against which the lofty issues of 1776 were rehearsed.

In England, millennial expectations receded after the 1650s; in the colonies, especially Puritan New England, they evolved into the eighteenth century as an orthodoxy, though without the revolutionary threat implicit in English sectarianism. New England society had earlier come close to being a theocracy; the sense of America as a religious experiment, as the new Israel, still gave stability and practical content to millenarian hopes. In the southern colonies, these traditions may have been refreshed by the Calvinism of Scots and Scots-Irish immigrants. The Great Awakening, in turn, was explicitly millenarian; when it lost its first impetus, England's wars of the 1740s and 50s against France and Spain renewed the identification of Antichrist with Catholicism and revitalised the old images of Catholic persecution. As a preacher warned, 'our inveterate and popish Enemies both without and within the Kingdom, are restless to enslave and ruin us'. If France won, 'Cruel *Papists* would quickly fill the *British Colonies*, and seize our Estates, abuse our Wives and Daughters, and barbarously murder us; as they have done the like in *France* and *Ireland*'.

In the 1740s and 50s, Britain overcame the major threats to her internal stability – threats to the religious and dynastic order. In the American colonies they survived; indeed they were exacerbated. Apart from the conflict of loyalist and republican, in the period following the Peace of Paris, a common thread ran through the conflicts which saw colonial Americans in armed conflict with each other: the clash of material interests between the pioneers, the settlers of the western backcountry, and the long-established settlers of the eastern seaboard with their control first of colonial, then of republican government. This applied to the march of the Paxton Boys against Philadelphia (1764); the Regulator movement in North and South Carolina (1768-71); the clashes in the Wyoming Valley of Pennsylvania between Pennamite and Yankee (1770-1); the disorders of the Green Mountain Boys in Vermont (early 1770s); Shays' Rebellion in Massachusetts (1786-7); the Whiskey Rebellion in Pennsylvania (1794); and Fries' Rebellion (1799). Such conflicts were once held to owe everything to the material grievances of the backcountry and equally little either to the pursuit of secular constitutional ideals or to formal sectarian allegiance. Yet these instances of civil disobedience can now be seen to share important features with other colonial insurrections since 1676, especially the religious catalyst; their ethnic composition brings their sectarian nature into sharp relief.

The wide availability of millennial thought meant that British legislation on the American colonies in the 1760s could at once be seen in an 'apocalyptical perspective'. The Stamp Act therefore quickly reversed a whole nexus of ideas which had grown up in a fervent identification of civil and religious liberty with British rule. George Grenville's stamps were described in the language of the Book of Revelation as 'the mark of the beast'; In cartoons, British policy was often personified as the devil. This paranoia had been expressed again in the New England controversy of 1763-5 over the threatened appointment of an Anglican bishop. In 1774 it received an immense boost: the Quebec Act, granting toleration to Canadian Catholics, was taken as proof of an imperial plot to promote popery. From the 1740s, American imagery had steadily strengthened the identity between tyranny and sin, civil liberty and grace. This was partly a consequence of a religious revivalist movement sufficiently dramatic and distinct to acquire a capitalised name: the Great Awakening.

Several decades before British political authority was systematically challenged in the colonies, a similar challenge had been launched against conventional ecclesiastical authorities of several denominations by the 'New Light' preachers of the religious revival. The significance of their appeal to personal revelation, a right of private judgement and a duty of secession from sinful congregations was interpreted by the established powers in the same terms as that of the rebels of 1776. The New Light clergy were 'Innovators, disturbers of the peace of the church, sowers of heresies and seditions'; they were 'foremost in propagating the Principles of Sedition, and Disobedience to Authority'. George Whitefield recorded in 1739 the unpopularity of the New Light ministers who graduated from William Tennent's famous Log College: 'Carnal ministers oppose them strongly; and, because people, when awakened by Mr. Tennent or his brethren, see through them, and therefore leave their ministry, the poor gentlemen are loaded with contempt, and looked upon as persons who turn the world upside-down'.

Few of the implications of New Light theology were brought to bear against British rule before the early 1760s: until the conclusion of the Seven Years' War, the threat to liberty, property and Protestantism clearly emanated from French Canada. In New England especially, Britain was depicted as the main bulwark of freedom against the antichrist of Rome. From the mid-1760s, however, colonists were free to redirect their rhetoric of Protestant virtue. In this they were encouraged by the perspective of still more recent immigrants from Scotland and Ireland, including the clergymen John Witherspoon and Alexander Craighead, who re-emphasised the Covenanter roots of political contractarianism. With-

'The Mitred Minuet' - an attack on the ill-timed Quebec Act of 1774, where the British government's provision to allow the Catholic church to keep its privileges there inflamed anti-Popish sentiment and suspicion in the colonies. The devil hovers over George III's ministers, Lords Bute and North, onlookers at the episcopal dance.

erspoon exercised his influence as President of Princeton from 1768 to 1794, Craighead in more humble surroundings as a minister in Mecklenburg County, North Carolina, from 1755 to his death in 1766. Craighead had already been expelled from ministering in two presbyteries for imposing the Solemn League and Covenant and the National Covenant: his affinities with the Cameronians made him a difficult neighbour. Among the Scots-Irish of the backcountry, however, he found a receptive audience. To them he appealed both by his preaching and his published works. Among the latter has been claimed the anonymous pamphlet *Renewal of the Covenants* (Philadelphia, 1743, 1748) which reviewed their history in Scotland and their violation under the persecution of Stuart and Hanoverian monarchs.

Like the Covenanters, Craighead preached 'a defensive War against all Usurpers of the Royal Prerogative of the glorious Lamb of God'. After his death, this message was sustained by other New Light clergy in the neighbourhood, like the influential David Caldwell: their teaching flowed directly into the Regulator movement. Although other denominations includ-

ing New England Congregationalism shared this religious impetus to political engagement, the popular movement which bore that name had a special place in the tradition of disorder. The history of colonial British America was punctuated with a series of backcountry rebellions against east coast authorities. The last and greatest of these occurred only shortly before the larger Revolution of 1776, for from 1768 until their military destruction at the battle of Alamance in May 1771 the piedmont of North and South Carolina was increasingly under the control of the self-styled Regulators, local activists usurping by force the authority of colonial magistrates and tax officials.

What prompted certain Americans to rebel? The old constitutional scenario of a sinister and concerted attempt by George III to resurrect monarchical absolutism is now untenable; so is the related notion that the ministry of Lord North rested on a revived Tory party. Nevertheless, the historiographical tradition which made a neo-Harringtonian libertarianism into the almost universal American idiom even before 1776 required that the trigger of revolution should be external to the colonies, a reassertion of authoritarian ideology in

1760s Britain. A fuller picture of the monarchical, Anglican nature of the early-Hanoverian regime removes the significant elements in this contrast between the years before and after 1760, and reopens the question of internal colonial triggers to the rebellion of 1776.

Before the 1760s, the main idioms of political discourse in mainland colonies had echoed English norms: they were determined by the dynastic and religious questions fought over by Englishmen since 1679. But why was it thought appropriate by some people to use Whig rhetoric against a Whig regime? After 1760, the pattern in the New World again corresponded closely to that in the Old. The external threats disappeared, together with the internal polarity they had induced. The confluence of former Whigs and Tories in support of George III simultaneously reawakened old fears and provided new targets for existing opposition rhetoric.

In both 1688 and 1766, the constitutional problems raised by questions of taxation, executive prerogative and parliamentary jurisdiction were turned from grievances into issues which evoked the passionate commitment of great numbers of ordinary men by their engagement with a much wider nexus of ideas and feelings. Contemporaries recognised the part played by religious enthusiasm in the American cause. 'Enthusiasm' now came to take on a wider secular meaning: John Adams echoed Shaftesbury's eulogy of 'noble enthusiasm' as a quality which 'raised the imagination to an opinion or conceit of something majestic and divine'. But its secular sense had most importance only to the small circle of men who formed part of the Jeffersonian Enlightenment. The political commitments of most men were still an aspect of their religion; and this was already taking forms which were both new and distinctively American.

Richard Price rightly sensed that the American colonies in 1776 were 'animated by piety'. They were, indeed, in the grip of one of the more momentous of religious revivalist movements. The evangelical phenomenon known in the colonies as the Great Awakening began slowly in the 1740s, under the inspiration of the New Light Presbyterians, a highly politicized élite associated in the foundation of Princeton. From the 1740s it grew to become a mass movement, turning into a 'landslide' in the decade following 1765. By 1776, the Great Awakening had inspired in many colonists a vision of an imminent millennium. The expectation of a future moral transformation was matched by a condemnation of the sinfulness, luxury and corruption of past life, and, especially, of English modes. It was the millenarian impulse which gave immediacy to the academic neo-Harringtonian critique of 'corruption', and the social constituency of the evangelical movement which gave these religious insights their populist focus as an attack on privilege and hierarchy, an assertion of divinely-sanctioned popular sovereignty against the divine right of the English monarchy.

In the decade before 1776, the rhetoric of American clergy subtly changed. The familiar jeremiad about the sins of God's chosen people and the need for a collective act of atonement was increasingly combined with an implication that that repentance had already been demonstrated by the resistance to tyranny, so that Providence was now enlisted in the rebel cause. The doctrine that God stood in a con-

tractual relation with his chosen people – a doctrine especially emphasised in New England Congregationalism and by Presbyterians – became more generally available to all Americans, and the burden of guilt for the breach of this eternal contract was by implication transferred to the mother country.

Indeed, argued Perry Miller, it was not the 'genial Anglicanism' of the established clergy nor the 'urbane rationalism' of the Washingtons, Jeffersons and Franklins that

> brought the rank and file of American Protestants into the war. What aroused a Christian patriotism that needed staying power was a realization of the vengeance God denounced against the wicked; what fed their hopes was not what God promised as a recompense to virtue, but what dreary fortunes would overwhelm those who persisted in sloth; what kept them going was an assurance that by exerting themselves they were fighting for a victory thus providentially predestined.

It has been suggested that colonial Americans were able to mobilise so quickly between 1773 and 1776 because a millennial tradition of thought was available for instant activation, overriding the tradition of a remedy for present corruption in the return to former virtue. Mobilisation on the scale of 1776 is evidence against religious imagery being mere rhetoric. A break in the tie with Britain, a renunciation of existing rationales for American society, demanded and was easily given an alternative rationale, a biblically-supported vision of a new future.

Within the millenarian vision, one component in particular still acted as an emotional catalyst and a political trigger: the fear of Popery. Its role was already an ancient one. The New England colonies were founded at a time of frenzied anti-Catholicism in England, and carried this inheritance as a lasting and vivid theme in their moral and political discourse. Laudian persecution of Puritans added the element of paranoia. Consequently, the imperial challenges of the 1670s and 80s produced an even more hysterical reaction in the colonies than in England. By the mid-Eighteenth century, the vocabulary of tyranny, slavery and arbitrary power was still grounded on the meanings of the key term 'popery'; but, under the impact of such early eighteenth century English texts as *Cato's Letters*, these meanings had been stretched to cover the exercise of

power by any established, episcopal church. Whatever its origin, this heightened emotional temperature acted to sweep up and distort patterns of argument which might otherwise have provided grounds for caution rather than insurrection.

American rhetoric in the 1760s and 1770s combined the same inconsistent elements as did that of England: beside contract theory and natural rights theory went the doctrine of the ancient constitution. As important as the specific form of the ancient constitution was the long record of sacrifice in its defence: colonists revered the 'ancestors [who] have liberally shed their blood to secure to us the rights we now contend for'; but such a rhetoric carried the implication that the constitutoin could only be maintained 'at the hazard of our lives and fortunes'. A theory of past achievement became itself an incitement to present excess: in the frenzy of an evangelical religious movement, the theory of the ancient constitution demanded sacrifice and atonement rather than negotiation, compromise or humility.

From soon after the accession of George III, English Dissenters cooperated with their colonial co-religionists to confirm and strengthen the Americans in their belief that a transatlantic conspiracy was being hatched against both civil and religious liberty. These issues were revitalised, for English Dissenters also, by the Anglican church's intermittent moves to appoint a bishop for the colonies. Only when viewed against the background of the history of English, Irish and Scots sectarian emigration to the colonies did this modest proposal assume the sinister shape of a bid to reimpose those claims which the Americans had fled their homelands to escape. The Wilkes affair and Anglican resistance to the Feathers Tavern petition against subscription to the Thirty-Nine Articles fell into place as episodes in the royal conspiracy.

It required the Dissenting perspective to arrange these unconnected incidents into a scenario of impending tyranny. Anglicans explained the innocence of a scheme for a bishop in America: as a memorandum of Shelburne re-emphasised in 1764, it was proposed to 'model every thing upon the most extensive Principles of the *Toleration*... No Coercive Powers are desired over the Laity'. But the ancient intolerance of New England Congregationalism was given a new object by the loyal behaviour of Anglican clergy during the Stamp Act crisis; by 1771 the clergy of New York and New Jersey, petitioning once more for a bishop, could warn that 'Independency in Religion will naturally produce Republicanism in the State'. Anglicanism had changed greatly from the persecutory creed it had been as recently as Anne's reign; colonial Dissenters still largely lived with their ancient shibboleths, nursing atavistic hatreds.

Yet the perspective of the Jeffersonian Enlightenment blocked any deeper understanding of the causes of rebellion. At the same time, a right of rebellion, once asserted so successfully, had become part of American culture. It could not be removed by Britain's recognition of the independence of thirteen of her colonies in 1783. Rebellions therefore continued, adding to fears that the new republic would break into its component parts, either between northern and southern or between eastern and western states. In Shays' Rebellion (1786), the Whiskey Rebellion (1794), and Fries' Rebellion

(1799), Americans fought Americans in a continuing conflict over the issues that had been at stake in 1776; but now it was a US Federal government which asserted its authority with the whisky excise of 1791, and the stamp and land taxes of 1798. This continuing conflict sets 1776 in the perspective of a civil war rather than a war of national liberation, a war to emancipate a pre-existing nation; and it reopens the question of its religious origins.

Evidence does survive of these later rebels identifying the cause of their east coast opponents with Antichrist. Many were active Presbyterians, and although their church officially disavowed rebellion, the religious element continued to do more than strengthen their group identity. Even Fries' Rebellion contained an echo of dynastic, anti-Anglican fears. The Presbyterianism of the Whiskey rebels, too, bound them closely into a transatlantic tradition. Opposition to internal taxes in England in the 1730s, as in the colonies in the 1760s and 1790s,

was articulated by the élite in the familiar terms of arbitrary power. Popular perceptions showed why such language was activated: according to Lord Hervey, during the Excise Crisis of 1733 'the universal cry of the kingdom was "No slavery, no excise, no wooden shoes"'. The *London Journal* claimed that the opposition had spread the effective rumour 'that a great many Pair of *Wooden Shoes* were lately *imported*, on purpose to be carried about the City on Poles or Sticks, as *Emblems* or *Signs* to the People, of what a dismal State they are coming to'. Popery and poverty (wooden shoes) were as much a popular identity as a literary trope, as the Gordon Riots of 1780 once more emphasised.

Social stability combined with political instability was the norm in early modern societies of western Europe. This is particularly apparent in England's Atlantic empire during the seventeenth and eighteenth centuries. Conflict, massacre, schism and sometimes successful rebellion were set against steady but irregular structural change and commercial development, always threatened by the stresses and outcomes of war or insurrection. Why was the intellectual tradition of Common Law and parliamentary representation activated, turned from a defensive to an offensive creed? Why were great numbers of men periodically seized by revolutionary frenzy? From Venner's rising in 1661 through 1688 and 1776 to the Irish rebellion of 1798, we find not a monocausal explanation but a common thread on both sides of the Atlantic in religion.

FOR FURTHER READING:
Ruth M. Bloch, *Visionary Republic: Millennial Themes in American Thought, 1756-1800* (Cambridge, 1985); Patricia U. Bonomi, *Under the Cope of Heaven: Religion, Society and Politics in Colonial America* (Oxford, 1986); Nathan O. Hatch, *The Sacred Cause of Liberty: Republican Thought and the Millennium in Revolutionary New England* (New Haven, 1977); Winthrop D. Jordan, *White over Black: American Attitudes towards the Negro, 1550-1812* (Chapel Hill, NC, 1968); Cushing Strout, *The New Heavens and New Earth* (New York, 1974).

Burning the Stamp Act in Boston, 1765 – several of its colonial opponents had described the actual stamps in apocalyptic terms as 'the mark of the beast'.

National Consolidation and Expansion

The Constitution has come to be a revered document in American history. With the exception of the Civil War, the government it established has survived intact until today. But the Constitution is skeletal in form, its provisions general and subject to interpretation. Those who participated in government during the early years had the task of fleshing it out into a workable system. Disagreement over how to do this caused a variety of struggles that resulted, among other things, in a two-party system the Founders had not anticipated. "James Madison and the Bill of Rights" provides an opportunity to trace the evolution of James Madison's thinking about the virtues and defects of a bill of rights.

The decades between the establishment of the new government in 1789 and the Civil War were marked by two major developments: westward expansion and the onset of industrialism. The nation's size was doubled by the Louisiana Purchase in 1803; Florida was acquired in the 1820s; Texas, California, and Oregon in the 1840s. The opening of new lands stimulated agricultural production, which was matched by urban and industrial growth. Railroads spanned the nation, creating ever-larger markets that in turn stimulated higher productivity. The United States on the eve of the Civil War was a colossus compared with the struggling nation of 1789.

All this was accomplished at high costs. Periods of prosperity were punctuated by depressions, farmers went broke because of bad weather or low prices, and urban workers often toiled long hours under deplorable conditions. The institution of slavery remained, making a mockery of the nation's stated ideals. The environment was despoiled. Natural resources were gobbled up with little thought of the future, and the byproducts of "progress" polluted water and fouled the air.

There was no inevitability about the way the United States developed under the new Constitution. The nagging question of slavery was highlighted when the nation's capital was located in Washington, D.C., which soon became the center of a thriving slave trade as described in "Slaves and Freedmen." An examination of the dynamics of women in Southern slavery is made in "The Lives of Slave Women." The role of the Supreme Court was vastly enhanced by John Marshall, as recounted in "The Great Chief Justice." "A Shadow of Secession?"

tells how the Hartford Convention of 1814 raised probing questions about the nature of the Union, and "The Jacksonian Revolution" analyzes what its author believes constituted a watershed in American history.

Expansion has been an almost constant theme in American history. Although the United States did not acquire Alaska until 1867, "Russia's American Adventure" makes clear that understanding Alaska's native culture requires knowledge of Russian influences during the 1820s and 1830s. "Lone Star Rising" discusses Texas as it was before and after annexation by the United States. "Eden Ravished" describes the way Americans plundered the vast domain they inhabited. Two final essays treat the theme of expansion: "El Presidente Gringo" describes how William Walker's forays into Central America influenced domestic politics and Latin American attitudes toward the United States; and "The Cry Was: Go West, Young Man, and Stay Healthy" describes the prevailing attitudes about western climate and life.

The growth of industry altered the lives of Americans in many ways. Failure of an effort to create a safe, healthy environment for young working women is the theme of "From Utopia to Mill Town." "The Secret Life of a Developing Country (Ours)" describes changes in manners and morals.

Reform movements have waxed and waned throughout the American experience. "Act One" analyzes an early effort by women to gain equal rights with men. Temperance advocates ascribed a great many social ills to the consumption of alcohol. "The War Against Demon Rum" tells how the "drys" shifted their focus from moral suasion to legislative prohibition.

Looking Ahead: Challenge Questions

The new government that began functioning in 1789 faced many challenges. What were Alexander Hamilton's contributions to economic and political developments? How did Chief Justice John Marshall influence the role of the Supreme Court in national affairs? What was the "Jacksonian Revolution"?

How did expansion influence the American people? How did it influence those who were its targets?

Industrial growth profoundly influenced the way people lived. New products and facilities made life easier and healthier for many, but did so at social and environmental costs. Discuss both aspects.

Movements for women's rights, temperance, and abolition failed to achieve their goals before the Civil War. What did these groups have in common and how did they differ?

James Madison and the Bill of Rights

JACK N. RAKOVE

Jack N. Rakove is director of the American studies program at Stanford University and the author of *The Beginnings of National Politics: An Interpretive History of the Continental Congress* (1979)

James Madison went to the Federal Convention of 1787 convinced that it faced no greater challenge than finding some means of checking "the aggressions of interested majorities on the rights of minorities and of individuals." He left it still fearful that the new Constitution would not effectually "secure individuals against encroachments on their rights." In his best known contribution to American political theory, *The Federalist*, No. 10, Madison again voiced his great concern that majorities were enacting laws "adverse to the rights of other citizens," and he went on to define the protection of the individual "faculties" of men as "the first object of government."

These and other statements suggest that Madison should have welcomed the addition of a Bill of Rights to the Constitution. And in fact Madison can rightly be regarded as the principal framer of the Bill of Rights which the First Federal Congress submitted to the states in 1789. Many congressmen felt that he was acting with undue haste in calling for quick action on the subject of amendments. Had Madison not pressed them to consider the amendments he had introduced early in the session, the Bill of Rights might never have been added to the Constitution

Yet even as he was shepherding the amendments through Congress in August 1789, Madison privately described his efforts as a "nauseous project." His acceptance of the need for a Bill of Rights came grudgingly. When the Constitution was being written in 1787, and even after it was ratified in 1788, Madison dismissed bills of rights as so many "parchment barriers" whose "inefficacy" (he reminded his good friend, Thomas Jefferson) was repeatedly demonstrated "on those occasions when [their] control is most needed." Even after Jefferson's entreaties finally led him to admit that bills of rights might have their uses, it still took a difficult election campaign against another friend, James Monroe, to get Madison to declare that, if elected to the House of Representatives, he would favor adding to the Constitution "the most satisfactory provisions for all essential rights."

To trace the evolution of James Madison's thinking about the virtues and defects of a bill of rights, then, is to confront the ambiguous mix of principled and political concerns that led to the adoption of the first ten amendments. Today, when disputes about the meaning of the Bill of Rights and its lineal descendant, the Fourteenth Amendment, have become so heated—when, indeed, we often regard the Bill of Rights as the essence of the Constitution—it is all the more important to fix the relation between the Constitution of 1787 and the amendments of 1789. To do this there is no better place to begin than with the concerns that troubled James Madison.

Enumerating Rights

Much of the contemporary debate and controversy about the rights-based decisions that the Supreme Court has made over the past three decades centers on the question of whether the judiciary should protect only those rights that enjoy explicit constitutional or statutory sanction, or whether it can act to establish new rights—as in the case of abortion—on the basis of its understanding of certain general principles of liberty. We cannot know how Madison would decide particular cases today. But one aspect of his analysis of the problem of rights seems highly pertinent to the current debate. Madison's deepest reservations about the wisdom of adopting any bill of rights reflected his awareness of the difficulty of enumerating all the rights that deserved protection against the "infinitude of legislative expedients" that could be deployed to the disadvantage of individuals and minorities. Madison's notion of rights was thus open-ended, but his ideas about which kinds of rights were most vulnerable changed over time. In 1787 he felt that the greatest dangers to liberty concerned the rights of property. The passage of paper money laws in various states revealed the depths of "injustice" to which these populist forces were willing to descend. Worse might be yet to come. At the Federal Convention, Madison told his fellow delegates that he foresaw a day when "power will slide into the hands" of "those who labour under all the hardships of life, and secretly sigh for a more equal distribution of its blessings." And even if the Constitution succeeded in checking the danger from a dispossessed proletariat, Madison thought that almost any act of legislation or taxation would affect rights of property. "What are many of the most important acts of legislation," he asked in *Federalist* 10, "but so many judicial determinations ... concerning the rights of large bodies of citizens?"

But the development of Madison's ideas of liberty long predated the specific concerns he felt about the economic legislation of the 1780s. His first known comments on political issues of any kind expressed his abhorrence at the persecution of religious dissenters in pre-Revolutionary Virginia; and his first notable action in public life had been to secure an amendment to the Virginia Declaration of Rights, the most influential of the bills of rights that had been attached to the state constitutions written at the time of independence. In 1785 Madison led the fight against a bill to provide public aid for all teachers of the Christian religion in Virginia; the *Memorial and Remonstrance Against Religious Assessments* that he published in conjunction with this campaign treated rights of conscience as a realm of behavior entirely beyond the regulation of civil authority.

Majority Misrule

We thus cannot doubt Madison's commitment to the cause of pro-

CONGRESS of the UNITED STATES.

In the HOUSE *of* REPRESENTATIVES,

Monday, 24th August, 1789,

RESOLVED, by the Senate and House of Representatives of the United States of America in Congress assembled, two thirds of both Houses deeming it necessary, That the following Articles be proposed to the Legislatures of the several States, as Amendments to the Constitution of the United States, all or any of which Articles, when ratified by three fourths of the said Legislatures, to be valid to all intents and purposes as part of the said Constitution—Viz.

ARTICLES in addition to, and amendment of, the Constitution of the United States of America, proposed by Congress, and ratified by the Legislatures of the several States, pursuant to the fifth Article of the original Constitution.

ARTICLE the FIRST.

After the first enumeration, required by the first Article of the Constitution, there shall be one Representative for every thirty thousand, until the number shall amount to one hundred, after which the proportion shall be so regulated by Congress, that there shall be not less than one hundred Representatives, nor less than one Representative for every forty thousand persons, until the number of Representatives shall amount to two hundred, after which the proportion shall be so regulated by Congress, that there shall not be less than two hundred Representatives, nor less than one Representative for every fifty thousand persons.

ARTICLE the SECOND.

No law varying the compensation to the members of Congress, shall take effect, until an election of Representatives shall have intervened.

ARTICLE the THIRD.

Congress shall make no law establishing religion or prohibiting the free exercise thereof, nor shall the rights of Conscience be infringed.

ARTICLE the FOURTH.

The Freedom of Speech, and of the Press, and the right of the People peaceably to assemble, and consult for their common good, and to apply to the Government for a redress of grievances, shall not be infringed.

The first four of twelve amendments to the Constitution proposed by the House of Representatives August 24, 1789. Chapin Library, Williams College, Williamstown, Mass.

tecting private rights and civil liberties against improper intrusion by the government. But all orthodox republicans in Revolutionary America shared such beliefs. What carried Madison beyond the conventional thought of his contemporaries was, first, his analysis of the sources of the dangers to individual and minority rights, and second, the solutions and remedies he offered.

Traditional republican theory held that the great danger to liberty lay in the relentless efforts of scheming rulers to aggrandize their power at the expense of ordinary citizens. The great safeguard against such threats was believed to lie in the virtue and vigilance of the people.

The skeptical Madison sought to overturn this received wisdom. In the weeks preceding the gathering of the Federal Convention in May 1787, Madison collected his thoughts in a memorandum on the "Vices of the Political System of the United States." As he saw it, the "multiplicity," "mutability," and most important, "the injustice" of the laws of the states had called "into question the fundamental principle of republican Government, that the majority who rule in such Governments are the safest Guardians both of public Good and of private rights." The experience of the states demonstrated, Madison concluded, that neither legislative majorities nor the popular majorities whom they represented could be expected to refrain "from unjust violations of the rights and interests of the minority, or of individuals," whenever "an apparent interest or common passion" spurred such majorities to act. Religion, honor, a sense of the public good—all the virtues a good republican might hope to see operate as restraints—seemed ineffective.

It is crucial to note that Madison directed his criticism against the character of lawmaking *within the individual states;* and the logic of his analysis further led him to conclude that the greatest dangers to liberty would continue to arise within the states, rather than from a reconstituted national government. The ill effects of majority rule far more likely would emerge within the small compass of local communities or states, where "factious majorities" could easily form, than in the extended sphere of a national republic that would "be broken into a greater variety of interests, of pursuits, of passions," whose very diversity and fluidity would check each other.

A Proposal for a National Veto

The solutions Madison offered to this problem operated at two levels. He reserved his most radical proposal—an absolute national veto over state laws "in all cases whatsoever"—for the continuing need to protect individual rights against majority misrule within the states. In effect, Madison hoped the national government would serve as a "disinterested and dispassionate umpire in disputes between different passions and interests" within the states.

But Madison was also prepared to concede that the wrong kinds of majorities might still coalesce within the new Congress that the Federal Convention would create. "Experience in all the States had evinced

a powerful tendency in the Legislature to absorb all power into its vortex," he reminded the Convention on July 21. Who could say whether Congress might not prove equally "impetuous"? To protect citizens against the danger of unjust *national* legislation, Madison favored establishing a joint executive-judicial council of revision armed with a veto over acts of Congress; he was also attracted to the idea of an independent and powerful Senate, insulated from both the state legislatures and the electorate, to counteract the excesses of the House of Representatives.

Madison justified all of these proposals in terms of the protection they would extend to individual and minority rights. But he went to the Convention convinced that bills of rights could add little if anything to the defense of civil liberty. None of the existing state bills of rights provided an effective check against legislative or popular excess. The problem was that bills of rights were not self-enforcing. The actual protection of the lofty principles they espoused required the existence of well-constituted governments. But if such governments did exist—or could be created—what need would they have for bills of rights?

Most of the framers at Philadelphia agreed that there was no need for adding a bill of rights to the new Constitution, but they rejected Madison's two pet proposals for a national veto and a Council of Revision. The Convention protected individual liberty only by placing a handful of prohibitions on the legislative authority of the states (notably laws impairing the obligation of contracts) or Congress (habeas corpus, ex post facto, bills of attainder). When George Mason belatedly insisted that the new Constitution required a much longer list of enumerated rights, his arguments were ignored.

The rejection of his pet scheme for a national veto on all state laws greatly disappointed Madison. During the first weeks after the Convention's adjournment, he seems to have feared that the new Constitution was fatally flawed because the

new government would still lack the authority to deal with the problem of "vicious" popular and legislative majorities in the *states*. Even though the supremacy clause of the Constitution established a basis for state and federal judges to overturn laws violating individual rights, he doubted whether the judiciary could ever muster the will or political strength to withstand majoritarian excesses or the ingenuity of ambitious legislators.

When it came to the dangers that liberty might face from the *national* government, however, he was far more optimistic. Though not entirely happy with the system of checks and balances that would shape relations among the three branches, Madison thought it would discourage the enactment of harmful legislation. Moreover, he continued to rely confidently on the theory of the advantages of multiple factions he had derived just prior to the Convention. "In the extended republic of the United States, and among the great variety of interests, parties, and sects which it embraces," he wrote in *The Federalist*, No. 51, "a coalition of a majority of the whole society could seldom take place upon any other principles than those of justice and the general good." State laws might still work wholesale injustice; national laws, he believed, would not.

Anti-Federalist Clamor

As Madison threw himself into the campaign to ratify the Constitution, however, he was forced to take seriously the growing clamor for the addition of a bill of rights—especially after Jefferson wrote him to affirm *his* conviction "that a bill of rights is what the people are entitled to against every government on earth, general or particular [i.e., national or local], and what no just government should refuse or rest on inference." Had the issue of amendments been confined to matters of rights alone, Madison might have readily agreed. But fearing that many diehard Anti-Federalists hoped to exploit the call for amendments to propose major changes in the Constitution or even to promote a second convention, Madison balked at accepting Jefferson's correction.

In October 1788—more than a year after the adjournment of the Convention, and a good four months after Virginia became the tenth state to ratify the Constitution—Madison wrote Jefferson to explain why, though now willing to see a bill of rights added to the Constitution, he found no other solid reason to support it than the fact "that it is anxiously desired by others." With other Federalists—notably James Wilson of Pennsylvania—he still thought that a bill of rights was superfluous because the federal government could exercise only those powers that were expressly delegated to it—and those powers did not extend to violating individual liberties. Moreover, Madison confessed his "fear that a positive declaration of some of the most essential rights could not be obtained in the requisite latitude." Better (in other words) not to have any bill of rights than to incorporate in the Constitution weak statements that might actually leave room for the violation of the very liberties they were meant to protect.

Again, however, Madison drew his greatest doubts about the value of a bill of rights from his analysis of the problem of majority tyranny. In a monarchical regime, Madison noted, such declarations might serve as "a signal for rousing and uniting the superior force of the community" against the government. But in a republic, where the greatest dangers to liberty arose not from government but from the people themselves, a bill of rights could hardly serve to rally the majority against itself. The most Madison would concede was that a bill of rights might help to instill in the people greater respect for "the fundamental maxims of free government," and thus "counteract the impulses of interest and passion." He was willing to entertain, too, the idea that a bill of rights would be useful in case "usurped acts of the government" threatened the liberties of the community— but in his thinking, that problem remained only a speculative possibility.

Like any intellectual, then, Madi-

James Madison, *age 82. Library of Congress.*

son valued consistency too highly to renounce ideas to which he was deeply and personally committed. But Madison, for all his originality as a political theorist, was also a working politician. His early disappointment with the Constitution had quickly given way to the belief, as he wrote in *The Federalist*, No. 38, that "the errors which may be contained in the Constitution ... [were] such as will not be ascertained until an actual trial shall have pointed them out." Amendments taking the form of a bill of rights might serve a vital *political* function—even though unnecessary on their merits—if they could be framed in such a way as to reconcile the moderate opponents of the Constitution without opening an avenue to a radical assault on the essential structure of the new government.

This sensitivity to the need to assuage popular opinion was reinforced by Madison's own experience in the first congressional elections of 1788–89, when he faced a difficult fight against James Monroe. With reports abroad that Madison "did not think that a single letter of [the Constitution] would admit of a change," he found it

necessary not only to return to Virginia from his seat in the Confederation Congress at New York and to travel around the district debating with Monroe, but more important, to issue public letters affirming his willingness to propose and support amendments guaranteeing such "essential rights" as "the rights of Conscience in the fullest latitude, the freedom of the press, trials by jury, security against general warrants &c." Even then, however, he was careful to note that he had "never seen in the Constitution ... those serious dangers which have alarmed many respectable Citizens."

Political Exigencies

Madison carried the election by a margin of 336 votes out of 2,280 cast. Four weeks into the first session of Congress, he informed his colleagues of his intention to bring the subject of amendments forward, but another month passed before he was at last able to present a comprehensive set of proposals on June 8, 1789.

Some congressmen thought that Madison was acting from political motives alone. Senator Robert Morris of Pennsylvania scoffed that Madison "got frightened in Virginia 'and wrote a Book'"—a reference to his public letters on amendments. But there was nothing disingenuous about Madison's June 8 speech introducing his plan of amendments. Having reconciled himself to political exigencies, Madison sought to achieve goals consistent with his private beliefs.

In typical scholarly fashion, he had culled from over two hundred amendments proposed by the state ratification conventions a list of nineteen potential changes to the Constitution. Two of his proposals concerned congressional salaries and the population ratio of the House; two can best be described as general statements of principles of government. The remaining amendments fell under the general rubric of "rights."

The most noteworthy aspects of Madison's introductory speech of June 8 is that it faithfully recapitulates the positions he had taken not only in his election campaign against Monroe but also in his correspondence with Jefferson. He took care to deal with the objections that could come from Anti-Federalists and Federalists alike, noting his reasons for originally opposing amendments, explaining why he had changed his mind, yet also leaving his listeners and readers with a clear understanding that he was acting on a mixture of political and principled motives. The central elements of his analysis of the problem of protecting rights in a republican government were all there: the difficulty of enumerating rights, the emphasis on the greater danger from popular majorities than acts of government, the risks of trusting too much to "paper barriers."

Two of his proposals deserve special notice. The first is the forerunner of the Ninth Amendment. In its graceless original wording, it read: "The exceptions here or elsewhere in the constitution, made in favor of particular rights, shall not be so construed as to diminish the just importance of other rights retained by the people; or as to enlarge the powers delegated by the constitution; but either as actual limitations of such powers, or as inserted merely for greater caution." Here Madison sought to prevent the enumeration of specific rights from relegating other rights to an inferior status—a concern that was consistent with both his open-ended notion of rights and his fear that any textually specific statement might inadvertently or otherwise create loopholes permitting the violation of liberties. As finally adopted by Congress and ratified by the states, this amendment came to read: "The enumeration in the Constitution, of certain rights, shall not be construed to deny or disparage others retained by the people."

Among all the provisions of the Bill of Rights, this somewhat mysterious formula has had perhaps the most curious history. Long ignored and disparaged because it did not identify the additional rights it implied should be protected, it was resurrected in the critical 1965 case of *Griswold* v *Connecticut*. In his

concurring opinion, Justice Arthur Goldberg invoked the Ninth Amendment to support the claim that state prohibition on contraception even for married couples violated a fundamental right of privacy that did not need to be specifically identified to be deserving of constitutional protection. If interpreted in Madisonian terms, this "forgotten" provision is immediately and enormously relevant to the current controversy over the extent to which judges can recognize claims of rights not enumerated in the text of the Constitution itself.

"No State Shall Violate . . ."

The second proposal of particular interest—and arguably the most important to Madison—held that "No state shall violate the equal rights of conscience, or the freedom of the press, or the trial by jury in criminal cases." All the other amendments that Madison enumerated elsewhere in his speech imposed limitations on the power of the national government alone. This amendment, by contrast, proposed adding to the prohibitions on state legislative authority already found in Article VI of the Constitution these further restraints in the three critical areas of religion, speech, and criminal law. Here, in effect, Madison belatedly hoped to salvage something of his original intention of creating a national government capable of protecting individual rights within (and against) the individual states, in a manner consistent with his belief that the greatest threats to liberty would continue to arise there, and not at the national level of government.

On this proposal Madison again met defeat. Not until the adoption of the Fourteenth Amendment in 1868 would the Constitution contain provisions that would establish a firm foundation upon which the

federal government could finally act as the James Madison of 1787–89 had hoped it would. But after a variety of procedural delays, Congress finally endorsed Madison's remaining provisions for the protection of individual liberty. All of the first ten amendments that we collectively describe as the Bill of Rights appeared, in seminal form, in Madison's speech of June 8. Among the rights he then insisted upon recognizing, Madison included: free exercise of religion; freedom of speech, of the press, and the right of assembly; the right to bear arms; and the protection of fundamental civil liberties against the legal and coercive power of the state through such devices as restrictions on "unreasonable searches and seizures," bail, "the right to a speedy and public trial" with "the assistance of counsel," and the right to "just compensation" for property.

Rethinking

Because the states retained the major share of legislative responsibility for more than another century, the Bill of Rights had little initial impact. Arguably only during the past forty years has it emerged as a central pillar of American constitutionalism—and thus as a central source of political controversy as well, as the current debate over the legitimacy of judicial "activism" in the enforcement and even creation of rights readily attests. But the question of what the prohibitions of the Bill of Rights finally mean can be answered only in part by appealing to the evidence of history.

Madison himself was one of the first to realize how ideas of rights had to be adjusted to meet changing political circumstances. His original breakthroughs in constitutional theory had rested on the conviction that in a republic the greatest dangers to liberty would arise

> *[Madison] proposed adding to the prohibitions on state legislative authority already found in Article VI . . . restraints in the three critical areas of religion, speech, and criminal law . . . . On this proposal, Madison again met defeat."*

"not from acts of government contrary to the sense of its constituents, but from acts in which the Government is the mere instrument of the major number of the constituents." He had further predicted that the greatest dangers to liberty would continue to arise within the states. Within a decade of the writing of the Constitution, however, the efforts of the Federalist administration of President John Adams to use the Sedition Act of 1798 to quell the opposition press of Madison's Republican party, in seeming defiance of the First Amendment, forced Madison to rethink his position. Now he saw more clearly how the existence of a bill of rights could serve to rally public opinion against improper acts of government; how dangers to liberty could arise at the enlightened level of national government as well as at the more parochial level of the states; and even how the political influence of the states could be used to check the excesses of national power.

Our ideas of rights and liberty have deep historical and philosophical roots which any good faith effort at interpretation must always take into account; and Madison's agency in drafting both the Constitution and its first ten amendments suggests that his views deserve particular attention and even respect. Yet just as his own efforts to understand both what the Constitution meant and how liberty was to be protected continued well after 1789—indeed literally to his death nearly a half century later—neither can ours be confined to recovering only some one meaning frozen at a mythical moment of supreme understanding. Such a moment has never existed and never will.

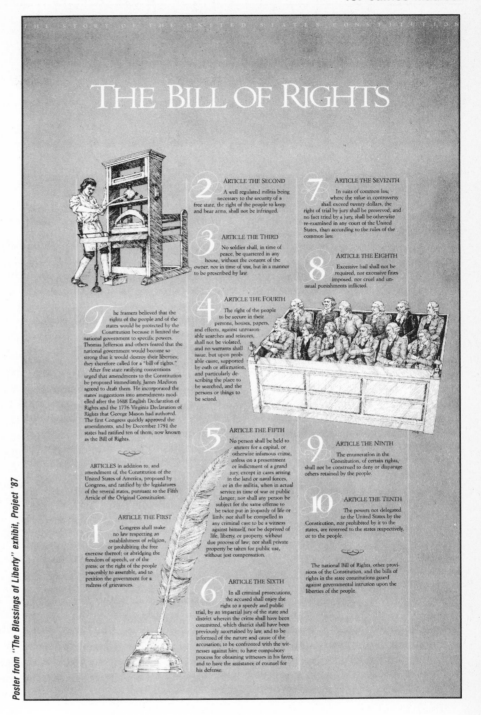

Poster from "The Blessings of Liberty" exhibit, Project '87

SLAVES AND FREEDMEN

Keith Melder

Keith Melder, 56, is a curator in the Division of Political History at the National Museum of American History. Born in Seattle, Washington, he received a B.A. (1954) from Williams College, and an M.A. (1958) and a Ph.D. (1964) from Yale. He is the editor of City of Magnificent Intentions: A History of the District of Columbia *(1983).*

The history of Washington, D.C., begins—not surprisingly—with a political deal.

On a June evening in 1790, Secretary of State Thomas Jefferson encountered Treasury Secretary Alexander Hamilton outside of the Alexander Macomb Mansion (on today's Broadway) in New York City, where President George Washington was living. Looking, as Jefferson said, "sombre, haggard, and dejected," Hamilton was troubled by a political dispute that threatened to sunder the Union: whether the federal government should assume the debts that the states had accrued during the long and costly War for Independence.

The issue, Jefferson later recalled, had "created greater animosities than I ever yet [had seen] take place on any occasion." Like most Northern politicians, Hamilton, the New Yorker, favored the debt assumption bill, which had been defeated in the new U.S. House of Representatives. Most Southerners, including Jefferson, did not. The two men paced "backwards and forewards before the president's door for half an hour," the Virginian said, before they decided to meet at his home, where they settled the dispute over dinner.

Jefferson later reported what happened:

It was finally agreed . . . [that] the vote [against federal assumption of the debts] should be rescinded . . . . But it was observed that this pill would be peculiarly bitter to the Southern states, and that some concomitant measure should be adopted to sweeten it a little to them. There had before been propositions to fix the seat of government either at Philadelphia, or at Georgetown permanently afterwards . . . [to] calm in some degree the ferment . . . . So two of the Potomac members [Alexander White and Richard Bland Lee] agreed to change their votes, and Hamilton undertook to carry the other point [that of convincing the Northerners to agree to placing the capital in the South].

Having chosen a Southern site, Congress still had to decide exactly where the capital would be. The Constitution determined that the District, which could not "exceed 10 miles square," would be formed "by cession of particular states." On July 16, 1790, Congress passed the Residence Act, which empowered the president to select a plot of land, "directed on the River Potomac, at some place between the mouths of the Eastern Branch [the Anacostia River] and the Connogochegue." George Washington chose a river site not far from his Mount Vernon, Virginia, estate.

In establishing the capital as a separate federal district, the nation's founders created a complicated and often vexing political regime: Congress (as Article I, Section 8 of the Constitution required) would retain "exclusive Legislation over such district in

From *The Wilson Quarterly*, New Year's 1989, pp. 77-83. Copyright © 1989 by The Woodrow Wilson International Center for Scholars.

all Cases whatsoever," even though taxpaying residents lacked representation on Capitol Hill.

And, by carving the new federal district out of two slave states (and by mandating that, at least until 1800, the laws of Maryland and Virginia would apply there), Congress guaranteed that the capital would be a place where, for a time, slavery and the slave trade would thrive. Washington would also become a place to which Southern black freedmen would migrate, and where, to the dismay of local whites, a lively black community would develop.

Whereas London, Paris, and Rome were all great cities before they became national capitals, Washington did not even exist before it was named the seat of the U.S. government. In 1790, the federal district enveloped two small, flourishing Potomac River tobacco ports that had been founded during the mid-18th century: Alexandria, Virginia (pop. 5,000), and Georgetown, Maryland (3,200).

With its two-story brick houses and bustling wharves, Alexandria was, as France's Duke de la Rochefoucauld-Liancourt observed in 1799, "the handsomest town in Virginia, and indeed . . . among the finest in the United States." Georgetown's position atop "several small hills," he added, rendered "its aspects pleasing." In addition, there were two small settlements in the territory: Carrollsburgh on the Eastern Branch (now called the Anacostia River) and Hamburg, a hamlet near where Rock Creek emptied into the Potomac.

From 1790 until his death in 1799, President Washington took a strong interest in the capital. He appointed three commissioners who would raise money for public buildings by selling off some parcels of land. They would later name the city "Washington." The president also assigned a temperamental French engineer, Pierre Charles L'Enfant, to design the city; L'Enfant's plan dispersed the various offices of government across the District, thus creating, as Charles Dickens was to observe in 1842, "a city of magnificent intentions." Andrew Ellicott and his deputy, black mathematician Benjamin Banneker, would survey and configure the 10-mile-square area

The capital, as envisioned by planner Pierre L'Enfant in 1793. Congress had considered locating the federal district on the Delaware River, near Trenton, N.J.

so that the corners of the square pointed north, south, east, and west.

Under the Residence Act of 1790, Philadelphia served as the seat of government until 1800.* The City of Brotherly Love was by then a metropolis with museums, taverns, book stores, and cobblestone streets. But the District was dominated by wooded hills and gnat-infested swamps. Pennsylvania Avenue was an often-muddied dirt track, obstructed by tree stumps and thorn bushes. The Capitol and the headquarters for the State and War departments were still unfinished, as was the sandstone "President's House"—which President Thomas Jefferson later called, "big enough for two emperors, one pope, and the grand lama."

The federal territory was inhabited mostly by white shopkeepers, teachers, manual laborers, and government clerks, who dwelled in modest quarters, such as the boarding houses on Jenkins Hill (Capitol Hill), or in row houses near the Navy Yard. In his *Early Recollections of Washington City* (1866), Christian Hines recalled seeing the first presidents "in and about the city." The chief executives, he wrote, "would ride around the suburbs and into the country unattended by either servants or escorts. Mr. Jefferson, in particular, was fond of being where any improvements were going on."

After arriving in Washington throughout 1800, members of Congress confronted a question that has yet to be answered to everyone's satisfaction: whether the Congress or the local citizenry should oversee the federal district.

As noted, the Constitution had empowered Congress to exercise "exclusive Legislation" over the 10-mile-square district.** But as James Madison suggested in *The Federalist* (no. 43), citizens could still be allowed "a

municipal legislature for local purposes, derived from their own suffrages."

In February of 1801, Congress, exercising its prerogative, divided the District into five administrative parcels: the counties of Washington (most of the land granted by Maryland) and Alexandria (most of the land granted by Virginia); the two self-governing municipalities of Georgetown and Alexandria; and the undeveloped city of Washington, which after 1802 would be in the hands of a presidentially appointed mayor and an elected City Council—which, in keeping with contemporary practices, was chosen, as the law states, by "free white male inhabitants of full age who [had] . . . paid taxes the preceding year."

At that time, there were no more than 14,000 inhabitants in the entire federal enclave. The whites were largely natives of adjoining Maryland and Virginia. There were some 4,000 blacks, over 80 percent of whom were slaves. Touring the United States in 1804, Irish poet Thomas Moore, observing Washington, wrote:

Even here beside the proud
Potomac's streams . . .
The medley mass of pride and misery
Of whips and charters,
manacles and rights
Of slaving blacks and democratic
whites . . .

The number of slaves in the District rose, especially after 1808, when Congress banned the importation of bondsmen from Africa, thereby creating a greater demand for domestic slaves. Now, planters in Georgia and the Carolinas began looking for bonded labor within the United States.

Tobacco farmers in Maryland and Virginia, where the croplands had been exhausted by overplanting and soil erosion, were happy to oblige. They brought their excess chattel to the District, where black men and women could be either rented to local businesses or sold South. A vigorous slave trade ensued. "Although Washington was not the largest slave market," historian John Hope Franklin has written, "it was the most notorious down to 1850."

The sudden boom in the slave business startled many Washingtonians. In 1809, President James Madison's secretary, Ed-

---

*In that year, the entire federal government included one president, one vice-president, 32 senators, 106 representatives, and 131 clerks and bureaucrats.

**Under the Constitution, only states—and thus not the federal district—would be entitled to representation on Capitol Hill. Yet in 1971, Congress decided to allow a nonvoting District "Delegate" in the U.S. House of Representatives. The Constitution did not allow District residents to choose presidential electors—until the 23rd Amendment was ratified in 1961.

ward Coles, was worried that foreign dignitaries would witness "such a revolting sight" on the streets of the capital as the "gangs of Negroes, some in chains, on their way to a Southern market." Just as unsettling to white Washingtonians was the steady increase in the number of free blacks. Some of them had purchased their freedom from local masters; others had been liberated by them. Meanwhile, free blacks migrated to the relatively tolerant capital from elsewhere in the South.

"We have already too many free Negroes and mulattoes in this city," one District resident would write to the *National Intelligencer*, "and the policy of our corporate authorities should tend to the diminution of this insolent class." The City Council enacted Black Codes in 1808, as Southern states had done, to control slaves and the growing number of freedmen, many of whom had migrated to the city from Maryland and Virginia.

The measures imposed, among other things, a $5 fine on any "Negro," or on any "loose, idle, disorderly person" found on the streets or "at a tippling or other house" after 10 P.M. Four years later, the council quadrupled that fine, imposed a $10 penalty on all blacks found playing games of "immoral tendency," and authorized 40 lashes for slaves caught at "nightly and disorderly meetings."

Washington's Black Codes, however, failed to discourage the immigration of free blacks to the District; the rules were, after all, still among the most lenient in the South. Whereas Maryland and Virginia required newly manumitted blacks to leave those states within a fixed amount of time—or forfeit their freedom—freedmen could reside in the District as long as they pleased. And when freedmen in Maryland and Virginia were wrongfully enslaved, they enjoyed no official recourse. But District law granted them a hearing in court.

As the number of free blacks in the District increased, so did the degree of distrust between the races. When the United States went to war with Britain in 1812, some white Washingtonians feared that "our enemy at home" might fight for the Redcoats. As it happened, when District Mayor James Blake asked all citizens to help build fortifications at the District line at Bladensburg, hundreds of blacks responded to the call.

In what became known as "the Bladensburg Races," the British punctured the city's flimsy defenses, routed the militia, and, under orders from Admiral George Cockburn, burned the White House, the Capitol, and the Treasury Building. But the efforts that blacks contributed to the battle did not go unrecognized. "The free people of color of this city," said the *National Intelligencer* in August 1814, acted as patriots, "manifesting by their exertions all the zeal of free men."

By the mid-19th century, there were at least three classes of blacks in Washington. At the bottom of the ladder stood the 30

The slave trade. Abolitionist Jessey Torrey charged that "kidnapped freemen . . . are annually collected at Washington . . . for transportation to slave regions."

percent who were slaves—most of whom worked as domestics. "Many of them," wrote one city official, "were favorite family servants, who came here with congressmen from the South and with the families of other public officers."

Working in proximity to their masters, most bondsmen in Washington enjoyed more freedom than rural field hands. Some even lived apart from their masters, frequently in wooden shanties. "A city slave is almost a free citizen," said Frederick Douglass, who had been a slave both in Baltimore and on Maryland's Eastern Shore. "He enjoys privileges altogether unknown to the whip-driven slave on the plantation."

On the next rung were freedmen, many of whom were mulattos—usually the offspring of white men and free black women. Free blacks often did the same work as slaves, but for (modest) wages. They labored as skilled craftsmen: carpenters, tailors, barbers, butchers, and shoemakers. Meanwhile, black women, both free and bonded, toiled as seamstresses, maids, cooks, and nurses. By all accounts, most blacks enjoyed some leisure time. They went fishing and swimming in the Potomac and duck hunting in the tidal marshes.

At the summit of black society stood a number of property-owning businessmen as well as civic and religious leaders. This upper class included George Fisher, who ran a blacksmith shop on East Capitol Street; Spencer Johnson, who made shoes at Pennsylvania Avenue and 21st Street; and the Rev. John F. Cook. Educated at the private, white-owned Columbia Institute, Cook became best known as the founder of the Union Seminary, a private high school for blacks, in 1834. He also started the Colored Presbyterian Church and, to shepherd black youths, organized the Young Men's Moral and Literary Society.

Within the black community, historian Constance Green has pointed out, everyone knew his place. "Lower-class Negroes looked up to superior colored persons as fully as the upper class looked down upon the inferior," she wrote. "... Negroes in Washington were employing the prefix Mr. or Mrs. in speaking of their most respected fellows, the ministers and teachers above all; the rest remained Tom and Sam or Mary and Sally."

Yet the local whites worried about living in what they feared might become a disorderly "colored" city. Such fears were inflamed in August of 1831, when a bondsman named Nat Turner led an abortive slave revolt in Southampton County, Virginia, leaving 51 whites dead. The Washington City Council reacted by making the Black Codes harsher: A black man who struck a white person was now subject to having his ears cut off.

Four years later, mob violence broke out when a lone slave attempted to murder Mrs. William Thornton, the widow of the architect of the U.S. Capitol. In a fit of vengeance that later would be called the "Snow Storm," outraged young whites ran through the streets, wrecking black homes and establishments—including John F. Cook's Union Seminary and a popular restaurant owned by a freedman named Beverly Snow.

And, in April 1848, a Northern abolitionist named Daniel Drayton helped more than 60 slaves from the District escape aboard a schooner, the *Pearl*. The getaway was well executed. But slaveowners quickly secured a steamship and pursued the fugitives, catching them at Point Lookout, located at the confluence of the Potomac River and Chesapeake Bay.

Such episodes helped make slavery in Washington a recurrent theme in Capitol Hill debates on the "peculiar institution." Abolitionist groups, such as the American Anti-Slavery Society, distributed broadsides showing slaves working near the Capitol, with the caption stating that "The Land of the Free" was also "The Home of the Oppressed." The New England Anti-Slavery Society charged that the District's slave traders were kidnapping free blacks and selling them to "inland pirates who purchase them for the western markets."

Across the Potomac, slaveowners in Alexandria County were so afraid that the abolitionists would prevail that, in 1846, they petitioned Congress to give the county back to Virginia. Ironically, they appealed to the democratic instincts of the politicians on Capitol Hill. "Whilst the principles of free government are yearly extending with the rapid march of civilization, and thrones and dynasties are yielding to their influence," said the Virginians, "here alone, in the 10 miles square, in and about the capital of this great country, there is no improvement, no advance in popular rights."

Congress granted the request—and thus reduced the federal district to the broken diamond shown on tourist maps today. (By the time President Lincoln signed a bill outlawing slavery in the District on April 16, 1862, Virginia had long since seceded from the Union.)

Even so, on the eve of the Civil War, many prominent black Washingtonians, despite the Black Codes and the daily indignities, could reflect on the previous 60 years with some satisfaction. The federal enclave had offered more tolerance and more opportunity than any city in the South.

Not only were nearly four out of five local blacks free, by 1860 over 10 percent of all blacks owned property; some 40 percent of black adults were literate and 1,100 black children were attending private schools. At the Union Seminary, black pupils studied composition, the scriptures, reading, "recitation," a manual of morals, and physiology. The black girls attending Miss Myrtilla Miner's high school, it was said, received a better education than did white girls attending any of the city's 30 public schools.

Black teachers and ministers had reason to hope that, with the support of their schools, churches, and small businesses, more freedmen in the District would begin to prosper, even amid poverty and racial discrimination.

But everything was to change after the early hours of April 12, 1861, when Confederate artillery under the command of General P. G. T. Beauregard fired on the federal garrison at Fort Sumter, which guarded the seaward approaches to Charleston, South Carolina. The Civil War had begun.

The Lives of Slave Women

DEBORAH GRAY WHITE

Deborah Gray White is associate professor of history and Africana studies at Rutgers University, New Brunswick, New Jersey. This chapter is adapted from her book, Ar'n't I a Woman? Female Slaves in the Plantation South, published in 1985 by W. W. Norton.

Slave women have often been characterized as self-reliant and self-sufficient, yet not every black woman was a Sojourner Truth or a Harriet Tubman. Strength had to be cultivated. It came no more naturally to them than to anyone else, slave or free, male or female, black or white. If slave women seemed exceptionally strong it was partly because they often functioned in groups and derived strength from their numbers.

Much of the work slaves did and the regimen they followed served to stratify slave society along sex lines. Consequently slave women had ample opportunity to develop a consciousness grounded in their identity as females. While close contact sometimes gave rise to strife, adult female cooperation and dependence of women on each other was a fact of female slave life. The self-reliance and self-sufficiency of slave women, therefore, must be viewed in the context not only of what the individual slave woman did for herself, but what slave women as a group were able to do for each other.

It is easy to overlook the separate world of female slaves because from colonial times through the Civil War black women often worked with black men at tasks considered by Europeans to be either too difficult or inappropriate for females. All women worked hard, but when white women consistently per-formed field labor it was considered temporary, irregular, or extraordinary, putting them on a par with slaves. Actress Fredericka Bremer, visiting the ante-bellum South, noted that usually only men and black women did field work; commenting on what another woman traveler sarcastically claimed to be a noble admission of female equality, Bremer observed that "black [women] are not considered to belong to the weaker sex."[1]

Bremer's comment reflects what former slaves and fugitive male slaves regarded as the defeminization of black women. Bonded women cut down trees to clear lands for cultivation. They hauled logs in leather straps attached to their shoulders. They plowed using mule and ox teams, and hoed, sometimes with the heaviest implements available. They dug ditches, spread manure fertilizer, and piled coarse fodder with their bare hands. They built and cleaned Southern roads, helped construct Southern railroads, and, of course, they picked cotton. In short, what fugitive slave Williamson Pease said regretfully of slave women was borne out in fact: "Women who do outdoor work are used as bad as men."[2] Almost a century later Green Wilbanks spoke less remorsefully than Pease in his remembrances of his Grandma Rose, where he implied that the work had a kind of neutering effect. Grandma Rose, he said, was a woman who could do any kind of job a man could do, a woman who "was some worker, a regular man-woman."[3]

It is hardly likely, though, that slave women, especially those on large plantations with sizable female populations, lost their female identity. Harvesting season on staple crop plantations may have found men and women gathering the crop in sex-integrated gangs, but at other times women often worked in exclusively or predominantly female gangs.[4] Thus women stayed in each other's company for most of the day. This meant that those they ate meals with, sang work songs with, and commiserated with during the work day were people who by virtue of their sex had the same kind of responsibilities and problems. As a result, slave women appeared to have developed their own female culture, a way of doing things and a way of assigning value that flowed from their perspective as slave women on Southern plantations. Rather than being squelched, their sense of womanhood was probably enhanced and their bonds to each other strengthened.

Since slaveowners and managers seemingly took little note of the slave woman's lesser physical strength, one wonders why they separated men and women at all. One answer appears to be that gender provided a natural and easy way to divide the labor force. Also probable is that despite their limited sensitivity regarding female slave labor, and the double standard they used when evaluating the uses of white and black female labor, slaveowners did, using standards only they could explain, reluctantly acquiesce to female physiology. For instance, depending on their stage of pregnancy, pregnant women were considered half or quarter hands. Healthy nonpregnant women were considered three-quarter hands. Three-quarter hands were not necessarily exempt from some of the herculean tasks performed by men who were full hands, but usually, when labor was being parceled out and barring a shortage of male hands to do the very heavy work or a rush to get that work completed, men did the more physically demanding work. A case in point was the most common differentiation where men plowed and women hoed.[5]

Like much of the field labor, nonfield labor was structured to promote cooperation among women. In the Sea Islands, slave women sorted cotton lint according to color and fineness and removed cotton seeds crushed by the gin into the cotton and lint. Fence building often found men splitting rails in one area and women doing the actual construction in another. Men usually shelled corn, threshed peas, cut potatoes for planting, and platted shucks. Grinding corn into meal or hominy was women's work. So too were spinning, weaving, sewing, and washing.[6] On Captain Kinsler's South Carolina plantation, as on countless others, "old women and women bearin' chillun not yet born, did cardin' wid handcards." Some would spin, others would weave, but all would eventually learn from some skilled woman "how to make clothes for the family . . . knit coarse socks and stockins."[7]

"When the work in the fields was finished women were required to come home and spin one cut a night," reported a Georgian. "Those who were not successful in completing this work were punished the next morning."[8] Women had to work in the evenings partly be-

---

A great deal of both field labor and nonfield labor was structured to promote cooperation among slave women.

---

cause slaveowners bought them few ready-made clothes. On one South Caro-

lina plantation each male slave received annually two cotton shirts, three pairs of pants, and one jacket. Slave women, on the other hand, received six yards of woolen cloth, six yards of cotton drilling, and six yards of cotton shirting a year, along with two needles and a dozen buttons.[9]

Perhaps a saving grace to this "double duty" was that women got a chance to interact with each other. On a Sedalia County, Missouri plantation, women looked forward to Saturday afternoon washing because, as Mary Frances Webb explained, they "would get to talk and spend the day together."[10] Quiltings, referred to by former slaves as female "frolics" and "parties," were especially convivial. Anna Peek recalled that when slaves were allowed to relax, they gathered around a pine wood fire in Aunt Anna's cabin to tell stories. At that time "the old women with pipes in their mouths would sit and gossip for hours."[11] Missourian Alice Sewell noted that sometimes women would slip away and hold their own prayer meetings. They cemented their bonds to each other at the end of every meeting when they walked around shaking hands and singing, "fare you well my sisters, I am going home."[12]

The organization of female slave work and social activities tended not only to separate women and men, but also to generate female cooperation and interdependence. Slave women and their children could depend on midwives and "doctor women" to treat a variety of ailments. Menstrual cramps, for example, were sometimes treated with a tea made from the bark of the gum tree. Midwives and "doctor women" administered various other herb teas to ease the pains of many ailing slaves. Any number of broths — made from the leaves and barks of trees, from the branches and twigs of bushes, from turpentine, catnip, or tobacco — were used to treat whooping cough, diarrhea, toothaches, colds, fevers, headaches, and backaches.[13] According to a Georgia ex-slave, "One had to be mighty sick to have the services of a doctor." On his master's plantation "old women were . . . responsible for the care of the sick."[14] This was also the case on Rebecca Hooks's former Florida residence. "The doctor," she noted, "was not nearly as popular as the 'granny' or midwife, who brewed medicines for every ailment."[15]

Female cooperation in the realm of medical care helped foster bonding that

led to collaboration in the area of resistance to abuses by slaveholders. Frances Kemble could attest to the concerted efforts of the black women on her husband's Sea Island plantations. More than once she was visited by groups of women imploring her to persuade her husband to extend the lying-in period for childbearing women. On one occasion the women had apparently prepared beforehand the approach they would take with the foreign-born and sympathetic Kemble, for their chosen spokeswoman took care to play on Kemble's own maternal sentiments, and pointedly argued that slave women deserved at least some of the care and tenderness that Kemble's own pregnancy had elicited.[16]

Usually, however, slave women could not be so outspoken about their needs, and covert cooperative resistance prevailed. Slaveowners suspected that midwives conspired with their female patients to bring about abortions and infanticides, and on Charles Colcock Jones's Georgia plantation, for example, this seems in fact to have been the case. A woman named Lucy gave birth in secret and then denied that she had ever been pregnant. Although the midwife attended her, she too claimed not to have delivered a child, as did Lucy's mother. Jones had a physician examine Lucy, and the doctor confirmed what Jones had suspected, that Lucy had indeed given birth. Twelve days later the decomposing body of a full-term infant was found, and Lucy, her mother, and the midwife were all hauled off to court. Another woman, a nurse, managed to avoid prosecution but not suspicion. Whether Lucy was guilty of murder, and whether the others were accessories, will never be known because the court could not shatter their collective defense that the child had been stillborn.[17]

The inability to penetrate the private world of female slaves is probably what kept many abortions and infanticides from becoming known to slaveowners. The secrets kept by a midwife named Mollie became too much for her to bear. When she accepted Christianity these were the first things for which she asked forgiveness. She recalled, "I was carried to the gates of hell and the devil pulled out a book showing me the things which I had committed and that they were all true. My life as a midwife was shown to me and I have certainly felt sorry for all the things I did, after I was converted."[18]

Health care is not the only example of how the organization of slave work and slave responsibilities led to female cooperation and bonding; slave women also depended on each other for child-care. Sometimes, especially on small farms or new plantations where there was no extra woman to superintend children, bondswomen took their offspring to the field with them and attended to them during pre-scheduled breaks. Usually, however, infants and older children were left in the charge of an elderly female or females. Josephine Bristow, for example, spent more time with Mary Novlin, the nursery keeper on Ferdinand Gibson's South Carolina plantation, than she spent with her mother and father, who came in from the fields after she was asleep: "De old lady, she looked after every blessed thing for us all day long en cooked for us right along wid de mindin'."[19] In their complementary role as nurses, they ministered to the hurts and illnesses of infants and children.[20] It was not at all uncommon for the children's weekly rations to be given to the "grannies" as opposed to the children's parents.[21] Neither the slaveowner nor slave society expected the biological mother of a child to fulfill all of her child's needs. Given the circumstances, the responsibilities of motherhood had to be shared, and this required close female cooperation.

Cooperation in this sphere helped slave women overcome one of the most difficult of predicaments — who would provide maternal care for a child whose mother had died or been sold away? Fathers sometimes served as both mother and father, but when slaves, as opposed to the master, determined maternal care, it was usually a woman who became a child's surrogate mother. Usually that woman was an aunt or a sister, but in the absence of female relatives, a non-kin woman assumed the responsibility.[22] In the case of Georgian Mollie Malone, for example, the nursery superintendent became the child's substitute mother.[23] When Julia Malone's mother was killed by another Texas slave, little Julia was raised by the woman with whom her mother had shared a cabin.[24] On Southern plantations the female community made sure that no child was truly motherless.

Because black women on a plantation spent so much time together, they inevitably developed some appreciation of each other's skills and talents. This intimacy enabled them to establish the criteria by which to rank and order themselves. The existence of certain "fe-

male jobs" that carried prestige created a yardstick by which bondswomen could measure each other's achievements. Some of these jobs allowed for growth and self-satisfaction, fringe benefits that were usually out of reach for the field laborer. A seamstress, for example, had unusual opportunities for self-expression and creativity. On very large plantations the seamstress usually did no field work, and a particularly good seamstress, or "mantua-maker," might be hired out to others and even allowed to keep a portion of the money she earned.[25] For obvious reasons cooks, midwives, and female folk doctors also commanded the respect of their peers. Midwives in particular often were able to travel to other plantations to practice their art. This gave them an enviable mobility and also enabled them to carry messages from one plantation to the next.

Apart from the seamstresses, cooks, and midwives, a few women were distinguished as work gang-leaders. On most farms and plantations where there were overseers, managers, foremen, and drivers, these positions were held by men, either black or white. Occasionally, however, a woman was given a measure of authority over slave work, or a particular aspect of it. For instance Louis Hughes noted that each plantation he saw had a "forewoman who . . . had charge of the female slaves and also the boys and girls from twelve to sixteen years of age, and all the old people that

were feeble."[26] Similarly, a Mississippi slave remembered that on his master's Osceola plantation there was a "colored woman as foreman."[27]

Clearly, a pecking order existed among bondswomen — one which they themselves helped to create. Because of age, occupation, association with the master class, or personal achievements, certain women were recognized by other women — and also by men — as important people, even as leaders. Laura Towne met an aged woman who commanded such a degree of respect that other slaves bowed to her and lowered their voices in her presence. The old woman, Maum Katie, was according to Towne a "spiritual mother" and a woman of "tremendous influence over her spiritual children."[28]

Sometimes two or three factors combined to distinguish a particular woman. Aunt Charlotte was the aged cook in John M. Booth's Georgia household. When Aunt Charlotte spoke, said Booth, "other colored people hastened to obey her."[29] Frederick Douglass's grandmother wielded influence because of her age and the skills she possessed. She made the best fishnets in Tuckahoe, Maryland, and she knew better than anyone else how to preserve sweet potato seedlings and how to plant them successfully. She enjoyed what Douglass called "high reputation," and accordingly "she was remembered by others."[30] In another example, when Elizabeth Botume went to the Sea Islands after the Civil War, she employed as a house servant a young woman named Amy who performed her tasks slowly and sullenly, until an older woman named Aunt Mary arrived from Beaufort. During slavery Amy and Aunt Mary had both worked in the house but Amy had learned to listen and obey Aunt Mary. After Aunt Mary arrived the once obstreperous Amy became "quiet, orderly, helpful and painstaking."[31]

The leadership of some women had a disruptive effect on plantation operations. Bennet H. Barrow repeatedly lamented the fact that Big Lucy, one of his oldest slaves, had more control over his female workers than he did: "Anica, Center, Cook Jane, the better you treat them the worse they are. Big Lucy the Leader corrupts every young negro in her power."[32] A self-proclaimed prophetess named Sinda was responsible for a cessation of all slave work for a considerable period on Butler Island in Georgia. According to a notation made

> *A slaveowner lamented that Big Lucy, one of his oldest slaves, had more control over his female workers than he did.*

by Frances Kemble in 1839, Sinda's prediction that the world would come to an end on a certain day caused the slaves to lay down their hoes and plows in the belief that their final emancipation was imminent. So sure were Sinda's fellow slaves of her prediction that even the lash failed to get them into the fields. When the appointed day of judgment passed uneventfully Sinda was whipped mercilessly. Yet, for a time, she had commanded more authority than either master or overseer.[33]

Bonded women did not have to go to such lengths in order to make a difference in each other's lives. The supportive atmosphere of the female community was considerable buffer against the depersonalizing regimen of plantation work and the general dehumanizing nature of slavery. When we consider that women were much more strictly confined to the plantation than men, that many women had husbands who visited only once or twice a week, and that slave women outlived slave men by an average of two years, we realize just how important the female community was to its members.

If we define a stable relationship as one of long duration, then it was probably easier for slave women to sustain stable emotional relationships with other bondswomen than with bondsmen. This is not to say that male-female relationships were unfulfilling or of no consequence. But they were generally fraught with more uncertainty about the future than female-to-female relationships, especially those existing between female blood kin. In her study of ex-slave interviews, Martha Goodson found that of all the relationships slaveowners disrupted, through either sale or dispersal, they were least likely to separate mothers and daughters.[34] Cody found that when South Carolina cotton planter Peter Gaillard divided his estate among his eight children, slave women in their twenties and thirties were twice as likely to have a sister with them, and women over 40 were four times more likely to have sisters with them than brothers. Similarly, daughters were less likely than sons to be separated from their mother. Over 60 percent of women aged 20 to 24 remained with their mothers when the estate was divided, as did 90 percent of those aged 25 to 29.[35] A slave song reflected the bonds between female siblings by indicating who took responsibility for the motherless female slave child. Interestingly enough, the one

designated was neither the father nor the brother:

A motherless chile see a hard time.
Oh Lord, help her on de road.
Er sister will do de bes' she kin,
Dis is a hard world, Lord, fer a
motherless chile.[36]

If female blood ties did indeed promote the most enduring relationships among slaves, then we should probably assume that like occupation, age, and personal achievement these relationships helped structure the female slave community. This assumption should not, however, obscure the fact that in friendships and dependency relationships women often treated non-relatives as if a consanguineous tie existed. This is why older women were called Aunt and Granny, and why unrelated women sometimes called each other Sister.[37]

While the focus here has been on those aspects of the bondswoman's life that fostered female bonding, female-to-female conflict was not uncommon. It was impossible for harmony always to prevail among women who saw so much of each other and who knew so much about one another. Lifelong friendships were founded in the hoe gangs and sewing groups, but the constant jockeying for occupational and social status created an atmosphere in which jealousies and antipathies smoldered. From Jesse Belflowers, the overseer of the Allston rice plantation in South Carolina, Adele Petigru Allston heard that "mostly mongst the Women" there was a "goodeal of quarling and disputing and telling lies."[38] The terms of a widely circulated overseer's contract advised rigorous punishment for "fighting, particularly amongst the women."[39] Some overseers followed this advice. According to Georgian Isaac Green, "Sometimes de women uster git whuppin's for fightin.'"[40]

Occasionally, violence between women could and did get very ugly. Molly, the cook in James Chesnut's household, once took a red hot poker and attacked the woman to whom her husband had given one of her calico dresses.[41] Similarly, when she was a young woman in Arkansas, Lucretia Alexander came to blows with another woman over a pair of stockings that the master had given Lucretia.[42] In another incident on a Louisiana cotton plantation, the day's cotton chopping was interrupted when a feisty field worker named Betty lost her tem-

per in the midst of a dispute with a fellow slave named Molly and struck her in the face with a hoe.[43]

The presence of conflict within interpersonal relationships between female slaves should not detract from the more important cooperation and dependence that prevailed among them. Conflict occurred *because* women were in close daily contact with each other and because the penalties for venting anger on other women were not as severe as those for striking out at men, either black or white. It is not difficult to understand how dependency relationships could become parasitical, how sewing and washing sessions could become "hanging courts," how one party could use knowledge gained in an intimate conversation against another.

Just how sisterhood could co-exist with discord is illustrated by the experience of some black women of the South Carolina and Georgia Sea Islands between 1862 and 1865. On November 7, 1861, Commodore S.F. DuPont sailed into Port Royal Sound, quickly defeated the Confederates, and put Union troops ashore to occupy the islands. Almost before DuPont's guns ceased firing, the entire white population left the islands for the mainland. A few house servants were taken with the fleeing whites but most of the slaves remained on the islands. The following year they and the occupying army were joined by a host of government agents and Northern missionaries. Several interest groups were gathered in the islands and each had priorities. As Treasury agents concerned themselves with the cotton, and army officers recruited and drafted black soldiers, and missionaries went about "preparing" slaves for freedom, the black Sea Islanders' world was turned upside down. This was true for young and middle-aged men who served in the Union army, but also for the women who had to manage their families and do most of the planting and harvesting in the absence of the men.[44]

During the three years of upheaval, black female life conformed in many ways to that outlined here. Missionaries' comments indicate that certain women were perceived as leaders by their peers. Harriet Ware, for instance, identified a woman from Fripp Point on St. Helena Island named Old Peggy as "the leader." This woman was important because she, along with another woman named Binah, oversaw church membership. Ware's housekeeper Flora told her, "Old

Peggy and Binah were the two whom all that came into the Church had to come through, and the Church supports them."[45]

On the Coffin's Point Plantation on St. Helena Island, a woman named Grace served her fellow women at least twice by acting as spokeswoman in disputes over wages paid for cotton production. On one occasion the women of the plantation complained to Mr. Philbrick, one of the plantation superintendents, that their wages were not high enough to permit them to purchase cloth at the local store. They were also upset because the molasses they bought from one of the other plantation superintendents was watered down. As Grace spoke in their behalf, the women shouted words of approval. At least part of the reason for Grace's ascendancy stemmed from the fact that she was among the older women of the island. She was also a strong and diligent worker who was able despite her advanced age to plant, hoe, and harvest cotton along with the younger women.[46]

Ample evidence exists of dependency relationships and cooperation among Sea Island women throughout the war years. In slavery sick and "lying-in" women relied on their peers to help them, and the missionaries found this to be the case on the islands during the Union occupation as well. For instance, Philbrick observed that it was quite common for the blacks to hire each other to hoe their tasks when sickness or other inconveniences kept an individual from it. In 1862 some of the Coffin's Point men were recruited by government agents to pick cotton elsewhere in the Sea Islands. This left many of the women at Coffin's Point completely responsible for hoeing the land allotted to each. Women who were sick or pregnant stood to lose their family's allotment since neglected land was reassigned to others. However, the women saw to it, according to Philbrick, that "the tasks of the lying-in women [were] taken care of by sisters or other friends in the absence of their husbands." No doubt these "other friends" were women, since in the same letter Philbrick noted that the only men left on the plantation were those too old to work in the cotton.[47]

Another missionary, Elizabeth Hyde Botume, related similar episodes of female cooperation. Regardless of the circumstances surrounding a pregnancy, it was common for the women of Port Royal to care for, and keep company with, expectant and convalescing mothers.

Several times Botume was approached by a spokeswoman seeking provisions for these mothers. Sometimes she gave them reluctantly because many of the women were not married. Usually, however, she was so impressed by the support that the pregnant women received from their peers that she suspended judgment and sent clothes and groceries for the mothers and infants. On one occasion she was approached by several women who sought aid for a woman named Cumber. The women were so willing to assist one of their own that Botume remarked abashedly: ". . . their readiness to help the poor erring girl made me ashamed."[48] These were not the only instances of cooperation among the black women. Some moved in with each other and shared domestic duties; others looked after the sick together.[49] With so many of the men away, women found ways of surviving together and cooperating. Predictably, however, along with the "togetherness" went conflict.

Many situations held possibilities for discord. Charles P. Ware, a missionary from Boston, wrote that the work in the crops would go more smoothly if only he could get the women to stop fighting. At least some of the fights were caused by disputes over the distribution of the former mistress's wardrobe. According to Ware, when a woman said, "I free, I as much right to ole missus' things as you," a fight was sure to erupt.[50] Harriet Ware witnessed a fight in which the women "fired shells and tore each other's clothes in a most disgraceful way." The cause of the fight was unknown to her but she was sure it was the "tongues of the women." Jealousy, she noted, ran rampant among the women, and to her mind there was "much foundation for it."[51]

The experiences of the Sea Islands women in the early 1860s comprised a special episode in American history, but their behavior conformed to patterns that had been set previously by bonded women on large plantations. Historians have shown that the community of the quarters, the slave family, and slave religion shielded the slave from absolute dependence on the master and that parents, siblings, friends, and relatives served in different capacities as buffers against the internalization of degrading and dependent roles. The female slave network served as a similar buffer for black women, but it also had a larger significance. Treated by Southern whites as if they

were anything but self-respecting women, many bonded females helped one another to forge their own independent definitions of womanhood, their own notions about what women should be and how they should act.

NOTES
1. Fredericka Bremer, *Homes of the New World*, 2 vols. (New York, 1853), 2: 519; Frances Anne Kemble, *Journal of a Residence on a Georgian Plantation*, ed. John A. Scott (New York, 1961 [1863]), p. 66. See also: Harriet Martineau, *Society in America*, 3 vols. (London, 1837), 2: 243, 311-12.
2. Benjamin Drew, *The Refugees: A North Side View of Slavery*, in *Four Fugitive Slave Narratives* (Boston, 1969), p. 92.
3. George Rawick, ed., *The American Slave, A Complete Autobiography*, 19 vols. (Westport, CT, 1972), Ga., vol. 13, pt. 4: 139.
4. Frederick Olmsted, *A Journey in the Seaboard Slave States* (New York, 1856), pp. 430-32; Olmsted, *The Cotton Kingdom*, ed. David Freeman Hawke (New York, 1971), p. 176; William Howard Russell, *My Diary North and South (Canada, Its Defenses, Condition and Resources)*, 3 vols. (London, 1865), 1: 379-80; Solomon Northup, *Twelve Years a Slave, Narrative of Solomon Northup* in Gilbert Osofsky, ed., *Puttin' on Ole Massa* (New York, 1969), pp. 308-09; Rawick, *American Slave*, Ark., vol. 10, pt. 5: 54; Ala., vol. 6: 46, 336; Newstead Plantation Diary 1856-58, entry Wednesday, May 6, 1857, Southern Historical Collection (SHC), University of North Carolina at Chapel Hill; Adwon Adams Davis, *Plantation Life in the Florida Parishes of Louisiana 1836-1846 as Reflected in the Diary of Bennet H. Barrow* (New York, 1943), p. 127; Frederick Olmsted, *A Journey in the Back Country* (New York, 1907), p. 152; *Plantation Manual*, SHC, p. 4; Eugene Genovese, *The Political Economy of Slavery: Studies in the Economy and Society of the Slave South* (New York, 1961), p. 133; Stuart Bruchey, ed., *Cotton and the Growth of the American Economy: 1790-1860* (New York, 1967), pp. 176-80.
5. See note 4.
6. J.A. Turner, ed., *The Cotton Planters Manual* (New York, 1865), pp. 97-98; Guion B. Johnson, *A Social History of the Sea Islands* (Chapel Hill, NC, 1930), pp. 28-30; Jenkins Mikell, *Rumbling of the Chariot Wheels* (Columbia, SC, 1923), pp. 19-20; Bruchey, *Cotton and the Growth of the American Economy*, pp. 176-80.
7. Rawick, *American Slave*, S.C., vol. 2, pt. 2: 114.
8. Ibid., Ga., vol. 13, pt. 3: 186.
9. *Plantation Manual*, SHC, p. 1.
10. Rawick, *American Slave*, Ok., vol. 7: 315.
11. George P. Rawick, Jan Hillegas, and Ken Lawrence, eds., *The American Slave: A Composite Autobiography, Supplement, Series 1*, 12 vols. (Westport, CT, 1978), Ga., Supp. 1, vol. 4: 479.
12. Rawick, *American Slave*, Mo., vol. 11: 307.
13. For examples of cures see: Ibid., Ark., vol. 10, pt. 5: 21, 125; Ala., vol. 6: 256, 318; Ga., vol. 13, pt. 3: 106.
14. Ibid., Ga., vol. 12, pt. 1: 303.
15. Ibid., Fla., vol. 17: 175; see also: Rawick *et al.*, *American Slave, Supplement*, Miss. Supp. 1, vol. 6: 317; Ga. Supp. 1, vol. 4: 444; John Spencer Bassett, *The Southern Plantation Overseer, as Revealed in His Letters* (Northampton, MA, 1923), pp. 28, 31.
16. Kemble, *Journal of a Residence on a Georgian Plantation*, p. 222.
17. Robert Manson Myers, ed., *The Children of Pride: A True Story of Georgia and the Civil War* (New Haven, CT, 1972), pp. 528, 532, 542, 544, 546.
18. Charles S. Johnson, ed., *God Struck Me Dead: Religious Conversion Experiences and Autobiographies of Negro Ex-Slaves* in Rawick, *American Slave*, vol. 19: 74.
19. Rawick, *American Slave*, S.C., vol. 2, pt. 1: 99.

20. Ibid., Ga., vol. 12, pt. 2: 112; S.C., vol. 2, pt. 2: 55; Fla., vol. 17: 174; see also Olmsted, *Back Country*, p. 76.

21. See, for instance, *Plantation Manual*, SHC, p. 1.

22. Rawick, *American Slave*, Ala., vol. 6: 73.

23. Rawick *et al.*, *American Slave, Supplement*, Ga. Supp. 1, vol. 4, pt. 3: 103.

24. Rawick, *American Slave*, Tex., vol. 5, pt. 3: 103.

25. Hughes, *Thirty Years a Slave*, p. 39; Rawick, *American Slave*, Fla., vol. 17: 158; S.C., vol. 2, pt. 1: 114; White Hill Plantation Books, SHC, p. 13.

26. Hughes, *Thirty Years a Slave*, p. 22.

27. Ophelia Settle Egypt, J. Masuoha, and Charles S. Johnson, eds., *Unwritten History of Slavery: Autobiographical Accounts of Negro Ex-Slaves* (Washington, 1968 [1945]), p. 41.

28. Laura M. Towne, *Letters and Diary of Laura M. Towne Written from the Sea Islands of South Carolina 1862-1884*, ed. Rupert Sargent Holland (New York, 1969 [1912]), pp. 144-45. See also: Kemble, *Journal of a Residence on a Georgian Plantation*, p. 55.

29. Rawick, *American Slave*, Ga. vol. 13, pt. 3: 190.

30. Frederick Douglass, *My Bondage and My Freedom* (New York, 1968 [1855]), p. 36.

31. Elizabeth Hyde Botume, *First Days Amongst the Contrabands* (Boston, 1893), p. 132.

32. Davis, *Plantation Life in the Florida Parishes*, p. 191. See also pp. 168, 173.

33. Kemble, *Journal of a Residence on a Georgian Plantation*, pp. 118-19.

34. Martha Graham Goodson, "An Introductory Essay and Subject Index to Selected Interviews from the Slave Narrative Collection," (Ph.D. diss., Union Graduate School, 1977), p. 33.

35. Cheryll Ann Cody, "Naming, Kinship, and Estate Dispersal: Notes on Slave Family Life on a South Carolina Plantation, 1786 to 1833," *William and Mary Quarterly* 39 (1982): 207-09.

36. Rawick, *American Slave*, Ala., vol. 7: 73.

37. Herbert G. Gutman, *The Black Family in Slavery and Freedom, 1750-1925* (New York, 1976), pp. 216-22.

38. J.H. Easterby, ed., *The South Carolina Rice Plantations as Revealed in the Papers of Robert W. Allston* (Chicago, 1945), p. 291.

39. Bassett, *The Southern Plantation Overseer*, pp. 19-20, 32.

40. Rawick, *American Slave*, Ga., vol. 12, pt. 2: 57.

41. C. Vann Woodward, ed., *Mary Chesnut's Civil War* (New Haven, CT, 1981), pp. 33-34.

42. Norman Yetman, *Voices from Slavery* (New York, 1970), p. 13.

43. J. Mason Brewer, *American Negro Folklore* (New York, 1968), p. 233.

44. Willie Lee Rose, *Rehearsal for Reconstruction: The Port Royal Experiment* (New York, 1964), p. 11.

45. Elizabeth Ware Pearson, ed., *Letters from Port Royal: Written at the Time of the Civil War* (New York, 1969 [1906]), p. 44.

46. Ibid., pp. 250, 303-04.

47. Ibid., p. 56.

48. Botume, *First Days Amongst the Contrabands*, p. 125.

49. See for instance: Ibid., pp. 55-56, 58, 80, 212.

50. Pearson, *Letters from Port Royal*, p. 1133.

51. Botume, *First Days Amongst the Contrabands*, pp. 210-11.

Under the leadership of John Marshall, the nation's highest tribunal became a court supreme in fact as well as in name.

The Great Chief Justice

Brian McGinty

Brian McGinty is a California attorney and writer.

He was a tall man with long legs, gangling arms, and a round, friendly face. He had a thick head of dark hair and strong, black eyes—"penetrating eyes," a friend called them, "beaming with intelligence and good nature." He was born in a log cabin in western Virginia and never wholly lost his rough frontier manners. Yet John Marshall became a lawyer, a member of Congress, a diplomat, an advisor to presidents, and the most influential and respected judge in the history of the United States. "If American law were to be represented by a single figure," Supreme Court Justice Oliver Wendell Holmes, Jr., once said, "sceptic and worshipper alike would agree without dispute that the figure could be but one alone, and that one John Marshall."

To understand Marshall's preeminence in American legal history it is necessary to understand the marvelous rebirth the United States Supreme Court experienced af-ter he became its chief justice in 1801. During all of the previous eleven years of its existence, the highest judicial court in the federal system had been weak and ineffectual—ignored by most of the nation's lawyers and judges and scorned by its principal politicians. Under Marshall's leadership, the court became a strong and vital participant in national affairs. During his more than thirty-four years as Chief Justice of the United States, Marshall welded the Supreme Court into an effective and cohesive whole. With the support of his colleagues on the high bench, he declared acts of Congress and of the president unconstitutional, struck down laws that infringed on federal prerogatives, and gave force and dignity to basic guarantees of life and liberty and property. Without John Marshall, the Supreme Court might never have been anything but an inconsequential junior partner of the executive and legislative branches of the national government. Under his guidance and inspiration, it became what the Constitution intended it to be—a court system in fact as well as in name.

From *American History Illustrated*, September 1986, pp. 8-14, 46-47. Reprinted through the courtesy of Cowles Magazines, publishers of *American History Illustrated*.

Jefferson and Marshall: Two Great Minds in Conflict

PROFILE PORTRAITS
BY M. FEVRET DE SAINT MEMIN
AMERICAN HISTORY ILLUSTRATED COLLECTION

Fellow Virginians Thomas Jefferson and John Marshall (next page) had contrasting philosophies regarding the roles of government. Jefferson believed in state sovereignty and in a limited role for national government.

BORN ON SEPTEMBER 4, 1755, in Fauquier County, Virginia, John Marshall was the oldest of fifteen children born to Thomas Marshall and Mary Randolph Keith. On his mother's side, the young Virginian was distantly related to Thomas Jefferson, the gentlemanly squire of Monticello and author of the Declaration of Independence. Aside from this kinship, there was little similarity between Marshall and Jefferson. A son of the frontier, Marshall was a backwoodsman at heart, more comfortable in the company of farmers than intellectuals or scholars. Jefferson was a polished aristocrat who liked to relax in the library of his mansion near Charlottesville and meditate on the subtleties of philosophy and political theory.

The contrast between the two men was most clearly drawn in their opposing political beliefs. An advocate of limiting the powers of central government, Thomas Jefferson thought of himself first and foremost as a Virginian (his epitaph did not even mention the fact that he had once been president of the United States). Marshall, in contrast, had, even as a young man, come to transcend his state roots, to look to Congress rather than the Virginia legislature as his government, to think of himself first, last, and always as an American. Throughout their careers, their contrasting philosophies would place the two men at odds.

Marshall's national outlook was furthered by his father's close association with George Washington and his own unflinching admiration for the nation's first president. Thomas Marshall had been a schoolmate of

Washington and, as a young man, helped him survey the Fairfax estates in northern Virginia. John Marshall served under Washington during the bitter winter at Valley Forge and later became one of the planter-turned-statesman's most loyal supporters.

Years after the Revolution was over, Marshall attributed his political views to his experiences as a foot soldier in the great conflict, recalling that he grew up "at a time when a love of union and resistance to the claims of Great Britain were the inseparable inmates of the same bosom;—when patriotism and a strong fellow feeling with our suffering fellow citizens of Boston were identical;—when the maxim 'united we stand, divided we fall' was the maxim of every orthodox American . . ." "I had imbibed these sentiments so thoughroughly [sic] that they constituted a part of my being," wrote Marshall. "I carried them with me into the army where I found myself associated with brave men from different states who were risking life and everything valuable in a common cause believed by all to be most precious; and where I was confirmed in the habit of considering America as my country, and Congress as my government."

After Washington's death, Marshall became the great man's biographer, penning a long and admiring account of Washington's life as a farmer, soldier, and statesman, expounding the Federalist philosophy represented by Washington and attacking those who stood in opposition to it. Jefferson, who detested Federalism as much as he disliked Marshall, was incensed by the biography, which he branded a "five-volume libel."

Marshall believed in a strong central government, in the Constitution as the key to the laws of the land, and in courts as the supreme custodians of those laws— views that would influence his shaping of the Supreme Court.

COURTESY OF THE CORCORAN
GALLERY OF ART, WASHINGTON, D.C.

FRONTIERSMAN THOUGH HE WAS, Marshall was no bumpkin. His father had personally attended to his earliest schooling, teaching him to read and write and giving him a taste for history and poetry (by the age of twelve he had already transcribed the whole of Alexander Pope's *Essay on Man*). When he was fourteen, Marshall was sent to a school a hundred miles from home, where future president James Monroe was one of his classmates. After a year, he returned home to be tutored by a Scottish pastor who had come to live in the Marshall house. The future lawyer read Horace and Livy, pored through the English dictionary, and scraped at least a passing acquaintance with the "Bible of the Common Law," William Blackstone's celebrated *Commentaries on the Laws of England*.

In 1779, during a lull in the Revolution, young Marshall attended lectures at the College of William and Mary in Williamsburg. He remained at the college only a few weeks, but the impression made on him by his professor there, George Wythe, was lasting. A lawyer, judge, and signer of the Declaration of Independence, Wythe is best remembered today as the first professor of law at any institution of higher learning in the United States. As a teacher, he was a seminal influence in the development of American law, counting among his many distinguished students Thomas Jefferson, John Breckinridge, and Henry Clay.

Marshall did not remain long at William and Mary. It was the nearly universal custom then for budding lawyers to "read law" in the office of an older lawyer or judge or, failing that, to appeal to the greatest teacher of all—experience—for instruction. In August 1780, a few weeks before his twenty-fifth birthday, Marshall appeared at the Fauquier County Courthouse where, armed with a license signed by Governor Thomas Jefferson of Virginia, he was promptly admitted to the bar.

His first cases were not important, but he handled them well and made a favorable impression on his neighbors; so favorable that they sent him to Richmond in 1782 as a member of the Virginia House of Delegates. Though he retained a farm in Fauquier County all his life, Richmond became Marshall's home after his election to the legislature. The general courts of Virginia held their sessions in the new capital, and the commonwealth's most distinguished lawyers crowded its bar. When Marshall's fortunes improved, he built a comfortable brick house on the outskirts of the city, in which he and his beloved wife Polly raised five sons and one daughter (four other offspring died during childhood).

Marshall's skill as a lawyer earned him an enthusiastic coterie of admirers and his honest country manners an even warmer circle of friends. He liked to frequent the city's taverns and grog shops, more for conviviality than for refreshment, and he was an enthusiastic member of the Barbecue Club, which met each Saturday to eat, drink, "josh," and play quoits.

Marshall liked to do his own shopping for groceries. Each morning he marched through the streets with a basket under his arm, collecting fresh fruits, vegetables, and poultry for the Marshall family larder. Years after

"If American law were to be represented by a single figure . . . the figure could be but one alone, and that one John Marshall."

his death, Richmonders were fond of recalling the day when a stranger came into the city in search of a lawyer and found Marshall in front of the Eagle Hotel, holding a hat filled with cherries and speaking casually with the hotel proprietor. After Marshall went on his way, the stranger approached the proprietor and asked if he could direct him to the best lawyer in Richmond. The proprietor replied quite readily that the best lawyer was John Marshall, the tall man with the hat full of cherries who had just walked down the street.

But the stranger could not believe that a man who walked through town so casually could be a really "proper barrister" and chose instead to hire a lawyer who wore a black suit and powdered wig. On the day set for the stranger's trial, several cases were scheduled to be argued. In the first that was called, the visitor was surprised to see that John Marshall and his own lawyer were to speak on opposite sides. As he listened to the arguments, he quickly realized that he had made a serious mistake. At the first recess, he approached Marshall and confessed that he had come to Richmond with a hundred dollars to hire the best lawyer in the city, but he had chosen the wrong one and now had only five dollars left. Would Marshall agree to represent him for such a small fee? Smiling good-naturedly, Marshall accepted the five dollars, then proceeded to make a brilliant legal argument that quickly won the stranger's case.

Marshall was not an eloquent man; not eloquent, that is, in the sense that his great contemporary, Patrick Henry, a spellbinding courtroom orator, was eloquent. Marshall was an effective enough speaker; but, more importantly, he was a rigorously logical thinker. He had the ability to reduce complex issues to bare essentials and easily and effortlessly apply abstract principles to resolve them.

Thomas Jefferson (himself a brilliant lawyer) was awed, even intimidated, by Marshall's powers of persuasion. "When conversing with Marshall," Jefferson once said, "I never admit anything. So sure as you admit any position to be good, no matter how remote from the conclusion he seeks to establish, you are gone. . . . Why, if he were to ask me if it were daylight or not, I'd reply, 'Sir, I don't know, I can't tell.'"

Though Marshall's legal prowess and genial manner won him many friends in Richmond, his political views did little to endear him to the Old Dominion's political establishment. While Jefferson and his followers preached the virtues of agrarian democracy, viewing with alarm every step by which the fledgling national government extended its powers through the young nation, Marshall clearly allied himself with Washington, Alexander Hamilton, and John Adams and the Federalist policies they espoused.

Marshall was not a delegate to the convention that met in Philadelphia in 1787 to draft a constitution for the United States, but he took a prominent part in efforts to secure ratification of the Constitution, thereby winning the special admiration of George Washington. After taking office as president, Washington offered Marshall the post of attorney general. Marshall declined the appointment, as he did a later offer of the prestigious post of American minister to France, explaining that he preferred to stay in Richmond with his family and law practice.

He did agree, however, to go to Paris in 1798 as one of three envoys from President John Adams to the government of revolutionary France. He did this, in part, because he was assured that his duties in Paris would be temporary only, in part because he believed he could perform a real service for his country, helping to preserve peaceful relations between it and France during a time of unusual diplomatic tension.

After Marshall joined his colleagues Elbridge Gerry and Charles Pinckney in Paris, he was outraged to learn that the French government expected to be paid before it would receive the American emissaries. Marshall recognized the French request as a solicitation for a bribe (the recipients of the payments were mysteriously identified as "X," "Y," and "Z"), and he refused to consider it.

Thomas Jefferson, who was smitten with the ardor and ideals of the French Revolution, suspected that Marshall and his Federalist "cronies" were planning war with France to promote the interests of their friends in England. But the American people believed otherwise. When they received news of the "XYZ Affair," they were outraged. "Millions for defense," the newspapers thundered, "but not one cent for tribute!" When Marshall returned home in the summer of 1798, he was welcomed as a hero. In the elections of the following fall, he was sent to Congress as a Federalist representative from Richmond.

Jefferson was not pleased. He declined to attend a dinner honoring Marshall in Philadelphia and wrote worried letters to his friends. Though he deprecated his fellow Virginian's popularity, alternatively attributing it to his "lax, lounging manners" and his "profound hypocrisy," Jefferson knew that Marshall was a potentially dangerous adversary. A half-dozen years before the Richmonder's triumphal return from Paris, Jefferson had written James Madison a cutting letter about Marshall that included words he would one day rue: "I think nothing better could be done than to make him a judge."

In Congress, Marshall vigorously supported the Federalist policies of President John Adams. Adams took note of the Virginian's ability in 1800 when he appointed him to the important post of secretary of state, a position that not only charged him with conduct of the country's foreign affairs but also left him in effective charge of the government during Adams's frequent absences in Massachusetts.

John Marshall's future in government seemed rosy and secure in 1800. But the elections in November of that year changed all that, sweeping Adams and the Federalists from power and replacing them with Jefferson and the Democratic Republicans.

After the election, but before Adams's term as president expired, ailing Supreme Court Chief Justice Oliver Ellsworth submitted his resignation. Casting about for a successor to Ellsworth, Adams sent John Jay's name to the Senate, only to have Jay demand that it be withdrawn. The thought of leaving the appointment of a new chief justice to Jefferson was abhorrent to Adams, and the president was growing anxious. He summoned Marshall to his office to confer about the problem.

"Who shall I nominate now?" Adams asked dejectedly. Marshall answered that he did not know. He had previously suggested that Associate Justice William Paterson be elevated to the chief justiceship, but Adams had opposed Paterson then and Marshall supposed that he still did. The president pondered for a moment, then turned to Marshall and announced: "I believe I shall nominate you!"

Adams's statement astounded Marshall. Only two years before, Marshall had declined the president's offer of an associate justiceship, explaining that he still hoped to return to his law practice in Richmond. "I had never before heard myself named for the office," Marshall recalled later, "and had not even thought of it. I was pleased as well as surprized [sic], and bowed my head in silence."

Marshall's nomination was sent to the Senate and promptly confirmed, and on February 4, 1801, he took his seat as the nation's fourth chief justice. As subsequent events would prove, it was one of the most important dates in American history.

WITH THOMAS JEFFERSON in the Executive Mansion and John Marshall in the chief justice's chair, it was inevitable that the Supreme Court and the executive branch of the government should come into conflict. Marshall believed firmly in a strong national government and was willing to do all he could to strengthen federal institutions. Jefferson believed as firmly in state sovereignty and the necessity for maintaining constant vigilance against federal "usurpations." In legal matters, Jefferson believed that the Constitution should be interpreted strictly, so as to reduce rather than expand federal power.

Marshall, in contrast, believed that the Constitution should be construed fairly so as to carry out the intentions of its framers. Any law or executive act that violated the terms of the Constitution was, in Marshall's view, a nullity, of no force or effect; and it was the peculiar prerogative of the courts, as custodians of the laws of the land, to strike down any law that offended the Supreme Law of the Land.

Jefferson did not question the authority of the courts to decide whether a law or executive act violated the Constitution, but he believed that the other branches of the government also had a duty and a right to decide constitutional questions. In a controversy between the Supreme Court and the president, for example, the Supreme Court could order the president to do whatever the Court thought the Constitution required him to do; but the president could decide for himself whether the Supreme Court's order was proper and whether or not it should be obeyed.

As he took up the duties of the chief justiceship, Marshall contemplated his role with uncertainty. The Supreme Court in 1801 was certainly not the kind of strong, vital institution that might have been expected to provide direction in national affairs. There were six justices when Marshall joined the Court, but none (save the chief justice himself) was particularly distinguished. One or two men of national prominence had accepted appointment to the Court in the first eleven years of its existence, but none had remained there long. John Jay, the first chief justice, had resigned his seat in 1795 to become governor of New York. During the two years that John Rutledge was an associate justice, he had regarded the Court's business as so trifling that he did not bother to attend a single session, and he finally resigned to become chief justice of South Carolina. The Court itself had counted for so little when the new capitol at Washington was being planned that the architects had made no provision for either a courtroom or judges' chambers, and the justices (to everyone's embarrassment) found that they had to meet in a dingy basement room originally designed for the clerk of the Senate.

How could Chief Justice Marshall use his new office to further the legal principles in which he believed so strongly? How could he strengthen the weak and undeveloped federal judiciary when most of the nation's lawyers and judges regarded that judiciary as superfluous and unnecessary? How could he implement his view of the Supreme Court as the final arbiter of constitutional questions when the President of the United States—his old nemesis, Thomas Jefferson—disagreed with that view so sharply? It was not an easy task, but John Marshall was a resourceful man, and he found a way to accomplish it.

His opportunity came in 1803 in the case of *Marbury v. Madison*. William Marbury was one of several minor federal judges who had been appointed during the closing days of John Adams's administration. When Jefferson's secretary of state, James Madison, refused to deliver the commissions of their offices, the judges sued Madison to compel delivery. In 1789, Congress had passed a law granting the Supreme Court authority to issue writs of mandamus, that is, legally enforceable orders compelling public officials to do their legal duties. Following the mandate of Congress, Marbury and the other appointees filed a petition for writ of mandamus in the Supreme Court.

Marshall pondered the possibilities of the case. He was sure that Marbury and his colleagues were entitled to their commissions, and he was just as sure that Jefferson and Madison had no intention of letting them have them. He could order Madison to deliver the commissions, but the secretary of state would certainly defy the order; and, as a practical matter, the Court could not compel obedience to any order that the president refused to acknowledge. Such an impasse would weaken, not strengthen, the federal union, and it would engender unprecedented controversy. No, there must be a better way. . . .

All eyes and ears in the capitol were trained on the lanky chief justice as he took his seat at the head of the high bench on February 24, 1803, and began to read the Supreme Court's opinion in *Marbury v. Madison*.

The evidence, Marshall said, clearly showed that Marbury and the other judges were entitled to their commissions. The commissions had been signed and sealed before John Adams left office and were, for all legal purposes, complete and effective. To withhold them, as Jefferson and Madison insisted on doing, was an illegal act. But the Supreme Court would not order the secretary of state to deliver the commissions because the law authorizing it to issue writs of mandamus was unconstitutional: the Constitution does not authorize the Supreme Court to issue writs of mandamus; in fact, it prohibits it from doing so. And any law that violates the Constitution is void. Since the law purporting to authorize the Supreme Court to act was unconstitutional, the Court would not — indeed, it could not — order Madison to do his legal duty.

If historians and constitutional lawyers were asked to name the single most important case ever decided in the United States Supreme Court, there is little doubt that the case would be *Marbury v. Madison*. Though the dispute that gave rise to the decision was in itself insignificant, John Marshall used it as a springboard to a great constitutional pronouncement. The rule of the case — that the courts of the United States have the right to declare laws unconstitutional — was immediately recognized as the cornerstone of American constitutional law, and it has remained so ever since.

MORE THAN A HALF-CENTURY would pass before the Supreme Court would again declare an act of Congress unconstitutional, but its authority to do so would never again be seriously doubted. Marshall had made a bold stroke, and he had done so in such a way that neither Congress, nor the president, nor any other public official had any power to resist it. By denying relief to Marbury, he had made the Supreme Court's order marvelously self-enforcing!

Predictably, Thomas Jefferson was angry. If the Supreme Court could not issue writs of mandamus, Jefferson asked, why did Marshall spend so much time discussing Marbury's entitlement to a commission? And why did the chief justice lecture Madison that withholding the commission was an illegal act?

The president thought for a time that he might have the chief justice and his allies on the bench impeached. After a mentally unstable federal judge in New Hampshire was removed from office, Jefferson's supporters in the House of Representatives brought a bill of impeachment against Marshall's colleague on the Supreme Court, Associate Justice Samuel Chase. Chase was a Federalist who had occasionally badgered witnesses and made intemperate speeches, but no one seriously contended that he had committed an impeachable offense (which the Constitution defines as "treason, bribery, or other high crimes and misdemeanors"). So the Senate, three-quarters of whose members were Jeffersonians, refused to remove Chase from office. Marshall breathed a deep sigh of relief. Had the associate justice been impeached, the chief had no doubt that he himself would have been Jefferson's next target.

Though he never again had occasion to strike down an act of Congress, Marshall delivered opinions in many cases of national significance; and, in his capacity as circuit judge (all Supreme Court justices "rode circuit" in the early years of the nineteenth century), he presided over important, sometimes controversial, trials. He was the presiding judge when Jefferson's political arch rival, Aaron Burr, was charged with treason in 1807. Interpreting the constitutional provision defining treason against the United States, Marshall helped to acquit Burr, though he did so with obvious distaste. The Burr prosecution, Marshall said, was "the most unpleasant case which has been brought before a judge in this or perhaps any other country which affected to be governed by law."

On the high bench, Marshall presided over scores of precedent-setting cases. In *Fletcher v. Peck* (1810) and *Dartmouth College v. Woodward* (1819), he construed the contracts clause of the Constitution so as to afford important protection for the country's growing business community. In *McCulloch v. Maryland* (1819), he upheld the constitutionality of the first Bank of the United States and struck down the Maryland law that purported to tax it. In *Gibbons v. Ogden* (1824), he upheld federal jurisdiction over interstate commerce and lectured those (mainly Jeffersonians) who persistently sought to enlarge state powers at the expense of legitimate federal authority.

Though Marshall's opinions always commanded respect, they were frequently unpopular. When, in *Worcester v. Georgia* (1832), he upheld the treaty rights of the Cherokee Indians against encroachments by the State of Georgia, he incurred the wrath of President Andrew Jackson. "John Marshall has made his decision," "Old Hickory" snapped contemptuously. "Now let him enforce it!" Marshall knew, of course, that he could not enforce the decision; that he could not enforce any decision that did not have the moral respect and acquiescence of the public and the officials they elected. And so he bowed his head in sadness and hoped that officials other than Andrew Jackson would one day show greater respect for the nation's legal principles and institutions.

Despite the controversy that some of his decisions inspired, the chief justice remained personally popular; and, during the whole of his more than thirty-four years as head of the federal judiciary, the Court grew steadily in authority and respect.

3. NATIONAL CONSOLIDATION AND EXPANSION

WELL INTO HIS SEVENTIES, Marshall continued to ride circuit in Virginia and North Carolina, to travel each year to his farm in Fauquier County, to attend to his shopping duties in Richmond, and to preside over the high court each winter and spring in Washington. On one of his visits to a neighborhood market in Richmond, the chief justice happened on a young man who had been sent to fetch a turkey for his mother. The youth wanted to comply with his mother's request, but thought it was undignified to carry a turkey in the streets "like a servant." Marshall offered to carry it for him. When the jurist got as far as his own home, he turned to the young man and said, "This is where I live. Your house is not far off; can't you carry the turkey the balance of the way?" The young man's face turned crimson as he suddenly realized that his benefactor was none other than the chief justice of the United States.

Joseph Story, who served as an associate justice of the Supreme Court for more than twenty years of Marshall's term as chief justice, spent many hours with the Virginian in and out of Washington. Wherever Story observed Marshall, he was impressed by his modesty and geniality. "Meet him in a stagecoach, as a stranger, and travel with him a whole day," Story said, "and you would only be struck with his readiness to administer to the accommodations of others, and his anxiety to appropriate the least to himself. Be with him, the unknown guest at an inn, and he seemed adjusted to the very scene, partaking

of the warm welcome of its comforts, wherever found; and if not found, resigning himself without complaint to its meanest arrangements. You would never suspect, in either case, that he was a great man; far less that he was the Chief Justice of the United States."

In his youth, Marshall had been fond of corn whiskey. As he grew older, he lost his appetite for spirits but not for wine. He formulated a "rule" under which the Supreme Court judges abstained from wine except in wet weather, but Story said he was liberal in allowing "exceptions." "It does sometime happen," Story once said, "the the Chief Justice will say to me, when the cloth is removed, 'Brother Story, step to the window and see if it does not look like rain.' And if I tell him that the sun is shining brightly, Judge Marshall will sometimes reply, 'All the better; for our jurisdiction extends over so large a territory that it must be raining somewhere.'" "You know," Story added, "that the Chief was brought up upon Federalism and Madeira, and he is not the man to outgrow his early prejudices."

In Richmond, Marshall held regular dinners for local lawyers, swapped stories with old friends, and tossed quoits with his neighbors in the Barbecue Club. An artist named Chester Harding remembered seeing the chief justice at a session of the Barbecue Club in 1829. Harding said Marshall was "the best pitcher of the party, and could throw heavier quoits than any other member of the club." "There were several ties," he added, "and, before long, I saw the great Chief Justice of the United States, down on his knees, measuring the contested distance with a straw, with as much earnestness as if it had been a point of law; and if he proved to be in the right, the woods would ring with his triumphant shout."

In 1830, a young Pennsylvania congressman and future president of the United States commented on Marshall's enduring popularity among his neighbors. "His decisions upon constitutional questions have ever been hostile to the opinions of a vast majority of the people in his own State," James Buchanan said, "and yet with what respect and veneration has he been viewed by Virginia? Is there a Virginian whose heart does not beat with honest pride when the just fame of the Chief Justice is the subject of conversation? They consider him, as he truly is, one of the great and best men which this country has ever produced."

John Marshall's Richmond home, completed in 1790, still survives and is open to the public. Completely restored and furnished following extensive archaeological and historical research, the elegant Federal-style two-story residence—the only eighteenth-century brick house still standing in Richmond—retains its original woodwork, floors, and paneling. Ninety percent of the home's furnishings, silver, and china are original to the Marshall family, and John Marshall's judicial robes and his wife Polly's wedding dress are also on display. Located at 818 Marshall Street, the John Marshall House is administered by the Association for the Preservation of Virginia Antiquities and is open Tuesday through Saturday, 11:00 AM to 4:00 PM. For further information, call (804) 648-7998.

MARSHALL WAS NEARLY EIGHTY YEARS OLD when he died in Philadelphia on July 6, 1835. His body was brought back to Virginia for burial, where it was met by the longest procession the city of Richmond had ever seen.

In the contest between proponents of strong and weak national government, Marshall had been one of the foremost and clearest advocates of strength. The struggle—between union and disunion, between federation and confederation, between the belief that the Constitution created a nation and the theory that it aligned the states in a loose league—was not finally resolved until 1865. But the struggle *was* resolved. "Time has been on Marshall's side," Oliver Wendell Holmes, Jr., said in

1901. "The theory for which Hamilton argued, and he decided, and Webster spoke, and Grant fought, is now our cornerstone."

Justice Story thought that Marshall's appointment to the Supreme Court contributed more "to the preservation of the true principles of the Constitution than any other circumstances in our domestic history." "He was a great man," Story said. "I go farther; and insist, that he would have been deemed a great man in any age, and of all ages. He was one of those, to whom centuries alone give birth."

John Adams and Thomas Jefferson both lived long and distinguished lives, but neither ever gave an inch in their differences of opinion over Marshall. Jefferson went to his grave bemoaning the "cunning and sophistry" of his fellow Virginian. Adams died secure in the belief that his decision to make Marshall chief justice had been both wise and provident. Years later, Adams called Marshall's appointment "the pride of my life." Time has accorded Thomas Jefferson a great place in the affections of the American people; but, in the controversy over John Marshall, the judgment of history has come down with quiet strength on the side of John Adams.

A Shadow of Secession?

THE HARTFORD CONVENTION, 1814

★ ★ ★ ★ ★ ★ ★

A separatist assembly of Federalist New England at the height of war-weariness provided precedence and philosophy for future defiance of the Union.

James M. Banner, Jr.

THE SUMMER OF 1814 WAS THE AMERICAN nation's worst time since the winter of 1778, when independence hung in the balance. Its second war with Great Britain was two years old; and after two years of military reverses, relieved only by the exploits of American seamen, the United States was verging on bankruptcy and defeat. Britain, having put Napoleon to rout, had begun to concentrate her superior forces in North America. By June, the Royal Navy held the entire east coast under blockade. A month later, Eastport and Moose Island, Maine, fell to invading forces. In August, the British reached Washington, burned the White House and Capitol, and sent President James Madison and the government fleeing in humiliation over the countryside. Early September brought news that Sir George Prevost had invaded New York at Lake Champlain and that Maine as far south as the Penobscot River had fallen under enemy control. The War of 1812, a war declared by the United States, seemed to be ending in disaster. And the possible consequences were not too far to seek: a permanent loss of territory, a forced dismemberment of the Union, worst of all the reimposition of British rule.

To these military setbacks was added commercial and financial ruin. Free trade with the world was at a standstill, and thousands looked in vain for work. In August, banks south of Connecticut suspended specie payment as the money supply ran short. As for the federal government, its coffers were almost dry: expenses far outran receipts, and few investors had enough confidence to subscribe to offerings of federal bonds. It was doubtful that the economic resources to continue the struggle could be found. Even if the war were to continue, a strategic portion of the nation's population – the Federalist Party majority of New England – meant in any case not to fight on. Assailing the folly and iniquity of 'Mr. Madison's War', they believed that the real moral and military threat to the republic was imperial France under the 'archfiend' Napoleon. Yet the Democratic-Republican administration had chosen war with Britain – the mightiest power of the time, source of American commercial prosperity, what Massachusetts Federalist Timothy Pickering called 'the world's last hope'.

The partisan cast to the Federalists' opposition to war surprised few contemporaries. Since their origin in the late 1790s, the Democratic-Republican and Federalist parties – the first political parties in the modern sense of the word – had differed sharply over the nation's position towards domestic and foreign policies. The Democratic-Republican Party, identified with its founders Thomas Jefferson and James Madison, represented the interests of the nation's predominantly agrarian economy, championed limited government, and sought to open all foreign markets to American goods and to maintain a studied neutrality in the conflicts of other nations. The Federalist Party of Alexander Hamilton and John Adams espoused a more active federal role in national life, spoke up for commercial, manufacturing and banking interests, and favoured a 'realistic' policy in foreign affairs – which in effect meant acceding to the military and commercial ascendancy of Britain.

Under presidents George

From *History Today*, September 1988, pp. 24-30. Reproduced by kind permission of History Today, Ltd., 83-84 Berwick Street, London W1V 3PJ, England.

Washington and John Adams in the 1790s, the Federalists had secured commercial tranquility with Britain and fought an undeclared war with France – thus coming to be seen as the 'British party' in American politics. Upon Jefferson's inauguration in 1801 and the resumption of the Napoleonic Wars in Europe, American relations with Britain had soured. British and American ships battled at sea. Jefferson attempted to embargo all trade with foreign nations in an unsuccessful effort to force Britain to lift restrictions on American trade with her colonies and Continental ports. And after Madison's succession to the presidency in 1809, relations between the two nations plunged further. Commerce-minded Federalists, especially in the northeast, saw their interests imperilled and their communities suffering unemployment and bankruptcy – all, they thought for the misbegotten principles of free neutral trade. After the Democratic-Republican administration led the nation into war in 1812, Federalist political opposition turned seditious, their tactics more desperate.

By 1814, then, it was clear to New England Federalists that the party of Jefferson and Madison was squandering the proven benefits of peace, however conditional they might be, for a conflict which brought on the corruptions of war and endangered the very existence of the fledgling nation. Nor was the administration preparing American defences against a foe fresh from triumph in Europe. So when, in September 1814, the call went out from Massachusetts for a winter convention of New England delegates in Hartford, Connecticut, not only had the military situation become desperate, American territory been taken, and the government been reduced to flight, but Federalist New England was on the point of open rebellion.

The roots of New England revolt, however, lay deeper in the past than recent partisan conflict. The Federalist opposition to war may have represented a crabbed sectionalism and the search of a defeated party for political advantage, but its significance also arose from venerable hopes and fears embedded in the nation's revolutionary and republi-

can heritage and from the advancing modernisation and democratisation of party politics, especially in Massachusetts.

These hopes and fears about the nation's fate expressed themselves most vividly in the venom with which Federalist accusations against political enemies were expressed. In part, the Federalists' supercharged rhetoric grew from their recent defeat at Jefferson's hands in 1800. In part, it originated from the sheer novelty of party politics, the absence as yet of any accepted standards of partisan behaviour. Above all, like most Americans, New England Federalists had deeply absorbed a set of republican political attitudes, born in eighteenth-century Britain and given coherence during the Revolution, which held that factions and parties subverted the best of regimes by introducing corruption, creating disunity, and debasing the quality of leadership. Of course, to the Federalists, theirs was not a party or faction but a union of men of principle, a collection of 'the wise and good' who stood above politics. It was Jefferson's opposition, in contrast, which was made up of 'unprincipled demagogues' and 'the most God-provoking Democrats this side of Hell'.

The master key to Federalists' protests against the war was their fear for the 'republican experiment' itself. The United States, they argued, was 'the world's last hope of a republick'. Believing that they bore a burden for all posterity, New England Federalists were exceptionally touchy, anxious, and fault-finding. These were, after all, perilous times: in the age of Austerlitz and Trafalgar, no nation seemed safe.

But what could preserve this unique American experiment? Republican ideology had always stressed the fragility and impermanence of republics. That 'it is the lot of free republican government to be but of short duration' was not a history lesson designed to make men carefree about their future. If anything, it made them inordinately vigilant in hunting down dangers to the nation and examining others' motives. It also made them measure all actions against the standards that republican theory considered to be essential for the preservation of republican society.

Of these standards, the first was public and private virtue. 'It has ever been an acknowledged maxim in the science of politics', a typical Federalist statement asserted, 'that virtue is the only permanent basis of a republic.' Social solidarity, harmony among classes and sections, a sense of comity and co-operation – all of which implied a homogeneity of race and religion – also, so they thought, underpinned republican society. 'The strength of a republick', declared Massachusetts Governor Caleb Strong, 'consists in the mutual dependence and agreement of its several parts.'

Compact territorial boundaries which enabled citizens to enjoy this harmony and brought them into closer contact with government also enhanced republican prospects. Federalists believed, after Montesquieu, that 'all history showed that great empires, whether monarchies or republics, had ultimately broken to pieces by their magnitude' – a view which underlay much of their protest against the Louisiana Purchase. No less important in their republican canon was the belief that excessive power, whether exemplified in the high-handed enforcement of Jefferson's 1807 embargo or in the waging of external war, endangered a fragile republican state.

Republican theory offered no guidelines about how to create these indispensable conditions. Yet in the view of New England Federalists, the Jeffersonians had violated all tenets of the republican creed. Corruption was everywhere in evidence, from the irreligion of Jefferson (a deist who observed no formal religion) to his appointment policies (which seemed to reward party fidelity rather than personal character). The harmony of neighbourhood and nation had been undermined by an open-door immigration policy which welcomed such 'offscourings' of Europe as the Irish and French and by anti-commercial policies which struck at the basic economic livelihood of maritime New England. The nation had taken on the aspects of an empire with its vast new western lands. And a war with the only nation which could hold off the hordes of Napoleonic France had been declared. What all this showed to Federalists was that the government had alienated itself from the people. 'We fear', declared a group of Massachusetts Federalists, 'that government has withdrawn from us.'

One other cultural tradition, this one perhaps even more deeply rooted than republicanism, also fueled the disaffection of Federalist New England: a belief in New England's special character and role. This idea of New England exclusiveness had it that the north-east was the home of the best talents, the highest moral integrity, the most advanced politics, and the people of the greatest ethnic homogeneity and social harmony in the nation. 'The God of nature, in his infinite goodness', one commentator typically wrote, 'has made the people of New England to excel every other people that ever existed in the world.'

It is easy enough to dismiss this kind of assertion as a response to Federalists' fear of their section's flagging role in the union. Yet the notion of exclusivity was something more. It was an idea which catalysed the thinking of many despondent New Englanders and which helped to overcome – just as it originated in – a growing sense of regional insecurity. Equally important, exclusivist beliefs made many conclude that, as the repository of all that was good in the republic, New England had to defend itself in order to save the future of republicanism everywhere. It was this potent combination of republican and exclusivist attitudes which led many people during the trying days of 1814 to talk of concerted protest, a separate peace with Great Britain, or, in the last extremity, disunion.

A crisis in internal Federalist party affairs also lay at the roots of the Hartford Convention. Two groups of men had been battling for control of the still young Federalist Party and for influence over a rapidly democratising electorate. One contained the professional politicians experienced in partisan life, the second a number of party figures excluded from the party's inner circle and an assortment of amateur politicians, especially Congregational ministers, who meant to direct the public mind.

Since 1800, provoked in part by the challenge of the Democratic-Republicans but also by the need to regulate

The Battle of Lake Erie, 1813 (captured by a contemporary artist) – an American victory that temporarily relieved British pressure from Canada.

their own factional conflicts, Federalists had created party organisations throughout New England. At their apex was the party's legislative caucus, composed of elected members of the legislature, which, among other functions, approved candidates for offices throughout the state and made major appointments to the party's state central committee. Beneath the caucus were county, town, and sometimes ward caucuses which served the same functions in lesser jurisdictions.

Parallel to the caucus system, a committee hierarchy had also come into being. Also broken into state, county, town, and ward divisions, the committees were in effect the agents of the caucuses, designed primarily to see to the election of party candidates through propaganda, fund-raising, and election-time activities. In practice, then, the party was broken roughly into two segments, one comprising the legislative and local caucuses, the other comprising committees of party workers, men who served the party outside electoral office and laboured in behalf of its candidates. As is apt to happen in any institution, members of the committees gradually identified themselves with the interests of the

party as a continuing organisation. Many of them served for long periods, while the elected representatives who made up the caucuses came and went. Committee politicians, coming to understand the party's affairs in the largest perspective, also gradually came to possess predominating influence in its councils.

The basic task of the committees was to get out the vote, and in this they succeeded remarkably. The competition of two organised parties struggling to win elections – a new feature of public life since the mid-1790s – stimulated an ever larger proportion of New England's qualified voters (which is to say, of the adult white males) to go to the polls to cast their ballots. In Massachusetts, where only about 33 per cent of the voters turned out for the gubernatorial election of 1800, 68 per cent did so in 1812. In New Hampshire, the level of voting was even higher, reaching 81 per cent in 1814. By the end of roughly the first decade of the nineteenth century, electoral democracy had been achieved in New England.

It was achieved, however, at considerable cost to the stability of Federalist politics. The comfortable élitism of the past, with its assurance of political control by educated and leisured men, began to give way, now that the vote had to be turned out, to more open, democratic, professional political methods. Large political rallies replaced the low-keyed requests for votes among neighbours; splashy handbills began to supplant discreet newspaper essays. And with the old élite methods disappeared the assured and durable respect of citizens for their political 'betters'. As party leaders soon found out, the people might get ahead of the party's ability to control them.

This problem of political control was especially difficult in Massachusetts. The old Puritan Commonwealth was the home of the most powerful Federalist Party and the most numerous Federalist constituency in the nation. It possessed a large and competitive Democratic-Republican opposition. Moreover, the Bay State contained a historically influential and proud group of clerics of the established Congregational faith. The combination of a large rank-and-file following led by a young but strong party organisation whose growth seemed to endanger ministers' public authority provided the makings of an internal party conflict which came to a head in 1814.

Men with party responsibility in Massachusetts – such as Harrison Gray Otis, the statesmanlike *beau ideal* of social Boston; William Sullivan, the young and hard-working party activist; and Thomas Handasyd Perkins, wealthy and well-placed man of affairs – had learned the need to compromise, to form coalitions, to fudge an issue to land a vote. Their aim was not simply to enunciate principle but to gain office. Moreover, as men of the worlds of the law and business, they trafficked in information, inhabited the parlours of prestige and wealth, and enjoyed association through their political and professional activities with other men elsewhere throughout the state and nation.

Among Congregational clerics of the state's established Church, as among their doctrinal and social allies, the Presbyterians and Episcopalians, Federalism was also the order of the day. Yet where politicians sought votes, ministers sought

the 'Truth'. Where politicians answered to a varied constituency, clergymen were responsible to single congregations. Politicians faced dismissal from office at every election; clerics' posts, though not permanent, were far more secure. And where party politicians were now part of a growing organisation, affected by its values and needs, clerics of the Congregational persuasion were relatively autonomous, answerable principally to their immediate parishioners.

In many ways, then, the political party had become the chief rival of the church, and politics had become the chief competitor of religion for the attention of the average citizen. The party enunciated the current attitudes of the day, dramatised conflicts of policy and purpose, and recruited many of the best talents. Its rallies were like religious services and its workers like ministers out on call. In short, there had developed a critical schism between the values, lives, and perspectives of Congregational clerics and Federalist politicians, partisan allies but both dominant in their own diverging spheres.

Among the clerics were men of impressive talents, such as Jedidiah Morse, Nathaniel Emmons, and Elijah Parish. Along with a small but

vocal group of lay figures and old-style politicians who clamoured for the immediate secession of New England, among whom Timothy Pickering was the best known, these clerics scorned the gradualism, the 'trimming', of the political men. Joined after June 1812 by a broadening mass of normally prudent but now increasingly angry and frustrated men and women throughout New England, these ministers and lay extremists began to demand immediate and radical action to redress New England's grievances.

Some, like Parish, told their congregations to 'proclaim an honourable neutrality... *Forbid this war to proceed in New-England*'. Others went further to urge New England to 'cut the connexion' with the southern states. Federalists of all stripes were coming to agree, in the words of an Essex County committee, that:

> Our common interests, liberties, and safety are now more injured, oppressed and endangered, by the doings of our own National Government, than they were when in 1775 we took arms to protect and defend them against the measures of the government of Great Britain.

Through sermons and personal visits, the clergy's views gained wide

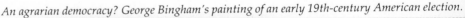

An agrarian democracy? George Bingham's painting of an early 19th-century American election.

currency and met increasingly favourable reception. And through a newspaper press broadened substantially since 1800, the attitudes of those radicals like Pickering who were urging nullification or disunion enjoyed wide note. Thus such had been the democratisation of the ballot and the modernisation of the Federalist Party structure that party chieftains found themselves exposed from below to mounting demands for concerted party action against Democratic-Republican misgovernment. As if to bring the message home, the spring legislative elections of 1814 returned an overwhelming Federalist majority in Massachusetts, one less inclined than before to heed counsels for moderation.

So when the summer crisis of 1814 broke upon the nation, the professional guardians of Federalist politics found the pressures for some sort of united party protest irresistible. The convening of extra-legal conventions, such as the Stamp Act and Continental Congresses, to correct grievances and reform government were part of the American tradition. Now, after being resisted for so long, such a course recommended itself to Massachusetts Federalist leaders as a way of channelling protest and dissent.

Early in 1814, after Madison's administration had closed the coasting trade to cut off a flourishing business in smuggling, Massachusetts rose to the verge of rebellion. Calls for a regional convention were debated in the state legislature, the General Court. By the late summer of 1814, with the entire nation humbled by its enemy, postponement was no longer possible. In early September, Governor Caleb Strong ordered the General Court into special session to adopt such measures as 'the present dangerous state of public affairs may render expedient'.

Although the Hartford Convention has always been regarded as a convention brought on by Federalists from the five New England states, it was basically a Massachusetts affair, originating in the special conditions of that state's Federalist politics and designed and led by leaders of the party there. Soon after Strong's call for the special session, Otis, Sullivan, Perkins, and other party leaders met in intensive consultation. Their chief aim, as Otis later attested, was to satisfy the 'high toned and menacing' public clamour and to prepare steps both 'constitutional and peaceable'. In the words of George Cabot, the party's elder statesman soon to be elected President of the Convention, every effort would be bent towards preventing the 'young hot-heads from getting into mischief'.

How successful the wily Otis and his astute colleagues could be in holding the region's emboldened Federalists to a prudent course immediately became evident. Beating down calls for such actions as cutting off the collection of federal customs duties – an act tantamount to nullification – Otis drafted a report for the General Court which called for a conference 'between those States the affinity of whose interests is closest' to propose constitutional amendments to 'lay the foundation for a radical reform in the national compact, by inviting to a future convention a deputation from all the States of the Union'. The legislature swiftly approved the report, 250-90. Soon after, it selected twelve delegates to Hartford and invited the other New England states to do likewise.

The Massachusetts delegation to the Hartford Convention, like those sent from Connecticut and Rhode Island, was composed, almost without exception, of professional men long active in party affairs and intimately linked with the party organisation. None of them were of 'impetuous temperament and fiery earnestness'. All could be counted upon for cautious action and a due regard for the interests of the party's electoral future. Moreover, most of the twenty-six delegates were official representatives of their state governments and thus under some restraint of action. Only the three delegates selected by *ad hoc* Federalist meetings in three counties of Vermont and New Hampshire represented the people alone. As if to make rash action even more unlikely, counsel flowed in from well-placed Federalists elsewhere, urging moderation and implying that extreme Convention action would seriously embarrass the party everywhere.

Not surprisingly, the Convention produced no call for secession. That its sessions were held in secret to allow greater freedom of debate, after the example of the Philadelphia Convention of 1787, has long given rise to charges that its members plotted disloyal action. But if treasonable words were ever spoken, the proceedings were rather bland. Moreover, the official Convention report was along the lines of what might have been anticipated from such men: a temperate document, disappointing to party radicals, which offered some predictable, if far-fetched, proposals for constitutional reform, along with carefully worded threats of stronger action if the report went unheeded.

Who was to expect otherwise? After all, the Convention, which first met on December 15th, remained under the control throughout of the Massachusetts delegation. George Cabot, early chosen its president, saw to it that Otis sat upon or headed all the important committees. And it was Otis who wrote the report which was finally adopted on January 3rd after three weeks of debate.

This document was a clear victory for moderate federalism and nicely captured two decades of New England Federalist political thought. After firmly rebuking extremist action, the report reminded its readers that Americans everywhere had hoped that the young republic would avoid 'the embarrassments of old and rotten institutions'. The lust for power, the misuse of executive authority, and 'unjust and ruinous wars' were 'the natural offspring of bad administration, in all ages and countries'. For:

> ...when abuses, reduced to a system, and accumulated through a course of years, have pervaded every department of government, and spread corruption through every region of the state; when these are clothed with the forms of law, and enforced by an executive whose will is their source, no summary means of relief can be applied without recourse to direct and open resistance.

Nevertheless, such drastic action like nullification or disunion, 'especially in a time of war', was justifiable only by 'absolute necessity'.

The report offered a brief for the right of a state to nullify such recent federal acts as those placing national officers in command of the state militias, enlisting minors without the consent of their parents, and drawing up draft quotas on the basis of the white population alone (rather than including black slaves, which would have increased recruitment in the South). Yet in drawing back from endorsing nullification, the Convention urged the government to permit the states to assume their own defence and to share the federal revenue by refunding a 'reasonable portion' of federal tax revenues to the states to defray defence costs.

Looking beyond the immediate crisis of the war, the report proposed seven constitutional amendments. Ostensibly designed to reclaim national harmony and forestal another war, they were designed to protect New England's influence better in the national councils. The first and most significant called for the apportionment of congressional representation and direct taxation according to the free white population of the states; another, arising from Louisiana's admission to statehood in 1812, would have required a two-thirds vote in Congress to admit new states. Both amendments looked to the reduction of the power of southern and western states. Two other amendments would have limited embargos to sixty days and required a two-thirds majority for their enactment. A fifth proposed the same two-thirds vote for declarations of war; a sixth, reflecting Federalist nativism, would have barred from Congress and other national offices all naturalised citizens; and the seventh, aimed at the succession of Virginia presidents, would have outlawed the election of presidents from the same state in successive terms.

Statesmanlike in tone, the report was warmly received in most Federalist circles – although the party's 'warm bloods' were disappointed, and the Democratic-Republicans accused the Convention of fomenting disloyalty, plotting treason, and undercutting the war effort. The governments of Massachusetts, Connecticut and Rhode Island officially adopted the report and appointed delegations to carry it to Washington. But events conspired to make a

mockery of the Convention's hopes. During the very weeks its members were deliberating, a peace treaty with Great Britain had finally been concluded at Ghent. And on January 8th 1815, long before anyone in the north-east could learn, General Andrew Jackson's forces put the British regulars to rout at New Orleans. By mid-February, the entire nation knew of the treaty and battle, and the report of the Convention was quickly buried under a torrent of ridicule. Yet had the Convention, after all, been for nothing?

To be sure, the meeting at Hartford

Playing the patriotic card; an 1807 Republican election poster against the 'British' Federalists.

The finifhing
STROKE.
Every Shot's a Vote,
And every Vote
KILLS A TORY!
DO YOUR DUTY, REPUBLICANS
Let your exertions this day
Put down the Kings
AND TYRANTS OF BRITAIN.
LAST DAY.
April, 1807.

put an end to the already waning national fortunes of the Federalist Party while giving a legitimacy to the notion of nullification which would haunt the nation later. Yet the Convention preserved the centrist course of New England federalism. Indeed, as the most notable instance since the Second Continental Congress of men organising to satisfy, direct, and control an aroused populace, it was a monument to the growth of electoral democracy. It was a victory for political management, for the 'system'.

But more than this, the Hartford Convention was another of the continuing attempts to define the meaning of the American experiment in a hostile and unstable world and to hold the nation to standards under

which it began. Men may debate how these standards are to be met, and the Convention may not have represented all that was best in the New England tradition. Yet the Federalists of New England were trying to raise, sincerely and anxiously, some enduring questions – some of them for the first time in the young republic's history – about the conduct of government and the quality of society, both in and out of war. As such, their concerns have never lost their timeliness. The Federalists of the Hartford Convention were, if nothing else, steadfast in their republican faith.

That faith, however, could have many consequences, take many forms. It was the dark legacy of the Hartford Convention not only to taint ineradicably the Federalist Party with disloyalty and irrelevance, from which it died by 1820, but also to provide precedent and philosophy for future acts of defiance toward policies of the national government. South Carolina's effort to nullify the collection of federal tariff duties in 1832 echoed the themes of regional interest and reserved constitutional rights laid down in 1814. More fatefully, those same principles of nullification remained alive in the South throughout the 1840s and 1850s, finally gaining enough acceptance by 1860 to justify the South's secession because of Abraham Lincoln's determination to prevent the further spread of black slavery in the United States. Thus it was that, in a small Connecticut town forty-six years before, were planted some of the seeds of the resort to arms that ensued, of the bloodiest war in the nation's history, of the manumission of the slaves, and of the survival of the American Union.

FOR FURTHER READING:
James M. Banner, Jr., *To the Hartford Convention: The Federalists and the Origins of Party Politics in Massachusetts, 1789-1815* (Alfred A. Knopf, 1970); Reginald Horsman, *The War of 1812* (Alfred A. Knopf, 1969); Linda K. Kerber, *The Federalists in Dissent: Imagery and Ideology in Jeffersonian America* (Cornell University Press, 1970); J. C. A. Stagg, *Mr. Madison's War: Politics, Diplomacy, and Warfare in the Early American Republic, 1783-1830* (Princeton University Press, 1983).

Russia's American Adventure

For more than a century, traders from imperial Russia pursued their dreams in Alaska

Lydia T. Black

Lydia T. Black started researching the Russian period in Alaska as an outgrowth of her fieldwork among the Aleuts, which she began in 1975. Born in Kiev, USSR, she has been able to bring her own cultural background to bear on the subject. A professor of anthropology at the University of Alaska, Fairbanks, Black previously taught at Providence College in Rhode Island.

On March 13, 1867, U. S. Secretary of State William H. Seward and Eduard Stoeckl, representing the Russian emperor Alexander II, signed the treaty by which the United States acquired Alaska, then part of the Russian empire. On October 18 of the same year, in Novoarkhangelsk (Sitka), the capital of Russian America, the imperial flag came down, and Gen. Lovell H. Rousseau formally accepted the vast territory for the United States. The ceremony did not go smoothly: the Russian flag became entwined in the ropes of the ninety-foot flagstaff, and it took considerable effort to bring it down. The episode is often cited in Alaska today—not always with amusement—when the imprint the Russians left on the land and its people is discussed.

Russian expansion to America had been initiated in the 1640s by private entrepreneurs ("the frontiersmen for the czar," one American scholar has called them), who reached the North Pacific from the Anadyr River basin, as well as by sailing south through the Bering Strait from the Arctic Ocean. The government followed on their heels. In the reign of Peter the Great (1682–1725), intercontinental expansion became a matter of policy. The first Russian port on the Pacific, Okhotsk, was founded, local shipbuilding was established, the sea route to the Kamchatka Peninsula was explored, and charting of the North Pacific began. Peter the

Great's design continued under his successors. In 1728 Commodore Vitus Bering sailed, with Capt. Alexei Chirikov, to the strait that bears his name. In 1732 another naval expedition made a landfall at Cape Prince of Wales, on the Alaskan side of the strait. And Bering and Chirikov again sailed across the North Pacific from Kamchatka to Alaska's Pacific shore, landing on Kayak Island and near modern Ketchikan in 1741 and returning along the Aleutian island chain. Three quarters of a century later, on the basis of these landfalls, international conventions determined the boundaries of Russian territory on the North American continent.

By the eighteenth century, many of the settlers in Kamchatka and Okhotsk were engaged in the fur trade, an ancient occupation in northern Russia. When Bering's men returned and reported that marine fur-bearing animals were plentiful on the Aleutian Islands to the east, some traders naturally extended their operations. If the risks were great, so were the potential rewards. There were not only riches to be gained but also honors to be received from the crown for exploring new territories.

The Aleutian Islands extend in a great arc from mainland Alaska to the Commander Islands, near the Kamchatkan coast. Many are either the tips of giant submarine volcanoes or more ancient geologic formations dominated by active volcanoes. The islands are treeless and originally supported few land animals—lemmings and mice, red foxes (and their commercially prized variants, the cross, black, and silver foxes) eastward of Umnak Island, and caribou and brown bear only on Unimak Island, off the Alaskan mainland. The human population was sparse, with the greatest concentration at the eastern end of the archipelago. The inhabitants spoke dialects of the Aleut language, at least two of which were so

distinct that they were mutually unintelligible. (Other Native American groups the Russians encountered included the Inupiaq and Yupik Eskimo on the northern and western coasts of the Alaskan mainland; Alutiiq on the Kodiak archipelago; the Chugach [Koniag], Eyak, Tlingit, Haida, and Tsimshian on the Northwest Coast; and various Athabaskan-speaking groups, which generally occupied interior regions but also had coastal settlements along the Cook Inlet.)

All the Aleuts depended on the sea for subsistence, and their technology was superbly adapted for exploitation of marine resources: seals, sea lions, whales, seabirds, and fish. Nevertheless, there were significant cultural differences among local groups. These were organized into several large, named political units, which defended their territories and engaged in warfare. Boys were trained to be warriors from early childhood, and war parties had a structured chain of command.

At the same time, Aleuts engaged in long-distance trade with mainland Alaskan groups, primarily to obtain caribou products, copper, and iron. On rare occasions, they even traded with Japanese, other Asiatic, and possibly European seafarers. As a result, they were ambivalent about the arrival of the Russian intruders. Periods of peaceful barter and amicable personal relations were punctuated by outbreaks of violence, depending on circumstances and the character of Russian and local native leaders. Often, no quarter was given by either side. In the eastern islands, in 1763, Aleuts destroyed four Russian ships and nearly all their crew members, more than 200 men.

The Russian traders were known as *promyshlenniki* (today the term translates as "industrialists," but was then used to refer to those who left their communities on some sort of commercial enter-

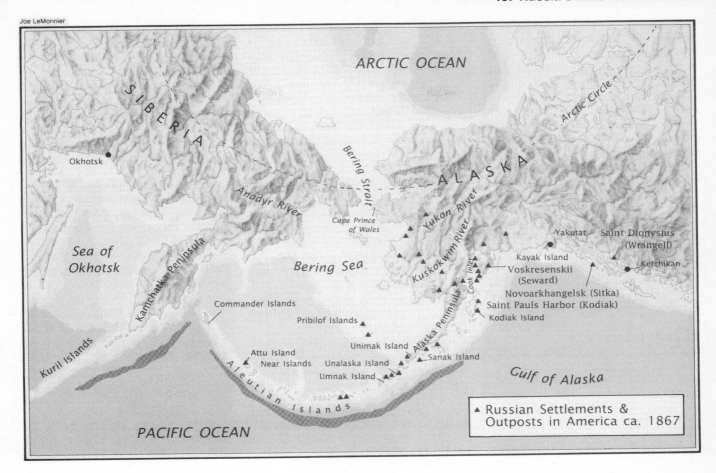

Joe LeMonnier

ARCTIC OCEAN

SIBERIA

ALASKA

Arctic Circle

Okhotsk

Bering Strait

Anadyr River

Yukon River

Cape Prince of Wales

Kuskokwim River

Yakutat

Saint Dionysius (Wrangell)

Sea of Okhotsk

Bering Sea

Kayak Island

Ketchikan

Voskresenskii (Seward)

Cook Inlet

Novoarkhangelsk (Sitka)

Kamchatka Peninsula

Saint Pauls Harbor (Kodiak)

Commander Islands

Kodiak Island

Pribilof Islands

Kuril Islands

Alaska Peninsula

Unimak Island

Attu Island

Near Islands

Unalaska Island

Sanak Island

Umnak Island

Gulf of Alaska

Aleutian Islands

PACIFIC OCEAN

▲ Russian Settlements & Outposts in America ca. 1867

prise). In the early period, most came from around the White Sea and other northern areas, the cradle of ancient polar navigation, the fur trade, and sea mammal hunting. A lesser but still sizable number came from Siberia and the Russian Far East and were often descended in part from native peoples, such as the Chukchi, Koryak, Yakut, Tungus, and Kamchadal. This is not always apparent in historical sources, since in Russia the ethnic ascription as well as civil estate was in the male line. A "Russian" from Kamchatka was thus very likely to have had a Kamchadal or Koryak mother. Moreover, in the early years of the Aleutian fur trade, many skippers enlisted Kamchatkan and Siberian natives as crew members. They were believed less likely to suffer scurvy and other diseases, and they understood the battle tactics of the Aleuts and were considered invaluable in conflicts.

For the *promyshlenniki,* neither the physical appearance of the local Alaskans nor their customs and manner of living were strange. Semisubterranean winter houses, summer fishing camps, skin boats, clothing made from the skins of sea mammals and birds, not to mention sub-

sistence on salmon, halibut, cod, seal and sea lion meat, and drift whale carcasses, were all familiar, taken for granted. The fur traders often adopted the Aleut life style, with modifications. They wore Aleut parkas and *kamleikas* (the water-proof shirt of sea mammal gut that is the prototype of modern rain gear), but added trousers, boots, and hats to their attire; they built semisubterranean dwellings and storage structures, but instead of using the roof entry and notched log ladders, they added doors, forerooms, and windows (made of translucent sea mammal gut, which the Aleuts used to cover their roof hatches).

The Aleuts in turn borrowed ideas and material items from the foreigners. Within ten years after first contact in the Near Islands, the Aleuts of Attu were extracting salt from seawater and using it to preserve fish. The steam bath, widespread in northern Europe and Asia, was quickly adopted and today survives as a native institution. Ironworking underwent a great change when the Russians introduced hot forging. Russian vessels usually carried a fully equipped forge and a blacksmith. In 1775, Ivan Solovev, leaving

Sanak Island, left his forge to the Aleut leader. Russian carpentry tools and the Russian ax came into vogue. The axes are spoken of to this day, and in one family a full set of carpenter's tools is lovingly preserved as a treasured possession.

In the eastern islands, Russians distributed Siberian-style fox traps and encouraged Aleuts to trap the native foxes (which were not hunted in precontact times). In the Near Islands, not only traps but also arctic foxes from the Commander Islands were imported. Ground squirrels, now distributed throughout most of the archipelago, were introduced as fodder for foxes. (Today, models of the Aleut fox trap are sold to tourists, while the U. S. Fish and Wildlife Service, which is responsible for the Aleutian Islands as part of the Alaska Maritime National Wildlife Refuge, is exterminating arctic foxes because they are not indigenous to the ecosystem.) By the early 1800s, the Russians had introduced vegetable gardening, pigs, goats, and cattle.

Shamanistic practices, such as healing and forecasting, were also familiar to the Russians. Although they were devout adherents of the Orthodox Church, their folk beliefs had features in common with the Aleut world view. Sometimes they called on local shamans for aid when sick. Similarly, when Aleuts appealed for help because their shamans had given up, the Russians would pray for them and perform rituals, such as lay baptism.

Russian laymen introduced Orthodoxy to the Aleuts many years before the arrival of clergy. The *promyshlenniki* often built chapels in their camps, and by the time the first missionaries arrived on Kodiak Island in 1794, the majority of people in the Aleutian chain and a number in the Kodiak archipelago and on the mainland considered themselves Orthodox Christians. The first church in Russian America, however, was built between 1795 and 1796 at Saint Pauls Harbor (the modern city of Kodiak).

The use of the Russian language also found ready acceptance. With international trade and negotiation so important, many Alaskan native men spoke several languages. Learning to speak the language of the newcomers was considered nothing special. Some Russians learned to speak Aleut, but most needed interpreters. Often they took young boys to their camps, where they were taught Russian, or sent them to school in their home ports. Aleut leaders sometimes volunteered their young kinsmen so that they would learn the language and gather as much intelligence about the foreigners as possible. More often, the boys were hostages, held at the Russian camps to insure peaceful relations with the Aleuts.

Holding hostages to guarantee safety and peace was an ancient practice both in Siberia and among native Alaskans. Russians always asked for hostages or took them by threat of force. Occasionally, a Russian was left as a hostage in a native community. In 1796, six Russians were left as hostages in the Tlingit settlement at Yakutat, on the Alaskan coast, to insure the safe return of the chief's son, who was sailing to visit the Russian community on Kodiak Island.

Because Aleut women were not valued very highly, the Russians preferred male hostages, neither so old as to become a danger within the Russian camp nor so young as to require special care. Russian men, perhaps fathers or elder brothers lonesome for home and family, often formed genuine attachments to their hostages. They introduced them to Orthodoxy, baptized them by lay baptism, and gave them Russian names. Such a godson was given a Russian Christian name and a name based on the godfather's Christian name, as well as his godfather's family name. This practice explains, more often than actual paternity, the prevalence of Russian surnames in Aleut communities of the Aleutian and Kodiak archipelagoes, as well as among other Alaskan groups that came under the Russian scepter. Sometimes slaves held by the Aleuts or young Aleuts without kin were adopted and taken to Russia.

British and "Bostonian" (American) sea otter and fur seal traders, who began operating on the Northwest Coast beginning in 1785, traded from their vessels only during the summer sailing season and seldom established shore camps. The Russian practice, in contrast, was to establish a winter camp, beaching the vessel in a convenient stream or lagoon. Such camps served for at least a year, but more often for several years and sometimes for as many as ten. Leaving a skeleton crew at the vessel, the Russians would disperse in small groups to hunt the furbearers. They also bartered with the Aleuts for additional furs.

As a rule, these hunting parties set up their own camps, often near established Aleut settlements. Occasionally, a solitary hunter or a small group of men took up residence within an Aleut community. Since the fur-trading vessels, according to available records, did not carry women, Russian-Aleut unions inevitably developed. While forcible abductions of women occurred, some women joined Russian camps willingly or at the behest of their male relatives.

By and large the *promyshlenniki* were God-fearing men, and a number sought to legalize their unions with native women and provide for their children to inherit their estates. Sometimes the unions were solemnized by following Aleut matrimonial customs. Often, in addition, a written contract would be drawn up and sworn to on the cross or the bible by the man concerned and the witnesses—other Russian *promyshlenniki*, Alaskan native leaders, and relatives of the bride. When the first clergymen came, one of their first tasks was to bless these marriages, making them fully legal and unbreakable.

Children of Russian–native unions often grew up bicultural, and as early as the 1760s, some *promyshlenniki* were teaching their young hostages, godchildren, and their own and their friends' childen to read and write. By the 1770s the Russian government issued charters that gave Aleuts rights as subjects of the empire and provided protection against any arbitrary violence on the part of the Russian skippers. Aleuts treasured such charters and other written documents and learned to write Russian themselves.

In the nineteenth century, Orthodox clergymen, of whom the most prominent in Alaska was Ioann Veniaminov (now Saint Innocent of the Aleutians), introduced writing systems for a number of Alaskan languages. The first publications in the new scripts were the Gospels and church service books, but the Aleuts also began to use the scripts for secular literature and everyday communication.

Despite the cultural exchanges, however, the Russian presence in the islands caused massive social dislocation. Participation in the fur trade changed the economic system of the Aleuts in short order. Aleuts often traveled long distances or resettled in order to gain access to Russian trading vessels or to particular trading partners. This facilitated the spread of diseases, both indigenous and newly introduced. The greatest scourges during the early period were venereal and intestinal infections and probably tuberculosis.

Smallpox may have touched the Tlingit sometime prior to 1786 (when a British skipper reported seeing some pockmarked individuals on the coast), but the disease did not really strike Alaska until 1835. Russian administrators attempted to check the epidemic by vaccination. Although many people were vaccinated, and in some islands the disease was prevented, the Russians were unsuccessful on the mainland and on Kodiak Island. Not only were they unable to reach many segments of the population, but the Alaskan natives often resisted vaccination because the procedure contradicted their theories of what causes disease. This was the case for the Tlingit, among whom casualties were extemely high, the Yupik, and the Kodiak islanders. Ironically, among the Yupik the belief persists that the Russians purposefully injected the natives with the disease, a belief based on the vaccination effort. The lesson was learned, however: a major American smallpox epidemic in the 1860s did not spread to Alaska, largely owing to the efforts of the clergy, who promoted a new vaccination program.

Systematic economic exploitation of the Aleuts, specifically in the eastern Aleutian Islands and in the Kodiak archipelago, developed toward the end of the eighteenth century. The fur trade changed from local entrepreneurs to large-scale capital enterprises, and as the competition increased, the skippers were pressed by the owners for profit. Always short of labor, they resorted to impressment of Aleuts, carrying them off to mainland Alaska, to the Pribilof Islands, and even resettling them in new outposts. This left the villages with the women, the old, and the young, who were often unable to insure their own subsistence.

In 1790, Aleut leaders on Unalaska Island bitterly protested these practices to an imperial navy expedition that had been sent by Catherine the Great. The Aleuts were careful to point out that not all skippers were to blame and named those with whom they liked to trade and for whom they liked to work. Those accused of the most grievous abuses were all in the employ of the merchant Grigorii Shelikhov.

Shelikhov had entered the Siberian fur trade in the 1770s. From the beginning, his interests extended from Kamchatka and the Kuril Islands to Alaska. Soon he held a controlling interest in many ventures, gradually squeezing out his partners and his competitors. By 1780, he had grandiose plans to build an empire on the American continent and was continually importuning the government for support of his "services to the state." Although the empress was more than skeptical, Shelikhov managed to enlist considerable official backing. In 1783 he sailed from Okhotsk for Russian America with permission to carry more than the usual armament on his three vessels.

For Shelikhov, acquisition of furs was a means of amassing capital to build his empire. He wanted to settle Alaska, build cities, industry, agriculture, cathedrals, schools—from the Northwest Coast to Bering Strait and beyond. To establish a permanent stronghold, he chose the most populous region known, Kodiak Island, bypassed by most skippers because of the highly organized strength of the indigenous inhabitants. Contrary to government policy, he directed an armed conquest, on the premise that what the government did not know was not going to hurt it. This was accomplished in a series of swift, sudden, and even by the standards of the time, brutal strikes.

Shelikhov left Kodiak in 1786, but by 1791 he had found a man eager to carry out his wishes—Aleksandr Baranov. An able leader and a skillful diplomat, Baranov used Kodiak islanders as his main labor force and impressed them into his "army." Although Shelikhov died in 1795, his company continued to operate and was granted a monopolistic, twenty-year charter by the emperor Paul I in 1799. Baranov then became the general manager of the Russian American Company, ruling as a de facto governor.

During Baranov's reign, with Europe in the grip of the Napoleonic wars, Russian ships could not regularly be spared to supply the needs of the colony. Taking matters into his own hands, Baranov began shipbuilding in Alaska. In 1796, the first three-masted ship was launched at Voskresenskii (now Seward). Smaller vessels were built at other locations, while several ships were bought from the Americans. A colonial merchant fleet came into existence. American skippers were tempted by Baranov to carry cargo from the eastern seaboard of the United States and from Canton, China, to the Russian settlements in Alaska in exchange for furs. A linkage with John Jacob Astor's enterprises was in the works.

Aided by his army of impressed Aleuts and various volunteer contingents, Baranov checked the British and American competition along the Northwest Coast and established Novoarkhangelsk as his capital in the Tlingit territory. He weathered the armed conflict with the Tlingit (who were aided by British and American ordnance and several American sailors), sent out exploring parties to the Columbia River, established Fort Ross in California in the face of Spanish opposition, and attempted to gain a foothold in Hawaii. His kayak fleets ranged to Baja California for sea otter, fur seal, and salt.

Baranov's achievements notwithstanding, adverse reports by the clergy and navy personnel resulted in his removal in 1818. Reform followed: native impressment ended, and in accordance with the Russian system of social ranking, in which each rank had different duties and rights, Aleuts were assigned a status equivalent to that of free peasants. In lieu of taxes and military service, a certain number of Aleuts from each village had to serve with the company, primarily as sea mammal hunters, and were paid set wages. Local Aleut leaders managed native affairs, including the selection of those who were to serve in the company.

In 1821, following negotiations, the Russian American Company received a second charter, which imposed new responsibilities. Fur seal and sea otter conservation measures were instituted and eventually enforced. In the fur seal rookeries in the Pribilof and Commander islands, only nonbreeding adult males were taken. Periodically, the harvest was dis-

continued for a number of years. Any use of firearms or establishment of settlements near sea otter hauling grounds was forbidden, and only a limited number of skins were taken per year. In areas where the Aleuts hunted sea otters and sold them to the company on an independent basis, there was some discontent, as furs in excess of the established quota for the district were not bought. Immature and female sea otter skins were also refused.

The company was obliged to provide services to the population, such as churches, medical outposts manned by paramedical specialists, and schools. Open to all, the bilingual and bicultural schools taught basic literacy skills, religious studies, mathematics, geography, history, music, and art. Educational opportunities were especially favorable for the members of a newly created Alaskan rank, or estate, called creoles. Creoles were persons who could claim descent in the male line from a Russian. Sometimes an Alaskan native was considered a creole if he occupied a position of responsibility within the company.

Likened to the burghers in Russia, the creoles could (and often did) become company officials or achieve military or naval officer rank. By the end of the Russian period, this class provided the backbone for the Russian Alaskan enterprise. They explored the Alaskan interior and North Slope, established trading posts and trading networks that crisscrossed the entire territory, and commanded company ships. They were managers, shipbuilders, artisans, medics, and physicians. Some served in the navy, others became artists or priests. High-ranking visitors from Saint Petersburg often ridiculed this class as social upstarts, while Russians of lower ranks resented the creoles' social mobility and the educational opportunities and other privileges granted them.

With the advent of U. S. sovereignty, the creoles suffered great degradation because Americans considered them contemptible "half-breeds." Today, the majority of their descendants are absorbed in the Alaskan native communities; others moved out of Alaska and blended with the "white" population of the other states.

Russians were never numerous in Alaska. At times there were fewer than 200. By 1830, the number was about 300 and slowly growing. From the 1840s to the end of Russian America in 1867, they numbered just under 600, of whom nearly 500 resided in Novoarkhangelsk or on Kodiak Island. There were no troops stationed in Alaska at all before the Crimean War (1853–1856). At that time the Russians, fearing the British would attack or incite Tlingit unrest, brought one hundred soldiers from Siberia to man Novoarkhangelsk's defenses. They were mostly employed in various tasks in the harbor and around the town and were not used to subjugate the natives.

The level of violence in Russian America after 1818 was remarkably low. Governmental policy prohibited retaliation against acts committed by Alaskan natives, maintaining a legal fiction that any such acts were the result of provocation by the company's employees. Gifts were exchanged to reestablish relations after a violent incident. Noninterference in native affairs was a matter of policy. The Russians were often called in as a neutral party to settle disputes between native groups and between the Tlingit and the Hudson's Bay Company trading post near modern-day Wrangell.

Crime was exceedingly rare among the Russian colonists as well. The general manager acted administratively when employees transgressed company regulations, but had no jurisdiction in either civil or criminal cases. When a crime was committed, the accused and the witnesses were shipped to Russia for judicial proceedings. There were no courts and no jails in Alaska during the Russian period.

In the beginning of the Russian period, the fur trade was the driving force of the colony, but by the middle of the nineteenth century the situation was changing. As fur markets in Europe diminished and the Chinese market collapsed, the company attempted economic diversification. Ice was shipped to San Francisco, coal to Vancouver and Victoria and to American ports farther south, and fish to places as far away as Hawaii. None of these ventures fared too well. Better coal was found in British Columbia and was less expensive to ship to the American cities. In the absence of canning technology, Alaskan salted fish found but a small market.

The Russians were aware of the region's iron, copper, and gold (although they never identified major gold deposits), but they never exploited these minerals. Historians do not agree if behind this inattention was ignorance of the true potential of the area or the fear that the territory would be overrun by fortune hunters from the United States and Canada. I incline to the latter view: in Russian documents, the California and Stikine River gold-rush stampedes are often mentioned with alarm as horrible examples of what might befall a country once greed is awakened on a mass scale.

Nevertheless, the Russian American Company's long-term economic prospects remained good. The Russian period ended because of a government move. In the wake of the Crimean War, the navy's capacity to protect Alaska from British expansion seemed doubtful. Besides, the government wanted to consolidate its position in the Amur region on the Chinese border. The decision was taken to retreat from Alaska. The United States, then friendly toward Russia, was invited to purchase the territory for a modest price.

The Russians in Alaska did not foresee nor desire this outcome. When the ceremony of transfer commenced on October 18, 1867, few Russians attended, aside from those present in an official capacity. An American witness commented:

Alaska is the fatherland—native soil.... They would be less than human were they to regard this cession of the country with any other than feelings of sadness.... Let me not be misunderstood. The Russian citizens of Sitka are loyal to their sovereign, and submit to his mandate peaceably and without complaint. There has been no repining, no exhibition of moroseness or ill-will toward our people. Yet it was impossible for the more patriotic of the resident population not to have a feeling of sorrow while seeing the flag under which they were born lowered from its time-honored position, never again to float over their island home.

Within three years after the transfer, the majority of Russians, some creoles, and even a few Alaskan natives chose to repatriate to Russia. A few Russians remained in Alaska, some intermarrying with the immigrants who flooded the territory from the United States and Europe. The newcomers came as businessmen, sea otter and fur seal hunters (under new laissez-faire policies), whalers, and finally, in unprecedented numbers, as gold seekers. Except in the Alaskan native communities, few families in Alaska today trace their descent to the Russian settlers.

Nevertheless, the Russian Orthodox Church retains a central place in Alaskan culture, and other aspects of local life, such as the cuisine and folk dancing, still bear a Russian stamp. Today, partly because Alaskan native groups have called for better teaching of their own history, a new generation is examining this heritage. Conferences, exhibits, documentaries, and efforts to preserve churches and other historic structures are reviving interest in Russian America, as are the inevitable tourism promotions. And when the state celebrates Alaska Day each October 18, citizens of Sitka gather to commemorate, and reenact, the transfer from Russian to U. S. sovereignty. At the end of the ceremony, the Russian American Company flag, which on holidays flies alongside the state flag and the Stars and Stripes, is raised on the hill where the general manager's house once stood.

For Additional Reading

For additional reading, the author recommends *Russian America: The Great Alaskan Venture, 1741–1867*, by novelist Hector Chevigny (Portland: Binford & Mort Publishing, 1979); *The Wreck of the Sv. Nikolai: Two Narratives of the First Russian Expedition to the Oregon Country, 1808–1810*, introduced by Kenneth S. Owens and translated by Alton S. Donnelly (Portland: Oregon Historical Society, 1985); and *Builders of Alaska: The Russian Governors, 1818–1867*, by Richard A. Pierce (Kingston, Ontario: The Limestone Press, 1985). *Crossroads of Continents: Cultures of Siberia and Alaska*, by William W. Fitzhugh and Aron Crowell (Washington, D.C.: Smithsonian Institution, 1988).

From Utopia to Mill Town

The Boston Associates wanted to build the perfect industrial community. But could they become more than Lords of the Loom?

Maury Klein

Tennessee native Maury Klein is presently a professor of history at the University of Rhode Island. A 1965 Ph.D. recipient from Emory University in Georgia, he has written a total of four books and several dozen articles and reviews. For further reading on Lowell, he suggests Steven Dunwell's THE RUN OF THE MILL *(1978) and* THE GOLDEN THREADS *(1949), by Hannah Josephson.*

They flocked to the village of Lowell, these visitors from abroad, as if it were a compulsory stop on the grand tour, eager to verify rumors of a utopian system of manufacturers. Their skepticism was natural, based as it was on the European experience where industry had degraded workers and blighted the landscape. In English manufacturing centers such as Manchester, observers had stared into the pits of hell and shrank in horror from the sight. Charles Dickens used this gloomy, putrid cesspool of misery as a model in *Hard Times*, while Alexis de Tocqueville wrinkled his nose at the "heaps of dung, rubble from buildings, putrid, stagnant pools" amid the "huge palaces of industry" that kept "air and light out of the human habitations which they dominate. . . . A sort of black smoke covers the city. . . . Under this half daylight 300,000 human beings are ceaselessly at work. A thousand noises disturb this damp, dark labyrinth, but they are not at all the ordinary sounds one hears in great cities."

Was it possible that America could produce an alternative to this hideous scene? It seemed so to the visitors who gaped in wonderment at the village above the confluence of the Concord and Merrimack rivers. What they saw was a planned community with mills five to seven stories high flanked by dormitories for the workers, not jammed together but surrounded by open space filled with trees and flower gardens set against a backdrop of the river and hills beyond. Dwelling houses, shops, hotels, churches, banks, even a library lined the streets in orderly, uncrowded rows. Taken whole, the scene bore a flavor of meticulous composition, as if a painting had sprung to life.

The contrast between so pristine a vision and the nightmare of Manchester startled the most jaded of foreigners. "It was new and fresh, like a setting at the opera," proclaimed Michel Chevalier, a Frenchman who visited Lowell in 1834. The Reverend William Scoresby, an Englishman, marveled at how the buildings seemed "as fresh-looking as if built within a year." The indefatigable Harriet Martineau agreed, as did J.S. Buckingham, who pronounced Lowell to be "one of the most remarkable places under the sun." Even Dickens, whose tour of America rendered him immune to most of its charms, was moved to lavish praise on the town. "One would swear," he added "that every 'Bakery,' 'Grocery' and 'Bookbindery' and every other kind of store, took its shutters down for the first time, and started in business yesterday."

If Lowell and its social engineering impressed visitors, the mill workers dazzled them. Here was nothing resembling Europe's *Untermenschen*, that doomed proletariat whose brief, wretched lives were squeezed between child labor and a pauper's grave. These were not men or children or even families as found in the Rhode Island mills. Instead Lowell employed young women, most of them fresh off New England farms, paid them higher wages than females earned anywhere else (but still only half of what men earned), and installed them in dormitories under strict supervision. They were young and industrious, intelligent, and entirely respectable. Like model citizens of a burgeoning republic they saved their money, went to church, and spent their leisure hours in self-improvement.

More than one visitor hurried home to announce the arrival of a new industrial order, one capable of producing goods in abundance without breaking its working class on the rack of poverty. Time proved them wrong, or at best premature. The Lowell experiment lasted barely a generation before sliding back into the grinding bleakness of a conventional mill town. It had survived long enough to tantalize admirers with its unfulfilled promise and to reveal some harsh truths

From *American History Illustrated*, October 1981, pp. 34-40, 48. Reprinted through the courtesy of Cowles Magazines, publisher of *American History Illustrated*.

about the incompatibility of certain democratic ideals and the profit motive.

The founding fathers of Lowell were a group known as the Boston Associates, all of whom belonged to that tight knit elite whose dominance of Boston society was exceeded only by their stranglehold on its financial institutions. The seed had been planted by Francis Cabot Lowell, a shrewd, far-sighted merchant who took up the manufacture of cotton cloth late in life. A trip abroad in 1810 introduced him to the cotton mills of Lancashire and to a fellow Boston merchant named Nathan Appleton. Blessed with a superb memory and trained in mathematics, Lowell packed his mind with details about the machinery shown him by unsuspecting mill owners. The Manchester owners jealously hoarded their secrets and patents, but none regarded the wealthy American living abroad for his health as a rival.

Once back in America, Lowell recruited a mechanical genius named Paul Moody to help replicate the machines he had seen in Manchester. After much tinkering they designed a power loom, cottonspinning frame, and some other machines that in fact improved upon the English versions. As a hedge against inexperience Lowell decided to produce only cheap, unbleached cotton sheeting. The choice also enabled him to use unskilled labor, but where was he to find even that? Manchester drew its workers from the poorhouses, a source lacking in America. Both the family system and use of apprentices had been tried in Rhode Island with little success. Most men preferred farming their own land to working in a factory for someone else.

But what about women? They were familiar with spinning and weaving, and would make obedient workers. Rural New England had a surplus of daughters who were considered little more than drains on the family larder. To obtain their services Lowell need only pay decent wages and overcome parental reservations about permitting girls to live away from home. This could be done by providing boarding houses where the girls would be subject to the strict supervision of older women acting as chaperones. There would be religious and moral instruction enough to satisfy the most scrupulous of parents. It was an ingenious concept, one that cloaked economic necessity in the appealing garb of republican ideals.

Lowell added yet another wrinkle. Instead of forming a partnership like most larger businesses, he obtained a charter for a corporation named the Boston Manufacturing Company. Capitalized at $300,000, the firm started with $100,000 subscribed by Lowell and a circle of his caste and kin: Patrick Tracy Jackson and his two brothers, Nathan Appleton, Israel Thorndike and his son, two brothers-in-law, and two other merchants. Jackson agreed to manage the new company, which chose a site at the falls on the Charles River at Waltham.

By late 1814 the first large integrated cotton factory in America stood complete, along with its machine shop where Lowell and Moody reinvented the power loom and spinner.

Production began in 1815, just as the war with England drew to a close. The mill not only survived the return of British competition but prospered in spectacular fashion: during the years 1817–1824 dividends averaged more than nineteen percent. Moody's fertile mind devised one new invention after another, including a warp-yarn dresser and double speeder. His innovations made the firm's production methods so unique that they soon became known as the "Waltham system." As Gilman Ostrander observed, "The Waltham method was characterized by an overriding emphasis upon standardization, integration, and mechanization." The shop began to build machinery for sale to other mills. Even more, the company's management techniques became the prototype on which virtually the entire textile industry of New England would later model itself.

Lowell did not live to witness this triumph. He died in 1817 at the age of forty-two, having provided his associates with the ingredients of success. During the next three years they showed their gratitude by constructing two more mills and a bleachery, which exhausted the available water power at Waltham. Eager to expand, the Associates scoured the rivers of New England for new sites. In 1821 Moody found a spot on the Merrimack River at East Chelmsford that seemed ideal. The river fell thirty-two feet in a series of rapids and there were two canals, one belonging to the Pawtucket Canal Company and another connecting to Boston. For about $70,000 the Associates purchased control of the Canal Company and much of the farmland along the banks.

From that transaction arose the largest and most unique mill town in the nation. In this novel enterprise the Associates seemed to depart from all precedent, but in reality they borrowed much from Waltham. A new corporation, the Merrimack Manufacturing Company, was formed with Nathan Appleton and Jackson as its largest stockholders. The circle of investors was widened to include other members of the Boston elite such as Daniel Webster and the Boott brothers, Kirk and John. Moody took some shares but his ambitions went no further; he was content to remain a mechanic for the rest of his life. The memory of Francis Cabot Lowell was honored by giving the new village his name.

The task of planning and overseeing construction was entrusted to Kirk Boott. The son of a wealthy Boston Anglophile, Boott's disposition and education straddled the Atlantic. He obtained a commission in the British army and fought under Wellington until the War of 1812 forced his resignation. For several years he studied engineering before returning home in 1817 to take up his father's business. A brilliant, energetic, imperious martinet, Boott leaped at the opportunity to take charge of

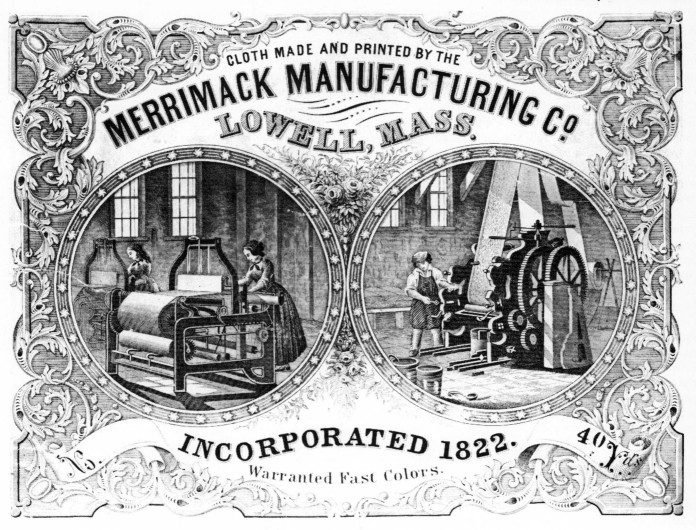

Merrimack trade label. Courtesy of the American Antiquarian Society.

the new enterprise. As Hannah Josephson observed, he became "its town planner, its architect, its engineer, its agent in charge of production, and the leading citizen of the new community."

The immensity of the challenge appealed to Boott's ordered mind. He recruited an army of 500 Irish laborers, installed them in a tent city, and began transforming a pastoral landscape into a mill town. A dam was put across the river, the old canal was widened, new locks were added, and two more canals were started. The mills bordered the river but not with the monotony of a wall. Three buildings stood parallel to the water and three at right angles in a grouping that reminded some of Harvard College. Trees and shrubs filled the space between them. The boarding houses, semi-detached dwellings two-and-a-half stories high separated by strips of lawn, were set on nearby streets along with the superintendents' houses and long brick tenements for male mechanics and their families. It was a standard of housing unknown to working people anywhere in the country or in Europe. For himself Boott designed a Georgian mansion ornamented with a formidable Ionic portico.

Lowell emerged as the nation's first planned industrial community largely because of Boott's care in realizing the overall concept. At Waltham the boarding houses had evolved piecemeal rather than as an integral part of the design. The Associates took care to avoid competition between the sites by confining Lowell's production to printed calicoes for the higher priced market. While Waltham remained profitable, it quickly took a back seat to the new works. The machine shop provided a true barometer of change. It not only produced machinery and water wheels for Lowell but also oversaw the construction of mills and housing. Shortly before Lowell began production in 1823, the Associates, in Nathan Appleton's words, "arranged to equalize the interest of all the stockholders in both companies" by formally purchasing Waltham's patterns and patent rights and securing Moody's transfer to Lowell. A year later the entire machine shop was moved to Lowell, leaving Waltham with only a maintenance facility.

3. NATIONAL CONSOLIDATION AND EXPANSION

The success of the Lowell plant prompted the Associates to unfold ambitious new plans. East Chelmsford offered abundant water power for an expanding industry; the sites were themselves a priceless asset. To use them profitably the Associates revived the old Canal Company under a new name, the Locks and Canals Company, and transferred to it all the land and water rights owned by the Merrimack Company. The latter then bought back its own mill sites and leased the water power it required. Thereafter the Locks and Canals Company sold land to other mill companies, leased water power to them at fixed rates per spindle, and built machinery, mills, and housing for them.

This organizational arrangement was as far advanced for the times as the rest of the Lowell concept. It brought the Associates handsome returns from the mills and enormous profits from the Locks and Canals Company, which averaged twenty-four percent in dividends between 1825 and 1845. As new companies like the Hamilton, Appleton, and Lowell corporations were formed, the Associates dispersed part of their stock among a widening network of fellow Brahmins. New partners entered their exclusive circle, including the Lawrence brothers, Abbott and Amos. Directories of the companies were so interlocked as to avoid any competition between them. In effect the Associates had created industrial harmony of the sort J.P. Morgan would later promote under the rubric "community of interest."

By 1836 the Associates had invested $6.2 million in eight major firms controlling twenty five-story mills with more than 6,000 employees. Lowell had grown into a town of 18,000 and acquired a city charter. It boasted ten churches, several banks to accommodate the virtue of thrift on the part of the workers, long rows of shops, a brewery, taverns, schools, and other appurtenances of progress. Worldwide attention had transformed it into a showcase. Apart from the influx of foreigners and other dignitaries, it had already been visited by a president the Associates despised (Andrew Jackson), and by a man who would try three times to become president (Henry Clay).

The Associates basked in this attention because they viewed themselves as benevolent, far-seeing men whose sense of duty extended far beyond wealth. To be sure the life blood of the New England economy flowed through their counting houses from their domination of banks, insurance companies, railroads, shipping, and mills elsewhere in New England. Yet such were the rigors of their stern Puritan consciences that for them acquisition was all consuming without being all fulfilling. Duty taught that no fortune was so ample that more was not required. Economist Thorstein Veblen later marveled at the "steadfast cupidity" that drove these men "under pain of moral turpitude, to acquire a 'competence,' and then unremittingly to augment any competence acquired."

Not content with being an economic and social aristocracy, the Associates extended their influence to politics, religion, education, and morality. Lowell fit their *raison d'etre* so ideally because it filled their coffers while at the same time reflecting their notion of an orderly, paternal community imbued with the proper values. The operatives knew their place, deferred to the leadership of the Associates, shared their values.

Or so they thought. In reality the homogeneity of Lowell had always been, like a painting, somewhere between an illusion and a contrivance. The planned community stopped just beyond the border of the mills and boarding houses. No provision had been made for the Irish who built the mills; they huddled together in a squalid settlement, the pioneer settlers of what became the town. Shopkeepers overwhelmed the space provided by the Associates until their stores and homes sprawled in the same indiscriminate manner of other towns. Gradually the growth of Lowell threw the Associates into the familiar role of dominant taxpayer demanding economy and reluctant to approve services that cost money.

While the town mushroomed in chaotic manner, the mills also underwent profound changes. Between 1836 and 1850 they doubled in number, reflecting the enormous growth of the industry as a whole. The press for space filled the breathing room around the original buildings with solid five-story walls that blotted out all view of the river. The rising tide of operatives overwhelmed the boarding houses and flooded into tenement neighborhoods, leading one observer to complain that "few cities are so crowded as Lowell."

During those same years the Associates had to contend with falling prices, a major depression, and by 1840, reduced dividends. Once docile stockholders grumbled about inefficiency and demanded changes. The Associates realized that to restore dividends to their accustomed levels, falling prices had to be offset by increased volume. This could be done by reducing wages on piecework and assigning each worker more looms or spindles to tend, practices known as speedup and stretch-out. The workday grew both harder and longer, about twelve-and-a-half hours, and working conditions harsher. As a final inspiration the Associates introduced the premium system whereby overseers and second hands received bonuses for getting more work than usual out of the operatives.

By 1860 the industrial utopia had given way to a grim mill town, and its operatives were fast sliding down into that abyss of misery and despair once reserved for the English working class. The Associates had lost their bloom as models of propriety and benevolence. Some called them "lords of the loom" and consigned them to the same terrace of Inferno as the South's "lords of the lash." How ironic it was for Nathan Appleton, the most beloved of souls with an unmatched reputation for philanthropy and civic virtue, that his mills were the first to be called "soulless corporations."

Robert Owen, that ardent utopian capitalist, had once declared, "I can make manufacturing pay without reducing those whom I employ to misery and moral degredation." The Associates had thought to do as much, but the lesson of buying cheap and selling dear was too deeply etched in their characters. The harsh truth was that benevolence cost money, and when the cost grew so dear as to compel a choice between ideals and dividends, idealism went the way of all utopias. Gradually their paternalism shriveled into the narrow, impersonal wage relationship typical of other factories. As for the workers, by 1845 they were, in Hannah

Josephson's words, "putting in more time under less agreeable working conditions, turning out more cloth and receiving less pay than when the industry was first established."

After that date they ceased even to be the same workers. The pride and joy of Lowell had always been its girls, those sturdy daughters of New England farms, but they were fast departing the mills. In their place came hordes of Irish immigrants fleeing the famine and desperate for work. Those who remained in the mills struggled helplessly against their declining position. Like Lowell itself the bloom had fled their cheeks, left them older and wiser about the ways of the world and its unfilled promises.

THE SECRET LIFE OF A DEVELOPING COUNTRY

(OURS)

JACK LARKIN

Jack Larkin is Chief Historian at Old Sturbridge Village. This article is adapted from his book *The Reshaping of Everyday Life in the United States, 1790–1840,* published by Harper & Row.

Forget your conventional picture of America in 1810. In the first half of the nineteenth century, we were not at all the placid, straitlaced, white-picket-fence nation we imagine ourselves to have been. By looking at the patterns of everyday life as recorded by contemporary foreign and native observers of the young republic and by asking the question that historians often didn't think to ask of another time—what were people really like? how did they greet one another on the street? how did they occupy their leisure time? what did they eat?—Jack Larkin brings us a detailed portrait of another America, an America that was so different from both our conception of its past life and its present-day reality as to seem a foreign country.

WE LOOKED DIFFERENT

Contemporary observers of early-nineteenth-century America left a fragmentary but nonetheless fascinating and revealing picture of the manner in which rich and poor, Southerner and Northerner, farmer and city dweller, freeman and slave presented themselves to the world. To begin with, a wide variety of characteristic facial expressions, gestures, and ways of carrying the body reflected the extraordinary regional and social diversity of the young republic.

When two farmers met in early-nineteenth-century New England, wrote Francis Underwood, of Enfield, Massachusetts, the author of a pioneering 1893 study of small-town life, "their greeting might seem to a stranger gruff or surly, since the facial muscles were so inexpressive, while, in fact, they were on excellent terms." In courtship and marriage, countrymen and women were equally constrained, with couples "wearing all unconsciously the masks which custom had prescribed; and the onlookers who did not know the secret would think them cold and indifferent."

Underwood noted a pervasive physical as well as emotional constraint among the people of Enfield; it was rooted, he thought, not only in the self-denying ethic of their Calvinist tradition but in the nature of their work. The great physical demands of unmechanized agriculture gave New England men, like other rural Americans, a distinctively ponderous gait and posture. Despite their strength and endurance, farmers were "heavy, awkward and slouching in movement" and walked with a "slow inclination from side to side."

Yankee visages were captured by itinerant New England portraitists during the early nineteenth century, as rural storekeepers, physicians, and master craftsmen became the first more or less ordinary Americans to have their portraits done. The portraits caught their caution and immobility of expression as well as recording their angular, long-jawed features, thus creating good collective likenesses of whole communities.

The Yankees, however, were not the stiffest Americans. Even by their own impassive standards, New Englanders found New York Dutchmen and Pennsylvania German farmers "clumsy and chill" or "dull and stolid." But the "wild Irish" stood out in America for precisely the opposite reason. They were not "chill" or "stolid" enough, but loud and expansive. Their expressiveness made Anglo-Americans uncomfortable.

The seemingly uncontrolled physical energy of American blacks left many whites ill at ease. Of the slaves celebrating at a plantation ball, it was "impossible to describe the things these people did with their bodies," Frances Kemble Butler, an English-born actress who married a Georgia slave owner, observed, "and above all with their faces. . . ." Blacks' expressions and gestures, their preference for rhythmic rather than rigid bodily mo-

American Comic Almanac, 1834

A dour face of the early 1800s.

tion, their alternations of energy and rest made no cultural sense to observers who saw only "antics and frolics," "laziness," or "savagery." Sometimes perceived as obsequious, childlike, and dependent, or sullen and inexpressive, slaves also wore masks—not "all unconsciously" as Northern farm folk did, but as part of their self-protective strategies for controlling what masters, mistresses, and other whites could know about their feelings and motivations.

American city dwellers, whose daily routines were driven by the quicker pace of commerce, were easy to distinguish from "heavy and slouching" farmers attuned to slow seasonal rhythms. New Yorkers, in particular, had already acquired their own characteristic body language. The clerks and commercial men who crowded Broadway, intent on their business, had a universal "contraction of the brow, knitting of the eyebrows, and compression of the lips . . . and a hurried walk." It was a popular American saying in the

I**n** marriage, couples wore "all unconsciously the masks which custom had prescribed."

1830s, reported Frederick Marryat, an Englishman who traveled extensively in the period, that "a New York merchant always walks as if he had a good dinner before him, and a bailiff behind him."

Northern and Southern farmers and city merchants alike, to say nothing of Irishmen and blacks, fell well short of the standard of genteel "bodily carriage" enshrined in both English and American etiquette books and the instructions of dancing masters: "flexibility in the arms . . . erectness in the spinal column . . . easy carriage of the head." It was the ideal of the British aristocracy, and Southern planters came closest to it, expressing the power of their class in the way they stood and moved. Slave owners accustomed to command, imbued with an ethic of honor and pride, at ease in the saddle, carried themselves more gracefully than men hardened by toil or preoccupied with commerce. Visiting Washington in 1835, the Englishwoman Harriet Martineau contrasted not the politics but the postures of Northern and Southern congressmen. She marked the confident bearing, the "ease and frank courtesy . . . with an occasional touch of arrogance" of the slaveholders alongside the "cautious . . . and too deferential air of the members of the North." She could recognize a New Englander "in the open air," she claimed, "by his deprecatory walk."

Local inhabitants' faces became more open, travelers observed, as one went west. Nathaniel Hawthorne found a dramatic contrast in public appearances only a few days' travel west of Boston. "The people out here," in New York State just west of the Berkshires, he confided to his notebook in 1839, "show out their character much more strongly than they do with us," in his native eastern Massachusetts. He compared the "quiet, silent, dull decency . . . in our public assemblages" with Westerners' wider gamut of expressiveness, "mirth, anger, eccentricity, all showing themselves freely." Westerners in general, the clergyman and publicist Henry Ward Beecher observed, had "far more freedom of manners, and more frankness and spontaneous geniality" than did the city or country people of the New England and Middle Atlantic states, as did the "odd mortals that wander in from the western border," that Martineau observed in Washington's political population.

WE WERE DIRTY AND SMELLY

Early-nineteenth-century Americans lived in a world of dirt, insects, and pungent smells. Farmyards were strewn with animal wastes, and farmers wore manure-spattered boots and trousers everywhere. Men's and women's working clothes alike were often stiff with

Freely moving pigs fed on the city's trash.

dirt and dried sweat, and men's shirts were often stained with "yellow rivulets" of tobacco juice. The locations of privies were all too obvious on warm or windy days. Unemptied chamber pots advertised their presence. Wet baby "napkins," today's diapers, were not immediately washed but simply put by the fire to dry. Vats of "chamber lye"—highly concentrated urine used for cleaning type or degreasing wool—perfumed all printing offices and many households. "The breath of that fiery bar-room," as Underwood described a country tavern, "was overpowering. The odors of the hostlers' boots, redolent of fish-oil and tallow, and of buffalo-robes and horse-blankets, the latter reminiscent of equine ammonia, almost got the better of the all-pervading fumes of spirits and tobacco."

Densely populated, but poorly cleaned and drained, America's cities were often far more noisome than its farmyards. Horse manure thickly covered city streets, and few neighborhoods were free from the spreading stench of tanneries and slaughterhouses. New York City accumulated so much refuse that it was generally believed the actual surfaces of the streets had not been seen for decades. During her stay in Cincinnati, the English writer Frances Trollope followed the practice of the vast majority of American city housewives when she threw her household "slops"—refuse food and dirty dishwater—out into the street. An irate neighbor soon informed her that municipal ordinances forbade "throwing such things at the sides of the streets" as she had done; "they must just all be cast right into the middle and the pigs soon takes them off." In most cities hundreds, sometimes thousands, of free-roaming pigs scavenged the garbage; one exception was Charleston, South Carolina, where buzzards patrolled the streets. By converting garbage into pork, pigs kept city streets cleaner than they would otherwise have been, but the pigs themselves befouled the streets and those who ate their meat—primarily poor families—ran greater than usual risks of infection.

PRIVY MATTERS

The most visible symbols of early American sanitation were privies or "necessary houses." But Americans did not always use them; many rural householders simply took to the closest available patch of woods or brush. However, in more densely settled communities and in regions with cold winters, privies were in widespread use. They were not usually put in out-of-the-way locations. The fashion of some Northern farm families, according to Robert B. Thomas's *Farmer's Almanack* in 1826, had long been to have their "necessary planted in a garden or other conspicuous place." Other countryfolk went even

Chamber pots were dumped in the streets.

further in turning human wastes to agricultural account and built their outhouses "within the territory of a hog yard, that the swine may root and ruminate and devour the nastiness thereof." Thomas was a long-standing critic of primitive manners in the countryside and roundly condemned these traditional sanitary arrangements as demonstrating a "want of taste, decency, and propriety." The better-arranged necessaries of the prosperous emptied into vaults that could be opened and cleaned out. The dripping horse-drawn carts of the "nocturnal goldfinders," who emptied the vaults and took their loads out for burial or water disposal—"night soil" was almost never used as manure—were a familiar part of nighttime traffic on city streets.

The humblest pieces of American household furniture were the chamber pots that allowed people to avoid dark and often cold nighttime journeys outdoors. Kept under beds or in corners of rooms, "chambers" were used primarily upon retiring and arising. Collecting, emptying, and cleaning them remained an unspoken, daily part of every housewife's routine.

Nineteenth-century inventory takers became considerably more reticent about naming chamber pots than their predecessors, usually lumping them with miscellaneous "crockery," but most households probably had a couple of chamber pots; genteel families reached the optimum of one for each bedchamber. English-made ceramic pots had become cheap enough by 1820 that few American families within the reach of commerce needed to go without one. "Without a pot to piss in" was a vulgar tag of long standing for extreme poverty; those poorest households without one, perhaps more common in the warm South, used the outdoors at all times and seasons.

The most decorous way for householders to deal with chamber-pot wastes accumulated during the night was to throw them down the privy hole. But more casual and unsavory methods of disposal were still in wide use. Farm families often dumped their chamber pots out the most convenient door or window. In densely settled communities like York, Pennsylvania, the results could be more serious. In 1801, the York diarist Lewis Miller drew and then described an event in North George Street when "Mr. Day an English man [as the German-American Miller was quick to point out] had a bad practice by pouring out of the upper window his filthiness . . . one day came the discharge . . . on a man and wife going to a wedding, her silk dress was fouled."

LETTING THE BEDBUGS BITE

Sleeping accommodations in American country taverns were often dirty and insect-ridden. The eighteenth-century observer of American life Isaac Weld saw "filthy beds swarming with bugs" in 1794; in 1840 Charles Dickens noted "a sort of game not on the bill of fare." Complaints increased in intensity as travelers went south or west. Tavern beds were uniquely vulnerable to infestation by whatever insect guests travelers brought with them. The bedding of most American households was surely less foul. Yet it was dirty enough. New England farmers were still too often "tormented all night by bed bugs," complained *The Farmer's Almanack* in 1837, and books of domestic advice contained extensive instructions on removing them from feather beds and straw ticks.

Journeying between Washington and New Orleans in 1828, Margaret Hall, a well-to-do and cultivated Scottish woman, became far more familiar with intimate insect life than she had ever

We were not "clean and decent" by today's standards; washing was difficult.

been in the genteel houses of London or Edinburgh. Her letters home, never intended for publication, gave a graphic and unsparing account of American sanitary conditions. After sleeping in a succession of beds with the "usual complement of fleas and bugs," she and her party had themselves become infested: "We bring

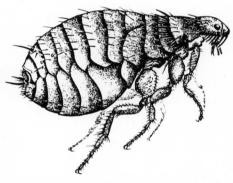

Insects infested many American beds.

them along with us in our clothes and when I undress I find them crawling on my skin, nasty wretches." New and distasteful to her, such discoveries were commonplace among the ordinary folk with whom she lodged. The American children she saw on her Southern journey were "kept in such a state of filth," with clothes "dirty and slovenly to a degree," but this was "nothing in comparison with their heads . . . [which] are absolutely crawling!" In New Orleans she observed women picking through children's heads for lice, "catching them according to the method depicted in an engraving of a similar proceeding in the streets of Naples."

BIRTH OF THE BATH

Americans were not "clean and decent" by today's standards, and it was virtually impossible that they should be. The furnishings and use of rooms in most American houses made more than the most elementary washing difficult. In a New England farmer's household, wrote Underwood, each household member would "go down to the 'sink' in the lean-to, next to the kitchen, fortunate if he had not to break ice in order to wash his face and hands, or more fortunate if a little warm water was poured into his basin from the kettle swung over the kitchen fire." Even in the comfortable household of the prominent minister Lyman Beecher in Litchfield, Connecticut, around 1815, all family members washed in the kitchen, using a stone sink and "a couple of basins."

Southerners washed in their detached kitchens or, like Westerners in warm weather, washed outside, "at the doors . . . or at the wells" of their houses. Using basins and sinks outdoors or in full view of others, most Americans found anything more than "washing the face and hands once a-day," usually in cold water, difficult, even unthinkable. Most men and women also washed without soap, reserving it for laundering clothes; instead they used a brisk rubbing with a coarse towel to scrub the dirt off their skins.

Gradually the practice of complete bathing spread beyond the topmost levels of American society and into smaller towns and villages. This became possible as families moved washing equipment out of kitchens and into bedchambers, from shared space to space that could be made private. As more prosperous households furnished one or two of their chambers with washing equipment—a washstand, a basin, and a ewer, or large-mouthed pitcher—family members could shut the chamber door, undress,

AMERICAN ANTIQUARIAN SOCIETY

Davy Crockett, like many Americans, preferred to wash himself in the great outdoors.

and wash themselves completely. The daughters of the Larcom family, living in Lowell, Massachusetts, in the late 1830s, began to bathe in a bedchamber in this way; Lucy Larcom described how her oldest sister started to take "a full cold bath every morning before she went to her work . . . in a room without a fire," and the other young Larcoms "did the same whenever we could be resolute enough." By the 1830s better city hotels and even some country taverns were providing individual basins and pitchers in their rooms.

At a far remove from "primitive manners" and "bad practices" was the genteel ideal of domestic sanitation embodied in the "chamber sets" — matching basin and ewer for private bathing, a cup for brushing the teeth, and a chamber pot with cover to minimize odor and spillage — that American stores were beginning to stock. By 1840 a significant minority of American households owned chamber sets and washstands to hold them in their bedchambers. For a handful there was the very faint dawning of an entirely new age of sanitary arrangements. In 1829 the new Tremont House hotel in Boston offered its patrons indoor plumbing: eight chambers with bathtubs and eight "water closets." In New York City and Philadelphia, which had developed rudimentary public water systems, a few wealthy households had water taps and, more rarely, water closets by the 1830s. For all others flush toilets and

bathtubs remained far in the future.

The American people moved very slowly toward cleanliness. In "the backcountry at the present day," commented the fastidious author of the *Lady's Book* in 1836, custom still "requires that everyone should wash at the pump in the yard, or at the sink in the kitchen." Writing in 1846, the physician and health reformer William Alcott rejoiced that to "wash the surface of the whole body in water daily" had now been accepted as a genteel standard of personal cleanliness. But, he added, there were "multitudes who pass for models of neatness and cleanliness, who do not perform this work for themselves half a dozen times — nay once — a year." As the better-off became cleaner than ever before, the poor stayed dirty.

WE DRANK AND FOUGHT WHENEVER WE COULD

In the early part of the century America was a bawdy, hard-edged, and violent land. We drank more than we ever had before or ever would again. We smoked and chewed tobacco like addicts and fought and quarreled on the flimsiest pretexts. The tavern was the most im-

portant gateway to the primarily male world of drink and disorder: in sight of the village church in most American communities, observed Daniel Drake, a Cincinnati physician who wrote a reminiscence of his Kentucky boyhood, stood the village tavern, and the two structures "did in fact represent two great opposing principles."

The great majority of American men in every region were taverngoers. The printed street directories of American cities listed tavernkeepers in staggering numbers, and even the best-churched parts of New England could show more "licensed houses" than meetinghouses. In 1827 the fast-growing city of Rochester, New York, with a population of approximately eight thousand, had nearly one hundred establishments licensed to sell liquor, or one for every eighty inhabitants.

America's most important centers of male sociability, taverns were often the scene of excited gaming and vicious fights and always of hard drinking, heavy smoking, and an enormous amount of alcohol-stimulated talk. City men came to their neighborhood taverns daily, and "tavern haunting, tippling, and gaming," as Samuel Goodrich, a New England historian and publisher, remembered, "were the chief resources of men in the dead and dreary winter months" in the countryside.

City taverns catered to clienteles of different classes: sordid sailors' grogshops near the waterfront were rife with brawling and prostitution; neighborhood taverns and liquor-selling groceries were visited by craftsmen and clerks; well-appointed and relatively decorous places were favored by substantial merchants. Taverns on busy

In the 1820s America was a bawdy and violent land. We drank more than we ever would again.

Backwoodsmen have a "knock down" in this 1841 woodcut from *Crockett's Almanack.*

highways often specialized in teamsters or stage passengers, while country inns took their patrons as they came.

Taverns accommodated women as travelers, but their barroom clienteles were almost exclusively male. Apart from the dockside dives frequented by prostitutes, or the liquor-selling groceries of poor city neighborhoods, women rarely drank in public.

Gambling was a substantial preoccupation for many male citizens of the early republic. Men played billiards at tavern tables for money stakes. They threw dice in "hazard," slamming the dice boxes down so hard and so often that tavern tables wore the characteristic scars of their play. Even more often Americans sat down to cards, playing brag, similar to modern-day poker, or an elaborate table game called faro. Outdoors they wagered with each other on horse races or bet on cockfights and wrestling matches.

Drink permeated and propelled the social world of early-nineteenth-century America—first as an unquestioned presence and later as a serious and divisive problem. "Liquor at that time," recalled the builder and architect Elbridge Boyden, "was used as commonly as the food we ate." Before 1820 the vast majority of Americans considered alcohol an essential stimulant to exertion as well as a symbol of hospitality and fellowship. Like the Kentuckians with whom Daniel Drake grew

up, they "regarded it as a duty to their families and visitors . . . to keep the bottle well replenished." Weddings, funerals, frolics, even a casual "gathering of two or three neighbors for an evening's social chat" required the obligatory "spirituous liquor"—rum, whiskey, or gin—"at all seasons and on all occasions."

Northern householders drank hard cider as their common table beverage, and all ages drank it freely. Dramming—taking a fortifying glass in the forenoon and again in the afternoon—was part of the daily regimen of many men. Clergymen took sustaining libations between services, lawyers before going to court, and physicians at their patients' bedsides. To raise a barn or get through a long day's haying without fortifying drink seemed a virtual impossibility. Slaves enjoyed hard drinking at festival times and at Saturday-night barbecues as much as any of their countrymen. But of all Americans they probably drank the least on a daily basis because their masters could

To get through a long day's haying without drink seemed an impossibility.

usually control their access to liquor.

In Parma, Ohio, in the mid-1820s, Lyndon Freeman, a farmer, and his brothers were used to seeing men "in their cups" and passed them by without comment. But one dark and rainy night they discovered something far more shocking, "nothing less than a *woman beastly drunk* . . . with a flask of whiskey by her side." American women drank as well as men, but usually much less heavily. They were more likely to make themselves "tipsy" with hard cider and alcohol-containing patent medicines than to become inebriated with rum or whiskey. Temperance advocates in the late 1820s estimated that men consumed fifteen times the volume of distilled spirits that women did; this may have been a considerable exaggeration, but there was a great dif-

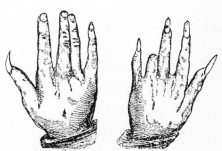

The hands of a celebrated gouger.

ference in drinking habits between the sexes. Americans traditionally found drunkenness tolerable and forgivable in men but deeply shameful in women.

By almost any standard, Americans drank not only nearly universally but in large quantities. Their yearly consumption at the time of the Revolution has been estimated at the equivalent of three and one-half gallons of pure two-hundred-proof alcohol for each person. After 1790 American men began to drink even more. By the late 1820s their imbibing had risen to an all-time high of almost four gallons per capita.

Along with drinking went fighting. Americans fought often and with great relish. York, Pennsylvania, for example, was a peaceable place as American communities went, but the Miller and Weaver families had a long-running quarrel. It had begun in 1800 when the Millers found young George Weaver stealing apples in their yard and punished him by "throwing him over the fence," injuring him painfully. Over the years hostilities broke out periodically. Lewis Miller remembered walking down the street as a teenaged boy and meeting Mrs. Weaver, who drenched him with the bucket of water she was carrying. He retaliated by "turning about and giving her a kick, laughing at her, this is for your politeness." Other York households had their quarrels too; in "a general fight on Beaver Street," Mistress Hess and Mistress Forsch tore each other's caps from their heads. Their husbands and then the neighbors interfered, and "all of them had a knock down."

When Peter Lung's wife, Abigail, refused "to get up and dig some potatoes" for supper from the yard of their

In
isolated areas it was not uncommon to meet men who had lost an eye in a fight.

small house, the Hartford, Connecticut, laborer recalled in his confession, he "kicked her on the side . . . then gave her a violent push" and went out to dig the potatoes himself. He returned and "again kicked her against the shoulder and neck." Both had been drinking, and loud arguments and blows within the Lung household, as in many others, were routine. But this time the outcome was not. Alice Lung was dead the next day, and Peter Lung was arrested, tried, and hanged for murder in 1815.

In the most isolated, least literate and commercialized parts of the United States, it was "by no means uncommon," wrote Isaac Weld, "to meet with those who have lost an eye in a combat, and there are men who pride themselves upon the dexterity with which they can scoop one out. This is called *gouging*."

THE SLAVE'S LOT

Slaves wrestled among themselves, sometimes fought one another bitterly over quarrels in the quarters, and even at times stood up to the vastly superior force of masters and overseers. They rarely, if ever, reduced themselves to the ferocity of eye gouging. White Southerners lived with a pervasive fear of the violent potential of their slaves, and the Nat Turner uprising in Virginia in 1831, when a party of slaves rebelled and killed whites before being overcome, gave rise to tighter and harsher controls. But in daily reality slaves had far more to fear from their masters.

Margaret Hall was no proponent of abolition and had little sympathy for black Americans. Yet in her travels south she confronted incidents of what she ironically called the "good treatment of slaves" that were impossible to ignore. At a country tavern in Georgia, she summoned the slave chambermaid, but "she could not come" because "the mistress had been whipping her and she was not fit to be seen. Next morning she made her appearance with her face marked in several places by the cuts of the cowskin and her neck handkerchief covered with spots of blood."

Southern stores were very much like Northern ones, Francis Kemble Butler observed, except that they stocked "negro-whips" and "mantraps" on their shelves. A few slaves were never beaten at all, and for most, whippings were not a daily or weekly occurrence. But they were, of all Americans, by far the most vulnerable to violence. All

A white master takes a baby from its mother.

slaves had, as William Wells Brown, an ex-slave himself, said, often "heard the crack of the whip, and the screams of the slave" and knew that they were never more than a white man's or woman's whim away from a beating. With masters' unchecked power came worse than whipping: the mutilating punishments of the old penal law including branding, ear cropping, and even occasionally castration and burning alive as penalties for severe offenses. In public places or along the road blacks were also subject to casual kicks, shoves, and cuffs, for which they could retaliate only at great peril. "Six or seven feet in length, made of cowhide, with a platted wire on the end of it," as Brown recalled it, the negro-whip, for sale in most stores and brandished by masters and overseers in the fields, stood for a pervasive climate of force and intimidation.

PUBLIC PUNISHMENT

The penal codes of the American states were far less bloodthirsty than those of England. Capital punishment was not often imposed on whites for crimes other than murder. Yet at the beginning of the nineteenth century many criminal offenses were punished by the public infliction of pain and suffering. "The whipping post and stocks stood on the green near the meetinghouse" in most of the towns of New England and near courthouses everywhere. In Massachusetts before 1805 a counterfeiter was liable to have an ear cut off, and a forger to have one cropped or partially amputated, after spending an hour in the pillory. A criminal convicted of manslaughter was set up on the gallows to have his forehead branded with a letter M. In most jurisdictions town officials flogged petty thieves as punishment for their crime. In New Haven, Connecticut, around 1810, Charles Fowler, a local historian, recalled seeing the "admiring students of [Yale] college" gathered

A man in the stocks awaits a flogging.

around to watch petty criminals receive "five or ten lashes . . . with a rawhide whip."

Throughout the United States public hangings brought enormous crowds to the seats of justice and sometimes seemed like brutal festivals. Thousands of spectators arrived to pack the streets of courthouse towns. On the day of a hanging near Mount Holly, New Jersey, in the 1820s, the scene was that of a holiday: "around the place in every direction were the assembled multitudes — some in tents, and by-wagons, engaged in gambling and other vices of the sort, in open day." In order to accommodate the throngs, hangings were usually held not in the public square but on the outskirts of town. The gallows erected on a hill or set up at the bottom of a natural amphitheater allowed onlookers an unobstructed view. A reprieve or stay of execution might disappoint a crowd intent on witnessing the deadly drama and provoke a riot, as it did in Pembroke, New Hampshire, in 1834.

RISE OF RESPECTABILITY

At a drunkard's funeral in Enfield, Massachusetts, in the 1830s — the man had strayed out of the road while walking home and fallen over a cliff, "his stiffened fingers still grasping the handle of the jug" — Rev. Sumner G. Clapp, the Congregationalist minister of Enfield, mounted a log by the woodpile and preached the town's first temperance

sermon before a crowd full of hardened drinkers. In this way Clapp began a campaign to "civilize" the manners of his parishioners, and "before many years there was a great change in the town; the incorrigible were removed by death, and others took warning." Drinking declined sharply, and along with it went "a general reform in conduct."

Although it remained a powerful force in many parts of the United States, the American way of drunkenness began to lose ground as early as the mid-1820s. The powerful upsurge in liquor consumption had provoked a powerful reaction, an unprecedented attack on all forms of drink that gathered momentum in the Northeast. Some New England clergymen had been campaigning in their own communities as early as 1810, but their concerns took on organized impetus with the

Liquor consumption provoked a powerful reaction: an unprecedented attack on drinking.

founding of the American Temperance Society in 1826. Energized in part by a concern for social order, in part by evangelical piety, temperance reformers popularized a radically new way of looking at alcohol. The "good creature" became "demon rum"; prominent physicians and writers on physiology, like Benjamin Rush, told Americans that alcohol, traditionally considered healthy and fortifying, was actually a physical and moral poison. National and state societies distributed anti-liquor tracts, at first calling for moderation in drink but increasingly demanding total abstinence from alcohol.

To a surprising degree these aggressive temperance campaigns worked. By 1840 the consumption of alcohol had declined by more than two-thirds, from close to four gallons per person each year to less than one and one-

half. Country storekeepers gave up the sale of spirits, local authorities limited the number of tavern licenses, and farmers even abandoned hard cider and cut down their apple orchards. The shift to temperance was a striking transformation in the everyday habits of an enormous number of Americans. "A great, though silent change," in Horace Greeley's words, had been "wrought in public sentiment."

But although the "great change" affected some Americans everywhere, it had a very uneven impact. Organized temperance reform was sharply delimited by geography. Temperance societies were enormously powerful in New England and western New York and numerous in eastern New York, New Jersey, and Pennsylvania. More than three-fourths of all recorded temperance pledges came from these states. In the South and West, and in the laborers' and artisans' neighborhoods of the cities, the campaign against drink was much weaker. In many places drinking ways survived and even flourished, but as individuals and families came under the influence of militant evangelical piety, their "men of business and sobriety" increased gradually in number. As liquor grew "unfashionable in the country," Greeley noted, Americans who wanted to drink and carouse turned increasingly to the cities, "where no one's deeds or ways are observed or much regarded."

Closely linked as they were to drink, such diversions as gambling, racing, and blood sports also fell to the same forces of change. In the central Massachusetts region that George Davis, a lawyer in Sturbridge, knew well, until 1820 or so gaming had "continued to prevail, more and more extensively." After that "a blessed change had succeeded," overturning the scenes of high-stakes dice and card games that he knew in his young manhood. Impelled by a new perception of its "pernicious effects," local leaders gave it up and placed "men of respectable standing" firmly in opposition. Racecourses were abandoned and "planted to corn." Likewise, "bear-baiting, cock-fighting, and other cruel amusements" began to dwindle in the Northern countryside.

AMERICAN ANTIQUARIAN SOCIETY

A popular temperance print of 1826 shows a drunkard's progress from a morning dram to loss of his home.

Elsewhere the rude life of the tavern and "cruel amusements" remained widespread, but some of their excesses of "sin and shame" did diminish gradually.

Over the first four decades of the nineteenth century the American people increasingly made churchgoing an obligatory ritual. The proportion of families affiliated with a local church or Methodist circuit rose dramatically, particularly after 1820, and there were fewer stretches of the wholly pagan, unchurched territory that travelers had noted around 1800. "Since 1830," maintained Emerson Davis in his retrospect of America, *The Half Century*, ". . . the friends of the Sabbath have been gaining ground. . . . In 1800, good men slumbered over the desecration of the Sabbath. They have since awoke. . . ." The number of Sunday mails declined, and the campaign to eliminate the delivery of mail on the Sabbath entirely grew stronger. "In the smaller cities and towns," wrote Mrs. Trollope in 1832, worship and "prayer meetings" had come to "take the place of almost all other amusements." There were still communities near the edge of settlement where a traveler would "rarely find either churches or chapels, prayer or preacher," but it was the working-class neighborhoods of America's larger cities that were increasingly the chief strongholds of "Sunday dissipation" and "Sabbath-breaking."

Whipping and the pillory, with their attentive audiences, began to disap-

pear from the statute book, to be replaced by terms of imprisonment in another new American institution, the state penitentiary. Beginning with Pennsylvania's abolition of flogging in 1790 and Massachusetts's elimination of mutilating punishments in 1805, several American states gradually accepted John Hancock's view of 1796 that "mutilating or lacerating the body" was less an effective punishment than "an indignity to human nature." Connecticut's town constables whipped petty criminals for the last time in 1828.

Slaveholding states were far slower to change their provisions for public punishment. The whipping and mutilation of blacks may have become a little less ferocious over the decades, but the whip remained the essential instrument of punishment and discipline. "The secret of our success," thought a slave owner, looking back after emancipation, had been "the great motive power contained in that little instrument." Delaware achieved notoriety by keeping flogging on the books for whites and blacks alike through most of the twentieth century.

Although there were important stirrings of sentiment against capital punishment, all American states continued to execute convicted murders before the mid-1840s. Public hangings never lost their drawing power. But a number of American public officials began to abandon the long-standing view of executions as instructive communal rituals. They saw the crowd's holiday

mood and eager participation as sharing too much in the condemned killer's own brutality. Starting with Pennsylvania, New York, and Massachusetts in the mid-1830s, several state legislatures voted to take executions away from the crowd, out of the public realm. Sheriffs began to carry out death sentences behind the walls of the jailyard, before a small assembly of representative onlookers. Other states clung much longer to tradition and continued public executions into the twentieth century.

SEX LIFE OF THE NATIVES

Early-nineteenth-century Americans were more licentious than we ordinarily imagine them to be.

"On the 20th day of July" in 1830, Harriet Winter, a young woman working as a domestic in Joseph Dunham's household in Brimfield, Massachusetts, "was gathering raspberries" in a field west of the house. "Near the close of day," Charles Phelps, a farm laborer then living in the town, "came to the field where she was," and in the gathering dusk they made love—and, Justice of the Peace Asa Lincoln added in his account, "it was the Sabbath." American communities did not usually document their inhabitants' amorous rendezvous, and Harriet's tryst with Charles was a commonplace event in early-nineteenth-century America. It escaped historical oblivion because she was unlucky, less in becoming pregnant than in Charles's refusal to marry her. Asa Lincoln did not approve of Sabbath evening indiscretions, but he was not pursuing Harriet for immorality. He was concerned instead with economic responsibility for the child. Thus he interrogated Harriet about the baby's father—while she was in labor, as was the long-customary practice—in order to force Charles to contribute to the maintenance of the child, who was going to be "born a bastard and chargeable to the town."

Some foreign travelers found that the Americans they met were reluctant to admit that such things happened in the United States. They were remarkably straitlaced about sexual matters in public and eager to insist upon the "purity" of their manners. But to take such protestations at face value, the unusually candid Englishman Frederick Marryat thought, would be "to suppose that human nature is not the same everywhere."

The well-organized birth and marriage records of a number of American communities reveal that in late-eighteenth-century America pregnancy was frequently the prelude to marriage. The proportion of brides who were pregnant at the time of their weddings had been rising since the late seventeenth century and peaked in the turbulent decades during and after the Revolution. In the 1780s and 1790s nearly one-third of rural New England's brides were already with child. The frequency of sexual intercourse before marriage was surely higher, since some couples would have escaped early pregnancy. For many couples sexual relations were part of serious courtship. Premarital pregnancies in late-eighteenth-century Dedham, Massachusetts, observed the local historian Erastus Worthington in 1828, were occasioned by "the custom then prevalent of females admitting young men to their beds, who sought their company in marriage."

Pregnancies usually simply accelerated a marriage that would have taken

Lovers await Cupid's dart in this woodcut.

place in any case, but community and parental pressure worked strongly to assure it. Most rural communities simply accepted the "early" pregnancies that marked so many marriages, although in Hingham, Massachusetts, tax records suggest that the families of well-to-do brides were considerably less generous to couples who had had "early babies" than to those who had avoided pregnancy.

"Bundling very much abounds," wrote the anonymous author of "A New Bundling Song," still circulating in Boston in 1812, "in many parts in country towns." Noah Webster's first *Dictionary of the American Language* defined it as the custom that allowed couples "to sleep on the same bed without undressing"—with, a later commentator added, "the shared understanding that innocent endearments should not be exceeded." Folklore and local tradition, from Maine south to New York, had American mothers tucking bundling couples into bed with special chastity-protecting garments for the young woman or a "bundling

Early-
nineteenth-century
Americans were more
licentious than we
imagine them to be.

board" to separate them.

In actuality, if bundling had been intended to allow courting couples privacy and emotional intimacy but not sexual contact, it clearly failed. Couples may have begun with bundling, but as courtship advanced, they clearly pushed beyond its restraints, like the "bundling maid" in "A New Bundling Song" who would "sometimes say when she lies down/She can't be cumbered with a gown."

Young black men and women shared American whites' freedom in courtship and sexuality and sometimes exceeded it. Echoing the cultural traditions of West Africa, and reflecting the fact that their marriages were not given legal status and security, slave communities were somewhat more tolerant and accepting of sex before marriage.

Gradations of color and facial features among the slaves were testimony that "thousands," as the abolitionist and former slave Frederick Douglass wrote, were "ushered into the world annually, who, like myself, owe their existence to white fathers, and those fathers most frequently their own masters." Sex crossed the boundaries of race and servitude more often than slavery's defenders wanted to admit, if less frequently than the most outspoken abolitionists claimed. Slave women had little protection from whatever sexual demands masters or overseers might make, so that rapes, short liaisons, and long-term "concubinage" all were part of plantation life.

As Nathaniel Hawthorne stood talking with a group of men on the porch of a tavern in Augusta, Maine, in 1836, a young man "in a laborer's dress" came up and asked if anyone knew the whereabouts of Mary Ann Russell. "Do you want to use her?" asked one of the bystanders. Mary Ann was, in fact, the young laborer's wife, but she had left him and their child in Portland to become "one of a knot of whores." A few years earlier the young men of York, Pennsylvania, made up a party for "overturning and pulling to the ground" Eve Geese's "shameful house" of prostitution in Queen Street. The frightened women fled out the back door as the chimney collapsed around them; the apprentices and young journeymen—many of whom had surely been previous customers—were treated by local officials "to wine, for the good work."

From medium-sized towns like Augusta and York to great cities, poor American women were sometimes pulled into a darker, harsher sexual world, one of vulnerability, exploitation, and commerce. Many prostitutes took up their trade out of poverty and domestic disaster. A young widow or a country girl arrived in the city and, thrown on her own resources, often faced desperate economic choices because most women's work paid too poorly to provide decent food, clothing, and shelter, while other women sought excitement and independence from their families.

As cities grew, and changes in transportation involved more men in long-distance travel, prostitution became more visible. Men of all ages, married and unmarried, from city lawyers to visiting country storekeepers to sailors on the docks, turned to brothels for sexual release, but most of the customers were young men, living away from home and unlikely to marry until their late twenties. Sexual commerce in New York City was elaborately graded by price and the economic status of clients, from the "parlor houses" situated not far from the city's best hotels on Broadway to the more numerous and moderately priced houses that drew artisans and clerks, and finally to the broken and dissipated women who haunted dockside grogshops in the Five Points neighborhood.

From New Orleans to Boston, city theaters were important sexual marketplaces. Men often bought tickets less to see the performance than to make assignations with the prostitutes, who sat by custom in the topmost gallery of seats. The women usually received free admission from theater managers, who claimed that they could not stay in business without the male theatergoers drawn by the "guilty third tier."

Most Americans—and the American common law—still did not regard abortion as a crime until the fetus had "quickened" or began to move perceptibly in the womb. Books of medical ad-

vice actually contained prescriptions for bringing on delayed menstrual periods, which would also produce an abortion if the woman happened to be pregnant. They suggested heavy doses of purgatives that created violent cramps, powerful douches, or extreme kinds of physical activity, like the "violent exercise, raising great weights . . . strokes on the belly . . . [and] falls" noted in William Buchan's *Domestic Medicine*, a manual read widely through the 1820s. Women's folklore echoed most of these prescriptions and added others, particularly the use of two American herbal preparations—savin, or the extract of juniper berries, and Seneca snakeroot—as abortion-producing drugs. They were dangerous procedures but sometimes effective.

REINING IN THE PASSIONS

Starting at the turn of the nineteenth century, the sexual lives of many Americans began to change, shaped by a growing insistence on control: reining in the passions in courtship, limiting family size, and even redefining male and female sexual desire.

Bundling was already on the wane in rural America before 1800; by the 1820s it was written about as a rare and antique custom. It had ceased, thought an elderly man from East Haddam, Connecticut, "as a consequence of education and refinement." Decade by decade the proportion of young women who had conceived a child before marriage declined. In most of the towns of New England the rate had dropped from nearly one pregnant bride in three to one in five or six by 1840; in some places prenuptial pregnancy dropped to 5 percent. For many young Americans this marked the acceptance of new limits on sexual behavior, imposed not by their parents or other authorities in their communities

Every Body's Album (PHILADELPHIA, 1836)

Just say no: Quaker lovers hold back.

but by themselves.

These young men and women were not more closely supervised by their parents than earlier generations had been; in fact, they had more mobility and greater freedom. The couples that courted in the new style put a far greater emphasis on control of the passions. For some of them—young Northern merchants and professional men and their intended brides—revealing love letters have survived for the years after 1820. Their intimate correspondence reveals that they did not give up sexual expression but gave it new boundaries, reserving sexual intercourse for marriage. Many of them were marrying later than their parents, often living through long engagements while the husband-to-be strove to establish his place in the world. They chose not to risk a pregnancy that would precipitate them into an early marriage.

Many American husbands and wives were also breaking with tradition as they began to limit the size of their families. Clearly, married couples were renegotiating the terms of their sexual lives together, but they remained resolutely silent about how they did it. In the first two decades of the nineteenth century, they almost certainly set about avoiding childbirth through abstinence; coitus interruptus, or male withdrawal; and perhaps sometimes abortion. These contraceptive techniques had long been traditional in preindustrial Europe, although previously little used in America.

As they entered the 1830s, Americans had their first opportunity to learn, at least in print, about more effective or less self-denying forms of birth control. They could read reasonably inexpensive editions of the first works on contraception published in the United States: Robert Dale Owen's *Moral Physiology* of 1831 and Dr. Charles Knowlton's *The Fruits of Philosophy* of 1832. Both authors frankly described the full range of contraceptive techniques, although they solemnly rejected physical intervention in the sexual act and recommended only douching after intercourse and coitus interruptus. Official opinion, legal and religious, was deeply hostile. Knowlton, who had trained as a physician in rural Massachusetts, was prosecuted in three different counties for obscenity, convicted once, and imprisoned for three months.

But both works found substantial numbers of Americans eager to read them. By 1839 each book had gone through nine editions, putting a combined total of twenty to thirty thousand copies in circulation. An American physician could write in 1850 that contraception had "been of late years so much talked of." Greater knowledge about contraception surely played a part in the continuing decline of the American birthrate after 1830.

New ways of thinking about sexuality emerged that stressed control and channeling of the passions. Into the 1820s almost all Americans would have subscribed to the commonplace notion that sex, within proper social confines, was enjoyable and healthy and that prolonged sexual abstinence could be injurious to health. They also would have assumed that women had powerful sexual drives.

Starting with his "Lecture to Young Men on Chastity" in 1832, Sylvester Graham articulated very different counsels

The sexual lives of Americans began to change, reshaped by a new emphasis on self-control.

about health and sex. Sexual indulgence, he argued, was not only morally suspect but psychologically and physiologically risky. The sexual overstimulation involved in young men's lives produced anxiety and nervous disorders, "a shocking state of debility and excessive irritability." The remedy was diet, exercise, and a regular routine that pulled the mind away from animal lusts. Medical writings that discussed the evils of masturbation, or "solitary vice," began to appear. Popular books of advice, like William Alcott's *Young Man's Guide*, gave similar warnings. They tried to persuade young men that their health could be ruined, and their prospects for success darkened, by consorting with prostitutes or becoming sexually entangled before marriage.

A new belief about women's sexual nature appeared, one that elevated them above "carnal passion." Many American men and women came to believe during the nineteenth century that in their true and proper nature as mothers and guardians of the home, women were far less interested in sex than men were. Women who defined themselves as passionless were in a strong position to control or deny men's sexual demands either during courtship or in limiting their childbearing within marriage.

Graham went considerably farther than this, advising restraint not only in early life and courtship but in marriage itself. It was far healthier, he maintained, for couples to have sexual relations "very seldom."

Neither contraception nor the new style of courtship had become anything like universal by 1840. Prenuptial pregnancy rates had fallen, but they remained high enough to indicate that many couples simply continued in familiar ways. American husbands and wives in the cities and the Northern countryside were limiting the number of their children, but it was clear that those living on the farms of the West or in the slave quarters had not yet begun to. There is strong evidence that many American women felt far from passionless, although others restrained or renounced their sexuality. For many people in the United States, there had been

a profound change. Reining in the passions had become part of everyday life.

SMOKING AND SPITTING

"Everyone smokes and some chew in America," wrote Isaac Weld in 1795. Americans turned tobacco, a new and controversial stimulant at the time of colonial settlement, into a crucially important staple crop and made its heavy use a commonplace — and a never-ending source of surprise and indignation to

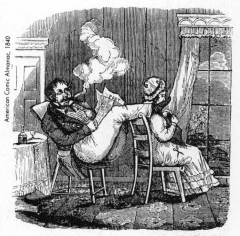

American Comic Almanac, 1840

On the home front: a smoker indulges.

visitors. Tobacco use spread in the United States because it was comparatively cheap, a homegrown product free from the heavy import duties levied on it by European governments. A number of slave rations described in plantation documents included "one hand of tobacco per month." Through the eighteenth century most American smokers used clay pipes, which are abundant in colonial archeological sites, although some men and women dipped snuff or inhaled powdered tobacco.

Where the smokers of early colonial America "drank" or gulped smoke through the short, thick stems of their seventeenth-century pipes, those of 1800 inhaled it more slowly and gradually; from the early seventeenth to the late eighteenth century, pipe stems became steadily longer and narrower, increasingly distancing smokers from their burning tobacco.

In the 1790s cigars, or "segars," were introduced from the Caribbean. Prosperous men widely took them up; they were the most expensive way to consume tobacco, and it was a sign of financial security to puff away on "long-nines" or "principe cigars at three cents each" while the poor used clay pipes and much cheaper "cut plug" tobacco. After 1800 in American streets, barrooms, stores, public conveyances, and even private homes it became nearly impossible to avoid tobacco chewers. Chewing extended tobacco use, particularly into workplaces; men who smoked pipes at home or in the tavern barroom could chew while working in barns or workshops where smoking carried the danger of fire.

"In all the public places of America," wrote Charles Dickens, multitudes of men engaged in "the odious practice of chewing and expectorating," a recreation practiced by all ranks of American society. Chewing stimulated salivation and gave rise to a public environment of frequent and copious spitting, where men every few minutes were "squirting a mouthful of saliva through the room."

Spittoons were provided in the more meticulous establishments, but men often ignored them. The floors of American public buildings were not pleasant to contemplate. A courtroom in New York City in 1833 was decorated by a "mass of abomination" contributed to by "judges, counsel, jury, witnesses, officers, and audience." The floor of the Virginia House of Burgesses in 1827 was "actually flooded with their horrible spitting," and even the aisle of a Connecticut meetinghouse was black with the "ejection after ejection, incessant from twenty mouths," of the men singing in the choir. In order to drink, an American man might remove his quid, put it in a pocket or hold it in his hand, take his glassful, and then restore it to his mouth. Women's dresses might even be in danger at fashionable balls. "One night as I was walking upstairs to valse," reported Margaret Hall of a

Yankee Notions (NEW YORK, 1852)

An expert spitter takes aim.

dance in Washington in 1828, "my partner began clearing his throat. This I thought ominous. However, I said to myself, 'surely he will turn his head to the other side.' The gentleman, however, had no such thought but deliberately shot across me. I had not courage enough to examine whether the result landed in the flounce of my dress."

The segar and the quid were almost entirely male appurtenances, but as the nineteenth century began, many rural and lower-class urban women were smoking pipes or dipping snuff. During his boyhood in New Hampshire, Horace Greeley remembered, "it was often my filial duty to fill and light my mother's pipe."

After 1820 or so tobacco use among women in the North began to decline. Northern women remembered or depicted with pipe or snuffbox were almost all elderly. More and more Americans adopted a genteel standard that saw tobacco use and womanliness—delicate and nurturing—as antithetical, and young women avoided it as a pollutant. For them, tobacco use

After 1800, in public and private it became nearly impossible to avoid tobacco chewers.

marked off male from female territory with increasing sharpness.

In the households of small Southern and Western farmers, however, smoking and snuff taking remained common. When women visited "among the country people" of North Carolina, Frances Kemble Butler reported in 1837, the "proffer of the snuffbox, and its passing from hand to hand, is the usual civility." By the late 1830s visiting New Englanders were profoundly shocked when they saw the women of Methodist congregations in Illinois, including nursing mothers, taking out their pipes for a smoke between worship services.

FROM DEFERENCE TO EQUALITY

The Americans of 1820 would have been more recognizable to us in the informal and egalitarian way they treated one another. The traditional signs of deference before social superiors—the deep bow, the "courtesy," the doffed cap, lowered head, and averted eyes—had been a part of social relationships in colonial America. In the 1780s, wrote the American poetess Lydia Huntley Sigourney in 1824, there were still "individuals . . . in every grade of society" who had grown up "when a bow was not an offense to fashion nor . . . a relic of monarchy." But in the early nineteenth century such signals of subordination rapidly fell away. It was a natural consequence of the Revolution, she maintained, which, "in giving us liberty, obliterated almost every vestige of politeness of the 'old school.'" Shaking hands became the accustomed American greeting between men, a gesture whose symmetry and mutuality signified equality. Frederick Marryat found in 1835 that it was "invariably the custom to shake hands" when he was introduced to Americans and that he could not carefully grade the acknowledgment he would give to new acquaintances according to their signs of wealth and breeding. He found instead that he had to "go on shaking hands here, there and everywhere, and with everybody." Americans were not blind to inequalities of economic and social power, but they less and less gave them overt physical expression. Bred in a society where such distinctions were far more clearly spelled out, Marryat was somewhat disoriented in the United States; "it is impossible to know who is who," he claimed, "in this land of equality."

Well-born British travelers encountered not just confusion but conflict when they failed to receive the signs of respect they expected. Margaret Hall's letters home during her Southern travels outlined a true comedy of manners. At every stage stop in the Carolinas, Georgia, and Alabama, she demanded that country tavernkeepers and their households give her deferential service and well-prepared meals; she received instead rancid bacon and "such an absence of all kindness of feeling, such unbending frigid heartlessness." But she and her family had a far greater share than they realized in creating this chilly reception. Squeezed between the pride and poise of the great planters and the social debasement of the slaves, small Southern farmers often displayed a prickly insolence, a considered lack of response, to those who too obviously considered themselves their betters. Greatly to their discomfort and incomprehension, the Halls were experiencing what a British traveler more sympathetic to American ways, Patrick Shirreff, called "the democratic rudeness which assumed or presumptuous superiority seldom fails to experience."

LAND OF ABUNDANCE

In the seventeenth century white American colonials were no taller than their European counterparts, but by the time of the Revolution they were close to their late-twentieth-century average height for men of

Americans were better nourished than the great majority of the world's peoples.

slightly over five feet eight inches. The citizens of the early republic towered over most Europeans. Americans' early achievement of modern stature—by a full century and more—was a striking consequence of American abundance. Americans were taller because they were better nourished than the great majority of the world's peoples.

Yet not all Americans participated equally in the nation's abundance.

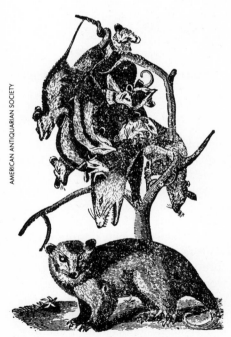

Possum and other game were dietary staples.

Differences in stature between whites and blacks, and between city and country dwellers, echoed those between Europeans and Americans. Enslaved blacks were a full inch shorter than whites. But they remained a full inch taller than European peasants and laborers and were taller still than their fellow slaves eating the scanty diets

afforded by the more savagely oppressive plantation system of the West Indies. And by 1820 those who lived in the expanding cities of the United States—even excluding immigrants, whose heights would have reflected European, not American, conditions—were noticeably shorter than the people of the countryside, suggesting an increasing concentration of poverty and poorer diets in urban places.

Across the United States almost all country households ate the two great American staples: corn and "the eternal pork," as one surfeited traveler called it, "which makes its appearance on every American table, high and low, rich and poor." Families in the cattle-raising, dairying country of New England, New York, and northern Ohio ate butter, cheese, and salted beef as well as pork and made their bread from wheat flour or rye and Indian corn. In Pennsylvania, as well as Maryland, Delaware, and Virginia, Americans ate the same breadstuffs as their Northern neighbors, but their consumption of cheese and beef declined every mile southward in favor of pork.

Farther to the south, and in the West, corn and corn-fed pork were truly "eternal"; where reliance on them reached its peak in the Southern uplands, they were still the only crops many small farmers raised. Most Southern and Western families built their diets around smoked and salted bacon, rather than the Northerners' salt pork, and, instead of wheat or rye bread, made cornpone or hoecake, a coarse, strong bread, and hominy, pounded Indian corn boiled together with milk.

Before 1800, game—venison, possum, raccoon, and wild fowl—was for many American households "a substantial portion of the supply of food at certain seasons of the year," although only on the frontier was it a regular part of the diet. In the West and South this continued to be true, but in the Northeast game became increasingly rare as forests gave way to open farmland, where wild animals could not live.

Through the first half of the eighteenth century, Americans had been primarily concerned with obtaining a sufficiency of meat and bread for their families; they paid relatively little attention to foodstuffs other than these two "staffs of life," but since that time the daily fare of many households had grown substantially more diverse.

COMING TO THE TABLE

Remembering his turn-of-the-century Kentucky boyhood, Daniel Drake could still see the mealtime scene at the house of a neighbor, "Old Billy," who "with his sons" would "frequently breakfast in common on mush and milk out of a huge buckeye bowl, each one dipping in a spoon." "Old Billy" and his family were less frontier savages than traditionalists; in the same decade Gov. Caleb Strong of Massachusetts stopped for the night with a country family who ate in the same way, where "each had a spoon and dipped from the same dish." These households ate as almost all American families once had, communally partaking of food from the same dish and passing around a single vessel to drink from. Such meals were often surprisingly haphazard affairs, with household members moving in and out, eating quickly and going on to other tasks.

But by 1800 they were already in a small and diminishing minority. Over the eighteenth century dining "in common" had given way to individualized yet social eating; as families acquired chairs and dining utensils, they were able to make mealtimes more important social occasions. Most Americans expected to eat individual portions of food at a table set with personal knives, forks, glasses, bowls, and plates. Anything that smacked of the old communal ways was increasingly likely to be treated as a sin against domestic decency. The clergyman Peter Cartwright was shocked at the table manners of a "backward" family who ate off a "wooden trencher," improvised forks with "sharp pieces of cane,"

and used a single knife, which they passed around the table.

"One and all, male and female," the observant Margaret Hall took note, even in New York's best society, ate "invariably and indefatigably with their knives." As a legacy of the fork's late arrival in the colonies, Americans were peculiar in using their "great lumbering, long, two-pronged forks," not to convey food to the mouth, as their English and French contemporaries did, but merely to keep their meat from slip-

Families began to sit down at mealtime.

ping off the plate while cutting it. "Feeding yourself with your right hand, armed with a steel blade," was the prevalent American custom, acknowledged Eliza Farrar's elaborate *Young Lady's Friend* of 1836. She added that it was perfectly proper, despite English visitors' discomfort at the sight of a "prettily dressed, nice-looking young woman ladling rice pudding into her mouth with the point of a great knife" or a domestic helper "feeding an infant of seventeen months in the same way."

Mrs. Farrar acknowledged that there were stirrings of change among the sophisticated in the 1830s, conceding that some of her readers might now want "to imitate the French or English . . . and put every mouthful into your mouth with your fork." Later in the nineteenth century the American habit of eating with the knife completely lost its claims to gentility, and it became another relic of "primitive manners." Americans gradually learned to use

Primitive manners succumbed to campaigns for temperance and gentility.

forks more dexterously, although to this day they hold them in the wrong hand and "upside down" from an Englishman's point of view.

The old ways, so startlingly unfamiliar to the modern reader, gradually fell away. Americans changed their assumptions about what was proper, decent, and normal in everyday life in directions that would have greatly surprised most of the men and women of the early republic. Some aspects of their "primitive manners" succumbed to campaigns for temperance and gentility, while others evaporated with the later growth of mass merchandising and mass communications.

Important patterns of regional, class, and ethnic distinctiveness remain in American everyday life. But they are far less powerful, and less central to understanding American experience, than they once were. Through the rest of the nineteenth century and into the twentieth, the United States became ever more diverse, with new waves of Eastern and Southern European immigrants joining the older Americans of Northern European stock. Yet the new arrivals—and even more, their descendants—have experienced the attractiveness and reshaping power of a national culture formed by department stores, newspapers, radios, movies, and universal public education. America, the developing nation, developed into us. And perhaps our manners and morals, to some future observer, will seem as idiosyncratic and astonishing as this portrait of our earlier self.

The Jacksonian Revolution

Robert V. Remini

Robert V. Remini is professor of history at the University of Illinois Circle Campus in Chicago, and author of a multivolume biography of Andrew Jackson.

"What?" cried the outraged North Carolina lady when she heard the dreadful news. "Jackson up for president? *Jackson? Andrew* Jackson? The Jackson that used to live in Salisbury? Why, when he was here, he was such a rake that my husband would not bring him into the house! It is true, he *might* have taken him out to the stable to weigh horses for a race, and might drink a glass of whiskey with him *there*. Well, if Andrew Jackson can be president, anybody can!"

Indeed. After forty years of constitutional government headed by presidents George Washington, John Adams, Thomas Jefferson, James Madison, James Monroe, and John Quincy Adams, the thought of Gen. Andrew Jackson of Tennessee—"Old Hickory" to his devoted soldiers—succeeding such distinguished statesmen came as a shock to some Americans in 1828. And little did they know at the time that Old Hickory would be followed in succession by the little Magician, Tippecanoe and Tyler, too, Young Hickory, and then Old Rough and Ready.

What had happened to the American political process? How could it come about that the Washingtons, Jeffersons, and Madisons of the world could be replaced by the Van Burens, Harrisons, Tylers, and Taylors? What a mockery of the political system bequeathed by the Founding Fathers!

The years from roughly 1828 to 1848 are known today as the Age of Jackson or the Jacksonian era. To many contemporaries, they initiated a "revolution," a shocking overthrow of the noble republican standards of the founders by the "common people," who in 1828 preferred as president a crude frontiersman like Andrew Jackson to a statesman of proven ability with a record of outstanding public service like John Quincy Adams.

Over the forty years following the establishment of the American nation under the Constitution, the United States had experienced many profound changes in virtually all phases of life. Following the War of 1812, the industrial revolution took hold and within thirty years all the essential elements for the creation of an industrial society

in America were solidly in place. At the same time, a transportation revolution got underway with the building of canals, bridges, and turnpikes, reaching a climax of sorts in the 1820s with the coming of the railroads. The standard of living was also improved by numerous new inventions. Finally, many of the older eastern states began to imitate newer western states by democratizing their institutions, for example, amending their constitutions to eliminate property qualifications for voting and holding office, thereby establishing universal white manhood suffrage.

The arrival of many thousands of new voters at the polls in the early nineteenth century radically changed American politics. In the past, only the wealthy and better educated were actively involved in government. Moreover, political parties were frowned upon by many of the Founding Fathers. Parties stood for factions or cliques by which greedy and ambitious men, who had no interest in serving the public good, could advance their private and selfish purposes. John Adams

From *The World & I*, January 1988, pp. 549-563. *The World & I*, a publication of The Washington Times Corporation.

spoke for many when he declared that the "division of the republic into two great parties . . . is to be dreaded as the greatest political evil under our Constitution."

But times had changed. An entirely new generation of politicians appeared at the outbreak of the War of 1812, men like Henry Clay, John C. Calhoun, Martin Van Buren, and Daniel Webster, who regarded political parties more favorably. Indeed, the party structure that had emerged before the end of President Washington's administration had been their corridor to power, since none of them could offer to their constituents a public record to match what the founders had achieved.

> # An entirely new generation of politicians appeared at the outbreak of the War of 1812.

None had fought in the Revolution. None had signed the Declaration or participated in the debates leading to the writing and adoption of the Constitution. Some of them—Martin Van Buren is probably the best example —actually considered parties to be beneficial to the body politic, indeed essential to the proper working of a democratic society. Through the party system, Van Buren argued, the American people could more effectively express their will and take measures to ensure that that will was implemented by their representatives. "We must always have party distinctions," he wrote, "and the old ones are the best. . . . Political combinations between the inhabitants of the different states are unavoidable and the most natural and beneficial to the country is that between the planters of the South and the plain Republicans of the North."

In supporting Andrew Jackson for the presidency in 1828 and trying to

win support from both planters and plain Republicans, Van Buren affirmed his belief in the American need for a two-party system. Jackson's election, he told Thomas Ritchie, editor of the Richmond *Enquirer*, "as the result of his military services without reference to party, and, as far as he alone is concerned, scarcely to principle, would be one thing. His election as the result of combined and concerted effort of a political party, holding in the main, to certain tenets and opposed to certain prevailing principles, might be another and far different thing."

Van Buren eventually formed an alliance with John C. Calhoun and a number of other southern politicians, and led the way in structuring a political organization around the presidential candidacy of Andrew Jackson. That organization ultimately came to be called the Democratic Party. Its leaders, including Jackson, Van Buren, Calhoun, and Thomas Hart Benton, claimed to follow the republican doctrines of Thomas Jefferson. Thus they opposed both a strong central government and a broad interpretation of the Constitution, and they regarded the states, whose rights must be defended by all who cared about preserving individual liberty, as a wholesome counterweight to the national government. Many of them opposed the idea of the federal government sponsoring public works, arguing that internal improvements dangerously inflated the power of the central government and jeopardized liberty. As president, Andrew Jackson vetoed the Maysville road bill and contended that the national government should avoid internal improvements as a general practice, except for those essential to the national defense.

The political philosophy these Democrats espoused was fundamentally conservative. It advocated economy in operating the government because a tight budget limited government activity, and Jackson swore that if ever elected president he would liquidate the national debt. True to his word, he labored throughout his administration to cut expenditures by vetoing several appropriations bills he tagged as exorbitant, and he finally succeeded in obliterating the national debt altogether in January 1835—a short-lived accomplishment.

The organization of the Democratic Party in its initial stages included a

central committee, state committees, and a national newspaper located in Washington, D.C., the *United States Telegraph*, which could speak authoritatively to the party faithful. In time it was said that the Democratic organization included "a chain of newspaper posts, from the New England States to Louisiana, and branching off through Lexington to the Western States." The supporters of Jackson's election were accused by their opponents of attempting to regulate "the popular election by means of organized clubs in the States, and organized presses everywhere."

Democrats took particular delight in celebrating the candidacy of Andrew Jackson. They found that Old Hickory's personality and military accomplishments made him an attractive and viable candidate for the ordinary voter. Indeed his career and personality stirred the imagination of Democratic leaders around the country and they devised new methods, or improved old ones, to get across the message that Andrew Jackson was a "man of the people." "The Constitution and liberty of the country were in imminent peril, and he has preserved them both!" his supporters boasted. "We can sustain our republican principles . . . by calling to the presidential chair . . . ANDREW JACKSON."

Jackson became a symbol of the best in American life—a self-made man, among other things—and party leaders adopted the hickory leaf as their symbol. Hickory brooms, hickory canes, hickory sticks shot up everywhere—on steeples, poles, steamboats, and stage coaches, and in the hands of all who could wave them to salute the Old Hero of New Orleans. "In every village, as well as upon the corners of many city streets," hickory poles were erected. "Many of these poles were standing as late as 1845," recorded one contemporary, "rotten momentoes [sic] of the delirium of 1828." The opponents of the Democratic Party were outraged by this crude lowering of the political process. "Planting hickory trees!" snorted the Washington *National Journal* on May 24, 1828. "Odds nuts and drumsticks! What have hickory trees to do with republicanism and the great contest?"

The Democrats devised other gimmicks to generate excitement for their ticket. "Jackson meetings" were held in every county where a Democratic organization existed. Such meetings were not new, of course. What was new was their audience. "If we go into one of these meetings," declared one newspaper, "of whom do we find them composed? Do we see there the solid, substantial, moral and reflecting yeomanry of the country? No. . . . They comprise a large portion of the dissolute, the noisy, the discontented, and designing of society." The Democratic press retorted with the claim that these so-called dissolute were actually the "bone and muscle of American society. They are the People. The real People who understand that Gen. Jackson is one of them and will defend their interests and rights."

The Jacksonians were also very fond of parades and barbecues. In Baltimore a grand barbecue was scheduled to commemorate the successful defense of the city when the British attacked during the War of 1812. But the Democrats expropriated the occasion and converted it into a Jackson rally. One parade started with dozens of Democrats marching to the beat of a fife and drum corps and wearing no other insignia save "a twig of the sacred [hickory] tree in their hats." Trailing these faithful Jacksonians came "gigantic hickory poles," still live and crowned with green foliage, being carted in "on eight wheels for the purpose of being planted by the democracy on the eve of the election." These poles were drawn by eight horses, all decorated with "ribbons and mottoes." Perched in the branches of each tree were a dozen Democrats, waving flags and shouting, "Hurrah for Jackson!"

"Van Buren has learned you know that the *Hurra Boys* were for Jackson," commented one critic, "and to my regret they constitute a powerful host." Indeed they did. The number of voters in the election of 1828 rose to 1,155,340, a jump of more than 800,000 over the previous presidential election of 1824.

The Hurra Boys brought out the voters in 1828, but at considerable cost. The election set a low mark for vulgarity, gimmickry, and nonsensical hijinks. Jackson's mother was accused of being a prostitute brought to America to service British soldiers, and his wife was denounced as an "adulteress" and bigamist. "Ought a convicted adulteress and her paramour husband

to be placed in the highest offices of this free and Christian land?" asked one editor. But the Democrats were no better, accusing John Quincy Adams of pimping for the czar of Russia.

The tone and style of this election outraged many voters who feared for the future of American politics. With so many fresh faces crowding to the polls, the old republican system was yielding to a new democratic style and that evolution seemed fraught with all the dangers warned against by the Founding Fathers. Jackson's subsequent victory at the polls gave some Americans nightmares of worse things to come.

At his inauguration people came

> # The tone and style of this election outraged many voters who feared for the future of American politics.

from five hundred miles away to see General Jackson, wrote Daniel Webster, "and they really seem to think that the country is rescued from some dreadful danger!" They nearly wrecked the White House in their exuberance. Their behavior shocked Joseph Story, an associate justice of the Supreme Court, and sent him scurrying home. "The region of KING MOB seemed triumphant," he wailed. But a western newspaper disagreed. "It was a proud day for the people," reported the *Argus of Western America*. "General Jackson is *their own* President."

Jackson himself was fiercely committed to democracy. And by democracy he meant majoritarian rule. "The people are the government," he wrote, "administering it by their agents; they are the Government, the sovereign power." In his first message to Congress as president, written in December 1829, Jackson announced: "The

majority is to govern." To the people belonged the right of "electing their Chief Executive." He therefore asked Congress to adopt an amendment that would abolish the College of Electors. He wanted all "intermediary" agencies standing between the people and their government swept away, whether erected by the Founding Fathers or not. "The people are sovereign," he reiterated. "Their will is absolute."

So committed was Jackson to the principle of popular self-rule that he told historian-politician George Bancroft that "every officer should in his turn pass before the people, for their approval or rejection." And he included federal judges in this sweeping generalization, even justices of the Supreme Court. Accordingly, he introduced the principle of rotation, which limited government appointments to four years. Officeholders should be regularly rotated back home and replaced by new men, he said. "The duties of all public officers are . . . so plain and simple that men of intelligence may readily qualify themselves for their performance." Otherwise abuse may occur. Anyone who has held office "a few years, believes he has a life estate in it, a vested right, & if it has been held 20 years or upwards, not only a vested right, but that it ought to descend to his children, & if no children then the next of kin—This is not the principles of our government. It is rotation in office that will perpetuate our liberty." Unfortunately, hack politicians equated rotation with patronage and Jackson's enemies quickly dubbed his principle "the spoils system."

But it was never meant to be a spoils system. Jackson wanted *every* office of government, from the highest to the lowest, within the reach of the electorate, arguing that "where the people are everything . . . there and there only is liberty." Perhaps his position was best articulated by Alexis de Tocqueville, the French visitor in the 1830s whose *Democracy in America* remains one of the most profound observations about American life in print. "The people reign in the American political world," declared Tocqueville, "as the Deity does in the universe. They are the cause and aim of all things; everything comes from them, and everything is absorbed in them." The "constant celebration" of the people, therefore, is what Jackson and the Democratic Party provided the nation during his eight years in office. It is what Jacksonian Democracy was all about.

As president, Jackson inaugurated a number of important changes in the operation of government. For example, he vetoed congressional legislation more times than all his predecessors combined, and for reasons other than a bill's presumed lack of constitutionality. More importantly, by the creative use of his veto power he successfully claimed for the chief executive the right to participate in the legislative process. He put Congress on notice that they must consider his views

> # Jackson himself was fiercely committed to democracy. And by democracy he meant majoritarian rule.

on all issues *before* enacting them into law or run the risk of a veto. In effect he assumed the right to initiate legislation, and this essentially altered the relationship between the executive and the Congress. Instead of a separate and equal branch of the government, the president, according to Jackson, was the head of state, the first among equals.

Jackson also took a dim view of the claim that the Supreme Court exercised the final and absolute right to determine the meaning of the Constitution. When the court decided in *McCulloch vs. Maryland* that the law establishing a national bank was constitutional, Jackson disagreed. In his veto of a bill to recharter the Second National Bank in 1832, he claimed among other things that the bill lacked authority under the Constitution, despite what the high court had decided. Both the House and the Senate, as well as the president, he continued, must decide for themselves what is and what is not constitutional

before taking action on any bill. The representatives of Congress ought not to vote for a bill, and the president ought not to sign it, if they, in their own good judgment, believe it unconstitutional. "It is as much the duty of the House of Representatives, of the Senate, and of the President to decide upon the constitutionality of any bill or resolution which may be presented to them for passage or approval as it is of the supreme judges when it may be brought before them for judicial decision." Jackson did not deny the right of the Supreme Court to judge the constitutionality of a bill. What he denied was the presumption that the Court was the final or exclusive interpreter of the Constitution. All three branches should rule on the question of constitutionality, Jackson argued. In this way the equality and independence of each branch of government is maintained. "The authority of the Supreme Court," he declared, "must not, therefore, be permitted to control the Congress, or the Executive when acting in their legislative capacities, but to have only such influence as the force of their reasoning may deserve." What bothered Jackson was the presumption that four men could dictate what 15 million people may or may not do under their constitutional form. To Jackson's mind that was not democratic but oligarchic. But that was precisely the intention of the Founding Fathers: to provide a balanced mix of democratic, oligarchic, and monarchical forms in the Constitution.

Of course Jackson was merely expressing his own opinion about the right of all three branches to pass on the constitutionality of all legislation, an opinion the American people ultimately rejected. The great fear in a democratic system—one the Founding Fathers knew perfectly well—was the danger of the majority tyrannizing the minority. Jackson would take his chances. He believed the American people were virtuous and would always act appropriately. "I for one do not despair of the republic," he wrote. "I have great confidence in the virtue of a great majority of the people, and I cannot fear the result. The republic is safe, the main pillars [of] virtue, religion and morality will be fostered by a majority of the people." But not everyone shared Jackson's optimism about the goodness of the electorate.

And in time—particularly with the passage of the Fourteenth Amendment—it fell to the courts to guard and maintain the rights of the minority.

Jackson summed up his assertion of presidential rights by declaring that he alone—not Congress, as was usually assumed—was the sole representative of the American people and responsible to them. After defeating Henry Clay in the 1832 election, he decided to kill the Second National Bank by removing federal deposits because, as he said, he had received a "mandate" from the people to do so. The Senate objected and formally cen-

> # Jackson wanted *every* office of government, from the highest to the lowest, within the reach of the electorate.

sured him, but Jackson, in response, merely issued another statement on presidential rights and the democratic system that had evolved over the last few years.

By law, only the secretary of the treasury was authorized to remove the deposits, so Jackson informed his secretary, William Duane, to carry out his order. Duane refused pointblank. And he also refused to resign as he had promised if he and the president could not agree upon a common course of action with respect to the deposits. Thereupon, Jackson sacked him. This was the first time a cabinet officer had been fired, and there was some question whether the president had this authority. After all, the cabinet positions were created by Congress and appointment required the consent of the Senate. Did that not imply that removal also required senatorial consent—particularly the treasury secretary, since he handled public funds that were controlled by Congress? The law creating the Treasury Department never called it an "executive" department, and it required its secretary to report to the Congress, not the president. None of this made a particle of difference to Andrew Jackson. All department heads were *his* appointees and they would obey *him* or pack their bags. The summary dismissal of Duane was seen by Jackson's opponents as a presidential grab for the purse strings of the nation. And in fact presidential control over all executive functions gave the chief executive increased authority over the collection and distribution of public funds.

THE JACKSONIAN REVOLUTION

By the close of 1833 many feared that Andrew Jackson was leading the country to disaster. Henry Clay regularly pilloried the president on the Senate floor. On one occasion he accused Jackson of "open, palpable and daring usurpation" of all the powers of government. "We are in the midst of a revolution," Clay thundered, "hitherto bloodless, but rapidly tending towards a total change of the pure republican character of the Government."

A "revolution"—that was how the opposition Whig Party characterized Jackson's presidency. The nation was moving steadily away from its "pure republican character" into something approaching despotism. What the nation was witnessing, cried Clay, was "the concentration of all power in the hands of one man." Thereafter Whig newspapers reprinted a cartoon showing Jackson as "King Andrew the First." Clad in robes befitting an emperor, he was shown wearing a crown and holding a scepter in one hand and a scroll in the other on which was written the word "veto."

Democrats, naturally, read the "revolution" differently. They saw it as the steady progress of the country from the gentry republic originally established by the Founding Fathers to a more democratic system that mandated broader representation in government and a greater responsiveness to popular will.

Andrew Jackson did not take kindly to Clay's verbal mauling. "Oh, if I live to get these robes of office off me," he snorted at one point, "I will bring the rascal to a dear account." He later likened the senator to "a drunken man in a brothel," reckless, destructive, and "full of fury."

Other senators expressed their opposition to this "imperial" president and seconded Clay's complaints. John C. Calhoun, who by this time had deserted to the enemy camp, adopted the Kentuckian's "leading ideas of revolution" and charged that "a great effort is now making to choke and stifle the voice of American liberty." And he condemned Jackson's insistence on taking refuge in democratic claims. The president "tells us again and again with the greatest emphasis," he continued, "that he is the immediate representative of the American people! What effrontery! What boldness of assertion! Why, he never received a vote from the American people. He was elected by electors . . . who are elected by Legislatures chosen by the people."

Sen. Daniel Webster and other Whigs chimed in. "Again and again we hear it said," rumbled Webster, "that the President is responsible to the American people! . . . And this is thought enough for a limited, restrained, republican government! . . . I hold this, Sir, to be a mere assumption, and dangerous assumption." And connected with this "airy and unreal responsibility to the people," he continued, "is another sentiment . . . and that is, that the President is the direct representative of the American people." The sweep of his language electrified the Senate. And "if he may be allowed to consider himself as the sole representative of all the American people," Webster concluded, "then I say, Sir, that the government . . . has already a master. I deny the sentiment, and therefore protest against the language; neither the sentiment nor the language is to be found in the Constitution of this Country."

Jackson's novel concept that the president served as the people's tribune found immediate acceptance by the electorate, despite the warnings of the Whigs. In effect, he altered the essential character of the presidency. He had become the head of government, the one person who would formulate national policy and direct public affairs. Sighed Senator Benjamin W. Leigh of Virginia: "Until the President developed the faculties of the Executive power, all men thought it inferior to the legislature—he manifestly thinks it superior: and in his hands [it] . . . has proved far stronger than the representatives of the States."

> Jackson took a dim view of the claim that the Supreme Court has the final right on the meaning of the Constitution.

JACKSON INTERPRETED

From Jackson's own time to the present, disagreement and controversy over the significance of his presidency has prevailed. In the twentieth century the disagreements intensified among historians. Confusion over the meaning of Jacksonian Democracy, varying regional support for democratic change, and the social and economic status of the Democrats and Whigs have clouded the efforts of scholars to reach reliable conclusions about the Old Hero and the era that bears his name.

Andrew Jackson himself will always remain a controversial figure among historians. That he can still generate such intense partisan feeling is evidence of his remarkable personality. He was an aggressive, dynamic, charismatic, and intimidating individual. And although modern scholars and students of history either admire or dislike him intensely, his rating as president in polls conducted among historians over the past thirty years varies from great to near great. He carries an enormous burden in winning any popularity contest because of his insistence on removing the eastern Indians west of the Mississippi River and on waging a long and vicious war against the Second National Bank of the United States.

His first biographer, James Parton, wrote a three-volume *Life of Andrew*

Jackson (1859, 1860), and came away with mixed feelings about the man and his democracy. At times Parton railed against the mindless mob "who could be wheedled, and flattered, and drilled," but at other times he extolled democracy as the mark of an enlightened society. What troubled Parton particularly was the spoils system. Rotation, he wrote, is "an evil so great and so difficult to remedy, that if all his other public acts had been perfectly wise and right, this single feature of his administration would suffice to render it deplorable rather than amiable."

William Graham Sumner's *Andrew Jackson* (1882) was relentlessly critical of his subject, deploring in particular Jackson's flawed moral charter and emotional excesses. Sumner and other early historians, such as Herman von Holst and James Schouler, constituted what one student of the Jacksonian age called a "liberal patrician" or "Whig" school of history. These individuals came from European middle- or upper middle-class families with excellent backgrounds of education and public service. Because their class had been ousted from political power, these historians were biased against Jacksonian Democracy, and their books reflect their prejudice.

The interpretation of Old Hickory and his adherents took a sharp about—face with the appearance in 1893 of the vastly influential article by Frederick Jackson Turner, "The Significance of the Frontier in American History." Turner argued that American democracy emerged from the wilderness, noting that universal white manhood suffrage guaranteed by the new western states became something of a model for the older, eastern states. Naturally Jackson and his followers were seen as the personification of this frontier democracy. The thesis was advanced and sometimes amplified by Charles A. Beard, Vernon L. Parrington, and other western and southern historians of the early twentieth century who were caught up in the reform movement of the Progressive era. They dubbed the Jacksonian revolution an age of egalitarianism that produced the rise of the common man. Jackson himself was applauded as a man of the people. Thus the liberal patrician school of historiography gave way to the Progressive school.

This interpretation dovetailed rath-er well with the views of Tocqueville. During his visit, Tocqueville encountered a widespread belief in egalitarianism but worried that majoritarian rule could endanger minority rights. There are so many sharp and accurate insights into American society and institutions in *Democracy in America* that it ought to be the first book anyone reads in attempting to understand the antebellum period of American history. Among other things, he catches the American just as he is emerging from his European and colonial past and acquiring many of the characteristics of what are generally regarded as typically American today.

Tocqueville's democratic liberalism, augmented by the works of the Progressive historians—especially Turner, Beard and Parrington—dominated historical thought about the American past for the next fifty years or more. Almost all the Progressive historians stressed the role of geographic sections in the nation, and Turner at one point even denied any class influence in the formation of frontier democracy. The only important negative voice concerning Jackson during this period came from Thomas P. Abernethy, whose *From Frontier to Plantation in Tennessee: A Study in Frontier Democracy* (1932) insisted that Jackson himself was a frontier aristocrat, an opportunist, and a land speculator who strongly opposed the democratic forces in his own state of Tennessee.

The virtual shattering of the Progressive school's interpretation of Jacksonian Democracy came with the publication of one of the most important historical monographs ever written concerning American history: *The Age of Jackson* (1945), by Arthur M. Schlesinger, Jr. This classic work virtually rivals in importance the frontier thesis of Frederick Jackson Turner. It is a landmark study and represents the beginning of modern scholarship on Jackson and his era.

Schlesinger argued that class distinctions rather than sectional differences best explain the phenomenon of Jacksonian Democracy. He interpreted Jackson's actions and those of his followers as an effort of the less fortunate in American society to combat the power and influence of the business community. The working classes in urban centers as well as the yeoman farmers, he argued, were the true wellsprings of the Jacksonian movement. Jacksonian Democracy evolved from the conflict between classes and best expressed its goals and purposes in the problems and needs facing urban laborers. Schlesinger singled out the bank war as the most telling example of the conflict and as the fundamental key to a fuller understanding of the meaning of Jacksonian Democracy. What attracted many historians to this path-breaking study, besides its graceful and majestic style, was Schlesinger's perceptive definition of Jacksonian Democracy and a precise explanation of its origins.

The reaction to Schlesinger's work was immediate and dramatic. It swept the historical profession like a tornado, eliciting both prodigious praise and, within a relatively short time, fierce denunciations. Bray Hammond, in a series of articles as well as his *Banks and Politics in America from the Revolution to the Civil War* (1957), and Richard Hofstadter, in his *The American Political Tradition and the Men Who Made It* (1948), contended that the Jacksonians were not the champions of urban workers or small farmers but rather ambitious and ruthless entrepreneurs principally concerned with advancing their own economic and political advantage. They were "men on the make" and frequently captains of great wealth. According to Hofstadter, the Jacksonians were not so much hostile to business as they were hostile to being excluded from entering the confined arena of capitalists. Where Schlesinger had emphasized conflict in explaining the Jacksonian era, Hofstadter insisted that consensus best

> Jackson declared that he alone —not Congress —was the sole representative of the American people.

characterized the period. The entrepreneurial thesis, as it was called, found strong support among many young scholars who constituted the Columbia University school of historians. In a series of articles and books produced by these critics, Jackson himself was described as an inconsistent opportunist, a strikebreaker, a shady land speculator, and a political fraud. Marvin Meyers, in his *The Jackson Persuasion* (1957), provides a slight variation on the entrepreneurial thesis by arguing that Jacksonians did indeed keep their eyes on the main chance but yearned for the virtues of a past agrarian republic. They hungered after the rewards of capitalism but looked back reverentially on the blessings of a simpler agrarian society.

A major redirection of Jacksonian scholarship came with the publication of Lee Benson's *The Concept of Jacksonian Democracy: New York as a Text Case* (1961). This work suggested a whole new approach to the investigation of the Jacksonian age by employing the techniques of quantification to uncover solid, factual data upon which to base an analysis. Moreover, Benson emphasized social questions and found that such things as ethnicity and religion were far more important than economics in determining how a person voted or which party won his allegiance. He dismissed Jacksonian rhetoric about democracy and the rights of the people as "claptrap" and contended that local issues in elections meant more to the voters than national issues. Andrew Jackson himself was dismissed as unimportant in understanding the structure and meaning of politics in this period. In time, some college textbooks virtually eliminated Jackson from any discussion of this period except to mention that he opposed social reforms and that his removal of the Indians was one of the most heinous acts in American history.

An ethnocultural school of historical writing soon emerged that rejected class difference as an important factor

> **That Andrew Jackson can still generate such intense partisan feeling is evidence of his remarkable personality.**

in political determinism. German and Irish Catholics, for example, were more likely to vote Democratic because of their ethnicity and religion than anything else. Besides, some argued, Whigs were not materially richer than Democrats. Edward Pessen, in a series of books and articles, took the argument one step further and insisted that Jacksonian America was not particularly egalitarian in terms of wealth, as Tocqueville had stated. He rejected the argument that the common man politically came into his own during the Jacksonian age. In a nice turn of phrase concluding his *Jacksonian America: Society, Personality, and Politics* (1969), Pessen declared that there was only "*seeming* deference to the common man by the uncommon men [the rich and powerful] who actually ran things."

By the end of the 1970s the ethnocultural approach had quieted down and was replaced by newer kinds of social analyses, most particularly by cultural Marxists who reemphasized class conflict in understanding voter preference. Other historians took a different approach and sought to describe what might be called a "political culture" for the period. However, many of the insights of Benson and the other students of the ethnocultural school have been incorporated into the whole to form a

more sophisticated analysis. Joel Silbey, Sean Wilentz, Harry L. Watson, and others have shown that the electorate normally develops a wide set of values based on class, religion, nationality, family, residence, and several other factors and then invariably votes to safeguard those values as they perceive them. Watson particularly has demonstrated by his study of North Carolina politics that national issues did in fact matter in general elections. Even Jackson has been somewhat restored to his former importance, if not his former heroic stature. My own three-volume life of Old Hickory, *Andrew Jackson and the Course of American Empire, 1767-1821; Andrew Jackson and the Course of American Freedom, 1822-1832; Andrew Jackson and the Course of American Democracy, 1833-1845* (1977, 1981, 1984) highlights Schlesinger's findings and Jackson's faith and commitment to liberty and democracy. I contend that Jackson was in fact a man of the people, just as the Progressive historians had argued, and that he actively attempted to advance democracy by insisting that all branches of government, including the courts, reflect the popular will. I also tried to show that, for a number of reasons, the president's policy of Indian removal was initiated to spare the Indian from certain extinction. And Francis Paul Prucha has argued persuasively that Indian removal was probably the only policy possible under the circumstances.

The study of the Jacksonian era is essential for any serious examination of the evolution of the American presidency. This has been widely recognized since the avalanche of articles and books triggered by the appearance of Schlesinger's monumental work. Jackson himself has never lost his ability to excite the most intense passions and interest among students of American history. No doubt scholars and popular writers will continue to debate his role as a national hero and as an architect of American political institutions.

Lone Star Rising
Texas Before & After the Alamo

Archie P. McDonald

*History professor, editor, and author Archie P. McDonald is
the current president of the Texas State Historical Association,
executive director and editor of the East Texas Historical Association, and editor of* Encyclopedia USA.

Thousands of years before the first European
arrived, Paleo-Americans and then American
Indians roamed the forests, prairies, and mountains of the vast territory that would one day become
defined as Texas. Not yet identified by its present borders, this Texas land blended the three major land forms
of North America: the Southern Forest, the Plains, and
the Western Desert and Mountain regions.

All who came to this vacant land gave it definition.
The Paleo-Americans hunted the plains for giant prey,
surviving on large bisons and other animals. The various tribes of American Indians—Caddo, Karankawa,
Atakapa, Coahuiltecan, and Comanche, to name but a
few—adapted to whatever environment they inhabited
and hunted, fished, and, in time, grew agricultural
crops. Indeed, New World Indian farmers developed the
majority of the world's edible crops. Texas Indians
lagged behind their kind to the south in what Europeans
called civilization, but they had thriving cultures in all
parts of their lands.

Then came the Europeans. The first Spaniard to see
Texas, Alonso Alvarez de Pineda, arrived in 1519. He
surveyed the coast, landed briefly at the mouth of the
Rio Grande, which was called *Rio de las Palmas* by his
expedition, and named the area *Amichel*. Within a year,
Diego de Camargo duplicated the voyage. In 1528, Alvar
Núñez Cabeza de Vaca, shipwrecked survivor of the
Narváez expedition, was blown ashore at Mulhado, or
Galveston, with eighty of his countrymen. Within a
year, only fifteen of them survived, and seven years later
there were only four, including de Vaca, who remained
to tell the Spanish patrol that found them of the wonders of Texas, especially stories from the Indians about
cities made of gold.

Such news quickened the interest of the Spaniards.
Viceroy Mendoza sent Marcos de Niza, a priest who
desired to take Christianity to the Northern Provinces,
to confirm the story. Whether by deceit or honest mistake, de Niza's report sustained de Vaca's stories. So in
1540, Francisco Vásquez de Coronado led a mighty
entrata (expedition) to locate the Cities of Gold. For two
years, his several hundred men trekked across Arizona,
New Mexico, Texas, Oklahoma, and Kansas in a fruit-
less search for the precious metal. Their failure to find
gold fixed the Spanish policy toward the north: thereafter they did not want to spend unnecessary funds on
the region, but neither did they want others, particularly
their French and English neighbors in North America,
to have it. Only when the Spanish felt their claims jeopardized did they send missionaries or soldiers to the area
as signposts of Spanish claims.

The first such effort was the result of the establishment of a plantation by Rene Robert Cavelier Sieur de
La Salle of Fort Saint Louis near Matagorda Bay in
1685. Governor Alonso de Léon launched eleven expeditions to locate the fort, only to find that La Salle's own
men had murdered their leader and that Karankawa
Indians had destroyed the fort.

In 1690 de Léon commissioned the Mission San Francisco de las Tejas, located nearly four hundred miles

Suggested additional reading: Texas: All Hail the Mighty State
(Eakin, 1983) and Travis *(Pemberton, 1977), both by Archie P.
McDonald.*

From *American History Illustrated*, March 1986, pp. 48-51. Reproduced through the courtesy of Cowles Magazines,
publishers of *American History Illustrated*.

northeast of the fort in the direction of French claims along the Mississippi River, as a signpost to the French. Father Damien Massanet headed the mission. The Indians showed an interest that quickly waned because of quarrels among the priests and presidio soldiers and because they did not find Christianity to their liking. All the clergy were gone within a few years.

Spanish interest in Texas languished until 1714, when the remarkable Frenchman Louis Juchereau de St. Denis walked from Natchitoches, Louisiana, to the Rio Grande. St. Denis proposed a trade relationship between the two nations along their frontier. Back came the missionaries, this time to found six missions in eastern Texas and western Louisiana, one as far east as Robiline, Louisiana. St. Denis established trade, however illegal it might have been, and once again the Spanish enforced their presence in Texas. Other missions, most notably San Antonio de Valero, also came into existence to fasten Spain's grip on her northern provinces, but few succeeded in converting many Indians.

Following the transfer of French territory west of the Mississippi River to Spain by the Peace of Paris Treaty in 1763, Spain no longer worried about penetrations of their territory from that nation, and they could not imagine that the Anglos could move all the way from the Appalachian barrier in less than several hundred years. So, following the advice of their investigator, the Baron de Rubi, they determined to pull back to the Rio Grande. The New Regulation of the Presidios in 1772 closed all missions beyond San Antonio and even ordered civilians to move there as well. In effect, Spain returned most of Texas to the Indians.

Most of the Spanish who had established farms and ranches in East Texas moved reluctantly; indeed, soldiers had to flush some of them out of the woods to compel them to go. No sooner had they arrived in San Antonio than their leader, Antonio Gil YBarbo, petitioned that they be allowed to return to their homes. They were permitted to move east, but no closer than one hundred leagues (approximately three hundred miles) from Natchitoches.

YBarbo led his settlers to the banks of the Trinity River, where they founded the community of Bucareli. They remained there through four years of floods and Comanche raids. Then, without authorization, they moved east to the site of the Mission Nuestra Senora de Guadalupe de los Nacogdoches, probably the only Spanish building still standing in eastern Texas. YBarbo later informed the authorities in San Antonio of his action, and in 1779 they recognized the *pueblo* of Nacogdoches and acknowledged YBarbo's leadership of the community.

The Spanish still did not want foreigners in their territory, but far more rapidly than either they or the Americans imagined, the first of frontiersmen from the United States began to filter into Texas in the 1790s. William Barr and Samuel Davenport established a trading post in Nacogdoches in 1798, and local officials made them citizens and permitted them to do business. Others just quietly slipped into the area unannounced and claimed land they would confirm later.

Some Americans came in conquest. The Spanish suspected Philip Nolan's forays into Texas to round up mustangs for sale in Louisiana masked his real purpose of scouting the area for General James Wilkinson, commander of the United States forces in the Old Southwest. Eventually they attempted to arrest Nolan and his men, and he was killed in a skirmish near Waco.

In 1812 Augustus Magee and Bernardo Gutierrez de Lara led the Army of the North across the Sabine to Nacogdoches, where they proclaimed Texas free from Spain. They published the first newspaper in Texas, the *Gaceta de Tejas*, while occupying the Stone Fort before moving on to La Bahia. Later Magee died, some said at the hands of Gutierrez, and then General Joaquín Arrendondo led an expedition north that purged Texas of the venture and its sympathizers.

So Texas remained substantially Spanish, save for a few isolated Americans who slipped by unnoticed or were tolerated, until the Adams-Onís Treaty of 1819. By its provisions, the United States gained Florida but forever renounced any claims to Texas. The anger of slave-state Americans, who wanted the opportunity to expand westward, brought forth two expeditions led by Dr. James Long of Natchez, Mississippi. Again Texas was declared independent, and again the Spanish prevailed. Long was killed, and Jane, his young bride, had to return to the United States. She later made her way back to Texas and would be honored with the designation of the "Mother of Texas" because of her ordeal in the wilderness after her husband's capture.

With such a stormy beginning, Anglo immigration to Texas seemed unlikely for years to come. But this was not the case. Moses Austin, an American lead miner and businessman who had moved to Missouri while that territory remained in Spanish hands, went broke in the panic of 1819. He remembered that years before, the Spanish had allowed William Morgan to lead a colony of Irishmen from New Jersey to establish a settlement at New Madrid, Missouri. Morgan had become the first *empresario* in Spain's North American territory.

Austin determined to duplicate Morgan's example in Texas to recoup his fortune. He traveled to San Antonio, where he was rebuffed by Spanish officials until an old friend, the Baron de Bastrop, vouched for him. Then Austin's request was forwarded to higher authority, and surprisingly, the reply was positive. But Moses Austin died before he could establish his colony. And before his son, Stephen Fuller Austin, could fully claim his inheritance, the Spanish government of Mexico fell to nationalist revolutionaries.

Over the next several years, Stephen Austin patiently worked with a succession of Mexican republicans, imperialists under Colonel Augustín de Iturbide, and States'-rights proponents following the coup that finally established the Constitution of 1824. In each case his rights were confirmed, only to be lost when the existing government fell. Finally, as one of the architects of a new Mexican government, he received permission to settle three hundred families on his grant. Later, more than thirty others received empresarial grants in Texas.

Austin established his colony along the coast, where it was approximately divided into three parts by the Brazos and Colorado rivers. It extended northward to the El Camino Real, or the highway connecting Nacogdoches and San Antonio. His colony was west of the eastern thickets and its fields could be cleared easily, yet it still had sufficient rainfall for the crops his Southern American immigrants already knew how to grow.

Life in Texas would remain difficult until the Civil War, with little noticeable difference between the colonial, republic, or early statehood periods. Most early immigrants walked to Texas, some carrying literally all their possessions, and others walking beside wagons. The more fortunate came by coastal boats from New Orleans. Some, such as Jared Groce, were wealthy, but most were short of cash. They all sought opportunity and cheap land. Each immigrant received a league of land (over 4,400 acres), and additional amounts could be obtained with little expense.

Food was abundant for skilled hunters or fishermen, but their diet remained limited and seasonal. Without modern methods of food preservation, the early Texans ate greens in the warm months and lived on meat and ground corn the rest of the year. They lived in log cabins, in time perhaps a dogtrot house, and when lumber became available, boarded over the logs to hide early poverty.

All were or became nominal Roman Catholics and Mexican citizens as the price of admission to Texas, considered to be formalities and a cheap enough price for the amount of land involved. It seemed a good life. Then the trouble came.

Some historians date the beginning of the Texas Revolution as early as the Fredonia Rebellion in 1826–27. Empresario Haden Edwards obtained lands around Nacogdoches, and, because of the presence of previous Spanish, Mexican, and Anglo land grantees, he had difficulty in establishing his claims. In despair he declared his area free of Mexico, but a single military expedition scattered his supporters.

From that moment some Mexican leaders, especially the extreme nationalists, resented the presence of Americans in Texas. They persuaded President Vincente Guerrero to abolish slavery in Mexico in 1829, a move aimed at the Americans in Texas who held slaves. The next year they secured the passage of the Law of April 6, 1830, which stopped American immigration, began the collection of customs, and forbade trade with the United States. Many Texans believed this to be in violation of the Mexican Constitution of 1824, which had handed such matters over to the individual states.

Real trouble began in 1832 when the commander of the Mexican garrison at Anáhuac, Juan (John) Davis Bradburn, arrested William Barret Travis and his law partner, Patrick Jack, for making trouble. Settlers from the various colonies assembled near Turtle Bayou and adopted resolutions pledging their loyalty to the Constitution of 1824 and their willingness to fight centralists, such as Bradburn, who had violated it.

The matter was settled when José de Las Piedras, Bradburn's superior, arrived at Anáhuac. Piedras fired Bradburn and released Travis and Jack. When Piedras returned to his duty station in Nacogdoches he tried to prevent a similar occurrence by ordering citizens in the area to surrender their guns. Instead they brought their weapons to town for a battle on August 2–3 that ended with the surrender of Piedras. Finally, John Austin had led a group from Anáhuac to Velasco to obtain a cannon for use against Bradburn. He had to shoot his way past soldiers commanded by Colonel Domingo Ugartechea.

These three disturbances of 1832 set in motion a series of events that led inevitably to revolution. Already, States'-rights proponents under General Santa Anna, at heart a centralist but willing to appear in any guise to obtain power, combated the government. Santa Anna's lieutenant, José Antonio Mexia, came to Texas to investigate the meaning of the disturbances. Stephen F. Austin entertained Mexia at a gala in his honor at Brazoria and succeeded in convincing the Mexican general that the Texans were merely standing up for the States'-rights constitution, and therefore supported Santa Anna.

Mexia returned convinced, but still the Americans felt the need to make a formal statement to the central government. In December 1832, delegates met at San Felipe de Austin and drafted a petition that requested the reopening of immigration from the United States, relief from paying customs, and, above all, separate statehood within the Mexican union. The political chief at San Antonio brusquely rejected their petition, and so a second convention was held in January 1833. This time a more militant atmosphere prevailed. The delegates drafted a similiar proposal, added a draft of a constitution for their proposed state, and convinced Stephen F. Austin to take their request to Mexico City.

Austin found the capital city in turmoil. Recent elections had placed Santa Anna and Valentine Gomez Farias in the presidency and vice-presidency of Mexico. Santa Anna allowed his liberal subordinate to attempt sweeping reforms of all three major power bases in the country—the landowners, the church, and the army. Farias was much too busy to worry about Texas, and after a time Austin grew impatient. What he intended as candor appeared to be a threat when he told Farias that he might as well accept Texas as a separate state because it already was one.

Austin wrote to the *ayuntamiento*, or governing council, at San Antonio, suggesting that they begin their government. Instead, the council turned the letter over to the central government, and Austin was arrested. During the more than eighteen months he remained in prison, Texans remained quiet in fear for Austin's life. Meanwhile, Santa Anna seized full power, deposed his vice president, and summoned a new congress that set aside the liberal Constitution of 1824. In its place Santa Anna established a Mexican government under his complete control.

The summer of 1835 proved eventful in Texas. Austin returned, neither formally charged of a crime nor pardoned, just released. And Captain Antonio Tenorio arrived at Anáhuac to resume the collection of customs. A protest group convinced William B. Travis to lead about thirty men to drive Tenorio from Texas. They had little trouble in doing so, but their action upset the Peace Party, a group that feared his action would bring down the wrath of the central government.

This in fact resulted when General Martín Perfecto de Cós, Santa Anna's brother-in-law who was headquartered in Saltillo, ordered Travis's arrest. But even the Peace Party would not suffer this, so Cós threatened to arrest all the Texans.

Then in October, the Mexican commander ordered the surrender of a cannon held by the citizens of Gonzales. They successfully defended their cannon under a makeshift flag bearing the words "Come and Take It." When others gathered to defend the cannon that no longer needed defending, they were easily led to drive Cós, who had moved up to San Antonio, from Texas. At first a kind of siege was effected, and finally in December a five-day battle erupted. Led by Ben Milam, who died in the battle, the Texans defeated Cós, who agreed to leave Texas and never return.

Santa Anna determined immediately to avenge this insult to Mexico. While the Texans remained disorganized, gloried in their victory, and contemplated ill-advised raids on Mexico, he started north. Arriving at the Rio Grande in January 1836, Santa Anna dispatched General José Urrea along a southerly route to capture, and eventually execute, about five hundred men under James Fannin. Meanwhile he personally led a larger force to recapture San Antonio. This resulted in the thirteen-day siege and fall of the Alamo on March 6.

Nearly four hundred men gathered at Gonzales in response to requests for aid from the Alamo's commander, William B. Travis. Leaderless, they did nothing. On March 1 a convention met at Washington-on-the-Brazos. The next day the delegates declared Texas free of Mexico, and in fifteen days more wrote a constitution for the Republic of Texas.

The convention designated Sam Houston the commander of their army, and he joined the volunteers at Gonzales on March 11. Learning of the fall of the Alamo, Houston led his men east, buying time for his army to grow larger. Then, on April 21, his men led him to battle on the plains at San Jacinto against Santa Anna, who had advanced ahead of his main army with less than one thousand men in an attempt to capture the Texans' government. The battle, which last only a few minutes, changed the destiny of nations. Immediately it confirmed the independence of Texas and eventually led to the Mexican-American War, when the infant and fragile republic became the twenty-eighth state of the American Union in 1845. When that war ended in 1848, Mexico was reduced in size by one-half, and the United States enlarged by one-quarter.

The Texans wrestled with the problems of independence under three presidents of the Republic. The first, Sam Houston, tried to keep the Republic's money problems and possible recapture by Mexico at bay by doing little. The second president, Mirabeau Buonaparte Lamar, made war on Indians and Mexico alike in an attempt to expand Texas's influence. When Houston won a second term in 1841, he returned to a policy of peace.

Houston and Lamar differed markedly over the issue of statehood. Houston attempted to gain admission to the Union during both of his terms because he thought it the only course that would keep Texas safe from Mexico. Lamar approached the problem differently: he boldly tried to expand the Republic and did not desire statehood at all.

In 1844 Anson Jones became president, and although the path to statehood was rough—marked by a rejected treaty in the United States Senate in 1844—the U.S. presidential election of 1844 placed James Knox Polk, an expansionist, in the White House. Even before Polk took the inaugural oath, retiring President John Tyler started the process that made Texas a state in the Union on December 29, 1845.

Statehood in the American Union did not at first dramatically change the life of the average Texan, but eventually Texans prospered and assumed positions of national political and economic leadership. In time Texas became the third largest state in population, and the national leader in fields such as petroleum production. But even today, Texas has retained its own special character, a legacy of its stormy and heroic past.

Eden Ravished

The Land, Pioneer Attitudes, and Conservation

Harlan Hague

Harlan Hague teaches history of the American West and American environmental history at San Joaquin Delta College, Stockton, California. He is the author of Road to California: The Search For a Southern Overland Route *and articles on western exploration and trails.*

IN O. E. RÖLVAAG'S *Giants in the Earth,* a small caravan of Norwegian immigrants stopped on the prairie, and the riders got down from their wagons. They scanned the landscape in all directions and liked what they saw. It was beautiful, all good plowland and clean of any sign of human habitation all the way to the horizon. After so much hoping and planning, they had finally found their place in the new land. One of the men, Per Hansa, still had difficulty comprehending what was happening:

"This vast stretch of beautiful land was to be his—yes, his. . . . His heart began to expand with a mighty exaltation. An emotion he had never felt before filled him and made him walk erect. . . . 'Good God!' he panted. 'This kingdom is going to be mine!'"

Countless others who went to the West reacted like Rölvaag's Per Hansa. They entered the Promised Land with high expectations, possessed the land and were possessed by it. They changed the land and in time were changed by it.

The influence of the West on the American mind has interested historians ever since Frederick Jackson Turner read his momentous essay in 1893 to a meeting of the American Historical Association. In the essay, Turner concluded: "The existence of an area of free land, its continuous recession, and the advance of American settlement westward, explain American development." Turner went on to describe in some detail the various ways the western environment changed the frontiersman, molding him into the American. The processes and result of this evolution were in the end, by implication, favorable.

Writing in the early 1890s, Turner did not detect one of the most important themes, if not the most important, of the westward movement, a theme which would have immense impact on the shaping of the American character. This was the belief that the resources of the West were inexhaustible. Henry Nash Smith, in his influential *Virgin Land,* caught the point that Turner missed:

"The character of the American empire was defined not by streams of influence out of the past, not by a cultural tradition, nor by its place in a world community, but by a relation between man and nature—or rather, even more narrowly, between American man and the American West. This relation was thought of as unvaryingly fortunate."

This cornucopian view of the West was the basis of the frontiersman's attitude toward and his use of the land.

The typical trans-Mississippi emigrant in the last half of the nineteenth century accepted the assumption of inexhaustible resources. Yet the view of the West as an everlasting horn of plenty had been proven false long before the post-Civil War exodus. For example, commercial hunting of the sea otter along the California coast, which had begun in 1784, reached its peak around 1815; by the mid-1840s, the numbers of the animals had declined alarmingly, and the otter was soon hunted almost to extinction. The beaver's fate was similar. Soon after Lewis and Clark told about the teeming beaver populations in western streams, trappers moved westward to harvest the furs. They worked streams so relentlessly that the beaver began to disappear in areas where it had always been plentiful. By 1840, the beaver had been trapped virtually to oblivion. No mountain man in the 1820s would have dreamed there could ever be an end to the hardy little animal. Yet unbridled exploitation had nearly condemned the beaver to extinction. The lesson was lost on Westerners.

Pioneers were not noticeably swayed by the arguments of the naturalists, who publicized the wonders of nature or went further and pled for its preservation. William Bartram, a contemporary of Jefferson, wrote eloquently about the beauty of American nature in his *Travels.* Originally published in 1791, his book was more popular in Europe than in the United States, which had yet to discover its aesthetic environment. John James Audubon had more influence in this country upon publication of his *Birds of America* series (1827–1844) and his subsequent call for protection of wildlife. Francis Parkman, while not famed as a naturalist, wrote firsthand accounts about the scenic West and the Indian inhabitants who lived in harmony with nature. It is no wonder that Parkman, who was enthralled with the outdoors, admired Indians and mountain men more than the settlers he encountered during his western travels.

There was indeed a whole body of romantic literature and art during the first half of the nineteenth century that might have persuaded Americans that environmental values could be measured in terms other than economic. William Cullen Bryant wrote with such depth of feeling about the simple pleasures of the outdoors that he is still known as one of our foremost nature poets. The founding spirit of transcendentalism, Ralph Waldo Emerson, wrote in his first book, *Nature:*

"In the presence of nature, a wild delight runs through the man. . . . In the woods, is perpetual youth. . . . In the woods, we return to reason and faith. . . . The currents of the Universal Being circulate through me; I am part or particle of God. . . . In the wilderness, I find something more dear and connate than in streets or villages."

Emerson's contemporary, Henry David Thoreau, was even less restrained in his adoration of untamed nature when he wrote: "In Wildness is the preservation of the World." At the same time, Thomas Cole and the Hudson River school of landscape painters captured on canvas the essence of nature that the romantic writers had recorded in prose and poetry. And farther west, beyond the Mississippi River, George Catlin, Karl Bodmer, and Alfred Jacob Miller were painting the exotic wilderness that increasingly drew the attention of Americans.

Unmoved by praise of the aesthetic quality of the environment, frontiersmen were even less impressed by warnings that its resources were not without end. Every American generation since the colonial period had been told of the virtue of using natural resources wisely. An ordinance of Plymouth Colony had regulated the cutting of timber. William Penn had decreed that one acre of trees be left undisturbed for every five acres cleared. In 1864, only a moment before the beginning of the migration that would cover the West within one generation, George Perkins Marsh published his book *Man and Nature,* the most eloquent statement up to that time of the disastrous result that must follow careless stewardship of the land. "Man has too long forgotten," he wrote, "that the earth was given to him for usufruct alone, not for consumption, still less for profligate waste." That is, man could and should both cherish and use the land, but he should not use it up. The significance in Marsh's warning was the recognition that the land could be used up.

While American ambassador to Italy, Marsh had theorized that ancient Rome's fall could be traced to the depletion of the empire's forests. He predicted a like fate for the United States if its resources were similarly squandered. Marsh's book appears to have been widely read by American intellectuals and probably favorably influenced the movements for national parks and forestry management. In it, indeed, were the seeds of the conservation movement of the early twentieth century. Yet it is unlikely that many frontiersmen read or were aware of—or at least they did not heed—Marsh's advice.

Pioneers heard a different drummer. They read descriptions about the West written by people who had been there. Lansford W. Hastings's glowing picture of California and Oregon thrilled thousands:

"In view of their increasing population, accumulating wealth, and growing prosperity, I can not but believe, that the time is not distant, when those wild forests, trackless plains, untrodden valleys, and the unbounded ocean, will present one grand scene, of continuous improvements, universal enterprise, and unparalleled commerce: when those vast forests, shall have disappeared, before the hardy pioneer; those extensive plains, shall abound with innumerable herds, of domestic animals; those fertile valleys, shall groan under the immense weight of their abundant products: when those numerous rivers shall team [sic] with countless steam-boats, steam-ships, ships, barques and brigs; when the entire country, will be everywhere intersected, with turnpike roads, rail-roads and canals; and when, all the vastly numerous, and rich resources, of that now, almost unknown region, will be fully and advantageously developed."

Once developed, hopeful emigrants learned, the area would become the garden of the world. In the widely-distributed *Our Western Empire: or the New West Beyond the Mississippi,* Linus P. Brockett wrote that "in no part of the vast domain of the United States, and certainly in no other country under the sun, is there a body of land of equal extent, in which there are so few acres unfit for cultivation, or so many which, with irrigation or without it, will yield such bountiful crops."

Other books described the routes to the Promised Land. The way west was almost without exception easy and well-watered, with plenty of wood, game, and grass.

There was not just opportunity on the frontier. Walt Whitman also saw romance in the westward migration:

Come my tan-faced children,
Follow well in order, get your weapons ready,
Have you your pistols? have you your sharp-edged axes?
    Pioneers! O pioneers!

For we cannot tarry here,
We must march my darlings, we must bear the brunt of danger,

We the youthful sinewy races, all the rest on us depend,
    Pioneers! O pioneers! . . .

    We primeval forests felling,
We the rivers stemming, vexing we and piercing deep the mines within,
We the surface broad surveying, we the virgin soil upheaving

3. NATIONAL CONSOLIDATION AND EXPANSION

Pioneers! O pioneers! . . .

Swift! to the head of the army!—swift! spring to your places, Pioneers! O Pioneers!

The ingredients were all there: danger, youth, virgin soil. Well might frontiersmen agree with Mark Twain who wrote that the first question asked by the American, upon reaching heaven, was: "Which way West?" Thoreau also thought a westward course the natural one:

"When I go out of the house for a walk . . . my needle . . . always settles between west and south-southwest. The future lies that way to me, and the earth seems more unexhausted and richer on that side. . . . westward I go free. . . . I must walk toward Oregon."

Emigrants felt this same pull but for different reasons. Thoreau's West was a wild region to be enjoyed for itself and preserved untouched, while the West to the emigrants was a place for a new start. The pioneers would conquer the wilderness and gather its immeasurable bounty. This did not imply that Westerners were oblivious to the beauty of the land. Many were aware of the West's scenic attractions but felt, with the influential artist Thomas Cole, that the wilderness, however beautiful, inevitably must give way to progress. In his "Essay on American Scenery," Cole described the sweet joys of nature—the mountains, lakes, rivers, waterfalls, and sky. The essay, dated 1835, is nostalgic. Cole closed his paean with an expression of "sorrow that the beauty of such landscapes are quickly passing away . . . desecrated by what is called improvement." But, after all, he added, "such is the road society has to travel." Clearly, Cole, like most of his nineteenth-century readers, did not question the propriety of "improvement" or the definition of "progress."

THE BELIEF in the inexhaustibility of western resources was superimposed on an attitude toward the land that Americans had inherited from generations past. In the Judeo-Christian view, God created the world for man. Man, was the master of nature rather than a part of it. The resources of the earth—soil, water, plants, animals, insects, rocks, fish, birds, air—were there for his use, and his proper role was to dominate. It was natural then for God's children to harvest the rich garden provided for them by their Creator. They went into the West to do God's bidding, to use the land as he willed, to fulfill a destiny.

This attitude of man-over-nature was not universal. Like most primitive cultures throughout history, it was not held by the American Indian. The Indian saw himself as a part of nature, not its master. He felt a close kinship with the earth and all living things. Black Elk, a holy man of the Oglala Sioux, for example, believed that all living things were the children of the sky, their father, and the earth, their mother. He had special reverence for "the earth, from whence we came and at whose breast we suck as babies all our lives, along with all the animals and birds and trees and grasses." Creation legends of many tribes illustrate the Indian's familial attachment to the earth and his symbiotic relationship with other forms of life.

The land to Indians was more than merely a means of livelihood for the current generation. It belonged not only to them, the living, but to all generations of their people, those who came before and those who would come after. They could not separate themselves from the land. Of course, there were exceptions. Some Indians fell under the spell of the white trader who offered them goods that would make their lives easier, not to say better. As they became dependent on white man's goods, the land and its fruits began to assume for them an economic value that might be bartered for the conveniences produced by the white man's technology. This is not to say that the Indian attitude toward the land changed. Rather it illustrates that some Indians adopted the white man's view.

To European-Americans, the western Indians' use of the land was just another proof of their savagery. The pioneers had listened to the preachers of Manifest Destiny, and they knew that the nomadic tribes must stand aside for God's Chosen People who would use the land as God intended.

And so they returned to Eden. While some went to California and some to Oregon, the most coherent migration before the rush for California gold began in 1849 was the Mormon exodus to Salt Lake Valley. The latter was not typical of the westward movement. The persecuted saints entered the West not so much for its lure as because of its inaccessibility. In 1830, the same year that the Mormon Church was founded, Joseph Smith announced a revelation which would lead eventually to—or at least foresaw—the great migration:

"And ye are called to bring to pass the gathering of mine elect . . . unto one place upon the face of this land . . . [which] . . . shall be on the borders by the Lamanites [Indians]. . . . The glory of the Lord shall be there, and it shall be called Zion. . . . The righteous shall be gathered out from among all nations, and shall come to Zion, singing with songs of everlasting joy."

Mormons who trekked to the Utah settlements in the late 1840s and 1850s knew they were doing God's bidding.

Other emigrants were just as sure that the Lord had prepared a place for them. "Truly the God in Heaven," wrote an Oregon-bound traveler in 1853, "has spread in rich profusion around us everything which could happify man and reveal the Wisdom and Benevolence of God to man." Oregon Trail travelers often noted in their journals that they were going to the "Promised Land." In A. B. Guthrie's *The Way West*, Fairman, who would be leaving Independence shortly for Oregon, proposed a toast "to a place where there's no fever." McBee, another emigrant, impatient to get started, responded:

" 'Y God, yes, . . . and to soil rich as anything. Plant a nail and it'll come up a spike. I heerd you don't never have to put up hay, the grass is that good, winter and all. And lambs come twice a year. Just set by and let the grass grow and the critters birth and get fat. That's my idee of farmin'."

It seems that most emigrants, in spite of the humor, did not expect their animals or themselves to wax fat in the new land without working. God would provide, but they must harvest.

Following close on the heels of the Oregon Trail farmers, and sometimes traveling in the same wagon trains, were the miners. This rough band of transients hardly thought of themselves as God's children, but they did nevertheless accept the horn-of-plenty image of the West. Granville Stuart wrote from the California mines that "no such enormous amounts of gold had been found anywhere before, and . . . they all believed that the supply was inexhaustible." Theirs was not an everflowing cornucopia, however, and each miner hoped to be in the right spot with an open sack when the horn tipped to release its wealth.

The typical miner wanted to get as rich as possible as quickly as possible so he could return home to family, friends, and a nabob's retirement. This condition is delightfully pictured in the frontispiece illustration in Mark Twain's *Roughing It*. A dozing miner is seated on a barrel in his cabin, his tools on the floor beside him. He is dreaming about the future: a country estate, yachting, carriage rides and walks in the park with a lady, an ocean voyage and a tour of Europe, viewing the pyramids. The dreams of other miners, while not so grand, still evoked pleasant images of home and an impatience to return there. This yearning is obvious in the lines of a miner's song of the 1850s:

> Home's dearest joys Time soon destroys,
> Their loss we all deplore;
> While they may last, we labor fast
> To dig the golden ore.
> When the land has yielded its riches:
> Then home again, home again,
> From a foreign shore,
> We'll sing how sweet our heart's delight,
> With our dear friends once more.

Miners' diaries often reflected these same sentiments, perhaps with less honeyed phrases but with no less passion.

A practical-minded argonaut, writing in 1852 from California to his sister in Alabama, explained his reason for going to the mines: "I think in one year here I can make enough to clear me of debt and give me a pretty good start in the world. Then I will be a happy man." What then? He instructed his sister to tell all his friends that he would soon be "back whare [sic] I can enjoy there [sic] company." Other miners thought it would take a little longer, but the motives were the same. A California miner later reminisced:

"Five years was the longest period any one expected to stay. Five years at most was to be given to rifling California of her treasures, and then that country was to be thrown aside like a used-up newspaper and the rich adventurers would spend the remainder of their days in wealth, peace, and prosperity at their eastern homes. No one talked then of going out 'to build up the glorious State of California.'"

The fact that many belatedly found that California was more than worked-out diggings and stayed—pronouncing the state glorious and themselves founding fathers—does not change their motives for going there.

There was a substantial body of miners, perpetually on the move, rowdies usually, the frontier fraternity boys, whose home was the mining camp and whose friends were largely miners like themselves. They rushed around the West to every discovery of gold or silver in a vain attempt to get rich without working. Though they had no visions of returning east to family and fireside, they did believe that the West was plentifully supplied with riches. It was just their bad luck that they had not found their shares. Their original reason for going to the mining camps and, though they might enjoy the camaraderie of their fellows, their reason for staying, was the same as that of the more genteel sort of miner who had come to the western wilderness, fully expecting to return to the East. More than any other emigrant to the West, the miner's motive was unabashed exploitation. For the most part, he did not conserve, preserve, or enrich the land. His intention, far from honorable, was rape.

THE CATTLEMAN was a transition figure between the miner who stripped the land and the farmer who, while stripping the land, also cherished it. The West to the cattleman meant grass and water, free or cheap. The earliest ranchers on the plains raised beef for the eastern markets and for the government, which had decreed that the cow replace the buffalo in the Plains Indians' life-style. The Indians, except for a few "renegades," complied, though they were never quite able to work the steer into their religion.

It was not long before word filtered back to the East that fortunes could be made in western stock raising. James Brisbin's *Beef Bonanza; or, How to Get Rich on the Plains*, first published in 1881, was widely read. Readers were dazzled by the author's minutely documented "proof" that an industrious man could more than double his investment in less than five years. Furthermore, there was almost no risk involved:

"In a climate so mild that horses, cattle, and sheep and goats can live in the open air through all the winter months, and fatten on the dry and apparently withered grasses of the soil, there would appear to be scarcely a limit to the number that could be raised."

Experienced and inexperienced alike responded. Getting rich, they thought, was only a matter of time, not expertise.

Entrepreneurs and capital, American and foreign, poured into the West. Most of the rangeland was not in private ownership. Except for small tracts, generally homesteaded along water courses or as sites for home ranches, it was public property. Though a cattleman might claim rights to a certain range, and though an association of cattlemen might try to enforce the claims of its members, legally the land was open, free, and available.

By the mid-1880s, the range was grossly overstocked. The injury to the land was everywhere apparent. While some began to counsel restraint, most ranchers continued to ravish the country until the winter of 1886–1887 forced them to respect it. Following that most disastrous of winters, which in some areas killed as much as 85 percent of range stock, one chastened cattle king wrote that the cattle business "that had been fascinating to me before, suddenly became distasteful. . . . I never wanted to own again an animal that I could not feed and shelter." The industry gradually recovered, but it would never be the same. More land was fenced, wells dug, and windmills installed. Shelters for cattle were built, and hay was grown for winter feeding. Cattle raising became less an adventure and more a business.

In some cattlemen there grew an attachment, if not affection, for the land. Some, especially after the winter of 1886–1887, began to put down roots. Others who could afford it built luxurious homes in the towns to escape the deficiencies of the countryside, much as twentieth-century townsmen would build cabins in the country to escape the deficiencies of the cities. Probably most cattlemen after the winter of 1886–1887 still believed in the bounty of the West, but a bounty which they now recognized would be released to them only through husbandry.

Among all those who went into the West to seek their fortunes, the frontier farmers carried with them the highest hopes and greatest faith. Their forebears had been told for generations that they were the most valuable citizens, chosen of God, and that their destiny lay westward. John Filson, writing in 1784 about frontier Kentucky, described the mystique of the West that would be understood by post-Civil War emigrants:

"This fertile region, abounding with all the luxuries of nature, stored with all the principal materials for art and industry, inhabited by virtuous and ingenious citizens, must universally attract the attention of mankind." There, continued Filson, "like the land of promise, flowing with milk and honey, a land of brooks of water, . . . a land of wheat and barley, and all kinds of fruits, you shall eat bread without scarceness, and not lack any thing in it."

By 1865 the Civil War had settled the controversy between North and South that had hindered the westward movement, the Homestead Act had been passed, and the Myth of the Garden had replaced the Myth of the Desert. By the grace of God and with the blessing of Washington, the frontier farmer left the old land to claim his own in the new:

Born of a free, world-wandering race,
Little we yearned o'er an oft-turned sod.
What did we care for the father's place,
Having ours fresh from the hand of God?

Farmers were attracted to the plains by the glowing accounts distributed by railroads and western states. Newspapers in the frontier states added their accolades. The editor of the *Kansas Farmer* declared in 1867 that there were in his state "vast areas of unimproved land, rich as that on the banks of the far famed Nile, . . . acres, miles, leagues, townships, counties,—oceans of land, all ready for the plough, good as the best in America, and yet lying without occupants." Would-be emigrants who believed this sort of propaganda could sing with conviction:

Oh! give me a home where the buffalo roam,
Where the deer and the antelope play;
Where never is heard a discouraging word,
And the sky is not clouded all day.

There was a reason for the sky's clarity, the emigrants learned when they arrived on the plains. It was not long before many had changed their song:

We've reached the land of desert sweet,
Where nothing grows for man to eat;

I look across the plains
And wonder why it never rains.

And, finally, sung to the cadence of a "slow, sad march":

We do not live, we only stay;
We are too poor to get away.

It is difficult to generalize about the experience of pioneer farmers. Those who continued their journeys to the Pacific Coast regions were usually satisfied with what they found. It was those who settled on the plains who were most likely to be disillusioned. Their experience was particularly shattering since they had gone to the West not just to reap in it but also to live in it. Most found not the land of milk and honey they expected, but, it seems, a life of drudgery and isolation.

The most persistent theme in the literature of the period is disenchantment. This mood is caught best by Hamlin Garland. In *Main-Travelled Roads,* Garland acknowledged two views of the plains experience when he wrote that the main-travelled road in the West, hot and dusty in summer, muddy and dreary in fall and spring, and snowy in winter, "does sometimes cross a rich meadow where the songs of the larks and bobolinks and blackbirds are tangled." But Garland's literary road is less cluttered: "Mainly it is long and wearyful, and has a dull little town at one end and a home of toil at the other. Like the main-travelled road of life it is traversed by many classes of people, but the poor and the weary predominate."

The opposite responses to the plains are more pronounced in O. E. Rölvaag's *Giants in the Earth,* one of the most enduring novels of the agricultural West. Per Hansa meets the challenge of the new land, overcomes obstacles and rejoices in each success, however small. He accepts the prairie for what it is and loves it. Meanwhile, his wife, Beret, is gradually driven insane by that same prairie. Where Per Hansa saw hope and excitement in the land, Beret saw only despair and loneliness. "Oh, how quickly it grows dark out here!" she cries, to which Per Hansa replies, "The sooner the day's over, the sooner the next day comes!" In spite of her husband's optimistic outlook, Beret's growing insanity dominates the story as it moves with gloomy intensity to its tragic end. It is significant that Per Hansa dies, a victim of the nature that he did not fear but could not subdue.

Willa Cather, the best-known novelist of nineteenth-century prairie farm life, treated relationships between people and their environment more sensitively than most. While her earlier short stories often dwell on themes of man against the harsh land, her works thereafter, without glossing over the severity of farm life, reveal a certain harmony between the land and those who live on it and love it. Her characters work hard, and suffer; but they are not immune to the loveliness of the land.

The histories of plains farming dwell more on processes than suffering, but accounts that treat the responses of the settlers to their environment generally verify the novelists' interpretations. According to the histories, the picture of desperation painted by Garland and Rölvaag applies principally to the earliest years of any particular frontier region. By the time sod houses acquired board floors and women were able to visit with other women regularly, Cather's images are more accurate.

The fact that pioneer farmers were not completely satisfied with what they found in the Promised Land does not alter their reasons for going there. They had gone into the West for essentially the same reason as the trappers, miners, and cattlemen: economic exploitation. Unlike their predecessors, they also had been looking for homes. Yet, like them, they had believed fervently in the Myth of Superabundance.

THE IRRATIONAL BELIEF that the West's resources were so great that they could never be used up was questioned by some at the very time that others considered it an article of faith. George Perkins Marsh in 1864 warned of the consequences of a too rapid consumption of the land's resources. In 1878, John Wesley Powell attacked the Myth of the Garden when he pointed out that a substantial portion of western land, previously thought to be cultivable by eastern methods, could be farmed successfully only by irrigation. Overgrazing of grasslands resulted in the intrusion of weeds and the erosion of soil, prompting many ranchers, especially after the devastating winter of 1886–1887, to contract their operations and practice range management. Plowing land where rainfall was inadequate for traditional farming methods resulted in wind and water erosion of the soil. Before the introduction of irrigation or dry farming techniques, many plains farmers gave up and returned eastward. The buffalo, which might have numbered fifty million or more at mid-century, were hunted almost to extinction by 1883. Passenger pigeons were estimated to number in the billions in the first half of the nineteenth century: around 1810, Alexander Wilson, an ornithologist, guessed that a single flock, a mile wide and 240 miles long, contained more than two billion birds. Yet before the end of the century, market hunting and the clearing of forest habitats had doomed the passenger pigeon to extinction. Examples of this sort led many people to the inescapable conclusion that the West's resources were not inexhaustible.

At the same time a growing number of people saw values other than economic in the West. Some plains farmers struggling with intermittent drought and mortgage could still see the beauty of the land. Alexandra in Cather's *O Pioneers!* could see it: "When the road began to climb the first long swells of the Divide, Alexandra hummed an old Swedish hymn. . . . Her face was so radiant" as she looked at the land "with love and yearning. It seemed beautiful to her, rich and strong and glorious. Her eyes drank in the breadth of it, until her tears blinded her."

Theodore Roosevelt wrote often of the "delicious" rides he took at his Badlands ranch during autumn and spring. He described the rolling, green grasslands; the prairie roses; the blacktail and whitetail deer; the songs of the skylark; the white-shouldered lark-bunting; and the sweet voice of the meadowlark, his favorite. Of a moonlight ride, he wrote that the "river gleams like running quicksilver, and the moonbeams play over the grassy stretches of the plateaus and glance off the wind-rippled blades as they would from water." Lincoln Lang, a neighbor of Roosevelt's, had the same feeling for the land. He called the Badlands "a landscape masterpiece of the wild, . . . verdant valleys, teeming with wild life, with wild fruits and flowers, . . . with the God-given atmosphere of truth itself, over which unshackled Nature, alone, reigned queen."

Even miners were not immune to the loveliness of the countryside. Granville Stuart, working in the California mines, was struck by the majestic forests of sugar pine, yellow pine, fir, oak, and dogwood. He described the songs and coloration of the birds and the woodpeckers' habit of storing acorns in holes that they meticulously pecked in tree limbs. He delighted in watching a covey of quail near his cabin each day. "Never was I guilty of killing one," he added. Bret Harte lived among the California miners, and his stories often turn to descriptions of the picturesque foothills of the Sierra Nevada. After the birth of "The Luck" in Roaring Camp, the proud, self-appointed godfathers decorated the baby's "bower with flowers and sweet-smelling shrubs, . . . wild honey-suckles, azaleas, or the painted blossoms of Las Mariposas. The men had suddenly awakened to the fact that there were beauty and significance in these trifles, which they had so long trodden carelessly beneath their feet."

3. NATIONAL CONSOLIDATION AND EXPANSION

Success of some sort often broadened the frontiersman's viewpoint. The miner, cattleman, or farmer who had succeeded in some way in his struggle with the land had more time and inclination to think about his relationship with it. Viewing his environment less as an adversary, the Westerner began to see what was happening to it.

At times, concern for the environment led to action. The mounting protests of Californians whose homes and farms had been damaged by the silt-laden runoff from hydraulic mining finally led to the outlawing of this mindless destruction of the land. Frederick Law Olmsted, who had designed New York's Central Park, initiated an era in 1864 when he and some friends persuaded Congress to grant to the state of California a piece of land in California's Sierra Nevada for the creation of a park, merely because the land, which included Yosemite Valley and the Mariposa Big Trees, was beautiful and the public would enjoy it. The idea took hold, and other parks soon followed, Yellowstone in 1872 being the first public "pleasuring ground" under federal management. The new art of landscape photography showed Easterners the wonders of the West, without the hardships of getting there, and revealed to many Westerners a land they inhabited but had never seen. With the improvement in transportation, principally railroads, more and more people ventured into the West to see these wonders firsthand.

A growing awareness that unrestrained exploitation was fast destroying the natural beauty of the West and that its resources, by the end of the nineteenth century widely acknowledged to be finite, were being consumed at an alarming pace led to considerable soul-searching. Frederick Jackson Turner, who had most eloquently described the influence that the great expanses of western land had on the shaping of American character, also hinted that the disappearance of available land was likely to cause some serious disruptions in American society. "The frontier has gone," he wrote, "and with its going has closed the first period of American history."

If the first phase of American history, in which a dominant theme was the advance of the frontier, ran from 1607 to 1890, the second phase began with the emergence of the conservation movement which would lead to the alteration of fundamental attitudes toward the land nurtured during the first phase. While based generally on concern for the environment, the movement split in the early twentieth century into two factions. One faction argued for wise management of the country's resources to prevent their being wasted. This "utilitarian conservation" was not a break with the frontier view of exploitation. It was a refinement. While the frontier view was one of rapid exploitation of inexhaustible resources, the utilitarian conservationists rejected the myth of inexhaustibility and advocated the careful use of finite resources, without rejecting the basic assumption that the resources were there to be exploited. This view of conservation led to the setting aside and management of forest reserves, soil and water conservation projects, and irrigation and hydroelectric programs.

The other faction, whose ideology has been called "aesthetic conservation," clearly broke with the frontier past when its members argued for the preservation of areas of natural beauty for public enjoyment. This group's efforts bore fruit in the establishment of national and state parks, monuments and wilderness areas. There are indications that the two factions are drawing closer together in the umbrella ecology movement of the 1970s, perhaps eventually to merge.

It is senseless to compare nineteenth-century frontier attitudes toward the land with today's more enlightened views. Faced seemingly with such plenty—billions of passenger pigeons, millions of buffalo, innumerable beaver, endless seas of grass, vast forests of giant trees, mines to shame King Solomon's—excess was understandable and probably inevitable. Excess in this case meant waste. Here the Turner thesis is most meaningful, for the belief in the inexhaustibility of resources in the West generated the unique American acceptance of waste as the fundamental tenet of a life-style. For this, the frontiersman is not entirely blameless. But certainly, he is less blameworthy than the neo-pioneer who continues, against reason and history, to cling hopefully to the myth of inexhaustibility. Yet there were examples, however few, and voices, however dim, that the frontiersman might have heeded. It remains to be seen whether Americans today have learned the lesson their ancestors, four generations removed, failed to comprehend.

BIBLIOGRAPHIC NOTE

There are few comprehensive surveys of the evolution of American attitudes toward the environment. Three useful sources are Stewart L. Udall, *The Quiet Crisis* (New York: Holt, Rinehart, 1963); Hans Huth, *Nature and the American: Three Centuries of Changing Attitudes* (Berkeley: University of California, 1957); and Roderick Nash, *Wilderness and the American Mind,* rev. ed. (New Haven: Yale University, 1973), the last particularly concerned with the American response to wilderness. Frederick Jackson Turner's frontier thesis, which inevitably must be considered in any study of the relationship between Americans and their environment, is in his *The Frontier in American History* (New York: Henry Holt,

1921). Invaluable to an understanding of what Americans thought the West was is Henry Nash Smith, *Virgin Land: The American West as Symbol and Myth* (New York: Vintage Books, 1950). The most influential book of the twentieth century in the development of a land ethic is Aldo Leopold, *A Sand County Almanac* (New York: Oxford University, 1949).

Selections from historical materials and literature were blended in this study to illustrate western emigrants' expectations for and responses to the new country. In addition to titles listed in the text, literary impressions of nature are in Wilson O. Clough, *The Necessary Earth: Nature and Solitude in American Literature* (Austin: University of Texas, 1964) and John Conron, *The American Landscape: A Critical Anthology of Prose and Poetry* (New York: Oxford University, 1974). Useful bibliographies of the literature of the westward movement are Lucy Lockwood Hazard, *The Frontier in American Literature* (New York: Thomas Y. Crowell, 1927) and Richard W. Etulain, *Western American Literature* (Vermillion, S.D.: University of South Dakota, 1972). Bibliographies of historical materials are in Ray Allen Billington, *Westward Expansion*, 4th ed. (New York: Macmillan, 1974), and Nelson Klose, *A Concise Study Guide to the American Frontier* (Lincoln: University of Nebraska, 1964).

ACT ONE

Lois W. Banner

Lois W. Banner, 47, is professor of history and of the Program for the Study of Women and Men in Society at the University of Southern California. Born in Los Angeles, she received a B.A. from the University of California, Los Angeles (1960) and a Ph.D. from Columbia University (1970). She is the author of Elizabeth Cady Stanton: A Radical for Women's Rights *(1980) and is co-editor of* Clio's Consciousness Raised: New Perspectives on the History of Women *(1976).*

On July 19, 1848, in the village of Seneca Falls, New York, some 300 people crowded into a small Methodist chapel, drawn by an announcement in the daily *Seneca County Courier*. The notice proclaimed something unheard of—a two-day "Woman's Rights Convention." Despite a request that men stay away until the second day, about 40 curious males showed up at the start.

The organizers of the convention—Lucretia Mott, a 55-year-old Quaker activist from Philadelphia, and Elizabeth Cady Stanton, 32, the wife of a local lawyer-politician—would be remembered later as the founders of the American women's rights movement. But on that day in 1848, they lacked the temerity to preside over their own meeting and instead persuaded Mott's husband, James, a merchant, to serve as chairman. Not until Stanton rose to speak did anyone get a sense of what was to come.

"I should feel exceedingly diffident . . . having never before spoken in public," she told the audience, " . . . did I not feel that the time had come for the question of woman's wrongs to be laid before the public, did I not believe that woman herself must do this work; for woman alone can understand the height, the depth, the length and the breadth of her degradation."

Stanton went on to read aloud the "Declaration of Rights and Sentiments" that she and several fellow organizers had drafted for the convention. A clever rewording of Thomas Jefferson's Declaration of Independence, its title borrowed from the 1833 covenant of William Lloyd Garrison's American Anti-Slavery Society, the broadside provoked 18 straight hours of debate among those present—farmers, local merchants, housewives, mill workers, abolitionists and sundry other reformers.

"We hold these truths to be self-evident," Stanton said, "that all men and women are created equal." Thus, Stanton positioned her declaration squarely within the American political tradition. But she underscored the radical roots of that tradition: "The history of man-

kind is a history of repeated injuries and usurpations on the part of man toward woman, having in direct object the establishment of an absolute tyranny over her. To prove this, let the facts be submitted to a candid world."

The facts Elizabeth Cady Stanton presented that day in Seneca Falls illustrated the social and legal liabilities attached to being a woman during the first 60 years of the republic.

As she pointed out, the status of the majority of American women at midcentury was vividly characterized by the common-law term "civil death." A throwback to British Colonial days (indeed to the Norman Conquest), civil death made married women, in effect, private property. Legally, they could not sign contracts, keep earnings, or control property.* Divorces were granted only in cases of nonsupport, desertion, or adultery; even then, fathers retained child custody. Single women had legal status, for they were expected to pay property taxes. But without the right to vote they incurred the very injury that provoked the American Revolution: taxation without representation.

Stanton's Declaration of Sentiments also deplored women's "social and religious degradation." Man, Stanton charged, had "deprived woman of a thorough education, all colleges being closed against her."† He "monopolized nearly all the profitable employments" and held women to a moral code by which *his* "delinquencies" were "deemed of little account." He "usurped the prerogative of Jehovah himself" and made women "willing to lead a dependent . . . life."

In its demand for suffrage—women's "inalienable right to the elective franchise"—the declaration must have appeared almost as revolutionary as another social tract of 1848, the *Communist Manifesto*. To the Seneca Falls group, this demand for the vote seemed so excessive that only the black abolitionist Frederick Douglass would take the floor in Stanton's support. Lucretia Mott warned her friend not to make their movement appear "ridiculous." Stanton's father, a New York State Supreme Court judge, was reportedly outraged. Her husband, Henry, ever the politician, quietly left town.

---

*In 1848, New York had passed the Married Woman's Property Act, the nation's first reform of civil death. It gave certain real estate and personal property rights to wives.

†Oberlin College (Ohio), founded in 1833 to train missionaries, was coeducational; Mount Holyoke (Massachusetts), founded for women in 1837, received collegiate status in 1883.

 From *The Wilson Quarterly*, Autumn 1986, pp. 90-98. Copyright 1986 by The Woodrow Wilson International Center for Scholars.

Home Rule

After two days of impassioned rhetoric, only one-third of Seneca Falls' conferees were persuaded to sign the declaration. Some later retracted their signatures. An editorial in the *Philadelphia Public Ledger and Daily Transcript* plainly showed what fears Stanton had aroused: "A woman is nobody. A wife is everything. A pretty girl is equal to ten thousand men, and a mother is, next to God, all powerful.... The ladies of Philadelphia... are resolved to maintain their rights as Wives, Belles, Virgins, and Mothers, and not as Women." Was not protection preferable to the risks inherent in equality? It was a question that would surface repeatedly for over a century.

Other American women had spoken out before Seneca Falls— the essays of Judith Sargent Murray, daughter of a Massachusetts sea captain, argued for equal rights 10 years before Mary Wollstonecraft's 1792 *A Vindication of the Rights of Women* appeared in England. By 1848, literate Americans of both sexes had pondered the "Woman Question," most of them apparently concluding, along with Thomas Jefferson, that "the tender breasts of ladies were not formed for political convulsion." But the Seneca Falls meeting became a mid–19th-century media event; the nation's newspapers, newly linked by telegraph, gave it plenty of play. Stanton saw that bad publicity ("the most shocking and unnatural incident ever recorded in the history of womanity," pronounced a typical newspaper editorial) was better than no publicity. "There is no danger of the Woman Question dying for want of notice," she wrote.

It was an era of national expansion, radical hopes, and conservative fears. Sutter's Creek in California yielded gold, President James K. Polk's generals won the Mexican War, and a new antislavery political party was formed—the Free-Soilers—all in 1848. Mid-century America abounded with middle-class reformers, usually led by clergymen, variously upset by urban dislocation in the industrializing North, slavery in the South, and immorality out West.

In upstate New York, where Stanton was raised, the opening of the Erie Canal in 1825 brought thousands of settlers and entrepreneurs. After them came Evangelical Protestant revivalists, with so many hellfire sermons that the area became known as "the burned-over district." Preachers set up tents to warn against money-grubbing, declaring that "all men may be saved if they will" and taking public confessions from largely female audiences. While at Emma Willard's Troy Female Seminary, the young Stanton went to hear the Rev. Charles Grandison Finney, a tall, charismatic ex-lawyer who claimed to have seen Christ in Rochester, New York. She became ill from all the emotional intensity, and thereafter distrusted religion.

As Stanton learned early, American middle-class society was organized around the popular notion of "separate spheres" for men and women. "Everything I liked and enjoyed," she wrote of her childhood, "was messy and injurious; ... and ... everything I disliked was just the thing." According to Sarah Hale—editor of the widely read *Godey's Lady's Book* and a kind of 19th-century Emily Post—"ladies" kept to "the chaste, disinterested circle of the fireside," where "purer, more excellent, more spiritual values" than "the contagion of moneymaking" prevailed. How much Stanton enjoyed such advice may be surmised by her depiction of home life in Seneca Falls: "How rebellious it makes me feel when I see Henry going about where and how he pleases," she wrote to a friend, while "I have been compelled ... to be ... a household drudge."

Sexual Politics

This was not quite the whole picture. Even household drudges could get out of the kitchen for a good cause—and there were plenty of those in the Northern states, from helping unwed mothers to hiding fugitive slaves. Indeed, social uplift became the main outlet for the talents of educated women such as Stanton. Inadvertently, reform organizations became a training ground for future women's rights leaders. Despite Stanton's contempt for the *spheres* ("A man has quite enough to do," she replied to one critic, "without being taxed to find out also where every woman belongs"), the custom of creating separate male and female groups within these organizations had a polarizing effect that led many women to seek greater equality.

The first social reform groups—"benevolence societies" such as the American Bible Society and the Home Missionary Society— bloomed in the early 1800s, and they tended to be highly conservative. Women raised money for missionaries laboring in the unruly West. They visited the poor, cared for orphans and widows, established schools, asylums, and workshops.

Over time, social reform took on a distinct coloration, the first sign of what Kate Millet would call "sexual politics." Uplift groups, such as the social purity and temperance movements, which campaigned against male carnality and drunkenness, signaled a widening rift between men and women over the state of the nation's manners and morals. By 1840, the American Female Moral Reform Society had over 500 auxiliaries and a weekly journal read by 20,000 subscribers. Its members battled prostitution by spying on prominent clients of brothels. In Utica, New York, "visiting committees" went into poor sections of town to solicit tales of men's sexual abuses at home. Meanwhile, temperance workers went on tour with stories of wife beating, child molesting, gambling, and other incarnations of "Demon Rum." Later in the century, it was common for temperance women to invade saloons in large "praying bands."

Most important to feminists were the antislavery organizations. In 1840, just before the convention at Seneca Falls, abolitionists split into factions, partly over whether women should speak out in "promiscuous" (mixed) company. The "political" wing, headed by several New Yorkers, among them Henry Stanton, favored gradual abolition and a no-talking policy for women. The radicals, led by William Lloyd Garrison, wanted an immediate end to slavery and had no qualms about letting women say so, giving many future feminists their first taste of political agitation.

It has been said that women abolitionists became feminists when they perceived the analogy between slavery and the plight of womankind. But Stanton and Mott became feminists when they saw how women were treated by certain male abolitionists. They met in 1840, at the first international antislavery convention in London. Mott had been dispatched by the Philadelphia Female Anti-Slavery Society; Stanton was simply accompanying her new husband. Forced, despite the objections of Garrison and Wendell Phillips, to keep silent in a curtained-off section of the hall, the two women vowed to retaliate when they returned to the United States.

National Strides

They envisioned the meeting at Seneca Falls as the first in a series of public forums on women's rights. Until the outbreak of the Civil War in 1861, conventions did take place almost every year. But the women's movement never attracted much of a popular following among women compared to temperance, abolition, and moral uplift. Its ideas were both too radical and too bourgeois, the product of upper-middle-class experience. Though they spoke of self-reliance, feminist leaders did not form their own independent organization for nearly two decades. And by relying on women in temperance and abolitionist groups to publicize their activities and provide a grass-roots structure, the feminists antagonized conservative reformers and may have discouraged would-be supporters. Moreover, by focusing on property rights, marriage reform, and suffrage, they failed to arouse much support from one of their natural constituencies, a fast-growing group of women workers with grievances of their own.

By 1850, women—often unmarried, first generation teen-agers or farmers' daughters—constituted nearly 25 percent of the country's expanding manufacturing work force. Even in the textile mills around Lowell, Massachusetts (touted for model industrial conditions), women worked 13-hour shifts in overcrowded rooms. Many got sick from the fumes of kerosene lamps. They sometimes slept six to a room, two to a bed, in nearby boarding houses. Theirs was a separate sphere in one sense: women's pay, less than one-half that of male workers, ranged from $1 to $3 per week; much of it went for room and board.

Some of these women staged strikes and made sporadic attempts to form labor organizations during the 1830s and '40s. Sarah Bagley, one of the nation's first trade unionists, founded the Female Labor Reform Association in New England. But such efforts eventually foundered for lack of funds, time, and support from men's labor organizations. Only after the Civil War would women's rights leaders take up the factory workers' cause.

In 1850, feminists from seven states met in Worcester, Massachusetts. Some were already prominent among social reformers: Mott, Lucy Stone, and Angelina Grimké, who left her Southern plantation to work against slavery; Paulina Wright Davis, a wealthy one-time moral reformer; Ernestine Rose, a Polish Jew active in the early temperance movement; Antoinette Brown, the first female Protestant minister. The leaders of this unusually large meeting—about 1,000 people came—set the agenda for subsequent conventions. They initiated petition campaigns in eight states for women's suffrage and established committees to report on women's educational, legal, and professional status.

Then as later, the press approached the Woman Question with hostility or scorn: "What do women want?" ran an editorial in the *New York Herald*. "They want... to be lawyers, doctors... generals in the field. How funny it would sound... that Lucy Stone, pleading a cause... gave birth to a fine bouncing boy in court!" Other editors wrote of "petticoat rebellions" or "hen conventions" arranged by "love-starved spinsters."

Stanton stayed in Seneca Falls until the last of her seven children reached adolescence—surrounded, as she wrote to Wendell Phillips, "by small craft which I am struggling to tug up life's stream." Even so, her exceptional eloquence guaranteed her a central role during the early years of the movement; she wrote impassioned letters that were read aloud at each feminist convention. She was further encouraged when, through Amelia Bloomer, a neighbor who published *The Lily*, a monthly temperance newspaper, she met Susan B. Anthony, a Quaker temperance activist. In contrast to the high-spirited, talkative Stanton, Anthony was sober and introspective, yet the two became lifelong friends.

Choosing Sides

This alliance proved essential to the women's movement. With Anthony's coaching, Stanton's ideas developed into powerful speeches and essays. Whereas all of the other feminist leaders had husbands and children to worry about, Anthony, unwed, could give all of her time to promoting the cause. Stanton fondly recalled how her friend would turn up with a briefcase full of slanderous diatribes by male politicians against women. "Whenever I saw that stately Quaker girl coming across my lawn," she wrote, "I knew that some happy convocation of the sons of Adam was to be set by the ears. She supplied the facts... I the philosophy."

In 1852, the New York State Men's Temperance Society invited women's groups to attend their annual meeting. However, they forbade the women to speak. Anthony, Mott, and other outraged delegates formed a rival New York State Women's Temperance Society, electing Stanton president. But Stanton's radical ideas—especially her insistence that women be permitted to divorce drunken husbands—dismayed conservatives. Even Bloomer took sides against Stanton. She was not re-elected.

Anthony quit the temperance group out of loyalty to her friend. It was the beginning of both women's commitment to direct political agitation. Stanton outlined their goals: the full rewards of citizenship, including the right to vote; property and marriage reforms for wives—especially the right to dissolve unhappy marriages in divorce. (All were controversial, yet suffrage proved hardest to attain.)

Anthony organized a plan of action. She enlisted 60 women, one from every county in New York State, to be "captains" of a petition campaign. In six weeks she had signatures from over 10,000 women—5,931 for married women's rights; 4,164 for woman suffrage. But it was grueling work. Often women slammed their doors against the canvassers, Anthony reported, saying they had husbands, thank God, to look after their interests.

A Slave's Appeal

The petition campaign culminated in the Albany women's rights convention of 1854, timed by Anthony to take place while the New York legislature was in session. As she had hoped, the legislature allowed Stanton to present the petitions to the Joint Judiciary Committee. But the response to her plea came in a committee report asserting that since "the ladies always have the best place and choicest titbit at the table... the warmest place in the winter and the coolest place in the summer... if there is any inequity or oppression in the case, the gentlemen are the sufferers."

On Christmas Day 1854, Anthony set out alone to bring back more petition signatures, with $50 loaned by Wendell Phillips. During one of the coldest winters in New York's history, she traveled by train, sleigh, and often on foot, carrying a carpetbag full of tracts by Stanton. Often hungry and exhausted, she stayed in unheated hotels and passed the hat to cover her expenses. By May, she had canvassed 54 of New York's 60 counties.

This effort, and repeated efforts over the next five years, failed to stir Albany's male politicians. Not until 1860, when Stanton reappeared before the Judiciary Committee with a speech entitled "A Slave's Appeal," would legislators finally listen, though not to pleas for suffrage or changes in divorce law. They amended the existing Married Women's Property Act to include child custody, control over earnings, and property rights for widows.*

However, marriage reform was not the most pressing issue in America by that time—not even to Stanton and Anthony. The country was on the verge of civil war over questions of slavery and states' rights, and these life-or-death issues consumed the attention of the reformers from whom feminists drew their support. Stanton and other leaders identified their aims with those of the abolitionists. At rallies sponsored by William Lloyd Garrison's American Anti-Slavery Society, women speakers argued that suffrage was a "natural right" both of white females and of the oppressed black race.

In 1857, the year the Supreme Court declared slavery permissible in the Dred Scott decision, Anthony started working as a paid organizer for Garrison. Stanton, whose husband allied himself with the conservative abolitionists, earlier had shared his fear that demanding an immediate end to slavery would provoke an unnecessary war. But by 1857 she had gone over to the radicals' cause, and in early 1861 she left home to join Anthony for a series of antislavery rallies in western New York. For suggesting that the newly elected president, Abraham Lincoln, commit himself to ending slavery, the two women often faced mobs throwing eggs and stones.

When the Civil War erupted in April 1861, all talk of women's rights abruptly stopped. Over Anthony's objections, Stanton and other feminists decided to devote themselves to supporting the war effort. They reasoned that a grateful government in Washington would reward their wartime loyalty with the right to vote. As Stanton later wrote, "It was a blunder." While she and others knitted socks and cared for the wounded, the New York legislature gutted its own 1860 marriage reform bill, banning joint child custody and revoking widows' property rights. Stanton and Anthony's wartime petition drive for universal enfranchisement would be seen by Congress as evidence of national support for black male suffrage only. The politics of postwar Reconstruction would divide the feminist movement over questions unrelated to women's rights. In the war's aftermath, feminists would have to start from scratch in many areas. But at least in a perverse way, the long, bloody conflict had advanced their cause: It showed how important civil rights could be.

---

*Fourteen other states passed bills from 1848 to 1860 giving women limited property rights.

This daring filibuster's odyssey as liberator and President of Nicaragua was brief—and bloody. His legacy is with us still.

El Presidente Gringo

William Walker and the Conquest of Nicaragua

Roger Bruns and Bryan Kennedy

Roger Bruns is director of publications of the National Historical Publications and Records Commission in Washington, D.C. His latest book is The Damndest Radical: The Life and World of Ben Reitman, *published by the University of Illinois Press. His article, ''Of Miracles and Molecules: The Story of Nylon'' appeared in the December 1988 issue of this magazine.*

A free-lance researcher who specializes in military history, Bryan Kennedy lives in the Washington, D.C. area.

HIS EYES—there was something about his eyes. They were gray, languid yet penetrating, the color seeming to spill out from a cavernous depth. William Walker had heard the ancient legend told by Central American Indians of a "Gray-eyed Man of Destiny," a savior who would bring peace and plentitude, a liberator whose coming they would hail and before whom they would lay offerings of fruit. Walker believed that he was that messiah, that man of destiny. "I am not ashamed to say," he declared, "that I am favored by the gods."

This preordination, Walker believed, was inextricably linked to America's destiny, its "manifest destiny," the inevitable hemispheric triumph of the "pure American race." The world's history, he said, was replete with examples of superior races overwhelming the inferior, of the drumbeat of human progress toward perfection, of the natural struggle between barbarism and civilization, of the clash of ancient, moldering cultures against the fresh breezes of enlightenment. That conviction would drive Walker south to Mexico, later to Central America. He saw himself as conqueror and prophet, an American Caesar.

Walker. To his enemies, the name conjured up no images of American destiny, no notions of progress and enlightenment. Rather it spoke of terrorism and invasion, of marauding bandits burning and killing, of towns overrun, of peoples humiliated and conquered.

In the small town of San Jacinto, Nicaragua stands a statue of a boy soldier who had slain one of Walker's invaders with a stone. The boy is still revered in Nicaragua, where he remains a symbol of resistance to foreign aggression. For Nicaragua, Walker is the devil never exorcised. His legacy lives on.

H E LOOKED an unlikely adventurer, an improbable conqueror. Barely more than 120 pounds, five-feet-five, with wispy blond hair, Walker was unimposing in stature, had a shrill, quavering voice, and often wore odd, ludicrously ill-matched clothing. But his innocuous appearance masked an intense, almost pathologically restless nature. Walker was seemingly always on a quest for excitement, violence, action. A driven romantic, hopelessly eccentric, he above all craved fame and recognition.

The usual image, the one that has grown with the legend, depicts a stern, rifle-carrying figure dressed in an over-large black parson's cape and broad, flat-brimmed black hat: a humorless, self-absorbed, puritanical, almost prudish zealot, impervious to danger, with a mind leaping and vaulting from apparent madness to brilliance.

He was born in 1824, the eldest son of a Scotch-born Nashville dry-goods merchant who had made a fortune in the insurance business. Walker's devout parents, members of the Disciples of Christ, a fundamentalist sect, encouraged William to prepare for the ministry,

From *American History Illustrated*, February 1989, pp. 15-20, 46-48. Reprinted through the courtesy of Cowles Magazines, publisher of *American History Illustrated*.

but he decided instead to study medicine. An academic prodigy, Walker graduated from the University of Nashville at age fourteen, then went north to the University of Pennsylvania where, at age nineteen, he obtained a medical degree.

Walker traveled to Europe for postgraduate work, becoming a proponent of the pain-relieving powers of hypnotic surgery. But disgusted by the wretched, ill-equipped hospitals of the early nineteenth century, and troubled by his inability to cure his mother's acute rheumatism, he gradually drifted away from medicine to the study of law. His penetrating, rapacious intellect mastered this new field as swiftly as it had the first. He was admitted to the bar in New Orleans and practiced briefly.

But Walker's restlessness soon drove him to yet another profession—journalism. In 1848 he became an editorial writer for the *New Orleans Crescent*. While working there, he fell in love with a deaf and mute woman named Ellen Martin.

When Martin contracted cholera and suddenly died, Walker was devastated. He escaped to San Francisco, taking a job with one of the city's newest papers, the *Daily Herald*.

Journalism ignited Walker's intellectual fires. He was stirred by the contentious debate over slavery then raging across the country; mesmerized by tales of gold; by stories of adventurers and pioneers; of Indians and Mexican banditos; of duels and shoot-outs. The seemingly gentle, courteous, and chivalrous young writer stood ready to break the chains of convention. The path of destiny beckoned.

The call came from the south.

DURING the United States' war with Mexico in 1847, Commodore Matthew C. Perry had written to Secretary of the Navy John Mason: "Destiny has doubtless decided that the vast continent of North America . . . shall in the course of time fall under the influence of Laws and institutions of the United States."

Perry's belief was hardly new. The idea that the United States would eventually annex the entire western hemisphere—from the Arctic snows to Cape Horn—had for years excited Americans, especially politicians and speculators. They shared an unbridled nationalism, the conviction that the moral and cultural superiority of the United States would gain for the country increasing dominance.

In this fever of expansionism, many Americans were drawn south to Latin America, with its rich lands and uncertain future. Torn by incessant wars, riddled by political intrigue and corruption, coveted by European colonial powers, the countries of Latin America tottered in confusion and instability. For reckless men on the run, for daring entrepreneurs, for adventurers of all types, the region was alluring. It was especially so for those imaginative if presumptuous freebooters known as "filibusters"—men who by force of arms sought to seize countries and establish themselves as rulers.

The idea was simple enough. Gather together the best available soldiers of fortune, equip them with weapons and supplies, rent a ship or two, sail to a Latin American country, usurp power, and become a dictator, president, king, or whatever title of government or royalty one chose. Fame and riches awaited the man bold enough, ingenious enough, to succeed.

Walker had heard of several such expeditions—and of the ignominious embarrassment and defeat of most. But these forays, Walker thought, had not been led by men of *his* caliber. Driven by wanderlust, embittered by his beloved's death, Walker was about to enter a world of club and iron, a world of short odds. It would become his obsession.

WALKER THE FILIBUSTER. In 1853 he recruited a force of about forty-five men, set sail for Lower California, and launched his career as a conqueror. His mission, he announced, was humanitarian: to protect American women and children living along the Mexican border from attacks by Apache Indians. He was acting, he said, to overcome oppression and bring the blessings of American civilization to these benighted Mexican provinces, to introduce democracy and stability to a troubled land.

From the early days of the excursion, Walker displayed the grandiloquent, pompous air that would mark his entire career. After his troops managed to capture La Paz, the small, sleepy capital of Baja California, Walker boldly issued a proclamation establishing the "Republic of Lower California." The new government came equipped with a flag designed by Walker, a constitution written by Walker, and a cabinet chosen by Walker from the ranks of his army of adventurers. Walker, of course, was President.

Word of his initial success attracted new recruits from California. Next, Walker's army moved eastward over rugged mountains and across the Colorado River to Sonora. When Walker announced the addition of this neighboring state to his paper nation, a San Francisco editor noted that "It would have been just as cheap and easy to have annexed the whole of Mexico at once, and would have saved the trouble of making future proclamations."

As President, Walker adopted an aloof, burdened posture. Here was a head of state with weighty problems crushing down on him, a man totally absorbed by the affairs of government, carrying on admirably in the face of insurmountable odds.

But although he issued a stream of orders and demands, the rigorous discipline Walker had sought to instill in his men began to slip out of his grasp. In a brazen effort to control his forces, he ordered the execution of two of his troops who had tried to flee the foundering enterprise. Nevertheless, as conditions continued to deteriorate, desertions became rampant.

The adventure came to an abrupt end. Chased out of Lower California, Walker managed to lead a few surviving members of his party back across the United States

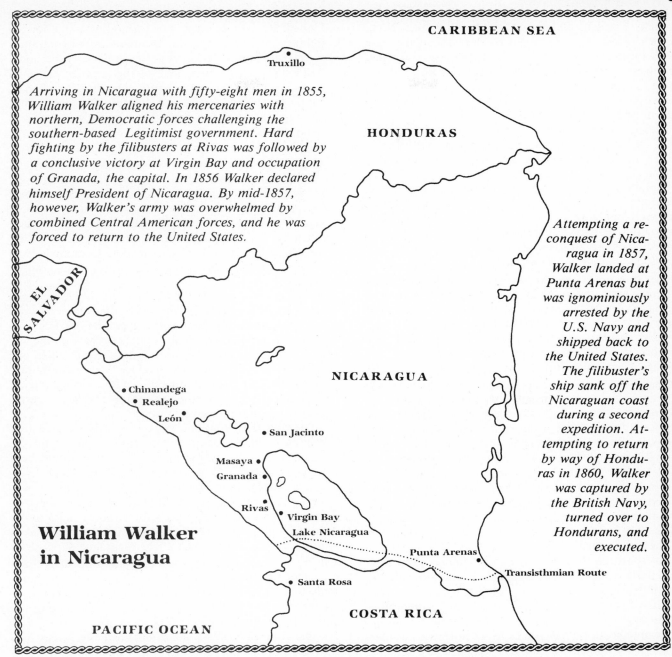

CARIBBEAN SEA

Truxillo

HONDURAS

Arriving in Nicaragua with fifty-eight men in 1855, William Walker aligned his mercenaries with northern, Democratic forces challenging the southern-based Legitimist government. Hard fighting by the filibusters at Rivas was followed by a conclusive victory at Virgin Bay and occupation of Granada, the capital. In 1856 Walker declared himself President of Nicaragua. By mid-1857, however, Walker's army was overwhelmed by combined Central American forces, and he was forced to return to the United States.

EL SALVADOR

Attempting a reconquest of Nicaragua in 1857, Walker landed at Punta Arenas but was ignominiously arrested by the U.S. Navy and shipped back to the United States. The filibuster's ship sank off the Nicaraguan coast during a second expedition. Attempting to return by way of Honduras in 1860, Walker was captured by the British Navy, turned over to Hondurans, and executed.

NICARAGUA

• Chinandega
• Realejo
• León

• San Jacinto

Masaya •
Granada •

Rivas •

• Virgin Bay
Lake Nicaragua

Punta Arenas

Transisthmian Route

William Walker in Nicaragua

• Santa Rosa

COSTA RICA

PACIFIC OCEAN

border near San Diego on May 8, 1854—his thirtieth birthday.

Most of Walker's troops had perished in Mexico from fever, starvation, or enemy bullets. The survivors had run out of provisions en route and barely escaped eradication by Mexican soldiers and Indians. They had marched nearly barefoot for hundreds of miles, leaving a trail of blood on the sun-baked desert sand. Walker himself limped across the border wearing one boot and one makeshift sandal. Only the pen of Cervantes, some said, could have done the scene justice.

Although the expedition had been, indeed, a quixotic fiasco, one from which Walker was fortunate to have escaped with his life, he seemed charged by the experience. Filibustering, he now realized, was his true calling.

On his return to San Francisco, Walker was hailed by some Americans as a hero. He was, in their eyes, a prime example of rugged individualism, a private, patriotic freedom-fighter exemplifying courage and fortitude. When he stood trial in November 1854 for violating neutrality laws, the patriot was acquitted by a jury that took only eight minutes to reach its verdict.

Filibustering, Walker saw, brought the adulation and recognition he craved. The Mexican venture had been only a warm-up for the real game. Next he targeted Nicaragua.

NICARAGUA: poor but fertile, a land of tropical fruit fields, clear lakes, and active volcanoes. For generations, explorers and sailors from many lands had roamed its forests and walked its shores. Spanish, French, English, Belgians, Dutch all valued Nicaragua's resources and recognized the vital significance of its location, nestled as it was between two oceans. The narrow isthmus, Napoleon III once wrote, "can become . . . the necessary route of the great commerce of the world and is destined to attain an extraordinary degree of prosperity and grandeur."

Nicaragua had endured a shaky independence since 1823. A succession of political chieftains jockeyed for power and control, leaving the population vulnerable and unstable.

Diplomats and politicians from England, France, and the United States tiptoed through endless negotiations, plotting, conniving, each warily watching the moves of his counterparts, each fearing that an enemy would gain control over this strategically important republic.

For the United States, Nicaragua had special significance; through it ran the favored transisthmian route for travelers between the U.S. Atlantic coast and California. By treaty Nicaragua had granted Americans the right to establish transit. Now, by river boat, lake steamer, and carriage, travelers were able to cross from one ocean to the other without a long and dangerous passage around South America.

The transit route was the brainchild of one of America's wealthiest men: Cornelius Vanderbilt, the "Commodore," who had made a fortune running steamboats on the Hudson River. Vanderbilt's sagacious business instincts had been whetted by the prospective profits from Nicaraguan investment. Promising to fill Nicaraguan leaders' pockets with gold, he had negotiated a contract for his Accessory Transit Company in 1849. Two years later he opened his isthmian route and began to run steamers from both U.S. coasts to Nicaraguan ports. The Accessory Transit Company enlarged the Vanderbilt fortune.

But soon the "Commodore" had competition. Two slick businessmen united to challenge Vanderbilt's control of Nicaraguan transit and began to earn substantial profits of their own. The "Commodore" would later get his revenge.

Meanwhile, in 1854 Byron Cole, a California business associate of Walker, traveled to Nicaragua to assess the economic and political opportunities there. He found two factions warring for power. The Democrats, a "people's party" headquartered in the north Nicaraguan town of León, were challenging the rule of the Legitimists, a Southern, aristocratic party based in Granada. Cole soon began to negotiate a deal with General Francisco de Castellon, leader of the Democrats. Cole promised to supply Castellon with American "colonists liable to military duty." In return, Castellon offered substantial payment and grants of land for each of the "colonists."

Cole returned to California to consult with Walker, and, after subsequent negotiations in which language suggesting military service was removed from the proposed accord, a deal was struck. The resulting agreement was a "colonization grant" that, according to civil

and military officials in San Francisco, did not violate United States neutrality laws forbidding unauthorized military intervention in the affairs of friendly nations.

Walker began recruiting "colonists"—the most battle-hardened, tough, skillful mercenaries he could find—men who thrived in battle, who lived for the kill, for the bottle, and for women. In May 1855, a year after his humiliating return from Mexico, he was ready to strike again.

WHEN WALKER and fifty-eight men arrived in Nicaragua in June 1855, landing at the northwest coast town of Realejo, the Democrats under General Castellon were supported in their bid for power by Nicaragua's northern neighbor, Honduras. They were, nevertheless, losing. A large force of Legitimists, led by General Ponciano Corral and aided by Guatemala, was preparing to march on the Democrats' stronghold at León.

Walker's arrogance soon became a mighty force in the Nicaraguan war. To *El Filibustrero*, the Democrats and General Castellon were hopeless as military tacticians—confused, bewildered, totally unable to carry on the war effort effectively. He began to ignore them. When one of the generals became offended by Walker's presumptuousness, the American threatened to leave Nicaragua. Castellon quickly promised to reinforce Walker's troops with two hundred native conscripts.

Viewing the situation, Walker quickly decided that waiting in the Democratic capital of León for the expected onslaught by the Legitimist troops would be a foolhardy, probably suicidal strategy. He decided, instead, to take the offensive.

"La Falange Americana" (the American Phalanx), as the Democrats called Walker's force, sailed south to the Pacific end of Vanderbilt's transit route and prepared to attack Rivas, a town near Lake Nicaragua supposedly held by a small Legitimist force. If the Americans could control the transit route, Walker reasoned, then supplies, money, and weapons could be procured from the United States and recruits mustered from among the Transit Company's passengers.

On June 29, 1855 Walker slammed his forces into Rivas. He had his own fifty-eight soldiers of fortune and about 150 native Nicaraguans supplied by the Democrats. The conscripts soon began to disappear, however, either through treachery or cowardice. The American invaders were left to face a force about ten times their number.

But the odds were not as one-sided as they appeared. The American mercenaries carried Mississippi rifles and V.C. Colt revolvers, and they were all crack shots. The native Nicaraguans carried muskets that were notoriously inaccurate, even at close range.

After a bold attack, "La Falange" found itself surrounded in a building on the town's outskirts. There, Walker's troops exchanged gunfire with the enemy for several hours. Finally, running out of ammunition and seemingly doomed, Walker played his usual hand: he charged. His men rushed into the streets, rifles blazing, and soon more than one hundred dead and wounded Nicaraguans littered the area. "La Falange" escaped, leaving behind six dead. Walker, later musing on the success of his brash tactics, wrote that "the Legitimists were not much in the humor of pursuing those who had taught them a first lesson in the use of a rifle."

José de Marcoleta, the Legitimist government's minister to the United States, complained bitterly to Secretary of State William Marcy of the devastation at Rivas: "The remains of buildings are still burning, and the ruins and ashes produced by the torch and hand of Walker are still smoking; the blood that has been shed is still warm; and years will elapse before the bitter tears will be dried which that brigand has caused to be shed by numberless families in both sections of the continent of America."

WALKER WITHDREW his force to Chinandega, a small town in northern Nicaragua, where he established his base of operations. Although his Democratic sponsors now wanted Walker to disperse his American troops throughout the Democratic army, *El Filibustero* refused. His cadre of about fifty men would better serve, he reasoned, as the terrifying nucleus of an army that could overrun all of Nicaragua.

He drilled his small army hard, and soon it was again ready to take the offensive. The filibusters sailed south again in August, landing on the coast west of Virgin Bay, another town on the transit route. Walker now commanded about forty-five mercenaries and 120 Nicaraguans. They soon confronted the enemy. Six hundred Legitimist troops bore down, testing the flanks of the small Democratic force. The Americans fired methodically and with deadly accuracy. Of the Legitimists, Walker wrote: "When they got within thirty or forty yards of the Americans their hearts seemed to fail them . . . either the quantity of liquor was insufficient, or it may have been too great, or it began to die out before the soldiers got close to their adversaries."

At battle's end, sixty dead Legitimists carpeted the outskirts of Virgin Bay. Two Nicaraguan Democrats had been killed, and several Americans wounded. A ball struck Walker, but he survived relatively unscathed. No wonder the press in the United States now began to call Walker and his fighters the "Immortals."

Walker did not wreak a conqueror's wrath upon the vanquished; instead, he instructed his men to bind the enemy's wounds. To captives who had fully expected to be bayoneted, Walker's orders seemed godlike. But this was a man on a divine mission. Cruel retribution, he believed, would have been unseemly. Walker was above that kind of barbarism. With this victory at Virgin Bay, he had tasted glory. Nothing, he was convinced, now stood between his band and ultimate triumph.

At dawn on October 13, a transit steamer carrying Walker and his warriors anchored near the Legitimist capital of Granada. Soon the "Immortals" stormed the town, taking it with barely a shot fired. To many Nicaraguans, Walker now appeared invincible.

The victor issued a "Manifesto Addressed to Nicaraguans." To those who had expected rape and pillage from invading marauders, Walker offered order and tranquility. There would be no "unutterable immoralities" under a Walker regime, he promised, but protection to laboring men; a fostering of the arts, science, and agriculture; a government liberal in principle, committed to preserving peace and the vital interests of the nation. "Here it is," he declared, "a democratic Government in its true sense."

Although Walker had convincingly taken power in Granada, his victory still left a large number of Legitimist troops under General Corral holding much of Nicaragua. Walker's solution was a call for a coalition government composed of leaders from both parties.

Walker's willingness to seek a peaceful reconciliation astonished both sides. Impressed at such open compromise, many of Walker's bitterest enemies were grudgingly beginning to respect the *gringo* leader with the floppy hat. And when some Nicaraguans attempted to persuade Walker to accept the presidency of the country, he declined the offer—an act that so impressed U.S. Minister to Nicaragua John Wheeler that he began to work in Walker's behalf without even asking for the U.S. State Department's consent.

Working long hours, Walker started a state newspaper called *El Nicaragüense*, designed a state seal, created a flag, and began organizing a new government. He was not yet *El Presidente*, but it seemed that anything in Nicaragua was his for the taking.

WALKER'S JUDICIOUS MANEUVERING took one perilous turn during these months. Vanderbilt's transit company, Walker perceived, was accruing large profits without turning any of it to the benefit of Nicaragua. Aligning himself with Vanderbilt's business rivals because of their association with his long-time friend Edmund Randolph, Walker revoked the charter of the Accessory Transit Company, a move both bold and ominous. Responding to this audacious move, the "Commodore" made plans to send guns and money to oust from Nicaragua the impudent invader.

As leaders of neighboring Central American countries became increasingly alarmed at Walker's success, U.S. Secretary of State William Marcy assured diplomats that his country had not officially recognized the Walker government. But Marcy's disclaimer did not ring true with leaders in Costa Rica, Guatemala, Honduras, and El Salvador. They suspected the U.S. government of engineering a covert operation, of launching a subversive move to take over Central America.

By December 1855, two months after the fall of Granada, Central American opposition to filibuster control began to coalesce. Walker's success in Nicaragua had, ironically, promoted Central American nationalism. Leaders of the various countries began to work together toward one common goal—to crush the *gringo* usurper.

Costa Rica was the first to act. On March 1, 1856, Costa Rican President Juan Rafael Mora declared war on the Yankees. When word reached Walker, he decided on a pre-emptive raid into Costa Rica. But the force of about two hundred men he sent across the border to the town of Santa Rosa was quickly routed.

Although Walker was sick with fever, he rallied his demoralized forces and attacked the town of Rivas, where the advancing Costa Rican forces had taken temporary residence. The "Immortals" fought a long, house-to-house brawl and then were forced to withdraw with more than one hundred casualties.

But again Walker survived. Cholera and antiwar sentiment on the home front forced the Costa Ricans to withdraw, and a feared invasion from Honduras never materialized. For his humane treatment of Costa Rican sick left behind, Walker was lionized by some American newspaper editors.

ENCOURAGED by the enthusiasm for his cause in the United States, Walker decided to dispense with the charade of a puppet government and become Nicaragua's *Presidente*. On June 29, 1856, Walker's paper, *El Nicaragüense*, announced that an enormous election turnout had given him the presidency. Although the origin of the votes he claimed begged explanation, the American took office. He ignored the fact that the Nicaraguan constitution expressly excluded from office all who were not native-born.

Back in the United States, Walker had become something of a folk hero—an intrepid American adventurer defying the odds and taking on all foreign enemies in the name of liberty, democracy, justice, and American values. Crowds of sympathizers cheered his exploits at public meetings; newspaper headlines applauded his victories and lamented his defeats. He was toasted at banquets. In New York, a musical entitled *Nicaragua or General Walker's Victories* opened at Purdy's National Theater in July 1856. With a cast of characters that included "General Walker, the Hope of Freedom" and "Ivory Black, superior nigger," the musical featured the "Filibuster Overture" as well as patriotic favorites such as "Columbia, the Pride of the Ocean," "Yankee Doodle," and, of course, "The Star Spangled Banner."

On assuming the presidency, Walker presented his Inaugural Address. Sleepless vigilance, untiring devotion to liberty, an ardent resolve, and dedication to peace and progress—the message of *El Presidente* struck familiar patriotic notes. The victory of the "Immortals" would, he declared, usher in a new era; it was the culmination of Nicaraguan revolution against Spanish monarchy finally achieved after many years. Other Central American countries, driven by jealousy and the political enmity of a host of "imbecile rulers," would be unable to impede Nicaragua's noble experiment in democracy. The new epoch would inaugurate freedom of speech (with the new additional official language of English as well as Spanish), social order, an increase in commerce, a maturation of the arts, a sweeping away of crusty institutions by the strong winds of intellectual and moral advancement. "And for carrying out these intentions with success, I humbly invoke the aid of Him, without whose assistance all Human exertions are but a bubble on a stormy sea."

Although he now held power, Walker nested on a precarious perch. Groping for allies, money, guns, and troops—and opposed by Guatemala, Honduras, El Salvador, Costa Rica, much of Nicaragua, and Cornelius Vanderbilt—Walker, on September 22, 1856, made a bold, calculated move. He issued a decree annulling legislation that had abolished slavery in Nicaragua several decades earlier.

Walker was making an overt appeal to the American South. Here in Nicaragua, Walker said, was a new outpost for the expansion of slavery. Here was the answer to Southern political leaders who sought a way to tip the balance of power between North and South. "Is it not time," he asked, "for the South to cease the contest for abstractions and to fight for realities? . . . How else can she strengthen slavery than by seeking its extension beyond the Union?"

To John Wheeler, the U.S. ambassador to Nicaragua, Walker's decree was sweet music. Wheeler was from North Carolina and a slave holder. He now saw Nicaragua breaking forth into a veritable Nirvana. He enthused over the arrival of eager white settlers, the sweet hum of new machinery, the cheerful roll of American carts through the streets. Only through slave labor, he saw, could the rich soil of Nicaragua be adapted to the culture of cotton, sugar, rice, and other staples. Wheeler and other Walker followers dashed off letters to friends in the Southern states seeking support for this new slave land.

The *Richmond Enquirer* declared, "This [is a] magnificent country General Walker has taken possession of in the name of the white race. . . . Here is a new state soon to be added to the South, in or out of the Union." Walker had succeeded in placing himself and Nicaragua deeply in the slavery debate. He hoped it would bolster his own government.

But his army was now meeting determined and sometimes fierce resistance. At San Jacinto Hill near Tipitapa, three hundred of Walker's fighters were routed. Their leader, Byron Cole, who had originally brought Walker to Nicaragua, was hanged by a group of peasants. And at San Jacinto a Nicaraguan named Andres Castro became a future national hero when he killed a filibuster with a rock.

At the town of Masaya, the "Immortals," numbering about eight hundred, fought a combined Central American force of about 2,300. Both sides suffered severe losses. Walker retreated to Granada.

With the Central American combined offensive gathering strength, Walker's position rapidly deteriorated. He had now lost many men in the field, while others were ravaged by cholera. Although the Puritan martinet continued to preach morality, many of his men succumbed to the bottle and other vices. Demoralized, many of the "Immortals" saw their chances for survival rapidly fading. But Walker seemed oblivious, his grip on reality ebbing as the situation grew more critical. He waited for reinforcements.

Walker's business friends in the United States—Vanderbilt's rivals—responded with Charles Frederick Henningsen, one of Europe's most skilled soldiers of fortune. Arriving in Granada, he brought men, rifles, howitzers, mortars, and years of fighting experience in Spain, Russia, and Hungary.

The Henningsen-trained "Immortals" attacked Virgin Bay with artillery support and, although outnumbered four-to-one, beat back the Costa Ricans. But following another engagement at Masaya, more than fifty American bodies lay scattered among those of hundreds of Guatemalans. The highly-skilled mercenary force, even with its reinforcements, began to crumble.

In mid-November 1856, Walker finally decided to abandon Granada. He informed Henningsen that the Americans would retreat to the volcanic island of Omotepe in Lake Nicaragua. He ordered Henningsen to stay behind with three hundred men and burn the 332-year-old city of Granada.

In a drunken haze, the smoke-blackened filibusters looted and torched the town they had supposedly come to civilize. For two days and nights flames and black clouds engulfed the ancient city. At the height of this orgy of destruction, the combined armies of Central America attacked Granada. Henningsen soon found himself trapped in the town's Guadalupe Cathedral.

Despite the added burdens of death and disease, Henningsen's men were able to blunt the enemy's attacks for two weeks. Finally, on December 12, just as the beleaguered force was running low on food and ammunition, its survivors, aided by a rescue party Walker sent, broke out of the cathedral and fled Granada. They left behind more than two hundred dead. In the smoking rubble Henningsen left a sign that read "Aqui Fué Granada" ("Here was Granada").

Walker later tried to justify his burning of the city. Its inhabitants, he insisted, had turned on the Americans, their leaders and protectors. They had become spies and had abetted the enemy. "By the laws of war," Walker wrote, "the town had forfeited its existence; and the policy of destroying it was as manifest as the justice of the measure."

With his battered forces strangling in confusion and disarray, Walker now held only a small area at the western end of the transit route. In several skirmishes in early 1857, the Central American forces, aided by money, men, and supplies from Vanderbilt, inflicted heavy casualties on Walker's remaining troops.

For the first time, desertions by the "Immortals" became a serious problem. A series of cleverly timed raids planned by Vanderbilt's agents enabled the Costa Ricans to seize all the transit steamers and the ports on the San Juan River, cutting off Walker's supply lines from the east. To survive, his men were forced to eat their horses and mules. Walker nevertheless exhorted his dying army to fight on, declaring that "The destiny of this region and the interests of humanity are confided to our care."

Although fighting continued sporadically through April 1857, it was clear that the filibuster force had been decimated. Now the only question was whether or not Walker would escape the country alive.

On May 1, 1857, Commander Charles E. Davis of the U.S. sloop-of-war *St. Mary's* negotiated safe passage out of Nicaragua for *El Filibustero*, his troops, and other Americans. Four hundred and sixty-three men returned to the United States.

Walker's losses had been staggering—according to some estimates, as high as five thousand dead and missing. Hundreds of survivors were left behind in Nicaragua, many of them wounded and sick, wandering the alien forests and fields.

WALKER RETURNED to the United States embittered, sulking, convinced that he had been betrayed. The regime of *El Presidente* Walker, it seemed, was at an end.

But in New Orleans, thousands of supporters gathered to cheer their hero. Invigorated by the public support, *El Filibustero* was soon planning a reconquest. He traveled to Mobile and then to New York, speaking to throngs of admirers, most of whom generously opened their pocketbooks.

His humiliating losses in Nicaragua now seemed only minor impediments to the cause, mere irritants. Thousands of new soldiers, Walker knew, could be found; more ships awaited outfitting. The unvanquished crusader would forge on.

For American politicians, the Walker factor continued to wedge stubbornly in the middle of the national debate over the extension of slavery. Many Southerners still hoped that the annexation of Nicaragua and other Central American nations could turn the balance of power squarely on the side of proslavery interests.

A U.S. Navy lieutenant wrote in 1857 that public sentiment in the South was strongly in favor of the filibuster expeditions. They were, he wrote, "a frequent theme of conversation . . . in the streets, and at the hotels; and further, that there seemed to be an idea pervading . . . that Washington rather winked at the fitting out and departure of these expeditions."

President James Buchanan and his advisors seemed perplexed by Walker. As the "Conqueror" traveled the country preparing for another assault on Central America, the Administration issued warnings, made public declarations, sent vague, often conflicting instructions to its diplomats and military commanders. Filibusterism was a violation of the neutrality laws, the Administration noted. Any individuals discovered to be engaged in preparing a military expedition against a foreign nation must be detained. The rhetoric, though lacking explicit instructions on how to stop Walker, sounded genuine, even tough.

And yet Walker went about his work with apparent impunity. Considering the popular appeal enjoyed by the "Conqueror" and the support he drew from many Southern Democratic politicians, Buchanan was reluctant to take vigorous action against him. Indeed, Walker himself met privately with the President in Washington in June 1857 and later claimed that Buchanan had encouraged him to return to Nicaragua.

3. NATIONAL CONSOLIDATION AND EXPANSION

ON NOVEMBER 14, 1857, aboard the steamer *Fashion*, Walker, with more than 150 men and a supply of arms, left Mobile for Central America. Additional ships and men prepared to leave from other ports. Eleven days later the "Immortals" landed at Punta Arenas, near San Juan del Norte. Walker had returned; the reconquest of Nicaragua had begun.

But before the campaign could get seriously underway, the invaders' plans were ignominiously squelched. Commodore Hiram Paulding, flag officer commanding the U.S. Home Squadron, took President Buchanan's instructions to heart. On December 8, 1857 a detachment of three hundred Marines and sailors arrested Walker and his officers and put them aboard the USS *Saratoga*. Paulding sent them back to the United States.

Many Southerners erupted in fury over the arrest. Georgia Senator Alexander Stephens urged that Paulding be court-martialed. The commodore, said Stephens, had no authority to make an arrest on foreign soil. More than two dozen other Southern senators agreed. Even Buchanan, although applauding Paulding's motives, lamented the Navy officer's breach of authority.

Northern politicians, in turn, denounced the Southern reaction. Walker, they charged, was a thug who had led a lawless band of highwaymen against a foreign nation in violation of the United States' neutrality laws. He was a criminal, not a hero. Walker, they claimed, was a tool of Southern slave interests.

Meanwhile, the indefatigable Walker, who had taken to signing his letters "Commander-in-Chief, Army of Nicaragua," was brought to New York and interrogated by U.S. marshals. There he met Secretary of State Lewis Cass. The Secretary had made no secret of his admiration for Walker and of his own support for the filibustering missions. He had earlier declared, "The difficulties which General Walker has encountered and overcome will place his name high on the roll of the distinguished men of his age."

In May 1858 Walker was tried in New Orleans for violating neutrality laws. Ten of the twelve jurors voted for acquittal, and he was released.

WALKER LOST NO TIME in planning yet another expedition. Touring the South, he sought new recruits. In Mississippi he appealed to mothers "to bid their sons buckle on the armor of war, and battle for the institutions, for the honor of the Sunny South."

The "Sunny South" listened and responded with both men and money.

In December 1858 Walker sailed from Mobile, departing without clearance papers from the port collector, in defiance of the federal government. Off British Honduras, about sixty miles from the Nicaraguan coast, his ship struck a reef and sank. Walker was rescued by a British warship and returned to the South on New Year's Day 1859, to another tumultuous welcome.

The intractable Walker made one more try. Traveling in small groups, ninety-seven filibusters rendezvoused in Honduras in the fall of 1860, where they hoped to join forces with former Honduras President Trinidad Cabañas, who was leading a Liberal revolt in that country. From there Walker hoped to invade Nicaragua and Costa Rica, and to reinstate the Central American federation.

Going on the offensive, Walker decided to attack a stone fortress that guarded the Honduran port of Truxillo. He planned to take the town, join Cabañas, and then take the country. Walker's raid was successful, and he raised the colors of the old Central American federation over the fort.

British authorities, upset when Walker declared Truxillo a free port (all customs revenue there had been previously assigned to the British government), felt compelled to intervene with military force. The warship *Icarus*, commanded by Captain Norvell Salmon, arrived at Truxillo, and Salmon ordered Walker to surrender. But Walker and his men fled in search of Cabañas's jungle encampment. A strong force of Honduran soldiers followed them.

The Hondurans eventually stopped Walker, trapping him in a swampy region near the Rio Negro. Salmon, in one of two British boats to sail up the river, again demanded Walker's surrender.

This time Walker did not resist.

The filibuster believed he was surrendering to a representative of the British government, but Salmon had other ideas. He turned Walker over to Honduran officials.

On September 12, 1860 a Honduran firing squad executed Walker, forever closing the infamous gray eyes.

AN EXCEEDINGLY COMPLEX MAN—beset by visions of fame and indestructability, harboring in his puritanical mind demons only he would ever see, obsessed by causes he only vaguely understood, possessing an acute intelligence somehow gone askew—Walker, with few devices beyond his own ambition, cunning, and drive, had made an extraordinary impact.

Walker's raids had exacerbated the debate in the United States over slavery's extension. That debate would soon end violently in the American Civil War.

But Walker's mark was etched most deeply in Central America. The Walker invasions left a chasm of distrust, misunderstanding, and bitterness. In October 1860, on the eve of the election that brought Abraham Lincoln to the White House, Luis Molina, Nicaragua's Chargé d'Affaires in Washington, talked of a conspiracy of the Southern states to destroy the "nationality and independence of the States of Central America," to conquer them and to introduce slavery. The conspiracy lived, he said, under the protection of the flag of the United States. Even with Walker's death, the despicable treachery would likely continue. Central America, he promised, would remain vigilant.

William Walker's legacy is with us still.

The War Against Demon Rum

With alcohol consumption on the rise in 19th-century America, the temperance cause took root.

Robert Maddox

Robert Maddox, of Pennsylvania State University, is a distinguished historian whose article "War In Korea: The Desperate Times" appeared in the July 1978 issue of AHI. For those interested in reading further on the subject of temperance he suggests The Origins of Prohibition *(1925), by John Allen Krout and* Ardent Spirits *(1973), by John Kobler.*

"Good-bye, John Barleycorn," cried the Reverend Billy Sunday to an approving crowd, "You were God's worst enemy. You were Hell's best friend. I hate you with a perfect hatred. I love to hate you." The date was January 16, 1920, the day when the Eighteenth Amendment to the Constitution went into effect. Drys across the nation celebrated happily, while drinkers cursed and contemplated a future without alcohol. Both were premature. John Barleycorn was by no means dead, though he did go underground for more than a decade. But on that first day, those who had worked on behalf of prohibition could congratulate themselves on a victory over what at times had seemed insurmountable odds.

From the first settlements at Jamestown and Plymouth Rock, Americans have brewed, fermented, and distilled everything they could. Though their drinking customs were from Europe, the colonists displayed remarkable ingenuity in devising additional reasons for having a cup of this or a mug of that. Writers of early travel accounts express surprise as to the amount of alcohol the colonists consumed. Everything from the crudest beers and ciders to the most elegant wines ran down American throats in amazing quantities.

During the colonial period there were few attempts to restrict the availability of alcohol, much less to prohibit it entirely. Public houses and taverns abounded. Even in Puritan New England, contrary to popular legend, the people had virtually unrestricted access to spirits of all kinds. Indeed, alcohol was seen as one of God's blessings, to be enjoyed as He intended. When taken in moderation, it was believed to be beneficial for both the mind and the body.

Drunkenness was another matter. Defined in one colony as "drinking with excess to the notable perturbation of any organ of sense or motion," public inebriation was dealt with harshly. The penalties varied from place to place but ranged from fines for first offenders to hard labor or whippings for chronic indulgers. Still, drunkenness was seen as a personal weakness or sin, and the guilty party had no one save himself to blame. Alcohol bore the repsonsibility scarcely more than did the fire which burned down a careless person's home.

A number of people, principally clergymen, spoke out or wrote locally distributed tracts denouncing the intemperate use of intoxicants. This was particularly true after the middle of the 17th century when rum and whiskey replaced the milder ciders and wines. To some it appeared their communities were in danger of drowning in alcohol. It was not until 1784 that any single temperance tract received wide attention. In that year the eminent Philadelphia physician, Dr. Benjamin Rush, published his "An Inquiry into the Effects of Spiritous Liquors on the Human Body and Mind." This pamphlet went through many editions and portions of the work were widely reprinted in newspapers and almanacs across the entire country.

The reception accorded Rush's tract undoubtedly reflected a growing concern about the problems concerning alcoholic consumption. Aside from its popularity, the pamphlet differed from earlier ones in several ways. First of all, as a physician-general in the Continental Army during the Revolution, Rush had had ample opportunity to observe the effects of drinking on soldiers. Thus his words had the backing of what appeared to be scientific examination, rather than mere moral exhortation. Rush denied the popular notions that drinking helped prevent fatigue, protected one against cold, and many other popular myths of the day. Quite the contrary, he argued, in general the consumption of alcohol helped *bring on* diseases of both the mind and of the body. Second, his pamphlet differed from previous ones in that he not only warned against excessive amounts of drink, but claimed that even moderate use over an extended period of time would have harmful effects. It is interesting to note, however, that Rush's

From *American History Illustrated*, May 1979. Reproduced through the courtesy of Cowles Magazines, publishers of *American History Illustrated*.

broadside was directed against distilled spirits only. Beers and light wines, he thought, *were* beneficial if taken in moderation.

How much effect, if any, Rush's pamphlet had on the consumption of alcohol at the time is uncertain. But it did inspire a number of reformers who took up the temperance cause in the years following. Perhaps the most important, and colorful, of these was the Reverend Lyman Beecher of East Hampton, Long Island. Father of thirteen children (including the famous Henry Ward Beecher and the even more famous Harriet Beecher Stowe), Beecher had been appalled by the drinking habits of his fellow students while at Yale and little he saw thereafter reassured him. Indeed, he came to believe, alcohol posed the greatest threat to the society's physical and spiritual well-being. Though males were the worst offenders, even women consumed impressive amounts. Nor were the clergy immune.

Beecher spoke of attending one convocation where, after a time, the room came to look and smell "like a very active grog shop." Worse yet were the amounts of alcohol given to children of all ages. Fairfax Downey, in a recent article about Beecher, tells the story of a 7-year-old girl who visited her grandmother in Boston. When she learned she would be given no spirits, she angrily notified her parents. "Missy," the grandmother learned, "had been brought up as a lady and must have wine and beer with every meal." Beecher was so concerned about the situation that he claimed he never gave a child even the smallest amount of money without adding the warning "not to drink ardent spirits or any inebriating liquor."

Beecher frequently lectured his congregation on the dangers of drink, and became even more active in the cause after taking the pastorate at Litchfield, Connecticut, in 1811. He was instrumental in forming one of the first temperance groups, the Connecticut Society for the Reformation of Morals. Among other things, the Society printed and distributed large numbers of Dr. Rush's pamphlet. In 1825 Beecher delivered six sermons on the temperance issue which later were published in pamphlet form. Widely reprinted in the years following, the "Six Sermons" according to one scholar, "were as widely read and exerted as great an influence as any other contribution to the literature of the reform."

The Reverend Beecher went beyond earlier temperance leaders in several respects. Like Dr. Rush, he believed that the sustained use of liquor was harmful even if one never actually got drunk. "Let it therefore be engraven upon the heart of every man," he wrote, "that the daily use of ardent spirits, in any form, or in any degree, is intemperance." Beecher's prescription was radical; he called for nothing less than total abstinence from distilled beverages. He differed from Rush on the question of drinking wine as well. Rush had recommended it; Beecher thought it a treacherous way station on the road to stronger potions. Under the influence of Beecher, and others like him, the

temperance movement had come a long way from mere denunciations of drunkenness.

The 1830's witnessed a remarkable growth of temperance societies. The United States Temperance Union (later renamed the American Temperance Union) was founded in 1833, though four years passed before it held its first national convention. Despite its increasing popularity, the cause suffered grievously from internal disunity. For some, temperance meant what the word itself meant: moderation. For others, such as Beecher, it had come to mean abstinence. And what was to be included in the list of harmful beverages: distilled spirits only, or wines and beers too? Finally, should temperance (however defined) be promoted exclusively by moral suasion, or should the societies enter the realm of politics? Members of the various groups wrangled over these questions in seemingly endless debates which did little to achieve effectiveness.

A new development took place after 1840. Until this time, the most visible leaders of the cause were opinion leaders such as clergymen, newspaper publishers, and college presidents. Beginning with a group which called itself the Washington Temperance Society, however, a new element came to the fore: reformed drinkers. These were men who, some way or another, had seen the light and who wanted to help save others. Who knew better the evils of drink than those who once had been in its clutches themselves? This "Washington revival," as it became known, spread throughout the country and produced a number of eloquent spokesmen for the temperance cause.

One of the most popular of the reformed drunkards was John H.W. Hawkins. Hawkins began drinking as a young lad while serving as an apprentice to a hatmaker. For more than twenty years he alternated between periods of excessive drinking and relative sobriety. Finally, as his bouts with alcohol became longer and more debilitating he was no longer able to provide for his family and became a public ward. According to his own account, Hawkins was redeemed when members of the Washington Temperance Society in Baltimore convinced him to sign a pledge of total abstinence. Possessing impressive oratorical talents, Hawkins went on to become one of the cause's most sought-after speakers. He later estimated that during his first ten years as a reformer he traveled more than 100,000 miles and delivered some 2,500 lectures.

John Bartholomew Gough was equally in demand. Gough too had begun drinking as a youngster, and his habit cost him job after job and several physical breakdowns. During one, when his seriously ill wife tried to nurse him through, the strain proved too much for her and she died. For some time after her death he rarely drew a sober breath. When finally converted by a friend, Gough pitched himself wholeheartedly into the cause. By several accounts he was a masterful speaker, able to manipulate the emotions of his audience as he wished. He boasted in his autobiography that singlehandedly he accounted for more than 15,000 converts to abstinence.

Things did not always go smoothly for Gough. Early in his career as a reformer he "fell off the wagon" and did so again at the height of his popularity in 1845. The latter occasion touched off quite a furor. While visiting New York City Gough disappeared for almost a week. After a desperate search, friends located him in a bawdy house in one of the seedier sections of the city. He was, it was obvious, recovering from a monumental drinking spree. The incident received wide publicity as the anti-temperance press had a field day at Gough's expense. He claimed innocence. An acquaintance, whose name he could not remember, had treated him to a glass supposedly containing only a soft drink. Having consumed the beverage, Gough claimed, he blanked out and did not know how he ended up where he did. How many people believed Gough's explanation—implying as it did that the liquor interests had conspired to do him in—is unknown, but he remained a popular speaker on the temperance circuit for another five years.

The temperance movement evolved one step more during the pre-Civil War years. It was becoming painfully evident to some that, despite the thousands of pamphlets issued, meetings held, and speeches delivered, the drinking habits of most Americans had not changed. Taverns and saloons prospered, men and women reeled about in the streets, and the gallons of drink consumed rose with each passing year. But what of all the converts? The usual evidence of success consisted of the number of signed pledges individuals or societies collected from "redeemed" individuals, who promised either moderation or total abstinence. There were two problems with this approach. First, even in the most rewarding years no more than a tiny percentage of the adult population signed such promises. Second, how valid were they? To be sure, an effective speaker such as Hawkins or Gough could cause people to struggle in the aisles to sign up. But when emotions cooled, it was obvious, many resumed their old habits. Indeed, as one anti-temperance joke had it, some individuals became so elated by taking the pledge that they could scarcely wait to celebrate by having a few drinks. Increasingly, therefore, temperance advocates sought to strengthen moral persuasion with legal enforcement.

Some reformers had advocated legal controls in the 1830's and 1840's, but they were always in the minority. True conversion could only come through education, the majority had argued, and there was great fear that the purity of the cause would become sullied by entangling it in partisan politics. But this position became increasingly untenable as time wore on; unaided moral suasion simply had not achieved the desired effects. Nor was local-option legislation sufficient. This tactic had been tried in many communities, but serious drinkers could always lay in a supply from nearby towns or cities. Some reformers, therefore, came to believe that nothing less than statewide prohibition could get the job done. A formidable undertaking to be sure, but the prospects were dazzling.

Neal Dow was a successful businessman who looked the part. He wore expensive clothes, a lace-trimmed vest, and kept the time by a fat gold watch reportedly costing more than $200. He was dynamic, aggressive, and exuded vitality. Although slight of stature, Dow feared no man and used his fists effectively when the occasion demanded it. He was also a devout reformer. Dow devoted his life to the temperance cause and, as early as the 1830's, had become convinced that state prohibition was the only answer.

Born and raised in Portland, Maine, Dow practiced the teachings of his temperance-minded parents with a vengeance. At the age of 18 he joined the volunteer fire department of Portland and before very long somehow convinced the group to stop serving alcohol at its social get-togethers. Later, as captain, he enraged many drinkers by allowing a liquor store to burn to the ground without turning a hose on it. Called before the city's board of alderman to account for his behavior, Dow claimed he had acted as he did to "save" adjacent buildings. On another occasion, when the casks of a wholesale dealer were erupting into fireballs, Dow remarked to an aide that it was a "magnificent sight." Small wonder that the liquor interests in Portland would have preferred another fire chief.

But Dow was after bigger game. Throughout the 1840's he worked tirelessly to bring the temperance issue into the political arena. At first he concentrated on turning Portland dry, but statewide legislation was his real goal. He was careful not to allow prohibition to become a partisan issue; he and his allies (he often used his own employees to do temperance work) supported all those who were "right" on the good cause. At last, in 1851, Dow won what had seemed an impossible victory. With many members of both houses indebted to him politically, he shepherded through the Maine legislature the first general prohibition law in American history. Dow, who was by this time mayor of Portland, prosecuted the new law to the best of his considerable abilities.

The Maine Law of 1851 served as rallying point for prohibitionists in other states. Dubbed "The Napoleon of Temperance," Dow became a hero to drys everywhere as the following song attests:

> Come all ye friends of temperance, and listen to my strain,
> I'll tell you how Old Alchy fares down in the State of Maine.
> There's one Neal Dow, a Portland man, with great and noble soul,
> He framed a law, without a flaw, to banish alcohol.

Unfortunately, as Dow himself admitted privately, alcohol was not "banished" from Maine, but flowed rather freely through illegal channels. Still, it was a step forward, and in the next four years two territories and eleven states enacted similar laws. Many people deserved the credit, if such it be, but no one more than Dow who advised and counseled his fellow reformers across the nation.

The hope that prohibition would become an irresistible tide proved illusory after the mid-1850's. The most important reason was the growing sectional struggle which culminated in the Civil War. As compared to the great issues of slavery and secession, prohibition seemed almost trivial except to the faithful. More than twenty-five years were to pass before another state would adopt prohibition. Equally ominous, though less obvious, was a simple statistic. During those years of temperance victories the per capita consumption of wine, whiskey, and beer *rose* from slightly over four gallons to almost six and one-half. Later prohibitionists ignored or downplayed the grim truth that laws in the books were ineffective so long as a sufficient number of people were willing to disobey them.

By the early 1870's, the temperance movement began stirring again. One of the most significant developments of this era was the role women played. Women always had constituted the backbone of the movement in terms of numbers, but men invariably held the positions of leadership. The first sign of change occurred in what became known as the "Women's Crusade." In communities across the nation groups of women assembled in front of saloons and taverns, vowing to remain until owners agreed to close. For hours, days, and even longer the women sang and prayed, and tried to discourage men from entering. Some places indeed did close, but usually only temporarily and the Crusade dwindled after a few years. Veterans of the Crusade were not about to quit, however, and in 1874 formed the Woman's Christian Temperance Union. This organization would play an important part in the drive for national prohibition.

The dominant force of the WCTU until her death in 1898 was Frances Willard. Born into a family dedicated to reform (her father was a member of the Washington Society), Willard was a zealous temperance advocate from youth. Endowed with a formidable intelligence and incredible energy, she received a good education and was a college faculty member at age 23. In 1871 Willard was named president of Northwestern Female College and, when that institution merged with Northwestern University, became dean of women. She subsequently resigned from this post, however, and thereafter dedicated herself to the temperance movement.

Under Willard the WCTU became the largest, best organized, and most powerful temperance organization in the country. It published tons of pamphlets, provided speakers, lobbied legislators. There were few aspects of society the organization failed to penetrate. Willard herself was a dynamo who, when not giving a speech or chairing a meeting, wrote letters and articles in behalf of the cause. Described by one individual as "organized mother love," the WCTU under Willard reached into every community.

Less important than Willard, though far more colorful, was Carry A. Nation ("carry a nation for temperance," she liked to say). A member of the WCTU, Nation circled in her own orbit and in fact was an embarrassment to some of the members. Having grown up in a family where eccentricity was the norm, Carry at age 19 married a man who drank himself to death very quickly. When the daughter of that union developed chronic illnesses of the cruelest sort, Carry concluded they were the results of her husband's addiction to alcohol and tobacco. These two substances became her lifelong enemies. Though she became involved in temperance work earlier, Carry made the full commitment after claiming to have received a direct communication from God during the summer of 1900.

Nation's methods were similar to the Women Crusaders—with a difference. She too prayed and sang that saloon keepers and their customers would repent. But in addition to her words she hurled bricks and bottles. Her favorite weapon came to be a hatchet which she wielded with remarkable verve for a middle-aged woman. "Smash! Smash! For Jesus' sake, Smash!" was her battle cry as she broke up saloons from Kansas to New York. Though she garnered a great deal of publicity, and caused some other women to take up their own hatchets, Carry's impact was not lasting. Indeed, in later years she became a curiosity, touring county fairs and carnivals. At age 64 she collapsed after a lecture and died a few months later in the summer of 1911.

The temperance movement took on new life with the founding of the Anti-Saloon League of America in 1895.

This temperance cartoon was captioned "Commit him for manslaughter in the greatest degree." ("Harper's Weekly," March 21, 1874)

As was the WCTU, it was misnamed. Just as "temperance" really meant abstinence, the Anti-Saloon League was dedicated to banning all alcohol rather than just that dispensed by saloons. It was an effective ploy because the term "saloon" conjured up all sorts of negative images: drunken fistfights, scarlet women, and husbands drinking away their wages. The word "League" was accurate, however, because the organization was nonsectarian and accepted any individuals or groups dedicated to prohibition.

The League's dedication to a single goal made it more effective than its predecessors. It took on no other reforms, rarely got bogged down in internal disputes, and appealed to everyone interested in the cause. The organization was pragmatic to say the least, and subordinated everything to its goal. "Ethics be hanged," as one of the leaders put it, and they very often were. The League regularly supported politicians who were known drinkers, for instance, provided they could be depended upon to vote dry. In the South, League speakers and pamphlets often played upon racial prejudices by describing in lurid terms how alcohol heightened the lust black males had for white women. Dedicated, unscrupulous as to means, the League was able to bring great pressure to bear upon politicians across the country.

During the first decade of the 20th century, the League, the WCTU, and other organizations, succeeded in getting a number of state legislatures to pass prohibitory laws of various kinds. By 1913 the League went on record as favoring a constitutional amendment to make prohibition nationwide. Bills were introduced in Congress and the issue aroused considerable debate, which spurred the drys on to greater efforts. When the 1914 elections were over, men committed to voting dry had gained in both houses of Congress. During the next session a prohibition bill introduced in the House won by a 197-190 majority. This was a good deal short of the two-thirds necessary to start the amendment process (three-fourths of the states have to concur), but still constituted a victory of which earlier temperance advocates could not have dreamed.

Would the prohibitionists ultimately have prevailed because of their own efforts? Or would the movement have peaked short of its goal, and then perhaps waned as had earlier temperance crusades? The answer is speculative. For it was the onset of World War I—and more particularly, American entry into the conflict—which assured a prohibitionist victory.

American participation in the war gave the drys two additional weapons which they employed with deadly effect. The first stemmed from the simple fact that various grains and sugar are the main ingredients of beer and liquor. At a time when Americans were being called upon to conserve food for the war effort, how could one defend the diversion of these materials into alcohol? Few politicians were prepared to defend themselves against charges that they were willing to see drunks get their liquor while boys in the trenches went hungry. That most breweries and many distilleries bore Germanic names provided a second boon to the drys. They were able to concoct all sorts of horror stories about German plots to undermine the war effort by encouraging soldiers and civilians to drink their vile products. Such allegations may seem absurd today, but they carried weight during a period when sauerkraut was renamed "victory cabbage."

Under these circumstances the prohibition movement was unstoppable. What was to become the Eighteenth Amendment was adopted by the Senate in August 1917 and by the House in December. The wets thought they had outmaneuvered their opponents when they worked in a seven-year time limit on the ratification process, but they were badly mistaken. The required number of states ratified within thirteen months of submission and the Eighteenth Amendment became law on January 16, 1919, (though it was not to take effect until one year from that date). The "Noble Experiment" would soon begin.

Last Stop on the Underground Railroad

MARY ANN SHADD IN CANADA

Cheryl MacDonald

Cheryl MacDonald has written biographies of Victorian diva Emma Albani and pioneer feminist Adelaide Hoodless, both published by Dundurn Press.

In October 1855 people in Philadelphia were talking about Mary Ann Shadd. The young black woman had been in the "City of Brotherly Love" several times before, usually to promote the *Provincial Freeman*, a Canadian-based abolitionist paper. That was her purpose again this fall, but she also took advantage of an opportunity to participate in a public debate against J.C. Wears, a prominent Philadelphian.

The topic was emigration, specifically the emigration of blacks. For five years, America's black population had feared the repercussions of the Fugitive Slave Law, which allowed slave hunters to pursue runaways into states where slavery was illegal. In some cases, free born blacks were also captured and sold into slavery. Many reacted by fleeing. Most went north to Canada, although there were groups whose preferred destinations were Africa or the Caribbean islands.

For her part, the dynamic young woman with "bright sharp eyes, that look right through you" favoured Canada, a point she made clear in the debate against Wears. Her knowledge of the subject was impressive, gained largely through her own experience. She had been in Canada since 1851; in 1852 she had published a pamphlet, *Notes of Canada West*, describing conditions blacks were likely to find north of the border.

The facts Shadd presented in the debate were similar to those in the 44-page pamphlet. Canada West offered more benefits than any other destination, she argued. Tropical Africa, she said, was "teeming. . .with the breath of pestilence, a burning sun and fearful maladies. . ." In the Southern States, blacks faced "the probability of worse than inquisitorial inhumanity". By contrast, Canada offered good soil, temperate conditions and a beneficial political climate.

Yes, there was prejudice:

> Coloured persons have been refused entertainment in taverns, (invariably of an inferior class,) and on some boats distinction is made; but in all cases, it is that kind of distinction that is made between poor foreigners and other passengers. . . . It is an easy matter to make out a case of prejudice in any country. We naturally look for it, and the conduct of many is calculated to cause unpleasant treatment, and to make it difficult for well-mannered persons to get comfortable accommodations. There is a medium between servility and presumption, that recommends itself to all persons of common sense, of whatever rank or complexion; and if coloured people would avoid the two extremes, there would be but few cases of prejudice to complain of in Canada. In cases in which tavern keepers and other public characters persist in refusing to entertain them, they can, in common with the travelling public, generally, get redress at law.

It was this last fact she emphasized when Wears asked her about racism. Certainly it existed, she conceded, but there was no law to support it, and so "it

By Cheryl McDonald. Originally published in *The Beaver*, February/March 1990, pp. 32-38.

Black American fugitives arriving in Canada.

was manageable, not like it is in the States."

Mary Shadd won the debate against Wears. Soon afterward, another triumph followed, when Philadelphians arranged a benefit evening, celebrating her as the first black woman in North America to edit a newspaper. Celebrities, including the "Black Swan", soprano Elizabeth Taylor Greenfield, were on hand to ensure the success of the event. When the last song was sung, the last dish of ice cream eaten, enough money had been raised to help Mary Shadd continue to publish her newspaper for a little while longer.

At this point, Mary Shadd's life was dominated by the newspaper. It had not always been so, although the abolition of slavery had been a constant theme in her development. Not that the Shadd family had personal experience with slavery. Both her parents were free born, and, according to a tradition, her father's people had never been slaves.

Abraham Shadd, a shoemaker by trade, actively fought for the abolition of slavery. His house was a station on the Underground Railroad; Shadd also sold subscriptions for the *Liberator*, an abolitionist newspaper, an activity that was just as dangerous as helping slaves to freedom. In 1837, Elijah P. Lovejoy, the publisher of the *Liberator* and a friend of the Shadd family, was killed by an Alton, Illinois mob that invaded his office, dumped his printing press into the river, and set fire to the building.

Shadd senior was also active in anti-slavery groups, and for a time served as president of the National Convention for the Improvement of Free People of Colour in the United States. He would later become

the first black person elected to public office in Canada West.

There was no doubt that the Shadds were an exceptional family. Isaac, the fourth child and eldest son, served in the Mississippi legislature from 1871 to 1874, part of that time as Speaker of the House. Abraham, a younger brother, practised law in Mississippi and Arkansas. But it was Mary, who rose above the dual barriers of race and sex, whose achievements were most notable.

Mary Ann Camberton Shadd was born 9 October 1823 in Wilmington, Delaware. It was a slave state, and, although the Shadds were free, there were few opportunities to educate their children. So, before Mary was ten, the family moved to West Chester, Pennsylvania, close to Philadelphia. There, according to family tradition, she was educated by Quakers.

At a time when it was illegal in many states to teach a slave to read or write, education was the Holy Grail for blacks who sought a better life. And, like the legendary Grail, it was an elusive goal when community prejudice often kept black children out of school even if the law provided for their education. For a girl like young Mary Shadd, brought up to work for the improvement of her people, education was an inevitable starting point. After finishing school at sixteen, she returned to Wilmington, where she opened a school for black children. Over the next few years, she taught in several other places, including Trenton, New Jersey, and New York City.

It was in New York that an incident took place which epitomizes Mary Shadd's character. Perhaps apocry-

Mary Ann Shadd.

phal, it nevertheless captures her formidable dignity and determination. According to the story, she was walking along Broadway, saw a trolley car, and flagged it down. It was a time when few black women dared to ride on trolleys, let alone signal one to stop. But, in Mary's case, "there was such an air of imperative command. . . that the large, coarse ruffianly driver" stopped his horses.

She was never one to back down from conflict. By the late 1840s, she was actively seeking it with letters to the editors of newspapers and, in 1849, a 12-page pamphlet, *Hints to the Coloured People of the North*. In many of her writings there is a note of urgency, an impatience with the long, drawn out process of committee discussion and resolutions, a plea for black people to take their destiny into their own hands. Typical was a letter to Frederick Douglass's *North Star*, in which she suggested blacks should become more involved in farming:

The estimation in which we would be held by those in power, would be quite different, were we producers and not merely as now, consumers. . . .We have been holding conventions for years — have been assembling together and whining over our difficulties and afflictions, passing resolutions on resolutions to any extent; but it does really seem that we have made but little progress, considering our resolves. . . .We should do more and talk less.

Within two years, Mary was following her own advice and trying to do more. In mid-September 1851, she visited Toronto, where she heard Martin Delany, a prominent black abolitionist, and John Scoble, an English supporter of the cause, speak on slavery. She also heard Henry Bibb, founder of *Voice of the Fugitive*, a newspaper based in Sandwich, not far from Windsor. Within days, Mary Ann was writing to her brother, Isaac, who was in Buffalo, that she liked Canada, and that she was on her way to Sandwich. After a stop in Buffalo, she boarded a steamer for the Detroit-Windsor area.

Windsor was a tiny community of perhaps 200 people at the time. Because of its proximity to Detroit, it was a terminal on the Underground Railroad. As more and more blacks moved into the area, prejudice against them grew. That was just one disadvantage the new arrivals faced — there were also housing shortages, poverty, disease, and the problems of adjusting to the climate and laws of a new country.

Mary Ann travelled to the area after hearing about the destitution and ignorance of the black refugees. She wanted to help, and, again, chose teaching as the way. Initially, she moved cautiously. Henry Bibb's wife had her own school, and before beginning to teach, Mary Shadd asked her permission.

At first, things went smoothly, but then Mary's principles got in the way. She strongly opposed segregation, would not teach in a segregated school, and for the same reason, had not renewed her membership in the African Methodist Episcopalian church. In her letter to the *North Star* in March 1849 she had hinted at the reasons. "What intellectually we most need . . . is the knowledge of the white man, a great amount of which by intercourse in public meetings, etc., we could glean. . ."

Again, Mary Shadd was fighting an uphill battle. At a school meeting, she was the only one to oppose segregation — strictly on a matter of principle, since schools for white children already existed, and in practice no white students attended schools run by blacks. Still, there was some support for her view in the community, enough to allow her to open a private school in an abandoned barracks. She charged 4 shillings a month for attendance at the drafty and badly furnished school, then dropped the fee to 3 shillings as the Bibbs brought increasing pressure against her.

As long as she had twenty paying pupils, Mary calculated there would be enough to cover the costs of running the school and her own living expenses. However, as enthusiasm gave way to parental apathy, payments dropped off. So she wrote to the American Missionary Society, an organization that had several missionaries and teachers working with fugitive blacks, asking for support for the school.

Her contact was George Whipple, secretary of the organization. Before he would proceed, Whipple wanted to know more about Schoolmistress Shadd. One ref-

"The Provincial Freeman": From anti-slavery to temperance.

of the problems facing abolitionists, free blacks and fugitive slaves alike. Sometimes, the problems arose from philosophical differences; sometimes, it was motivated by greed for power and money. Like modern patients and prisoners, freshly released from institutions after years of having all their needs seen to, newly freed blacks had awesome adjustments to make in their way of living. With little education, many were easy prey for unscrupulous leaders, whether white or black.

To Mary Ann Shadd, Henry Bibb was one such unscrupulous leader. One of his jobs was gathering money for the Refugee Home Society, a segregated community funded by donations and designed to give fugitives a place to live and develop farming skills. But Shadd pointed out in 1852 that, with only 22 families on the Refugee Home Society's 100,000 acres, no real community existed. Worse, the Bibbs appeared to be growing rich on the donations they collected.

Another prominent black she censured was Josiah Henson, founder of Dawn, a settlement for blacks where Henson opened the British American Institute, one of

erence came from Reverend Alexander McArthur, who described her as

> a young (light coloured) lady of fine education, refined address and christian deportment. . . .well qualified to fill the situation in question. . . and possessing an energy of character & enlargement of views well fitting her for the work of teaching amongst such people as this.

Mary eventually got $125 for support of the school, but by this time it had temporarily closed, due to cold weather and lack of firewood.

When she learned of the American Missionary Society's support, Mary discussed it with her colleagues. Already frustrated with community apathy, and remembering how swiftly payments had trickled to almost nothing, she feared that news of the supplement might be interpreted as a signal to stop payments altogether. So she purposely kept news of the grant a secret.

Four months later, the *Voice of the Fugitive* reported the grant, and Mary was forced to defend her decision. It was just one more act in the bitter rivalry between Mary, the Bibbs, and their respective factions, a drama that has been amply documented in the Jim Bearden and Linda Jean Butler biography, *The Life and Times of Mary Shadd Cary*. The struggle was characteristic

Henry Bibb.

the earliest vocational schools in North America. Believed by many of his contemporaries to be the prototype for Harriet Beecher Stowe's Uncle Tom, Henson was a stubborn, ambitious and eloquent man, often accused of mishandling community funds entrusted to his care. While some felt his only flaw was lack of managerial skill, others suspected him of worse faults. Mary Ann Shadd detested him, possibly because he was too much like other ministers she had known. She described them as members of a "corrupt clergy". . .

> inculcating ignorance as a duty, superstition as a true religion. . . .their gross ignorance and insolent bearing, together with the sanctimonious garb and by virtue of their calling, a character for mystery they assume. . .

In her war against men like Bibb and Henson, Mary Ann won the battle over the American Missionary Society's unreported support of her school. At a public meeting, she was even thanked for her work. But Mary Shadd was not a woman who could be bought off with pleasant words. In a series of anonymous articles for the *Western Evangelist*, she attacked the Refugee Home Society. And, in the same month, she teamed up with the Reverend Samuel Ringgold Ward.

A noted orator and minister who had once led a white congregation, Ward came to Windsor as a speaker for the Anti-Slavery Society. Like Mary, he opposed segregation, and, with her and some others, formed the Windsor Anti-Slavery Society. One of their goals was to create a newspaper which would provide a different viewpoint from the *Voice of the Fugitive*.

Ostensibly, Ward was editor of the *Provincial Freeman* but he was usually away on speaking engagements. In fact, Mary Shadd, whose official capacity was business manager, was publisher, editor and subscription agent. By this time, she had been dismissed by the Missionary Society. She believed her race, her sex, and her refusal to sacrifice principles had all hurt her cause, and afterwards she seldom lost an opportunity to criticize "Yankee Missionaries, such as we have met in Canada, with smooth words and hearts full of negrohate."

However, she had little time to brood. She travelled throughout Canada West and the northern United States, speaking on abolition and emigration, and encouraging her listeners to subscribe to the *Provincial Freeman*. It was a far from easy task. With little money, she could only afford the cheapest fares on trains or steamers, and, as a black woman travelling alone, she was often in danger of insult or physical violence.

She persisted, and, for a time, it seemed the newspaper might prosper. In 1854, she moved it to Toronto, then a town of 47,000, with the largest black community in the province. At first, she kept her identity as editor secret, using initials rather than her name. There were still strong biases against women working in male-dominated fields, although the seeds of the North American women's movement had been sown at Seneca Falls, New York, in July 1848. It didn't take

American slave hunters capture a runaway.

long, though, before people suspected her identity, and while some took exception to a female's control of a newspaper, there were others who regarded Mary Shadd as "one of the best editors in the province even if she did wear petticoats".

The newspaper contained a potpourri of news articles from other sources. An introduction in an early issue noted:

The *Provincial Freeman* will be devoted to the elevation of the Coloured People; and in seeking to effect this object, it will advocate the cause of TEMPERANCE....

Many articles dealt with abolition, emigration to Canada, and local events. As time went on, Mary's brother Isaac and her sister Amelia also worked for the paper. In 1854, Amelia served as editor while Mary toured western Ontario, sending back letters whenever she could. From London she wrote on 25 July:

Attended the meeting held by the voters last night, at Chatham, at which I saw quite a large number of females. I like that new feature in political gatherings, and you will agree with me, that much of the asperity of such assemblies will be softened by their presence.

She was back in Toronto in time for Emancipation Day, 1 August, and a report of the event appeared on 5 August. Starting with a prayer meeting at 5 a.m. in the Sayer Street Chapel, Toronto blacks paraded to the lake shore to meet the *Arabian*, carrying visitors from Hamilton. Rain delayed the proceedings a little bit, but addresses followed, along with a procession moving to the music of Scott's Brass Band. There was a sermon at the cathedral, then dinner at Government Grounds and more speeches, including an address to the Queen, which began:

We, the Coloured Inhabitants of Canada, most respectfully, most gratefully and most loyally approach your Gracious Majesty, on this, the anniversary of our *death* to *Slavery*, and our *birth* to *Freedom*. ....Our hearts are wholly your Majesty's. ...

The speeches were followed by a resolution to meet in Hamilton in 1855 and several toasts, including one to the queen, one to the *Provincial Freeman*, and a final one to "Our wives and Sweethearts".

Soon afterward, Mary was off on tour again. After her triumphant benefit in Philadelphia, she returned to Canada. In January, she married Thomas Cary, a Toronto barber, at her sister's home in St. Catharines. Within a week, she was back on the road, promoting the *Provincial Freeman*.

Eventually, public opinion forced Mary to stop editing the paper. She was replaced by a "gentleman Editor", who published the newspaper from the Chatham area. Mary continued to be the motivating force behind the publication, though, and she moved to Chatham as well. Aside from the newspaper, there was another attraction — by this time, her parents and siblings had emigrated to Canada.

Although she and Thomas were frequently separated because of business concerns, their first child, a daughter, was born in August 1857. Around this time, publication of the *Provincial Freeman* stopped, partly because of Mary's family obligations, partly because the newspaper was deeply in debt. Thomas continued to work in Toronto, sending money whenever he could, baby Sarah was left in the care of her 19-year-old aunt, and Mary went on the road yet again to find new subscribers. In June 1858, the paper resumed publication, and, around this time, Thomas joined the staff.

Getting the paper out became more and more difficult as war clouds gathered over the United States. Mary also had other concerns. In November 1860, Thomas died after a long illness. By this time, there was another child to care for, a son named Linton. Mary followed the Civil War with interest, and, beginning around January 1864 helped recruit Canadian blacks for the Union army. After the war, she returned to the United States. In 1868, she obtained a teaching certificate in Detroit, then moved to Washington, D.C., where she taught and later worked as the principal of a public school.

Like her brothers, Abraham and Isaac, she also studied law. Although there is no record of her being admitted to the bar, she is listed in the senior class of 1872 at Howard Law School. She was also deeply involved in the women's movement, and addressed the national convention of the Women's Suffrage Association in 1878.

Mary Shadd Cary died in Washington, D.C. in 1893. In her lifetime, she had either been loved as a crusader for justice or hated as a "mischief maker". She was often tactless, fiercely attacking those whose ideas did not coincide with her own. But there was no doubt she had the courage of her convictions. An episode recounted by her daughter illustrates this.

One Sunday, ignoring national boundaries, slave hunters pursued a black youth into Chatham, where they caught him. Enraged, Mary tore the boy away from them, ran to the courthouse and rang the bell, warning the whole town. As a crowd gathered, the hunters fled. Mary Shadd Cary had won one more battle.

The cry was: Go West, young man, and stay healthy

Bil Gilbert

The author writes often for Smithsonian *and has recently completed a biography of Mountain Man Joe Walker titled* Westering Man.

In the 1840s Americans by thousands headed toward the Great Plains, seeking not only land and gold, but also a cure for Great Pains

Josiah Gregg is remembered as the author of *Commerce of the Prairies*, an account of his experiences during the 1830s as an early trader and traveler on the Santa Fe Trail. The book remains a primary historical document, and one that can still be read with pleasure, because Gregg was an intelligent, accurate observer with an easy literary style. But it is the reasons why he migrated that are especially instructive, since his motives were typical of many of those who pioneered in the West.

Gregg was born in Missouri in 1806. He grew into a sickly child whose survival was often in doubt. On the assumption that he was too frail to bear the hard work of the frontier, his family—which did well in farming and trade—encouraged him to read law. Gregg soon found he had little taste for it. Besides, he found himself sick so much of the time that he could not have practiced anyway.

By 1831, at age 25, he was virtually an invalid. His book describes the "morbid condition" that afflicted him. He was "so debilitated" that he could rarely walk "beyond the narrow precincts of my chamber. In this hopeless condition, my physicians advised me to take a trip across the prairies, and, in the change of air and habits which such an adventure would involve, to seek that health which their science had failed to bestow."

A carriage loaded with pills

Gregg immediately arranged to join a caravan then forming near Independence, Missouri, and bound for Santa Fe. He felt too poorly to walk far or sit on his horse, so he arrived at the rendezvous in a carriage, loaded with pills, powders and other "such commodities as I deemed necessary for my comfort and health." The assumption was that if he reached New Mexico at all, it would be in this vehicle, traveling more or less as a litter patient. After only a week on the trail, though, Gregg abandoned his carriage and medicines. Thereafter he rode a horse, worked, ate and slept on the ground just like the teamsters, traders and scouts of the caravan. "When we reached the buffalo range," he recalled, "I was not only as eager for the chase as the sturdiest of my companions, but I enjoyed far more exquisitely my share of the buffalo than all the delicacies which were ever devised to provoke the most fastidious appetite."

For the rest of his life, Gregg was healthy and vigorous. After nine years in the Santa Fe trade, he became a front-line correspondent in the Mexican War. In 1849 he took a troop of prospective gold miners overland to California. Gregg died of starvation early in 1850 while leading a party of explorers in the then unknown mountains of northern California. He was only 44, but his premature end was not caused by any constitutional infirmity.

Neither the doctors who originally suggested that Gregg take to the wilderness to cure his chronic ailments, nor the patient who accepted that advice, were unusual in the 1830s. As he wrote at the trailhead where his first Santa Fe caravan assembled, "The prairies have become very celebrated for their sanative effects. . . . Most chronic diseases, particularly liver complaints, dyspepsias, and similar affections, are often radically cured; owing, no doubt, to the peculiarities of diet, and the regular exercise incident to prairie life, as well as to the purity of the atmosphere of those elevated unembarrassed regions."

Gregg shared these opinions with a large number of men of letters who went West hoping to cure themselves. According to historian Archibald Hanna, one reason there are so many books about the West is that so many writers went West for the cure. An incomplete list of such authors, their ailments and works, includes: Washington Irving (nervous depression), *A Tour on the Prairies*; Francis Parkman (severe headaches), *The Oregon Trail*; Matthew Field (gastric ulcers), *Prairie and Mountain Sketches*; Lewis Garrard (general puniness), *Wah-to-yah and the Taos Trail*; William Hamilton (fevers), *My Sixty Years on the Plains*.

Though their testimonials helped to popularize notions about the remarkable curative effects of life in the far West, the notion of a healthy West was not the exclusive property of pallid young men with literary leanings. The belief was general among explorers, fur trappers, traders, miners, stockmen and covered-wagon pioneers—all classes, in fact, that took part in the westward migration. The truth seems to be that many pioneers thought of the whole trans-Mississippi country as a kind of miraculous, all-purpose spa full of restorative properties. The belief was particularly strong during pre-Civil War decades when most of the genuine pioneering took place. A compelling reason was the simple fact that conditions in the heavily-settled parts of the East tended to be so bad that many people desperately wanted to escape from them.

Except for a few scattered localities, health records were not generally kept until the latter part of the 19th century. But historians estimate the national life expectancy in 1840 at approximately 39 years—about 30 fewer than it is now. The mortality rate in the large cities, about 30 deaths per year per thousand, was more than three times higher than today's.

Early 19th-century Americans suffered from all our current afflictions, plus a great number of lethal and disabling ills since eliminated or reduced to minor problems. They were commonly laid low by cholera, diphtheria, lockjaw, rabies, smallpox and typhus, not to mention milk fever, the mysterious disease that killed Nancy Hanks Lincoln. Not until this century was it discovered that milk fever was caused by cows feeding on white snakeroot and other plants containing the toxin tremetol.

At a conservative estimate, well over half the population south and west of New England probably suffered at one time or another from malaria, then commonly called "the ague." Entire families, and even communities, were sometimes laid low with malarial chills and fevers, headaches, nausea and exhaustion. In Indianapolis in 1822 it was reported that out of a population of 1,000, some 900 people were shaking with the ague. The next year, 90,000 of the 165,000 settlers in the 17 counties around Columbus, Ohio, had malaria. A Kentuckian, who had been driven out of Missouri by the fever there, met another health seeker on the road who was headed toward the town of Boone's Lick for safety, and tried to discourage him: "The people die there like rotten sheep. They have filled one graveyard already and have begun upon another. Well, go on, but I can tell you, *you will shake!*"

By 1830, the U.S. population had tripled to 13 million—nearly all of it still east of the Mississippi. During the same period, medicine, and the techniques for disposing of waste and protecting the purity of food and drink, improved very little. In the cities more and more people lived in closer quarters. Bad air, water, food and filth diseases became chronic plagues. With the advent of the Industrial Revolution conditions worsened. Suggestions that employers or communities had some legal or ethical responsibility for the health and safety of employees or citizens were generally regarded as subversive. The occupational accident rate was high, often with gruesome results. Such antique-sounding but serious ailments as brass-founder's fever, hatter's shakes and file-cutter's paralysis were common among working people. The term "mad as a hatter" had its origin in a real neurologic disease caused by mercury poisoning.

Wealth increased steadily although, paradoxically, much evidence suggests that dietary standards declined. Out of necessity colonial families often foraged for wild foods, and so fed on fresh meat and vegetables. By 1830 supplies of such foods, as well as the taste for them, had decreased in many localities. Meals were monotonous and often non-nutritious. Coastal residents were more sophisticated, and had easier, cheaper access to varied foods. But the standard fare of inland Americans was corn and hog meat. The former was ordinarily served as mush, grits or bread; the latter was salted. Everything that possibly could be fried *was* fried, and in lard. "I had never undergone such gastronomic privations as in the western [i.e., the present Midwest] parts of America," wrote German Prince Maximilian of Wied-Neuwied in 1843. Maximilian was an early naturalist (SMITHSONIAN, October 1976) and one of many foreign travelers who complained about American food.

The quality of the grub may have been bad, but the quantities put away were impressive. "Americans," journalist Robert Tomes admitted in an 1856 issue of

Harper's Magazine, "are not epicures, but gluttons. They swallow, but don't eat; and, like the boa constrictor, bolt everything. . . . It startles a foreigner to see with what voracity even our delicate women dispose of the infinite succession of dishes on the public tables."

An early report in the *Medical Repository*, a principal journal of the day, commented on the national eating habits: "The inhabitants are almost constantly in a state of repletion, by stuffing and cramming, and by the use of stimulating drink. The consumption of animal food is probably much greater in the Fredonian [United] states, than in any other civilized nation. . . ."

If anything, Americans drank worse than they ate. Coffee was dear. So was tea. Besides, in the early days, it was scorned as British and therefore unpatriotic. With good reason both milk and water were commonly suspected of being contaminated or outright lethal. The most popular alternatives in early 19th-century America were corn whiskey and hard apple cider. In his excellent study, W. J. Rorabaugh speculates that the unsavory general diet probably had something to do with prodigious boozing. Only raw whiskey, he reasoned, could cut through the layers of grease that coated American palates. Many Americans drank morning, noon and night and paid for it with dyspepsia, liver and bilious complaints, delirium tremens, terrible hangovers and other forms of crapulence.

Dr. Daniel Drake, probably the most prominent physician west of the Appalachians in the 1830s and '40s, suggested that even more bizarre consequences resulted from the obesity and drunkenness of his countrymen. Reporting to a professional meeting, Drake said he knew of several cases in which fat men had so stuffed themselves with grease and alcohol that they became literally flammable and had more or less exploded when sparks from a fire fell on them. He described the phenomenon as "spontaneous combustion."

Physicians were often part of the health problem. The first half of the 19th century was a time of total medical chaos. Homeopaths, "hydropathists, botanics," allopaths fiercely contended with each other, usually to the detriment of the patient. The dominant school of medicine was still the "heroic" one, the term applying to the theory of treatment rather than to the character of the practitioner. Doctors regularly administered massive doses of drugs—quinine and calomel being the favorites—and practiced bleeding on a grand scale.

The official aim was to relieve "inflammation," but the technique was usually used with little or no relation to the disease. In 1806, for example, a man named John Shaw, trying to sink a well in Knoblick, Kentucky, accidentally blew himself up with blasting powder. When found, Shaw was covered with dirt, had lost several fingers, and suffered fractures of the leg, arm and skull. Through the latter, brain matter oozed. After removing some skull fragments from the wound,

the attending physician proceeded to bleed his patient 16 times in the next ten hours. Shaw, if not his doctor, seems to have been a hero, for he survived.

There were, of course, competent and compassionate individual physicians, among them Daniel Drake, despite his odd notions about spontaneous combustion. But there were so many quacks that, cynics suggested, one of the best reasons for migrating to the trans-Mississippi country was to escape the clutches of the medical profession. When you added to that the growing suspicion that some of the worst scourges might be connected with heavily settled places and the style of life in them, seeking a cure by migrating to the unsettled West made good sense.

Malaria may have had more direct influence on the westering movement than any other single disease. Although quinine was available by the 1820s, treatment for malaria was not really effective until much later. In the 1840s a professional colleague practicing in Louisiana wrote Drake that during an outbreak of ague in that city he had drawn "blood enough to float, and given calomel enough to freight, the steamboat *General Jackson*." Since it was common knowledge that malaria (mal-aria from "bad air") was prevalent in wet, fetid, low-lying areas, an obvious thing to do was to get out and find higher, drier ground and sweeter air. People who fled the swampy bottomlands to escape the ague (as well as all that bloody medical attention) almost invariably moved West toward new and perhaps healthier land.

Real estate speculators and promoters in underpopulated territories were quick to lure settlers by touting the healthfulness of their regions. In the late 1830s boosters in then "frontier" Wisconsin claimed physicians had found their territory "distressingly healthy." Before malaria spread there, along with a heavy influx of settlers, Missouri was extolled as a place where undertakers had to shoot and kill to get customers. Antoine Robidoux, a Rocky Mountain trapper and trader in the 1820s and '30s, became interested in guiding emigrant parties to California. Trying to drum up more trade he blithely told prospective pioneers that "there was but one man in California that had ever had a chill there, and it was a matter of so much wonderment to the people of Monterey that they went eighteen miles into the country to see him shake."

Whether they liked it or not, early travelers in the West were treated with buffalo meat—a specific as highly thought of as mung-bean sprouts are today. Frontiersmen ate buffalo regularly, up to 15 pounds per sitting. It was said among them that if a man "could eat buffalo all his days he need never go under," i.e., die. The custom was to consume peculiar parts of the buffalo, including the hot blood, raw liver and whole intestines, all good sources for vitamin C. These eating habits may help to explain why, though the early mountain men and plainsmen were almost exclusively carnivores, they seldom suffered from scurvy.

Rufus Sage, a young Connecticut man, went West in 1841. He was sickly and yearned to write a book. A few years later he turned out *Rocky Mountain Life: or, Startling Scenes and Perilous Adventures in The Far West*. Sage spent several years living as a genuine mountain man and enthusiastically described the taste and tonic effects of buffalo: "The agreeable odor exhaled from the drippings of the frying flesh, contained in the pan, invited the taste. . . . Catching up the vessel, a testing sip made way for the whole of its contents, at a single draught—full six gills! Strange as it may seem, I did not experience the least unpleasant feeling as the result of my extraordinary potation."

The stomach, he continued, "never rebels against buffalo-fat. . . . And then, in point of *health*, there is nothing equal to buffalo-meat. It, alone, will cure dyspepsy, prevent consumption, amend a broken constitution, put flesh upon the bones of a *skeleton*, and restore a dead man again *to life*!—if you will give credence to one half of the manifold virtues he [the voyageur] carefully names in your hearing."

Whether or not it was because of their "buffler" buffets, the mountain men were among the most durable and romantic figures in the pantheon of native heroes. In their own time they were great celebrities, admired for their physical prowess, who served as living advertisements for the virtues of Western life. George Catlin, perhaps the most talented and widely traveled of early frontier painters, noted that in the 1830s he had met hundreds of mountain men who "lived exactly upon the Indians' system, continually exposed to the open air." He added that never in his life had he seen "a more hardy and healthy race."

Maybe the healthiest of all mountain men was Joe Walker. Coming out of Tennessee to Missouri in 1819 as a teen-age veteran of the Appalachian Indian wars, he roamed the West for 50 years as trapper and surveyor. Walker was the first to lead an overland party to California through the Sierras. He brought the first wagon train to the state and led the first settlers into central Arizona through the Apache territories. In the 1840s when the covered wagons began to roll in earnest, Walker was so celebrated that meeting him was considered an event worth noting in diaries and letters back home. When Walker was in his fifties, Richard May of Missouri reported: "Mr. Walker steps with the elasticity of a youth but this much may be said of any one that has lived in these mountains a few years."

In LeRoy Hafen's monumental study, *The Mountain Men*, Richard J. Fehrman contributed an essay dealing with the vital statistics of 292 mountain men who constituted more or less the crème de la crème of this class. Their average life span, he found, was 64 years, 22 years more than the national average in their own day and only a few years short of the current life expectancy for American males. Of course, comparing mountain men with the hordes of emigrants who followed them West is a bit misleading. The emigrants were householders, including some children and old people, many of them ailing in the first place, while the mountain men knew the land, lived alone or in small bands, and were rarely exposed to contagious diseases. They were also sheltered involuntarily from one of the most common afflictions of other men—drunkenness. Except for one hell-roaring drunk a year, when they came in to sell their furs, they lived in places where booze was extremely scarce, and what they drank they had to pack in with them.

Thousands of westbound travelers, seeking health or wealth or a new life, were willing to suffer on the road. Indeed, it took a brave family to make the attempt. But even as regards those hardships, especially the Indian slaughters that figure so heavily in books and films, the way West appears to have been a good deal healthier—and a good deal less lethal—than we presently suppose.

In his definitive study of the overland migration, *The Plains Across* (SMITHSONIAN, June 1979), John Unruh concluded that during the 1840-60 period, when most of the wagons rolled, an estimated 10,000 migrants out of some 300,000 died from all causes. Admittedly, the pioneer companies were largely made up of adults who were usually on the trains for only three or four months. Nevertheless, their mortality rate while actually making the crossing was far lower than the national average at that time.

Medically speaking, it was the Indians who suffered most from the arrival of those pre-Civil War wagon trains full of Eastern health seekers. Indian doctoring was based on herbal cures whose effectiveness modern science is only now beginning to understand and credit. But Indian medicine men could do little for a people with almost no immunity to European diseases. Not merely smallpox and cholera, to which white men had by then developed some immunity, as well as some medical skill in handling, but simpler ills like measles and the common cold often helped lay the Indians low. It was not surprising that by 1850, as Unruh wrote, "A Fort Laramie observer reported that frightened natives were deserting the [wagon] trails in hopes of avoiding the deadly peril."

In that connection, Unruh also made another statistical discovery that tends to astonish those who share the common vision of Western wagon roads littered with burning prairie schooners and white bodies stuck full of arrows. After sifting through the tall tales, he estimated that from 1840 to 1860 the deaths of only 362 of the 300,000 overland emigrants could be attributed to Indians. At that rate, murder and mayhem were surely less common along the Western trails than in the Eastern settlements—then or now.

The Civil War and Reconstruction

In many ways the Civil War was the central event in United States history. Nearly as many men died in that conflict as in all the other American wars combined. Great issues were involved—among them the nature of the Union and the fate of slavery. Brother literally fought against brother, and blacks fought with and against whites. That the war still lives in the American consciousness can be seen in the enormous interest aroused by a popular multipart television documentary on the Civil War in late 1990.

Sectional differences had been obvious at the Constitutional Convention, and they continued to plague the new government. None proved more troublesome than the issue of slavery. Attempts were made in 1820 and 1850 to strike a compromise, but these arrangements merely delayed a final accounting. As the 1850s wore on, both national parties came apart despite efforts to keep the matter offstage. Southerners began talking openly of secession if the newly created Republican party gained the presidency. Following the election of 1860, both the lame-duck president, James Buchanan, and Abraham Lincoln tried to avoid bloodshed when Southern states began leaving the Union. At last, convinced that preservation of the Union overrode all other considerations, Lincoln took steps that gave the South no choice but to give in or fight. The war began.

"Dred Scott in History" shows how a Supreme Court ruling on the constitutionality of slavery poured fuel on the sectional fires already burning in the late 1850s. Abraham Lincoln's nomination on the Republican ticket, analyzed in "How We Got Lincoln," made what followed almost inevitable. The Democratic party had split apart at its convention, virtually assuring a Republican victory that so many Southerners had warned would lead to secession.

"There in the Heat of July, Was the Shimmering Capitol" recounts the events in 1864 when the South was all but beaten, yet Jubal Early's ragged army had Washington, D.C., within its grasp. Brian Holden Reid and Bruce Collins address the problem of the Confederacy morale and the use of guerrilla warfare in "Why the Confederacy Lost." The essay "A Union Officer at Gettysburg" provides an eyewitness account of the Battle of Gettysburg, including Pickett's famous charge.

The status of blacks, over which the war ultimately came to be fought, is treated in the final three articles. "The Hard Fight Was Getting Into the Fight at All" describes the obstacles and humiliations blacks had to overcome in order to fight on the Union side, and the proud record they compiled thereafter. "What Did Freedom Mean?" provides personal recollections by former slaves and masters on conditions after emancipation. "The New View of Reconstruction" considers the efforts in the postwar period to achieve full equality for black people. These efforts failed, the author argues, but provided an "animating vision" for the future.

Looking Ahead: Challenge Questions

Analyze the importance of the Dred Scott decision in preventing accommodation over the slavery question.

Why was William Henry Seward's statement about an "irrepressible conflict" so damaging to his candidacy in 1860?

Discuss those issues over which the Civil War was fought. Was there any merit for the Southerners' claim that they were fighting for "liberty" just as their revolutionary forefathers had done?

Racism was not the exclusive property of the South. Discuss Northern resistance to blacks fighting in the Union army, and the gradual abandonment of blacks during Reconstruction.

DRED SCOTT
IN · HISTORY

Walter Ehrlich

Dr. Walter Ehrlich is Associate Professor of History and Education at the University of Missouri–St. Louis.

Dred Scott v. *John F. A. Sanford* stands as one of the most memorable and important cases in the history of the United States Supreme Court. Except for the celebrated *Marbury* v. *Madison,* which in 1803 established the Supreme Court's power to invalidate federal laws, perhaps more has been written about *Dred Scott* than about any other action of the American judiciary, either state or federal. Most of that literature deals with the controversial final decision, rendered on March 6, 1857, by Chief Justice Roger Brooke Taney. To comprehend the full significance and impact of that decision, it is imperative to understand clearly what the issues were; and to understand the issues necessitates an almost step-by-step unfolding of the litigation itself. It did indeed have a singular history.[1]

Dred Scott, *by Louis Schultze, 1881. Courtesy of the Missouri Historical Society, St. Louis.*

---

[1] *For the best account of the case's chronology, especially in the Missouri courts, see Walter Ehrlich,* **They Have No Rights: Dred Scott's Struggle for Freedom** *(Greenwood Press, 1979). For further information, see Don E. Fehrenbacher's* **The Dred Scott Case: Its Significance in American Law and Politics** *(Oxford University Press, 1978) and David Potter's* **The Impending Crisis, 1848-1861** *(Harper and Row, 1976).*

Born in Southampton County, Virginia, in the late 1790's or early 1800's, the property of Peter Blow, Dred Scott came with his master to Missouri, via Huntsville and Florence, Alabama, settling finally in St. Louis in 1830. Very little is known about the slave's early life. He was "raised" with the Blow children and apparently was close to them, performing menial labor one might associate with household slaves. Yet when Peter Blow found himself strapped financially, he sold Scott to Dr. John Emerson, a physician then

From *Westward,* Vol. 1, No. 1, Winter 1983, pp. 5-10. Published by The Jefferson National Expansion Memorial Historical Association. Reprinted by permission of the author.

residing in St. Louis. This was sometime before December 1, 1833, when Emerson embarked on a military career that took him, among other places, to Illinois and Wisconsin Territory (now Minnesota). Scott was with his master in both places until 1842, even though slavery was prohibited in Illinois by that state's constitution and in the northern Louisiana Purchase territory by the Missouri Compromise of 1820. Scott, however, made no effort to secure his freedom.

While Scott was in this service to Dr. Emerson, two weddings occurred which affected the slave's life. The first was Scott's, in 1836 or 1837, to Harriet Robinson, whose master, Major Lawrence Taliaferro, transferred her ownership to Emerson. This marriage was unique in American slave history, for it was a legal civil ceremony performed by a justice of the peace. Dred and Harriet Scott had two daughters; Eliza was born in October, 1838, aboard the steamboat "Gipsey" while it was on the Mississippi River in "free," "northern" waters, and Lizzie was born about 1845 at Jefferson Barracks in Missouri. (Eliza never married. Lizzie married Wilson Madison of St. Louis, and through them exist the present descendants of Dred Scott.) The other wedding was Emerson's, on February 6, 1838, to Eliza Irene Sanford, whose brother later played a major role in Dred Scott's legal struggles for freedom.

In 1842 Dr. Emerson was posted to Florida where American military forces fought against the Seminole Indians. He left his wife and the slaves in St. Louis with Mrs. Emerson's father. The doctor returned from the wars in 1843, but died shortly thereafter at the age of forty, leaving a young widow with an infant daughter and the Dred Scott family.

The whereabouts of the slaves during these St. Louis years is unclear, except that they were hired out to various people, a frequent experience for city-dwelling slaves. Then on April 6, 1846, Dred and Harriet Scott sued their mistress Irene Emerson for freedom, initiating litigation in the local Missouri state circuit court that would take eleven years before culminating in the celebrated decision of the Supreme Court of the United States on March 6, 1857.

But what brought on that suit for freedom in 1846, when Scott had been "eligible" in free territory since 1833? The evidence is not exactly clear, but some facts are obvious. From 1833 to 1846 Scott was unaware of the law. (It should be noted that he was illiterate and had to mark an "X" for his signature, not uncommon for slaves.) Only after he returned to St. Louis was he apprised of the possibility of being free. But why, and by whom? Again all the details are not known, but it is now undeniable why the case was *not* brought. It was *not* instituted for political or financial reasons as many later imputed. The evidence is indisputable that Dred Scott filed suit for one reason and one reason only, to secure freedom for himself and his family, and nothing else.

But who told him now what he had been unaware of for thirteen years? Again the evidence could be stronger, but it points persuasively to several people. One was a white abolitionist lawyer, Francis Butter Murdoch, recently moved to St. Louis from Alton, Illinois, where as city attorney he had prosecuted criminal offenders on both sides in the infamous and bloody Elijah P. Lovejoy riots and murders. Another was Reverend John R. Anderson, himself a former slave and the black pastor of the Second African Baptist Church of St. Louis, in which Harriet Scott was a devout member. Like Murdoch, Anderson was an emigre from racial-torn Alton.

The exact sequence of events remains somewhat fuzzy; but it was Murdoch, on April 6, 1846, who posted the necessary bonds and filed the required legal papers which initiated the suit. Then, within a few months and before any further legal action occurred, Murdoch left for the west coast, where he lived the rest of his days in California. Having thus initiated the suit, he dropped out completely.

Now another group of Dred Scott's benefactors emerged: the sons and sons-in-law of Peter Blow, those "boys" with whom the slave had been "raised." Murdoch's departure left their ex-slave and childhood companion in limbo. Now the former owners stepped in, posted bonds, secured attorneys, and took over the process of seeking his

freedom. They were to carry it through to the very end.

They anticipated no difficulty. According to the facts of the case and the legal precedents in Missouri, there is no question that Dred Scott was entitled to freedom; indeed, that it was such a patently open-and-shut case may even explain why the Blow family so readily came to their former slave's rescue. At any rate, two totally unexpected developments now changed the situation.

The first was the decision on June 30, 1847, in the trial court, denying Scott his freedom and ordering a new trial—not because of the law or the facts, but because of a legal technicality invalidating certain evidence introduced by Scott's attorney. The slave's freedom, which otherwise unquestionably would have been granted in 1847, now had to await a new trial. The second unexpected development was that it took three long years, until 1850, before that second trial finally occurred, a delay caused by events over which none of the litigants had any control. With that legal technicality of 1847 corrected, the court now, on January 12, 1850, unhesitatingly granted the slave his freedom. That should have ended the case.

But during that three-year delay more unexpected developments came into play. The first was Mrs. Emerson's departure from St. Louis and marriage to Dr. Calvin Clifford Chaffee, a Massachusetts abolitionist completely unaware of the litigation involving his new wife. When she left St. Louis, her local affairs were supervised for her by her businessman-brother, John F. A. Sanford. Among those affairs was the pending slave case.

A second development was monetary. Because Scott's eventual status was still undecided, the court had assigned the local sheriff as custodian of all wages the Scott family might earn, which would then accordingly be turned over to either a free Dred Scott or to his owner. The accrued wages, though by no means an inordinate amount, nevertheless made ownership of the slaves in 1850 much more worthwhile than it had been in 1846 or 1847. The result was, therefore, that Mrs. Emerson (actually her attorney hired for her by her brother Sanford) immediately appealed to the Missouri Supreme Court to reverse the freedom decision of the lower court.

This set the stage for the most consequential development yet, the injection of slavery as a political issue. Up to this point the legality or morality of slavery had never entered into the case to any degree. But by the early 1850's, stimulated by national discord over the seemingly uncompromisable slavery issues, and exacerbated by local Missouri factionalism centering on Senator Thomas Hart Benton, some judges of the Missouri Supreme Court took it upon themselves to reinterpret and reverse Missouri's longstanding legal principle of "once free always free," that a slave once emancipated in free territory would remain free even after returning voluntarily to the slave state of Missouri. By sheer coincidence, the case just appealed to the Missouri high court contained the necessary circumstances for such a ruling. This singularly irregular political partisanship on the part of the judges was abetted by an equally dissolute legal brief introduced at the last moment by Mrs. Emerson's attorney, Lyman D. Norris, a document characterized more by its vituperative pro-slavery tirades than by its legal reasoning.

The result was that on March 22, 1852, the Missouri Supreme Court reversed the lower court's decision and remanded Dred Scott to slavery. What the court now said in effect was, even though the law of a free state and a free United States territory may have emancipated a slave, the slave state of Missouri no longer would accept that status within its own borders. In other words, "once free always free" became "maybe once free, but now back to slavery." It was a radical change in Missouri law, overturning precedent and clearly endorsing the extreme pro-slavery point of view. What had been a simple and genuine emancipation case seeking only freedom for a slave under longstanding law and principle had been transformed into a matter focusing on the most divisive issue the nation had ever experienced.

This was precisely why the case appealed to the Supreme Court of the United States: to clarify "once free always free" and to determine to what degree, if at all, a state could reverse freedom once granted through the implementation of the Northwest Ordinance of 1787, prohibiting slavery in the Northwest Territory, and the Missouri Compromise of 1820. Note that this did not question the validity of granting freedom in a free state or territory; the power to prohibit slavery or to manumit slaves taken into free territory was universally recognized. In question was whether that freedom *once granted* could be lost by returning to a slave state. It was a highly controversial and delicate political and moral issue which the United States Supreme Court had deliberately side-stepped even when the opportunity to decide had been present. The Court had shown that judicial restraint as recently as 1850, in *Strader* v. *Graham*. Instead of deciding on the merits in that particular case, the Court took a procedural approach: it fell back on a long-standing and safe (albeit unpopular to some) principle that the Court simply would abide by the decision of a state's supreme court as the definitive arbiter of that state's law, in this instance Kentucky.

Some time before the Missouri high court rendered its drastic decision, Dred Scott's situation came to the attention of Roswell M. Field, one of St. Louis' leading lawyers. A native of Vermont and an abolitionist, Field for some time had articulated the need for clarification of "once free always free." He realized *Dred Scott* v. *Irene Emerson* could be the vehicle through which to appeal to the Supreme Court for that clarification. But he also was aware of the *Strader* case. *Strader* v. *Graham* had gone to the Supreme Court of the United States on

---

*S*ince it was rendered, the Dred Scott case has been one of the most discussed and written about court cases in American history. This booklet, containing the Supreme Court decision in the Dred Scott case, was published in 1857. It is preserved in the Jefferson National Expansion Memorial archives, located in St. Louis' Old Courthouse.

---

direct appeal from the high court of Kentucky. If Dred Scott's case were appealed the same way, directly, the Court could easily evade the controversial and delicate merits by using *Strader* as a precedent and then simply fall back on the Missouri decision, foredooming Scott to slavery. The only way Scott might attain his freedom was to get the Supreme Court to examine the case's merits; and the only way to do that was to institute a case in a lower *federal* court and appeal from it to Washington. In that way *Strader* might not be a precedent and it could open the door for an examination of the substantive issues.

Thus was born *Dred Scott* v. *John F. A. Sanford* in the federal Circuit Court of the United States, docketed in St. Louis in 1853 and tried on May 15, 1854.[2] Sanford was named defendant for two reasons. The first was to make the case eligible for the federal court system. A long-time resident of St. Louis, Sanford had moved to New York, though he still maintained business and social ties in St. Louis. Scott as a citizen

[2]*Contrary to widespread St. Louis tradition that all the local Dred Scott trials occurred in the historic Old Courthouse, this trial was conducted elsewhere, in an inauspicious upstairs room in what was then the Papin Building on First Street between Chestnut and Pine Streets. Normally the federal courts sat free of charge in the Old Courthouse. But since that structure was state-owned, state courts had priority on use of the courtrooms, and if there was no room available then the United States marshall simply had to make other arrangements. This was the situation in May, 1854, and so the private room in the Papin Building was rented.*

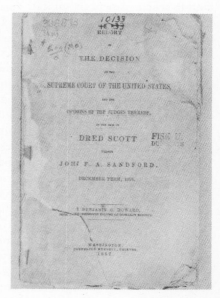

A lthough her name does not enjoy the widespread recognition of her husband's, Harriet Scott's (above) freedom was tied to the fate of her husband's court cases. The Scott's two daughters (right) Eliza, left, and Lizzie, were also affected by the litigation involving their parents.

of Missouri suing Sanford as a citizen of New York created a federal case on the grounds of diversity of citizenship. The second reason for naming Sanford as defendant was as executor of his brother-in-law's estate and thus the virtual, if not real, owner who was "holding" Scott in slavery.

As an interesting and fascinating side issue, the presumption of Sanford as executor was in fact not true. Sanford had been named in Dr. Emerson's will as executor, but by a unique set of circumstances he never legally qualified. For some curious and unknown reasons, though, neither he nor, apparently, his attorneys realized this, and he accordingly managed the estate as though he was indeed the executor. When Dred Scott sued Sanford, therefore, the latter could not and did not deny that he was at least "holding" Scott as a slave, and so whether he was the executor or the actual owner made no difference. What counted legally was that he was "holding" Scott as a slave.

And so *Dred Scott v. John F. A. Sanford* was instituted to clarify "once free always free." But again a new issue unexpectedly appeared. Sanford's attorney Hugh A. Garland (his partner Lyman D. Norris had died) now claimed

that Scott was not a citizen of Missouri and therefore could not sue in a federal court. The reason, argued Garland, a native of Virginia with pro-slavery proclivities, was that Scott was "a negro of African descent." Now injected into the case was the right of a black man to be a citizen of the United States. As if "once free always free" was not delicate enough!

More was to come. It was a foregone conclusion that the lower federal court decision would be appealed to the Supreme Court, as of course it was. Moving to the highest court in the land brought more changes. One was that both sides acquired outstanding and nationally-reputed attorneys and spokesmen for their political and legal points of view. Another was that the case was now publicized throughout the country as one involving important and highly controversial issues.

Yet another change transformed this case from the obscure freedom suit it had been in 1846 to the *cause celebre* which it now became. It will be recalled that *Scott* v. *Sanford* came into the federal courts to seek clarification of "once free always free," and that the original right and power to emancipate a slave in a free state or territory was universally ac-

cepted. Now that too was changed, when Sanford's attorneys, Senators Henry S. Geyer of Missouri and Reverdy Johnson of Maryland, introduced the extreme pro-slave doctrine that slaves were private property protected by the Constitution and therefore Congress did not have the power to abolish or forbid slavery in the first place. In other words, the Missouri Compromise, and presumably any similar slavery prohibition, was unconstitutional. Applied specifically to this case, the issue was no longer whether Missouri could remand Dred Scott to slavery; the issue was whether he had ever been free in the first place.

This, then, was the case and these the issues thrust before the Supreme Court of the United States. At any other time these matters would have been difficult enough to deal with, for they could not be divorced from their political and sociological implications. In the tense and discordant national atmosphere of the 1850's, those political and sociological implications made an acceptable solution virtually impossible. In addition, the pressures on the Court were appalling. It was precisely because the issues were so delicate that many looked to the Supreme Court as the only institution which could solve them, indicative of the esteem in which the Court was held.

Nevertheless, it appeared that judicial restraint would prevail, as the Court found a way to skirt the divisive substantive questions. Even though *Dred Scott* had come up from a lower federal rather than a state supreme court, *Strader* v. *Graham* still would be used as a precedent, and how the state (Missouri) supreme court had ruled on its own state law would be acceptable to the United States Supreme Court. This was a safe and long-accepted principle, and most important it would avoid dealing with the volatile substantive slavery questions. Justice Samuel Nelson of New York was assigned the task, and he began to write what apparently would be a very bland Court's Opinion.

Then all the unbridled forces of the time came to a head. The exact sequence of events is not absolutely clear, but the key event was the proposal by Justice James M. Wayne of Georgia that the decision be changed to include the two controversial issues Nelson was deliberately omitting, the citizenship of blacks and the constitutionality of the Missouri Compromise. Though Wayne made the specific proposal, responsibility for precipitating the drastic step falls on at least four of his colleagues, Chief Justice Taney and Associate Justices John McLean, Benjamin R. Curtis and Peter V. Daniel. At any rate, a bare majority, all from slave states, concurred with Wayne. Chief Justice Taney would write the new Court Opinion. As delivered on March 6, 1857, it is the famous—or infamous—"Dred Scott Decision."

Dred Scott was declared to be still a slave, for several reasons. (1) Although blacks could be citizens of a given state, they could not be and were not citizens of the United States with the concomitant right to sue in the federal courts. Dred Scott's suit therefore was dismissed because the Court lacked jurisdiction. (2) Aside from not having the right to sue in the first place, Scott was still a slave because he never had been free to begin with. Slaves were property protected by the Constitution, and Congress exceeded its authority when it passed legislation forbidding or abolishing slavery in the territories. The Missouri Compromise was such an exercise of unconstitutional authority and was accordingly declared invalid. (3) Whatever the status of an erstwhile slave may have been while he was in a free state or territory, if he voluntarily returned to a slave state, his status there depended upon the law of that slave state as interpreted by its own courts. In Scott's case, since the Missouri high court had declared him to be still a slave, that was the status and law which the Supreme Court of the United States would accept and recognize. "Once free always free" went by the wayside.

In the tense sectional-ridden atmosphere of the time, it is no wonder that the decision triggered a violent reaction. The Court had sought to solve the volatile slavery issue; instead, what it did has been recorded as the most ill-advised and unfortunate moment in its history. It unleashed irreconcilable passions, both North and South, that merged with those already building toward civil war. The press, the pulpit, the political stump and the halls of Congress now reverberated with scathing condemnations as well as vigorous defenses of the Court's action.

*D*red Scott's *final resting place is in St. Louis' Calvary Cemetery. The descendents of Scott's last owner, Taylor Blow, paid to have this monument erected in 1957.*

The intrusion of the Court into the slavery issue created an unprecedented political dilemma. *Dred Scott* appeared to give constitutional sanction to slavery. If so, that compromised the new anti-slave Republican party, whose very *raison d'etre* now seemed undermined. Existence as a national political party demanded respect for the law; but that existence also demanded the overturn of *Dred Scott* law. The political realities of the time offered little likelihood of either. Undoing *Dred Scott,* therefore, involved a hard new look at existing American institutions. To many in both North and South, any compromise over slavery now was impossible. The attack on slavery consequently was bound to involve action and measures more radical and drastic than anything the American democratic process had ever before experienced, and in like manner, the defense of slavery was destined to become equally inflexible. Once the Court had spoken, the two sections, irrevocably moved down a road that could lead only to disaster. *Dred Scott* might well have been the point of no return.

Anti-slavery forces now rose in righteous anger, determined to prevent the next fearful step, the legalizing of slavery everywhere. For that was the frightful specter which *Dred Scott* foreshadowed. If slaves were property protected in the territories, which was the consequence of the Missouri Compromise being declared unconstitutional, then they were also property which could be protected in the states. One more decision like *Dred Scott* and slavery would be a national institution. "Slavery national" rather than "freedom national" loomed on the horizon.

Forces intent on ridding the nation of slavery now mounted an unprecedented assault. Ironically, *Dred Scott* and Chief Justice Taney showed the way. Pro-slave states' rights Jeffersonian agrarians, for all their political philosophy, had utilized *national* institutional machinery to strengthen slavery. If that machinery was strong enough to *legalize* slavery throughout the nation (as some feared it now would), was it not also strong enough to *destroy* slavery throughout the nation? If Republicans could just hold the line on slavery and prevent any further expansion, all they had to do was gain control of the national machinery *without weakening it institutionally.* They could then use it to reverse whatever gains agrarianism and slavery had made. (After all, slavery was not the only concern of the new Republican party.) Gaining control of the executive and legislative branches had to come first; "proper" appointments to the federal judiciary would eventually follow.

In the meantime, the Court had to be prevented from legalizing slavery nationally, not by subverting its institutional decision-making power, but by diminishing its influence and prestige *temporarily.* This was done by a vicious assault upon the *Dred Scott* decision. The charge of *obiter dictum* rang throughout the country, meaning once the Court had decided Dred Scott could not sue for lack of jurisdiction, then any incidental opinion on issues having no bearing upon the case was uncalled for. Legal scholars today overwhelmingly agree that Taney's rulings were not *obiter dicta,* but many contemporaries were convinced otherwise.

Taney and his concurring colleagues were derided and ridiculed to such a degree, not only for their legal abilities but also for personal matters, that confidence gradually eroded in their ability to render unbiased judgments. At the same time, Republicans and abolitionists heightened the fear of a "slave-power conspiracy" that purportedly included even members of the Supreme Court. This vicious attack on the Court was the spearhead of an unprecedented furious campaign to gain control over the national government, and then to run it under a centralized-power philosophy. It succeeded; in 1860, Abraham Lincoln

was elected President of the United States.

The *Dred Scott* decision played a most significant role in those troubled days in still another way. As noted, individual judges were singled out for abuse and vilification because of their legal opinions. Inevitably, the assault on these individuals affected the institution itself, degrading it as a partisan body no longer capable of rendering justice without bias. Prior to *Dred Scott* there was a willingness—even an eagerness—to look to the Court to solve difficult constitutional problems, including slavery; after *Dred Scott,* confidence in the Court on such issues evaporated. Perhaps never before in the history of the United States was there so much need for the stabilizing influence, the sobriety, and the sound guidance that a respected Court might have provided. But it was no longer there. True, it would return later, but too late. Instead, bloodshed and violence prevailed.

The Dred Scott case, then, was of momentous consequence. Originating as an obscure open-and-shut freedom litigation, it literally was dragged by circumstances into prominence and notoriety. Little could that slave anticipate, when his benevolent friends went into St. Louis' Old Courthouse to seek his freedom, that they were unleashing one of the most exciting and traumatic episodes in American constitutional history.

POSTSCRIPT: With the Taney pronouncement caught up in the dramatic events that exploded into bloody civil war, historians have largely overlooked what happened to Dred Scott the person. According to the Court, of course, he remained a slave. But whose? A careful examination of the record

revealed that he still belonged to Mrs. Emerson, now Mrs. Chaffee, whose husband was a prominent Massachusetts abolitionist. Incredulously, though, Chaffee did not learn of his wife's association with the now-famous slave until only a few weeks before the Court rendered its final decision. His embarrassment was compounded because Massachusetts law considered his wife's property as his. The law also prevented him from freeing the slave until the pending legal action had been concluded. Once the Court announced its decision, however, Chaffee issued a quitclaim transferring ownership to Taylor Blow in St. Louis. (Dred Scott and his family had remained in St. Louis throughout the entire litigation.) Then, on May 26, 1857, in accordance with Missouri law, Taylor Blow formally freed Dred Scott, his wife Harriet, and their two daughters. That action occurred in the same courtroom in St. Louis where the case had started eleven years earlier in 1846. And so, despite the Supreme Court decision, Dred Scott and his family now were free.

Dred Scott worked as a porter in a St. Louis hotel for more than a year. But his popularity and new-found fame were short-lived. On September 17, 1858, he died of tuberculosis (some called it consumption). He was buried in the Wesleyan Cemetery just outside the St. Louis city limits. In 1867, as the city expanded westward, the cemetary was abandoned. Through the efforts again of Taylor Blow, Dred Scott's remains were reinterred in Calvary Cemetery in what is now northern St. Louis. For a long time the grave remained unmarked. In 1957, through the generosity of Taylor Blow's granddaughter, a stone marker was installed. It stands there today as a historical monument, a reminder of one of the most famous episodes in America's legal and constitutional history.

HOW WE GOT LINCOLN

Every presidential election is exciting when it happens. Then the passing of time usually makes the outcome seem less than crucial. But after more than a century and a quarter, the election of 1860 retains its terrible urgency.

Peter Andrews

Peter Andrews is an American Heritage contributing editor. His account of the epic defense of Wake ran in the July/August 1987 issue of American Heritage.

In the crowded months between the beginning of the 1860 presidential campaign and the attack on Fort Sumter, it is easy now to see the emergence of Abraham Lincoln as something preordained, as though the issues had manufactured a figure commensurate with their importance. Or at the least, one might imagine a dramatic, hard-fought campaign with Northern and Southern states rallying around their respective candidates. But that's not quite how it happened.

There is drama enough in the 1860 campaign, but most of it does not spring from the election itself. The moment Lincoln was nominated, the issue was settled: He would become the President; he would be faced with the dissolution of the federal Union. The crucial steps on Lincoln's road to the White House came earlier, during the most important party convention in our history — a convention that seemed, at the time, certain to nominate William Henry Seward as Republican party candidate for President of the United States.

The senator from New York cut an odd, slight figure. Spare and angular, Seward looked, one newspaper said, like "a jay bird with a sparrow hawk's bill." His unprepossessing appearance aside, Seward seemed like a man very much in control of his political life as he marched down the Republican side of the Senate chamber on May 7, 1860. Taking his seat, Seward produced a large quantity of snuff and a yellow handkerchief that he waved expansively as he amused his fellow Republicans with a joke or two. There were few things in life Seward enjoyed more than being the focus of attention. The senators who watched him perform understood that they were looking at the next President of the United States. And no one in the chamber was more certain of this than Seward himself.

Four days earlier the Democratic party convention in Charleston had done an extraordinary thing. Deliberately, the delegates had thrown away the forthcoming presidential election. They had met to confirm Sen. Stephen A. Douglas of Illinois, the only Democrat who could have reached out beyond the slaveholding South and gathered up enough electoral votes from the border states to win. But insurrection had been in the air at Charleston. The smooth-talking Democrat from Alabama, William Yancey, who took pride in being known as "the Prince of the Fire-Eaters," had his mind not on success within the political system but on secession from the Union. With Yancey calling the shots, the convention turned away from Douglas and refused to nominate anybody. The party would eventually put up two candidates, Douglas and Vice-President John Breckinridge, while a hastily formed splinter group calling itself the Constitutional Union party nominated John Bell of Tennessee.

Yancey had what he wanted. The fragmented Democrats would most likely lose to a Republican committed to abolition. The South would have no choice but to secede.

So the way was left open for the Republicans. A political organization that had been stitched together five years earlier by grafting snippets of Free-Soilers, Know-Nothings, Abolitionists, and runaway Democrats onto the carcass of the old, moribund Whig party had the Presidency within its grasp for the first time. In 1856, with no reasonable chance of victory, the Republicans had nominated the romantic adventurer John Frémont, and lost. Now it was time for a seasoned man of politics. That man was Seward.

The senator had every right to be confident. He was a traditional politician of the day and had played the political game in the traditional manner. He had spoken out on the questions Republicans wanted addressed. He had led them where they wanted to go. Seward had paid his dues, and now it was time to collect.

He had the credentials. An early organizer of the party, Seward led the antislavery forces in Congress despite his uninspiring public-speaking style. Indeed, he frequently gave the impression of talking to himself. The great orators such as Daniel Webster and John C. Calhoun had ignored his speeches. But Seward had a keen mind and once, in a moment of inspiration, he described the issue between slave and free as an "irrepressible conflict." The phrase went into the political language of the day, and Seward's followers liked to call themselves "the Irrepressibles."

He had the following. No American politician of the time could claim more devoted supporters. To a party based on opposition to slavery, Seward was more than simply a leader. He was, as the contemporary journalist Isaac Bromley put it, "the central figure of the whole movement, its prophet, priest, and oracle." A presidential election without Seward, Bromley concluded, "would be the play without Hamlet."

He had the money. With a war chest full of dollars culled from New York State political organizations, Seward's campaign manager, Thurlow Weed, had been able to collar Republican leaders by promising "oceans of money" to underwrite not only Seward's campaign but theirs as well.

He had the votes. To secure the nomination, Seward would need 233 delegates. He had 170 in his pocket as he sat in the Senate. If there had been a national primary at the time, Seward would certainly have won it. The Republicans held a number of straw votes before the convention showing him an easy winner. One from Michigan gave him 210 votes and all other candidates 30, while another from the Northwest showed him with 127 and 44 for the rest.

Always meticulous in such matters, Seward started working on a draft of the resignation speech he would give to the Senate upon receiving the nomination. But the smooth senator from New York found himself heading into some very rough territory.

In a neat piece of symbolism for the emerging importance of the party's Western reach, the Republican convention was set for Chicago. It was not much of a city. Writing in the mid-1850s, the historian James Parton said that of all American prairie towns, Chicago "was the most repulsive to every human sense." Cattle still crowded the sidewalks, and stables were routinely emptied into Lake Michigan, which provided the city's drinking water. Consumption, cholera, and smallpox were commonplace; Chicago had the highest death rate in the nation. But it was an energetic place. When engineers decided the city streets had to be raised twelve feet to bring them safely above river level, every building in town was jacked up and twelve hundred acres were filled in.

By 1860 Chicago had made itself into a convention city of fifty-seven hotels, eight of them considered deluxe by the town's relaxed standards. And just for the Republicans the city had erected the first building in America specifically constructed to hold a political convention: an immense two-story wooden structure called the Wigwam and billed as "the largest audience room in the United States." Completed only four days before the convention opened, the eighteen-thousand-square-foot Wigwam could accommodate somewhere between six and fifteen thousand people. With more than twenty thousand Republicans coming to town, it was going to be a tight fit.

Chicago was a good town in which to practice a little political bushwhacking, and Seward, although he carried the cachet that goes with being the front-runner, made an appealing target. He was so confident of the righteousness of his causes that he seemed indifferent to the intensity of the resentment he aroused.

Once when Senator Douglas, exasperated during an all-night Senate session, used the word *nigger*, Seward snapped, "Douglas, no man who spells Negro with two *g*s will ever be elected President of the United States." The line played well back home, but it made Seward enemies. Although there was no evidence to support the charge, many suspected Seward, among other Northern Republicans, of complicity in John Brown's raid on Harpers Ferry the year before. One Richmond newspaper carried an advertisement offering fifty thousand dollars for the head of the "traitor" William Seward.

Several highly placed Republicans disliked the senator as well, and all of them were coming to Chicago. If Seward was to be stopped, the Wigwam was the place where it could be done.

The Republicans began streaming into Chicago in crowds that made the railroad depots "beat like great hearts with their living tide," according to one correspondent. They came in such numbers that some 130 of them had to sleep on pool tables in hotel billiard rooms. They were a rough, contentious group who smelled victory and started their celebrating early. The New York Republicans in particular, said one witness, "can drink as much whiskey, swear as loud and long, sing as bad songs, and 'get up and howl' as ferociously as any crowd of Democrats. . . ."

The imperious Thurlow Weed, nicknamed "Lord Thurlow," led the pack. He set up headquarters at the Richmond House with an abundant supply of good cigars and champagne, and a willingness to promise anything required to secure the remaining 60 votes Seward needed. To back him up with muscle and yelling power for marching in parades and shouting in floor demonstrations, Weed had brought in a gang of roughnecks, among them the former American heavyweight champion Tom Hyer (who in fact was considered by many to be the best-mannered man at the convention).

There were other candidates in the contest besides Seward, but Weed discounted them. Salmon Chase of Ohio yearned to be President, but he seemed too proud to campaign actively for it. Judge Edward Bates of St. Louis, backed by powerful forces within the party, had been tainted by his association with the Know-Nothings and their chauvinistic policies against the foreign-born and Roman Catholics, two important voting blocs with long memories. Simon Cameron, the party boss of Pennsylvania, had presi-

dential ambitions, but Cameron was essentially a deal-maker who could be made content as long as he got something for himself out of the convention. The field was filled out with favorite-son candidates such as William Dayton of New Jersey and Abraham Lincoln of Illinois.

Surveying it all, Weed calculated that although Lincoln was a marginal candidate, he would require scrutiny. In an attempt to give some regional balance to the campaign, Weed offered him second place on the ticket. The offer was tempting, but Lincoln and his advisers refused. They were after bigger game.

Fifty-one years old, Abraham Lincoln was a made-over Whig with considerable local experience and some small national distinction. Born in Kentucky, and raised in Indiana and Illinois, he had worked as a land surveyor and won election as a captain of militia during the Black Hawk War before turning to law. He served for eight years in the Illinois legislature as a Clay Whig and generally could be relied upon to vote down the line with his party. Elected to Congress in 1846, he was turned out after one term, largely because of his opposition to the Mexican War, and afterward returned to Springfield to practice law.

Lincoln attained national recognition ten years later when he ran for the Senate against Douglas. His opening speech declared, famously, that "a house divided against itself cannot stand." It became part of the national conscience, but it cost Lincoln the election. Douglas used the phrase to paint Lincoln as an abolitionist, and Leonard Swett, one of Lincoln's closest advisers, later commented that Lincoln had defeated himself in the first sentence of his first speech. During his famous series of debates with Douglas, Lincoln attempted to backpedal. "I am not . . . in favor of making voters or jurors of Negroes," he said in Charleston, Illinois, "nor of qualifying them to hold office. . . ." But the political damage had been done.

Nevertheless, Lincoln made his national mark. He carried the antislavery issue about as far as most Republicans wished it taken and he had emerged as the leading Republican in Illinois.

Lincoln was woven of genuine homespun — he said "jist" for "just" and "sich" for "such" — but he was no political naif. He had toiled hard for the party and done the scut work of driving Frémont's campaign wagons in 1854. He knew the names of hundreds of precinct and county workers and was careful to keep in contact with them. Lincoln was fiercely ambitious for political advancement. His long-time legal associate, Henry C. Whitney, said Lincoln picked his companions for what they could do for him. Noting that Lincoln used to play billiards with a somewhat disreputable Illinois attorney from time to time, Whitney remarked that "it was the only non-utilitarian thing" he ever saw Lincoln do.

Lincoln and Seward never confronted each other. The struggle was fought out by their supporters in Chicago. Lincoln awaited word of the results in Springfield, while the senator remained in his hometown of Auburn, New York. In a letter to Lincoln marked "Profoundly private," Dr. Charles Ray, editor of the Chicago *Tribune*, laid it out simply enough: "You need a few trusty friends here to say words for you that may be necessary to be said. . . . A pledge or two may be necessary when the pinch comes."

The trusty friends behind Lincoln were solid, practical men of good sense and considerable diligence. Judge David Davis, who had known the candidate since they had both been circuit-riding lawyers in Illinois, served as Lincoln's campaign manager. Weighing close to three hundred pounds, Davis gave the appearance of a sleepy mountain, but he was quick-witted and possessed of a nice political judgment. Charles Ray and his fellow editor Joseph Medill were ready to put the *Tribune* at Lincoln's disposal. The state auditor Jesse Dubois was in Lincoln's camp, as were Judge Stephen Logan, who had once been Lincoln's law partner, and Norman Judd, a prominent railroad attorney who had been instrumental in setting up the Douglas debates.

They compared their man with Seward and were not unhappy. On the principal issue, Lincoln's record was as good. And for a national campaign he was considered less radical.

Seward's ringing "irrepressible conflict" had become something of an embarrassment to someone who hoped to win a national election without goading the South into insurrection. Seward admitted to a Washington hostess that if the Lord forgave him this time, he would never again put together two such high-sounding words. Lincoln had said almost as much in his "House Divided" speech, but coming from a minor Illinois politician its implications did not fall as stridently upon the ear as they did from a powerful New York senator.

If Lincoln did not have the public record of Seward, that meant also that he did not have as much to defend. There is nothing like being a political front-runner to find out who really doesn't like you, and the more Judge Davis poked around Seward's record, the more possible roadblocks to Seward's nomination he found. For-

mer Democrats, new to the Republican party, were unhappy with Seward's contention that blacks should have the vote. Then there were the Know-Nothings, whom Seward had consistently mocked. They were particularly powerful in states such as New Jersey, where the Republicans had no real organization of their own. Indiana and Pennsylvania were also strong Know-Nothing country. The big Northern businessmen, usually a source of strength for Seward, were getting shy about his prominence as a lightning rod for Southern hatred ever since Harpers Ferry and were beginning to worry about their commercial trade with the South. And, oddly for such a moral man, Seward had a hint of corruption about him. Weed had not always been scrupulous about how he raised money for Seward, sometimes resorting to little more than shakedowns from Republican officeholders and the promoters of New York City street railways who relied on Weed to guide their franchises through the legislature. Horace Greeley's New York *Tribune* said that when Seward was governor, the New York legislature was "not merely corrupt but shameless."

Greeley's animosity was difficult to understand. By rights, the two New Yorkers should have been political allies, but they had fallen out somewhere along the line over a matter of political patronage, and now Greeley remained implacable in his opposition to Seward's candidacy.

And then there was the image question. In many ways, Seward, a wealthy corporation lawyer, was in the classic old Whig mold of a wellborn moralist telling the people what was good for them whether they wanted to hear it or not. These Whigs had a poor record in winning the White House. The only two Presidents they had been able to elect were dusted-off generals, Harrison and Taylor, who had run on their war records while the Whig leadership made fools of themselves wearing coonskin caps and drinking hard cider, trying to look like men of the people.

But with Lincoln, the Republicans could have a man who really was from humble origins and looked comfortable in the part. Lincoln carefully cultivated his populist appeal. During the Douglas debates, when Douglas and his party arrived in a line of carriages, Lincoln trailed behind in a wagon hauled by oxen. His rail-splitter image was an inspired piece of political flackery conjured up by his supporters. When Lincoln secured the presidential pledge from the state convention on May 9, a group of men dressed as farmers carried in a pair of rails supposedly split by the candidate in 1830. Lincoln went along with the gag — up to a point. "I cannot say whether I made those rails or not, but I am quite sure I have made a great many as good," he said amid applause so great that part of the canvas roof covering the meeting hall collapsed.

Lincoln would do nicely if they could put him over. And that was a question of mathematics. Could Seward be stopped short of 230 delegates and could Lincoln then pick them up before the convention rallied to someone else?

Lincoln had already demonstrated one quality vital to a presidential candidate: he was lucky. Chicago had been chosen as a compromise site before Lincoln was considered a serious candidate. If he had been seen as a contender, the city would have been unacceptable to Seward's people; and if any other place had been chosen, it is unlikely Lincoln's Illinois team could have swung the nomination.

Months before, Lincoln had astutely indicated the basic strategy to be taken. Writing to a delegate from Ohio to thank him for his support, Lincoln said, "If I have any chance, it consists mainly in the fact that the whole opposition would vote for me, if nominated. (I don't mean to include the pro-slavery opposition of the South, of course.) My name is new in the field, and I suppose I am not the first choice of a very great many. Our policy, then, is to give no offense to others — leave them in a mood to come to us if they shall be compelled to give up their first love. . . ."

Davis, having established Lincoln's campaign headquarters in a two-room suite at the Tremont House, had three immediate jobs to do:

First, Seward had to be stopped from winning on the first ballot. Everything depended on that. As far as Davis was concerned, anyone who wouldn't vote for Seward was a Lincoln man. At least for one round.

Second, Lincoln had to be built into something more than a favorite-son candidate. Favorite sons would be blown away by the second ballot. Lincoln needed votes from outside Illinois to demonstrate his depth. Davis had hoped for a solid second-place finish from Lincoln on the first ballot — no easy task, because Chase, Cameron, and Bates were all coming to Chicago with more delegates than Lincoln.

Finally, Davis had to play a waiting game and secure as many second-ballot pledges for Lincoln as possible. Once Seward was stalled, it was imperative that Lincoln forge ahead before the convention could gather around someone else.

Davis dispatched his men to meet the various conventioneers as they arrived. Samuel Parks, who was born in Vermont, went to that delegation and Swett went to see his old friends from Maine. Every delegation Davis could get to was visited by Lincoln's men. They carried with them a pair of powerful messages from Davis.

Although they were careful not to disparage Seward, they drove home the point that he was not as solid as he looked. With only New England firmly in the Republican column, the national election would be won or lost in New Jersey, Indiana, Illinois, and Pennsylvania, where Know-Nothing sentiment remained high. The Republicans had to win three of those four doubtful states or lose it all. And these were precisely the four marginal states where Seward was weakest.

Something Seward had said in 1852 now returned to haunt him. When the Whigs of his state wanted to give the venerable Henry Clay a third chance for the Presidency, Seward had written a New York congressman saying, "it is not a question of who we should prefer but whom can we elect." Now the same hard political judgment was to be used against Seward. Even if he was the best man, his party could not elect him.

The second message was the Davis counter to Weed's "oceans of money." Davis had hardly any money at all. He later calculated the total expense of nominating Lincoln, including everything from band music to railroad tickets for delegates, at less than seven hundred dollars. With no cash, Davis did the next best thing he could think of. In effect he established a futures market in Lincoln's cabinet and sold it off chair by chair.

He had to start by securing his own Illinois delegation. Not all of the 22 delegates were solid for Lincoln. Men from the northern part of the state, about a third of the state delegates, were for Seward. Davis handled that by binding the state to vote as a unit.

Lincoln swiftly won Indiana's 26 delegates. Dr. Ray checked in with Medill at the Tremont House to tell him the news that Indiana was committed to Lincoln down the line. Asked how this was done, Ray replied, "By the Lord, we promised them everything they asked." After the election Indiana's Caleb Smith was appointed Secretary of the Interior and William Dole was given the post of Commissioner of Indian Affairs, where the hours were good and the money excellent.

As Chicago filled up with Republicans, and with the balloting only two days away, Lincoln still trailed Seward by as many as 90 votes, but Davis was happy. Lincoln's cause was moving forward, and he would likely have the solid second-place finish Davis wanted for his man.

The convention took over the city. Seward's men, led by a brass band with bright white and scarlet feathers in their hats, trooped up and down the streets playing the Seward campaign song, "Oh Isn't He a Darling?," as if the election was already over. Inside the hotels the delegates talked politics. As Murat Halstead of the Cincinnati *Commercial* described the scene, "Men gather in little groups, and with their arms about each other, and chatter and whisper as if the fate of the country depended upon their immediate delivery of the mighty political secrets with which their imaginations are big. . . . There are now at least a thousand men packed together in the halls of the Tremont House, crushing each other's ribs, tramping each other's toes, and titillating each other with the gossip of the day; and the probability is, not one is possessed of a single political fact not known to the whole; which is of the slightest consequence to any human being."

It was an insistent crowd that surged up to the Wigwam on Wednesday, May 16, for the opening of the convention. One man, a Mr. Johns, delegate-at-large from Iowa, described as "a plain, homespun western farmer, but sound to the core," had walked 150 miles to get to the railroad that would bring him to Chicago. The doors opened and the flood of delegates, newsmen, and spectators poured in. The press tables had the latest in telegraphic equipment but only sixty seats for nine hundred applicants. The standing-room-only delegate floor for forty-five hundred was filled within five minutes. The galleries, which would accommodate gentlemen only in the company of ladies, caused considerable problems for the all-male convention. Schoolgirls were offered a quarter for their company, and one woman, who was offered a half-dollar, refused because she had already accompanied six gentlemen inside and was afraid the police would object if she came in a seventh time. One enterprising Republican attempted to bring in an Indian woman who was selling moccasins on the street but was rebuffed by the guards, who held that an Indian woman could not be a lady.

The first day of the convention was given over to forming committees and listening to prayers and speeches blessing various Republican endeavors. David Wilmot gave a stem-winder of an anti-slavery speech and there was a small flap over the seating of Horace Greeley. Shut out from the New York delegation by Seward, Greeley had managed to get himself seated as a delegate from Oregon. No one seemed to mind very much. There would always be room for Horace Greeley at a Republican convention, although some wag played a joke on the editor by pinning a Seward campaign badge on the back of his coat. George Ashmun of Massachusetts was named president of the convention and presented with a gavel made of wood from Com. Oliver Hazard Perry's flagship *Lawrence*. Knowing a cue when he saw one, Ashmun told the convention, "I have only to say today that all the auguries are that we shall meet the enemy and they shall be ours."

The most spirited debate was whether or not to accept the Chicago Board of Trade's invitation to take a boat ride on Lake Michigan later in the day. After some discussion it was agreed to go, and the convention adjourned until the next day, when the platform was to be adopted and the candidates voted upon.

Davis did not go on the boat ride. Nor did Weed. Both men worked furiously on the Kansas delegation. First the Kansans went over to see Weed for a smoke and a glass of champagne and a spot of politics. Weed surprised and delighted them by knowing most of their names and pouring the wine with a generous hand. As he told them how Seward was unbeatable, one Kansan said the expansive host reminded him of Byron's Corsair — "The mildest mannered man that ever scuttled a ship or cut a throat."

Arriving back at their hotel, the Kansans were greeted by a beatific Horace Greeley all pink and sleek, "looking like a well-to-do farmer fresh from his clover field." Greeley came quickly to the point: ". . . you couldn't elect Seward if you could nominate him. . . . to name Seward, is to invite defeat. He cannot carry New Jersey, Pennsylvania, Indiana, or Iowa, and I will bring to you representative men from each of these states who will confirm what I say."

If Greeley had been fronting for Lincoln's men, which he was not (he still had hopes for Bates), he would have been hard put to define their position more clearly. Davis manipulated him masterfully. "We let Greeley run his Bates machine," Swett wrote later, "but got most of them for a second choice."

And for harder cases, Davis had stronger methods.

Gideon Welles, with a Santa Claus beard and an ill-fitting wig, came to Chicago heading up a badly split Connecticut delegation. He was not particularly well disposed toward Seward but was undecided about which way to jump until Lincoln's people talked to him about a cabinet position. Welles went to work and was later named Secretary of the Navy.

At some point Davis got to the influential Blair family of Maryland, which had been politically prominent since the days of Andrew Jackson. With the promise of Maryland's votes on the second ballot, Montgomery Blair was ticketed to be Postmaster General.

Thursday the seventeenth was largely given over to adopting the party platform, and had it not been for the excitement in the air of selecting the next President of the United States, a dreary day's work it would have been. The platform promised something for everyone except, perhaps, the slaveholding Southerners. There was a protective tariff to keep Greeley and Pennsylvania happy. There was a homestead law for the farmers and a Pacific railroad for the West. But there was little fire in the document. The 1856 platform had been given over almost entirely to the question of slavery. The 1860 platform included the issue as one of many before the voters, and not necessarily the most important one. The homestead and tariff planks received more cheers than the plank calling for the limiting of slavery.

So timid were the framers on the question of slavery that they turned down a proposed amendment by Joshua Giddings, an old campaigner in the abolitionist struggle, to reaffirm the line from the Declaration of Independence that "all men are created equal." Giddings, feeling "everything lost, even honor," stormed off the floor. His departure, however, was an empty gesture, for he was back a few minutes later when the New York delegation had the phrase inserted into the platform. As Giddings came back to his seat, William Evarts, Seward's floor manager from New York, commented, "Well, at least we saved the Declaration of Independence."

Unaware of the extent of the headway Davis was making off the convention floor, Seward's people were riding high. The delegates called to start the balloting, and if it had proceeded, Seward, still the leading candidate, would probably have been the party's nominee. But fate and Judge Davis intervened. The convention clerks said the tally sheets were prepared but, for some reason, were not at hand. After some desultory debate, the convention agreed to go to supper and reconvene in the morning.

Davis, "nearly dead from fatigue," would have one more night.

There was a great deal to do, and Davis was the sort of man who had a good eye for the detail as well as the big picture. To ensure that Lincoln was well represented on the floor with demonstrators, a large number of counterfeit tickets were printed and several Lincoln men stayed up all night forging signatures on them. And if Seward was going to have some shouters on the floor, so would Lincoln. Davis rounded up a group of strong-lunged men, including one Dr. Ames, reportedly possessed of lungs so hearty he could be heard across Lake Michigan, and even a stray Democrat who apparently had nothing better to do the next day.

Nobody slept very much that night. Seward's band serenaded the streets as politicians crisscrossed the city. Weed reportedly uncorked three hundred bottles of champagne, and Halstead saw Henry Lane of Indiana, "pale and haggard, with cane under his arm, walking as if for a wager," going from one caucus to another trying to bring it home for Lincoln.

Greeley was making the rounds as well. His Bates boom had fizzled and at 11:40 P.M. Greeley telegraphed the New York *Tribune*, saying, "My conclusion, from all that I can gather to-night is, that, the opposition to Gov. Seward cannot concentrate on any candidate, and that he will be nominated."

Davis, however, was far from finished. After Greeley left, he met with members of the New Jersey and Pennsylvania delegations and produced a tabulation showing Lincoln a solid second with many more votes than any other candidate except Seward. Both states said they would caucus and get back to Davis. New Jersey agreed to go along that night, but Pennsylvania would let him know in the morning.

A few hours before the convention was to reconvene on Friday, Judge Joseph Casey from Harrisburg arrived with the deal. Simon Cameron would deliver Pennsylvania on the second ballot if he could be named Secretary of the Treasury. A wire went off to Lincoln saying things looked good if Cameron could be accommodated. Lincoln sent back a startling telegram: "I authorize no bargains and will be bound by none." The wording was simple enough, but what did Lincoln mean by it? He knew Davis was in Chicago making deals for him. That's why Davis was there in the first place. Besides, Lincoln also had said earlier that he wanted that "big Pennsylvania foot" to come down on the scale for him. Surely he did not mean to back off just because the going was getting a little rough. The most likely explanation is that Lincoln expected Davis to continue dealing in his name while he covered himself for the record. The "Rail Splitter" was developing the long view.

As his agents discussed the telegram, Davis cut in sharply, "Lincoln ain't here." The candidate, he went on, "don't know what we have to meet, so we will go ahead, as if we hadn't heard from him, and he must ratify it." Dr. Ray agreed. "We are after a bigger thing than that; we want the Presidency and the Treasury is not a great stake to pay for it."

The extent of just how much Davis actually committed in Lincoln's name has been the subject of debate ever since. When Davis and his team later presented Lincoln with the due bill for political services rendered in Chicago, he responded, "Well, gentlemen, where do I come in? You seem to have given everything away."

The results, however, are certain. Pennsylvania dutifully swung over to Lincoln on the second ballot, and its leader was awarded a seat in Lincoln's cabinet. The sticky-fingered Cameron didn't get the Treasury, however. That went to Salmon Chase of Ohio. Cameron was named Secretary of War and after one inept and corrupt year in office was shipped off to Moscow as the U.S. ambassador to Russia.

On Friday morning the Seward people received their first setback at the door. When Seward's brass band arrived with a thousand supporters, they found they couldn't get in. Their places had been taken by Lincoln men with forged tickets.

The nomination of the candidates was swiftly done with, and it was obvious that only Seward and Lincoln had any clear vocal support. When Seward's name was seconded, his depleted backers gave a good account of themselves. Trying to describe it stretched Halstead to the journalistic limit. He wrote: "The effect was startling. Hundreds of persons stopped their ears in pain. The shouting was absolutely frantic, shrill and wild. No Camanches, no panthers ever struck a higher note, or gave screams with more infernal intensity."

Then it was Lincoln's turn. "Imagine all the hogs ever slaughtered in Cincinnati giving their death squeals together, a score of big steam whistles going," Halstead wrote, "and you conceive something of the same nature. I thought the Seward yell could not be surpassed; but the Lincoln boys were clearly ahead. . . ."

When the shouting finally petered out, it was time to begin the balloting, and things began to unravel quickly for Seward. Maine, voting first, gave Seward 10 and Lincoln 6. Abolitionist New England, which was supposed to be solid for Seward, was starting to crack. New Hampshire cast one wistful vote for Frémont, one for Chase,

one for Seward, and 7 for Lincoln. As Evarts tallied up the New England bloc, it showed 32 for Seward, 19 for Lincoln, and the remaining 30 spread out among the field. A lead, but not the kind to start parades for.

When New York was called, its 70 votes gave Seward a tally of 102 to only 19 for Lincoln. But then the senator ran into trouble. New Jersey held its 14 votes for Dayton and Pennsylvania gave Seward 1½ and Lincoln 4, and kept 47½ for Cameron. Virginia, which Seward had counted on, gave him only 8 and Lincoln 14. Henry Lane's eyes glittered when Indiana threw all 26 for Lincoln. By the end of the first ballot Seward led with 173½, some 60 votes shy of the 233 needed to win; Lincoln held a surprisingly strong 102. It was now the two-man fight Davis had wanted, and the victory would go to the one who gained more on the second ballot.

Again it began badly for Seward. Lincoln picked up 2 more votes from New Hampshire, and Vermont abandoned its favorite son and cast all 10 for Lincoln. "This was a blighting blow upon the Seward interest," Halstead wrote. "The New Yorkers started as if an Orsini bomb had exploded." Welles never did deliver Connecticut entirely to Lincoln, but the state stayed out of the Seward column, giving 4 to Lincoln and spreading its other 8 among Bates, Chase, and Cassius Clay, the old war-horse from Kentucky. But when Pennsylvania weighed in with 48 for Lincoln, the rout was on. The results of the second ballot showed Seward hanging on with 184½ and Lincoln with 181.

The third ballot was carried out "amid excitement that tested the nerves." Lincoln crept forward. Massachusetts took 4 of its Seward votes and gave them to Lincoln. Lincoln picked up a 3-vote lead from New Jersey and 4 more from Pennsylvania. Ohio came in with 29 for Lincoln, a gain of 15. He picked up 4 more when Oregon deserted Bates. Up and down the line it was almost all Lincoln. But would it be enough to put him over on this ballot? As the people in the hall tallied up the results, one newspaperman wrote, "a profound stillness suddenly fell upon the Wigwam; the men ceased to talk and the ladies to flutter their fans; one could distinctly hear the scratching of pencils and the ticking of telegraph instruments on the reporters' tables."

The tally showed Seward sagging to 181 and Lincoln at 231½. Another vote and a half would do it.

It was time for one last squeeze. Sometime during the first ballot Medill had wormed his way into the Ohio delegation and sat next to its floor leader, D. K. Cartter. Medill whispered to Cartter that Salmon Chase had only to come to Lincoln and he "can have anything he wants." When the suspicious Cartter asked how he could be certain, Medill assured him by saying, "I know and you know I wouldn't promise if I didn't know."

Cartter, pockmarked and stammering, stood up on a chair and called for attention. "I-I a-a-rise, Mr. Chairman, to a-a-nounce the ch-change of f-four votes, from Mr. Chase to Abraham Lincoln."

It was done.

There was a moment's silence," Halstead noted. "The nerves of the thousands, which through the hours of suspense had been subjected to terrible tension, relaxed, and as deep breaths of relief were taken, there was a noise in the Wigwam like the rush of a great wind, in the van of a storm — and in another breath, the storm was there. There were thousands cheering with the energy of insanity."

One of the secretaries with a tally sheet in his hand shouted over the crowd what they already knew, "Fire the Salute — Abe Lincoln is nominated!" With tears on his cheeks, Evarts, as Seward's floor manager, moved to have the nomination made unanimous. A huge charcoal portrait of Lincoln was brought in for the convention to admire, and one exulting group of his supporters tried to seize the New York banner as a trophy but was fought off.

The Seward crusade was over. It was left to Austin Blair of Michigan to make, in elegiac tones, the speech of the day: "Michigan, from first to last, has cast her vote for the great Statesman of New York. She has nothing to take back. She has not sent me forward to worship the rising sun, but she has put me forward to say that, at your behests here to-day, she lays down her first, best loved candidate to take up yours . . . she does not fear that the fame of Seward will suffer, for she knows that his fame is a portion of the history of the American Union; it will be written, and read,

and beloved long after the temporary excitement of this day has passed away, and when Presidents themselves are forgotten in the oblivion which comes over all temporal things. We stand by him still. . . ." Other Seward supporters wanted to eulogize their man, but the convention was in a mood to celebrate and cut them off.

Back home, each candidate received the word by telegram. Always the pessimist, Lincoln had assumed he would lose and that the convention, after failing to nominate Seward on the first ballot, would turn to either Bates or Chase. When the wire arrived telling him of his victory, Lincoln accepted congratulations from his friends and said, "There is a lady over yonder on Eighth Street who is deeply interested in this news; I will carry it to her."

In Auburn, Seward read the telegram: "Lincoln nominated third ballot." There was no change of expression on his face. "Well," he said, "Mr. Lincoln will be elected and has some of the qualities to make a good President."

Earlier that evening Seward's friends had dragged a cannon up near his house to be used when the good news arrived. Quietly the six-pounder was wheeled away, and a few hours later, still primed with Seward shot and powder, it fired a salute to Abraham Lincoln, the next President of the United States.

TO FIND OUT MORE

As always with historians of this period, Carl Sandburg and Bruce Catton may be read for both information and pleasure, although the latter was certainly more scrupulous with his research. *The Prairie Years* in Sandburg's multivolume biography of Lincoln and "The Crowd at the Wigwam" and "Railsplitter" chapters in Catton's *The Coming Fury* contain excellent accounts of the convention. Readers interested in more detail should consult William Baringer's comprehensive *Lincoln's Rise to Power*. The best primary source is contained in Murat Halstead's eyewitness account *The Caucuses of 1860*. — **P.A.**

There, in the heat of July, was the shimmering Capitol

*The year was 1864 and the South was all
but beaten, yet Jubal Early's ragged
army had Washington, D.C. within its grasp*

Thomas A. Lewis

**Thomas A. Lewis' second book on the valley campaign of
1864,** The Guns of Cedar Creek, *was published by Harper & Row in 1988.*

It may be altogether fitting and proper that the battle-
field has come to this. A ragged half-block of grass
surrounded by brick tenements and row houses, it lies
between the main business district of Washington,
D.C. and the burgeoning suburb of Silver Spring,
Maryland. When I visited there last, I was greeted by
a couple of hundred feet of eroding breastworks and
concrete replicas of a half-dozen gun platforms, awash
in fast-food wrappers and broken glass. Instead of
uniformed guides there were the flat stares of four men
pulling frequently on a large wine bottle.

It is not hard to be reminded here of lost causes and
wasted lives; of how events often reel crazily away from
the people who set them in motion, battering down
winners and thrusting losers toward greatness. So what
is left of Fort Stevens may be precisely the right memorial for the curious confrontation that occurred here,
and for the weary men who led it.

To Lieut. Gen. Jubal Early of the Confederate States
Army, at least for a little while that day, it must have
seemed that the war was young again. In the noonday
heat of July 11, 1864, the commander of the battle-
hardened II Corps of Robert E. Lee's Army of North-

ern Virginia sat his horse on a rise of ground in Maryland and saw, shimmering in the heat waves just six
miles to the south, the luminous dome of the United
States Capitol. Immediately in front of him were the
frowning works of Washington's formidable ring of
defensive entrenchments. A glance told him, he wrote
later, that they were "but feebly manned."

It was a year and a week after the fateful Confederate defeat at Gettysburg, four months after the advent
of Ulysses S. Grant as the Federal General in Chief,
and a month since Grant's armies had begun hammer-
ing at Petersburg, south of Richmond. For some time,
in other words, there had been for the South precious
little glory in this war and even less fun. The proud
young men strutting to the music of the bands were no
more; now sad-eyed, leather-skinned, worn-out infantrymen stumbled barefoot through the heat and dust
until they dropped. The caped and ostrich-feathered
officers, happily risking all for home and country,
were dead, replaced by bitter shells of men playing out
a losing hand.

And yet, by God, here at midday on a Monday in
July was the balding, foulmouthed, tobacco-chewing,

prophet-bearded Jubal Early, at the gates of the Federal capital. He had taken command of the men who had earned immortality as Stonewall Jackson's "foot cavalry," had marched them far enough and fought them hard enough to rival the memory of their dead commander, and now he stood on the brink of legend himself. He was going to take Washington City—its Treasury, its arsenals, its Capitol building, maybe even its President.

Even better, he was going to lift some of the crushing burden from the shoulders of his chief, Robert E. Lee. Beleaguered, almost surrounded, his sources of food and reinforcement slowly being choked off, his great heart failing under the agonizing pressure, Lee had asked Jubal Early to attempt two things, each of them a tremendous challenge.

First, reclaim the Shenandoah Valley from the Federal army that had managed, for the first time in the war, to occupy the granary of the Confederacy.

Then, if he could, invade the North again, as Lee had done in the campaigns of Antietam and Gettysburg, and raise such an uproar that Grant would be forced to detach part of his army to protect Maryland, Pennsylvania and Washington City; or attack Lee in his fortifications and risk suffering more of the slaughter that had stunned his army at Cold Harbor.

There were political as well as military benefits to be gained. The Union, heartily tired of war, would be electing its President in November. The likely Democratic candidate, George McClellan, was promising a negotiated peace while Abraham Lincoln was promising to finish the war no matter how long it took. If Early could embarrass Lincoln, deepen the war-weariness and brighten McClellan's prospects, he might assure the survival of the Confederacy.

The role of savior did not fit snugly on the tall form of the man they called "Old Jube." Thin and fierce, stooped by what he said was rheumatism, a confirmed bachelor at 48, he had a tongue that (when it was not caressing a plug of tobacco) rasped like a steel file on most sensibilities and a sense of humor that enraged as often as it amused. His adjutant general, Maj. Henry Kyd Douglas, admired Early's fighting abilities but saw him with clear eyes: "Arbitrary, cynical, with strong prejudices, he was personally disagreeable." It is remarkable, then, that before the war he had been a moderately successful politician and lawyer in his native Franklin County, in southwestern Virginia.

Professional soldiering seems not to have appealed to Jubal Early; he resigned from the U.S. Army in 1838, just one year after graduation from West Point, and went back only briefly in 1846 to do his duty in the Mexican War. He had argued caustically against secession and for the Union until his state seceded, whereupon he became an equally caustic supporter of the Confederacy and a colonel in its army.

It soon became clear that he was that rare commod-ity, a forceful and courageous leader of men in battle. This had been so at First and Second Bull Run, Antietam, Fredericksburg and Chancellorsville. As his commands increased in size, however, his touch became less sure and his luck more spotty. Yet such was General Lee's confidence that in 1864 Early had been given command of one of the three corps in the Army of Northern Virginia.

And now here he was, on the brink of history, about to quench the boundless thirst for recognition that glittered ceaselessly from his black eyes. Pursuant to Lee's instruction, he had chased one Federal army away from Lynchburg, Virginia, and clear into the West Virginia mountains where it disappeared. He met another near Frederick, Maryland, on the Monocacy River, and swept it aside. On fire with the glory of it all, forgetting his limited objective, Early now rasped out his orders to Maj. Gen. Robert Rodes, commander of the leading division: throw out a skirmish line; move forward into the enemy works; attack the capital of the United States.

Abraham Lincoln himself visited the fort and watched the sinuous dust clouds raised by enemy columns approaching from the northwest. "In his long, yellowish linen coat and unbrushed high hat," an Ohio soldier who had seen him at the fort wrote, "he looked like a care worn farmer in time of peril from drouth and famine." Far away to the south, the relentless Grant had refused to be distracted from his slow strangulation of Lee's army. On the whole, Lincoln approved; he had, after all, tried for three long years to find a general who would devote himself to destroying the enemy armies instead of striking attitudes and defending Washington. But it must have occurred to the President, that afternoon, that maybe Grant had gone too far.

A few months before, there had been 18,000 trained artillerymen manning the 900 guns and guarding the 37 miles of fortifications that ringed Washington. Grant had taken those men for harsher duty in the trenches in front of Petersburg, and now, on the threatened north side of the barrier Potomac, there were on the line no more than 4,000 frightened home guardsmen and militiamen.

Paroxysms of hysteria in the city

Reinforcements were on the way, to be sure. As soon as he realized what Early was up to, Grant dispatched two veteran VI Corps divisions—11,000 strong—and diverted to Washington 6,000 men of XIX Corps. The transports were not far downstream from the city, Lincoln knew, but Jubal Early had arrived. His 4,000 cavalry and artillerymen were harassing the Federal line for miles in either direction; he had 10,000 infantrymen and 40 cannon, and his skirmishers were already chasing the Federal pickets back into the fortifications.

Confronted by what they had so long feared—actual danger—the civilians of Washington went into paroxysms of hysteria, telling each other that a Confederate army "50,000 strong" was laying waste to Maryland and Pennsylvania. Military and political functionaries, meanwhile, went berserk.

Everyone took charge of everything. The military department was commanded by Maj. Gen. Christopher Augur; but the Army Chief of Staff, Henry Halleck, ordered Maj. Gen. Quincy Gillmore to take charge in the emergency; but the Secretary of War, Edwin Stanton, had called in Maj. Gen. Alexander McCook to handle the crisis; but General in Chief Grant had sent Maj. Gen. E.O.C. Ord to save the situation.

When yet another general, who for some reason was relaxing in a New York City hotel, sent word that he would be available for duties commensurate with his rank, Chief of Staff Halleck blew up. "We have five times as many generals here as we want," he responded, "but are greatly in need of privates. Anyone volunteering in *that* capacity will be thankfully received."

Everyone thought of something. Halleck had the hospitals checked for potentially useful walking wounded, so they could be formed up and marched toward the fortifications. On the way they probably stumbled into a ragged formation of clerks from the offices of the Quartermaster General, Brig. Gen. Montgomery Meigs, who had decided that now was the time for them to exchange their pencils for rifles. Someone else made preparations for destroying the bridges over the Potomac River. A steamboat was fired up and held ready to get the President away.

A restless tattoo of musketry

But the President was singularly serene. "Let us be vigilant," he telegraphed to an overwrought Baltimore committee, "but keep cool. I hope neither Baltimore nor Washington will be sacked." Yet on that sultry afternoon, with the earth trembling to the bark of the big guns, with the acrid smell of black powder hanging in the stifling air and a restless tattoo of musketry sounding along the lines, keeping cool could not have been easy.

Both the Federal defenses and the Confederate threat looked stronger than they were. "Undoubtedly we could have marched into Washington," wrote one of Early's division commanders, Maj. Gen. John B. Gordon. "I myself rode to a point on those breastworks at which there was no force whatsoever. The unprotected space was broad enough for the easy passage of Early's army without resistance."

Just beyond this inviting gap lay the legislative and administrative heart of the enemy government. What is more, there was the Federal Navy yard, with its ships to burn; the United States Treasury with its millions of dollars in bonds and currency, the seizure of which would have had catastrophic effects on the Northern economy; warehouse after warehouse of medical supplies, food, military equipment, ammunition—all scarce and desperately needed in the Confederacy. In short, a rich city, virgin to war, awaiting plunder.

Not to mention the incalculable humiliation to the Union if such a rape of its capital occurred. Maj. Gen. Lew Wallace (later the author of *Ben Hur*) had been stiffened to make his desperate stand against Early on the Monocacy, he wrote afterward, by a vision of "President Lincoln, cloaked and hooded, stealing from the back door of the White House just as some gray-garbed Confederate brigadier burst in the front door."

But for the moment, at least, the enormous prize was out of reach. The problem was not a lack of will or courage or even firepower; the problem was something that civilians and historians rarely think of as part of war—simple fatigue. Early's foot soldiers were just too tired to walk that far.

During the hottest and driest summer anyone could remember they had marched about 250 miles from Lynchburg in three weeks. They had fought hard at the Monocacy on July 9, then after burying their dead had marched again at dawn, struggling 30 miles in the searing heat to bivouac near Rockville, Maryland. The night of the 10th brought so little relief from the heat that the exhausted men were unable to sleep. On the 11th, with the sun burning more fiercely than ever, they had begun to give out.

General Early rode along the loosening formations, telling staggering, sweating, dust-begrimed men that he would take them into Washington that day. They tried to raise the old Rebel Yell to show him they were willing, but it came out cracked and thin. The mounted officers reluctantly slowed their pace, but before midday the road behind the army was littered with prostrate men who could go no farther.

Thus when Early ordered General Rodes to attack, both men—on horseback—were far ahead of the plodding columns. While Early fumed and spat tobacco juice, his officers struggled to get men and guns in position. They managed to mount a skirmish line to chase in the Federal pickets, but putting together a massed line of battle was beyond them. The afternoon wore on, and to Early every hour was the equivalent of a thousand casualties.

It was not the fault of his men. General Gordon later wrote of them that they possessed "a spirit which nothing could break."

Nor was it a failure of the officers; Jubal Early had for subordinate commanders some of the best generals in the Confederacy. John Gordon and John Breckinridge were, like Early, lawyers and politicians who lacked his West Point training but had shown a remarkable ability to lead men in combat. Breckinridge was a former Vice President of the United States and a candidate for President in 1860, who came in second to Lincoln in the electoral vote; now he was second in command of an army advancing on the U.S. capital. Stephen Dodson Ramseur, a major general at 27, possessed a ferocity in battle that usually got results.

No one embodied more of the paradoxes of this war than John Breckinridge. A passionate and lifelong champion of the Union and the Constitution, he had been convinced for years that slavery could not and should not survive; but he also believed that it was unconstitutional for the national government to prohibit slave states from participating in the country's booming Western expansion—the settlement of the territories.

For his constitutional arguments he was ostracized in the Senate and described as a traitor to the United States; back in Kentucky he pleaded with his state to stay out of the spreading civil war. Union military authorities ordered his arrest. Thus John Breckinridge had been left with nowhere to go but into the armies marching against the Union, on behalf of slavery.

Such were the men who stood at Jubal Early's side that afternoon. Before he could form his gasping troops and launch his attack, Early saw "a cloud of dust in the rear of the works toward Washington, and soon a column of the enemy filed into them on the right and left, and skirmishers were thrown out in front." Artillery fire opened from a number of batteries.

The Confederates had managed to take a few prisoners, who freely admitted that their lines were being held by "counter jumpers, hospital rats and stragglers." But the men just arriving were veterans, perhaps reinforcements from Grant. Jubal Early was bold, but he was not foolhardy; however tempting the prize, he would not commit to battle without knowing what he was facing. As he wrote later, "It became necessary to reconnoiter."

The Federal regiment that had impressed Early was from Grant's Army of the Potomac, but it was alone. Meanwhile, however, Abraham Lincoln had spotted something really interesting in his spyglass, and driven eagerly south to the Sixth Street wharves.

Marching off in the wrong direction

He arrived in midafternoon, and stood quietly gnawing on a chunk of hardtack while Maj. Gen. Horatio Wright assembled the first 650 arrivals from VI Corps and marched them off—in the wrong direction—toward Georgetown. With great shouting and clatter, some staff officers got the men turned around and headed up 11th Street, toward the enemy.

A Vermonter named Aldace Walker marched with VI Corps that day. He thought it was still morning, and had his dates confused, but he remembered how the presence of the capable Old Sixth brought "intense relief to the constitutionally timid Washingtonians. . . . Citizens ran through the lines with buckets of ice-water, for the morning was sultry; newspapers and eatables were handed into the column, and our welcome had a heartiness that showed how intense had been the fear."

The official welcome was less clear-cut. To his dis-

gust, Wright was ordered to hold his men in reserve, even though the raw troops at Fort Stevens were being severely pummeled by Early's guns and skirmishers, and were already showing signs of caving in. In the end, the only thing the soldiers did that night (and this only because Wright insisted on it) was to move out in front of the fortifications to restore a picket line and push back enemy skirmishers. "The pseudo-soldiers who filled the trenches around the fort were astounded at the temerity displayed by these war-torn veterans in going out before the breastworks," Walker remembered scornfully, "and benevolently volunteered most earnest words of caution."

Apparently the Federal high command did little that night but further confuse each other. Charles Dana, an Assistant Secretary of War and an old friend of Grant's, sent a despairing wire to the commanding general Tuesday morning: "General Halleck will not give orders except as he receives them; the President will give none, and until you direct positively and explicitly what is to be done, everything will go on in the deplorable and fatal way in which it has gone on for the past week."

On Monday night, Early and his division commanders gathered at their captured headquarters, "Silver Spring," the imposing mansion of the prominent Washington publisher and politician Francis Preston Blair (a cousin and former political patron of John Breckinridge). There the Confederate officers had dinner, a council of war and a party. Men were still straggling in from their hellish march, and it seemed a precious opportunity had been lost the previous afternoon. But the Federal works were still not manned in strength, and Early ordered an assault at first light.

A sound of revelry by night

His officers raided Francis Blair's wine cellar and talked about what they would do next day. They joked about escorting John Breckinridge back to his former place as presiding officer of the Senate. Outside, soldiers speculated about how they would divide up the contents of the Treasury. According to General Gordon, one private was asked what they would do when they took the city, and said the situation reminded him of a family slave whose dog chased every train that came by. The old man wasn't worried about losing his dog, said the soldier, he was worried about what the dog was going to do with a train when he caught one.

It was all good fun, but soon daylight was coming.

General Early was up before dawn, surveying the Federal fortifications with his field glasses. The trenches and the parapets teemed with blue uniforms—not the dark, new blue of fresh, untested cloth, but the faded sky-blue of well-used material. Everywhere he saw fluttering battle flags bearing the Greek Cross of VI Corps. The door to Jubal Early's niche in history had just slammed shut.

"I had, therefore, reluctantly to give up all hopes of capturing Washington, after I had arrived in sight of the dome of the Capitol," he wrote. But they could not give any sign of flinching with that many soldiers ready to pour after them. They would stay in place, look as dangerous as they knew how, and as soon as darkness covered them head back to Virginia. The Federals, meanwhile, made ready to fight a climactic battle for the city. They did it in the time-honored Washington way—with endless meetings. The day wore on, the baking heat returned, the sharpshooters let fly at anything that stirred, the cannon boomed from time to time—and nobody moved.

The citizens of Washington regained their courage. Ladies and gentlemen of society and rank declared a holiday and swarmed out to picnic and cheer the intrepid defenders. Some perhaps had been among the picnickers who, three years before, had gone to cheer the boys going into battle at Bull Run, but if they remembered the bloody stampede that had engulfed the tourists on that day, they gave no sign.

At midafternoon they were joined by the President and Mrs. Lincoln, who arrived at Fort Stevens in a carriage. General Wright went out to greet the Commander in Chief and casually asked if he would like to see the fight; the various chieftains had at last agreed to try a reconnaissance in force, to press the Confederates back and see just how strong they were. General Wright intended his question to be purely rhetorical, but as he wrote later, "A moment after, I would have given much to have recalled my words."

Delighted at the prospect of seeing actual combat for the first time, Lincoln bounded up to the parapet and stood looking over the field, his familiar, top-hatted form an inviting target for Confederate sharpshooters. While Wright begged the President to take cover, a trooper in Lincoln's cavalry escort saw bullets "sending little spurts and puffs of dust as they thudded into the embankment on which he stood." Thus for the first and only time in history a President of the United States came under fire in combat.

Behind the breastworks, a busy young captain from Massachusetts named Oliver Wendell Holmes jr. glanced up, saw a tall, awkward civilian standing in the spray of bullets and snapped, "Get down, you damn fool, before you get shot." Only then did the future Supreme Court Justice realize that he was berating the President.

Meanwhile a VI Corps brigade, about 2,000 strong, was sneaking out of Fort Stevens and taking position in a wooded area 300 yards east of what is now Wisconsin Avenue, just behind the line of Federal skirmishers and out of sight of the enemy. Their orders were to make a surprise charge at the Confederate positions on the wooded ridge less than a mile from Fort Stevens, where the Walter Reed hospital now stands.

Lincoln watched these maneuvers intently, standing fully exposed on top of the parapet, oblivious to the leaden hail. General Wright stood at the President's side, along with C.C.V. Crawford, the surgeon of one of the attacking regiments. Suddenly, a round ricocheted off a nearby soldier's rifle and into Crawford's thigh. Gravely wounded, he was carried to the rear.

General Wright, beside himself, ordered everyone off the parapet, and when the President ignored him threatened to have a squad of soldiers forcibly remove Lincoln from danger. "The absurdity of the idea of sending off the President under guard seemed to amuse him," Wright recalled, and more to put an end to the fuss than anything else, Lincoln finally agreed to sit behind the parapet and thus place most of his frame behind cover. But he kept leaping to his feet to see what was happening.

When the attacking regiments were in position, the guns of Fort Stevens opened a sustained fire on the enemy positions. The 36th shot, fired at about 6 P.M., was the signal for the picket line to plunge forward. Behind it, appearing as if from nowhere, surged thousands of howling Federals.

"I thought we were 'gone up,' " one of Early's staff officers remembered. But these were men familiar with death, and they opened a fire so hot that the Federals came to a halt and sent for reserves. The enemy, the Federal division commander reported, "was found to be much stronger than had been supposed."

There was cheering from the spectators and joking in the rear echelons, but this was no game; Aldace Walker remembered it as a "bitter little contest." Every regimental commander in the leading Federal brigade was shot down; a hundred Confederate dead were later found lying on the field between Fort Stevens and the Blair house. Heavy fighting continued until 10 P.M., even though General Wright ordered his men to hold their ground but not to storm the Confederate lines.

Major Douglas found Jubal Early in Francis Blair's mansion after dark, getting ready to pull out. "He seemed in a droll humor, perhaps one of relief," Douglas recalled, "for he said to me in his falsetto drawl: 'Major, we haven't taken Washington, but we've scared Abe Lincoln like hell!' " And so with hollow laughs they began a long retreat, away from legend and glory, into Virginia, where Appomattox waited.

A half-mile north of the crumbling remains of Fort Stevens, the asphalt and concrete environs of Georgia Avenue are interrupted by another unremarkable, postage-stamp square of green. Hardly larger than a townhouse lot, it is a National Cemetery, wherein are buried a few of the men for whom this "bitter little contest" was the last. Some earnest monuments to the men of New York and Ohio are crowded together here, but the most imposing thing one sees on entering is a bronze plaque. It memorializes not the dead, but an 1875 order prohibiting picnicking on, and otherwise defacing, their graves. Forgetfulness came quickly.

Family and Freedom:
BLACK FAMILIES IN THE AMERICAN CIVIL WAR

Ira Berlin
Francine C. Cary
Steven F. Miller
Leslie S. Rowland

NO EVENT IN AMERICAN HISTORY matches the drama of emancipation. More than a century later, it continues to stir the deepest emotions, and properly so. Emancipation accompanied the military defeat of the world's most powerful slaveholding class. It freed some four million slaves, a larger number than were emancipated in all other New World slave societies combined.

Born of a bloody civil war that raged for four long years (1861-65), emancipation accomplished a profound social revolution. It destroyed forever a way of life based upon the ownership of human beings, restoring to the former slaves proprietorship of their own persons, liquidating without compensation private property valued at billions of dollars, and forcibly substituting the relations of free labour for those of slavery. In designating the former slaves as citizens, emancipation placed citizenship upon new ground, defined it in the national Constitution and thenceforth removed it beyond the jurisdiction of the states. By obliterating the sovereignty of master over slave, emancipation handed a monopoly of sovereignty to the newly consolidated nation-state. The freeing of the slaves simultaneously overturned the old regime of the South and set the entire American nation upon a new course.

With emancipation in the South, the United States enacted its part in a world-wide drama. Throughout the western world and beyond, the forces unleashed by the American and French revolutions and by the industrial revolution worked to undermine political regimes based upon hereditary privilege and economic systems based upon bound labour. Slavery had already succumbed in the Northern states and in the French and British Caribbean before the Civil War, and it would shortly do so in its remaining strongholds in Spanish and Portuguese America. Almost simultaneously with the great struggle in the United States, the vestiges of serfdom in central and eastern Europe yielded to the pressure of the age. Only small pockets in

First published in *History Today*, January 1987, pp. 8-15. Reprinted by permission.

Africa and Asia remained immune, and their immunity was temporary. The fateful lightning announced by the victorious Union army was soon to strike (if it had not already struck) wherever men and women remained in bonds of personal servitude.

For all systems of bondage, emancipation represented the moment of truth. The upheaval stripped away the patina of routine, exposing the conflicts that had smouldered beneath the surface of the old order. Throwing off habitual restraints, freed men and women reconstituted their lives in ways that spoke eloquently of their hidden life in bondage, revealing clandestine institutions and long cherished values. In confronting new restraints, they abandoned their customary caution in favour of direct speech and action, alive to the realisation that they were setting radically new precedents for themselves and for future generations.

Because they thrust common people into prominence, moments of revolutionary transformation have long occupied historians. While those who enjoy political power and social authority speak their minds and indulge their inclinations freely and often, their subordinates generally cannot. Only in the upheaval of accustomed routine can ordinary men and women give voice to the assumptions that guide their world as it is and as they wish it to be.

Encompassing in full measure the revolutionary implications of all transitions from bondage to freedom, emancipation in the American South has left behind an unparalleled wealth of documentation permitting direct access to the thoughts and actions of the freed men and women themselves. As the Civil War became a war for liberty, the lives of slaves and ex-slaves became increasingly intertwined with the activities of both the Union and Confederate governments. Following the war, agencies of the federal government, especially the army and the Freedmen's Bureau, figured prominently in the reconstruction of Southern economy and society. The records created and collected by these governmental agencies and now housed in the National Archives of the United States provide an unrivalled manuscript source for

The newly-found voices of the slaves caught up in the American Civil War, and heard through letters to their families, are a testimony to their tenacity and unity in the struggle for emancipation.

understanding the passage of black people from slavery to freedom.

In these archival files, alongside official reports, hundreds of letters and statements by former slaves give voice to people whose aspirations, beliefs, and behaviour have gone largely unrecorded. Not only did extraordinary numbers of ex-slaves, many of them newly literate, put pen to paper in the early years of freedom, but hundreds of others, entirely illiterate, gave depositions to government officials, placed their marks on resolutions passed at mass meetings, testified before courts-martial and Freedmen's Bureau courts, and dictated letters to more literate blacks and to white officials and teachers. The written record thus created constitutes an unparalleled outpouring from people caught up in the emancipation process.

The Freedmen and Southern Society Project (University of Maryland) is a collaborative effort to draw upon these remarkable records to write a documentary history of emancipation in the American South. During three years of systematic research in the National Archives, the project editors made an initial selection of more than 40,000 documents (about 2 per cent of the items they examined). These documents serve as the basis for *Freedom: A Documentary History of Emancipation, 1861-1867*, a multi-volume history combining interpretative essays with documents. Two volumes have reached print thus far, both published

by Cambridge University Press: *The Destruction of Slavery* (1985) and *The Black Military Experience* (1982). Subsequent volumes will be concerned with the wartime genesis of free labour; land, labour, and capital in the postwar South; race relations, law, and justice; and black community life, including family, religion, education, and politics.

What follows is a sample of documents regarding one aspect of the story of emancipation – slave families in the wartime struggle for freedom. As slaves, black people had worked hard to maintain the sanctity of their family life. Despite enormous difficulties, they managed to create a dense network of kinship which stood at the centre of black society, not only performing the tasks of reproduction and socialisation that commonly fall to familial institutions but also giving meaning and direction to the lives of people who had no legal right to their own person or their progeny. The Civil War opened the way for slaves to put their family life on a firmer footing. When the opportunity arose, they hastily gathered their children, their parents, and other kin and fled toward safe – and, they hoped, free – ground. But the war created difficulties as well as opportunities for black families. Slaves had to balance the possibility of escape against the harsh retribution that would surely face family members left behind. Often they concluded that the only way to achieve their family's freedom was to strike out alone, with the hope of returning later as liberators. In short, wartime emancipation put black families to the test. The documents presented below reflect the dimensions of the ordeal.

The documents are transcribed exactly as written, with no correction of spelling, punctuation, capitalisation, or syntax. Extra space marks the end of unpunctuated sentences. Italicised words which are enclosed in brackets have been added by the editors; letters or words in ordinary roman type and enclosed in brackets indicate conjectural readings of illegible passages.

The free-born can perhaps never know the triumph and pain felt by the slave who gained liberty. John Boston, a Maryland slave, seized freedom early in the war by

This day i can adress you thank god as a free man...

Shield and motto of a Black regiment. Liberty, with the fasces — symbol of authority — hands the Union Flag to the regimental sergeant.

Upton Hill [*Virginia*] January the 12 1862 My Dear Wife   it is with grate joy I take this time to let you know Whare I am i am now in Safety in the 14th Regiment of Brooklyn this Day i can Adress you thank god as a free man I had a little truble in giting away But as the lord led the Children of Isrel to the land of Canon So he led me to a land Whare fredom Will rain in spite Of earth and hell Dear you must make your Self content i am free from al the Slavers Lash and as you have chose the Wise plan Of Serving the lord i hope you Will pray Much and i Will try by the help of god To Serv him With all my hart I am With a very nice man and have All that hart Can Wish But My Dear I Cant express my grate desire that i Have to See you i trust the time Will Come When We Shal meet again And if We dont met on earth We Will Meet in heven Whare Jesas ranes Dear Elizabeth tell Mrs Own[ees] That i trust that She Will Continue Her kindness to you and that god Will Bless her on earth and Save her In grate eternity My Acomplements To Mrs Owens and her Children may They Prosper through life I never Shall forgit her kindness to me Dear Wife i must Close rest yourself Contented i am free i Want you to rite To me Soon as you Can Without Delay Direct your letter to the 14th Reigment New york State malitia Uptons Hill Virginea In Care of Mr Cranford Comary Write my Dear Soon As you C Your Affectionate Husban Kiss Daniel For me

John Boston
Give my love to Father and Mother

escaping to a Union army regiment, where he obtained employment as the servant of a Northern officer. This route out of slavery held less promise for women, children, and old people, who were regarded as encumbrances by an army on the march. John Boston therefore fled alone, to share with the family he left behind not only the triumph of his new freedom, but also its pain.

When circumstances permitted, slave families attempted to escape bondage together. The risks were enormous because slaveowners mobilised to prevent flight and recapture runaways, but proximity to

Union army lines or to federally controlled territory like the District of Columbia could improve the chances. From the first days of the war, the District served as a haven for fugitive slaves from adjacent portions of Maryland and Virginia. However, freedom remained insecure even for those who successfully reached its borders. A military labourer who had fled slavery with his family described the re-enslavement and punishment of his mother, wife, and infant child.

Black men and women who reached freedom behind Union lines did not rest satisfied with their own liberty. Like

former slaves in other parts of the Union-occupied Confederacy, black military labourers in eastern Virginia organised an expedition to liberate families and friends left behind. Union General Edward A. Wild, whose brigade of black troops comprised ex-slaves from Virginia and North Carolina, assigned several of his soldiers to accompany the dangerous raid and reported its outcome to his superior officer. Slaves who gained freedom under the auspices of the Union army were not thereby assured of maintaining either their families or their liberty. The members

[*Washington, DC*] 6th day of Feb. 1864 Grandison Briskoe being duly sworn says he is about 25 years of age was born in Maryland & has been married to his wife since 1861 Came to reside with his wife in this City in April – 4th day of April 1862 & has resided in said City Since that period of time except a part of the time he has been in the Service of the United States all the time & is now in Said Service in Virginia – That his wife & his mother were taken away from Washington in April (on the 7th day) 1862 & as fugitive Slaves & taken to Piscatawa to Broad Creek to their master's [farm?] whose name is John Hunter & My mothers masters name was & is Robert Hunter – They were both taken to the barn & severely whipped Their clothes were raised & tied over their heads to keep their screams from disturbing the neighborhood & then were tied up & whipped very severely whipped and then taken to Upper Marlborough to jail My wife had a Child about nine month's old which was taken from her & died soon after. Some six or eight months after my wife was imprisoned she had a Child but the inhuman master & mistress though the[y] knew she was soon to be Confined or give birth to a Child made no arrangements provided no Clothing nor anything for the Child or mother I have sent them Clothing & other articles frequently until the first or near the first of January 1864 Since which the new jailor has refused to allow them to receive any thing from me

They have been in prison for the Crime of Coming to Washington to reside, ever since about the fourth of April 1862 now a year & ten months. They are confined in Jail at Upper Marlborough Prince George's County Maryland

Grandison Briscoe

of an Alabama slave family found themselves re-enslaved, separated, and sold to new masters in Kentucky, a Union state where slavery remained untouched by the Emancipation Proclamation or other wartime emancipation measures.

The recruitment of black soldiers into the Union army beginning late in 1862 helped speed both emancipation and Union vic-

Newport-News, [Va.]. Sept. 1st, 1864. Sir, I have the honor to report that some Government employees (colored) came up here from Fort Monroe and Hampton Hospitals, having been allowed a short leave of absence for the purpose of getting their families if possible. I told them I had no boats, but would help them with men. They reappeared the next day with sailboats. I sent with them a Captain and 15 men (dismounted Cavalry). The families were in and about Smithfield. I gave them strict instructions to abstain from plundering – to injure no one if possible – to get the women and children merely, and come away as promptly as possible. They were to land in the night. They followed these directions closely: but became delayed by the numbers of women and children anxious to follow, whom they packed in extra boats, picked up there, and towed along. They also had to contend against a head tide, and wind calm. So that their progress down Smithfield Creek in the early morn was exceedingly slow. The inhabitants evidently gathered in from some concerted plan of alarm or signals.

'Reading the Proclamation', J.W. Watts' emotive engraving of 1864.

Slave into Soldier: two photographs of Hubbard Pryor during the Civil War.

For, 3 miles below, the party were intercepted by a force of irregular appearance, numbering about 100 – having horses and dogs with them; – armed variously with shot guns, rifles, &c, and posted behind old breastworks with some hurried additions. They attacked the leading boats, killed a man and woman, and wounded another woman therein. The contrabands then rowed over to the opposite bank and scattered over the marshes. How many more have been slaughtered we know not. Two (2) men have since escaped to us singly. – When the rear boats, containing the soldiers, came up, the Captain landed, with the design of attacking the rebels. But then the firing revealed their full numbers. He found they outnumbered him, more than 6 to 1, and that the *revolvers* of our Cavalry, in open boats or on the open beach, would stand no chance against their rifles behind breastworks. He embarked again, and they made their way past the danger, by wading his men behind the boats, having the baggage and bedding piled up like a barricade. They then had a race with 3 boats, which put out from side creeks to cut them off. But for the coolness and ingenuity of Capt. Whiteman, none would have escaped. None

of the soldiers are known to have been severely wounded; but 3 are missing in the marshes and woods. We have since learned that there are signal Stations in that neighborhood – which ought to be brooken up. I would also earnestly recommend the burning of a dozen or 20 houses in accordance with *your* General Order No. 23. Very respectfully Your obt. Servant

Edwd A. Wild

tory. In the Union's own slave states (Delaware, Maryland, Missouri, and Kentucky), where the Emancipation Proclamation had no force, recruitment itself constituted the chief route to freedom. But it also created numerous difficulties for black soldiers' families, who remained legally slaves. Masters manipulated their slaves' family ties to try to deter the men from enlisting, and then turned their wrath upon the relatives of slave men who joined the Union army despite threats. When Martha Glover, a Missouri slave, wrote the following letter to her husband soon after he enlisted, her troubles had in fact only begun. Six weeks later, her master was apprehended while transport-

ing her and her three youngest children to Kentucky for sale.

Mexico Mo. Dec 30th 1863
My Dear Husband I have received your last kind letter a few days ago and was much pleased to hear from you once more. It seems like a long time since you left me. I have had nothing but trouble since you left. You recollect what I told you how they would do after you was gone. they abuse me because you went & say they will not take care of our children & do nothing but quarrel with me all the time and beat me scandalously the day before yesterday – Oh I never thought you would give me so much trouble as I have got to bear now. You ought not to left me in the fix I am in & all these little helpless children to take care of. I was invited to a party to night but I could not go I am in too much trouble to want to go to parties. the children talk about all you the time. I wish you could get a furlough & come to see us once more. We want to see you worse than we ever did before. Remember all I told you about how they would do me after you left – for they do worse than they ever did & I do not know what will become of me & my poor little children. Oh I wish you had staid with me & not gone till I could go with you for I do nothing but grieve all the time about you. write & tell me when you are coming.
Tell Isaac that his mother come & got his clothes she was so sorry he went. You need not tell me to beg any more married men to go. I see too much trouble to try to get any more into trouble too – Write to me & do not foget me & my children– farewell my dear husband from your wife

Martha

Slave men who enlisted in the Union army assumed that their military service should assure their families' freedom as well as their own. When Joseph Harris, a sergeant in the 82nd US Colored Infantry, found himself stationed in Florida, far from his

Barrancas Fa. Dec 27. 1864
Sir I beg you the granterfurction of a Small favor will you ples to Cross the Mississippia River at Bayou Sar La. with your Command & jest on the hill one mile from the little town you will finde A plantation called Mrs Marther. H. Turnbull & take a way my Farther & mother & my brothers wife with all their Childern & U take them up at your Hed Quarters. & write to me Sir the[y] ar ther & I will amejeately Send after them. I wishes the Childern all in School. it is

beter for them then to be their Surveing a mistes. Sir it isent mor then three or four Hours trubel I have bain trying evry sence I have bin in the servis it is goin on ner 3. years & Could never get no one to so do for me   now I thinks it will be don for you is my Gen. I wishes evry day you would send after us. our Regt. ar doing all the hard fightin her we have disapointe the Rebes & surprizeed theme in all. importan pointes they says they wishes to Captuer the 82nd Regt that they woul murdar them all they Calls our Regt the Bluebellied Eagles Sir my Farthers Name Adam Harris he will Call them all to gether. & tel him to take Cousan Janes Childarn with hime

Joseph. J. Harris
Sir I will remain Ob your Soldiar in the U.S.A.

[*Louisville, Ky. August 14?, 1865*] Amy Moore Colored, being duly Sworn deposeth and Says, that in the Summer of 1863 [*1862*] the United States Soldiers under command of Major McMillen came to her masters house in Huntsville Alabama, (her master and his family having left them) and carried away deponent together with her mother and three Sisters, that they brought us all to Nashville Tenn where we were put on board of a transport and Started for Cincinnati Ohio that when we arrived at Louisville Ky we were arrested by a man who Said he was a watchman and taken to the Slave pen on Second Street Louisville Ky and kept there two or three days when we were taken to the Depot of the Louisville and Nashville Rail Road and there another watchman

took charge of us and took us to Shepherdsville Ky and kept us confined several weeks when we were sold at auction by the Sherriff of Bullett County Ky. Dr. McKay bought deponent and paid for her the sum of Five Hundred (500) dollars *James Funk* bought deponents mother and youngest Sister paying Six Hundred (600) dollars for the two, and Soon after Sold her mother to *Judge Hoegner* who now holds her as a Slave *James Shepherd* bought my Sister Nora and *Richard Deets* bought my sister Ann, and further deponent saith that she and her mother and Sisters have been held as Slaves Since the above Sale and Still continue to be so held.

her
Amy X Moore
mark

Louisiana home and unable to accomplish his family's liberation, he sought the assistance of General Daniel Ullmann, who had supervised the recruitment of several black regiments in Louisiana.

The transformation of slaves into soldiers altered the expectations of both former slaves and slaveowners. Once black men donned the Union uniform, nothing was the same. When Private Spotswood Rice, a Missouri ex-slave, learned that the woman who owned his daughter Mary refused to permit the child to visit him and charged that he had tried to 'steal' her, he exploded in anger. His letters, the first to his enslaved daughters and the second to

Chaplain Warren of the Freedman's bureau officiating at a military wedding, Vicksburg.

Mary's mistress, suggest how military service made loving fathers into fierce liberators.

[*St. Louis, Missouri, September 3, 1864*] My Children I take my pen in hand to rite you A few lines to let you know that I have not forgot you and that I want to see you as bad as ever now my Dear Children I want you to be contented with whatever may be your lots be assured that I will have you if it cost me my life on the 28th of the mounth. 8 hundred White and 8 hundred blacke solders expects to start up the rivore to Glasgow and above there thats to be jeneraled by a jeneral that will give me both of you when they Come I expect to be with, them and expect to get you both in return. Dont be uneasy my children I expect to have you. If Diggs dont give you up this Government will and I feel confident that I will get you Your Miss Kaitty said that I tried to steal you But I'll let her know that god never intended for man to steal his own flesh and blood. If I had no cofidence in God I could have confidence in her But as it is If I ever had any Confidence in her I have none now and never expect to have And I want her to remember if she meets me with ten thousand soldiers she [*will?*] meet her enemy I once [*thought*] that I had some respect for them but now my respects is worn out and have no sympathy for Slaveholders. And as for her cristianantty I expect the Devil has Such in hell You tell her from me that She is the frist Christian that I ever hard say that aman could Steal his own child especially out of human bondage

You can tell her that She can hold to you as long as she can I never would expect to ask her again to let you come to

me because I know that the devil has got her hot set againsts that that is write now my Dear children I am a going to close my letter to you Give my love to all enquiring friends tell them all that we are well and want to see them very much and Corra and Mary receive the greater part of it you sefves and dont think hard of us not sending you any thing I you father have a plenty for you when I see you Spott & Noah sends their love to both of you Oh! My Dear children how I do want to see you

*

[*St. Louis, Missouri, September 3, 1864*] I received a leteter from Cariline telling me that you say I tried to steal to plunder my child away from you now I want you to understand that mary is my Child and she is a God given rite of my own and you may hold on to hear as long as you can but I want you to remembor this one thing that the longor you keep my Child from me the longor you will have to burn in hell and the qwicer youll get their for we are now makeing up a bout one thoughsand blacke troops to Come up tharough and wont to come through Glasgow and when we come wo be to Copperhood rabbels and to the Slaveholding rebbels for we dont expect to leave them there root neor branch but we thinke how ever that we that have Children in the hands of you devels we will trie your [*vertues?*] the day that we enter Glasgow I want you to understand kittey diggs that where ever you and I meets we are enmays to each orthere I offered once to pay you forty dollars for my own Child but I am glad now that you did not accept it Just hold on now as long as you can and the worse it will be for you you never in you life befor I came down hear did you give Children any thing not eny thing whatever not even a dollers worth of expencs   now you call my children your pro[per]ty not so with me   my Children is my own and I expect to get them and when I get ready to come after mary I will have bout a powrer and autherity to bring hear away and to exacute vengencens on them that holds my Child   you will then know how to talke to me   I will assure that and you will know how to talk rite too   I want you now to just hold on to hear if you want to   iff your conchosence tells thats the road go that road and what it will brig you to kittey diggs   I have no fears about geting mary out of your hands   this whole Government gives chear to me and you cannot help yourself

Spotswood Rice

Fearing that their families would be abused by angry masters, slave volunteers brought their wives, children, and other relatives with them to the Union recruitment centres. In the Union-occupied Confederacy, many of the black soldiers' families joined earlier fugitive slaves in 'contraband camps' established by the army for ex-slaves not suited to military labour or armed service. Others were employed on plantations supervised by Union authorities, or took up residence in the shantytowns that proliferated near military posts. Some Union army officers, however, had little regard for the family ties of black soldiers and labourers and — deeming the women, children, and old people a nuisance — periodically evicted them from military camps. Private Joseph Miller, who had recently enlisted in the 124th US Colored Infantry, testified to the cruel fate of his family when they were forced out of Camp Nelson, Kentucky.

Camp Nelson Ky, November 26, 1864
Personally appered before me E. B W Restieaux Capt. and Asst. Quartermaster Joseph Miller a man of color who being duly sworn upon oath says

I was a slave of George Miller of Lincoln County Ky. I have always resided in Kentucky and am now a Soldier in the service of the United States. I belong to Company I 124 U.S.C. Inft now Stationed at Camp Nelson Ky. When I came to Camp for the purpose of enlisting about the middle of October 1864 my wife and children came with me because my master said that if I enlisted he would not maintain them and I knew they would be abused by him when I left. I had then four children ages respectively ten nine seven and four years. On my presenting myself as a recruit I was told by the Lieut. in command to take my family into a tent within the limits of the Camp. My wife and family occupied this tent by the express permission of the aforementioned Officer and never received any notice to leave until Tuesday November 22" when a mounted guard gave my wife notice that she and her children must leave Camp before early morning. This was about six O'clock at night. My little boy about seven years of age had been very sick and was slowly recovering My wife had no place to go and so remained until morning. About eight Oclock Wednesday morning November 23" a mounted guard came to my tent and ordered my wife and children out of Camp The morning was bitter cold. It was freezing hard. I was certain that it would kill my sick child to take him out in the cold. I told the man in charge of the guard that it would be the death of my boy I told him that my wife and children had no place to go and I told him I was a soldier of the United States. He told me that it did not make any difference. He had orders to take all out of Camp. He told my wife and family that if they did not get up into the wagon which he had he would shoot the last one of them. On being thus threatened my wife and children went into the wagon My wife carried her sick child in her arms. When they left the tent the wind was blowing hard and cold and having had to leave much of our clothing when we left our master, my wife with her little one was poorly clad. I followed them as far as the lines. I had no Knowledge where they were taking them. At night I went in search of my family. I found them at Nicholasville about six miles from Camp. They were in an old meeting house belonging to the colored people. The building was very cold having only one fire. My wife and children could not get near the fire, because of the number of colored people huddled together by the soldiers. I found my wife and children shivering with cold and famished with hunger They had not recieved a morsel of food during the whole day. My boy was dead. He died directly after getting down from the wagon. I know he was Killed by exposure to the inclement weather I had to return to camp that night so I left my family in the meeting house and walked back. I had walked there. I travelled in all twelve miles Next morning I walked to Nicholasville. I dug a grave myself and buried my own child. I left my family in the Meeting house – where they still remain And further this deponent saith not

his
(Signed) Joseph   Miller
mark

The war ended when the Confederacy surrendered in April 1865, but many black soldiers were not mustered out of service for months or even years. As former masters returned home and reasserted their authority, black soldiers' families became special objects of abuse.

One Louisiana black soldier received the following letter from his wife about the difficulties forced upon his family in his absence. A sympathetic officer granted the soldier a furlough to attend to his family

'Contrabands' coming into a Union Camp, by A.R. Ward, 1862.

Flight to Freedom: Fugitive slaves with a Black military escort in Virginia.

and then, in the second letter, warned the newly organised Freedmen's Bureau that Union military authorities were unwittingly assisting erstwhile slaveowners in their persecution of black soldiers' families.

General Wild and his brigade of Black troops liberating slaves in North Carolina.

Roseland Plantation
[*St. Charles Parish, La.*] July 16th 1985

My Dear Husband I received a letter from you week before last and was glad to hear that you were well and happy.

This is the fifth letter I have written you and I have received only one – Please write as often as you can as I am always anxious to hear from you. I and the children are all well – but I am in a great deal of trouble as Master John Humphries has come home from the Rebel army and taken charge of the place and says he is going to turn us all out on the Levee unless we pay him (8.00) Eight Dollars a month for house rent – Now I have no money of any account and I am not able to get enough to pay so much rent, and I want you to get a furlough as soon as you can and come home and find a place for us to live in. and besides Amelia is very sick and wants you to come home and see her if possible   she has been sick with the fever now over two weeks and is getting very low – Your mother and all the rest of your folks are well and all send their regards & want to see you as soon as you can manage to come – My mother sends her compliments & hopes to see you soon

My children are going to school, but I find it very hard to feed them all, and if you can not come I hope you will send me something to help me get along

I get all the work I can and am doing the best I can to get along, but if they turn me out I dont know what I shall do – However I will try & keep the children along until you come or send me some assistance

Thank God we are all well, and I hope we may always be so Give my regards to all the boys. Come home as soon as you can, and cherish me as ever Your Aff wife   Emily Waters

*

Fort St. Philip. La. Aug. 1st, 1865
Sir. I am an officer in a co. of 140 men. – have been with them continually Since their organization as a Co., and most of the time the Sole officer with them. Feeling an interest in the advancement and prosperity of the colored race and always sympathizing with them in their trials and Sufferings, which are now very great, owing to the peculiar condition of the country, and their people, those under my immediate charge have learned to look to me for consolation in regard to many matters not Strictly military. I always do what I can but frequently that is nothing at all. One of the most frequent complaints brought to me is the mistreatment of Soldiers wives, and in Some cases their ejectment for non-payment of rent by *returned rebels* who seem to be resuming their old positions all over the country. This of course is inhuman as well as contrary to Genl. Orders. No. 99. Hd Qrs. Dept. of the Gulf. June 30th, 1865, which declares that the families of Soldiers in the Service of the Gov't. either on land or water, Shall not be ejected for rent past due, and no collections of rent forced until further orders. . . .

My object in writing you this letter is to call your attention to a Mr. John Humphrey, who I am told is a returned rebel officer, now living on Roseland Plantation, St. Charles Parish, who is Said to have made innumerable threats and at least one attempt to put out the family of one of my Soldiers. – *for non-payment of rent*. – I gave the man a furlough and he got home just in time to find a *Provost Guard* at his house for the purpose of ousting his wife and children. These look like Strange proceedings viewed at this distance with my understanding of the law. The fact is, persecution is the order of the day amongst these returned rebels, against the colored race in general, and Soldiers families *in particular*. And I am grieved to Say that many wearing the U.S. uniform are too easily bought body and Soul over to the evil designs and purposes of these same individuals. It seems to me that your Bureau and its agents are the "forlorn hope" of the colored people. – These rebels Strongly object to these agents, and declare that they will only keep up a confusion and disturbance, continually. That means that they do not intend to manifest the "good faith" for which Genl. Howard hopes, but intend to take Such a course with the colored people as will *oblige* the interference of the agents of your Bureau.

These are my views, although I owe you an apology for expressing them at Such length. If it pleases you I shall be glad to lay the frequent cases which arise in my Co. before you, as I know your voice is very potent With respect I am Your Most Obt. Servt.

Hugh P. Beach.

FOR FURTHER READING:
Freedom: A Documentary History of Emancipation, 1861-1867, Series 1, vol. I, *The Destruction of Slavery*, eds. Ira Berlin, Barbara J. Fields, Thavolia Glymph, Joseph P. Reidy and Leslie Rowland; Series 2, *The Black Military Experience*, eds. Ira Berlin, Joseph P. Reidy and Leslie S. Rowland (Cambridge University Press, 1985 and 1982); W.E.B. DuBois, *Black Reconstruction in America 1860-1880* (1935, reprinted Atheneum, 1969); Herbert G. Gutman, *The Black Family in Slavery and Freedom, 1750-1925* Pantheon, 1976); Leon F. Litwack, *Been in the Storm So Long: The Aftermath of Slavery* (Knopf, 1979); Willie Lee Rose, *Rehearsal for Reconstruction: The Port Royal Experiment* (Oxford University Press, 1976).

WHY THE CONFEDERACY LOST

Brian Holden Reid opens our two-headed debate on the American Civil War by arguing that the South failed to use revolutionary methods to full advantage.

The will to win; a Confederate print of Robert E. Lee and his colleagues stressing pride in the Southern military tradition.

MAO TSE-TUNG ONCE REMARKED THAT A revolutionary war is not a dinner party. A revolutionary war may be defined as the seizure of political power by armed force. The American Civil War was a good example of a revolutionary war – but one in which the side seeking to seize political power – the Southern Confederacy – failed to use revolutionary methods to its full advantage. What was the reason for this failure, and why did the Confederacy allow itself to be ground down in a war of attrition in a conflict in which the war aim on the Union side was nothing less than the unconditional surrender of the Confederate armies and the destruction of their warmaking potential? As nation states existed, according to Hobbes, either to maintain internal order or protect themselves from external aggression, this is the criterion by which to assess the strength of

Southern society to resist invasion and the imposition on it of political measures, including ultimately the emancipation of slavery, which it had gone to war to resist. Indeed it could be suggested that by 1864-65 the

Confederacy had no other justification for its existence other than to maintain armed forces in the field.

It was Napoleon, who was in a position to know, who said that in war moral factors are to the physical

From *History Today*, November 1988, pp. 32-41. Reproduced by kind permission of History Today, Ltd., 83-84 Berwick Street, London W1V 3PJ, England.

as three is to one. The study of social factors in the American Civil War presents a curious paradox. It is undoubtedly true that the Confederacy secured from its soldiers extraordinary courage, dedication and endurance, and the *élan* of Southern soldiers, their dash in the attack, the rebel 'yell', were legendary. But there is another side to the coin: defeatism, desertion, war weariness, doubts about the validity of the Southern cause and guilt over slavery. These factors need to be taken into account and given their due weight beside the more glorious elements in histories of the Confederacy's gallant struggle against great odds. They certainly need to be related to a fundamental problem which emerges from a study of the South's participation in the Civil War. In the Confederate states the war opened decisively and abruptly in April and July 1861 with the bombardment of Fort Sumter and the victory at the First Battle of Bull Run. These events were celebrated with great popular enthusiasm. The war ended just as abruptly with the surrender of General Robert E. Lee at Appomattox in April 1865, but without a glimmer of enthusiasm – a gritty determination to fight on irrespective of the odds. Why was this? Why did the war not continue, perhaps in some irregular form? Popular support for opening a war is usually a gauge for some measure of support for continuing it after defeat appears inevitable. Why did the South fail to field guerrilla columns like the resolute Boer commandos of 1899-1902? It may be that Southern nationalism as a socially binding force in war was more apparent than it was real.

There are two ways in which one state can exert power over another using military force. They have been well codified by the German military writer, Hans Delbruck, and developed as a tool to analyse the American Civil War by Major General J.F.C. Fuller. The first is the strategy of annihilation. In accordance with the strategy, the enemy's armies are destroyed by rapid manoeuvre and battle. This strategic form conforms to a more limited type of war and may be equated with the modern generic term, *blitzkrieg*. The second category is the strategy of

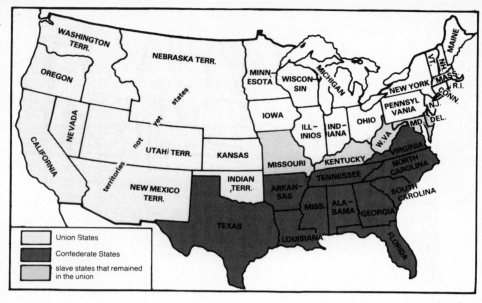

exhaustion or attrition: belligerents attempt to wear one another down in a long drawn out struggle. It was in the South's interests, if its independence could not be secured quickly, to persuade the North that it could not win because of the unacceptable human and material cost. Or alternatively, the North could destroy the South because Confederate resources were insufficient to prevent Union armies occupying large areas of territory and their war-making potential; the South would also find it difficult to prevent the creeping disintegration of its armed forces through war weariness and despondency. The strategy of exhaustion adheres more to an unlimited kind of war – 'total war'. In both forms of strategy, geographical, economic and moral factors are crucially important. 'Whereas in the first', commented General Fuller, 'the aim is the decisive battle, in the second battle is but one of several means, such as manoeuvre, economic attack, political persuasion and propaganda, whereby the political end is attained.'

There is a long tradition in American writing which contends that the South had a distinct military tradition, that the South was a singularly militaristic region of the United States. Marcus Cunliffe, in his influential and penetrating study, *Soldiers and Civilians: The Martial Spirit in America, 1775-1865* (1968), has shown convincingly that this view has been greatly exaggerated and that elements of a supposed Southern milit-

ary tradition were shared by the North. Nonetheless, these martial attitudes are important because they assist in delineating the Southern reaction to strategic reverses irrespective or whether they were unique to this region or not. They can be distinguished with reference to three main themes.

Firstly, optimism mixed with fatal dread. As General J.E.B. Stuart told George C. Eggleston in 1861:

I regard it as a foregone conclusion . . . that we shall ultimately whip the Yankees. We are bound to believe that anyhow; but the war is going to be a long and terrible one, first we've only just begun it, and very few of us will see the end.

There is a contradiction in Stuart's view: war consists in 'whipping' the enemy. But this does not appear to be sufficient. Faith in an eventual Confederate victory rested on the moral strength of the Southern cause – not on the political and economic strength of the Confederacy. Yet the view propounded by Stuart did not take into account the effects on morale of a strategy of attrition. As he observed in 1864, 'I would rather die than be whipped', a wish that was, alas, fulfilled at the Battle of Yellow Tavern later that year.

Secondly, a romantic nineteenth-century heritage. This attitude dominated the Southern outlook and was personified by Stuart again, although many others saw themselves as dashing cavaliers – gentlemen at war. As gentlemen they were chivalrous, like knights of the Middle Ages, a spirit that was captured by groups such as the 'Knights of the Golden Spurs'. This romantic spirit fed on the novels of Sir Walter Scott, which were immensely popular in the South. It persuaded many that war could be viewed in a distinctly glamorous, even sentimental light, so that campaigns took on the character of a 'quest', indeed a light-hearted 'lark'. Thus warfare came to be regarded as a game on an extended scale, such as Stuart's 'Ride Around McClellan's Army', which captured the South's imagination in June 1862.

Thirdly, these attitudes engendered an enigmatic sense of triumph. The enemy would be 'whipped', but his forces remained in the field despite the demonstrable superiority of Southern arms. The victories of Robert E. Lee reminded some Southern observers of the pyrrhic triumphs of Hannibal. Thus the final test would depend on the will of God.

These factors operated to sustain Southern morale while military operations appeared to favour the Confederacy. None of them, however, served to stiffen morale in a war of exhaustion. Despite their enigmatic asides to the contrary, most Southerners had expected a short war, or at least a longer war which conformed to the strategy of annihilation. This view contrasts clearly with the Boers of South Africa, for instance, who did not think in such European-orientated and romantic terms and were inured to the hardihood of the veldt.

Nevertheless a number of factors did operate in the South's favour. The Confederacy occupied a vast geographical area – certainly twice the size of South Africa which the British army had occupied with such difficulty in 1900-02. Clearly an army of occupation would have problems in holding down such an enormous area. Indeed it should be recalled that Sherman's 'March to the Sea' did not constitute an occupation of territory, only a raid in which his forces traversed three Southern states, destroying warmaking potential *en route*, but making no effort to hold them down. Secondly, the Confederate armies, despite setbacks, were still in being in 1864-65. Their organisation, equipment and performance in set-

piece battles were a considerable advance over comparable efforts in the American Revolution. Here was a considerable source of experienced manpower if Confederate commanders had chosen to disperse their forces in guerrilla groups throughout the countryside and in the back-country. Such a move would have been aided by the diffusion of the population over a great area and low wooded terrain, highly suitable for guerrilla warfare.

Finally, the importance of military time can hardly be underestimated in calculating the Confederacy's chances of survival. Time was on the side of the Confederacy, not in the sense that it required time to organise its resources (indeed time would dissipate these), but rather in that the South had to defer a military decision in the North's favour and assert its independence in the eyes of foreign powers. In other words, show to the world, and not least the federal government, that it could not be extinguished. Guerrilla action in the Carolinas against Lord Cornwallis in 1780-81 had achieved precisely this in the Revolution. But by 1865 a consensus had developed that the war should be ended. There had been a number of voices calling for the Confederacy to adopt a guerrilla strategy, the most famous being John Hunt Morgan, but these were a minority. How had this consensus taken such a firm hold? During the Boer War a mere 60,000 Boers had held at bay the might of the British Empire for two years, despite a much greater disparity of resources and the disadvantage of operating in a smaller theatre of operations.

In considering why the South collapsed so decisively, it should be recalled that loyalty in wartime is usually shaped and inspired by a state's war aims. But it was not altogether clear *what* the South was fighting for. Was it defence of property rights as exemplified by the defence of slavery? Or was it the independence of the Southern states? In pursuit of independence and as a vital aid to the maintenance of its armed forces by saving manpower, the Davis Administration began to emancipate slaves in 1865 in return for their joining the Confederate army. Considering the gigantic gamble represented by secession and

the impassioned rhetoric that had marked the Confederate states' ordinances of secession from the Union, and the fatal (and greatly exaggerated) threat that Southerners perceived faced the South's 'peculiar institution' after the election of the Lincoln Administration in 1860, this desperate action five years later surely forms a *reductio ad absurdum* of the Confederate position and strengthened the voices of those who had claimed in 1861 that slavery was better protected *within* the Union than without.

In addition, there can be no doubt that Southern morale was volatile. It oscillated between extremes of depression and exultation. By 1864, after extensive territory – especially in the west – had been given up, a widespread feeling developed that so much had been sacrificed for nothing. As Mary Chestnut wrote in her diary:

> Think of all those young lives sacrificed! If three for one be killed, what comfort is that? What good will that do? '... The best and bravest of one generation swept away!'... literally in the tide of blood.

Many Southerners could not understand that the South could afford to trade space for time, so long as her armed forces retained their fighting power. Southern morale had not the sophistication or endurance to sustain the blows inflicted by a strategy of exhaustion. Every withdrawal, even if it made military sense, depressed and caused consternation. One newspaper editor commented:

> Courts of Heaven resound with one great prayer; the supplications of a sorrowing people for the return of *peace* . . . appalled at the dire calamities which war has inaugurated, the heart of a nation pants for relief.

Many Southerners were prone to think that withdrawals or defeats in battle were a heavenly sign of the Lord's displeasure with the sins of the South. This only served to weaken morale. Typical comments in the newspapers and the pulpits include, 'Without special interposition we are a ruined people', and 'God will avenge himself on this American people, if this unnatural fratricidal butchery continues much longer'.

Confederate nationalism was a fragile reed. In a war against fellow Americans very few negative reference points existed for it to feed upon. Americans were not divided by any linguistic differences or fundamental cultural divergences of the type which so clearly differentiated the Boers from the British during the Boer War. The appeal of the Southern military tradition can be explained as an attempt to mark Southerners out as different from other Americans, inaccurately as it turns out. The only fundamental divergence that can be found concerns views about Negro slavery. But even here the Confederate Constitution imitated the Federal Constitution faithfully, save for additional clauses enshrining the protection of slavery. Yet by 1865, because of the pressure of Federal advances, the Confederate Government was beginning to emancipate slaves.

Finally, there was a widespread fear of what recourse to an uncontrolled revolutionary war would do to Southern society. This was especially strong among Confederate generals such as Robert E. Lee and Joseph E. Johnston, who were very keen to negotiate acceptable terms of surrender before guerrilla action developed on any sizeable scale. Irregular war might lead to the arming of blacks, and confirm the very worst Southern fears of race wars which had haunted whites before 1861. In the end, Southern leaders were not prepared to inflict guerrilla warfare on their people, who were in any case not prepared to carry its burdens.

In 1863 President Jefferson Davis claimed that Confederates:

... Have added another to the lessons taught by history for the instruction of man; ... they have afforded another example of the impossiblity of subjugating a people determined to be free.

Actually, the opposite was the case: the Confederacy showed that whatever advantages had accrued to it, a rebellion may be crushed if the rebels show insufficient *will* to seek and secure their independence. Southerners simply lacked a sense of national identity during the war years. They staked a claim for independence which mortgaged too heavily their moral and psychological resources.

WHY THE SOUTHERN CONFEDERACY collapsed in April 1865 is naturally a

---

***Bruce Collins** looks at the factors that made guerrilla warfare, Boer-style, an unlikely option for the South.*

---

question long debated by historians. Recent work on the subject has emphasised the lack of internal cohesion and sustained political will. It does not wholly concur in W.E. Gladstone's celebrated judgment of October 1862:

Jefferson Davis and other leaders of the South have made an army; they are making, it appears, a navy; and they have made what is more than either, they have made a nation.

Instead, it sees feebleness of national spirit and fragmentation of political power as key contributors to Confederate defeat. In assessing this weakening of morale, Dr Holden Reid has particularly focused on comparisons with the Boers' struggle against the British in 1899-1902 and on asking why the Confederates, unlike the Boers, failed to continue their fight for independence by guerrilla action once regular warfare had failed. The comparison of Confederates and Boers is most instructive, for the Boers resembled Southerners in conducting a farming people's war against fellow whites. The South African struggle may have been an imperial conflict but it was not a 'colonial war' in the classic nineteenth-century sense, where British regulars and allied levies overwhelmed non-European forces, often defective in training and/or weaponry. Boers and Southerners saw themselves as gallant individualists trying to preserve a traditional agrarian order against spreading industrialism and 'cosmopolitan' ideas. In many ways African subordination was less an issue for the Boers than slavery was for the Southerners, but Boers distrusted British policymakers' attitudes towards Africans. More generally, Boers and Confederates typically appear as opponents to national consolidation, advocates of localism, and upholders of increasingly anachronistic values. If one is thinking of nation-building and the

role of war in it, and of morale, the comparison of Boers and Confederates is far from being strained.

Yet comparison in detail reveals important contrasts which in turn help explain Confederate collapse. The Boers undertook extensive, prolonged guerrilla campaigns against the British from late 1900 to May 1902 partly because that style of warfare matched their conceptions of armed struggle. The Boers had no experience of formal warfare worth the name; small-scale frontier policing operations were all they had engaged in. No West Point of the high veldt turned out regular officers. Although very well equipped in 1899-1900, they saw no virtue in giving battle in classic style. Their preferred dispositions against British regulars in the field took the form of large-scale ambushes, with the aim of doing damage from a distance rather than rushing enemy lines and seizing enemy positions. Even at the height of their success, their military organisation creaked. At councils of war, at least in theory, corporals and cornets could outvote commandants. More important, the Boers lacked the manpower to sustain big battles once the British reinforced in strength. Their male population of arms-bearing age totalled only about 55,000. Their manpower losses in fighting *throughout* the war (about 7,000 killed) probably failed to match Confederate losses at Antietam. In terms of their training, past experience, and numbers, guerrilla warfare offered their *only* viable means of resistance once the British – to the surprise of some leading Boers – assembled an overwhelmingly superior army in South Africa during the winter of 1899-1900. From that point the Boers had little choice but to act, as was said at the time, as 'the gadfly of regular armies'. This was especially the case after no fewer than 13,900 men (of 35,000 initially raised) accepted Lord

Roberts' terms for laying down their arms during March-July 1900. But when the Boers switched to guerrilla action they did so under existing leaders and with existing forces. The total number of *bittereinders* who did not surrender until the war's end in 1902 (17,000) represented about half the strength of the initial Boer mobilisation in 1899. They formed not so much a stubborn rump, as a principal campaign force.

The Confederates possessed a very different military background and very different military aspirations. Nothing in their past prepared them for Antietam, Gettysburg or the Virginia campaign from May 1864. Formal warfare American-style was, like General Zachary Taylor's nickname, rough and ready. The greatest battle fought on Southern soil before 1861 was New Orleans in 1815, a bizarre and triumphant affair of assorted American contingents against British regulars. Indian warfare required planning, manpower, and commitment to more than just brief forays, but, again, it scarcely imbued officers or men with European military codes of behaviour. Yet Southerners entertained more formal ideas of warfare than the Boers. The crucial difference lay in the Mexican war of 1846-48 and in military education. The Southern states had provided a disproportionate contribution in manpower to the Mexican campaign, which required fairly elaborate planning and logistical organisation. And Confederate generals were mostly West Point graduates. They believed in decisive battle. They boasted that Southerners enjoyed superior classic military skills to Northerners. Guerrilla warfare was neither desirable nor necessary; and it was scarcely honourable. To the Boers, it was formal warfare that seemed alien or aberrant.

Confederates' distrust of guerrilla warfare stemmed also from the nature of the war they waged. While secession was a revolutionary act, in overthrowing the constitutional Union established in 1787-89, politicians, not generals, created the Confederacy and they extended its area in the spring of 1861 because the North challenged its legitimacy, not because they conquered any territory. In that sense, the Civil War did not fit a major pattern of twentieth-century revolutionary wars in which armed struggle carries a political movement to power and then helps consolidate that movement's dominant position. The Confederates achieved their initial objectives by political means; they fought the war defensively to secure Northern recognition of their independence. This fact partly explains also why the Confederate government lacked sweeping domestic powers. Accustomed to controlling their individual states' affairs, presiding over properly administered state governments, and imbued with highly articulated ideas of state rights, Confederate leaders distrusted central authority. They also distrusted unstructured power. Ultimately they would rather work within a political structure dominated by their enemies than take their chance with informal government appended to and supported by guerrilla movements.

But did such reluctance to resort to informal means after 1865 suggest a lack of will? Like all armies, including the Northern, the Confederate forces suffered from periodic losses of confidence, desertions, and soldiers' resentment against their officers. These characteristics have to be seen against the nature of the war, one not lightly called the first modern war for its heavy casualties sustained in frontal infantry assaults upon well-secured positions strengthened by artillery, and for its mass mobilisation of manpower. Desertions did not soar until autumn 1864, and did not reach epidemic proportions until early 1865, just before the surrender in April. The last returns of the Confederate armies gave 160,200 officers and men present, and no fewer than 198,500 absent from the flag. But by October 1864, the Confederate military cause was hopeless. The trans-Mississippi states of Arkansas, Louisiana and Texas had been virtually cut off from the rest of the Confederacy by the end of 1862. Those states in 1860 contained 1¾ million of the 9 million people of the Confederacy. Their isolation was no mean loss. The Confederacy was further fragmented when Sherman's army invaded Georgia and, on September 2nd, 1864, entered Atlanta. No Confederate army stood between Sherman and Lee's forces in Virginia. Sherman began marching northwards into South Carolina and subsequently into North Carolina in January 1865. The Confederate gov'ernment controlled very little territory by then. No wonder men slipped away to rejoin and perhaps rescue their families and homesteads.

This final collapse must be seen against the preceding years of armed resistance. It was remarkable that the South fought for so long. By the end of 1862 the Confederate position was already grim. The border South had not seceded. Much of Tennessee had been lost. The Federals had captured the Confederacy's principal city and port, New Orleans. They also seized Norfolk, Virginia's main port, and blockaded the key remaining Confederate ports of Charleston, Mobile and Savannah. The international front offered no comfort, since no country recognised the Confederacy as a belligerent. One wonders if Northern refusal to recognise Confederate independence would have survived equivalent pressure; an effective Confederate blockade of the Atlantic seaboard ports, Confederate capture of New York City and Chicago, Confederate control of a belt of land cutting off everything west of Indiana from the rest of the North, and the establishment of pro-Confederate governments in southern Pennsylvania, southern Ohio, and southern Indiana. Given the panic and dismay Northerners evinced when faced with far more limited Confederate advances, it seems improbable.

The collapse of morale during the winter of 1864-65 must be seen against several facts. First, during the war about one in every three Confederate males of military age died in, or as a result of, war service. Many more received injury. That amounted to an unprecedented level of blood-letting in a major modern war. When one adds that by early 1865 very large tracts of the Confederacy had been invaded, it is little wonder that morale sank. Those still in arms had every reason to feel hopeless. For their part, the Boers did not sustain a level of casualties anywhere approaching that withstood by the Confederates. And their guerrilla campaign petered out when the British army devastated their farms and livestock and removed civilians into concentration camps. If, as in so many historical instances, we are to judge whether the jug was half full or half empty, it is surely right to conclude that, by any standard of comparison, the Confederate measure of resistance looks more full than empty. Bell Wiley, the pre-eminent historian of Johnny Reb, warts and all, concluded:

> Few if any soldiers have had more than he of *élan*, of determination, of perseverance, and of the sheer courage which it takes to stand in the face of withering fire.

This certainly was a view shared by the Confederates' opponents. Grant in his memoirs recorded:

> Up to the battle of Shiloh, I, as well as thousands of other citizens, believed that the rebellion against the government would collapse suddenly and soon, if a decisive victory could be gained over any of its armies.

Sherman justified the scorched earth campaigns of 1864-65 on the grounds that:

> We are not only fighting hostile armies, but a hostile people and must make old and young, rich and poor, feel the hard hand of war, as well as organized armies.

It was this combination of civilian depredations, loss of military manpower, and loss of territory that wrecked the Confederate, just as it wrecked the Boer, war effort.

But the loss of an attainable political objective was also vital. When the Boers' Assembly of the People debated submission to the British in May 1902, one of their generals, Jan Smuts, took as his theme the keynote of Lincoln's Second Inaugural: 'to bind up the nation's wounds'. From a military point of view, he told the Assembly, the contest could continue, for 'We have still 18,000 men in the field, veterans, with whom you can do almost any work'. But the Assembly had to consider not merely this army, but the Afrikaner people, those in concentration camps as well as the free, those who had already given their lives, and 'those who will live after we are gone'. Independence was an honourable objective; 'But we may not sacrifice the Afrikaner people for that independence'. The Boers' prolongation of the war after 1900 had been aimed

at sapping British morale. Their dramatic raid into Cape Colony failed, however, to stir the 'Dutch' population there to revolt. And, in Britain, although strong Liberal attacks on General Kitchener's concentration camps – 'methods of barbarism' according to Campbell-Bannerman – surfaced in 1901, they failed to dent the Conservative Government's commitment to the war. By 1865, the Confederates faced a similar prospect of sacrificing the white South for an independence which could clearly not be attained. Invading the North had been tried and had failed to produce significant results. Confederate recourse to guerrilla fighting in 1865 would probably have stiffened Northern opinion even further politically against the Confederates and it is unlikely that the North would have refused the expenditure necessary to suppress guerrilla bands; the war, after all, had already cost enormous sums. Moreover, the last obvious chance for the Confederates to score a political settlement had already passed, just as the Boers' political strategy crumbled in 1902. For the Confederacy the last, best hope was the presidential election of 1864. If Lincoln had lost (and as late as August, before Atlanta fell on September 2nd, his prospects appeared by no means certain), some form of negotiated settlement might have been secured. Once Lincoln won re-election, then the Confederates had virtually no realistic political objective for which to fight. It was by no means illogical that Southern morale slumped after Atlanta's fall (the occasion of much public relief among Northerners) and after Lincoln's electoral victory in early November. Sherman set off from Atlanta on his march to the sea, and then inland, a few days after the Republicans' victory.

Behind these military and political events was a further cause of Confederate distress. However staunchly Confederate soldiers continued to fight the Yankees, their self-sacrifice could not stem the erosion of slavery at home. A recent study of wartime Georgia (by Clarence Mohr) shows how slavery became increasingly undermined, despite state politicians' efforts to maintain it in full force. Raids by the Federal navy drove coastal slave owners with their

valuable chattels inland. Inflation drove up land prices and made it difficult for these migrants to purchase fresh lands. Inflation also cut back on paternalism as clothing and other items became 'luxuries' for slave owners to bestow upon their work forces. The absence of white males on military service weakened racial control of the slaves. Rising demand for manufactured goods and urban services encouraged the hiring-out of slaves in towns, where, again, racial control became increasingly difficult. Slaves themselves exploited these openings to weaken the oppressive institution. Some ministers of religion began even to urge reform in the laws governing slavery. Finally, acute manpower shortages fostered proposals that slaves be armed and sent to war. As Howell Cobb, a former governor of Georgia and the United States Secretary of the Treasury, remarked in January 1865, 'If slaves will make good soldiers, our whole theory of slavery is wrong'. Georgia's experience was repeated throughout the South. If the very institution which Southerners left the Union to preserve against ultimate extinction was crumbling around them, it surely made more sense to uphold some vestige of white supremacy at home than to struggle for political objectives that, with Lincoln's re-election, were palpably unattainable. More generally, when the war ended, this collapse of traditional racial order was matched by the decline of settled relations between whites. Returning ex-soldiers indulged in a good deal of looting and lawlessness. Many Southerners saw any form of government as preferable to threatened anarchy.

Unfolding political circumstances also reduced possible pressures to continue resistance. Almost immediately after the Confederate surrender, Lincoln's assassination placed the vice-president, Andrew Johnson, in the White House. Johnson, a Tennessee Democrat before 1861, had been a wartime Unionist. While he often opposed the slave-holding planters as a social and political caste, his position towards the ex-Confederate leaders during 1865 shifted from hostility towards accommodation. So, too, Southern Unionists appointed to office within the shattered Confederacy lacked the numerical support and the ideological venom to press radical reform. Thus the political prospects in the former confederacy in the eight months following surrender resembled somewhat those obtaining in 1907-08 in South Africa. The ex-Confederates faced a leader who was no longer their wartime adversary, but a politician more amenable to their arguments. And many former secessionists accepted the need for cautious, conciliatory Southern leadership to restore the Southern economy and to safeguard social stability. Former Confederate leaders were soon winning elections to Congress. Interestingly enough, when Radical Republicans found this sort of reconstruction unacceptable and changed the very lenient rules of Andrew Johnson's political game, Southerners did indeed resort to armed resistance in 1868-71. But this took the form of widespread terrorism, directed by the Ku Klux Klan against black voting and office-holding.

Some efforts to continue the contest were made after Lee's surrender to Grant on April 9th. Jefferson Davis sought to fight on, possibly from across the Mississippi, but made it only to Georgia before being captured by Federal soldiers on May 10th. By then, it should have been clear that the Confederacy had fought itself to a standstill. Even the pugnacious Nathan Bedford Forrest refused to go on. 'To make men fight under such circumstances', he said in early May from southwest Alabama, 'would be nothing but murder'. His force was massively outnumbered, even for informal conflict. 'Any man who is in favor of a further prosecution of this war is a fit subject for a lunatic asylum'. Given the whole range of social, political and military events in the previous six months, that was surely an apposite judgement.

FOR FURTHER READING:

Marcus Cunliffe, *Soldiers and Civilians: The Martial Spirit in America, 1775-1865* (Little, Brown, 1968); George M. Frederickson, 'Blue Over Gray : Sources of Success or Failure in the Civil War', in G.M. Frederickson (ed), *A Nation Divided* (Minneapolis, 1975); Richard Beringer et al, *Why the South Lost the Civil War* (University of Georgia Press, 1986); Clarence L. Mohr, *On the Threshold of Freedom* (University of Georgia Press, 1986); James M. McPherson, *Battle Cry of Freedom* (Oxford University Press, 1988); Brian Holden Reid and John White, '"A Mob of Stragglers and Cowards" : Desertion from the Union and Confederate Armies', *The Journal of Strategic Studies*, VIII (March, 1985); Michael C.C. Adams, *Our Masters the Rebels* (Harvard University Press, 1978); Bruce Collins, *White Society in the Antebellum South* (Longman, 1985); Thomas Pakenham, *The Boer War* (Weidenfeld & Nicolson, 1979); W.K. Hancock, *Smuts*, Vol. I *The Sanguine Years 1870-1919* (Cambridge University Press, 1962)

This infantry lieutenant was in the thick of fighting during the Federal repulse of Pickett's Charge. The narrative he later wrote ranks as a classic eyewitness account of the Civil War's most crucial engagement.

A Union Officer at Gettysburg

Frank Aretas Haskell

No Civil War combat has been the subject of more continuing interest, study, or historical literature than the fighting that shook the countryside near Gettysburg, Pennsylvania, on July 1-3, 1863. During that three-day battle, General Robert E. Lee's Army of Northern Virginia wrestled with Federal forces under Major General George C. Meade. And no action in the war was to prove more crucial, or fateful in its consequences, than the frontal assault made on the afternoon of July 3 by some thirteen thousand Confederate infantrymen, commanded in part by Major General George Pickett.

Among those defending the Union positions in front of Cemetery Ridge that day was a thirty-five-year-old infantry lieutenant named Frank Aretas Haskell. A member of

Major General John Gibbon's staff, Haskell chanced to find himself near the focal point of Pickett's Charge, and he played a role in turning back the Confederate attack.

Several weeks after the battle, Haskell wrote a long and detailed narrative of what he had seen and experienced during the Gettysburg campaign. "Many things cannot be described by pen or pencil," he wrote; "such a fight [as Pickett's Charge] is one. Some hints and incidents may be given, but a description or picture, never." Despite Haskell's disclaimer, it can be argued that no other participant in Gettysburg wrote a better account of what happened there. Haskell's narrative has become acclaimed as a classic; his story of Pickett's Charge appears on the following pages.

FOR THE SAKE OF TELLING ONE THING AT A TIME I have anticipated events somewhat, in writing of this fight. I shall now go back to the starting point, four o'clock this morning, and, as other events occurred during the day second to none in the battle in importance, which I think I saw as much of as any man living, I will tell you something of them, and what I saw, and how the time moved on.

As the sun arose today the clouds became broken, and we had once more glimpses of sky and fits of sunshine—a rarity—to cheer us. From the crest, save to the right of the Second Corps, no enemy, not even his outposts, could be discovered along all the position where he so thronged upon the Third Corps yesterday. All was silent there. The wounded horses were limping about the fields; the ravages of the conflict were still perfectly visi-

From *American History Illustrated*, Summer 1988, pp. 12-21, 46-48. Reproduced through the courtesy of Cowles Magazines, publishers of *American History Illustrated*.

ble—the scattered arms and the ground thickly dotted with the dead—but no hostile foe.

The men were roused early, in order that their morning meal might be out of the way in time for whatever should occur. Then ensued the hum of an army not in ranks, [with the men] chatting in low tones, and running about and jostling among each other, rolling and packing their blankets and tents. They looked like an army of rag-gatherers while shaking these very useful articles of the soldier's outfit, for rain and mud in conjunction have not had the effect to make them very clean, and the wear and tear of service have not left them entirely whole. But one could not have told by the appearance of the men that they were in battle yesterday and were likely to be again today. They packed their knapsacks, boiled their coffee, and munched their hard bread, just as usual.

A native of Tunbridge, Vermont, Frank Aretas Haskell graduated from Dartmouth College in 1854. He practiced law in Madison, Wisconsin until June 1861, when he accepted a commission in the 6th Wisconsin Infantry. During the Battle of Gettysburg he served as a first lieutenant on the staff of General John Gibbon. This portrait shows Haskell several months after his experiences at Gettysburg.

As early as practicable the lines all along the left are revised and reformed, this having been rendered necessary by yesterday's battle, and also by what is anticipated today. It is the opinion of many of our generals that the rebel will not give us battle today, that he had enough yesterday; that he will be heading toward the Potomac at the earliest practicable moment, if he has not already done so. But the better and controlling judgment is that he will make another grand effort to pierce or turn our lines; that he will either mass and attack the left again, as yesterday, or direct his operations against the left of our center, the position of the Second Corps, and try to sever our line.

The losses were quite heavy yesterday, [and] some regiments are detached to other parts of the field—so there are less than six thousand men now in the two divisions, who occupy a line of about a thousand yards. Most of the way along this line upon the crest was a stone fence, constructed from small rough stones, a good deal of the way badly fallen down; but the men had improved it and patched it with rails from the neighboring fences, and with earth, so as to render it in many places a very passable breastwork against musketry and flying fragments of shell. These works are so low as to compel the men to kneel or lie down generally to obtain cover.

Near the right of the Second Division, and just by [a] little group of trees, this stone fence made a right angle, and extended thence to the front about twenty or thirty yards, where with another less than a right angle it followed along the crest again. The lines were conformed to these breastworks and to the nature of the ground upon the crest, so as to occupy the most favorable places. In some places a second line was so posted as to be able to deliver its fire over the heads of the first line behind the works, but such formation was not practicable all of the way. But all the force of these two divisions was in line, in position, without reserves, and in such a manner that every man of them could have fired his piece at the same instant.

I could not help wishing all the morning that this line of the divisions of the Second Corps were stronger; it was, so far as numbers constitute strength, the weakest part of our whole line of battle. What if, I thought, the enemy would make an assault here today, with two or three heavy lines, would he not sweep through that thin six thousand? But I was not General Meade, who alone had power to send other troops there; and he was satisfied with that part of the line as it was. He was early on horseback this morning, and rode along the whole line, looking to it himself, and with glass in hand sweeping the woods and fields in the direction of the enemy, to see if aught of him could be discovered.

Save the operations upon the right, the enemy, so far as we could see, was very quiet all morning. Occasionally the outposts would fire a little, and then cease. Movements would be discovered which would indicate the attempt on the part of the enemy to post a battery; our Parrotts would send a few shells to the spot, then silence would follow.

Between ten and eleven o'clock, over in a peach orchard some little show of the enemy's infantry was discovered. A few shells scattered the gray-backs; they again appeared, and it becoming apparent that they were only posting a skirmish line, no further molestation was offered them. A little after this some of the enemy's flags could be discerned over near the same quarter, above the top, and behind a small crest of a ridge. There seemed to be two or three of them— possibly they were guidons—and they moved too fast to be carried on foot. Possibly, we thought, the enemy is posting some batteries there. We knew in about two hours from this time better about the matter.

Eleven o'clock came. Not a sound of a gun or musket can be heard on all the field. The sky is bright with only the white fleecy clouds floating over from the west; the July sun streams down its fire upon the bright iron of the muskets in stacks upon the crest, and the dazzling brass of the Napoleons. The army lolls and longs for the shade, of which some get a hand's breadth from a shelter tent stuck upon a ramrod. The silence and sultriness of a July noon are supreme.

Now it so happened that just about this time of day a very original and interesting thought occurred to General Gibbon and several of his staff; that it would be a very good thing, and very good time, to have something to eat. When I announce to you that I had not tasted a mouthful of food since yesterday noon, and that all I had had to drink since that time, but the most miserable, muddy, warm water, was a little drink of whiskey that General Meade's aide-de-camp gave me last evening, and a cup of strong coffee that I gulped down as I was first mounting this morning, and further that, save the four or five hours in the night, there was scarcely a moment since that time but that I was in the saddle, you may have some notion of the reason of my assent to this extraordinary proposition.

We all came down to the little peach orchard where we had stayed last night, and, wonderful to see and tell, ever mindful of our needs, had it all ready, had our faithful John. There was an enormous pan of stewed chickens, and the potatoes and toast, all hot, and the bread and the butter, and tea and coffee.

General Hancock [was] of course invited to partake, and without delay we commenced operations. Stools are not very numerous—two in all—and these the two generals have by common consent. Our table was the top of the mess chest. By this the generals sat; the rest of us sat upon the ground and held our plates upon our laps. We were just well at it, when General Meade rode down to us from the line, accompanied by his staff, and by General Gibbon's invitation they dismounted and joined us. For the general commanding the Army of the Potomac, George, by an effort worthy of the person and the occasion, finds an empty cracker-box for a seat. The staff officers must sit upon the ground with the rest of us. Soon Generals Newton and Pleasanton, each with an aide, arrive. By an almost superhuman effort a roll of blankets is found, which, upon a pinch, is long enough to seat these generals both, and room is made for them. And, fortunate to relate, there was enough cooked for

us all, and from General Meade to the youngest second lieutenant we all had a most hearty and well-relished dinner. The generals ate and, after, lighted cigars, and under the flickering shade of a very small tree discoursed of the incidents of yesterday's battle, and of the probabilities of today.

And so the time passed on, each general now and then dispatching some order or message by an officer or orderly, until about half past twelve, when all the generals, one by one, rode off their several ways; and General Gibbon and his staff alone remained. We dozed in the heat, and lolled upon the ground, with half-open eyes. Our horses were hitched to the trees, munching some oats. A great lull [rested] upon all the field. Time was heavy, and for want of something better to do, I yawned and looked at my watch; it was five minutes before one o'clock. I returned my watch to its pocket, and thought possibly that I might go to sleep, and stretched myself upon the ground accordingly.

WHAT SOUND WAS THAT? There was no mistaking it! The distinct, sharp sound of one of the enemy's guns, square over to the front, caused us to open our eyes and turn them in that direction, when we saw directly above the crest the smoke of the bursting shell, and heard its noise. In an instant, before a word was spoken, as if that was the signal gun for general work, loud, startling, booming, the report of gun after gun, in rapid succession, smote our ears, and their shells plunged down and exploded all around us.

We sprang to our feet. In briefest time the whole rebel line to the west was pouring out its thunder and its iron upon our devoted crest. The wildest confusion for a few moments obtained among us. The shells came bursting all about. The servants ran terror-stricken for dear life, and disappeared. The horses hitched to the trees, or held by the slack hands of orderlies, neighed out in fright and broke away and plunged riderless through the fields.

The general at the first had snatched his sword, and started on foot to the front. I called for my horse; nobody responded. I found him tied to a tree nearby, eating oats, with an air of the greatest composure, which under the circumstances, even then struck me as exceedingly ridiculous. He alone, of all beasts or men near, was cool. He delayed me by keeping his head down, so I had time to see one of the horses of our mess wagon struck and torn by a shell. The pair plunge—the driver has lost the rein; horses, driver, and wagon go into a heap by a tree. Two mules close at hand, packed with boxes of ammunition, are knocked all to pieces by a shell.

General Gibbon's groom has just mounted his horse, and is starting to take the general's to him, when the flying iron meets him and tears open his breast; he drops dead; and the horses gallop away.

No more than a minute since the first shot was fired, and I am mounted and riding after the general. The mighty din that now rises to heaven and shakes the earth is not all of it the voice of rebellion; for our guns, the guardian lions of the crest, have opened their fiery jaws and begun to roar.

I [overtake] the general halfway up to the line. Before we reach the crest his horse is brought by an orderly. Leaving our horses just behind a sharp declivity of the ridge, on foot we go up among the batteries.

The men of the infantry have seized their arms, and behind their works, behind every rock, in every ditch, wherever there is any shelter, they hug the ground, silent, quiet, unterrified, little harmed. The enemy's guns, now in action, are in position at their front of the woods, along a ridge, and toward their right, behind a small crest in the open field, where we saw the flags this morning.

Their line is some two miles long, concave on the side toward us, and their range is from one thousand to eighteen hundred yards. A hundred and twenty-five rebel guns, we estimate, are now active, firing twenty-four-pound, twenty-, twelve-, and ten-pound projectiles, solid shot and shells, spherical, conical, spiral. The enemy's fire is chiefly concentrated upon the position of the Second Corps.

From the cemetery to Round Top, with over a hundred guns, and to all parts of the enemy's line, our batteries reply, of twenty- and ten-pound Parrotts, ten-pound projectiles as various in shape and name as those of the enemy. Captain Hazard, commanding the Artillery Brigade of the Second Corps, was vigilant among the batteries of his command, and they were all doing well. We had nothing to do, therefore, but to be observers of the grand spectacle of battle.

Who can describe such a conflict as is raging around us? To say that it was like a summer storm, with the crash of thunder, the glare of lightning, the shrieking of the wind, and the clatter of hailstones, would be weak. The thunder and lightning of these two hundred and fifty guns, and their shells, when smoke darkens the sky, are incessant, all-pervading, in the air above our heads, on the ground at our feet, remote, near, deafening, ear-piercing, astounding; and these hailstones are massy iron charged with exploding fire. Those guns are great infuriate demons, not of the earth, whose mouths blaze with snaky tongues of living fire, and whose murky breath, sulphur-laden, rolls around them and along the ground, the smoke of Hades. These grimy men, rushing, shouting, their souls in frenzy, plying the dusky globes and the igniting spark, are in their league, and but their willing ministers.

We thought that at the second Bull Run, at the Antietam, and at Fredericksburg on the 11th of December, we had heard heavy cannonading; they were but holiday salutes compared with this.

Besides the great ceaseless roar of the guns, which was but the background of the others, a million various minor sounds engaged the ear. The projectiles shriek long and sharp. They hiss, they scream, they growl, they sputter—all sounds of life and rage; and each has its different note, and all are discordant. Was ever such a chaos of sound before?

We note the effect of the enemy's fire among the batteries and along the crest. We see the solid shot strike axle, or pole, or wheel, and the tough iron and heart of oak snap and fly like straws. The great oaks there by Woodruff's guns heave down their massy branches with a crash, as if the lightning had smote them. The shells swoop down among the battery horses, standing there apart: a half-dozen horses start, they tremble, their legs stiffen, their vitals and blood smear the ground.

And these shot and shells have no respect for men either. We see the poor fellows hobbling back from the crest, or unable to do so, pale and weak, lying on the ground, with the mangled stump of an arm or leg dripping their lifeblood away, or with a cheek torn open or a shoulder smashed. And many, alas! hear not the roar as they stretch upon the ground with upturned faces and open eyes, though a shell should burst at their very ears.

Strange freaks these round shot play! We saw a man coming up from the rear with his full knapsack on, and some canteens of water held by the straps in his hands. He was walking slowly, and with apparent unconcern, though the iron hailed around him. A shot struck the knapsack, and it and its contents flew thirty yards in every direction; the knapsack disappeared like an egg thrown spitefully against the rock. The soldier stopped, and turned about in surprise, put up one hand to his back to assure himself that the knapsack was not there, and then walked slowly on again unharmed, with not even his coat torn.

Near us was a man crouching behind a small disintegrated stone, which was about the size of a common water bucket. He was bent up, with his face to the ground, in the attitude of a pagan worshipper before his idol. It looked so absurd to see him thus, that I went and said to him: "Do not lie there like a toad—why not go to your regiment and be a man?" He turned up his face with a stupid, terrified look upon me, and then without a word turned his nose again to the ground. An orderly that was with me at the time told me a few moments later, that a shot struck the stone, smashing it into a thousand fragments, but did not touch the man, though his head was not six inches from the stone.

All the projectiles that came near us were not so harmless. Not ten yards away from us a shell burst among some small bushes, where sat three or four orderlies, holding horses. Two of the men and one horse were killed. Only a few yards off a shell exploded over an open limber box in Cushing's battery, and almost at the same instant another shell over a neighboring box. In both the boxes the ammunition blew up with an explosion that shook the ground, throwing fire and splinters and shells far into the air and all around, and destroying several men.

We watched the shells bursting in the air, as they came hissing in all directions. Their flash was a bright gleam of lightning radiating from a point, giving place in a thousandth part of a second to a small, white, puffy cloud, like a fleece of the lightest, whitest wool. These clouds were very numerous. We could not often see the shell before it burst, but sometimes, as we faced toward the enemy, and looked above our heads, the approach would be heralded by a prolonged hiss, which always seemed to me to be a line of something tangible, terminating in a black globe, distinct to the eye, as the sound had been to the ear. The shell would seem to stop and hang suspended in the air an instant, and then vanish in fire and smoke and noise.

We saw the missiles tear and plow the ground. All in rear of the crest for a thousand yards, as well as among the batteries, was the field of their blind fury. Ambulances passing down the Taneytown road with wounded men were struck. The hospitals near this road were riddled. The house which was General Meade's headquarters was shot through several times, and a good many horses of officers and orderlies were lying dead around it. Riderless horses, galloping madly through the fields, were brought down by these invisible horse-tamers. Mules with ammunition, pigs wallowing about, cows in the pastures, whatever was animate or inanimate in all this range, were no exception to their blind havoc.

The percussion shells would strike and thunder, and scatter the earth, and their whistling fragments, the Whitworth bolts, would pound and ricochet, and bowl far away sputtering, with the sound of a mass of hot iron plunged in water: and the great solid shot would smite the unresisting earth with a sounding "thud," as the strong boxer crashes his iron fist into the jaws of his unguarded adversary.

Such were some of the sights and sounds of this great iron battle of missiles. Our artillery men upon the crest budged not an inch or intermitted; but, though caisson and limber were smashed, and guns dismantled, and men and horses killed, there, amidst smoke and sweat, they gave back without grudge nor loss of time in the sending, in kind whatever the enemy sent—an iron greeting to the rebellion, the compliments of the wrathful Republic.

An hour has droned its flight since first the roar began. There is no sign of weariness or abatement on either side. So long it seemed, that the din and crashing around began to appear the normal condition of nature there, and fighting man's element.

The general proposed to go among the men and over to the front of the batteries, so at about two o'clock he and I started. We went along the lines of the infantry as they lay there flat upon the earth a little to the front of the batteries. They were suffering little and were quiet and cool. How glad we were that the enemy were no better gunners, and that they cut the shell fuses too long. To the question asked the men: "What do you think of this?" the replies would be, "Oh, this is bully"; "We are getting to like it"; "Oh, we don't mind this." And so they lay under the heaviest cannonade that ever shook the continent, and among them a thousand times more jokes than heads were cracked.

We went down in front of the line some two hundred yards, and, as the smoke had a tendency to settle upon a higher plane than where we were, we could see near the ground distinctly all over the field, as well back to the crest where were our own guns as to the opposite ridge where were those of the enemy. No infantry was in sight save the skirmishers, and they stood silent and motion-

less—a row of gray posts through the field on one side, confronted by another of blue.

Under the shade of some elm trees, where we could see much of the field, we made seats of the ground and sat down. Here all the more repulsive features of the fight were unseen by reason of the smoke. We could see no men about the batteries. On either crest we could see the great flaky streams of fire of the opposing guns, and their white banks of swift convolving smoke; but the sound of the discharges was drowned in the universal ocean of sound. Over all the valley the smoke, a sulphur arch, stretched its lurid space; and through it always, shrieking on their unseen courses, thickly flew a myriad of iron deaths.

A shell struck our breastwork of rails up in sight of us, and a moment afterwards we saw the men bearing some of their wounded companions away from the same spot; and directly two men from there came down toward where we were and sought to get shelter in an excavation nearby, where many dead horses, killed in yesterday's fight, had been thrown. General Gibbon said to these men, more in a tone of kindly expostulation than of command: "My men, do not leave your ranks to try to get shelter here. All these matters are in the hands of God, and nothing that you can do will make you safer in one place than another."

The men went quietly back to the line at once. The general then said to me: "I am not a member of any church, but I have always had a strong religious feeling; and so, in all these battles, I have always believed that I was in the hands of God, and that I should be unharmed or not, according to his will. For this reason, I think it is, I am always ready to go where duty calls, no matter how great the danger."

Half past two o'clock, an hour and a half since the commencement, and still the cannonade did not in the least abate; but soon thereafter some signs of weariness and a little slacking of fire began to be apparent upon both sides. First we saw Brown's battery retire from the line, too feeble for further battle. Its position was a little to the front of the line. Its commander was wounded, and many of its men were so, or worse; some of its guns had been disabled, many of its horses killed; its ammunition was nearly expended. Other batteries in similar case had been withdrawn before to be replaced by fresh ones, and some were withdrawn afterwards.

Soon after the battery named had gone the general started to return, passing toward the left of the division, and crossing the ground where the guns had stood. The stricken horses were numerous, and the dead and wounded men lay about, and as we passed these latter, their low, piteous call for water would invariably come to us, if they had yet any voice left. I found canteens of water near—no difficult matter where a battle has been—and held them to livid lips; and even in the faintness of death the eagerness to drink told of the terrible torture of thirst.

But we must pass on. Our infantry was still unshaken, and in all the cannonade suffered little. The batteries had been handled much more severely. A great number

"Who can describe such a conflict as is raging around us? To say that it was like a summer storm, with the crash of thunder, the glare of lightning, the shrieking of the wind, and the clatter of hailstones, would be weak."

of horses have been killed—in some batteries more than half of all. Guns had been dismounted, a great many caissons, limbers, and carriages had been destroyed, and usually from ten to twenty-five men to each battery had been struck, at least along our part of the crest. Altogether the fire of the enemy had injured us much, both in the modes that I have stated, and also by exhausting our ammunition and fouling our guns, so as to render our batteries unfit for further immediate use.

The scenes that met our eyes on all hands among the batteries were fearful. In the number of guns active at one time, and in the duration and rapidity of their fire, this artillery engagement up to this time must stand alone and pre-eminent in this war. It has not been often, or many times, surpassed in the battles of the world. Two hundred and fifty guns, at least, rapidly fired for two mortal hours!

Of the injury of our fire upon the enemy, except the facts that ours was the superior position, if not better served and constructed artillery, and that the enemy's artillery hereafter during the battle was almost silent, we knew little. Of course during the fight we often saw the enemy's caissons explode, and the trees, rent by our shot, crashing about his ears; but we can from them alone infer but little of general results.

At three o'clock the last shot hummed and bounded and fell, and the cannonade was over. The purpose of General Lee in all this fire of his guns was to disable our artillery and break up our infantry upon the position of the Second Corps, so as to render them less an impediment to the sweep of his own brigades and divisions over our crest and through our lines. He probably supposed our infantry was massed behind the crest and the batteries; and hence his fire was so high and the fuses to his shells were cut so long, too long. The rebel general failed in some of his plans in this behalf.

The artillery fight over, men began to breathe more freely, and to ask: "What next, I wonder?" The battery men were among their guns, some leaning to rest and wipe the sweat from their sooty faces; some were handling ammunition boxes and replenishing those that were empty. Some batteries from the artillery reserve were moving up to take the places of the disabled ones; the smoke was clearing from the crest. There was a pause between acts, with the curtain down, soon to rise upon the great final act and catastrophe of Gettysburg.

We had passed by the left of the Second Division coming from the front; when we crossed the crest, the enemy was not in sight, and all was still. We walked slowly along in rear of the troops, by the ridge, cut off now from a view of the enemy or his position, and were returning to the spot where we had left our horses. General Gibbon had just said that he inclined to the belief that the enemy was falling back, and that cannonade was only one of his noisy modes of covering the movement. I said that I thought that fifteen minutes would show that, by all his bowling, the rebel did not mean retreat.

We were near our horses when we noticed Brigadier-General Hunt, chief of artillery of the army, near Woodruff's battery, swiftly moving about on horseback, and apparently in a rapid manner giving some orders about the guns. In a moment afterwards we met Captain Wessels, [judge advocate of the division] and the orderlies who had our horses. Captain Wessels was pale, and he said, excited: "General, they say the enemy's infantry is advancing!"

W E SPRANG INTO OUR SADDLES; a score of bounds brought us upon the all-seeing crest. To say that none grew pale and held their breath at what we saw and they then saw, would not be true. Might not six thousand men be brave and without shade of fear, and yet, before a hostile eighteen thousand, armed, and not five minutes' march away, turn ashy white?

None on that crest need now be told that *the enemy is advancing!* Every eye could see his legions, an overwhelming, resistless tide of armed men sweeping upon us! Regiment after regiment, and brigade after brigade, move from the woods and rapidly take their places in the lines forming the assault. Pickett's proud division, with some additional troops, holds their right; Pettigrew's (Heth's) their left. The first line, at short interval, is followed by a second, and that a third succeeds; and columns between support the lines.

More than half a mile their front extends; more than a thousand yards the dull gray masses deploy, man touching man, rank pressing rank, and line supporting line. Their red flags wave; their horsemen gallop up and down; the arms of eighteen thousand men, barrel and bayonet, gleam in the sun—a sloping forest of flashing steel. Right on they move in perfect order, without impediment of ditch or wall or stream, over ridge and slope, through orchard and meadow and cornfield, magnificent, grim, irresistible.

All was orderly and still upon the crest; no noise and no confusion. The men had little need of commands; for the survivors of a dozen battles knew well enough what this array in front portended, and they would be prepared to act when the right time should come. The click of the locks as each man raised the hammer to feel with his finger that the cap was on the nipple; the sharp jar as a musket touched a stone upon the wall when thrust, in aiming, over it; and the clinking of the iron axles, as the guns were rolled up by hand a little further to the front, were quite all the sounds that could be heard.

Cap boxes were slid around to the front of the body; cartridge boxes opened; officers opened their pistol holsters. Such preparations [and] little more, was needed. The trefoil flags, colors of the brigades and divisions, moved to their places in rear; but along the lines in front, the grand old ensign that first waved in battle at Saratoga, in 1777, and which these people coming would rob of half its stars, stood up as the sergeants sloped its lance toward the enemy.

General Gibbon rode down the lines, cool and calm, and in an unimpassioned voice he said to the men: "Do not hurry, men, and fire too fast; let them come up close before you fire, and then aim low and steadily."

The coolness of their general was reflected in the faces of his men. Five minutes had elapsed since first the enemy had emerged from the woods—long enough for us to note and weigh some of the elements of mighty moment that surrounded us: the disparity of numbers between the assailants and the assailed; that, few as were our numbers, we could not be supported or reinforced until support would not be needed, or would be too late, that upon the ability of the two trefoil divisions to hold the crest, and repel the assault, depended not only their own safety or destruction, but also the honor of the Army of the Potomac and defeat or victory at Gettysburg. Should these advancing men pierce our line, and become the entering wedge that would sever our army asunder, what hope there be afterward?

Our skirmishers open a spattering fire along the front, and, fighting, retire upon the main line. Then the thunders of our guns and their sounding shells smite the enemy.

The general said I had better go and tell General Meade of this advance. To gallop to General Meade's headquarters, to learn there that he had changed them to another part of the field, [to send a dispatch] to him by the Signal Corps, and to be again upon the crest, were but the work of a minute.

All our available guns are now active, and as the range grows shorter and shorter they change to shrapnel, and from shrapnel to canister; but in spite of shells and shrapnel and canister, without wavering or halt, the hardy lines of the enemy continue to move on. The rebel guns make no reply to ours, and no charging shout rings out today, as is the rebel wont; but the courage of these silent men amid our shot seems not to need the stimulus of other noise.

The enemy's right flank sweeps near Stannard's bushy crest, and his concealed Vermonters rake it with a well-delivered fire of musketry. The gray lines do not halt or reply, but withdrawing a little from that extreme they still move on. And so across all that broad, open ground they have come, nearer and nearer, nearly half the way, with our guns bellowing in their faces, until now a hundred yards, no more, divide our ready left from their advancing right.

First Harrow's breastworks flame, then Hall's, then Webb's. As if our bullets were the fire coals that touched off their muskets, the enemy in front halts and his countless level barrels blaze back upon us. The rattling storm soon spreads to the right, and the blue trefoils are vying with the white. All along each hostile front, a thousand yards, with narrowest space between, the volleys blaze and roll.

When the rebel infantry had opened fire our batteries soon became silent, and this without their fault, for they were foul by long previous use. They were the targets of the concentrated rebel bullets, and some of them had expended all their canister; but they were not silent before Rorty was killed, Woodruff had fallen mortally wounded, and Cushing, firing almost his last canister, had dropped dead among his guns. The conflict is left to the infantry alone.

UNABLE TO FIND MY GENERAL when I returned to the crest after transmitting his message to General Meade, I gave up hunting as useless and [rode] toward the right of the Second Division, with purpose to watch the progress of the battle, then to be ready to take part, according to my own notions. The conflict was tremendous, but I had seen no wavering in all our line. Wondering how long the rebel ranks, deep though they were, could stand our sheltered volleys, I had come near my destination, when—great heaven! were my senses mad?—the larger portion of Webb's brigade—my God, it was true—there by the group of trees and the angles of the wall, was breaking from the cover of the works, and without order or reason, with no hand uplifted to check them, was falling back, a fear-stricken flock of confusion! The fate of Gettysburg hung upon a spider's single thread!

A great, magnificent passion came on me at the instant. My sword that had always hung idle by my side, the sign of rank only, in every battle, I [now] drew. All rules and proprieties were forgotten, all considerations of person and danger and safety despised; for, as I met the tide of those rabbits, the damned red flags of the rebellion began to thicken and flaunt along the wall they had just deserted, and one was already waving over the guns of the dead Cushing. I ordered those men to "*halt*," and "*face about*," "*fire*," and they heard my voice, and gathered my meaning, and obeyed my commands.

On some unpatriotic backs the flat of my sabre fell, not lightly; and at its touch their love of country returned, and with a look at me as if I were the destroying angel, they again faced the enemy.

General Webb soon came to my assistance. He was on foot, but he was active, and did all that one could do to repair the breach or to avert its calamity. The men that had fallen back, facing the enemy, soon regained confidence and became steady.

This portion of the wall was lost to us, and the enemy [had] gained the cover of the reverse side, where he now stormed with fire. But Webb's men, with their bodies in part protected by the abruptness of the crest, now sent back in the enemy's faces as fierce a storm. Some scores of venturesome rebels that, in their first push at the wall, had dared to cross at the further angle, and those that had desecrated Cushing's guns, were promptly shot down, and speedy death met him who should raise his body to cross it again.

At this point little could be seen of the enemy, by reason of his cover and the smoke, except the flash of his muskets and his waving flags. Those red flags were accumulating at the wall every moment, and they maddened us as the same color does the bull.

Webb's men were [now] falling fast, and he is among them to direct and encourage; but however well they may now do, with that walled enemy in front, with more than a dozen flags to Webb's three, it soon becomes apparent that in not many minutes they will be overpowered, or that there will be none alive for the enemy to overpower.

Webb has but three regiments, all small—and he must have speedy assistance or this crest will be lost. Oh! where is Gibbon, where is Hancock, some general, anybody, with the power and will to support this wasting, melting line? I thought of Hays upon the right; but from the smoke and roar along his front, it was evident he had enough upon his hands. Doubleday upon the left was too far off, and too slow.

As a last resort I resolved to see if Hall and Harrow could not send some of their commands to reinforce Webb. I galloped to the left in the execution of my purpose, and as I attained the rear of Hall's line, from the nature of the ground there and the position of the enemy, it was easy to discover the reason and the manner of this gathering of rebel flags in front of Webb. The enemy, emboldened by his success in gaining our line by the group of trees and the angle of the wall, was concentrating all his right against, and was further pressing that point. There was the stress of his assault—there would he drive his fiery wedge to split our line. In front of Harrow's and Hall's brigades he had been able to advance no nearer than when he first halted to deliver fire; and these commands had not yielded an inch.

To effect the concentration before Webb, the enemy would march the regiment on his extreme right of each of his lines, by the left flank, to the rear of the troops, still halted and facing to the front, and so continuing to draw in his right. When they were all amassed in the position desired, he would again face them to the front, and advance to the storming. This was the way he made the wall before Webb's line blaze with his battle flags, and such was the purpose then of his thick-crowding battalions.

Not a moment must be lost. Colonel Hall I found just in rear of his line, sword in hand, noting all that passed, and directing the battle of his brigade. The fire was constantly diminishing now in his front. "How is it going?" Colonel Hall asked me as I rode up. "Well, but Webb is hotly pressed, and must have support, or he will be overpowered. Can you assist him?" "Yes." "You cannot be too quick." "I will move my brigade at once." He gave the order, and in briefest time I saw five friendly colors hurrying to the aid of the imperilled

three.

To Webb's brigade, pressed back as it had been from the wall, the distance was not great from Hall's right. The regiments marched by the right flank. Colonel Hall superintended the movement in person. The movement, as it did, attracting the enemy's fire, and executed in haste, as it must be, was difficult; but in reasonable time Hall's men were fighting gallantly side by side with Webb's before the all-important point.

I did not stop to see all this movement of Hall's but from him I went further to the left, to the First Brigade. General Harrow I did not see, but his fighting men would answer my purpose as well. [All of the] men that I could find, I took over to the right at the *double quick*.

As we were moving to the other brigades of the division, from my position on horseback I could see that the enemy's right, under Hall's fire, was beginning to stagger and to break. "See," I said to the men, "see the '*chivalry*,' see the gray-backs run!" The men saw, and as they swept to their places by the side of Hall's and opened fire, they roared, and this in a manner that said more plainly than words—*the crest is safe!*

CHANGES OF POSITION and new phases having occurred, some further description is necessary. Before the Second Division the enemy is massed, the main bulk of his force covered by the ground that slopes to his rear, with his front at the stone wall. Between his front and us extends the very apex of the crest. All there are left of the White Trefoil Division—yesterday morning there were three thousand eight hundred; this morning there were less than three thousand; at this moment there are somewhat over two thousand—are below, or behind the crest, in such a position that by the exposure of the head and upper part of the body they can deliver their fire in the enemy's faces along the top of the wall. By reason of the disorganization incidental, in Webb's brigade, to his men having broken and fallen back, in the two other brigades to their rapid and difficult change of position under fire, and in all the division, to severe and continuous battle, formation of companies and regiments in regular ranks is lost; but commands, companies, regiments, and brigades are [blended] and intermixed—an irregular, extended mass—men enough, if in order, to form a line of four or five ranks along the whole front of the division.

The twelve flags of the regiments wave defiantly at intervals along the front; at the stone wall, at unequal distances from ours of forty, fifty or sixty yards, stream nearly double this number of battle flags of the enemy.

These changes accomplished on either side, and the concentration complete, although no cessation or abatement of the general din of conflict since the commencement had at any time been appreciable, now it was as if a new battle, deadlier, stormier than before, had sprung from the body of the old.

The jostling, swaying lines on either side boil and roar, and dash their foamy spray, two hostile billows of a fiery ocean. Thick flashes stream from the wall; thick volleys answer from the crest. No threats or expostulation now; only example and encouragement. All depths of passion are stirred, and all combative fire, down to their deep foundations. Individuality is drowned in a sea of clamor; and timid men, breathing the breath of the multitude, are brave. The frequent dead and wounded lie where they stagger and fall. Webb, Hall, Devereux, Mallon, Abbott, among the men where all are heroes, are doing deeds of note.

Now the loyal wave rolls up as if it would overleap its barrier, the crest; pistols flash with the muskets. My "Forward to the wall" is answered by the rebel counter-command, "Steady, men," and the wave swings back. Again it surges, and again it sinks. These men of Pennsylvania, on the soil of their own homesteads, the first and only ones to flee the wall, must be the first to storm it.

"Sergeant, forward with your color. Let the rebels see it close to their eyes once more before they die." The color sergeant of the Seventy-second Pennsylvania, grasping the stump of the severed lance in both his hands, waved the flag above his head, and rushed toward the wall. "Will you see your color storm the wall alone?" One man only started to follow. Almost half-way to the wall, down go color bearer and color to the ground—the gallant sergeant is dead.

The line springs; the crest of the solid ground, with a great roar, heaves forward its maddened load—men, arms, smoke, fire, a fighting mass; it rolls to the wall: flash meets flash; the wall is crossed; a moment ensues of thrusts, yells, blows, shots, an undistinguished conflict, followed by a shout, universal, that makes the welkin ring again; and the last and bloodiest fight of the great battle of Gettysburg is ended and won.

The hard fight was getting into the fight at all

After 130 years, Americans are finally learning about the late, anguishing role black soldiers played in the Civil War

Jack Fincher

It was a charge to remember, that doomed three-quarter-mile rush down a naked beach and up the bristling earthworks of Fort Wagner. When it was over nearly half the 54th Massachusetts, a black regiment of 600 volunteers, had been killed, wounded or captured. Col. Robert Gould Shaw, 25, the pride of his Yankee abolitionist family, fell at the head of his men and was buried in a common sandy grave "with his niggers," as Confederates who buried him would put it.

For some five million Americans who have lately seen the film *Glory*, as well as the recent monumental public television history of the Civil War, the 54th's brave action has stirred interest in what was, for decades, too often ignored—the role of black men in the war that ended slavery. Some 130 years ago, too, Americans were stirred by that demonstration of black courage. "If this Massachusetts Fifty-Fourth had faltered when its trial came," the New York *Tribune* would write, 200,000 black troops "for whom it was a pioneer would never have been, put into the field."

But crucial as that moment in mid-July 1863 was, the men of the 54th were not the only pioneers. Black courage in battle had been proved in the American Revolution and in the War of 1812, though white Americans kept refusing to credit it. During the Civil War, the hardest problem for black men was not in being brave; it was in getting a chance to fight at all. At every step, they were confronted with racial scorn and fear, created by the long existence of slavery itself.

Few events offer a better way into the agonies and ambiguities involved than a scene that *Glory* didn't show. Only a few days before the black troops of the 54th stormed Rebel ramparts outside Charleston, South Carolina, other blacks—one related to a member of the 54th—had been killed in the streets of New York City by white rioters.

Most of this was the work of immigrants protesting President Lincoln's latest call for a new federal draft. Union armies had just won their two greatest victories of the war. On July 3, 1863, Lee was defeated at Gettysburg, ending Northern fears that England and France might recognize the South as an independent nation. The next day Vicksburg fell, after 47 days of siege, all but cutting the South in two and threatening to make the Mississippi a Union canal. As usual, casualties had been appalling, and volunteers had long since proved insufficient. But the draft had certain loopholes. Anyone could be exempted from service till the next draft call by paying the government $300, or exempted till war's end by hiring a substitute to fight in his place.

Economics and racism thus combined to make scapegoats of free blacks. Predictably, it had been rumored they were just waiting to step into the jobs left behind when white New York conscripts marched away. The nation was already two years into a war that would claim as many lives as all other U.S. wars including Vietnam. Yet as everyone knew, only a handful of blacks had done any fighting.

4. CIVIL WAR AND RECONSTRUCTION

"This is a white man's war!"

How this came to be so is a tortuous chronicle of politics and racism. When the war started, most men in the North, including military officers, thought that blacks couldn't fight. Early in the war blacks who tried to form a defensive home guard in Cincinnati were threatened by a mob and dispersed by police. Whites shouted at them, "We want you damned niggers to keep out of this, this is a white man's war!" But in political terms, the successful effort to keep blacks from fighting for the Union and their freedom was to a large extent the work of Abraham Lincoln, the man now rightly known to history as the Great Emancipator.

Well into the fighting, Lincoln hoped to save the country from the appalling destruction of a long war, somehow bringing the Southern states back, through a negotiated cease-fire and some informal plan for

Before-and-after pictures like these—of a drummer boy in a new black regiment—encouraged enlistment.

the gradual and recompensed emancipation of slaves. Yankee abolitionists were still seen as zealots and troublemakers. Political support for the war was shaky in the North, and most of it came from people who wanted to save the Union, not get killed to free the slaves. Preserving the Union was Lincoln's rallying cry. Well into 1862, he made his priorities clear: "If I could save the Union without freeing any slave, I would do it; and if I could save it by freeing all the slaves I would do it; and if I could save it by freeing some and leaving others alone, I would also do that." Meanwhile it was all-important to keep the slave-owning Border States, Kentucky, Missouri, Delaware and Maryland, from joining the South. (In Maryland's case, he would demonstrate his deadly seriousness on this subject by sending federal troops to shut down a session of the State Legislature meeting in Frederick when representatives seemed about to vote for secession.)

Blacks petitioned the President early on for a chance to fight and flocked to enlist. Everywhere they were rejected. Even after Congress had authorized black troops, when Indiana offered to contribute two black regiments, Lincoln replied, "To arm the negroes would turn 50,000 bayonets from the loyal Border States against us that were for us."

The great antislavery leader Frederick Douglass called upon Lincoln to use blacks in the war. "Once let the black man get upon his person the brass letters, U. S., let him get an eagle on his button, and a musket on his shoulder," Douglass declared, "and there is no power on earth which can deny that he has earned the right to citizenship in the United States." As new calls for volunteers were made, he struck pungently at what he saw as the illogic and unfairness of Lincoln's position. The government keeps screaming "Men, men! send us men!" he wrote. The edifice of state was burning, but the government would let only "Indo-Caucasian hands" help put out the fire.

Pressure from blacks eager to fight, from abolitionists and from a few Army officers who needed men, as well as changing circumstances, eventually altered Lincoln's policy. Along the way, convoluted legal questions involving the Constitution and slaves as property had to be got around. According to the Supreme Court's 1857 Dred Scott decision and the Fugitive Slave Act, slaves were beings without the rights of citizens, property that had to be returned to owners, no matter what.

After secession but before the war had started at Fort Sumter, Lincoln tried to limit the rift between the states by pledging in his First Inaugural Address that the government would not interfere with slavery where it already existed. Constitutional law naturally applied in more dramatic and perplexing terms to the thousands of slaves who soon began fleeing their white masters and taking refuge behind Union lines.

War had hardly begun, in May 1861, when Benjamin Butler, a worldly political general from Massachusetts, adopted the dodge of treating escaped slaves not as returnable property but as captured "contraband of war." On August 30, Gen. John C. Frémont, a hero for his role in claiming California, and the defeated Republican candidate for President on an antislavery platform in 1856, tried to expand the franchise. Caught in a mini civil war in Missouri, he put the whole state under martial law and declared that slaves of anyone who took up arms against the Union were forfeit—and forever free. Lincoln sacked him. In December, Secretary of War Simon Cameron publicly declared that a time would come when the government would not only have the right but the duty to use freed slaves in the war to suppress rebellion. Cameron had been a loose cannon in other ways, too. Now, Lincoln banished him as U.S. Minister to Russia.

In the new year Lincoln's new Secretary of War, Edwin Stanton, reiterated the Administration's position: blacks, slave or free, were not to fight. But in May 1862, in the Sea Islands and along the coasts of South Carolina, Georgia and Florida, which Union forces had occupied with little resistance, Maj. Gen. David Hunter proclaimed martial law, telling all slaves in his jurisdiction that they were free. In South Carolina he began recruiting them, sometimes at gunpoint. Without approval from Washington, however, the experiment was abandoned.

Throughout the year, casualties kept mounting. So did the political drumbeat from black newspapers and abolitionists, and from officers tantalized by a source of soldiery nearby, yet unable to make use of it. Though George B. McClellan had mostly managed to avoid fighting, other generals had engaged the enemy, with bloody results. In the spring of 1862 at the Battle of Shiloh on the Tennessee River, nearly 100,000 men fought for two days, with 23,000 casualties. It was a draw, with a slight edge to a chunky, unshaven, cigar-smoking general named Ulysses S. Grant. After Shiloh, General Grant gave up all hope of saving the Union with just a few victories and some kind of political compromise. It would take total war and "complete conquest" of the South. And that meant many more men to kill or be killed.

Down in New Orleans, where the North established a large bridgehead at the mouth of the Mississippi, astute and well-connected General Butler had lately become military governor of New Orleans. For weeks he had dickered with Washington about how to deal with the problem of using blacks in the war. Now he took action, knowing that at last he might receive official approval. On August 22, Butler shrewdly recruited as part of the federal forces in the area the 1,400-man Louisiana State Guard, an elite force of free black volunteers. They had formed the guard themselves, but the South never called them to combat (SMITHSONIAN, March 1979). When Union forces took

New Orleans the guard refused to follow the retreating Confederate Army.

Feeling such pressures, Lincoln came to the same conclusion as Grant, and was at last sure that the war could not be won without the abolition of slavery. In the summer of 1862 he secretly told his Cabinet about the Emancipation Proclamation. It would be announced after the next successful battle, to take effect in January 1863. Even so, freedom would be limited to slaves in areas in open rebellion against the Union. Slavery was still firmly in place in the Border States and Tennessee, and in Union-occupied portions of Virginia and Louisiana.

The dam was broken, however. Congress passed a new Militia Act, permitting the President to use "as many persons of African descent" as he needed "for suppression of the Rebellion." It also repealed a 1792 ordinance barring "persons of color" from serving in the militia. Free blacks and ex-slaves would be recruited, but they were regarded as laborers and their pay was not to be as much as that of white soldiers—$10 a month less clothing expenses, rather than $13 plus clothing expenses. They were not to have black officers, either.

When Frederick Douglass confronted Lincoln personally about these discrepancies, he was told that the whole idea of blacks as soldiers would be hard for the country to digest. Once that had happened, matters such as pay would be reconciled. About 100 blacks did eventually get commissions in the Union Army; 2,000 became noncommissioned officers.

In September, at Antietam Creek in Maryland, the Union Army under General McClellan finally gave Lincoln something like the victory he needed. Five days after the battle, the President made public his preliminary Emancipation Proclamation. In response, the South declared that captured slaves in Yankee uniforms, as well as their white officers taken in battle, would be executed. Hundreds of Northern soldiers deserted rather than serve with blacks; two Illinois regiments had to be disbanded as a result.

Nevertheless, the recruiting of blacks in Northern states went on apace. Wherever the Union armies were operating, teams of recruiters were authorized to offer $100 to $300 enlistment bounties. This was the period in which Gov. John Andrew of Massachusetts created the celebrated 54th Regiment, mostly composed of literate freemen, recruiting young Col. Robert Gould Shaw as its commanding officer.

Frederick Douglass proved right about the effect of weapons and uniforms on ex-slaves. Especially to men who risked terrible punishment, perhaps death, to escape—who stumbled on foot through the dark toward distant guns in the hope the guns were in friendly hands—the soldierly ritual that followed enlistment had considerable power. Each man was stripped and bathed, his old clothes burned, his Army blues put on.

One white soldier described the process: "Put a United States uniform on his back and the *chattel* is a *man*." Black recruit Elijah Marrs, who escaped slavery in Kentucky to join the Union Army, remembered the moment more simply: "I felt freedom in my bones."

Many were treated well and trained well. But many were brutalized, even by Army standards—until some said they were no better off than slaves. Many got inferior equipment and medical care. They died of diseases in the field at nearly twice the rate of whites. Of some 180,000 black men to serve in the Army, only about 2,800 died in combat; 34,000 were taken by disease.

The matter of inferior pay was somehow harder to bear, perhaps because it involved both hardship and principle. One of *Glory's* most dramatic scenes, in which the young Colonel Shaw joins his men in tearing up their pay chits rather than take less money than whites, did not actually take place. But Shaw did write Governor Andrew that his regiment would refuse pay until the matter was corrected. In this Shaw was an exception. All over the country white officers backed their troops in the struggle for equal pay, but ultimately urged them to take what they could and get on with the war. So did many black leaders. But some soldiers remained adamant. "Do we not fill the same ranks?" a private wrote. "Do we not take up the same length of ground in the grave yard?"

The government continued to welch on pay (it did not make amends until 1864 and then only partially). The situation was ripe for some kind of martyr. In 1863, after rumors of the New York draft riots and the Fort Wagner charge had spread throughout the Army, William Walker, a black sergeant in the 3d South Carolina Volunteers, became one. He ordered his men to stack arms because they would "not do duty any longer for $7 per month." It was clear that he had no idea of the gravity of his act in an army in wartime. Tried and convicted, Walker was executed for mutiny.

The 180,000 black soldiers in uniform by war's end represented nearly 10 percent of all Union forces. This at a time when blacks accounted for only 1 percent of the North's population, as opposed to 13 percent of the whole country, the same percentage as today. Despite their own zeal to volunteer, and objections from their own officers and abolitionist leaders, relatively few were ever allowed to see action. Black soldiers drew excessive fatigue duty, backbreaking work behind the lines that took time away from the training on which their lives might depend in battle. One private from Louisiana actually wrote a letter of complaint to the President: "Instead of the musket It is the Spad[e] and the Wheelbarrow and the Axe."

The first real clash between black troops officially recruited into the Union Army and Confederate soldiers did not take place until the war was almost half over. The time was January 1863. The outfit was the 1st South Carolina Infantry. The commander, by no coincidence,

was Thomas Higginson, a Boston abolitionist already renowned for supporting the idea of blacks as potential combat soldiers. The mission: to free slaves and confiscate lumber at the head of the St. Mary's River on the border between Georgia and Florida.

Shortly after midnight, at the head of a hundred handpicked infantry, Higginson marched through thick forest toward a Confederate camp—and a skirmish that, partly because of his eloquence, has become known to history as the Battle of the Hundred Pines.

"Nobody knows anything about these men who has not seen them in battle," Higginson wrote in his remarkable memoir, *Army Life in a Black Regiment.* "I find that I myself knew nothing." In the dark his troops met some Rebels. "They were as cool and wary," Higginson reported, "as if wild turkeys were the only game," and they fought with a "fiery energy" he had seen matched only by French Zouaves. A brief firefight followed, in which one soldier was killed and seven wounded, as against ten of the enemy killed, including their lieutenant. The rest were routed. Glowingly, Higginson reported, "No officer in this regiment now doubts that the key to the successful prosecution of this war lies in the unlimited employment of black troops."

These views were intended for Northern newspapers, but other observers confirmed them. The enthusiasm, loyalty and humor of black troops were all noted. White commanders, accustomed to having their authority resented, were pleased by the touching allegiance many enlistees showed them. Black volunteers in South Carolina were on their own home ground and new to war. When the bugle sounded for battle, they didn't go on sick call in droves to avoid fighting, as now often happened in battle-weary white outfits.

On the other side of the war, on the lower Mississippi, where Adj. Gen. Lorenzo Thomas had been raising black regiments from escaped slaves, officers also had a high regard for the new troops. Col. Robert Cowden, later the commanding officer of the 59th U.S. Colored Infantry, noted that the Army had to get rid of "plantation manners," including "awkward bowing and scraping, with hat under arm, and with averted look." Once uniformed and trained the men were good soldiers, he reported, except that, because their only free time as slaves had been during the hours of darkness, they were used to leaving camp at night. Strict discipline was needed, said Cowden, so that they would retire at 9 P.M. and "*stay retired* till reveille."

Stereotyping was common. When given a chance to fight, black troops seemed to excel at quick, all-out, headlong assault—which was encouraged because of the psychological effect it was supposed to have on Confederate fears of uncontrollable slave "savagery." As a result, the notion grew that black soldiers were of little use in tough, rearguard action but charged with a "terrible fierceness." This general impression persisted, despite a brave showing in two bitter fights that occurred far away on the Mississippi.

Complete control of the great river required the capture of Port Hudson in Louisiana, another Rebel bastion on the river, 250 miles south of Vicksburg. A short march north from Baton Rouge, Port Hudson was defended by 6,000 Confederate troops in heavily fortified positions and had been under siege for weeks that spring. On May 27, 1863, among those forces ordered to make the almost impossible assault were elements of the 1st and 3d Louisiana Regiments, both black. But the 1st had been the Louisiana State Guard, the only regiment with black officers, most notably Capt. André Callioux, a Paris-educated Louisiana landowner who proudly called himself the blackest man in New Orleans.

Six times, a thousand black soldiers of the 1st and 3d charged across an open field against high battlements. Six times, they were driven back by rifle and mortar fire, grapeshot and canister. After each charge Callioux led them forward again, the last time with his arm smashed at the elbow by a rifle ball. There were 212 casualties, with nearly 40 killed, including André Callioux. Except for undeniably demonstrating courage and discipline, these men fell in vain.

Less than two weeks later, on June 7 at Milliken's

An unknown soldier with a cigar gravely posed for a formal portrait with his wife before going to war.

Bend, 1,400 Union soldiers—the remains of two white companies and three black regiments—took the brunt of a charge by 1,500 Texans. In close combat marked by terrible bloodshed, the men beat back the Rebels. Word went out: the novice black soldiers had held their ground defensively against a seasoned assault.

After the battle, Capt. M. M. Miller, of the 9th Regiment of Louisiana Volunteers of African Descent, wrote his aunt back in Galena, Illinois, "I never more wish to hear the expression 'the niggers won't fight.'" "The bravery of the Blacks in the battle at Milliken's Bend," Assistant Secretary of War Charles Dana optimistically concluded, "completely revolutionized the sentiments of the Army." The stage was now set for the doomed 54th Massachusetts and Robert Gould Shaw to demonstrate black courage on a national scale.

By the time Shaw's regiment arrived, Northern forces in South Carolina were at last able to turn their attention to the necklace of heavily fortified islands that adorned Charleston harbor, and to Fort Sumter, where the war had started. The key to the Confederate defense was Fort Wagner. When the attack was planned no black troops appeared on the order of battle. "Our whole experience, so far, has been in loading and discharging vessels," Shaw wrote two weeks before the battle. "I feel very much disappointed." He complained to Brig. Gen. George C. Strong, arguing that "the colored soldiers should be associated as much as possible with the white troops, in order that they may have other witnesses besides their own officers to what they are capable of doing."

Shaw's connections, as well as his logic, were not lost on his superiors. Orders arrived on July 8: be ready to move at an hour's notice. Ten days later, the 54th Massachusetts was poised before Fort Wagner. Three brigades would mount the attack, and Shaw had offered the 54th as its spearhead.

"We may as well get rid of them"

Seasoned brigade commanders thought a charge up an open beach against defenses as forbidding as Fort Wagner's was foolhardy, but the assault commander, Maj. Gen. Truman Seymour—"a devil of a fellow for dash"—overruled them. The fort, he thought, would be softened by a massive daylong artillery bombardment. Beyond that, according to later testimony before the American Freedmen's Inquiry Commission, Seymour told the operating commander, Maj. Gen. Quincy Gillmore: "Well, I guess we will . . . put those damned niggers from Massachusetts in the advance; we may as well get rid of them one time as another."

All during the day of July 18, Union artillery banged away at the fort. Shortly after 6:30 P.M., 600 men of the 54th formed two wings and moved slowly up Morris Island beach. Just beyond reach of Confederate artillery, they lay down. Shaw dismounted and sent his horse cantering to the rear.

At 7:45, the bombardment stopped and the attack signal came. Shaw spoke to his soldiers: "Move in quick time until within a hundred yards of the fort, then, double-quick and charge!" Off they rushed into history, as 1,700 Confederate riflemen—almost six times as many as Union military intelligence had said were in Fort Wagner—clambered from their shell-battered bombproofs and raced to the ramparts (only eight of them died from the Union bombardment). Confederate batteries, mostly silent during the day to save ammunition, now opened up from the harbor's other islands.

Just before battle, Sgt. Robert Simmons, one of Shaw's men, sent a prophetic note to the members of his family, who only three days before had been under violent racist assault back in New York City: "God bless you all! Good-bye!" Despite a moat, some wire and a rifle pit, Shaw and a few of his men actually reached the parapets of the fort before being cut down by fire. The rest, less than half of the assault force, were driven back. For having carried the regimental colors despite multiple wounds, Sgt. William Carney became the first black to win the Medal of Honor. "The old flag never touched the ground, boys!" he shouted.

As so often happens with military disasters, the most elementary things had been left undone. "There was no provision for cutting away obstructions, filling the ditch, or spiking the guns," Regimental Historian Luis F. Emilio wrote afterward. "No engineers or guides accompanied the column; no artillery-men to serve captured guns; no plan of the work was shown company officers. . . ."

The attack once again indisputably showed black courage in battle. It also had other effects. One involved the treatment of prisoners. When the Confederate Army refused to exchange prisoners captured during the siege, word spread that those taken alive had been put to hard labor and might be sentenced to death.

If Northern admiration for the gallant 54th was enormous, Northern outrage at mistreatment of prisoners matched it. Within a fortnight Lincoln announced the Union would answer atrocity man for man. Sporadic eye-for-an-eye retribution set in, reaching some sort of apogee on April 12, 1864, at Fort Pillow, Tennessee. There, Gen. Nathan Bedford Forrest and 1,500 Confederate cavalrymen overwhelmed a 570-man, racially mixed garrison, driving survivors into the Mississippi, which was soon, in Forrest's words, "dyed with the blood of the slaughtered for 200 yards." After their surrender, scores of the black soldiers and some of the white soldiers were murdered. For black soldiers, "Remember Fort Pillow!" became a rallying cry, giving them a reason both to fight to the death and to offer no quarter. As another fallout from Fort Wagner, Fort Pillow deeply impressed on white enlisted men the danger of fighting alongside blacks in battle.

Retaliations escalated well into 1864, as the Union realized that victory would require the destruction of the South. Union general William T. Sherman laid waste to Georgia. Grant, at last promoted to commander of all Union armies, smashed away at Lee in Virginia with overwhelming numbers. The appalling series of battles of attrition that resulted became known as the Wilderness to Petersburg Campaign. In six weeks of fighting, Northern casualties amounted to 65,000; Southern, 35,000.

In the North, meanwhile, the 1864 Presidential campaign was being waged, with the Democrats running George McClellan against Lincoln on a "stop the war" platform. Though the war, begun as a fight to save a political union, had become a crusade to free blacks from slavery, the continued carnage with no sign

Engraving used in the first history of blacks in war, published in 1888 by a black Union soldier named Joseph Wilson, depicts Yankee cavalrymen herding Rebel captives along the streets of a Southern town.

of victory made the Democrats' cause popular, especially in the Midwest, where Yankee abolitionists were still far from loved and dying to free slaves was not exactly popular.

All through the late summer Lincoln was sure he would be defeated, especially without some dramatic military victory to show for the years of killing. But Grant's attempt to wear out Lee and take Richmond ended in the siege not of the Southern capital but of Lee's prime remaining supply depot, Petersburg, Virginia, 20 miles away. During the resulting stalemate, another legacy of the fatal charge of the 54th Massachusetts— government sensitivity to the political implications of consigning black soldiers to slaughter— contributed to one of the more bloody and bizarre blunders of the war.

After five days of Union failure to take Petersburg, Lt. Col. Henry Pleasants, a former mining engineer from the Pennsylvania coal country, offered a daring plan: to tunnel under the Rebel lines and set off a huge blast of dynamite—enough to blow an opening so big that the superior numbers of the North could sweep past dazed and demoralized defenders and wheel toward Richmond.

A 510-foot tunnel, one of the longest of its kind ever dug, was created by troops of the 48th Pennsylvania Infantry, many of them coal miners by trade. On July 27, its two 40-foot lateral galleries beneath Rebel lines were packed with four tons of fused and tamped gunpowder.

Maj. Gen. Ambrose Burnside's four divisions had been chosen to provide "shock troops" to exploit the general chaos that would follow the blast. He selected for special training Gen. Edward Ferrero's black 4th Division. They were new men, untested in battle; his white soldiers were by then exhausted from the Wilderness fighting. Two days before the detonation and long after the 4th had mastered its plan for an attack on both sides of the area that was to be exploded, Burnside's superior, Maj. Gen. George Meade, the victor at Gettysburg, abruptly vetoed the plan. Grant backed Meade. "It would then be said," he later testified before Congress, "that we were shoving those people ahead to get killed because we did not care anything about them."

Burnside allowed the white division that would lead the attack to be chosen by lot. Tragically, the short straw fell to Brig. Gen. James Ledlie's 1st Division. Ledlie was a drunk, an incompetent and a coward whom Grant once described as "the poorest division commander that General Burnside had." The 1st Division was a collection of former artillerymen for whom Burnside had little regard, labeling them "worthless."

When the explosion went off, the resulting havoc was beyond anyone's expectations. Most of a Confederate regiment and several artillery pieces disappeared entirely. The fort was blown apart. Confederates on both sides of the crater ran in horror. "Stones, timbers, arms, legs, guns unlimbered and bodies unlimbed" rained back down into the dust-filled, sulfurous crater, 170 feet long, 80 feet wide and 30 feet deep. Ledlie was back in a medical tent, drinking, as his 1st Division stumbled blindly forward through a narrow opening in the Union trenches and into the reeking crater. Caught there, they did not fan out to either side as the plan had intended them to, but having lost critical momentum and nerve, sought cover in the crater and huddled clinging to the shattered, blood-wet earth. Brigades from the 2d and 3d Divisions followed, to be lost in the smoke and confusion. By the time the black 4th Division was sent forward, the Confederates had recovered and were mounting a counterattack. The 4th was caught in a withering fire. Buckling at last, the black soldiers also retreated, many falling into the crater.

When the smoke had cleared, the Union had lost 3,798 men killed, wounded or missing.

Reports of the fiasco provided one of the sorriest footnotes of the war. Some Confederate soldiers had followed the 4th down into the crater and killed wounded blacks who were trying to surrender. They, too, remembered Fort Pillow. That was predictable. But there was worse news from the Union side. It was asserted that white Union soldiers bayoneted Union blacks to preserve themselves from Confederate vengeance. According to George Kilmer, a white artilleryman from New York, "Men boasted in my presence that blacks had thus been disposed of."

A lengthy court of inquiry also confirmed that the black division had lost far more men than any of the white divisions. As to white soldiers killing black soldiers, that was never looked into. No one was ever court-martialed.

Grant later said, "General Burnside wanted to put his colored division in front and I believe if he had done so it would have been a success." Nevertheless, in military myth the Battle of the Crater was such a disaster that it cast a general pall over the reputation for bravery that blacks had thus far earned. It was left for General Butler, the first to make use of the "contraband" label, and a man who had once belittled black soldiers for alleged awkwardness in gun handling, to fashion a long-overdue tribute. Fittingly, it came after another battle—at New Market Heights, Virginia. There, after having been ordered to remove the caps from the nipples of their guns so they could not fire them (officers believed that stopping to shoot might slow the momentum of the charge), nine black regiments victoriously stormed a Confederate redoubt at bayonet point, suffering 1,000 casualties.

"In a space not wider than the clerk's desk and three hundred yards long, lay the dead bodies of five hundred and forty-three of my colored comrades," Butler wrote, "and as I looked on their bronzed faces upturned in the shining sun, as if in mute appeal against the wrongs of the country for which they had given their lives, whose flag had only been to them a flag of stripes, on which no star of glory had ever shone for them—feeling I had wronged them in the past, I swore to myself a solemn oath . . . 'to defend the rights of those men who have given their blood for me and my country that day and for their race forever.'"

Before 1864 was out, the all-black XXV Army Corps was formed. The largest black unit ever in American military history, it was commanded by Gen. Godfrey Weitzel who, as a lieutenant, had asked to be relieved of an expedition with black troops because he thought leading them into the South would stir bloody slave insurrections. In the black corps hopes ran high of playing a major role in the spring campaign of 1865 that would end by vanquishing Lee. But then the XXV Corps was dismantled. Divisions were split off, brigades scattered, regiments ordered to temporary duty with white units, the corps' command fragmented and removed to secondary rear echelons. Grant already

had 110,000 men in the field to Lee's 50,000. But with some justice, a member of the corps lamented bitterly, "It was clearly not intended that the colored troops should win any glory. . . ."

On the great day when Union troops finally marched into the Confederate capital at war's end, they were led by black detachments from the XXV Corps. A Chicago *Tribune* editorialist reflected on the encouraging fact that representatives of a formerly enslaved race "bore the banner of freedom" into the birthplace of the rebellion. But he also rhapsodized about "sable warriors . . . rolling up the whites of their visual orbs, and exhibiting an untarnished display of nature's dentistry" as they entered Richmond. Immediately thereafter, wonder of wonders, the XXV Corps was reconstituted—and shipped to the Texas border with Mexico. Grant's order left little doubt what fate awaited them there: "You should take a fair quantity of intrenching tools. . . ."

What Did Freedom Mean?

The Aftermath of Slavery as Seen by Former Slaves and Former Masters in Three Societies

Dean C. Brink

Dean Brink is chairman of the history department at Roosevelt High School in Seattle Washington.

"Most anyone ought to know that a man is better off free than as a slave, even if he did not have anything," said the Reverend E. P. Holmes, a black Georgia clergyman and former house servant, to a Congressional committee in 1883. "I would rather be free and have my liberty. I fared just as well as any white child could have fared when I was a slave, and yet I would not give up my freedom."(1) Holmes was just one of over six million individuals held in bondage in the Western Hemisphere who were freed either by force and violence (as in Haiti between 1793-1803 and the United States between 1861-1865) or by government decree (as in Jamaica in 1838, Cuba in 1886, and Brazil in 1888). Four million of these slaves lived in the Southern United States. In Russia, two years before Lincoln issued the Emancipation Proclamation, Czar Alexander II freed fifty million serfs. Certainly the abolition of slavery was one of the most revolutionary and far-reaching developments of the nineteenth century.

Undoubtedly most of these former slaves would echo the Reverend Holmes statement that "I would not give up my freedom." But what did freedom mean? One way for the student of history to begin to answer this question is to analyze the accounts of former slaves and former masters on the ending of slavery in several societies. The accounts presented here illustrate some of the difficulties of adjusting to freedom. The first set of readings consists of the observations of former masters--two from the Southern United States, where the masters were white and the slaves were black, and one from Zaria, a region in northern Nigeria, where both slaves and masters were black. The second set of readings is a collection of letters written by former slaves to their former masters during the first years of Reconstruction in the South. A final set of readings contains the recollections of former slaves in Cuba and the Southern United States many years after abolition.

A Freedmen's Bureau station issuing rations to the old and sick. Although the Bureau, with the help of Union troops, tried to protect the civil rights of Southern blacks, brutal riots against blacks occurred in Memphis and New Orleans in 1866.

Reprinted from *OAH Magazine of History*, Vol. 4, No. 1., Winter 1989, pp. 35-46. Copyright © 1989 by the Organization of American Historians.

Accounts of Former Masters

Frances B. Leigh was the daughter of the acclaimed British actress Frances (Fanny) Kemble and Peter Butler, a Georgia planter. At the beginning of the Civil War, Butler had nearly one thousand slaves on two plantations. In 1866, Frances Leigh returned to Georgia with her father to manage the plantations. She described her experiences in *Ten Years on a Georgia Plantation Since the War* (1883).

The year after the war between the North and South, I went with my father to look after our property in Georgia and see what could be done with it.

The whole country had of course undergone a complete revolution. The changes that a four years' war must bring about in any country would alone have been enough to give a different aspect to everything; but at the South, besides the changes brought by the war, our slaves had been freed. . . . The South was still treated as a conquered country. The white people were disfranchised, the local government in the hands of either military men or Northern adventurers, the latter of whom, with no desire to promote either the good of the country or the people . . . encouraged the negroes in all of their foolish and extravagant ideas of freedom, set them against their masters, . . . in order to secure for themselves some political office which they hoped to obtain through the negro vote. . . .

We had, before the North, received two letters from Georgia, one from an agent of the Freedmen's Bureau, and the other from one of our neighbors both stating very much the same thing, which was that our former slaves had all returned to the island and were willing and ready to work for us, but refused to engage themselves to anyone else, even to their liberators, the Yankees; but they were very badly off, short of provisions, and would starve if something were not done for them at once. . . .

On Wednesday, when my father returned, he reported that he had found the negroes all on the place, not only those who were there five years ago, but many who were sold three years before that. . . . They received him very affectionately, and made an agreement with him to work for one half the crop. . . . Owing to our coming so late, only a small crop could be planted, enough to make seed for another year and clear expenses. . . . Most of the plantations were lying idle for want of hands to work them, so many of the negroes had died; . . . Many had taken to the Southwest, and other[s] preferred hanging about the towns, to working regularly on the plantations; so most people found it impossible to get any laborers, but we had as many as we wanted and nothing could induce our people to go anywhere else. My father . . . could attend to nothing but the planting, and we agreed that he should devote himself to that, while I looked after some furniture. . . .

The prospect of getting in the crop did not grow more promising as time went on. The negros talked a great deal about their desire and intention to work for us, but their idea of work . . . is very vague, some of them working only half a day and some even less. I don't think one does a full day's work, and so of course not half of the necessary amount is done and I am afraid never will be again, and so our properties will soon be utterly worthless, for no crop can be raised by such labor as this, and no negro will work if he can help it, and is quite satisfied to scrape along doing an odd job here and there to earn money enough to buy a little food. . . .

My father was quite encouraged at first, the people seemed so willing to work and said so much about their intentions of doing so; but not so many days after they started, he came in quite disheartened, saying that half of the hands had left the fields at one o'clock and the rest by three o'clock, and this just at our busiest time. Half a day's work will keep them from starving, but won't raise a crop. Our contract with them is for half the crop; that is, one half to be divided among them, according to each man's rate of work, we letting them have in the meantime necessary food, clothing, and money for their present wants (as they have not a penny) which is to be deducted from whatever is due to them at the end of the year.

This we found the best arrangement to make with them, for if we paid them wages, the first five dollars they made would have seemed like so large a sum to them, that they would have imagined their fortunes made and refused to work any more. But even this arrangement had its objections, for they told us, when they missed working two or three days a week, that they were losers by it as well as ourselves, half the crop being theirs. But they could not see that this sort of work would not raise any crop at all. . . . They were quite convinced that if six days' work would raise a whole crop, three days work would raise half a one, with which they as partners were satisfied, and so it seemed as if we should have to be too. . . .

In May 1867, Leigh and her father moved to their second plantation on a sea island off the coast of Georgia. Her account continues.

The rice plantation becoming unhealthy early in May, we removed to St. Simon's, a sea island on the coast, about fifteen miles from Butler's Island where the famous Sea Island cotton had

The Lilly Library

A Currier and Ives print, "Freedom to the Slaves," depicts Lincoln breaking the chains of bondage for a slave family.

formerly been raised. This place had been twice in the possession of the Northern troops during the war, and the negroes had consequently been brought under the influence of Northerners, some of whom had filled the poor people's minds with all sorts of vain hopes and ideas, among others that their former masters would not be allowed to return, and the land was theirs, a thing many of them believed, and they had planted both corn and cotton to a considerable extent. To disabuse their minds of this notion my father determined to put in a few acres of cotton. . . .

My father spent . . . time in talking to the negroes, of whom there were about fifty on the place, making arrangements with them for work, more to establish his right to the place than from any good work we expected to do this year. We found them in a very different frame of mind from the negroes on Butler's Island. . . . They were perfectly respectful, but quiet, and evidently disappointed to find they were not the masters of the soil and that their friends the Yankees had deceived them. . . .

In all other ways the work went on just as it did in the old times. The force, of about three hundred, was divided into gangs, each working under a head man--the old negro drivers. . . . To make them do odd jobs was hopeless, as I found when I . . . tried to make them clear up the grounds about the house, cut the undergrowth and make a garden. . . . Unless I stayed on the spot all the time, the instant I disappeared they disappeared as well. . . . And I generally found that if I wanted a thing done I first had to tell the negroes to do it, then show them how, and finally do it myself. Their way of managing not to do it was very ingenious, for they were always perfectly good tempered, and received my orders . . . and then always somehow or other left the thing undone. . . .

In August of 1867 my father died, and . . . I went down to the South to carry on his work, . . . but before anything else could be done the negroes had to be settled with for the past two years, and their share of the crops divided according to the amount due each man. . . .

Notwithstanding their dissatisfaction with the settlement, six thousand dollars was paid out among them, many getting as much as two or three hundred a piece. The result was that a number of them left me and bought land of their own, and at one time it seemed doubtful that I should have hands at all left to work. The land they bought, and paid forty, fifty dollars and even more for an acre, was either within the town limits, for which they got no title, and from which they were soon turned off, or out in the pine woods, where the land was so poor they could not raise a peck of corn to the acre. . . .

Most frightfully cheated the poor people were. But they had got their land, and were building their little log cabins on it, fully believing that they were to live on their property and incomes the rest of their lives, like gentlemen.(2)

Mary Boykin Chestnut was a woman of wit and intelligence who kept an intimate diary of life in the Confederacy during the Civil War. The daughter of one of South Carolina's finest families, she was married to James Chestnut, an aide to Jefferson Davis and a Brigadier General of the Confederacy. These two entrees are from *Mary Chestnut's Civil War*, the most recent edition of her diary.

May 2, 1865

Old Mr. Chestnut had a summer resort for his invalid negroes and especially for women with ailing babies. Myrtilla, an African, was head nurse then. She was very good, very sensible, very efficient, and her language a puzzle to me always. She went off with the Yankees. "Old Aunt Myrtilla run away," said Smith with a guffaw. Ellen (said)

"She was a black angel--she was so good."

"Yes," said Smith, "her arms hung back of her jis' like wings. She was always more like flying than walking--the way she got over ground."

"And Marster did treat her like a lady. She had a woman to wash and cook for her. You think the Yankees gwine do that for her? And then, she is that old--she is so old--I thought she only wanted in this world a little good religion to die with."

And now from Orangeburg comes the most pathetic letters. Old Myrtilla begs to be sent for. She wants to come home. Miss C, who feels terribly any charitable distress which can be relieved by other people, urges us to send for "poor old Myrtilla."

"Very well," says her brother. "You pay for the horses and the wagon and the driver, and I will send."

And that ended the Myrtilla tragedy as far as we were concerned, but poor old Myrtilla, after the first natural frenzy of freedom subsided, knew all too well on which side her bread was buttered--and knew too, or found out, where her real friends were. So in a short time old Myrtilla was on our hands to support once more. How she got back we did not inquire. (3)

June 12, 1865

> *Captain Barnwell came to see us. . . . He gave us an account of his father's plantation from which he had just returned.*
>
> *"Our negroes are living in great comfort. They were delighted to see me with overflowing affection. They waited on me as before, gave me breakfast, splendid dinners, etc. But they firmly and respectfully informed me: 'We own this land now. Put it out of your head that it will ever be yours again.'"(4)*

Baba was a Hausa woman who lived in the Nigerian states of Kano and Zaria between 1890 and 1951. The Hausa are a group of west African peoples who speak a similar language. They are traditionally village farmers who adhere to the Islamic faith. When the British abolished slavery in Zaria in 1901, Baba was a young girl. Her father owned about 200 slaves. She described her experiences in an autobiography, *Baba of Karo: A Woman of the Moslem Hausa.* (1964).

> *When I was a maiden the Europeans first arrived. Ever since we were quite small the malams (scholars of the Koran) had been saying that the Europeans would come with a thing called a train, they would come with a thing called a motorcar, . . . They would stop wars, they would repair the world, they would stop oppression and lawlessness, we should live at peace with them. We used to go and sit quietly and listen to the prophecies. . . .*
>
> *I remember when a European came to Karo on a horse, and some of his foot soldiers went into the town. Everyone came to look at them, but . . . everyone at Karo ran away--"There's a European, there's a European!" He came from Zaria with a few black men, two on horses and four on foot. . . . Later we heard that they were in Zaria in crowds, clearing spaces and building houses. . . .*
>
> *The Europeans said that there were to be no more slaves; if someone said 'Slave!' you could complain to the* alkali *(a judge) who would punish the master who said it, the judge said "That is what the Europeans have decreed!" The first order said that any slave, if he was younger than you, was your younger brother, if he was older than you he was your elder brother--they were all brothers of their master's family. No one could use the word 'slave' anymore. When slavery was stopped, nothing much happened at our* rinji *(a slave village) except that some slaves whom we had bought in the market ran away. Our father went to his farm and worked, he and his son took up large hoes; they loaned out their small farms. Tsoho our father and Kadiri my brother . . . and Babambo worked, they farmed guineacorn and millet and groundnuts and everything; before this they had supervised the slaves' work--now they did their own. When the midday food was ready, the women of the compound would give us children the food, one of us drew water, and off we went to the farm to take the men their food at the foot of the tree; I was about eight or nine at the time, I think. (5)*

Letters of Former Slaves to Former Masters

Because they were kept illiterate while in bondage, few former slaves were able to record their thoughts about the meaning of freedom or their hopes and aspirations for life in a society without slavery. Still, some letters from former slaves to former masters exist, and they reflect the memories and emotions that they had about slavery, freedom, and the ties that bound master and slave together. These three letters express some of the feelings and attitudes that millions of other illiterate former slaves may have held. (6)

Montgomery, February 10, 1867

> *My Dear Old Master,--I am anxious to see you and my young masters and mistresses. I often think of you, and remember with pleasure how kind you all were to me. Though freedom*

has been given to the colored race, I often sigh for the good old days of slave-times, when we were all so happy and contented. . . . I am tolerably pleasantly situated. I hired to a Mr. Sanderson, who treats me very well. I am very well and hope I may have an opportunity of coming to see you all next Christmas. I am still single and don't think very much about a beaux. I don't think the men in these days of freedom are of much account. If I could find one whom I think a real good man, and who would take good care of me, I would get married. Please, dear old master, ask some of my young mistresses to write me.

My kind and respectful remembrances to all.

Your former servant and friend,

Alice Dabney

February 5, 1867

Mas William,

I guess you will be somewhat surprised to receive a letter from me. I am well & doing just as well as I could expect under the circumstances, one blessing is that I have plenty to eat & have plenty of work to do, & get tolerable fair prices for my work. I have but two small children, they are good size boys, able to plow & help me out a great deal. I still work at my trade. I once thought I wanted to come back to that old country, but I believe I have given up that notion. Give my respects to old Mas Henry & his family Miss Jane & all the family.

Tell Austin howdy for me & tell him I want him to write me & give me all the news of that old country who has married who had died give me all the news I am anxious to hear from them all tell Austin to give them all my love to all I havent time to mention all ther names, but I wish to hear from all remember me to Coleman especially. As I am in a great hurry I will close please send me word, direct your letters to Camden in the Case or in the name of S. B. Griffin, Camden, Washita County, Arksas.

I remains as ever Respt
Your humble Servent
Jake

President Abraham Lincoln entering the city of Richmond, Virginia, former capital of the Southern States, April 4, 1865. He is said to have told the masses of freed slaves, "You must kneel to God only, and thank Him for the liberty you will hereafter enjoy. I am but God's humble instrument."

Dayton, Ohio, August 7, 1865

To My Old Master, Colonel P.H. Anderson
Big Spring, Tennessee

Sir: I got your letter and was glad to find you had not forgotten Jourdon, and that you wanted me to come back and live with you again, promising to do better for me than anyone else can. I have often felt uneasy about you. I thought the Yankees would have hung you long before this for harboring Rebs they found at your house. . . . Although you shot at me twice before I left you, I did not want to hear of your being hurt, and am glad you are still living. . . .

I am doing tolerably well here; I get $25 a month, with victuals and clothing; have a comfortable home here for Mandy (the folks here call her Mrs. Anderson), and the children, Milly, Jane and Grundy, go to school and are learning well. . . . Now if you will write and say what wages you will give me, I will be better able to decide whether it would be to my advantage to move back again.

As to my freedom, which you say I can have, there is nothing to be gained on that score, as I got my free papers in 1864. . . . Mandy says she would be afraid to go back without some proof that you are sincerely disposed to treat us justly and kindly--and we have concluded to test your sincerity by asking you to send us our wages for the time we served you. This will make us forget and forgive old scores, and rely on your justice and friendship in the future. At $25 a month for me, and $2 a week for Mandy, our earnings would amount to $11,680. Add to this the interest for the time our wages have been kept back and deduct what you paid for our clothing and three doctor's visits for me, and pulling a tooth for Mandy, and the balance will show that we are in justice entitled to. Please send the money by Adams Express. . . . We trust the good Maker has opened your eyes to the wrongs which you and your fathers have done to me and my fathers, in making us toil for you for generations without recompense. . . . Surely there will be a day of reckoning for those who defraud the laborer of his hire.

In answering this letter please state if there would be any safety for my Milly and Jane, who are now grown up and both good-looking girls. . . . You will also please state if there are any schools opened for colored children in your neighborhood, the great desire of my life now is to give my children an education, and have them form virtuous habits.

P.S.--Say howdy to George Carter, and thank him for taking the pistol from you when you were shooting at me.

From your old servant,
Jourdan Anderson

Recollections of Former Slaves

Esteban Montejo was a runaway slave who spent ten years hiding in the forests of central Cuba before slavery was abolished. He described his experiences after slavery had ended in *The Autobiography of a Runaway Slave* (1973). He was over one hundred years old at the time.

All my life I have liked the forest, but when slavery ended I stopped being a runaway. I realized from the way people were cheering and shouting that slavery had ended, an so I came out of the forest. They were shouting, 'we are free now.' But I didn't join in, I thought it might be a lie. I don't know . . . anyway, I went up to a plantation and let my head appear little by little till I was out in the open. . . . When I left the forest and began walking, I met an old woman carrying two children in her arms. I called to her, and when she came up I asked her, 'Tell me, is it true we are no longer slaves?' She replied, 'No, son, we are now free.' I went walking the way I was going and began looking for work. . . .

After this time in the forest I had become half savage. I didn't want to work anywhere, and I was afraid they would shut me up again. I knew quite well that slavery had not ended completely. A lot of people asked me what I was doing and where I came from. Sometimes I told them, 'My name is Stephen and I was a runaway slave.' Other times I said I had been working on a certain plantation and could not find my relations. I must have been about twenty at the time.

Since I didn't know anyone I walked from village to village for several months. I did not suffer from hunger because people gave me food. You only had to say you were out of work and someone would always help you out. But you can't carry on like that forever. I began to realize that work had to be done in order to eat and sleep in a barracoon (barracks for housing slaves) at least. By the time I decided to cut cane, I had already covered quite a bit of ground. . . .

The first plantation I worked on was called Purio. I turned up there one day in the rags I stood in and a hat I had collected along the way. I went in and asked the overseer if there was work for me. He said yes. I remember he was Spanish, with moustaches, and his name was Pepe. There were overseers in these parts until quite recently, the difference being that they didn't lay about them as they used to do under slavery. But they were men of the same breed, harsh, overbearing. There were still barracoons after Abolition, the same as before. Many of them were newly built of masonry, the old ones having collapsed under the rain and storms. The barracoon at Purio was strong and looked as if it had been recently completed. They told me to go and live there. I soon made myself at home for it wasn't too bad. They had taken the bolts off the doors and the workers themselves had cut holes in the walls for ventilation. They had no longer to worry about escapes or anything like that, for the Negroes were free now, or so they said. But I could not help noticing that bad things still went on. There were bosses who still believed that the blacks were created for locks and bolts and whips, and treated them as before. It struck me that many Negroes did not know that things had changed, because they kept saying, 'Give me your blessing, my master."

Those ones never left the plantation at all. I was different in that I disliked having anything to do with the whites. They believed they were the lords of creation. . . .

The work was exhausting. You spent hours in the fields and it seemed as if the work would never end. It went on and on until you were worn out. The overseers were always bothering you. Any worker who knocked off for long was taken off the job. I worked from six in the morning. The early hour didn't bother me since in the forest it had been impossible to sleep late because of the cocks crowing. There was a break at eleven for lunch, which had to be eaten in the workers' canteen, usually standing because of the crowd of people squashed in. This was the worst and hottest time. Work ended at six in the afternoon. Then I would take myself off to the river, bathe for a while, and go back to get something to eat. . . .

The Negroes who worked at Purio had almost all been slaves; they were so used to life in the barracoon they did not even go out to eat. When lunch-time came they shut themselves up in their rooms to eat, and the same with dinner. They did not go out at night. They were afraid of people, and they said they would get lost if they did, they were convinced of this. I wasn't like that--if I got lost I always found myself again. . . .

On Sundays all the workers who wanted to could work overtime. This meant that instead of resting you went to the fields and cleared, cleaned or cut cane. Or if not that, you stayed in, cleaning out the troughs or scraping the boilers. . . . As there was nothing special to do that day, all the workers used to go and earn themselves extra money. . . .

In those days you could get either permanent or temporary work on the plantations. Those employed on a permanent basis had to keep a time-table. This way they could live in the barracoons and did not need to leave the plantations for anything. I preferred being a permanent worker myself.

The barracoons were a bit damp, but all the same they were safer than in the forest. There were no snakes, and all us workers slept in hammocks which were very comfortable. Many of the barracoons were made of sacking. The one tiresome thing about them was the fleas; they didn't hurt, but you had to be up all night scaring them off with the Spanish broom, which gets rid of fleas and ticks. . . .

The Lilly Library

A slave.

After months of work on the plantation of Purio, Montejo left to go work at a sugar mill on a plantation at Ariosa.

But life grew wearisome on the plantations. It was boring to see the same people and fields day after day. The hardest thing was to get used to one place for a long time. I had to leave Purio because life seemed to have stopped still there. I started walking South, and I got to San Agustin Ariosa sugar-mill, near the villiage of Zulueta. At first I did not intend to stop there because I preferred walking . . . but as luck would have it I found myself a mistress there and so I stayed. . . .

I stayed a long time at Ariosa. . . . The plantation was of medium-size, owned by a man called Ariosa, a pure-blooded Spaniard. It was one of the first plantations to become a mill, and a large-gauge line ran through it, bring the cane direct from the fields into the boiler-house. It was much the same as everywhere else. There were the usual yes-men and toadies to masters and overseers alike. This was on account of the hatred which has always existed between the groups of slaves, because of ignorance. This is the only reason for it. The freed slaves were generally very ignorant and would lend themselves to anything. It happened that if some fellow became a nuisance, his own brothers would undertake to kill him for a few centenes. . .

They didn't give work to just anyone . . . and at Ariosa you had to work hard. (The overseers) watched you the whole time, and they would book you for nothing at all. I remember a criminal by the name of Camilo Polavieja, who became Governor of Cuba in the Nineties. No one liked him. He said the workers were cattle and he kept the same views he had during slavery. Once he ordered all the workers (to have cards). . . . The cards were slips of paper . . . with the worker's address on. Anyone caught without his card got a good belting across the shoulders. . . . It was always given in a gaol, because that's where they took you if you were caught without your card. The card cost twenty-five cents . . . and it had to be renewed every year. . . .

There were lots of workers at Ariosa, I think it must have been one of the biggest plantations . . . The owner was an innovator and made many changes in the mills. Some plantations gave very bad food because the cooks didn't care, but Ariosa wasn't like that, you ate well there. . . .

When the dead season came everything stopped. . . . There was less work and fewer duties at this time, and naturally this led to boredom. . . .

The women carried on as usual, there was no such thing as dead time for them. They washed the men's clothes, mended and sewed. . . . They had plenty of other things to do, like raising pigs and chickens. . . . There was no freedom. (7)

In the 1930s the Federal Writers' Project of the Works Progress Administration (WPA) sent teams of interviewers into the South to interview surviving former slaves. The results of the interviews of over two thousand ex-slaves were compiled in the Slave Narrative Collection. Two-thirds of those interviewed were over eighty years of age and the interviews gave them an unparalleled opportunity to describe their lives both under slavery and after emancipation. These four narratives are taken from *Life Under the "Peculiar Institution": Selections from the Slave Narrative Collection* (1970) by Norman P. Yetman. (8)

4. CIVIL WAR AND RECONSTRUCTION

1. Mary Anderson, age 86
   Interviewed near Raleigh, North Carolina

   I was born on a plantation near Franklinton, Wake County, North Carolina, May 10, 1851. I was a slave belonging to Sam Brodie, who owned the plantation at this place. . . .

   We had good food, plenty of warm clothes, and comfortable houses. . . . The plantation was very large and there was about two hundred acres of cleared land that was farmed each year. . . . There were about one hundred and sixty-two slaves on the plantation . . . .

   The War was begun and there were stories of fights and freedom. The news went from plantation to plantation and while the slaves acted natural and some even more polite than usual, they prayed for freedom.

   Then one day I heared something that sounded like thunder and Marster and Missus began to walk around and act queer. The grown slaves were whispering to each other. Sometimes they gathered in little gangs in the grove. . . .

   In a day or two everybody on the plantation seemed disturbed and Marster and Missus were crying. Marster ordered all of the slaves to come to the Great House at nine o'clock. . . . Then Marster said, "Good morning," and Missus said, "Good morning, children." They were both crying. Then Marster said, "Men, women, and children, you are free. You are no longer my slaves. The Yankees will soon be here." . . .

   The slaves were awfully excited. The Yankees stayed there, cooked, ate, drank, and played music until about night. . . .

   When they left the country, lots of the slaves went with them and soon there were none of Marster's slaves left. They wandered around from place to place, fed and working most of the time at some other slave owner's plantation and getting more homesick every day.

   The second year after the surrender our Marster and Missus got on their carriage and went and looked up all the Negroes they heard of who belonged to them. Some who went off with the Yankees were never heard from again. . . . Some were so glad to get back they cried, 'cause fare had been mighty bad part of the time they were rambling around and they were hungry.

2. Frank Bell, age 86
   Interviewed at St. Louis, Missouri

   I was owned by Johnson Bell and born in New Orleans . . . and my master . . . was real mean to me. . . . When war come, Master swear he not gwine to fight, but the Yankees they capture New Orleans and throws Marster in a pen and guards him. He gets a chance and escapes.

   When war am over he won't free me, says I'm valuable to him in his trade. He say, "Nigger, you's supposed to be free but I'll pay you a dollar a week and if you run off I'll kill you." So he makes me do like before the War, but gives me a dollar a month, 'stead week. He says I cost more'n I'm worth, but he won't let me go. Times I don't know why I didn't die before I'm growed, sleepin' on the ground, winter and summer, rain and snow.

   Master helt me long after the War. If anybody get after him, he told them I stay 'cause I wants to stay, but told me if I left he'd kill him another nigger. I stayed till he gits in a drunk brawl one night . . . and . . . got killed.

   Then I am left to live or die, so I wanders from place to place. I nearly starved to death before I'd leave New Orleans, 'cause I couldn't think Master am dead and I afraid. Finally I gets up nerve to leave town. . . .

   Then I gets locked up in jail. I didn't know what for, never did know. One of the men says to me to come with him and takes me to the woods and give me an ax. I cuts rails till I nearly falls, all with chain locked round feet, so I couldn't run off. He turns me loose and I wanders again. Never had a home. Works for me long 'nough to get fifty, sixty cents, then starts roamin' again, like a stray dog.

   After a long time I marries Feline Graham. . . . We has one boy and he farms and I lives with him. I worked at a sawmill and farms all my life, but never could make much money.

3. Elidge Davison, age 86
   Interviewed at Madisonville, Texas

My birth was in Richmond . . . in Old Virginny. . . . Massa and Missus were very good white folks and was good to the black folks. . . . Us work all day till just before dark. Some times us got a whipping. . . . Massa learn us to read and us read the Bible. He learn us to write too. . . .

I 'member plenty about the War, 'cause the Yankees they march on to Richmond. . . . When the War over Massa call me and tells me I'se free as he was. 'Cause them Yankees win the War. He gives me five dollars and say he'll give me that much a month iffen I stays with him, but I starts to Texas. I heared I wouldn't have to work in Texas, 'cause everything growed on trees and the Texans wore animal hides for clothes. I didn't get no land or mule or cow. There warn't no plantations divided that I knowed about. . . .

It about a year before I gets to Texas. I walks nearly all the way. . . . Sometimes I work for folks along the way and gets fifty cents and start again. I get to Texas and try to work for white folks and try to farm. I couldn't make anything at any work. I made five dollars a month for I don't know how long after the War. Iffen the woods wasn't full of game us . . . all starve to death them days.

4. Henri Necaise, age 105
Interviewed in Mississippi

I was thirty-one years old when I was set free. My Marster din't tell us about bein' free. De way I found out about it, he started to whip me once and de young marster up and says, "You ain't got no right to whip him now; he's free." Den Marster turn me loose. . . .

. . . Dey went out and turned us loose, just like a passel of cattle, and didn't show us nothin' or give us nothin'. Dey was acres and acres of land not in use, and lots of timber in dis country. Dey should-a give each one of us a little farm and let us get out timber and build houses. . . .

I never did look for to get nothin' after I was free. I had dat in my head to get me eighty acres of land and homestead it. As for the government making me a present of anything, I never thought about it. . . .

I did get me this little farm, but I bought it and paid for it myself. I got de money by workin' for it. . . .

Many of the major developments or experiences in American history are local topics for comparative study and analysis--the Revolution, the frontier experience, slavery and race relations, to name just a few. The growing body of research by scholars into the aftermath of emancipation in different societies now offers teachers and students an opportunity to study Reconstruction from a comparative perspective. The following suggestions from a lesson in comparative history are based on the assumption that students will have a good knowledge of American slavery and race relations including events during the Civil War leading to emancipation. The lesson can be used to introduce a unit on Reconstruction.

To begin, tell your students that you are going to have them assume the role of a slave who has been freed as a result of the Civil War. "It is 1866 and you have been free for nearly a year. What is freedom like? How is it different from slavery? You have the opportunity to write your former master a letter. What would you tell him or her about being free?" Spend a day having students read their letters in class, giving them the opportunity to draw comparisons about their descriptions of freedom. Have them speculate whether their letters would reflect the feelings of slaves who were freed at the time of the Civil War.

Next, tell your students that they will read "eyewitness accounts" about the aftermath of slavery by former masters and former slaves in three different societies--the United States, Cuba, and Zaria. Divide the class into small groups of equal size and give each group a different set of accounts--accounts by former masters, letters of former slaves, and recollections of former slaves. Appoint a discussion leader and tell each group to read and analyze the accounts and agree on three generalizations about what freedom meant to either former masters or former slaves. Students should consider such matters as attitudes toward work, changing roles of masters and slaves, how and when slaves learned about freedom, attitudes toward land ownership, and so on. Allow several days for this activity, and when each group has reported and defended its generalizations, lead a class discussion about the difficulties of adjusting to freedom and whether the attitudes about freedom stated by students in their letters were shared by the writers of the accounts they have just analyzed.

Finally, present to your students some of the insights about the aftermath of slavery in several societies from Thomas J. Pressly's article, "Reconstruction in the Southern United States: A Comparative Perspective." This might include a discussion of the common desire for

Teachers and students now have an opportunity to study Reconstruction from a comparative perspective.

land ownership by former slaves and the extent to which it was obtained, the reasons why former masters were able to retain their control after abolition, and the degree of political power, health care, and education gained by former slaves. Encourage the students to use the eyewitness accounts they have analyzed to support some of the ideas you have presented to them.

At this point you might turn to a more detailed study of the Reconstruction Era. By reading, analyzing, and discussing accounts about the aftermath of emancipation in different settings, students will be able to develop a better understanding about the problems associated with the ending of slavery in the nineteenth century United States. ■

NOTES

1. Foner, Eric. *Nothing But Freedom: Emancipation and Its Legacy*, 7. Baton Rouge: LSU Press, 1983.
2. Leigh, Frances B. *Ten Years on a Georgia Plantation Since the War*, 1-3, 13-16, 24-28, 32-33, 56-57, 73-74, 78-79. London: Richard Bentley & Son, 1883.
3. Vann Woodward, C., ed. *Mary Chestnut's Civil War*, 805-806. New Haven: Yale University Press, 1981.
4. Ibid., 827.
5. Smith, Mary B. *Baba of Karo: A Woman of the Moslem Hausa*, 66-68. New York: Praeger, 1964.
6. These letters are reprinted in Litwack, Leon F. *Been In The Storm So Long: The Aftermath of Slavery*, 333-335. New York: Vintage Books, 1979.
7. Montejo, Esteban. *The Autobiography of a Runaway Slave*, 59-60, 63-69, 83-85, 91-92, 171. New York: Vintage Press, 1973.
8. Yetman, Norman R. *Life Under the "Peculiar Institution": Selections From The Slave Narrative Collection*, 15, 17-18, 21-23, 91-93, 237-239. New York: Holt, Rinehart and Winston, Inc., 1970.

The New View of Reconstruction

Whatever you were taught or thought you knew about the post–Civil War era is probably wrong in the light of recent study

Eric Foner

Eric Foner is Professor of History at Columbia University and author of Nothing but Freedom: Emancipation and Its Legacy.

IN THE PAST twenty years, no period of American history has been the subject of a more thoroughgoing reevaluation than Reconstruction—the violent, dramatic, and still controversial era following the Civil War. Race relations, politics, social life, and economic change during Reconstruction have all been reinterpreted in the light of changed attitudes toward the place of blacks within American society. If historians have not yet forged a fully satisfying portrait of Reconstruction as a whole, the traditional interpretation that dominated historical writing for much of this century has irrevocably been laid to rest.

Anyone who attended high school before 1960 learned that Reconstruction was an era of unrelieved sordidness in American political and social life. The martyred Lincoln, according to this view, had planned a quick and painless readmission of the Southern states as equal members of the national family. President Andrew Johnson, his successor, attempted to carry out Lincoln's policies but was foiled by the Radical Republicans (also known as Vindictives or Jacobins). Motivated by an irrational hatred of Rebels or by ties with Northern capitalists out to plunder the South, the Radicals swept aside Johnson's lenient program and fastened black supremacy upon the defeated Confederacy. An orgy of corruption followed, presided over by unscrupulous carpetbaggers (Northerners who ventured south to reap the spoils of office), traitorous scalawags (Southern whites who cooperated with the new governments for personal gain), and the ignorant and childlike freedmen, who were incapable of properly exercising the political power that had been thrust upon them. After much needless suffering, the white community of the South banded together to overthrow these "black" governments and restore home rule (their euphemism for white supremacy). All told, Reconstruction was just about the darkest page in the American saga.

Originating in anti-Reconstruction propaganda of Southern Democrats during the 1870s, this traditional interpretation achieved scholarly legitimacy around the turn of the century through the work of William Dunning and his students at Columbia University. It reached the larger public through films like *Birth of a Nation* and *Gone With the Wind* and that best-selling work of myth-making masquerading as history, *The Tragic Era* by Claude G. Bowers. In language as exaggerated as it was colorful, Bowers told how Andrew Johnson "fought the bravest battle for constitutional liberty and for the preservation of our institutions ever waged by an Executive" but was overwhelmed by the "poisonous propaganda" of the Radicals. Southern whites, as a result, "literally were put to the torture" by "emissaries of hate" who manipulated the "simple-minded" freedmen, "inflaming the negroes' egotism" and even inspiring "lustful assaults" by blacks upon white womanhood.

In a discipline that sometimes seems to pride itself on the rapid rise and fall of historical interpretations, this traditional portrait of Reconstruction enjoyed remarkable staying power. The long reign of the old interpretation is not difficult to explain. It presented a set of easily identifiable heroes and villains. It enjoyed the imprimatur of the nation's leading scholars. And it accorded with the political and social realities of the first half of this century. This image of Reconstruction helped freeze the mind of the white South in unalterable opposition to any movement for breaching the ascendancy of the Democratic party, eliminating segregation, or readmitting disfranchised blacks to the vote.

NEVERTHELESS, THE demise of the traditional interpretation was inevitable, for it ignored the testimony of the central participant in the drama of Reconstruction—the black freedman. Furthermore, it was grounded in the conviction that blacks were unfit to share in political power. As Dunning's Columbia colleague John W. Burgess put it, "A black skin means membership in a race of men which has never of itself succeeded in subjecting passion to reason, has never, therefore, created any civilization of any kind." Once objective scholarship and modern experience rendered that assumption untenable, the entire edifice was bound to fall.

The work of "revising" the history of Reconstruction began with the writings of a handful of survivors of the era, such as John R. Lynch, who had served as a black congressman from Mississippi after the Civil War. In the 1930s white scholars like Francis Simkins and Robert Woody carried the task forward. Then, in 1935, the black historian and activist W.E.B. Du Bois produced *Black Reconstruction in America,* a monumental reevaluation that closed with an irrefutable indictment of a historical profession that had sacrificed scholarly objectivity on the altar of racial bias. "One fact and one alone," he wrote, "explains the attitude of most recent writers toward Reconstruction; they cannot conceive of Negroes as men." Du Bois's work, however, was ignored by most historians.

It was not until the 1960s that the full force of the revisionist wave broke over the field. Then, in rapid succession, virtually every assumption of the traditional viewpoint was systematically dismantled. A drastically different portrait emerged to take its place. President Lincoln did not have a coherent "plan" for Reconstruction, but at the time of his assassination he had been cautiously contemplating black suffrage. Andrew Johnson was a stubborn, racist politician who lacked the ability to compromise. By isolating himself from the broad currents of public opnion that had

nourished Lincoln's career, Johnson created an impasse with Congress that Lincoln would certainly have avoided, thus throwing away his political power and destroying his own plans for reconstructing the South.

The Radicals in Congress were acquitted of both vindictive motives and the charge of serving as the stalking-horses of Northern capitalism. They emerged instead as idealists in the best nineteenth-century reform tradition. Radical leaders like Charles Sumner and Thaddeus Stevens had worked for the rights of blacks long before any conceivable political advantage flowed from such a commitment. Stevens refused to sign the Pennsylvania Constitution of 1838 because it disfranchised the state's black citizens; Sumner led a fight in the 1850s to integrate Boston's public schools. Their Reconstruction policies were based on principle, not petty political advantage, for the central issue dividing Johnson and these Radical Republicans was the civil rights of freedmen. Studies of congressional policy-making, such as Eric L. McKitrick's *Andrew Johnson and Reconstruction,* also revealed that Reconstruction legislation, ranging from the Civil Rights Act of 1866 to the Fourteenth and Fifteenth Amendments, enjoyed broad support from moderate and conservative Republicans. It was not simply the work of a narrow radical faction.

EVEN MORE STARTLING was the revised portrait of Reconstruction in the South itself. Imbued with the spirit of the civil rights movement and rejecting entirely the racial assumptions that had underpinned the traditional interpretation, these historians evaluated Reconstruction from the black point of view. Works like Joel Williamson's *After Slavery* portrayed the period as a time of extraordinary political, social, and economic progress for blacks. The establishment of public school systems, the granting of equal citizenship to blacks, the effort to restore the devastated Southern economy, the attempt to construct an interracial political democracy from the ashes of slavery, all these were commendable achievements, not the elements of Bowers's "tragic era."

Unlike earlier writers, the revisionists stressed the active role of the freedmen in shaping Reconstruction. Black initiative established as many schools as did Northern religious societies and the Freedmen's Bureau. The right to vote was not simply thrust upon them by meddling outsiders, since blacks began agitating for the suffrage as soon as they were freed. In 1865 black conventions throughout the South issued eloquent, though unheeded, appeals for equal civil and political rights.

With the advent of Radical Recon-

Until recently, Thaddeus Stevens had been viewed as motivated by irrational hatred of the Rebels (left). Now he has emerged as an idealist in the best reform tradition.

NEW YORK PUBLIC LIBRARY, PRINT ROOM

LIBRARY OF CONGRESS

struction in 1867, the freedmen did enjoy a real measure of political power. But black supremacy never existed. In most states blacks held only a small fraction of political offices, and even in South Carolina, where they comprised a majority of the state legislature's lower house, effective power remained in white hands. As for corruption, moral standards in both government and private enterprise were at low ebb throughout the nation in the postwar years—the era of Boss Tweed, the Credit Mobilier scandal, and the Whiskey Ring. Southern corruption could hardly be blamed on former slaves.

Other actors in the Reconstruction drama also came in for reevaluation. Most carpetbaggers were former Union soldiers seeking economic opportunity in the postwar South, not unscrupulous adventurers. Their motives, a typically American amalgam of humanitarianism and the pursuit of profit, were no more insidious than those of Western pioneers. Scalawags, previously seen as traitors to the white race, now emerged as "Old Line" Whig Unionists who had opposed secession in the first place or as poor whites who had long resented planters' domination of Southern life and who saw in Reconstruction a chance to recast Southern society along more democratic lines. Strongholds of Southern white Republicanism like east Tennessee and western North Carolina had been the scene of resistance to Confederate rule throughout the Civil War; now, as one scalawag newspaper put it, the choice was "between salvation at the hand of the Negro or destruction at the hand of the rebels."

At the same time, the Ku Klux Klan and kindred groups, whose campaign of violence against black and white Republicans had been minimized or excused in older writings, were portrayed as they really were. Earlier scholars had conveyed the impression that the Klan intimidated blacks mainly by dressing as ghosts and playing on the freedmen's superstitions. In fact, black fears were all too real: the Klan was a terrorist organization that beat and killed its political opponents to deprive blacks of their newly won rights. The complicity of the Democratic party and

the silence of prominent whites in the face of such outrages stood as an indictment of the moral code the South had inherited from the days of slavery.

By the end of the 1960s, then, the old interpretation had been completely reversed. Southern freedmen were the heroes, the "Redeemers" who overthrew Reconstruction were the villains, and if the era was "tragic," it was because change did not go far enough. Reconstruction had been a time of real progress and its failure a lost opportunity for the South and the nation. But the legacy of Reconstruction—the Fourteenth and Fifteenth Amendments—endured to inspire future efforts for civil rights. As Kenneth Stampp wrote in *The Era of Reconstruction*, a superb summary of revisionist findings published in 1965, "If it was worth four years of civil war to save the Union, it was worth a few years of radical reconstruction to give the American Negro the ultimate promise of equal civil and political rights."

As Stampp's statement suggests, the reevaluation of the first Reconstruction was inspired in large measure by the impact of the second—the modern civil rights movement. And with the waning of that movement in recent years, writing on Reconstruction has undergone still another transformation. Instead of seeing the Civil War and its aftermath as a second American Revolution (as Charles Beard had), a regression into barbarism (as Bowers argued), or a golden opportunity squandered (as the revisionists saw it), recent writers argue that Radical Reconstruction was not really very radical. Since land was not distributed to the former slaves, they remained economically dependent upon their former owners. The planter class survived both the war and Reconstruction with its property (apart from slaves) and prestige more or less intact.

Not only changing times but also the changing concerns of historians have contributed to this latest reassessment of Reconstruction. The hallmark of the past decade's historical writing has been an emphasis upon "social history"—the evocation of the past lives of ordinary Americans—and the downplaying of strictly political events. When applied

to Reconstruction, this concern with the "social" suggested that black suffrage and officeholding, once seen as the most radical departures of the Reconstruction era, were relatively insignificant.

RECENT HISTORIANS have focused their investigations not upon the politics of Reconstruction but upon the social and economic aspects of the transition from slavery to freedom. Herbert Gutman's influential study of the black family during and after slavery found little change in family structure or relations between men and women resulting from emancipation. Under slavery most blacks had lived in nuclear family units, although they faced the constant threat of separation from loved ones by sale. Reconstruction provided the opportunity for blacks to solidify their preexisting family ties. Conflicts over whether black women should work in the cotton fields (planters said yes, many black families said no) and over white attempts to "apprentice" black children revealed that the autonomy of family life was a major preoccupation of the freedmen. Indeed, whether manifested in their withdrawal from churches controlled by whites, in the blossoming of black fraternal, benevolent, and self-improvement organizations, or in the demise of the slave quarters and their replacement by small tenant farms occupied by individual families, the quest for independence from white authority and control over their own day-to-day lives shaped the black response to emancipation.

In the post–Civil War South the surest guarantee of economic autonomy, blacks believed, was land. To the freedmen the justice of a claim to land based on their years of unrequited labor appeared self-evident. As an Alabama black convention put it, "The property which they [the planters] hold was nearly all earned by the sweat of *our* brows." As Leon Litwack showed in *Been in the Storm So Long*, a Pulitzer Prize–winning account of the black response to emancipation, many freedmen in 1865 and 1866 refused to sign labor contracts, expecting the federal government to give them land. In some localities, as one Alabama overseer

EDWARD S. ELLIS, *The History of Our Country*, VOL. 5, 1900

Reconstruction governments were portrayed as disastrous failures (left) because elected blacks were ignorant or corrupt. In fact, postwar corruption cannot be blamed on former slaves.

SCHOMBERG CENTER, NEW YORK PUBLIC LIBRARY

reported, they "set up claims to the plantation and all on it."

In the end, of course, the vast majority of Southern blacks remained propertyless and poor. But exactly why the South, and especially its black population, suffered from dire poverty and economic retardation in the decades following the Civil War is a matter of much dispute. In *One Kind of Freedom*, economists Roger Ransom and Richard Sutch indicted country merchants for monopolizing credit and charging usurious interest rates, forcing black tenants into debt and locking the South into a dependence on cotton production that impoverished the entire region. But Jonathan Wiener, in his study of postwar Alabama, argued that planters used their political power to compel blacks to remain on the plantations. Planters succeeded in stabilizing the plantation system, but only by blocking the growth of alternative enterprises, like factories, that might draw off black laborers, thus locking the region into a pattern of economic backwardness.

I F THE THRUST OF recent writing has emphasized the social and economic aspects of Reconstruction, politics has not been entirely neglected. But political studies have also reflected the postrevisionist mood summarized by C. Vann Woodward when he observed "how essentially nonrevolutionary and conservative Reconstruction really was." Recent writers, unlike their revisionist predecessors, have found little to praise in federal policy toward the emancipated blacks.

A new sensitivity to the strength of prejudice and laissez-faire ideas in the nineteenth-century North has led many historians to doubt whether the Republican party ever made a genuine commitment to racial justice in the South. The granting of black suffrage was an alternative to a long-term federal responsibility for protecting the rights of the former slaves. Once enfranchised, blacks could be left to fend for themselves. With the exception of a few Radicals like Thaddeus Stevens, nearly all Northern policy-makers and educators are criticized today for assuming that, so long as the unfettered operations of the marketplace afforded blacks the opportunity to advance through diligent labor, federal efforts to assist them in acquiring land were unnecessary.

Probably the most innovative recent writing on Reconstruction politics has centered on a broad reassessment of black Republicanism, largely undertaken by a new generation of black historians. Scholars like Thomas Holt and Nell Painter insist that Reconstruction was not simply a matter of black and white. Conflicts within the black community, no less than divisions among whites, shaped Reconstruction politics. Where revisionist scholars, both black and white, had celebrated the accomplishments of black political leaders, Holt, Painter, and others charge that they failed to address the economic plight of the black masses. Painter criticized "representative colored men," as national black leaders were called, for failing to provide ordinary freedmen with effective political leadership. Holt found that black officeholders in South Carolina mostly emerged from the old free mulatto class of Charleston, which

shared many assumptions with prominent whites. "Basically bourgeois in their origins and orientation," he wrote, they "failed to act in the interest of black peasants."

In emphasizing the persistence from slavery of divisions between free blacks and slaves, these writers reflect the increasing concern with continuity and conservatism in Reconstruction. Their work reflects a startling extension of revisionist premises. If, as has been argued for the past twenty years, blacks were active agents rather than mere victims of manipulation, then they could not be absolved of blame for the ultimate failure of Reconstruction.

Despite the excellence of recent writing and the continual expansion of our knowledge of the period, historians of Reconstruction today face a unique dilemma. An old interpretation has been overthrown, but a coherent new synthesis has yet to take its place. The revisionists of the 1960s effectively established a series of negative points: the Reconstruction governments were not as bad as had been portrayed, black supremacy was a myth, the Radicals were not cynical manipulators of the freedmen. Yet no convincing overall portrait of the quality of political and social life emerged from their writings. More recent historians have rightly pointed to elements of continuity that spanned the nineteenth-century Southern experience, especially the survival, in modified form, of the plantation system. Nevertheless, by denying the real changes that did occur, they have failed to provide a convincing portrait of an era characterized above all by drama, turmoil, and social change.

Building upon the findings of the past twenty years of scholarship, a new portrait of Reconstruction ought to begin by viewing it not as a specific time period, bounded by the years 1865 and 1877, but as an episode in a prolonged historical process—American society's adjustment to the consequences of the Civil War and emancipation. The Civil War, of course, raised the decisive questions of America's national existence: the relations between local and national authority, the definition of citizenship, the balance between force and consent in generating obedience to authority. The war and Reconstruction, as Allan Nevins observed over fifty years ago, marked the "emergence of modern America." This was the era of the completion of the national railroad network, the creation of the modern steel industry, the conquest of the West and final subduing of the Indians, and the expansion of the mining frontier. Lincoln's America—the world of the small farm and artisan shop—gave way to a rapidly industrializing economy. The issues that galvanized postwar Northern politics—from the question of the greenback currency to the mode of paying holders of the national debt—arose from the economic changes unleashed by the Civil War.

Above all, the war irrevocably abolished slavery. Since 1619, when "twenty negars" disembarked from a Dutch ship in Virginia, racial injustice had haunted American life, mocking its professed ideals even as tobacco and cotton, the products of slave labor, helped finance the nation's economic development. Now the implications of the black presence could no longer be ignored. The Civil War resolved the problem of slavery but, as the Philadelphia diarist Sydney George Fisher observed in June 1865, it opened an even more intractable problem: "What shall we do with the Negro?" Indeed, he went on, this was a problem "*incapable* of any solution that will satisfy both North and South."

As Fisher realized, the focal point of Reconstruction was the social revolution known as emancipation. Plantation slavery was simultaneously a system of labor, a form of racial domination, and the foundation upon which arose a distinctive ruling class within the South.

Its demise threw open the most fundamental questions of economy, society, and politics. A new system of labor, social, racial, and political relations had to be created to replace slavery.

The United States was not the only nation to experience emancipation in the nineteenth century. Neither plantation slavery nor abolition were unique to the United States. But Reconstruction was. In a comparative perspective Radical Reconstruction stands as a remarkable experiment, the only effort of a society experiencing abolition to bring the former slaves within the umbrella of equal citizenship. Because the Radicals did not achieve everything they wanted, historians have lately tended to play down the stunning departure represented by black suffrage and officeholding. Former slaves, most fewer than two years removed from bondage, debated the fundamental questions of the polity: What is a republican form of government? Should the state provide equal education for all? How could political equality be reconciled with a society in which property was so unequally distributed? There was something inspiring in the way such men met the challenge of Reconstruction. "I knew nothing more than to obey my master," James K. Greene, an Alabama black politician later recalled. "But the tocsin of freedom sounded and knocked at the door and we walked out like free men and we met the exigencies as they grew up, and shouldered the responsibilities."

You never saw a people more excited on the subject of politics than are the negroes of the south," one planter observed in 1867. And there were more than a few Southern whites as well who in these years shook off the prejudices of the past to embrace the vision of a new South dedicated to the principles of equal citizenship and social justice. One ordinary South Carolinian expressed the new sense of possibility in 1868 to the Republican governor of the state: "I am sorry that I cannot write an elegant stiled letter to your excellency. But I rejoice to think that God almighty has given to the poor of S. C. a Gov. to hear to feel to protect the humble poor without distinction to race or color. . . . I

am a native borned S. C. a poor man never owned a Negro in my life nor my father before me. . . . Remember the true and loyal are the poor of the whites and blacks, outside of these you can find none loyal."

Few modern scholars believe the Reconstruction governments established in the South in 1867 and 1868 fulfilled the aspirations of their humble constituents. While their achievements in such realms as education, civil rights, and the economic rebuilding of the South are now widely appreciated, historians today believe they failed to affect either the economic plight of the emancipated slave or the ongoing transformation of independent white farmers into cotton tenants. Yet their opponents did perceive the Reconstruction governments in precisely this way—as representatives of a revolution that had put the bottom rail, both racial and economic, on top. This perception helps explain the ferocity of the attacks leveled against them and the pervasiveness of violence in the postemancipation South.

The spectacle of black men voting and holding office was anathema to large numbers of Southern whites. Even more disturbing, at least in the view of those who still controlled the plantation regions of the South, was the emergence of local officials, black and white, who sympathized with the plight of the black laborer. Alabama's vagrancy law was a "dead letter" in 1870, "because those who are charged with its enforcement are indebted to the vagrant vote for their offices and emoluments." Political debates over the level and incidence of taxation, the control of crops, and the resolution of contract disputes revealed that a primary issue of Reconstruction was the role of government in a plantation society. During presidential Reconstruction, and after "Redemption," with planters and their allies in control of politics, the law emerged as a means of stabilizing and promoting the plantation system. If Radical Reconstruction failed to redistribute the land of the South, the ouster of the planter class from control of politics at least ensured that the sanctions of the criminal law would not be employed to discipline the black labor force.

Some scholars exalted the motives of the Ku Klux Klan (left). Actually, its members were part of a terrorist organization that beat and killed its political opponents to deprive blacks of their rights.

AN UNDERSTANDING OF this fundamental conflict over the relation between government and society helps explain the pervasive complaints concerning corruption and "extravagance" during Radical Reconstruction. Corruption there was aplenty; tax rates did rise sharply. More significant than the rate of taxation, however, was the change in its incidence. For the first time, planters and white farmers had to pay a significant portion of their income to the government, while propertyless blacks often escaped scot-free. Several states, moreover, enacted heavy taxes on uncultivated land to discourage land speculation and force land onto the market, benefiting, it was hoped, the freedmen.

As time passed, complaints about the "extravagance" and corruption of Southern governments found a sympathetic audience among influential Northerners. The Democratic charge that universal suffrage in the South was responsible for high taxes and governmental extravagance coincided with a rising conviction among the urban middle classes of the North that city government had to be taken out of the hands of the immigrant poor and returned to the "best men"—the educated, professional, financially independent citizens unable to exert much political influence at a time of mass parties and machine politics. Increasingly the "respectable" middle classes began to retreat from the very notion of universal suffrage. The poor were no longer perceived as honest producers,

the backbone of the social order; now they became the "dangerous classes," the "mob." As the historian Francis Parkman put it, too much power rested with "masses of imported ignorance and hereditary ineptitude." To Parkman the Irish of the Northern cities and the blacks of the South were equally incapable of utilizing the ballot: "Witness the municipal corruptions of New York, and the monstrosities of negro rule in South Carolina." Such attitudes helped to justify Northern inaction as, one by one, the Reconstruction regimes of the South were overthrown by political violence.

IN THE END, THEN, neither the abolition of slavery nor Reconstruction succeeded in resolving the debate over the meaning of freedom in American life. Twenty years before the American Civil War, writing about the prospect of abolition in France's colonies, Alexis de Tocqueville had written, "If the Negroes have the right to become free, the [planters] have the incontestable right not to be ruined by the Negroes' freedom." And in the United States, as in nearly every plantation society that experienced the end of slavery, a rigid social and political dichotomy between former master and former slave, an ideology of racism, and a dependent labor force with limited economic opportunities all survived abolition. Unless one means by freedom the simple fact of not being a slave, emancipation thrust blacks into a kind of no-man's land, a partial freedom that

made a mockery of the American ideal of equal citizenship.

Yet by the same token the ultimate outcome underscores the uniqueness of Reconstruction itself. Alone among the societies that abolished slavery in the nineteenth century, the United States, for a moment, offered the freedmen a measure of political control over their own destinies. However brief its sway, Reconstruction allowed scope for a remarkable political and social mobilization of the black community. It opened doors of opportunity that could never be completely closed. Reconstruction transformed the lives of Southern blacks in ways unmeasurable by statistics and unreachable by law. It raised their expectations and aspirations, redefined their status in relation to the larger society, and allowed space for the creation of institutions that enabled them to survive the repression that followed. And it established constitutional principles of civil and political equality that, while flagrantly violated after Redemption, planted the seeds of future struggle.

Certainly, in terms of the sense of possibility with which it opened, Reconstruction failed. But as Du Bois observed, it was a "splendid failure." For its animating vision—a society in which social advancement would be open to all on the basis of individual merit, not inherited caste distinctions—is as old as America itself and remains relevant to a nation still grappling with the unresolved legacy of emancipation.

abolitionists, 53, 75, 76, 114, 117, 143, 144, 158, 159, 161, 163, 171, 175, 177, 178, 182, 183, 215, 216, 218, 221

Adams, John, 29, 39, 50, 71, 86, 87, 88, 89, 91, 92, 93, 123–124

Adams, John Quincy, 29, 123

Adams, Samuel, 47, 50

aesthetic conservation, 140

Alamo, Texas before and after the, 130–133

Alaska, Russian traders in, 98–102

Albion's Seed (Fischer), American regionalism theory of, 28–31

Americas, discovery of the, 6–9

Annapolis Convention, 49

annihilation, Civil War as war of, 200

Antietam, Civil War battle at, 202, 203, 209, 217

Antifederalists, 48, 68–69, 70

Antinomians, 26, 27

Appalachia, regional characteristics of, 29, 30

Appleton, Nathan, 104, 105, 106–107

Appomattox, Confederate surrender at, 189, 200

Arnold, Benedict, 44

Articles of Confederation, 47, 51, 52

attrition, Civil War as war of, 199, 200

Austin, Stephen, 131–132, 133

Banneker, Benjamin, 74

bathing, custom of, in the early nineteenth century, 111–112

Beecher, Henry Ward, 109–110

Benton, Thomas Hart, 124, 172

Bibb, Henry, 160, 161

Bill of Rights, 56; James Madison and, 66–71

blacks: 28, 31, 205; as Civil War soldiers, 215–222; families of, in Civil War, 190–198; see also, freedmen; slavery; Underground Railroad

Boer War, as compared to the Civil War, 201–205

Boott, Kirk, 104–105

Boston Associates, development of planned mill community in Lowell, MA, by, 103–107

Boston Tea Party, 37, 38

Brown, John, 178

Buchanan, James, 90, 151, 152

buffalo: 137, 139; healthful effects of eating, 166, 167

Bull Run, Battle of, 186, 189, 200, 209

bundling, 117, 118

Burr, Aaron, 89

Calhoun, John C., 124, 127, 177

Canada, underground railroad to, 158–163

capital punishment, 114–115, 116

carpetbaggers, 235, 237

Catherine the Great, Russia's, 34, 38, 101

Catholicism, feelings against, and the American Revolution, 58–63

Catlin, George, 135, 167

cattlemen, Western, 137, 138, 140

Chancellorsville, Battle of, 186

Chase, Salmon, 178, 183, 184

child care, cooperative, among black slave women, 78–83

Civil War: 29, 77, 78, 80, 132, 143, 152, 155, 156, 163, 165, 167, 226; black families in, 190–198; black soldiers in, 215–222; and Confederate attack on Washington, D.C., 185–189; why the Confederacy lost the, 199–205; see also, Reconstruction

class distinctions, importance of, in Jacksonian democracy, 128, 129

Clay, Henry, 86, 106, 124, 126, 127, 180

Columbus, Christopher, 6–9

Commerce of the Prairies (Gregg), 164–165

conservation, land, and pioneer attitudes, 134–141

Constitution, U.S.: 8, 35, 37, 39, 40, 72, 74, 87, 89, 91, 123, 124, 173, 174, 188, 190, 202, 216; writing of, 50–57; see also, Bill of Rights

convicts, as indentured servants, 22, 23, 24

cornucopian view of the West, pioneers', 134–141

Cortés, Hernando, 7–8

Cotton, John, 25, 26

courtship and marriage customs, in the early nineteenth century, 109

covenant of works, vs. covenant of grace, 25

covert operations, during the Revolutionary War, 41–45

creoles, 101, 102

Culper spy network, 43, 44, 45

cultural cross-fertilization, in the New World, 6–9, 98–102

Dare, Virginia, 15

Davis, Jefferson, 202, 205, 226

Declaration of Independence, 8, 24, 34, 35, 38, 40, 47, 50, 52, 54, 85, 86, 124, 142, 182

Delaware Valley, regional characteristics of, 30

Democratic party, 124, 125, 126, 129, 179, 204, 220, 237

Democratic-Republicans, 88, 92, 93, 94, 96, 97

developing country, America as, in the early nineteenth century, 108–122

Dickinson, John, 52, 53

Douglas, Stephen A., presidential campaign of, 176–184

Douglass, Frederick, 76, 80, 117, 160, 216, 217

Dred Scott decision, 144, 170–175, 216

Du Bois, W. E. B., 236, 240

Early, Jubal, and Confederate attack on Washington, D.C., 185–189

Eighteenth Amendment, 153, 157

electoral college, 56, 125, 176, 187

Elizabeth I, England's, 10, 11, 15, 25

Ellsworth, Oliver, 52, 55

Emancipation Proclamation, 193, 217, 223

England: 47, 54; indentured servants from, 20–24; Roanoke, Virginia, Colony of, 10–16; as source of American regionalism, 28–31

Enlightenment, Jeffersonian, 62, 63

entrepreneurial thesis, Hofstadter's, of Jacksonian democracy, 129

equality, in social relationships of the early nineteenth century, 120–121

espionage, in the Revolutionary War, 41–45

ethnocultural approach, to historical writing, 129

etiquette, in the early nineteenth century, 108–122

Europeans, reaction of, to American Revolution, 34–38

executive power, Jackson's use of, 123–128

Federalists: 51, 69, 70, 71, 85, 86, 87, 88, 89, 90; and the Hartford Convention, 92–97

Fifteenth Amendment, 236, 237

filibusterer, William Walker as, 145–152

Fischer, David Hackett, American regionalism theory of, 28–31

Forrest, Nathan Bedford, 205, 220

Fort Pillow, Civil War battle at, 220, 221

Fourteenth Amendment, 70, 126, 236, 237

France: 15, 37, 54, 59, 60, 93, 131; see also, French Revolution

Franklin, Benjamin, 38, 50, 53, 55, 56, 57

freedmen, black: 161, 191, 197, 223–234, 235–240; in Washington, D.C., 72–78

Free-Soilers, 143, 177

French Revolution, 34, 35, 39, 40, 87

Fries' Rebellion, 60, 63

frontier thesis, Turner's, of American history, 128, 134, 140

Fugitive Slave Law, 158, 216

fur trade, Russian, in Alaska, 98–102

gambling, in the early nineteenth century, 113, 115, 143

Garland, Hamlin, 138, 139

Garrison, William Lloyd, 142, 143, 144

George III, England's, 34, 35, 36, 38, 60, 62

Gerry, Elbridge, 51, 53, 56, 87

Gettysburg, PA, Civil War battle at: 185–189, 203, 215, 221; eyewitness account of, 206–215

Giants in the Earth (Rölvaag), 138–139

Glory, 215, 217, 219–220

Gough, John Bartholomew, 154–155

Grant, Ulysses S., 91, 185, 186, 188, 217, 222

Great Awakening, 59, 60, 62

Great Compromise, 52, 55, 56

Greeley, Horace, 115, 120, 179, 181, 182

Gregg, Josiah, 164–165

Grenville, Sir Richard, 11, 12, 13, 14, 15

guerrilla action, in the Civil War, 201, 202, 203

Hale, Nathan, 42, 43

Hamilton, Alexander, 47, 49, 50, 72, 86, 91, 92

Hariot, Thomas, 11, 12, 13, 14, 15

Harper's Ferry, 178, 179

Harrison, William Henry, 123, 179

Hartford Convention, 92–97

Haskell, Frank Aretas, eyewitness account of Civil War battle at Gettysburg by, 206–215

Hawkins, John H. W., 154, 155

health, effects of emigration to the West on, 164–167

Henry, Patrick, 48, 49, 50, 51, 87

Henson, Josiah, 161–162

Holmes, Oliver Wendell, 84, 90–91

Homestead Act, 138

House of Representatives, 54, 56, 66, 68, 89

Houston, Sam, 133

Hutchinson, Anne, 25–27

hygiene, personal in the early nineteenth century, 110, 111–112

indentured servants, 20–24
Indians: Alaskan, 98–102; and Europeans in the New World, 8, 9, 10–16, 17, 19, 27, 59; Nicaraguan, 145, 146, 147; in Texas, 130, 133; Western, 134, 136, 137, 167, 239

Jackson, Andrew, 89, 97, 106, 123–129, 182
Jackson, Stonewall, 186
James I, England's, 15, 16, 25
Jamestown, Virginia, British colony at, 14, 16, 153
Jay, John, 43, 44, 45, 88
Jefferson, Thomas: 29, 40, 47, 49, 50, 56, 62, 63, 66, 68, 69, 70, 72, 74, 92, 93, 123, 142, 143, 174; and John Marshall, 85, 86, 87, 88, 91
Johnson, Andrew, 204, 205, 235, 236

King, Rufus, 48, 52–53
Know-Nothing political party, 177, 178, 180
Ku Klux Klan, 205, 237

Lane, Ralph, 11, 12, 13, 14
Lee, Robert E., 185, 186, 200, 201, 202, 203, 206, 211, 215, 222
liberty, regional versions of, 29, 30
Life Under the "Peculiar Institution": Selections from the Slave Narrative Collection (Yetman), 231–233
Lincoln, Abraham: 39, 40, 77, 97, 144, 152, 201, 204, 215, 216, 217, 220, 223, 225, 228, 235, 236, 239; and Confederate attack on Washington, D.C., 186, 187, 188; election of, 176–184
liquor: use of, in the early nineteenth century, 112, 113, 114, 115, 119–120, 166, 167; see also, temperance
Lost Colony, at Roanoke, Virginia, 10–16
Lowell, MA, planned mill community in, 103–107, 143

Madison, James: 48, 49, 74–75, 88, 92, 93, 123; and the Bill of Rights, 66–71; and the Constitution, 50, 51, 52, 53, 54, 55, 56, 57
Manifest Destiny, 17, 19, 136, 145
manners, in the early nineteenth century, 120–122
Marbury v. Madison, 88–89, 170
Maria Theresa, Austria's, 34, 38
Marshall, John, as chief Supreme Court justice, 84–91
Mason, George, 48, 50, 51, 53, 56, 68
McClellan, George, 186, 201, 217, 220
Meade, General George C., and the Civil War battle at Gettysburg, 206–215, 221
Merrimack Manufacturing Company, 104, 105
Mexico: 146, 147, 178, 186; Texas and, 130–133, 222
midwives, black slave women as, 79, 80
mill town, planned, in Lowell, MA, 103–107
millenarianism, and the American Revolution, 58, 60, 62
miners, Western, 137, 140
Missouri Compromise of 1820, 172, 173, 174
Monroe, James, 66, 69, 70, 86, 123
Morris, Gouverneur, 52, 53, 55–56

Morris, Robert, 51, 52, 69
Mott, Lucretia, 142, 143

Nation, Carry A., 156
natural liberty, 30
New England, regional characteristics of, 28
New Jersey Plan, 52, 53
New Light movement, 60, 61, 62
Nicaragua, William Walker and the conquest of, 145–152
Northwest Ordinance of 1787, 172, 174
nutrition, in the early nineteenth century, 121–122, 165

ordered liberty, 29
Oregon Trail, 136, 137
original intent, in the Constitution, 50, 57
Otis, Harrison Gray, 95, 96

Parkman, Francis, 134–135, 240
parks, origin of national, 135, 140
Parton, James, 127–128
Paterson, William, 52, 54, 88
Phillips, Wendell, 143, 144
Pickering, Timothy, 92, 95, 96
Pilgrims, 10, 17–19
Pinckney, Charles, 51, 87
pioneer attitudes: and land conservation, 134–141; toward healthfulness of the West, 164–167
planned community, mill town of Lowell, MA, as, 103–107
plantations, Southern, 29, 31, 109, 117, 121
Plymouth Colony, MA, Pilgrims at, 17–19, 135, 153
political parties, rise of, 123–124
Polk, James K., 133, 143
premarital pregnancies, in the early nineteenth century, 117, 118, 119
privateering, 11, 12, 14, 15, 16
Progressive school of historiography, 128, 129
promyshlennik, Russian, 98–99, 100
prostitution, in the early nineteenth century, 117–118, 119
Provincial Freeman, 162, 163
punishment, public, in the nineteenth century, 114–115, 116
Puritans, 7, 18, 29, 59, 106, 153

Quakers, 28, 29, 30, 42, 45, 51, 144, 159

Radical Reconstruction, 236–237, 239, 240
Radical Republicans, 235, 236
Raleigh, Sir Walter, 10, 14, 15–16
Randolph, Edmund, 48, 51, 54, 55, 56
reciprocal liberty, 30
Reconstruction, new view of, 235–240
Regulator movement, 60, 61
religion, American Revolution as war of, 58–63
Republican party, 71, 174, 175, 176, 177, 178, 179, 180, 181, 217, 237
Residence Act of 1790, 72, 74
Revolutionary War: 17, 20, 39–40, 72, 86, 124, 215; espionage in the, 41–45; European reaction to, 34–38; as war of religion, 58–63
Roanoke, Virginia, lost British colony at, 10–16
romantic spirit, of the Confederacy, 200–201

Rush, Benjamin, 115, 153–154
Russia, traders from, in Alaska, 98–102
Rutledge, John, 53, 55, 88

sanitation, in the early nineteenth century, 110–111, 165
Sante Fe Trail, 164, 165
scalawags, 235, 237
Schlesinger, Arthur M., views of, on Andrew Jackson, 128–129
scorched earth policy, Sherman's, 204
Sedition Act of 1798, 71
Seneca Falls, NY, women's rights conference at, 142, 143, 162
servants, indentured, 20–24
Seward, William H., 98, 176, 177–178, 179, 183
sexuality, in the early nineteenth century, 116–119
Shad, Maryanne, 158–163
Shaw, Robert Gould, 215, 217, 218
Shays' Rebellion, 49, 63
Sherman, Roger, 52, 55, 56
Sherman, William T., 201, 203, 220
slavery: 7, 13, 21, 22, 24, 40, 46, 47, 50, 53, 59, 62, 63, 97, 109, 132, 143, 167, 188, 215, 217; aftermath of, 223–234; in the early nineteenth century, 113, 114, 116, 117, 119, 121; in Nicaragua, 146, 150, 151, 152; in Washington, D.C., 72–78; women in, 78–83; see also, abolition; Dred Scott decision; freedmen
social relationships, in the early nineteenth century, 120–121, 122
South, regional characteristics of, 28, 30, 31
Spain: 47, 48, 54, 59, 60; as New World explorers, 8, 10, 11, 12, 15, 16, 19, 130, 131
spies, in the Revolutionary War, 41–45
spoils system, 125, 128
Stamp Act, 60, 63, 96
Standish, Miles, 17, 18, 19
Stanton, Elizabeth Cady, 142–144
Stevens, Thaddeus, 236
Stono Rebellion, 59
Story, Joseph, 90, 91, 125
Stowe, Harriet Beecher, 162
Strader v. Graham, 172, 174
Stuart, J. E. B., 200, 201
suffrage, women's, 142, 144, 163
Supreme Court: 66, 125, 126; John Marshall as chief justice of, 84–91, 144; see also, Dred Scott decision

Tallmadge, Benjamin, 43, 44
taverns, in the early nineteenth century, 112–113, 116, 155
Taylor, Zachary, 123, 179, 203
temperance movement, 115, 143, 144, 153–157, 163
Texas, before and after the Alamo, 130–133
textile industry, and planned mill community in Lowell, MA, 103–107, 143
Thoreau, Henry David, 135, 136
tobacco, use of, in the early nineteenth century, 112, 119–120
Treaty of Paris, 46, 47, 48
Truth, Sojourner, 78
Tubman, Harriet, 78

Turner, Frederick Jackson, frontier thesis of, 128, 134, 140
Turner, Nat, 76, 114
Twain, Mark, 136, 137
Tyler, John, 123, 133

Underground Railroad, 158–163
utilitarian conservation, 140

Van Buren, Martin, 123, 124, 125
Vanderbilt, Cornelius, and Nicaragua, 148, 149, 150–151
Vicksburg, Civil War battle at, 215, 219
Virginia, lost British colony in Roanoke, 10–16
Virginia Plan, 51–52, 54, 56

Walker, William, and the conquest of Nicaragua, 145–152
Waltham system, 104
War of 1812, 75, 92, 123, 124, 125, 215
Washington, D.C.: Confederate attack on, 185–189; slaves and freedmen in, 72–77
Washington, George: 29, 45, 49, 50, 55, 85, 86, 87, 92–93, 123, 124; and espionage during the Revolutionary War, 41–45
Way West, The (Guthrie), 136–137
Wears, J. C., 158–159
Webster, Daniel, 18, 91, 104, 124, 125, 127, 177

Weed, Thurlow, 178, 180, 181
Welles, Gideon, 181–182, 183
werowance, 12
West, settlement of, 164–167
Whigs, 61, 127, 128, 129, 177, 178, 179
Whiskey Rebellion, 60, 63
White, John, 11, 12, 13, 14, 15
Whitman, Walt, 135–136
Wilson, James, 52, 55, 56, 69
Winthrop, John, 25, 26, 27
women: lives of slave, 78–83; in planned mill community of Lowell, MA, 103–107; rights of, 142–144, 162
writ of mandamus, 89

Credits/ Acknowledgments

Cover design by Charles Vitelli

1. The New Land
Facing overview—The Library of Congress.

2. Revolutionary America
Facing overview—The Library of Congress. 58—From *The Political Register,* 1969. 59—HT Archives. 61—From *The London Magazine,* 1774. 63—Courtesy of The Library of Congress.

3. National Consolidation and Expansion
Facing overview—Courtesy of the Chicago Historical Society. 73, 75—Reproduction for the Collections of the Library of Congress. 94—HT Archives. 95—HT Archives. 97—From *The Pageant of America.* 110—(left) Anderson Collection, Print Room, New York Public Library; (right) Sears Roebuck Catalog. 111—The Bettmann Archive. 112, 113—American Antiquarian Society. 114—

Legion of Liberty, (Albany, 1845), New York Public Library. 115—Anderson Collection, Print Room, New York Public Library. 116—American Antiquarian Society. 122—Free Library of Philadelphia. 147—Randi Busillo. 162—The Library of Congress.

4. Civil War and Reconstruction
Facing overview—The Library of Congress. 192, 194—Courtesy of The Freedom & Southern Society Project Collection. 193, 195, 196, 197—Courtesy of The Library of Congress. 199—The Library of Congress/Weidenfeld Archives. 200—HT Map by Ken Wass. 207—Courtesy of The State Historical Society of Wisconsin. 216—John B. Leib/MOLLUS-U.S. Military History Institute. 219—Granger Collection. 220—Culver Pictures. 223, 228—The Bettmann Archive.

ANNUAL EDITIONS ARTICLE REVIEW FORM

■ NAME: _____ DATE: _____

■ TITLE AND NUMBER OF ARTICLE: _____

■ BRIEFLY STATE THE MAIN IDEA OF THIS ARTICLE: _____

_____

_____

_____

■ LIST THREE IMPORTANT FACTS THAT THE AUTHOR USES TO SUPPORT THE MAIN IDEA:

_____

_____

_____

_____

_____

■ WHAT INFORMATION OR IDEAS DISCUSSED IN THIS ARTICLE ARE ALSO DISCUSSED IN YOUR TEXTBOOK OR OTHER READING YOU HAVE DONE? LIST THE TEXTBOOK CHAPTERS AND PAGE NUMBERS:

_____

_____

_____

_____

_____

_____

■ LIST ANY EXAMPLES OF BIAS OR FAULTY REASONING THAT YOU FOUND IN THE ARTICLE:

_____

_____

_____

_____

■ LIST ANY NEW TERMS/CONCEPTS THAT WERE DISCUSSED IN THE ARTICLE AND WRITE A SHORT DEFINITION:

_____

_____

_____

_____

_____

ANNUAL EDITIONS: AMERICAN HISTORY, Vol. I
Pre-Colonial Through Reconstruction
Article Rating Form

Here is an opportunity for you to have direct input into the next revision of this volume. We would like you to rate each of the 37 articles listed below, using the following scale:

1. **Excellent: should definitely be retained**
2. **Above average: should probably be retained**
3. **Below average: should probably be deleted**
4. **Poor: should definitely be deleted**

Your ratings will play a vital part in the next revision. So please mail this prepaid form to us just as soon as you complete it.
Thanks for your help!

Rating	Article	Rating	Article
	1. A New World . . . and a New Era in World History		21. The Jacksonian Revolution
	2. Roanoke Lost		22. Lone Star Rising: Texas Before and After the Alamo
	3. Who Were the Pilgrims?		23. Eden Ravished
	4. Colonists in Bondage: Indentured Servants in America		24. Act One
	5. Anne Hutchinson: "A Verye Dangerous Woman"		25. El Presidente Gringo: William Walker and the Conquest of Nicaragua
	6. Remapping American Culture		26. The War Against Demon Rum
	7. The Shot Heard Round the World		27. Last Stop on the Underground Railroad: Mary Ann Shadd in Canada
	8. Life, Liberty, and the Pursuit of Happiness: America's Modest Revolution		28. The Cry Was: Go West, Young Man, and Stay Healthy
	9. General George Washington, Espionage Chief		29. Dred Scott in History
	10. 'It Is Not a Union'		30. How We Got Lincoln
	11. Philadelphia Story		31. There, in the Heat of July, Was the Shimmering Capitol
	12. The American Revolution: A War of Religion?		32. Family and Freedom: Black Families in the American Civil War
	13. James Madison and the Bill of Rights		33. Why the Confederacy Lost
	14. Slaves and Freedmen		34. A Union Officer at Gettysburg
	15. The Lives of Slave Women		35. The Hard Fight Was Getting Into the Fight at All
	16. The Great Chief Justice		36. What Did Freedom Mean? The Aftermath of Slavery as Seen by Former Slaves and Former Masters in Three Societies
	17. A Shadow of Secession? The Hartford Convention, 1814		37. The New View of Reconstruction
	18. Russia's American Adventure		
	19. From Utopia to Mill Town		
	20. The Secret Life of a Developing Country (Ours)		

(Continued on next page)

ABOUT YOU

Name_____ Date_____

Are you a teacher? ☐ Or student? ☐

Your School Name _____

Department _____

Address _____

City_____ State _____ Zip _____

School Telephone #_____

YOUR COMMENTS ARE IMPORTANT TO US!

Please fill in the following information:

For which course did you use this book? _____

Did you use a text with this Annual Edition? ☐ yes ☐ no

The title of the text? _____

What are your general reactions to the Annual Editions concept?

Have you read any particular articles recently that you think should be included in the next edition?

Are there any articles you feel should be replaced in the next edition? Why?

Are there other areas that you feel would utilize an Annual Edition?

May we contact you for editorial input?

May we quote you from above?

AMERICAN HISTORY, Vol. I 11th Ed.
Pre-Colonial Through Reconstruction